Arab-Israeli Conflict

Arab-Israeli Conflict

THE ESSENTIAL REFERENCE GUIDE

Priscilla Roberts, Editor

 ABC-CLIO

Santa Barbara, California • Denver, Colorado • Oxford, England

Library of Congress Cataloging-in-Publication Data

Roberts, Priscilla Mary.
    Arab-Israeli conflict : the essential reference guide / Priscilla Roberts, Editor.
        pages cm
    Includes index.
    ISBN 978-1-61069-067-6 (hardback) — ISBN 978-1-61069-068-3 (ebook)
1. Arab-Israeli conflict.   I. Title.
    DS119.7.R575   2014
    956.04—dc23   2014005600

ISBN: 978-1-61069-067-6
EISBN: 978-1-61069-068-3

18   17   16   15   14   1   2   3   4   5

This book is also available on the World Wide Web as an eBook.
Visit www.abc-clio.com for details.

ABC-CLIO, LLC
130 Cremona Drive, P.O. Box 1911
Santa Barbara, California 93116-1911

This book is printed on acid-free paper ∞

Manufactured in the United States of America

In Loving Memory of Dave Roberts
1932–2012
A Life Well Lived

Contents

PRIMARY SOURCE DOCUMENTS

APPENDIX: HISTORICAL DILEMMAS IN THE ARAB-ISRAELI CONFLICT

Overview of the Arab-Israeli Conflict

On November 29, 1947, the General Assembly of the United Nations (UN), to which Great Britain has transferred responsibility for determining the fate of Palestine, voted to partition the British Mandate into Jewish and Arab states. The Arabs of Palestine, supported by the Arab League, adamantly opposed the partition, and the first of four major wars began following news of the UN vote. The first war of 1947–1949 contains two identifiably separate conflicts: the Arab-Jewish communal war of November 30, 1947–May 14, 1948, which included volunteer forces from other Arab states as well as Palestinian Arabs, and the Israeli War of Independence, which began on May 15, 1948, a day after the ending of the British Mandate and with the founding of the State of Israel. It ended with the last truce agreement with Syria on July 30, 1949. The three other conflicts ensued in 1956 (the Sinai War, or Suez Crisis), 1967 (the Six-Day War), and 1973 (the October War, Ramadan War, or Yom Kippur War). In these four conflicts, Israeli forces eventually triumphed. Each threatened to bring about superpower intervention, and the four wars also had profound implications throughout the Middle East and beyond. Beyond these wars, however, were ongoing terrorist attacks against Israel; cross-border raids, some of them quite large; a successful

Israeli air strike on the Iraqi Osiraq nuclear reactor (1981); and large Israeli incursions into southern Lebanon (1982).

The 1948 war began following the announcement of the UN General Assembly's endorsement of Resolution 181 on November 29, 1947, calling for the partition of Palestine into Jewish and Arab states. While Jewish authorities in Palestine accepted the resolution, the Arabs—including the Palestinians and the Arab League—rejected it. In response to passage of the UN resolution, Arabs began attacking Jews throughout Palestine, and the incidents expanded so that from December 1947 to April or May 1948 an intercommunal war raged between Jewish and Arab residents of Palestine.

The Jewish community in Palestine then numbered some 600,000 people, while the Palestinians consisted of more than 1.2 million. However, Palestinian numerical advantage counted for little on the battlefield. The Palestinians had no national institutions of any kind, let alone a cohesive military. They were fragmented with divided elites and were unprepared for the violence, expulsions, and loss of their property. Probably most of the Palestinians did not want to go to war, hoping that their Jewish neighbors would retreat. Perhaps only 5,000 Palestinians took part in the fighting against the

Map of the growth of Jewish settlements in Palestine from 1880 to 1914.

Jews. These essentially guerrilla forces were poorly trained, poorly equipped, and ineffectively organized.

The Arab League pledged support to the Palestinians but through its Military Committee actually usurped the conflict from the Palestinians. The Military Committee and the mufti Haj Amin al-Husseini argued over the conduct of the war as each sought to control operations. The Military Committee failed, however, to provide the Palestinians with the money and weapons that the Arab rulers had pledged and sent its own commanders to Palestine to oversee the war. Such internal conflicts further weakened the overall Arab effort.

The Jews, on the other hand, were much better equipped and more organized. Jewish society was both Western and industrialized, having all the institutions of a modern state. In fact, structurally the establishment of the Jewish state required only the formal transformation of the pre-statehood institutions to government entities, parliament, political parties, banks, and a relatively well-developed military arm, known as the Haganah. The Haganah was organized during the civil war as a full-fledged army, with nine brigades with a total of some 25,000 conscripts. By May 1948, there were 11 brigades, with nearly 35,000 men. With the Jewish forces taking the offensive in early April 1948, the Palestinians had no chance but to counterattack and by early May had been defeated.

During this time, and even before the Jews' final campaign, hundreds of thousands of Palestinians were driven from or fled their homes and became refugees. By the end of the war, there would be 750,000 to 1 million or more Palestinian refugees. Many of them escaped from the battle zone, but others were forcibly expelled and deported by Jewish forces during the actual fighting.

On May 14, 1948, with the formal establishment of the State of Israel, Israeli forces secured control over all the territory allocated to it by the UN in addition to a corridor leading to Jerusalem and the Jewish part of Jerusalem, which according to the Partition Resolution was to have been internationalized. With the official termination of British rule in Palestine earlier that day, David Ben-Gurion, Israel's first elected prime minister, declared the establishment of the State of Israel. This declaration was followed by the advance of four Arab armies toward Palestine bent on a campaign to extinguish Israel.

The resulting war was, in many respects, primitive. Some 35,000 Israeli soldiers faced 35,000–40,000 Arab soldiers. Both sides were subjected to a UN Security Council arms embargo, but it was the Arabs who suffered the most from this. The Arab armies secured their weapons from Britain for Egypt, while Jordan and Iraq, which had no access to other markets, were forced into this arrangement under treaties with Britain. With the embargo in place, the Arabs were unable to replace damaged or destroyed weapons, and they had only limited access to ammunition. However, while the Jews received no military equipment from the West, they did manage in early 1948 to sign a major arms contract with the Czech government, thereby purchasing various weapons but mostly small arms and ammunition.

The strength of the Arab armies was in infantry. Their few tanks were mostly Egyptian. Even then, only a few dozen were operative. Despite an initial effort to create a unified command structure, the movements of the four Arab armies on Palestine were not coordinated. In April 1948, General Nur al-Din Mahmud, an Iraqi officer, was appointed by the Arab League to command the Arab forces. Mahmud submitted a plan that focused on northeastern Palestine, where the invading forces would try to sever eastern Galilee from the Hula Valley to Lake Kinneret (the Sea of Galilee) from Israel. That would be achieved through the coordinated advance of the Syrian, Lebanese, Iraqi, and Jordanian forces in the northern part of Palestine, while the Egyptian army would move northward to Yibna, which was inside the designated Arab state. The Egyptians were not to advance into the Jewish state's territory, at least not in the first stage, but rather were to create a diversion that would lure Israeli forces into their sector and reduce Israeli pressure on the main Arab push in the north.

Jordan's King Abdullah had different plans for his army, however. He planned to occupy the area designated for the Palestinian Arab state, west of the Jordan River (the West Bank). For that reason he rebuffed Mahmud's plan and ordered the commander of the Arab Legion to act independently and occupy the West Bank. That was done, with the Arab Legion completing its mission in a few days. With that, each Arab army acted in isolation, while at the last minute Lebanon refrained from participation in the war.

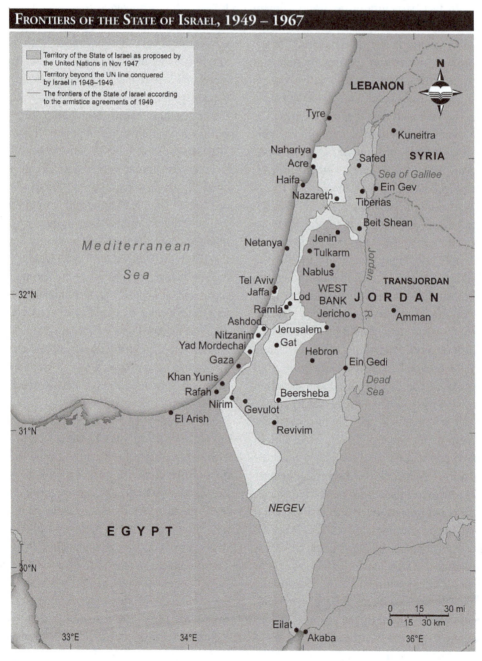

Map of the Israeli frontiers from 1949 to 1967 in the Arab-Israeli Wars.

Syrian and Iraqi forces fought in the northern part of Israel, the Jordanian Arab League in the central sector, and the Egyptian army in the southern sector.

The Egyptian government dispatched to Palestine 5,500 soldiers organized into two infantry brigades, accompanied by nearly 4,500 irregulars. Iraq dispatched to Palestine some 4,500 soldiers, while Syria sent 6,000. Jordan deployed almost all of its army, some 6,500 men. In addition, some 3,000 irregulars fought alongside the Arab armies.

At that time, Israel fielded more than 30,000 soldiers. The fighting was divided into two parts: the first from May 15 to June 10 and the second from July 9 to the end of the war. The first stage saw the Jews on the defensive, while in the second half of the war they took the offensive. In the indecisive first phase, small Iraqi and Syrian forces invaded Israel in the north but were repelled following a few days of fighting.

Jordanian forces concentrated on the occupation of the West Bank, while the main Egyptian expeditionary force moved northward along the coastline, reaching its final staging area near Yibna, within the area designated to the Arab state. Another part of the Egyptian force split from the main force. It crossed the Negev Desert from west to east and moved toward Samaria through Hebron up to the southern outskirts of Jerusalem. Neither Egyptian force encountered any Israeli forces during their movements.

In the north, the Syrian and the Iraqi armies tried to execute their part in Mahmud's plan, which was no longer valid. Acting in an uncoordinated manner, small forces of both armies invaded Israel in an area south of the Kinneret but were thwarted by the Israelis. The Syrian army retreated, to return about a week later and attack two Israeli settlements near the Israeli-Syrian border and occupy them. Israeli counterattacks failed, and the

Syrian forces withdrew only at the end of the war as part of the truce agreement between the two states. The Iraqi forces retreated too and returned to the Jordanian-occupied West Bank. The Iraqi troops acted in coordination with the Jordanian army, allowing the Jordanian command to send troops from around Samaria, now held by the Iraqis, to the Israeli-Jordanian battlefield. Iraqi forces departed the West Bank at the end of the war, with Iraq refraining from signing a truce agreement with Israel.

In this initial stage, the Israelis were concentrated along the road to Jerusalem. Both the Jordanians and the Israelis completely misread the other's intentions. The Israelis assumed that the Arab Legion planned to invade Israel, and the Jordanians feared that the Israelis intended to drive the Arab Legion from the West Bank.

In fact, all the Israelis sought was to bring the Jewish part of Jerusalem under Israeli control and, toward that end, to gain control over the road from the coast to Jerusalem. The Israelis feared that the Arab Legion would cut the road to Jerusalem and occupy all of Jerusalem, and to prevent this from occurring they reinforced Jerusalem. The Jordanians interpreted the dispatch of Israeli troops to Jerusalem as an attempt to build up a force to take the offensive against them. This mutual misunderstanding was the cause of the fierce fighting between Israeli and Jordanian forces that ended with the Jordanians repulsing the Israeli troops and holding on to bases in the Latrun area, the strategic site along the Tel Aviv–Jerusalem road.

Israeli-Jordanian fighting ended when the Israeli government acknowledged its inability to drive out Jordanian forces that blocked the road to Jerusalem and when the two governments realized that the other posed no risk. In November 1948, Jewish and Jordanian military commanders in Jerusalem concluded an agreement that formalized the positions established with the de facto cease-fire of the previous July.

With the end of the fighting with Jordan, the Israelis launched the final phase of the war. In a two-stage operation in October and December 1948, the Israeli army drove the Egyptian forces from the Negev. The Israeli effort to force out the Egyptians along the coast was only partially successful, however. The Egyptians remained in the Gaza Strip. Indeed, the Gaza Strip remained under Egyptian control until 1967.

Concurrent with the October operations in the south, other Israeli troops stormed the high ground in central Galilee, controlled by the Arab League's Arab Liberation Army. After brief fighting, the Israelis occupied all of Galilee. In early January 1949, a cease-fire came into effect, and shortly thereafter negotiations on armistice agreements began.

The second major confrontation between Israel and the Arabs was the Sinai War, or Suez Crisis, of October 1956. This time, France, Britain, Israel, and Egypt were involved in the fighting. The Israeli-Egyptian portion of the war, which in Israel was known as Operation KADESH, was part of a larger picture. During 1949–1956, there was constant unrest along the Israeli-Egyptian demarcation line as well as between Israel and Jordan. Infiltrators regularly crossed the border from the Egyptian-controlled Gaza Strip, from the Sinai, and from the West Bank. Some were Palestinian refugees seeking to return to their homes or to visit relatives who remained inside Israel; some hoped to harvest their fields on the Israeli side of the border; some came to steal; and a few went to launch terrorist attacks against Israeli targets.

These infiltrations had an enormous impact on Israel. Economic damage mounted, and border-area residents, many of them newly arrived immigrants, were unprepared for the challenge. Israel feared the political implications of the infiltrations, as estimates of their numbers were thousands per month. Consequently, Israeli security forces undertook harsh measures against the infiltrators, regardless of the motives for crossing the border. Israeli soldiers often ambushed infiltrators, killing them and launching reprisal attacks. As a result, tensions along the Israeli borders increased, chiefly along the frontiers with Jordan and Egypt.

While the cross-border tensions provided the background context, the war occurred for two main reasons. First, Egyptian president Gamal Abdel Nasser had absorbed a large number of Palestinian refugees into Egypt and was responsible in a legal sense for those in the Gaza Strip. Rather than allowing the Palestinians free rein to attack Israel, he sought to simultaneously support their cause yet limit the Israeli response to their actions in unspoken rules of engagement, which the Israelis hoped to overturn. Nasser was a fervent Arab nationalist who also aspired to lead and unite the Arab world, a potentiality that deeply troubled Prime Minister Ben-Gurion. Ben-Gurion attributed the Arab defeat in 1948 to a great extent to their divisions. Thus, he was fearful of a unified Arab world under Nasser's leadership. The third immediate reason for the war was the Egyptian-Soviet arms arrangement (normally referred to as the Czech Arms Deal), announced in September 1955. The agreement assured Nasser of the modern weapons that Ben-Gurion was certain Nasser intended to use in an all-out attack against Israel.

Israeli fears were mitigated by an Israeli-French arms agreement completed in June 1956, one month before Nasser nationalized the Suez Canal on July 26, provoking an acute international crisis that culminated with the 1956 war. Shortly after the beginning of the crisis, France invited Israel to take part in planning a joint military attack on Egypt.

For Israel, while there was no specific reason for such an offensive move, fear of Nasser's intentions seemed sufficient justification. Tensions between Israel and Egypt since 1949, and especially since 1954, had significantly diminished. In the summer of 1956, exchanges of fire along the armistice line had largely ceased. More importantly, Nasser, expecting a fierce Anglo-French reaction to the nationalization of the Suez Canal, reduced the Egyptian troop deployment along the Israeli-Egyptian border to reinforce the Suez Canal.

While Egypt had blockaded the Straits of Tiran, closing it to Israeli ships, that by itself could not be reason for war, as there was no Israeli commercial maritime transportation along that route. Nevertheless, Ben-Gurion feared that Nasser was planning to unite the Arab world against Israel, and thus the invitation from two major powers to take part in a combined military effort was too much to resist. In a meeting at Sèvres, France, during October 22–25, 1956, French, British, and Israeli negotiators worked out the details of the war.

According to the plan that was worked out, Israeli parachutists would land a few miles east of Suez. France and Britain would then issue an ultimatum to both parties to remove their military forces from the canal. Expecting an Egyptian refusal, French and British forces would then invade Egypt to enforce the ultimatum. In the meantime, Israeli forces would storm the Sinai Peninsula. Their goal was to join up with the parachutists in the heart of the Sinai and to open the Straits of Tiran.

Israel deployed the 7th Armored Brigade, with two tank battalions; the 27th and 37th

Mechanized Brigades; the 202nd Parachute Brigade; and the 1st, 4th, 9th, 10th, 11th, and 12th Infantry Brigades. The agreement with the British and French was the determining factor in the Israeli plan of attack. Instead of storming the Egyptian positions in front of them, a paratroop battalion was dropped on October 29, 1956, at the eastern gates of the Mitla Pass, some 30 miles east of the Suez Canal. Simultaneously, the paratroop brigade, commanded by Lieutenant Colonel Ariel Sharon, moved into the Sinai to join with the battalion waiting deep in the Sinai. The other Israeli forces had to wait until the Anglo-French attack on Egypt began.

Israeli commanders in the field were unaware of the agreement with the British and the French. Fearing for the parachute brigade and seeking a resolute and decisive victory over Egyptian forces, Major General Assaf Simhoni, commander of the southern command, ordered his forces to move ahead, with the armored brigade leading. The armored brigade stormed the Egyptian positions, with the remainder of the forces ensuring the defeat of the Egyptians. Israeli forces completed the occupation of the Sinai and the Gaza Strip within three days. During the fighting, nearly 170 Israeli soldiers were killed and 700 were wounded. The Egyptians suffered thousands of deaths, far more wounded, and more than 5,500 prisoners.

Israel did not enjoy for long the territorial achievements it gained in the war. Under enormous pressure from the United States and the Soviet Union, it was forced to remove its forces from the Sinai and the Gaza Strip. However, the terms of the Israeli evacuation of the Sinai aimed to provide it the security it was lacking: UN observers were deployed along the armistice demarcation lines to ensure that they would not be crossed by infiltrators. One result of the stationing of UN forces was the nearly complete cessation of infiltration from the Gaza Strip to Israel. It was also agreed that the Sinai would be demilitarized, removing with that the threat of an Egyptian surprise attack against Israel. The Dwight D. Eisenhower administration provided assurances that it would no longer allow closure of the Straits of Tiran. Finally, the performance of Israeli forces in the war marked a dramatic change in the history of the Israel Defense Forces (IDF). The IDF went from being an unsophisticated, infantry-based army to an efficient, modernized, and mechanized military force. The lessons of the Sinai War certainly paved the way toward the Israelis' impressive achievement in the Six-Day War of June 6–11, 1967.

While the immediate cause of the Six-Day War may be unclear, the long-term catalysts are more obvious. On May 15, 1967, Nasser sent his army into the Sinai. This set the stage for a dramatic three weeks that culminated in an Israeli attack and the total defeat of Egyptian, Jordanian, and Syrian forces. It also resulted in the loss of territories by these three Arab countries.

Tensions along the Israeli-Syrian and the Israeli-Jordanian borders formed the long-term cause of the war. There were three issues of contention. The first was the Israeli-Syrian struggle over the sovereignty of several pieces of land along their mutual border. According to the Israeli-Syrian armistice agreements, these areas were demilitarized. The Syrians insisted that sovereignty of the areas was undecided, while the Israelis believed that because the areas were on their side of the international border, they were under Israeli sovereignty. Consequently, Israel insisted that it had the right to cultivate the controversial pieces of land, to Syria's dismay. In a number of instances, the Syrians tried, by armed force, to prevent Israeli settlers from farming the land. The

second point of controversy lay in Syrian attempts to prevent Israel from diverting water from the Jordan River. Encouraged by the Arab League, the Syrians had tried since 1964 to divert the headwaters of the Jordan River inside Syria. Israel reacted fiercely to this, and until the Syrians finally abandoned the project, many clashes took place between the two nations' armed forces. The third issue was the continuing grievances of the Palestinians. Their desire to regain their land and find a solution for their displaced refugees was an ever-present theme in the politics of the neighboring Arab states and the Palestinian refugee community.

In 1964, Palestinian engineer and nationalist Yasser Arafat established Fatah, a political organization dedicated to liberating Palestine within the rubric of the Palestine Liberation Organization (PLO), also established in that year by the Arab League to provide a political representative body for the Palestinians. Over the next few years, other militant, political, and representative Palestinian organizations were established. In January 1965, Fatah planted a bomb near an Israeli water-pumping station. The Israelis defused the bomb, but Fatah celebrated this as the first Palestinian terrorist attack. Palestinian attacks continued throughout 1965, 1966, and 1967. Despite the relatively low scale of the attacks, Israel responded aggressively, blaming Jordan for funding the terrorists and Syria for harboring and encouraging them.

The extent and ferocity of Israeli-Syrian clashes increased during 1967, culminating in an aerial battle between Israeli and Syrian forces that took place in April 1967. Israeli pilots shot down six Syrian planes during one of the dogfights. In the course of a public address, IDF chief of staff Lieutenant General Yitzhak Rabin threatened war against Syria.

A month later, in May 1967, Nasser ordered his forces into the Sinai. The reasons for this action are in dispute. The common assumption is that Moscow warned both the Egyptian and Syrian governments that Israel was massing military forces along the Israeli-Syrian border and planning to attack Syria. Because Egypt and Syria were bound by a military pact signed on November 4, 1966, Nasser sent his army into the Sinai to force the Israelis to dilute their forces in the north and to forestall what he assumed was an imminent attack on Syria.

The Israelis responded to the entry of Egyptian forces into the Sinai with the calling up of IDF reserve forces. Nasser subsequently increased Israeli concerns when he ordered the UN observers along the Israeli-Egyptian border to concentrate in one location. UN secretary general U Thant responded by pulling UN forces out of the Sinai altogether. Next, Nasser again closed the Straits of Tiran, yet another violation of the agreements that had led to the Israeli withdrawal from the Sinai in 1957. Besides that, Jordan and Egypt signed a military pact on May 30, 1967. This further increased the Israeli sense of siege.

Israeli military doctrine called for preemptive strikes in case of a concentration of Arab forces along its borders. All that was necessary was U.S. permission, and the Lyndon B. Johnson administration gave that in early June. The war began at dawn on June 5, 1967, with preemptive Israeli air strikes on Egyptian and then Syrian, Jordanian, and Iraqi air bases. The purpose of the attack was to neutralize the Arab air forces and remove the threat of air strikes on Israel. This would also, at a later stage, allow the Israeli air force to provide close air support to its forces on the ground.

Catching the vast bulk of the Egyptian aircraft on the ground as their pilots were at breakfast, some 250 Israeli aircraft destroyed the backbone of the Arab air forces within an hour, and by the end of the day they had been almost completely wiped out. More than 300 of a total of 420 Egyptian combat aircraft were destroyed that day. The Israelis then turned to destroy the far smaller Jordanian and Syrian air forces.

About an hour after the start of the air raids against Egypt, at about 8:30 a.m. Israeli time, the IDF launched its ground offensive. Three Israeli divisions attacked Egyptian forces in the Sinai and within four days had destroyed the Egyptian army in the Sinai and occupied the Peninsula.

Israeli operational plans were initially restricted to the Egyptian front. The IDF high command had developed plans to take the fighting to the Jordanian and Syrian fronts, but on the morning of June 5 it had no wish to go to war with these two Arab states.

There were, however, unexpected developments. As the Israeli troops stormed into the Sinai, Jordanian artillery shelled the suburbs of Jerusalem and other targets in Israel. The Israeli government hoped that Jordan's King Hussein would stay out of the fray and refrain from engaging in serious fighting. That did not happen. Jordanian troops stormed the UN headquarters in Jerusalem, inducing fears that the next step would be an attempt to take over Israeli-held Mount Scopus, an enclave within eastern Jerusalem, a Jordanian-held territory. To prevent that, Israeli forces moved ahead to secure a road to Mount Scopus, and the Jerusalem area became a battlefield. In addition, Israeli troops moved in northern Samaria, from which long-range Jordanian artillery was shelling Israeli seaside cities. A full-fledged war was now in progress that lasted two days and ended with the complete Israeli victory over Jordanian forces. Israel then occupied the West Bank and eastern Jerusalem.

In the north, Syrian forces began to move westward toward the Israeli border but did not complete the deployment and, for unknown reasons, returned to their bases. For five long days the Syrians shelled Israeli settlements from the Golan Heights overlooking the Jordan River Valley. Hoping to avoid a three-front war, the Israelis took no action against the Syrians, despite the heavy pressure imposed on them by the settlers who had come under Syrian artillery fire. It was only in the last day of the war, with the fighting in the south and center firmly under control, that Israeli troops stormed the Golan Heights, taking it after only a few hours of fighting.

The end of the war saw a new Middle East in which Israel controlled an area three times as large as its pre-1967 territory. It had also firmly established itself as a major regional power. Israel also found itself in control of nearly 2 million Arabs in the West Bank, many of whom were refugees from the 1948–1949 war. The 1967 Six-Day War, known as the Naksa in the Arab world, was considered an utter defeat not only for the Arab armies but also for the principles of secular Arab nationalism as embodied in their governments. The defeat led to a religious revival.

Militarily, the 1967 Six-Day War marked a major military departure. First, it was a full-fledged armor war in which both sides, but chiefly the Egyptians and Israelis, deployed hundreds of tanks. Second, Cold War imperatives were clearly evident on the battlefield, with Israel equipped with sophisticated Western weapons and enjoying the full political support of the United States, while the Egyptians and the Syrians had the military and political support of the Soviet Union.

The next major Arab-Israeli conflict occurred six years later: the 1973 Yom Kippur War, also known as the War of Atonement and the Ramadan War. The years between 1967 and 1973 were not peaceful ones in the Middle East. Nasser refused to accept the results of the Six-Day War and rejected Israeli terms for negotiations of direct peace talks that would end in a peace agreement in return for giving up the Sinai. The Jordanians and the Syrians, as well as the rest of the Arab world, also rejected Israel's terms, instead demanding compliance with UN Resolution 242 (November 22, 1967) that called for the "withdrawal of Israeli armed forces from territories occupied in the recent conflict" and the "termination of all claims or states of belligerency and respect for and acknowledgement of the sovereignty, territorial integrity, and political independence of every state in the area."

UN Resolution 242 became the main reference for any agreement in the region, but it has never been enforced. The Israelis argue that it called for the withdrawal of Israeli armed forces from "territories occupied" and not from "the territories occupied," and thus it need not return to all the pre–June 6, 1967, lines as the UN has instead argued. Tel Aviv held that this was a matter for discussion with the Arab states involved. In addition, the resolution was not tied to any demand for the parties to begin direct peace talks, as Israel consistently required. The result was stalemate.

Israel launched settlement endeavors and placed Jewish settlers in the occupied territories, seeking to perpetuate with that its hold on the territories, while the Arab side again resorted to violence. The first to endorse violence were the Palestinians. Disappointed by the Arab defeat, some of the Palestinians changed their strategy, declaring a revolution or people's movement. Prior to 1967 they had used terror attacks as a trigger that might provoke war, which they hoped would end in an Arab victory. Now they decided to take their fate into their own hands and launch their own war of liberation against what they called the Zionist entity. The result was a sharp increase in the extent and ferocity of Palestinian terrorist attacks on Israel and in the level of tensions between the Arab states and the Palestinians.

In 1968, the Palestinians internationalized their struggle by launching terrorist attacks against Israeli and Jewish targets all over the world. Nasser now also decided to take a path of aggression. Frustrated by his inability to bring about a change in Israel's position, he began a campaign under the slogan of "what was taken by force would be returned by force." Following low-level skirmishes along the Suez Canal and adjoining areas, from June 1968, Egyptian forces began shelling and raiding Israeli troop deployments across the canal. The Israelis responded with artillery fire and retaliatory attacks. The violence escalated as Israel struck deep inside Egypt with its air force. Before long, this midlevel-intensity conflict became known as the War of Attrition and continued until 1970.

With the growing intensity of Israeli air attacks on Egypt, pilots from the Soviet Union took an active part in the defense of Egypt. The increased involvement of the Soviet military in the conflict deeply worried both the Israelis and the United States. Through the mediation of U.S. secretary of state William Rogers, a cease-fire agreement was concluded in August 1970, and the fighting subsided. However, shortly after the signing of the agreement, the Egyptians began placing surface-to-air (SAM) batteries throughout the Suez Canal area.

During 1970–1973, Rogers and UN mediator Gunnar Jarring introduced peace plans that were rejected by both the Israelis and the Egyptians. Following Nasser's death in September 1970, his successor, Anwar

Sadat, was determined to change the status quo. Toward that end, he acted on two fronts: he called for a gradual settlement that would lead to Israeli withdrawal from the Sinai without a full peace agreement, and he expelled the Soviet advisers brought in by Nasser and resumed negotiations with the United States, which Nasser had ended in 1955.

The failure of Sadat's diplomatic efforts in 1971 led him to begin planning a military operation that would break the political stalemate along the Israeli-Egyptian front. Sadat believed that even a minor Egyptian military success would change the military equilibrium and force a political settlement that would lead to a final settlement. In devising his plan, he carefully calculated Israeli and Egyptian strengths and weaknesses. He believed that Israel's strength lay in its air force and armored divisions, well trained for the conduct of maneuver warfare. Egyptian strengths were the ability to build a strong defense line and the new SAM batteries deployed all along the canal area and deep within Egypt. Sadat hoped to paralyze the Israeli air force with the SAMs and hoped to counter the Israelis' advantage in maneuver warfare by forcing them to attack well-fortified and defended Egyptian strongholds.

In an attempt to dilute the Israeli military forces on the Sinai front, Sadat brought in Syria. A coordinated surprise attack on both the Syrian and Egyptian fronts would place maximum stress on the IDF. But above anything else, the key to the plan's success lay in its secrecy. Were Israel to suspect that an attack was imminent, it would undoubtedly launch a preventive attack, as in 1967. This part of the plan was successful.

Israeli ignorance of effective deceptive measures undertaken by Egypt contributed to Israel's failure to comprehend what

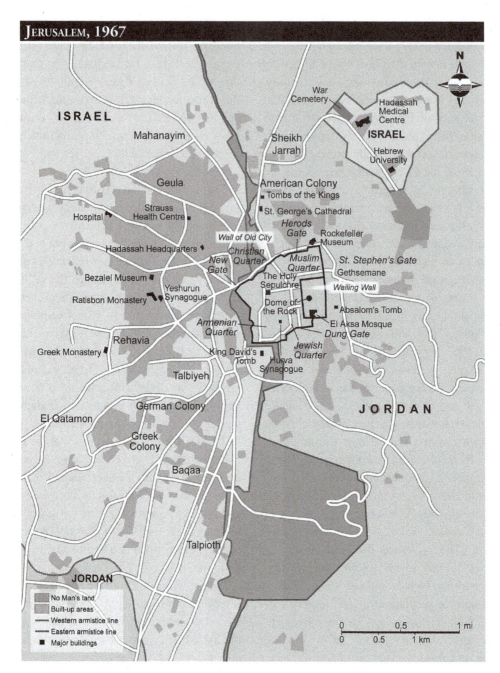

Map of Jerusalem in 1967.

was happening. One deception consisted of repeated Egyptian drills along the canal that simulated a possible crossing. The Israelis thus became accustomed to large Egyptian troop concentrations at the canal and interpreted Egyptian preparations for the actual crossings as just another drill. Even the Egyptian soldiers were told that it was simply a drill. Only when the actual crossing was occurring were they informed of its true nature. Even with the actual attack, however, the real intent of Egyptian and Syrian forces remained unclear to the Israelis, and they initially refrained from action.

Beginning at 2:00 p.m. on October 6, 1973, Egyptian and Syrian artillery and aircraft, and later their ground forces, launched major attacks along the Suez Canal and the Golan Heights. On the Israeli-Egyptian front, Egypt amassed a force of nearly 800,000 soldiers, 2,200 tanks, 2,300 artillery pieces, 150 SAM batteries, and 550 aircraft. Egypt deployed along the canal five infantry divisions with accompanying armored elements supported by additional infantry and armored independent brigades. This force was backed by three mechanized divisions and two armored divisions. Opposing this force on the eastern bank of the Suez Canal was one Israeli division supported by 280 tanks.

This Israeli force was no match for the advancing Egyptian troops. The defenders lacked reinforcements, as reserves were called on duty only after the outbreak of the war. They also did not have air support, as Egyptian SAMs proved deadly effective against Israeli aircraft.

The attacking Egyptians got across the canal and swept over the defending Israelis. It took less than 48 hours for the Egyptians to establish a penetration three to five miles deep on the east bank of the Suez Canal. They then fortified the area with more troops. Two divisions held the seized area, which was defended also by the SAM batteries across the canal. With that, the Egyptians had achieved their principal aims and a psychological victory.

The Israelis rushed reinforcements southward and launched a quick counteroffensive on October 8 in an attempt to repel the invading Egyptians troops. Much to Israeli surprise, it was a failure. Undermanned, unorganized, and underequipped Israeli troops moved against a far bigger and more well-organized and well-equipped force protected by highly effective handheld antitank missiles. The Egyptians crushed the Israeli counteroffensive.

Map of the growth of Jewish settlements in the West Bank and Gaza Strip from 1967 to 1978.

Following this setback, the Israeli General Staff decided to halt offensive actions on the Suez front and give priority to the fighting in the north on the Golan Heights, where in the first hours of the war little stood between massive numbers of invading Syrian armor and the Jewish settlements. Syria deployed two infantry divisions in the first line and two armored divisions in the second. This force had 1,500 tanks against only two Israeli armored brigades with 170 tanks. The Syrian forces swept the Golan Heights, crushing the small Israeli forces facing them. The few Israeli forces there fought desperately, knowing that they were the only force between the Syrians and numerous settlements. The Israeli forces slowed the Syrians and bought sufficient time for reserves of men and tanks to be brought forward. The Syrians also had an ineffective battle plan, which played to Israeli strengths in maneuver warfare. After seven days of fighting, Israeli troops thwarted the Syrian forces beyond the starting point of the war, across the pre–October 1973 Purple Line, and then drove a wedge into Syrian territory. Only then did the IDF again turn to the Egyptian front, where the goal remained driving Egyptian troops from the Sinai.

Sadat also overruled his ground commander and continued the advance. This took his forces out of their prepared defensive positions and removed them from the effective SAM cover on the other side of the canal, working to the Israelis' advantage. Israeli troops also located a gap between the two Egyptian divisions defending the occupied area that had gone unnoticed by the Egyptian command. Israeli forces drove through the gap and crossed the canal. The IDF hoped to achieve two goals. The first and most immediate goal was to create a SAM-free zone over which Israeli aircraft could maneuver free from the threat of missile attack. The second goal was to cut

off Egyptian troops east of the canal from their bases west of the canal. After nearly a week of fighting, the Israelis accomplished almost all of their objectives. Nonetheless, Soviet and U.S. pressure led to a cease-fire before the Israelis could completely cut off the two Egyptian divisions in the east from their bases.

Neither the Soviets nor the Americans wanted to see the Egyptians completely defeated. They also assumed that the Egyptian achievement would allow progress in the political process, just as Sadat had wanted. As a result, the war ended with Israeli and Egyptian forces entangled, the latter on the eastern side of the canal and the former on Egyptian soil.

Syrian president Hafez al-Assad's chief motivation in joining Sadat in the war against Israel was to recapture the Golan Heights. Al-Assad had no diplomatic goals and no intention of using the war as leverage for a settlement with Israel. The fighting in the north with Syria ended with the IDF positioned only about 25 miles from Damascus, while no Syrian forces remained within Israeli-held territory. It was only in 1974, after a disengagement agreement, that Israeli forces withdrew from Syrian territory beyond the Purple Line.

The 1973 war in effect ended in 1977 when Sadat visited Israel and the consequent 1979 Israeli-Egyptian peace treaty was signed. Turmoil continued, however, chiefly from the unresolved Palestinian problem, which was at the root of the Arab-Israeli conflict. Militant Palestinians refused to recognize the existence of the State of Israel, while Israel refused to treat with the Palestinian leadership. Terrorist attacks against Israel continued, and with a sharp increase in such attacks against the northern settlements from Lebanon, the Israeli government ordered IDF invasions of southern Lebanon in 1978 and 1982. The first

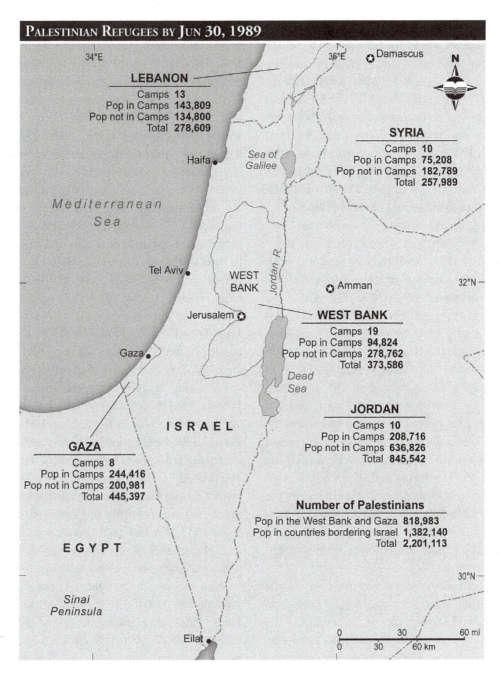

PALESTINIAN REFUGEES BY JUN 30, 1989

LEBANON
Camps **13**
Pop in Camps **143,809**
Pop not in Camps **134,800**
Total **278,609**

SYRIA
Camps **10**
Pop in Camps **75,208**
Pop not in Camps **182,789**
Total **257,989**

WEST BANK
Camps **19**
Pop in Camps **94,824**
Pop not in Camps **278,762**
Total **373,586**

JORDAN
Camps **10**
Pop in Camps **208,716**
Pop not in Camps **636,826**
Total **845,542**

GAZA
Camps **8**
Pop in Camps **244,416**
Pop not in Camps **200,981**
Total **445,397**

Number of Palestinians
Pop in the West Bank and Gaza **818,983**
Pop in countries bordering Israel **1,382,140**
Total **2,201,113**

Map of the Palestinian refugees by June 30, 1989 in the Arab-Israeli Wars.

invasion of 1978 was extremely costly in terms of civilian loss of life for the Lebanese, who were unable to mount an armed response to the Israelis. The Israelis also began to involve themselves in the ongoing civil war in Lebanon in order to further their own objectives.

Following increasing Palestinian rocket attacks from southern Lebanon, the Israelis began a large-scale invasion there on June 6, 1982. The stated goals of the operation were halting rocket attacks from that area against northern Israel and eliminating the

Palestinian fighters there. Ultimately, Israel committed some 76,000 men and considerable numbers of tanks, artillery, and aircraft to the operation. Minister of Defense Ariel Sharon and Prime Minister Menachem Begin had more ambitious goals, however. They also hoped to destroy the PLO and other Palestinian resistance in Lebanon altogether and to dismantle its political power. They also sought to force Syria from Lebanon and to influence Lebanese politics.

Begin and Sharon informed the cabinet that their goal was merely to eradicate PLO bases in southern Lebanon and push back PLO and Syrian forces some 25 miles, beyond rocket range of Galilee. Once the operation began, however, Sharon changed the original plan by expanding the mission to incorporate Beirut. Within days, the IDF advanced to the outskirts of Beirut. The PLO merely withdrew ahead of the advancing IDF on West Beirut. Sharon now mounted a broader operation that would force the PLO from Beirut, and for some 10 weeks Israeli artillery shelled West Beirut, killing both PLO members and scores of civilians. Fighting also occurred with Syrian forces in the Bekáa Valley area, but most of this combat was in the air. Not until June 2000 did Israel withdraw all its forces from southern Lebanon.

Israel achieved none of its goals in the invasion of Lebanon except for the eviction of the PLO from Beirut to Tunis and the deaths of many Palestinians and Lebanese. The Lebanese political scene was more turbulent than ever, and the PLO was certainly not eliminated. The Lebanese saw Israel as an implacable enemy, and an even more radical Islamic resistance took up hostilities against Israeli occupying troops and their Lebanese allies. That resistance eventually grew into Hezbollah, backed by Syria and Iran.

In December 1987, Palestinians began a protest movement, now known as the First Intifada, against Israeli rule in an effort to establish a Palestinian homeland through a series of demonstrations, improvised attacks, and riots. This intifada produced widespread destruction and human suffering, yet it also helped create a Palestinian national consciousness and made statehood a clear objective. It also cast much of Israeli policy in a negative light, especially with the deaths of Palestinian children, and thus helped rekindle international efforts to resolve the Arab-Israeli conflict. It also helped return the PLO from its Tunisian exile. Finally, it cost the Israeli economy hundreds of millions of dollars. The First Intifada ended in September 1993 with the signing of the historic Oslo Accords and the creation of the Palestinian Authority (PA).

Following torturous negotiations, the Israelis and Palestinians reached limited agreement at Oslo in September 1993 in the so-called Declaration of Principles. This eventually led to the establishment of the PA and limited Palestinian self-rule in the West Bank and the Gaza Strip. Nonetheless, the agreement was not fully implemented, and mutual Palestinian-Israeli violence continued, placing serious obstacles in the path of a general Arab-Israeli peace settlement.

With the advent of rightist Likud Party governments in Israel in the late 1990s, the Israeli-Palestinian peace process was essentially put on hold. Many politicians in Likud—but especially Prime Minister Benjamin Netanyahu—rejected the so-called land-for-peace formula. In the summer of 2000, U.S. president Bill Clinton hosted talks at Camp David between Israeli prime minister Ehud Barak and PLO chairman Yasser Arafat in an attempt to jump-start the moribund peace process. After 14 days of intense negotiations, the summit ended in an impasse.

The failure of the talks disheartened Clinton in the waning days of his presidency and led to bitter recriminations on both sides that the other had not negotiated in good faith.

Not surprisingly, the Palestinians reacted with great negativity to the failure of the Camp David talks. Their frustration was heightened by Arafat's false contention that Israel—and not the Palestinian side—had sabotaged the peace process. A new dimension to Palestinian outrage was added when Likud Party chairman Ariel Sharon visited the Temple Mount (Haram al-Sharif) on September 28, 2000. His presence there ignited Palestinian anger that began as a stone-throwing demonstration. Before long, a full-blown Palestinian uprising, known as the Second (al-Aqsa) Intifada, was under way. The uprising resulted in the deaths of many Israelis and Palestinians.

In recent years, momentous changes within the PLO and the PA have wrought more uncertainty for both the Palestinians and the Israelis. Arafat's death in November 2004 resulted in a sea change within the Palestinian leadership. Mahmoud Abbas was chosen to succeed Arafat. Like Arafat, Abbas was a member of Fatah. In January 2005, Abbas was elected president of the PA. In the meantime, terror attacks against Israelis and Israeli interests continued, and Abbas seemed powerless to stop the violence. Just a year after he ascended to the presidency, he suffered a stinging reversal when the Islamist party and organization Hamas won a majority of seats in the January 2006 Palestinian legislative elections. This led to the appointment of a Hamas prime minister. Most of the West promptly shunned the Hamas-led government and cut off all funding to the Palestinians. As violence continued and the lack of foreign aid hobbled the PA, bloody clashes between Fatah and

Hamas took place, mostly in Gaza. In June 2007, Hamas took over Gaza completely, so that effectively the PA controlled only the West Bank. Western governments resumed their aid to the PA, while radical Iran provided substantial financial assistance to the Hamas rulers in Gaza. Despite signing subsequent reconciliation agreements in 2011 and 2012, which included provisions for a united government and new elections, in late 2013, Fatah and Hamas were still far apart.

With increasing violence that included the kidnapping of an Israeli soldier in Gaza and a cross-border raid mounted by Hezbollah from Lebanon in July 2006 that killed three IDF soldiers and captured two others, the cabinet of Israeli prime minister Ehud Olmert again attacked southern Lebanon as well as Gaza. The fighting along the Israel-Lebanese border raged for 32 days between mid-July and mid-August. The incursion was largely limited to artillery and to air strikes that nonetheless included sections of Beirut and key bridges and lines of communication. Finally, some IDF ground troops were also sent in. Hezbollah responded by launching thousands of rockets into Israel. A great deal of Lebanese infrastructure that had been rebuilt since 1982 was destroyed in the countering Israeli strikes, and Israel's hopes that it might influence Lebanese politics again proved illusory. Indeed, Hezbollah, whose ability to launch rockets into northern Israel appeared undiminished despite the strikes, appeared to have strengthened its position in Lebanese politics and also to have gained prestige in the Arab world for seemingly fighting toe-to-toe with the IDF.

In early 2007, there were renewed calls for a concerted effort to jump-start the peace process. In June 2009, less than six months after taking office, U.S. president Barack Obama appealed for the implementation of the peace agreements between Israel and the Palestinians, but his words had little impact. Benjamin Netanyahu, the hard-line Likud politician who became prime minister of Israel in March 2009, authorized new Israeli settlements in the West Bank and despite participating in U.S.-brokered peace talks in September 2010, showed little interest in genuine compromise with the Palestinians. In June 2009, Netanyahu did publicly endorse the concept of a Palestinian state, but only on condition that it remained demilitarized. Fearing that Shiite Iran might launch a nuclear strike against Israel, Netanyahu also repeatedly urged the United States to move decisively to end Iran's nuclear program, by military force if necessary. In November 2012, persistent Hamas rocket attacks on southern Israel from Gaza led to eight days of retaliatory Israeli air strikes against targets in Gaza, ended by an Egyptian-brokered cease-fire.

David Tal and Spencer C. Tucker

Causes of the Arab-Israeli Conflict

Establishing precise parameters for the Arab-Israeli conflict is difficult. The wars are usually given as beginning with the Arab-Jewish Communal War (1947–1948) or the Israeli War of Independence (1948–1949). These wars in effect extend to the present, for some of the Arab confrontation states, most notably Syria, have yet to sign peace treaties with Israel.

But beginning the conflict in 1948 or even 1947 gives a false impression, as there had long been episodes of violence and armed clashes between Arabs and Jews in Palestine, especially in the 1920s and 1930s. These events were sparked by Arab fears over significant Jewish immigration to Palestine and land purchases there. Animosity thus found expression in the Arab Riots of 1920 and the Arab Revolt of 1936–1939.

Of course, strife was hardly new to this region. Palestine had been a battleground since the beginning of recorded history. History's first reliably recorded battle took place in 1457 BC at Megiddo, at the head of present-day Israel's Jezreel Valley. When Egyptian forces under the command of Pharaoh Thutmose III decisively defeated a Canaanite coalition under the king of Kadesh, the Canaanites withdrew to the city of Megiddo, which the Egyptians then brought under siege. Certain fundamentalist Christians identify Megiddo as the site of Armageddon, where according to the Book of Revelation the final great battle between good and evil will take place.

With its location on the eastern Mediterranean coast, ancient Palestine formed an important communication route between larger empires such as Egypt, Assyria, Babylon, and Persia. As such, it was destined for a stormy existence. These empires as well as Alexander the Great, the Seleucid Empire, the Romans, the Byzantines, the Abbasid caliphate, the Tartars, the Mongols, the Mamluks, the Ottoman Turks, and finally the British all fought for control of Palestine. Sometime around 1200 BC the Jews established and then maintained an independent Jewish state there. Ultimately, more powerful states prevailed, and the Jews were largely expelled from their own land by the occupiers in what became known as the Diaspora. Jews settled in most of the world's countries and on almost every continent.

In the 19th century, nationalism swept Europe. Sentiment for a national state also touched the Jews, who longed for a state of their own, one that would be able to protect them from the persecutions (pogroms) that occurred in the late 19th and early 20th centuries, most notably in Russia. Zionism, or the effort to reestablish a Jewish state in Palestine, attracted a great many Jews—religious and nonreligious—and a number of them went to Palestine as immigrants.

During World War I, the British government endeavored to win the support of both Arabs and Jews in the war against the Central Powers, including the Ottoman Empire. While at the same time supporting the Arab Revolt against Ottoman Turkey, the British government in the Balfour Declaration of November 1917 promised to work for the establishment of a Jewish homeland in Palestine. In retrospect, British policies were at once shortsighted and contradictory and helped sow the seeds of even more Arab-Jewish enmity when the war ended in 1918. Britain and France both secured League of Nations mandates in the Middle East after the war. France obtained Syria and Lebanon, while Britain took control of Palestine (which included what is today Israel/ Palestine and Jordan) and Iraq.

Increasing Jewish immigration, however, as well as ongoing Jewish purchases of Arab land increasingly inflamed Arab leaders in Palestine, who feared that if immigration could not be halted, the growing Jewish minority in Palestine would become a majority. In this position, the Arab leadership had the strong support of the Arab governments of the region. In what became an increasingly violent atmosphere, the British government found it impossible to please both sides. London, worried about its overall position in the Middle East with the approach of a new world war, increasingly tended to side with the Arabs. This meant restrictions on both Jewish immigration and land purchases in Palestine, but this came at precisely the time when German leader Adolf Hitler challenged the post–World War I status quo in Europe and was carrying out a fervent anti-Semitic policy.

Finding it impossible to secure agreement between the two sides, London announced plans for the partition of Palestine. The Arabs rejected this partitioning, insisting on independence for Palestine as one state under majority (Arab) rule. Concerned about their overall position in the Middle East, the British then withdrew from their pro-Zionist policy and in May 1939 issued a white paper that severely restricted the immigration of Jews to Palestine and forbade the purchase of Arab lands in Palestine by Jews.

Following World War II, Jews in Palestine conducted a campaign against the British policy there that mixed diplomatic campaign with armed struggle. Revelations of the intensity of Nazi Germany's genocidal efforts to eliminate the entire Jewish population of Europe during the war generated considerable international sympathy for Zionist calls for the creation of a Jewish state in Israel. Finding it more and more difficult to contain the growing violence in Palestine, coupled with the support of President Harry S. Truman's administration in the United States for the Jewish position, London turned the future of Palestine over to the new United Nations (UN).

David Tal and Spencer C. Tucker

Consequences of the Arab-Israeli Conflict

The fundamental consequence of the Arab-Israeli conflicts was the creation of a near irresoluble international dispute, with rival and almost irreconcilable claims to the territory of Palestine/Israel on the part of the original Arab inhabitants on the one hand, and the Israeli occupants on the other. The Palestinian Arabs, many of whom were driven out of their original homes in the communal warfare of the late 1940s and the 1948 Israeli War of Independence, could generally count upon receiving fierce sympathy and some level of military and financial support from other Arab states. As refugees, however, they often proved a destabilizing factor in their host countries, with radicalized Palestinians becoming particularly disruptive political forces in such relatively small states as Lebanon and Jordan. Support for the Palestinians and opposition to first Zionism and then Israel nonetheless became an article of faith for all Arab states in the Middle East, a process that intensified with the creation of the state of Israel in 1948 and repeated Israeli military victories over various coalitions of Arab nations. For several decades, Arab states refused to recognize Israel and denied its right to existence.

Israel, by contrast, generally looked to Western nations for help, initially receiving massive economic assistance and political backing from sympathetic Jewish supporters in North America and Europe. This was particularly the case with the United States. The Jewish lobby rapidly became extremely influential in United States politics, ensuring that the safeguarding of Israel's continued existence and national security was soon perceived as a key American national interest, one that most American politicians of either political party hesitated to question, for fear of the damage that Jewish opponents might wreak on their own careers. Despite the radical sympathies of some of its founding fathers, Israel swiftly aligned itself with the United States in the Cold War, presenting itself as a bulwark of democracy in the Middle East, as well as a pillar of U.S. security. From the early 1960s onward, Israel was the recipient of substantial military aid from the United States, with the two countries effectively unofficial allies. While conservative Arab states, notably Saudi Arabia, continued to align themselves with the United States, from the 1950s onward American identification with Israel was a factor in propelling more radical regimes, including those of Egypt, Syria, and Iraq, to lean toward the Soviet Union during the Cold War. This was particularly the case during the 1967 Six-Day War and the 1973 Yom Kippur War, when U.S. intelligence information and arms shipments to Israel were partly responsible for Arab defeats in those conflicts. Arab bitterness and resentment over U.S. support for Israel in the October 1973 war also resulted in the imposition of an Arab oil embargo on Western states that had been involved in resupplying Israel during the conflict, a measure that had massively detrimental economic consequences for those nations affected. Palestinian and Arab anger over Israel's very existence also led to terrorist attacks not just on Israeli targets, such as athletes at the 1972 Olympic Games, but also on sometimes less well protected Western objectives, such as airliners, hotels, and nightclubs.

With the upsurge in radical Islam in the Arab world from the 1970s onward, Western and particularly U.S. support for Israel gave added fuel to Muslim antagonism toward and the jihad (holy war) against what was seen as the decadent and infidel West, an outlook much in evidence in the charters and manifestoes of such pro-Palestinian organizations as the Muslim Brotherhood, Hamas, and Hezbollah, as well as Al Qaeda, the radical Islamic organization founded by the wealthy Saudi activist Osama bin Laden. The Iranian revolution of the late 1970s, in which the Muslim cleric Ayatollah Ruhollah Khomeini emerged as supreme leader, also perceived the West, especially the "great Satan" of the United States, as its foremost enemy, an outlook that led in 1979 to the seizure and imprisonment as hostages of diplomats from the U.S. embassy in Teheran. In the 1990s, Muslim radicals from Al Qaeda attacked American warships and embassies around the world. On September 11, 2001, Al Qaeda operatives successfully hijacked four airliners, destroying the World Trade Center twin towers in New York and hitting and damaging the Department of Defense Pentagon building headquarters in Washington, D.C. Muslims launched attacks on other Western targets after 2000, including British trains, buses, and airports, Spanish trains, and nightclubs patronized by foreigners in Bali, Indonesia. All these events had a strongly detrimental impact on popular Western opinions of the Islamic faith, contributing to public distrust and dislike of Muslims and widespread fears that a "clash of civilizations" between Christianity and Islam was inevitable.

From the Six-Day War of 1967 onward, after Israel annexed substantial additional Arab territories, including the West Bank of the River Jordan and the Gaza Strip, there were proposals—including resolutions passed by the United Nations—envisaging a bargain whereby, in return for receiving recognition from the Arab states, Israel would relinquish these territories, to become the basis of a Palestinian state that would serve as the homeland for Palestinian refugees. From the late 1960s onward, American presidents and secretaries of state, officials from the United Nations, and numerous prominent European figures, made heroic efforts to negotiate a lasting settlement of the Arab-Israeli conflict. On both sides, however, intransigence was deeply entrenched. When the Palestinian Liberation Organization, the foremost body representing Palestinian interests, renounced terrorism and violence and joined such negotiations, other more extremist Islamic organizations, notably Hamas and Hezbollah, denounced all efforts to compromise with Israel. Even when Arab leaders, as in Egypt and Jordan, were willing to negotiate with Israel, the ordinary man or woman on the Arab "street" was often far less sympathetic. In Israel itself, conservatives often sought to sabotage peace negotiations, with politicians from the right-wing Likud party in particular encouraging the extension of Israeli settlements in the West Bank territories that were expected to provide the physical foundation for any Palestinian state.

The Palestinian Authority, established in 1994 under the Oslo Accords to assume ever-increasing authority in the West Bank and Gaza, proved unable to prevent widespread suicide bombing attacks by individual Palestinians against Israeli targets. In 2005, Israel left Gaza, handing over control to Palestinian representatives. Palestinian elections in early 2006 returned a Hamas majority, leaving Gaza under Hamas administration, while the more moderate Palestinian Fatah organization held sway in the West Bank. Gaza soon became a base for rocket and other attacks on Israel, provoking several relatively brief but fierce Israeli military interventions. In late 2013, Israeli Palestinians were divided, with Hamas's writ still running in Gaza while the relatively moderate Palestinian president Mahmoud Abbas remained in power in the West Bank. Radical Hezbollah elements sworn to oppose Israel were a significant political force in Lebanon, while the anti-Israeli Muslim Brotherhood was gaining strength in the ongoing civil war in Syria. In July 2013, U.S. secretary of state John Kerry prevailed upon Abbas and Israel's prime minister Benyamin Netanyahu to begin direct talks, with the objective of reaching a complete settlement of all matters dividing the West Bank Palestinian Authority and Israel within nine months. Whether this initiative would succeed in achieving this ambitious objective remained an open question. Since the 1970s, massive U.S. and international involvement had undoubtedly brought some progress, often at glacial speed, toward resolving the bitter Arab–Israeli–Palestinian conflict. Given the intransigent stance of Hamas and many Israelis, however, it seemed probable that movement on this intractable problem would be relatively slow. For several more decades, the Arab-Israeli conflicts and the issues to which they had given rise seemed likely to continue to preoccupy the international community and to complicate U.S. and Western dealings with the states and peoples of both the Middle East and the Islamic world.

Priscilla Roberts

A

Abbas, Mahmoud

Born: March 26, 1935

First prime minister of the Palestinian Authority (PA) during March–October 2003 and president of the PA since January 2005. Mahmoud Abbas (Abu Mazen) was born on March 26, 1935, in Safed, British Mandatory Palestine. During the Israeli War of Independence (1948–1949), his family fled Palestine and settled in Syria. Abbas graduated from the University of Damascus and studied law in Egypt and Syria before earning a PhD in history in 1982 from the Oriental College, more often known as the People's Friendship University, in Moscow.

Abbas was the civil service director of personnel for Qatar when he began his involvement in Palestinian politics in the mid-1950s. He was one of the founders of Fatah (1957) and was part of the leadership of Yasser Arafat's Palestine Liberation Organization (PLO) in exile in Jordan, Lebanon, and Tunisia during the 1960s through the 1980s. During this time, Abbas cultivated relationships with left-wing and pacifist Jewish groups. He joined the Palestinian National Council (PNC) in 1968. According to Muammad Daod Awda, Abbas was the funding source for Black September's attack on Israeli athletes at the 1972 Summer Olympics in Munich, Germany. Abbas asserts that he was unaware of the intended use of the funds.

Abbas assumed the leadership of the PLO's Department for National and International Relations in 1980. He began his leadership of the PLO's Negotiations Affairs Department that same year. In May 1988, he assumed chairmanship of the division treating the occupied territories. When PLO support for Iraq's 1990 invasion of Kuwait harmed relationships with Arab states that joined the U.S.-led coalition in the 1991 Persian Gulf War, it was Abbas who repaired the damage. He was also the major architect of the 1993 Oslo Accords between the PLO and Israel. In 1996, he was elected secretary general of the PLO Executive Committee, headed the first session of the Israeli-Palestinian final status negotiations, led the Central Election Commission for the Palestinian Legislative Council (PLC), and then was elected to the PLC.

On March 19, 2003, Arafat appointed the more moderately and pragmatically perceived Abbas as the first prime minister of the PA. Arafat's unwillingness to share significant power, persistent conflicts with militant Palestinian groups such as Hamas and Islamic Jihad, Israeli targeted assassinations of Palestinian militants, and a perceived lack of support from the United States led Abbas to resign as prime minister on September 4, 2003, effective October 7, 2003.

Following Arafat's death, Abbas became chairman of the PLO on November 11, 2004. His authority and attempts to reengage the Road Map for Peace were challenged by most of the militant Palestinian groups, however. On January 15, 2005, he became president of the PA. A May 2005 pledge of $50 million and continued support of a free Palestinian state from the United States coupled with the Israeli withdrawal

Palestinian leader Mahmoud Abbas. The chairman of the Executive Committee of the Palestinian Liberation Organization (PLO) since November 2004, Abbas has been president of the Palestinian National Authority (PNA) since January 2005. (European Community)

from Gaza on August 23, 2005, led Abbas to set PLC elections for January 25, 2006. When Hamas fared well in local elections in December 2005, Abbas sought to postpone the PLC elections. Ultimately, however, he proceeded with the scheduled January elections, in which Hamas won a majority of the seats in the PA Parliament and reduced Abbas's Fatah party to minority status.

Although Abbas remains as the PA president, Hamas controls the parliament, governmental services, and the security forces. Israel has made it clear that Abbas and the PA are expected to fulfill all agreements made prior to the 2006 elections, including the agreement to disarm Palestinian militants. The United States and many European countries withdrew their financial support of the PA in view of Hamas's refusal to disavow its commitment to the destruction of Israel. This financial crisis and Hamas's

militancy continue to challenge Abbas's leadership and presidency.

On March 17, 2007, Abbas brokered a Palestinian unity government that included members of both Hamas and Fatah in which Hamas leader Ismail Haniyeh became prime minister. Yet, beginning in May, violence between Hamas and Fatah escalated in the Gaza Strip. Following the Hamas takeover of Gaza on June 14, Abbas dissolved the Hamas-led unity government and declared a state of emergency. On June 18, having been assured of European Union support, he dissolved the National Security Council and swore in an emergency Palestinian government. That same day, the United States ended its 15-month embargo on the PA and resumed aid in an effort to strengthen Abbas's government, which was now limited to the West Bank. On June 19, Abbas cut off all ties and dialogue with Hamas, pending the return of Gaza. In a further move to strengthen the perceived moderate Abbas, on July 1 Israel restored financial ties to the PA.

In March 2008, after Israel threatened retaliation against rocket attacks from Gaza, Abbas suspended peace talks with Israel. In January 2009, on the expiration of his term as president, Abbas unilaterally extended his tenure, initially by a year, then indefinitely. In late 2013 he remained president, though Hamas-controlled Gaza refused to recognize his authority. He continued high-profile diplomatic activities intended to bolster his quest for an independent Palestinian state, hosting a visit in May 2009 by Pope Benedict XVI, who endorsed this objective, and visiting sympathetic nations, including Canada, Bolivia, and Japan. In July 2013, U.S. secretary of state John Kerry prevailed upon Abbas and Israel's Prime Minister Benyamin Netanyahu to begin direct talks, with the objective of reaching a complete settlement of all matters dividing the West Bank Palestinian Authority and Israel within nine months. Despite difficulties over new Israeli settlements, in November 2013, Abbas expressed faith that this timetable was attainable.

Richard M. Edwards

Further Reading

Abbas, Mahmoud. *Through Secret Channels: The Road to Oslo; Senior PLO Leader Abu Mazen's Revealing Story of the Negotiations with Israel.* Reading, UK: Garnet, 1997.

Cook, Jonathan. *Disappearing Palestine: Israel's Experiments in Human Despair.* London: Zed Books, 2008.

Daoud, Abu. *Memoirs of a Palestinian Terrorist.* New York: Arcade Publishing, 2002.

Gelvin, James M. *The Israel-Palestine Conflict: One Hundred Years of War.* 3rd ed. Cambridge: Cambridge University Press, 2014.

Ghanem, Assad. *Palestinian Politics after Arafat: A Failed National Movement.* Bloomington: Indiana University Press, 2010.

Klein, Menachem. *The Shift: Israel/Palestine from Border Struggle to Ethnic Conflict.* Translated by Chaim Weitzman. New York: Columbia University Press, 2010.

Makovsky, David. *Making Peace with the PLO: The Rabin Government's Road to the Oslo Accord.* Boulder, CO: Westview, 1996.

Morris, Benny. *One State, Two States: Resolving the Israel/Palestine Conflict.* New Haven: Yale University Press, 2009.

Pappé, Ilan. *A History of Modern Palestine: One Land, Two Peoples.* Cambridge: Cambridge University Press, 2003.

Parsons, Nigel Craig. *The Politics of the Palestinian Authority: From Oslo to Al-Aqsa.* 2nd ed. London: Routledge, 2012.

Pearlman, Wendy. *Violence, Nonviolence, and the Palestinian National Movement.* Cambridge: Cambridge University Press, 2011.

Rubin, Barry. *Revolution until Victory? The Politics and History of the PLO.* Reprint ed. Cambridge: Harvard University Press, 2003.

Schanzer, Jonathan. *State of Failure: Yasser Arafat, Mahmoud Abbas, and the Unmaking of the Palestinian State.* Basingstoke: Palgrave Macmillan, 2013.

Al Jazeera

The most popular news agency in the Arab world and its first large nongovernment-operated news network. Founded in 1996, Al Jazeera (Jazira) has become well known for its willingness to report on topics that are controversial in both the Middle East and in the Western media. Al Jazeera is based in Qatar but is staffed by an international body of reporters. It claims to be the only uncensored news agency in the Middle East. However, its commitment to presenting material and interviews that countered U.S. foreign policy in the Middle East and at times were sharply critical of Middle Eastern leaders or governments made it a focus of official displeasure from many governments, including those of the United States and Israel.

A computer screen image of Arab TV station Al Jazeera's English-language channel as made available on the Livestation Internet website. (AP Photo)

The Arabic term *al-Jazeera* (meaning "the island") is a colloquial reference to the Arabian Peninsula. Its origins are rooted in a response to the censorship and control in the Arab media on the part of political commentators and reporters and the recognition of the new market available through satellite television.

Although popular with many in the region, the British Broadcasting Corporation (BBC) has discontinued much of its programming there in recent years. Many of the journalists employed by the BBC were eager to continue broadcasting and, together with Sheikh Hamad bin Thamer al-Thani, approached the emir of Qatar for money to establish a new network. Al-Thani, a cousin of Emir Sheikh Hamad ibn Khalifa al-Thani, convinced the Qatari ruler to provide a grant of $150 million. This became the start-up money for Al Jazeera. The network continues to receive financial assistance from Qatar and is further funded by advertising revenue and by distributing its exclusive news feeds.

Despite the subsidy from Qatar, Al Jazeera set out to maintain a strict independence from censorship, which was previously almost unknown in the region. Al Jazeera chose as its corporate motto "the right to speak up." It also proclaimed to the world that it sought in its reporting "objectivity, accuracy, and a passion for truth."

Broadcasting via satellite since November 1996, Al Jazeera quickly became the most-watched media outlet in the Arab world. Unfettered by the official censorship of government-sponsored news reporting, Al Jazeera earned a reputation among its audience as a network committed to presenting multiple sides of any debate.

Al Jazeera became the first major news outlet in the Arabic-speaking Middle East to regularly present interviews with official Israeli spokesmen as well as with banned Islamist organizations and feminist groups. Al Jazeera has also been openly critical of events that illustrate dictatorial or authoritarian actions by the governments of Saudi Arabia, Egypt, Syria, and Iraq. Such diversity of opinion and outspoken criticism of oppression made Al Jazeera a popular force in the latter part of the 1990s. Broadening its appeal beyond the Arabic-speaking world, from 2006 onward a sister channel, Al Jazeera English, offered 24-hour broadcasts in English, an enterprise providing coverage that gained substantial audiences and credibility, as well as several prestigious press awards.

In 2001, Al Jazeera captured the attention of news audiences far beyond the Arabic-speaking world. When the dramatic terror attacks of September 11, 2001, were carried out against the United States, Al Jazeera broadcast footage of Osama bin Laden and Sulayman Abu Ghaith praising the carnage. Many in the West previously unfamiliar with Al Jazeera now immediately perceived the network as a mouthpiece for Al Qaeda. Al Jazeera vehemently rejected this charge, stating that it had merely presented news footage obtained in the interest of showing all sides in a major story. Nevertheless, the broadcast initiated a new barrage of attacks, particularly by the U.S. government, against Al Jazeera.

These were exacerbated by Al Jazeera's broadcasts of scenes of suffering experienced by Afghan civilians in the wake of the November 2001 invasion of their country by U.S. military forces, and its coverage of Iraqi resistance activities to the American military presence after the 2003 U.S. invasion. Although news organizations around the world purchased the rights to broadcast the footage from Al Jazeera, the George W. Bush administration was extremely critical of the network. The administration was outraged when Al Jazeera broadcasts claimed that it sponsored the perpetuation of terrorist ideals. News organizations throughout the world, however, were impressed with the unparalleled quality of the Afghan war coverage by Al Jazeera. Indeed, its feeds were widely purchased for rebroadcast.

Under attack from both the United States and Iraq in the days before the launch of the Iraq War, Al Jazeera became a symbol for what some viewed as hypocrisy in both Iraq and the United States over press freedom. As the invasion of Iraq progressed in 2003 and the occupation of Iraq took hold, Al Jazeera continued to provide some of the world's most controversial and in-depth reporting, and its feeds were rebroadcast on every continent. Despite its headquarters in Baghdad and Kabul being bombed by U.S. forces and pressure being exerted by Washington on the Qatari government to shut it down, Al Jazeera's reporting on Afghanistan and Iraq remained the most comprehensive in the world, and was often the only journalism focusing on the heart-wrenching experiences of local people coping with disaster. Al Jazeera continued to broadcast controversial missives from insurgents, including footage of Westerners held hostage, until the Iraqi interim government, with U.S. encouragement, banned the network from the country in September 2004.

Through extreme adversity and international controversy, Al Jazeera continues to be one of the most-watched news networks in the world, promoting itself as one of the only truly free voices in the Middle East. In 2008, and again in 2009, Israel imposed sanctions on Al Jazeera, charging that its coverage was biased in favor of the radical Hamas Palestinians who controlled Gaza. In 2009, the Palestinian National Authority briefly closed Al Jazeera's West Bank offices, after the organization publicized claims that President Mahmoud Abbas had been responsible for the death of Yasser Arafat. Al Jazeera reported in depth on the Arab Spring protests of 2010–2011, leading Egyptian security forces to close its offices in January 2011. In July 2013, 22 staff members at its Egyptian bureau resigned, claiming that Al Jazeera's coverage was biased in favor of the recently ousted Muslim Brotherhood president, Mohammed Morsi. By early 2013, comparable allegations that Al Jazeera reporting supported Muslim Brotherhood insurgents in Syria's ongoing civil war were also rife. Al Jazeera's readiness to oppose authoritarian governments and publicize dissent made it almost certain that for the indefinite future, its operations would continue to generate controversy across various fronts.

Nancy L. Stockdale

Further Reading

El-Nawawy, Mohammed, and Adel Iskander. *Al Jazeera: The Story of the Network that Is Rattling Governments and Redefining Journalism.* Boulder, CO: Westview, 2003.

Lynch, Marc. *Voices of the New Arab Public: Iraq, al-Jazeera, and Middle East Politics Today.* New York: Columbia University Press, 2006.

Miles, Hugh. *Al Jazeera: How Arab TV News Challenges America.* New York: Grove, 2005.

Rushing, Josh, with Sean Elder. *Mission Al-Jazeera: Build a Bridge, Seek the Truth, Change the World.* New York: Palgrave Macmillan, 2007.

Seib, Philip. *The Al Jazeera Effect: How the New Global Media are Reshaping World Politics.* Washington, DC: Potomac Books, 2008.

Seib, Philip, ed. *Al Jazeera English: Global News in a Changing World.* New York: Palgrave Macmillan, 2012.

Zayani, Mohamed, ed. *The Al Jazeera Phenomenon: Critical Perspectives on the New Arab Media.* Boulder, CO: Paradigm Publishers, 2005.

Zayani, Mohamed, and Sofiane Sahraoui. *The Culture of Al Jazeera: Inside an Arab Media Giant.* Jefferson, NC: McFarland, 2007.

Al Qaeda

International radical Islamic organization, the hallmark of which is the perpetration of terrorist attacks against Western interests in the name of Islam. In the late 1980s Al Qaeda (Arabic for "base" or "foundation") fought with the mujahideen against the Soviet occupation of Afghanistan. The organization is, however, best known for the September 11, 2001, terrorist attacks in the United States, the worst such attacks in the history of that nation. The founding of Al Qaeda, which comprises salafi (purist) Sunni Muslims, is shrouded in controversy.

Al Qaeda was created sometime between 1987 or 1988 by Sheikh Abdullah Azzam, a mentor to Osama bin Laden, who became the head of the group after Azzam's

Osama bin Laden (second from left) and his top lieutenant, Ayman al-Zawahiri (second from right), are shown at an undisclosed location with two unidentified men in this image, which was broadcast by Al Jazeera on October 7, 2001. (AP Photo)

assassination in November 1989. Azzam was a professor at King Abd al-Aziz University in Jidda, Saudi Arabia. Bin Laden attended that university, where he met and was strongly influenced by Azzam.

Al Qaeda grew out of the Mujahideen Services Bureau that Azzam established in Peshawar. Bin Laden funded the organization and was considered the deputy director. This organization recruited, trained, and transported Muslim volunteers from any Muslim nation into Afghanistan to fight the jihad (holy war) against the Soviet armies in the 1980s. Radical groups such as the Gamaat Islamiya and the Egyptian Islamic Jihad developed the credo for Al Qaeda, basing their beliefs in turn on many ideas including those of Sayyid Qutb, an executed member of the Muslim Brotherhood, and Abd al-Salam al-Faraj whose influential pamphlet *al-Farida al-Gha'iba* (The Missing Duty) asserted the primacy of armed jihad to overthrow apostate Muslim governments. Azzam adopted and expanded on these arguments, and bin Laden applied them to the government of Saudi Arabia, which he believed was too closely allied with the West. Thus, armed struggle should combat the far as well as the near enemy in order to create a new Islamic society. Following the mysterious death of Sheikh Azzam in November 1989, perhaps at bin Laden's behest, bin Laden took over the leadership of Al Qaeda. He continued to work toward Azzam's goal of creating an international organization comprising mujahideen (soldiers) who would fight the oppression of Muslims throughout the world. Al Qaeda actually has several goals: to destroy Israel, to rid the Islamic world of the influence of Western civilization, to reestablish an authentic form of government throughout the world, to fight against any government viewed as contrary to the ideals of Islamic law and religion, and to aid Islamic groups trying to establish an Islamic form of government in their countries.

The organization of Al Qaeda has a *majlis al-shura*, or consultative council form of leadership. From late 1989 until his death in May 2011, the *emir al-mu'minin* (commander of the faithful) was bin Laden, followed by several other generals, and then additional leaders of related groups. Some sources say there were 24 related groups as part of the consultative council. The council consists of four committees: military, religious–legal, finance, and media. Each leader of these committees was reportedly selected personally by bin Laden and reported directly to him. After bin Laden's death, Ayman al-Zawahiri, the organization's former Deputy Operations Chief, succeeded him as commander. Experts currently differ over just how centralized the organization still remains, or whether it has fragmented into several largely independent groups. All levels of Al Qaeda are highly compartmentalized, and secrecy is the key to all operations.

Al Qaeda's ideology has appealed to both Middle Eastern and non–Middle Eastern Muslim groups. There are also a number of radical Islamic terrorist groups who initiated an association with Al Qaeda via public declarations, such as Al Qaeda fi Bilad al-Rafidhayn (in the land of the two rivers, meaning Iraq) and Al Qaeda fi Jazirat al-Arabiyya (of the Arabian Peninsula). Nevertheless, Al Qaeda continues to be the central force of world terrorism because of the media attention given to its occasional pronouncements.

The genesis of Al Qaeda's great antipathy toward the West—in particular the United States—can be traced back to the Persian Gulf War (1991), precipitated by the Iraqi invasion of Kuwait in August 1990. Bin Laden, originally a well-to-do Saudi Arabian, allegedly offered to commit Al Qaeda mujahideen fighters to the defense of Saudi Arabia in case of an Iraqi move on that nation. The Saudi government declined the offer and instead decided to permit the stationing of thousands of U.S. and coalition soldiers in Saudi Arabia during the run-up to the war. This move enraged bin Laden, who perceived the presence of foreign troops in Saudi Arabia as a blatant acknowledgment of the political linkage between his government and the United States. He portrayed this as a religious failing. Saudi Arabia is home to both Mecca and Medina, the holiest of places in all of Islam. When he condemned the stationing of troops in Saudi Arabia, bin Laden was expelled from the kingdom and had his citizenship revoked. He then took up temporary residence in the Sudan.

Once in Sudan, bin Laden began training Al Qaeda fighters and is believed to have carried out an abortive assassination attempt against Egyptian president Hosni Mubarak in 1994. Under intense international pressure led by the United States, Sudan expelled bin Laden and Al Qaeda leadership in late 1996. From Sudan, they traveled directly to Afghanistan, where the Islamic fundamentalist Taliban regime had already ensconced itself. The Taliban not only protected Al Qaeda but in all probability helped arm it and by doing so gave to it an air of legitimacy, at least in Afghanistan. In 1998, bin Laden joined forces with leaders from the Egyptian Islamic Jihad and several other radical organizations, all of whom vowed to wage a holy war against Israel and its allies. In August of that year, Al Qaeda carried out what are thought to be its first overseas attacks against Western interests. That month saw the car bombing of the U.S. embassies in Dar es Salaam, Tanzania, and Nairobi, Kenya. More than 200 people died in the attacks, and another 4,000 were wounded. In October 2000, Al Qaeda also carried out an attack on the U.S. Navy's guided missile destroyer *Cole* in the Yemeni port of Aden in which 17 sailors perished.

No attacks by Al Qaeda are known to have occurred against Israel, but the group's most horrific deed was the September 11, 2001, attacks on the United States that killed an estimated 2,976 people. The attacks were carried out by the hijacking of four jetliners, two of which were flown into New York City's World Trade Center, destroying both towers. A third jetliner was crashed into the Pentagon outside Washington, D.C., while a fourth, supposedly bound for the White House, crashed in a western Pennsylvania field, killing all onboard.

In the aftermath of these attacks, what U.S. president George W. Bush termed the war on terror achieved significant success in tracking down and either capturing or killing the Al Qaeda leadership. The most spectacular coup was a May 2011 raid by U.S. Special Forces personnel on a compound in Abbottabad, Pakistan, in which Osama bin Laden was killed.

Bin Laden was able to enlist many of the radical Islamic terrorist groups under the umbrella of Al Qaeda, so that its leadership spread throughout the world, and its influence penetrated many religious, social, and economic structures in most Muslim communities. While most Arab and Muslim governments tried to distance themselves from Al Qaeda and its operations, the group undoubtedly enjoys support among significant elements of the populations of these countries. The membership of Al Qaeda remains difficult to determine because of its decentralized organizational structure.

American and British officials tried to justify the 2003 Anglo-American invasion of Iraq with unfounded allegations that President Saddam Hussein of Iraq had close ties to Al Qaeda. Ironically, after his overthrow, Al Qaeda was believed to be supporting the growing insurgency in Iraq, which became a full-blown civil war during 2006. Al Qaeda adherents are normally members of the Sunni branch of Islam, and are highly intolerant of the rival Shiite sect, whose worshippers constitute the majority of the population in Iraq, Iran, and Syria. (Al Qaeda is equally hostile to liberal Islam and Sufism.) In Iraq, for several years Al Qaeda activists therefore mounted numerous suicide attacks on Shiite mosques, shrines, and holy places, with death tolls in double or even treble figures not uncommon.

As Al Qaeda was driven from some of its once safe havens in the 2000s, the organization turned to Yemen, which growing political disorder transformed into a sanctuary for all varieties of Muslim insurgents. As early as the late 1990s, Al Qaeda had mounted operations in Yemen. Although President Ali Abdullah Saleh assured U.S. president George W. Bush of Yemen's support in the War on Terror, in June 2004 a Shia insurgency against the government began. When fuel prices soared in 2005, violent protests ensued. In 2007 and 2008, suicide bombers attacked foreign tourists and businesses, diplomats, and Yemeni government officials and police. In Saudi Arabia, the conservative government was largely successful in suppressing Al Qaeda activities, driving its operatives to take refuge in Yemen. In 2009, Al Qaeda personnel in Yemen and Saudi Arabia merged, to form Al Qaeda in the Arabian Peninsula (AQAP), many of whose members had previously been imprisoned at the U.S. Guantánamo Bay facility.

Besides launching attacks on Saudi and Yemeni targets, AQAP called for renewed holy war against Israel and the imposition of a blockade on all sea traffic with Israel. In 2009 and 2010, Yemen's government launched a new offensive against the Shiite insurgents, a campaign in which AQAP groups assisted Yemeni military forces. From 2009 onward, the United States launched air strikes and drone attacks against suspected AQAP targets in Yemen. In February 2012, on the day a new president took office in Yemen, AQAP mounted a suicide attack on the presidential palace, killing 26. President Barack Obama deployed U.S. military, intelligence, and Special Forces personnel to Yemen and stepped up economic assistance. By late 2012 the government had largely succeeded in driving back AQAP forces, but the situation in Yemen remained precarious.

Al Qaeda militants were also active in the civil war that began in Syria in 2011, supporting the insurgents who sought to overthrow the government of President Bashar al-Assad. While their destabilizing presence was no longer welcome in Saudi Arabia, in Syria they received considerable financial and logistical support from the Saudi government, which sought to restrain the growing power of both Syria and its ally, Iran. Given the region's complicated politics, it seems likely that Al Qaeda will for the indefinite future remain a significant force in Middle Eastern politics. If circumstances permit, Al Qaeda adherents will undoubtedly seize any opportunity that may be offered to try to overturn any Palestinian-Israeli settlement.

Harry Raymond Hueston

Further Reading

Atwan, Abdel Bari. *After bin Laden: Al Qaeda, the Next Generation*. New York: New Press, 2012.

Bergen, Peter L. *Holy War, Inc.* New York: Touchstone, 2002.

Berner, Brad K. *The World According to Al Qaeda*. Charleston, SC: Booksurge, 2005.

Burke, Jason. *Al-Qaeda: The True Story of Radical Islam*. New York: I.B. Tauris, 2004.

Chaliand, Gérard, and Arnaud Blin, eds. *The History of Terrorism: From Antiquity to al Qaeda*. Berkeley: University of California Press, 2007.

Clark, Victoria. *Yemen: Dancing on the Heads of Snakes*. New Haven, CT: Yale University Press, 2010.

Gerges, Fawaz A. *The Rise and Fall of Al-Qaeda*. New York: Oxford University Press, 2011.

Gray, John. *Al Qaeda and What It Means to Be Modern*. New York: New Press, 2003.

Gunaratna, Rohan. *Inside Al Qaeda*. New York: Columbia University Press, 2002.

Habeck, Mary. *Knowing the Enemy: Jihadist Ideology and the War on Terror*. New Haven, CT: Yale University Press, 2007.

Hueston, Harry R., and B. Vizzin. *Terrorism 101*. 2nd ed. Ann Arbor, MI: XanEdu, 2004.

Hull, Edmund J. *High-Value Target: Countering Al Qaeda in Yemen*. Washington, DC: Potomac Books, 2011.

Ibrahim, Raymond, ed. *The Al Qaeda Reader: The Essential Texts of Osama Bin Laden's Terrorist Organization*. Louisville, KY: Broadway Press, 2007.

Johnsen, Gregory D. *The Last Refuge: Yemen, Al-Qaeda, and America's War in Arabia*. New York: Norton, 2012.

Riedel, Bruce. *The Search for Al Qaeda: Its Leadership, Ideology, and Future*. Rev. ed. Washington, DC: Brookings Institution, 2010.

Rose, Gideon, and Jonathan Tepperman, eds. *The U.S. vs. al Qaeda: A History of the War on Terror*. New York: Council on Foreign Relations, 2011.

Schmitt, Eric, and Tom Shanker. *Counterstrike: The Untold Story of America's Secret Campaign against Al Qaeda*. New York: Times Books, 2011.

Silber, Mitchell D. *The Al Qaeda Factor: Plots against the West*. Philadelphia: University of Pennsylvania Press, 2011.

Soufan, Ali H., with Daniel Freedman. *The Black Banners: The Inside Story of 9/11 and the War Against al-Qaeda*. New York: Norton, 2011.

Van Linschoten, Alex Strick, and Felix Kuehn. *An Enemy We Created: The Myth of the Taliban-Al Qaeda Merger in Afghanistan*. New York: Oxford University Press, 2012.

Wright, Lawrence. *The Looming Tower: Al-Qaeda and the Road to 9/11*. New York: Knopf, 2006.

Zuhur, Sherifa. *A Hundred Osamas: Islamist Threats and the Future of Counterinsurgency*. Carlisle Barracks, PA: Strategic Studies Institute, U.S. Army War College, 2006.

Algeria

Northwest African nation, almost 920,000 square miles in area. Algeria is bordered to the west by Morocco and Mauritania, to the north by the Mediterranean Sea, to the east by Tunisia and Libya, and to the south by Niger and Mali. Algeria was originally peopled by Berbers (who still make up a sizable national minority) but is now predominantly Arab. In 1830, France seized Algiers, and from then until 1847 it expanded its North African holdings to the interior in a protracted war that created modern Algeria, which was absorbed into France's metropolitan administrative structure in 1848.

French colonizers and their descendants (known as colons) dispossessed native Algerians of the best arable lands and monopolized political power. The non-European population worked the colons' lands or eked out a meager living in the less hospitable areas. By 1945, Algeria's population included approximately 900,000 colons. Arabs totaled perhaps eight times that number.

The postwar era saw the rapid growth of a militant nationalist movement opposed adamantly by the colons, who were determined that Algeria should remain part of France. In May 1945, Muslims throughout Algeria demonstrated against colonial rule. When French colonial police fired on the protesters in Sétif, they responded by attacking Europeans. In retaliation, the military carried out reprisals that killed thousands of Algerian Muslims. This massacre accelerated the conflict that culminated in the brutal Algerian War during 1954–1962.

From the beginning of the war, the Front de Libération Nationale (FLN) appealed to the United Nations (UN) for support of the nationalist cause, while France appealed to the United States and its European allies for assistance in its colonial claim. The Americans initially urged a negotiated peace, hoping to avoid a confrontation with France without antagonizing Arab nations. Convinced that Egypt was providing substantial assistance to the FLN, the French government joined with the governments of Britain and Israel in an attempt to overthrow Egyptian president Gamal Abdel Nasser in 1956. The ensuing Suez Crisis miscarried, thanks to U.S. government opposition. Exercised over the French role in the Suez Crisis, the United States then adopted a less compromising line with France, determined to prevent a wider conflict between Arab nationalists and France (and Britain). The Algerian War also split the communist bloc, with the People's Republic of China (PRC) supporting the Algerian nationalists and the Soviet Union keeping its distance.

The war actively influenced French politics and led to social and political turmoil in metropolitan France that toppled the Fourth French Republic in May 1958 and brought to power General Charles de Gaulle, who

Abdelaziz Bouteflika became Algeria's first civilian president in more than 30 years after winning the April 1999 elections in which all other candidates withdrew on the eve of the poll to protest fraud in early voting. (UN Photo)

created the Fifth French Republic. De Gaulle, then president of France, having exhausted other options, signed the Evian Agreements of March 1962 that granted Algeria its independence effective July 3. Within the span of a few months, most of the more than 1 million colons as well as some 91,000 harkis, pro-French Muslims who had served in the French army, immigrated to France.

The FLN-led Algerian government, headed by Prime Minister Muhammad Ben Bella, promptly confiscated the colons' abandoned property and established a decentralized socialist economy and a one-party state. The government collectivized land and began an aggressive campaign to industrialize the country.

Ben Bella's attempt to consolidate his power, combined with popular discontent with an inefficient economy, sparked a bloodless military coup by Defense Minister Houari Boumédienne in June 1965. In 1971,

the government endeavored to stimulate economic growth by nationalizing the oil industry and investing the revenues in centrally orchestrated industrial development. In the years that followed his seizure of power, Boumédienne's military-dominated government took on an increasingly authoritarian cast. The military expanded rapidly during the 1970s and 1980s, and by 1985 the army numbered 110,000, the air force 12,000, and the navy 8,000 men.

Algeria's leaders sought to retain their autonomy, joining their country to the Non-Aligned Movement. Boumédienne phased out French military bases. Although Algeria denounced perceived U.S. imperialism and supported Cuba, the communists in South Vietnam, Palestinian nationalists, and African anticolonial fighters, it maintained a strong trading relationship with the United States. At the same time, Algeria cultivated economic ties with the Soviet Union, which provided Algeria with important military material and training.

When the Spanish relinquished control of Western Sahara in 1976, Morocco attempted to annex the region. This led to a 12-year war with Algeria, which supported the guerrilla movement fighting for the region's independence. Diplomatic relations with the United States warmed after Algeria negotiated the release of U.S. hostages in Iran in 1980 and Morocco fell out of U.S. favor by allying with Libya in 1984.

Before independence, Algeria had a Jewish population of around 140,000, concentrated in the larger cities and towns. After independence the numbers declined to 6,500, with 130,000 moving to France and a further 25,681 immigrating to Israel from 1948 onward. In the early postindependence period, Algeria was too absorbed in its own internal problems to take much interest or participate actively in the Arab-Israeli conflict, although as an Arab state it did lend strong verbal support to the Palestinians. During the 1973 Yom Kippur War, Algeria did not commit ground troops, but it did supply two squadrons of MiG-21 fighters and a squadron of Su-7B fighter-bombers to Egypt. These aircraft were simply incorporated into Egyptian units.

Algeria had close and longstanding ties with the Palestine Liberation Organization (PLO), whose leaders viewed Algeria's struggle against France as a model for themselves. From the 1970s onward it welcomed visits by PLO leader Yasser Arafat and provided military training and arms to PLO fighters. In 1974, a Palestinian embassy was established in Algeria. After the 1979 Camp David Accords making peace between Egypt and Israel were signed, Algeria broke diplomatic relations with Egypt.

In 1976, a long-promised constitution that provided for elections was enacted, although

Algeria remained a one-party state. When Boumédienne died in December 1978, power passed to Chadli Bendjedid, the army-backed candidate. Bendjedid retreated from Boumédienne's increasingly ineffective economic policies, privatizing much of the economy and encouraging entrepreneurship. However, accumulated debt continued to retard economic expansion. Growing public protests from labor unions, students, and Islamic fundamentalists forced the government to end restrictions on political expression in 1988.

The Islamic Salvation Front (Front Islamique du Salut, FIS) proved the most successful of the host of new political parties founded. Bendjedid resigned after large victories by the FIS in local elections in June 1990 and national elections in December 1991, and a new regime under Mohamed Boudiaf imposed martial law, banning the FIS in March 1992. In response, Islamist radicals began a guerrilla war in which more than 160,000 people perished during 1992–2002, most of them innocent civilians. By 2002, the fighting was largely over, thanks to government action and an amnesty program, although some violence continued thereafter. Elections resumed in 1995, and in April 1999, following several short-term leaders representing the military, Abdelaziz Bouteflika was elected president.

In late December 2010 countrywide protests and demonstrations began, demanding political, constitutional, social, and economic reform. In late February 2011 Bouteflika responded by lifting the 19-year-old state of emergency and enacting legislation giving greater freedom in terms of political parties, electoral reform, and the representation of women. Parliamentary elections that international monitors considered relatively free took place in May 2012. The FLN won 221 seats, the military-backed National

Rally for Democracy 70, and the Islamic Green Alliance 47.

Its own political turmoil notwithstanding, in the international arena, Algeria remained staunchly aligned with the Palestinian cause. When the First Intifada erupted in the occupied territories in 1987, Algeria convened an emergency Arab League meeting that offered financial aid to the insurgents. When the PLO issued a Declaration of Independence on November 15, 1988, Algeria became the first country to recognize this new state, doing so the same day. Algeria strongly endorsed both the 1993 Oslo Accords and the 2002 Arab Peace Initiative, which demanded Israel's withdrawal from all the occupied territories and the establishment of an independent Palestinian state. Like most Arab leaders, Algerian presidents Liamine Zeroual and Abdelaziz Bouteflika both sought to encourage the peace process.

By late 2013, Algeria still had not opened diplomatic relations with Israel. In October 2009, the government cancelled a deal to purchase arms from France, on the grounds that some of this weaponry might include Israeli-made parts. Algeria condemned Israel's 2008–2009 invasion and subsequent blockade of Gaza, as well as the November 2012 Operation PILLAR OF DEFENSE, as breaches of international law, and urged the UN to take action to end "Israeli aggression against Gaza." In November 2012, Algeria voted in favor of UN General Assembly Resolution 67/19 granting Palestine non-member observer state status in the UN.

Elun Gabriel and Spencer C. Tucker

Further Reading

Evans, Martin. *Algeria: France's Undeclared War.* New York: Oxford University Press, 2012.

Le Sueur, James D. *Algeria since 1989: Between Terror and Democracy.* London: Zed Books, 2010.

Lowi, Miriam R. *Oil Wealth and the Poverty of Politics: Algeria Compared.* Cambridge: Cambridge University Press, 2009.

Phillips, John, and Martin Evans. *Algeria: Anger of the Dispossessed.* New Haven: Yale University Press, 2008.

Roberts, Hugh. *The Battlefield: Algeria 1988–2002, Studies in a Broken Polity.* London: Verso, 2003.

Ruedy, John. *Modern Algeria: The Origins and Development of a Nation.* 2nd ed. Bloomington: Indiana University Press, 2005.

Stora, Benjamin. *Algeria, 1830–2000: A Short History.* Translated by Jane Marie Todd. Ithaca, NY: Cornell University Press, 2001.

Willis, Michael. *Politics and Power in the Maghreb: Algeria, Tunisia and Morocco from Independence to the Arab Spring.* New York: Columbia University Press, 2012.

Arab League

The Arab League, also called the League of Arab States, is a voluntary organization of Arabic-speaking nations. It was founded at the end of World War II with the stated purposes of improving conditions in Arab countries, liberating Arab states still under foreign domination, and preventing the formation of a Jewish state in Palestine.

In 1943, the Egyptian government proposed an organization of Arab states that would facilitate closer relations between the nations without forcing any of them to lose self-rule. Each member would remain a sovereign state, and the organization would not be a union, a federation, or any other sovereign structure. The British government supported this idea in the hopes of securing the Arab nations as allies in the war against Germany.

In 1944, representatives from Egypt, Iraq, Lebanon, Yemen, and Saudi Arabia met in Alexandria, Egypt, and agreed to form a

Saudi Arabian foreign minister Prince Saud ibn Faisal al-Saud (right) speaks to the press as Lebanese foreign minister Mahmud Hammud (center) and Arab League secretary general Amre Moussa (left) listen during a press conference given on the final day of the Arab League Summit in Beirut on March 28, 2002. (AFP/Getty Images)

federation. The Arab League was officially founded on March 22, 1945, in Cairo. The founding states were Egypt, Iraq, Lebanon, Saudi Arabia, Transjordan, and Syria. Subsequent members include Libya (1953), Sudan (1956), Tunisia (1958), Morocco (1958), Kuwait (1961), Algeria (1962), South Yemen (1967, now Yemen), Bahrain (1971), Oman (1971), Qatar (1971), United Arab Emirates (1971), Mauritania (1973), Somalia (1974), Djibouti (1977), and Comoros (1993).

The original goals of the Arab League were to liberate all Arab nations still ruled by foreign countries and to prevent the creation of a Jewish state in Palestine as well as to serve the common good, improve living conditions, and guarantee the hopes of member states. In 1946, Arab League members added to their pact a cultural treaty under which they agreed to exchange professors, teachers, students, and scholars in order to encourage cultural exchange among member nations and to disseminate Arab culture to their citizens.

The Arab League's pact also stated that all members would collectively represent the Palestinians so long as Palestine was not an independent state. With no Palestinian leader in 1945, the Arab states feared that the British would dominate the area and that Jews would colonize part of Palestine. In response to these fears, the Arab League created the Arab Higher Committee (AHC) to govern Palestinian Arabs in 1945. This committee was replaced in 1946 by the Arab Higher Executive, which was again reorganized into a new Arab Higher Executive in 1947.

The State of Israel was declared on May 14, 1948. The next day Egypt, Iraq,

Lebanon, Saudi Arabia, Syria, and Transjordan responded with a declaration of war on Israel. Yemen also supported the declaration. Secretary General Abdul Razek Azzam Pasha declared that the Arab League's goal was to conduct a large-scale massacre and extermination. Although King Abdullah of Jordan (he officially changed the name of Transjordan to Jordan in April 1949) claimed to be the legitimate power in Palestine, the Arab League did not wish to see Jordan in control of the area and thus established its own government on behalf of the Palestinians, the All-Palestine State of October 1, 1948. The mufti of Jerusalem, Haj Amin al-Husseini, was its leader, and Jerusalem was its capital. Although ostensibly the new government ruled Gaza, Egypt was the real authority there. In response, Jordan formed a rival temporary government, the First Palestinian Congress, which condemned the government in Gaza. The Israeli War of Independence ended in 1949, with Jordan occupying the West Bank and East Jerusalem and Egypt controlling Gaza.

In 1950, the Arab League signed the Joint Defense and Economic Cooperation Treaty, which declared that the members of the league considered an attack on one member country to be an attack on all. The treaty created a permanent military commission and a joint defense council.

During the 1950s, Egypt effectively led the Arab League. In 1952, a military coup in Egypt nominally headed by General Muhammad Nagib overthrew King Farouk, but within two years Colonel Gamal Abdel Nasser assumed rule of the nation. A strong proponent of Arab unity, he called for a union of all Arab nations, including Palestine. Nasser ended the All-Palestine government in Palestine, formed the United Arab Republic with Syria, and called for the defeat of Israel.

In 1956, Nasser nationalized the Suez Canal, precipitating the Suez Crisis that brought an Israeli invasion of the Sinai followed by short-lived British and French invasions of Egypt. U.S. economic and political pressures secured the withdrawal of the invaders. Far from toppling Nasser, as the allied British, French, and Israeli governments had hoped, these pressures both strengthened Nasser's prestige in the Arab world and raised the stature of Pan-Arabism and the Arab League.

In the 1960s the Arab League pushed for the liberation of Palestine, and in 1964 it supported creation of the Palestine Liberation Organization (PLO), which was dedicated to attacks on Israel. Following the Six-Day War of 1967, which ended in extensive territory losses for Egypt, Jordan, and Syria, the Arab League met at Khartoum that August and issued a statement in which its members vowed not to recognize, negotiate with, or conclude a peace agreement with Israel. Egypt also agreed to withdraw its troops from Yemen.

The Arab League suspended Egypt's membership in 1979 in the wake of President Anwar Sadat's visit to Jerusalem and agreement to the 1978 Camp David Peace Accords. The league also moved its headquarters from Cairo to Tunis. When the PLO declared an independent State of Palestine on November 15, 1988, the Arab League immediately recognized it. Egypt was readmitted to the league in 1989, and the headquarters returned to Cairo. In the 1990s, the Arab League continued its efforts to resolve the Israeli-Palestine dispute in the Palestinians' favor.

At an Arab League meeting in Beirut in March 2002, Crown Prince Abdullah of Saudi Arabia put forward the Arab Peace Initiative, a comprehensive proposal for a permanent settlement. This called for complete Israeli withdrawal from the occupied territories, the creation of an independent Palestinian state with East Jerusalem as its capital, and a "just solution" to the problem of Palestinian refugees. In return, all Arab states would sign permanent peace treaties with Israel, recognizing its existence. The Arab League unanimously accepted this proposal, albeit with reservations on the part of some states, including Syria, on the right of the Palestinians to continue armed resistance.

In 2003, the Arab League voted to demand the unconditional removal of U.S. and British troops from Iraq. The lone dissenting voice was the tiny nation of Kuwait, which had been liberated by a U.S.-led coalition in the 1991 Persian Gulf War. Meeting in Riyadh, Saudi Arabia, in March 2007, the Arab League again called for the withdrawal of U.S. military forces from Iraq, at that time beset by insurgencies that were approaching civil war.

At this same meeting, hosted by Abdullah, now king of Saudi Arabia, the Arab League reaffirmed its commitment to the Arab Peace Initiative. UN secretary general Ban Ki-moon and European foreign policy commissioner Xavier Solana, both of whom attended this meeting, also endorsed it, as did President Mahmoud Abbas of the Palestinian Authority, though the Hamas representative abstained. Little progress on the Arab Peace Initiative occurred during the first administration of U.S. president Barack Obama, but in July 2013 U.S. secretary of state John Kerry sought to revive it, persuading Israel and Palestine to reopen negotiations aimed at reaching a final settlement within nine months. The Arab League supported this initiative. In late 2013, it remained unclear whether these talks would be more successful than earlier efforts to bring about a final status agreement between Israel and the West Bank Palestinian Authority.

Amy Hackney Blackwell

Further Reading

Hourani, Albert, and Malise Ruthven. *A History of the Arab Peoples*. 2nd ed. Cambridge: Harvard University Press, 2010.

McHugo, John. *A Concise History of the Arabs*. London: Saqi, 2013.

Rogan, Eugene. *The Arabs: A History*. 2nd rev. ed. New York: Penguin, 2012.

Smith, Charles D. *Palestine and the Arab-Israeli Conflict: A History with Documents*. 8th ed. New York: Bedford/St. Martin's Press, 2012.

Toffolo, Cris E. *The Arab League*. New York: Chelsea House, 2008.

Arab Spring

The term "Arab Spring" refers to a wave of popular protests and demonstrations, beginning in Tunisia in December 2010, which swept rapidly throughout North Africa and the Middle East in 2011 and 2012. Although responding in part to economic difficulties, including rising fuel and food costs and high unemployment, protesters generally also rebelled against repressive, authoritarian, and corrupt governments, demanding more open political systems. Most expressed frustration with regimes that were often effectively one-party systems or family dictatorships.

The precise form and course of protests varied across different countries, as did the responses of different governments. Jordan, Algeria, Iraq, Kuwait, and Morocco all experienced significant protests and unrest, which resulted in the implementation of a range of political, economic, and social reforms and constitutional changes. In Tunisia and Egypt, expressions of popular discontent were so widespread and intense that within weeks they forced the president then in power from office and brought the overhaul of the political system. In Yemen, the process was slower, extending over the

Thousands of Syrians wave their national flag and hold portraits of President Bashar al-Assad (portrait L) and Lebanon's Hezbollah chief Hassan Nasrallah (portrait R) during a rally to show support for their leader, who faced unprecedented domestic pressure amid a wave of dissent, in Damascus on March 29, 2011. (AFP/Getty Images)

better part of a year, and further complicated by long-term sectarian violence from two rival groups of Muslim insurgents, one Shiite, the other the Sunni Al Qaeda in the Arab Peninsula.

While many Arab governments eventually made at least some concessions to protesters, others were determined to repress all dissent, using whatever force might be needed for the purpose. In both Libya and Syria, opposition to the entrenched one-party governments of Colonel Muammar Gaddafi and President Bashar al-Assad was met by government military crackdowns. In both cases, a brutal and violent civil war was the result. In Libya, estimates of the numbers killed between February and October 2011 ranged from several thousand to 50,000 or more. United Nations declaration of a "no-fly zone" and air strikes by Western NATO forces played a significant part in the

relatively swift resolution of the war, which ended in Gaddafi's capture and execution.

In Syria, civil war began in March 2011 and was still continuing in late 2013. The Syrian conflict proved a magnet for Islamic militia forces of different complexions, while the international community divided over whether to support the government or the rebels. Militia units from Hezbollah and the Muslim Brotherhood, long-time allies of the Syrian government and its president, Bashar al-Assad, rallied to its support, as did Russia and Iran. Al Qaeda forces with backing from Saudi Arabia, by contrast, threw their lot in with the rebels. While calling on al-Assad to negotiate, the United States declined to intervene militarily. By September 2013 over 120,000 Syrians had reportedly been killed, while 6.5 million were refugees, 2 million of whom sought safety outside Syria. By late 2013 the balance appeared to be tilting in favor of the rebels, but the outcome was still far from certain.

Initially, many outside commentators, especially Westerners, hailed the Arab Spring with delight, believing that it would usher in the swift and near painless spread of democracy throughout the Middle East and Arab world. Many also hoped that any new governments that emerged would be liberal in outlook, committed to supporting human and civil rights, including women's rights and religious freedom, political transparency, democracy, equality, and the cause of peace. Yet it soon became clear that the governments that emerged from the upheavals of 2011 might well be strictly limited in terms of democracy and liberal values, and that the reforms that were implemented, far from representing a wholesale remodeling of the entire political, social, and economic fabric, would often be rather limited in scope.

Moreover, not all the political forces unleashed by the Arab Spring were liberal or secular in nature. In Egypt, Jordan, and Algeria, for example, for decades governments had sought to discourage sectarian Islamic political parties, for fear that allowing religious extremists too much influence might prove politically destabilizing, both domestically and externally. In Egypt, in particular, the overthrow of President Hosni Mubarak in February 2011 opened the way for Mohamed Morsi, an official of the Muslim Brotherhood, to gain the presidency in July 2012. Within months, he sought to implement drastic increases in his own powers, which many feared marked the beginning of a new dictatorship. After several months of ever larger demonstrations in which millions of Egyptians ultimately participated, in July 2013, the Egyptian military finally ousted Morsi, installing a caretaker president until a new constitution could be drafted and new elections held. In Jordan and Algeria, constitutional reforms meant that Islamic political parties also made some gains. Given that sectarian extremism enjoyed significant political support among the general population on the "Arab street," greater democracy might even inflame such issues as the ongoing Israeli-Palestinian disputes.

In some cases, especially in Libya and Syria, and perhaps Yemen, the fighting and violence that characterized the Arab Spring were in themselves destabilizing, unleashing tribal and other antagonisms and rivalries that were liable to continue indefinitely. And, just as in Iraq and Afghanistan in the early 21st century, in those states outside groups and elements that participated in the fighting might well stay on and become political forces to reckon with in their host countries. The initial optimism that the Arab Spring betokened an era in which democracy and liberalism would spread swiftly and benignly throughout the Middle East, transforming the region permanently for the better, soon came to seem premature and misplaced. While change might indeed be on the agenda, progress in the broad direction of civil society was, it seemed, likely to be slow and somewhat erratic in nature.

Priscilla Roberts

Further Reading

Achcar, Gilbert. *The People Want: A Radical Exploration of the Arab Uprising.* Translated by G. M. Goshgarian. Berkeley: University of California Press, 2013.

Ahmari, Sohrab, and Nasser Weddady, eds. *Arab Spring Dreams: The Next Generation Speaks Out for Freedom and Justice from North Africa to Iran.* New York: Palgrave Macmillan, 2012.

Al-faqih, Abdullah. *Liberalization and Democratization in Egypt, Jordan, and Yemen: Beginnings, Development, and Decline.*

Saarbrücken, Germany: VDM Verlag Dr. Müller, 2013.

Amar, Paul, and Vijay Prashad, eds. *Dispatches from the Arab Spring: Understanding the New Middle East*. Minneapolis: University of Minnesota Press, 2013.

Beinin, Joel, and Frederic Vairel, eds. *Social Movements, Mobilization, and Contestation in the Middle East and North Africa*. Stanford: Stanford University Press, 2011.

Bradley, John R. *After the Arab Spring: How Islamists Hijacked the Middle East Revolts*. New York: Palgrave Macmillan, 2012.

Council on Foreign Relations and Foreign Affairs. *The New Arab Revolt: What Happened, What It Means, and What Comes Next*. New York: Council on Foreign Relations, 2011.

Dabashi, Hamid. *The Arab Spring: The End of Postcolonialism*. London: Zed Books, 2012.

Danahar, Paul. *The New Middle East: The World after the Arab Spring*. London: Bloomsbury, 2013.

Darwish, Nonie. *The Devil We Don't Know: The Dark Side of Revolutions in the Middle East*. New York: Wiley, 2012.

Dawisha, Aweed. *The Second Arab Awakening: Revolution, Democracy, and the Islamist Challenge from Tunis to Damascus*. New York: Norton, 2013.

Feiler, Bruce. *Generation Freedom: The Middle Eastern Uprisings and the Remaking of the Modern World*. New York: William Morrow, 2011.

Gelvin, James L. *The Arab Uprisings: What Everyone Needs to Know*. New York: Oxford University Press, 2012.

Haddad, Basham, Rosie Bsheer, and Ziad Abu Rish, eds. *The Dawn of the Arab Uprisings: End of an Old Order?* London: Pluto Press, 2012.

Jamshidi, Maryam. *The Future of the Arab Spring: Civic Entrepreneurship in Politics, Art, and Technology Startups*. New York: Butterworth-Heinemann, 2013.

Korany, Bahgat, and Rabab El Mahdi, eds. *Arab Spring in Egypt: Revolution and Beyond*. Cairo: The American University in Cairo Press, 2012.

Lynch, Marc. *The Arab Uprising: The Unfinished Revolutions of the New Middle East*. New York: PublicAffairs, 2012.

McCarthy, Andrew C. *Spring Fever: The Illusion of Islamic Democracy*. Jackson, TN: Encounter Books, 2013.

Mirak-Weissbach, Muriel. *Madmen at the Helm: Pathology and Politics in the Arab Spring*. Reading, UK: Ithaca Press, 2012.

Noueihed, Lynn, and Alex Warren. *The Battle for the Arab Spring: Revolution, Counter-Revolution and the Making of a New Era*. New Haven, CT: Yale University Press, 2012.

Owen, Roger. *The Rise and Fall of Arab Presidents for Life*. Cambridge, MA: Harvard University Press, 2012.

Pargeter, Alison. *The Muslim Brotherhood: From Opposition to Power*. New ed. London: Saqi Books, 2013.

Peters, Joel, ed. *The European Union and the Arab Spring: Promoting Democracy and Human Rights in the Middle East*. Lanham, MD: Lexington Books, 2012.

Petras, James. *The Arab Revolt and the Imperialist Counterattack*. 2nd ed. Atlanta, CA: Clarity Press, 2012.

Pollack, Kenneth M., et al. *The Arab Awakening: America and the Transformation of the Middle East*. Washington, DC: Brookings Institution Press, 2011.

Prashad, Vijay. *Arab Spring, Libyan Winter*. Oakland, CA: AK Press, 2012.

Ramadan, Tariq. *Islam and the Arab Awakening*. New York: Oxford University Press, 2012.

Telhami, Shibley. *The World through Arab Eyes: Arab Public Opinion and the Reshaping of the Middle East*. New York: Basic Books, 2013.

Thompson, Elizabeth F. *Justice Interrupted: The Struggle for Constitutional Government in the Middle East*. Cambridge, MA: Harvard University Press, 2013.

Totten, Michael J. *The Road to Fatima Gate: The Beirut Spring, the Rise of Hezbollah, and the Iranian War against Israel*. New York: Encounter Books, 2011.

Wickham, Carrie Rosefsky. *The Muslim Brotherhood: Evolution of an Islamist Movement.* Princeton, NJ: Princeton University Press, 2013.

Wright, Robin. *Rock the Casbah: Rage and Rebellion across the Islamic World.* Updated ed. New York: Simon and Schuster, 2012.

Arab-Jewish Communal War

The fighting that erupted on November 30, 1947, between Arabs and Jews in the British Mandate for Palestine is often included as part of the Israeli War of Independence (1948–1949), but this first phase of fighting between Arabs and Jews began well before the Jewish proclamation of independence on May 14, 1948. It erupted on November 30, 1947, immediately following announcement of the United Nations (UN) General Assembly vote approving the partition plan for Palestine. The month before, the Arab League had urged its member states to begin training volunteers for a possible military campaign to prevent the establishment of a Jewish state.

In this first phase of fighting, the Jews were faced with a wave of violence by elements of the Arab Palestinian population, assisted by irregular Arab forces from the neighboring states. The Arab military effort was only loosely coordinated. The Arab Higher Committee announced a general strike, and Arab mobs soon responded by attacking Jewish buses and other vehicles. An Arab mob destroyed the old commercial center of Jerusalem, while Arabs also fired on and broke into Jewish shops in Haifa, Jaffa, and other places. By December, the Arab and Jewish sectors were clearly segregated. Marginal or mixed areas in the cities were quickly evacuated by one side or the other. From the beginning, the fighting to control the lines of communication was especially fierce.

The UN vote on partition was also the signal for violence against Jews within the Arab states. In Aleppo, Syria, Arab demonstrators torched 300 Jewish homes and 11 synagogues. In Aden, Yemen, 76 Jews were slain.

When the fighting began, the principal Jewish military force was the Haganah. Illegally constituted during the British Mandate, this self-defense force consisted of a small fully mobilized nucleus and a larger militia element. The Haganah high command could call on a standing military force of four battalions of the Palmach (commando units) numbering some 2,100 men in all, along with 1,000 reservists who could be called up on short notice, and the Hel Sade (HISH, field army) of about 1,800 men, with another 10,000 reservists. The Haganah could also count on perhaps 32,000 members of the Hel Mishmar (HIM, garrison army), most of whom were older persons assigned to the defense of fixed locations such as towns and cities. Finally, there were Gadna (Youth Battalions) consisting of young people who were receiving some military training with the plan that when they were older they would join the HISH or Palmach. Military equipment was inadequate. The Haganah could count on about 15,000 rifles of a bewildering number of types, some light machine guns, and several dozen medium machine guns and 3-inch mortars. The Haganah's secret arms workshops were also producing the largely stamped Sten submachine gun as well as hand grenades and explosives.

Two other organizations must be mentioned. These were the Irgun Tsvai Leumi (National Military Organization) of about 5,000 members and Lohamei Herut Israel

Crouched atop the roof of a Jerusalem railroad station, members of the Arab Liberation Army guard the main rail corridor to Bethlehem and Southern Palestine on May 7, 1948, only seven days before the declaration of the state of Israel. (Bettmann/Corbis)

(Fighters for the Freedom of Israel), also known as Lehi or the Stern Gang, with about 1,000 men. These two elements operated very much on their own at the start of the fighting. Indeed, there was no love lost between them and the Haganah, and there had even been armed clashes. During the fighting, however, both organizations disbanded, and their members joined the Haganah to form the new Tz'va Haganah L'Yisrael (Israel Defense Forces, IDF). From the start, David Ben-Gurion, chairman of the Jewish Agency Executive, had charge of both political and defense matters.

The British government manifested a pronounced partiality for the Arab side. This could be seen in its refusal to lift embargoes on Jewish immigration into Palestine and the acquisition of weapons. British authorities refused to recognize the right of the Haganah to exist and disarmed Haganah

members when they could be found. At the same time, Britain continued to sell arms to both Iraq and Transjordan with the full knowledge that these might be used against the Jews in Palestine. Also, Arab leaders were occasionally notified in advance of British military evacuations, enabling Arab irregulars to seize control for themselves of such strategically located sites as police stations and military posts.

The early Arab military attacks of the communal war within Palestine were uncoordinated. They took the form of hit-and-run raids against isolated Jewish settlements with the aim of destroying Jewish property. The attacks were mounted entirely by Palestinian Arabs, although they did receive some financial assistance and arms from the Arab states. Arab efforts early on were, however, handicapped by ongoing tensions between the Nashashibi and Husseini factions.

On September 16, 1947, the Political Committee of the Arab League, meeting in Sofar, Lebanon, had appealed for economic reprisals against both Britain and the United States and for arms and money for the Palestinian Arabs. Following the UN partition vote, Iraqi premier Salih Jabr called for a meeting of Arab leaders in Cairo on December 12. There he called on the Arab states to intervene militarily in Palestine, but Egypt and Saudi Arabia were opposed, and King Abdullah of Jordan disliked even the mention of Arab volunteers. Eventually, the Arab leaders adopted a resolution calling for 10,000 rifles and other light weapons and 3,000 Arab volunteers to be sent into Palestine through Syria with the sum of £1 million to be allocated for the defense of Palestine.

The Cairo decision led to the formation of the Arab Liberation Army (ALA), to be commanded by Iraqi staff officer General Sir Ismail Safwat Pasha. He immediately set up his headquarters outside of Damascus. Field command went to Fawzi al-Qawuqji, guerrilla leader of the Arab Revolt of 1936. Most ALA members were in fact mercenaries. They included a large number of Syrian Arabs along with some Yugoslav Muslims, Circassians from the Caucasus region, Poles, Germans, and Spaniards. In late January 1948, members of the ALA began infiltrating across the Syrian border into Palestine, and al-Qawuqji set up his headquarters in Tiberias in the Galilee region of north-central Palestine. By the end of February 1948, there were perhaps 5,000 members of the ALA in Palestine, and by the end of March their numbers had grown to perhaps 7,000.

In the spring the Arab forces, including the ALA, divided Palestine into three major fronts. The northern sector contained by far the largest Arab force, some 7,000 men under al-Qawuqji and the Syrian Adib al-Shishakli. Another 5,000 were in the central sector, the largest number of whom were under the command of Abd al-Qadr al-Husseini, a nephew of the mufti of Jerusalem. Some 2,000 Arab fighters, most of them Muslim Brotherhood volunteers from Egypt, were located in the southern sector of the Negev Desert.

In the winter and early spring of 1948, the Arab forces launched a series of largely uncoordinated military attacks. These fell on Jewish quarters in the cities, chiefly Jerusalem, as well as the more isolated kibbutzim in the Hebron Hills area. The outnumbered but disinterested British authorities did nothing to inhibit the Arabs, who were soon able to cut key roads, including those between Tel Aviv and Jerusalem, Haifa and western Galilee, Tiberias and eastern Galilee, and Afula and the Beit She'an Valley. The Jewish farms in the Negev were also soon isolated.

Jewish authorities, who had expected to have more time to prepare, were caught off guard by these Arab military moves. Perhaps the most ominous situation was that facing the Jews in Jerusalem, who were now without ammunition and other military supplies and were also cut off from food. The Arabs controlled the low hills dominating the Tel Aviv–Jerusalem Road into the city and were able to destroy at will the Jewish truck convoys attempting to reach Jerusalem. The difficulty of the military situation facing the Jews was compounded by the decision taken by Ben-Gurion and the Jewish Agency Executive to defend every bit of territory allocated to the future Jewish state under the partition plan as well as Jewish settlements, which in accordance with the plan would be allocated to the Arab state. This decision meant that already meager Haganah resources would have to be dispersed throughout Palestine in a defensive stance, making concentration into larger units for offensive operations impossible. Resupply operations of isolated Jewish settlements through Arab areas such as Galilee and the Negev would be particularly difficult, as would the resupply of Jewish enclaves in the cities, including Jerusalem.

On January 10, 1948, 900 members of the ALA attacked K'far Szold in Upper Galilee but were beaten back. The next day other attacks occurred throughout Palestine against isolated Jewish settlements in the same region but also in the Hebron Hills, the Judean Mountains, and the Negev. The Arabs also managed to get car bombs into the Jewish quarters of Haifa and Jerusalem. Among their successful targets were the offices of the *Jerusalem Post* and the Jewish Agency headquarters in Jerusalem. Jewish road traffic was largely limited to armored cars or armed convoys. Despite efforts to send the convoys at odd times and by circuitous routes, Arab military action soon brought this traffic to a complete halt.

In view of their inability to capture even one Jewish settlement, in March the Arabs decided to concentrate the bulk of their military effort against Jewish road traffic while at the same time not entirely abandoning attacks on the Jewish settlements or enclaves. The Jews did manage to get an armored convoy to isolated Gat and to destroy an Arab armaments convoy near Haifa. At the same time, however, the Arabs registered success in their effort to isolate Jerusalem. From late March they employed land mines for the first time, completely cutting off the coastal road to the Negev. The Arabs also ambushed at Nebi Daniel a large armored Jewish convoy bound for Jerusalem, destroying or capturing all its vehicles. To the north they also destroyed a Jewish convoy bound from Haifa to the isolated Y'hi'am settlement.

By the end of March the situation facing the Jews appeared grim. The Jewish section of Jerusalem was cut off from the coast, and settlements near the city were isolated from Jerusalem. The Negev and settlements of western Galilee were similarly cut off. On the other hand, Jewish forces were now fully mobilized. Some 21,000 men between the ages of 17 and 25 were now under arms. Progress had also been made in the manufacture of light weapons and explosives, and additional weapons were en route to Palestine from Czechoslovakia. Some 50 light liaison aircraft were in service, performing reconnaissance and transport of some light weapons and key personnel to isolated areas. Arab strength was also increasing, however.

Worried about weakening UN and U.S. support for the implementation of partition, the Jewish leadership was determined to take the offensive. This was made possible by the increased strength of the Haganah and the continued evacuation of British military personnel from Palestine. In considering their options, Ben-Gurion and the other Jewish leaders assigned top priority to opening the supply route to Jerusalem.

Code-named Operation NACHSHON, this plan to secure both sides of the Tel Aviv–Jerusalem supply corridor involved the concentration of some 1,500 Jewish troops, armed in large part with weapons that had arrived from Czechoslovakia on April 1, 1948. The operation commenced on April 6. Fighting was intense, especially at Kastel, which changed hands several times before the Arabs finally abandoned it on April 10. Abd el-Kadr al-Husseini, the Arab commander of the Jerusalem area, was killed in fighting on April 9. The operation, which ended on April 15, saw three large Jewish convoys reach the city.

At the same time, the ALA attempted to take the Jewish settlement of Mishmar

Ha'Emek. The Arabs opened artillery fire on the settlement on April 4, but the defenders repulsed subsequent ground assaults. On April 12, Haganah forces counterattacked, and the Arab forces retreated. This Arab artillery was then relocated to shell the Jewish sector of Jerusalem in early May. During April 12–14, a Druse mercenary battalion attempted, without success, to take the Ramat Yohanan settlement.

Emboldened by its successes, the Haganah stepped up its offensive, cutting the port of Tiberias in two on April 18 and forcing an Arab evacuation there. On April 21, as British forces were evacuating Haifa, the Haganah began an assault on that city, taking it in two days. Most of the Arab residents left for Lebanon by land and sea, their leaders promising a speedy return. Success here made possible the resupply of Jewish settlements in Upper Galilee, and contact was reestablished with Safed.

On May 1, Arab forces struck back with an assault on the Jewish settlement of Ramot Naftali, previously under siege. Lebanese artillery and tanks took part, but the attack was again defeated. On May 6, Jewish forces opened an assault against the Arab part of Safed but were themselves repulsed. The assault was renewed on the night of May 9–10, and this time Jewish forces were successful. The Arab inhabitants fled the city, and Palmach fighters captured a key mountain citadel there. Many other Arab residents in the general area of Safed now also fled, with the result that by mid-May all the Jewish settlements in Upper Galilee were connected. On April 29, part of the Golani Brigade seized Tzemah as well as a nearby police fort. Other former British police installations were taken, and the city of Akko and villages north to the Lebanese border were also secured by May 17.

In Operation HAMETZ, so named because it began on the eve of Passover (*hametz* means "leaven"), Jewish forces cleared Arab villages around Tel Aviv–Jaffa. On April 29, following Jewish encirclement of Jaffa, which was to be included in the Arab part of Palestine under the partition plan, many of its 70,000 Arab residents fled. The city itself surrendered on May 13 after the final British evacuation.

With the British stepping up their final evacuation, Arab forces again seized control of the Tel Aviv–Jerusalem Road. The Harel Brigade of the Palmach was shifted to Operation JEBUSI to reopen the supply corridor. The Harel Brigade was forced by a British ultimatum, backed by artillery, to withdraw from initial captures, and a Jewish attempt to secure the Jericho Road also failed. On the night of April 28–29, a struggle for control of the Monastery of St. Simon began. Jewish reinforcements from the Jerusalem Brigade tipped the balance. On May 11, in Operation MACCABEE, another effort was made to open the road to Jerusalem, but only one convoy of several dozen vehicles made it through before the Arabs again closed the road on May 17.

With the last British forces quitting Jerusalem on May 14, Jewish forces began Operation KILSHON (pitchfork) to prepare for an attack by the Arab Legion. It succeeded to the extent that the Jewish area of the city was made into a continuous whole for the first time, but it also failed to cut a supply corridor to the Jewish quarter of the Old City. Meanwhile, isolated Jewish settlements near Jerusalem were abandoned as indefensible, and the Arab Legion also registered several successes, including the capture of the entire Etzyon Block.

In six weeks of heavy fighting before the proclamation of the State of Israel and the invasion by regular Arab armies, Jewish fighters had secured Haifa, Jaffa, Safed, and Tiberias. They had also captured about 100 Arab villages and had surrounded Akko. Most of the main roads were again open to Jewish traffic. For all practical purposes, the Palestinian Arab military forces had been defeated. The ALA had suffered heavy losses, and Jewish armed strength had now increased to 30,000 men. The arms shipments from Czechoslovakia had filled many deficiencies, including antitank and antiaircraft weapons, but the Jews still lacked fighter aircraft, field artillery, and tanks. On May 15, 1948, moreover, regular Arab armies invaded Israel, beginning the Israeli War of Independence, which continued until July 20, 1949, and the signing of the last armistice agreement with Syria.

Spencer C. Tucker

Further Reading

Bregman, Ahron. *Israel's Wars: A History Since 1947*. 3rd ed. New York: Routledge, 2010.

Dupuy, Trevor N. *Elusive Victory: The Arab-Israeli Wars, 1947–1974*. Garden City, NY: Military Book Club, 2002.

Gelvin, James M. *The Israel-Palestine Conflict: One Hundred Years of War*. 3rd ed. Cambridge: Cambridge University Press, 2014.

Herzog, Chaim. *The Arab-Israeli Wars: War and Peace in the Middle East from the War of Independence to Lebanon*. Westminster, MD: Random House, 1984.

La Guardia, Anton. *War without End: Israelis, Palestinians, and the Struggle for a Promised Land*. Revised and updated ed. New York: St. Martin's Press, 2003.

Lucas, Noah. *The Modern History of Israel*. New York: Praeger, 1975.

Sachar, Howard M. *A History of Israel: From the Rise of Zionism to Our Time*. 3rd ed. New York: Knopf, 2007.

Sa'di, Ahmad H., and Lila Abu-Lughod, eds. *Nakba: Palestine, 1948, and the Claims of Memory*. New York: Columbia University Press, 2007.

Smith, Charles D. *Palestine and the Arab-Israeli Conflict: A History with Documents*. 8th ed. New York: Bedford/St. Martin's Press, 2012.

Arafat, Yasser

Born: August 24, 1929
Died: November 11, 2004

Palestinian nationalist and leader of the Palestine Liberation Organization (PLO) for 36 years (1969–2004). Yasser Arafat, officially named Mohammed Abdel Raouf Arafat al-Qudwa al-Husseini, was born on August 24, 1929. Arafat always stated that he was born in Jerusalem, but Israeli officials began to claim in the 1970s that he was born in Cairo to discredit him. There is also some dispute about his date of birth, which is occasionally given as August 4, 1929. He went by the name Yasser as a child.

Arafat's father was a Palestinian Egyptian textile merchant. Neither Arafat nor his siblings were close to their father. His mother, Zahwa, also a Palestinian, was a member of a family that had lived in Jerusalem for generations. She died when Arafat was five years old, and he then lived with his mother's brother in Jerusalem. Arafat vividly remembered British soldiers invading his uncle's house one night, destroying possessions and beating its residents. When Arafat was nine years old his father brought him back to Cairo, where his older sister raised him.

As a teenager in Cairo, Arafat became involved in smuggling arms to Palestine to aid those struggling against both the British authorities and the Jews living there. He attended the University of Fuad I (later Cairo University) in Cairo but left to fight in Gaza against Israel in the Israeli War of Independence of 1948–1949. When the Arabs lost the war and Israel was firmly established,

From 1969 until his death in November 2004, Yasser Arafat was the leader of the Palestine Liberation Organization and the most widely known Palestinian nationalist leader. (AP Photo)

Arafat was inconsolable. He briefly attended the University of Texas but then returned to Cairo University to study engineering. He spent most of his time with fellow Palestinian students spreading his hopes for a free Palestinian state.

Arafat became president of the Union of Palestinian Students, holding that position from 1952 to 1956. He joined the Muslim Brotherhood in 1952. He finally graduated from college in 1956 and spent a short time working in Egypt. During the 1956 Suez Crisis he served as a second lieutenant in the Egyptian army. In 1957, he moved to Kuwait, where he worked as an engineer and formed his own contracting company.

In 1958, Arafat founded the Fatah organization, an underground guerrilla group dedicated to the liberation of Palestine. In 1964,

he quit his job and moved to Jordan to devote all his energies to the promotion of Palestinian nationhood and to organize raids into Israel. The PLO was founded that same year.

In 1968, the Israel Defense Forces (IDF) attacked Fatah at the small Jordanian village of Al Karameh. The Palestinians eventually forced the Israelis back, and Arafat's face appeared on the cover of *Time* magazine as the leader of the Palestinian movement. In consequence, Palestinians embraced Fatah, and Arafat became a national hero. He was appointed chairman of the PLO the next year and within four years controlled both the military (the Palestine Liberation Army, or PLA) and political branches of the organization.

By 1970, Palestinians had assembled a well-organized unofficial state within Jordan.

However, King Hussein of Jordan deemed them a threat to security and sent his army to evict them. Arafat enlisted the aid of Syria, while Jordan called on the United States for assistance. On September 24, 1970, the PLO agreed to a cease-fire and agreed to leave Jordan. Arafat moved the organization to Lebanon, which had a weak government that was not likely to restrict the PLO's operations. The PLO soon began launching occasional attacks across the Israeli border.

Arafat did not approve of overseas attacks because they gave the PLO a bad image abroad. He publicly dissociated the group from Black September, the organization that killed 11 Israeli athletes at the 1972 Munich Olympics, although there is now evidence of his involvement. In 1974, he limited the PLO's attacks to Israel, the Gaza Strip, and the West Bank. Although Israel claimed that Arafat was responsible for the numerous terrorist attacks that occurred within the country during the 1970s, he denied responsibility. In 1974, he spoke before the United Nations (UN) General Assembly as the representative of the Palestinian people and condemned Zionism but offered peace, which won him praise from the international community.

During the Lebanese civil war, the PLO initially sided with the Lebanese National Front against the Lebanese forces, who were supported by Israel and backed by Defense Minister Ariel Sharon. As such, when Israeli forces invaded southern Lebanon, the PLO ended up fighting against the Israelis and then the Syrian militia group Amal. Thousands of Palestinians, many of them civilians, were killed during the struggle, and the PLO was forced to leave Lebanon in 1982 and relocate to Tunisia, where it remained until 1993.

During the 1980s, Iraq and Saudi Arabia donated millions of dollars to Arafat to help him rebuild the PLO. Arafat approved the First Intifada (1987) against Israel. In 1988, Palestinians declared Palestinian statehood at a meeting in Algiers. Arafat then announced that the Palestinians would renounce terrorism and recognize the State of Israel. The Palestinian National Council elected Arafat president of this new, unrecognized state in 1989.

Arafat and the Israelis conducted peace negotiations at the Madrid Conference in 1991. Although negotiations were temporarily set back when the PLO supported Iraq in the 1991 Persian Gulf War, over the next two years the two parties held a number of secret discussions. These negotiations led to the 1993 Oslo Peace Accords in which Israel agreed to Palestinian self-rule in the Gaza Strip and the West Bank. Arafat also officially recognized the existence of the State of Israel. Despite the condemnation of many Palestinian nationalists who viewed Arafat's moves as a sellout, the peace process appeared to be moving in a positive direction in the mid-1990s. Israeli troops withdrew from the Gaza Strip and Jericho in May 1994. Arafat was elected leader of the new Palestinian Authority (PA) in January 1996 with 88 percent of the vote in elections that were by all accounts free and fair (but with severely limited competition because Hamas and other opposition groups refused to participate).

Later that same year, Benjamin Netanyahu of the Likud Party became prime minister of Israel, and the peace process began to unravel. Netanyahu, a hard-line conservative, condemned terrorism and blamed Palestinians for numerous suicide bombings against Israeli citizens. He also did not trust Arafat, who he charged was supporting terrorists. Arafat continued negotiations with the Israelis into 2000. That July, with Ehud Barak having replaced Netanyahu as Israeli prime minister, Arafat traveled to the United States to meet with Barak and President Bill Clinton at the Camp David Summit. Despite generous concessions by Barak, Arafat refused to compromise, and a major chance at peace was lost.

On the collapse of the peace process, the Second (al-Aqsa) Intifada began. From the beginning of the Second Intifada in 2000, Arafat was a besieged man who appeared to be losing influence and control within the Palestinian and larger Arab communities. His inability or unwillingness to stop Palestinian terrorist attacks against Israel resulted in his virtual captivity at his Ramallah headquarters from 2002. In declining health by 2004, the PLO leader was beginning to look increasingly like a man past his time.

Flown to France for medical treatment, Arafat died on November 11, 2004, at Percy Military Hospital outside Paris, France. For a time, there were much intrigue and conspiratorial conjecture concerning his mysterious illness and death. Rumors persist that he was assassinated by poisoning, although it is equally likely that he succumbed to unintentional food poisoning. An autopsy conducted by Swiss scientists in November 2012 suggested that his death might have been due to polonium poisoning. He is buried at his former headquarters in the city of Ramallah.

Amy Hackney Blackwell

Further Reading

Abu Sharif, Bassam. *Arafat and the Dream of Palestine: An Insider's Account.* New York: Palgrave Macmillan, 2009.

Aburish, Said K. *Arafat: From Defender to Dictator.* New York: Bloomsbury, 1998.

Hart, Alan. *Arafat: A Political Biography.* Rev. ed. London: Sidgwick and Jackson, 1994.

Karsh, Efraim. *Arafat's War: The Man and His Battle for Israeli Conquest.* New York: Grove Press, 2003.

Rubin, Barry, and Judith Colp Rubin. *Yasir Arafat: A Political Biography.* New York: Oxford University Press, 2003.

Said, Edward W. *Peace and Its Discontents: Essays on Palestine in the Middle East Process.* New York: Vintage Books, 1995.

Schanzer, Jonathan. *State of Failure: Yasser Arafat, Mahmoud Abbas, and the Unmaking of the Palestinian State.* Basingstoke: Palgrave Macmillan, 2013.

Walker, Tony, and Andrew Gowers. *Arafat: The Biography.* London: Virgin Books, 2005.

Wallach, Janet, and John Wallach. *Arafat: In the Eyes of the Beholder.* Rev. and updated ed. New York: Citadel Books, 1997.

B

Begin, Menachem

Born: August 16, 1913
Died: March 9, 1992

Prime minister of Israel (1977–1983) and recipient (with Egyptian president Anwar Sadat) of the 1978 Nobel Peace Prize, awarded for the Camp David Accords that resulted in the 1979 Israel-Egypt Peace Treaty. Menachem Wolfovitch Begin was born to an Ashkenazic Jewish family in Brest-Litovsk (Brisk), Russia (now Belarus), on August 16, 1913. He fled with his family to Vilnius, Poland, to escape the battling German and Russian armies in World War I. Begin's father was an ardent Zionist, and Begin was a member of the Hashomer Hatzair scout movement until age 13 and joined Vladimir Jabotinsky's Betar youth movement at age 16. Betar was a subset of the Zionist revisionist movement committed to the creation of a Jewish state on both sides of the Jordan River. Begin took up the leadership of the Organization Department of Betar for Poland in 1932.

Begin graduated from the University of Warsaw with a law degree in 1935 and assumed the leadership of Betar Czechoslovakia in 1936. He returned to Warsaw in 1937 and was imprisoned for a short time because of his Zionist activities. He became head of Betar in Poland in 1938. Under his overall leadership, some 100,000 members engaged in self-defense, weapons, agricultural, and communications training. Members of Betar also transported to Palestine immigrants declared illegal by the British

government. Begin advocated the establishment of a Jewish national homeland in Palestine by conquest and pushed this position at the 1938 Betar convention.

In 1939, Begin fled Warsaw when the Germans invaded Poland. He managed to cross into eastern Poland, which the Soviets invaded two weeks later, and thus avoided the roundup of Jews by the Nazis. Both his parents and a brother died in Nazi concentration camps during the war. In 1940, he was arrested by the Soviets and sent to a concentration camp in Siberia. He was released following the agreement establishing a Polish army to fight the Germans that followed the German invasion of the Soviet Union in June 1941.

Begin duly enlisted in the Free Polish Army in exile and was sent for training in 1942 to the British Mandate for Palestine. He left the army there in 1943 and joined the Jewish national movement in Palestine. He openly criticized the Jewish Agency for Palestine and worldwide Zionism as too timid in their approach to a Jewish state. In 1942, he had joined Irgun Tsvai Leumi (National Military Organization) and commanded the movement from 1943 to 1948. Under Begin's leadership, Irgun declared war on the British and resumed attacks on Palestinian Arab villages and British interests. The declaration came in February 1944.

The British had already classified Irgun as a terrorist organization. The Jewish Agency for Palestine, Haganah, and Histadrut had all declared its operations as terrorist acts. Nevertheless, Irgun's operations were so successful under Begin that the British

Israel's prime minister Menachem Begin on November 13, 1978. (AP Photo/Max Nash)

launched an extensive manhunt for him. He avoided capture by disguising himself as an Orthodox rabbi. Meanwhile, he directed the Irgun bombing of the British military, police, and civil headquarters at Jerusalem's King David Hotel on July 22, 1946, that killed 91 people. Begin and Irgun claimed to have issued three warnings in an attempt to limit casualties.

In anticipation of and following the partitioning of Palestine in 1947, Irgun and Haganah increasingly coordinated. Israel declared its independence on May 15, 1948, and announced the absorption of Haganah into its national military, the Israel Defense Forces (IDF), effective May 18, 1948. All other armed forces were banned. Irgun signed an agreement to be absorbed by the IDF on June 1, 1948, which formally occurred in September 1948. Begin also played a key role in the *Altalena* incident of June 23, 1948.

After Israel's independence, Begin led Israel's political opposition from 1948 to

1977, reforming what remained of Irgun into the rightist Herut (Freedom) Party with himself as its head. In 1965, Herut merged with the Liberal Party, creating the Gahal Party, which formed the understructure of the future Likud (Unity) Party. Just prior to the June 1967 Six-Day War, he joined the National Unity government's cabinet as a minister without portfolio. The government was dissolved on August 1, 1970.

The Likud Party's May 17, 1977, victory in the national elections for the ninth Knesset allowed Begin, the chairman of Likud since 1970, to form the new government. On June 21, he became Israel's sixth (and first non-Labor) prime minister. Domestically, Begin moved to turn the Israeli economy away from the centralized, highly planned enterprise that characterized it under Labor. The prime minister also actively promoted immigration to Israel, especially from Ethiopia and the Soviet Union. Finally, he sought infrastructure improvements, advances in education, and the renewal of Israel's poorest neighborhoods.

It was in the realm of foreign policy, however, that Begin most asserted himself. One of his first acts as prime minister was to challenge King Hussein of Jordan, President Hafez al-Assad of Syria, and President Sadat of Egypt to meet with him to discuss peace. Sadat, but not the others, accepted the challenge and arrived in Israel on November 19, 1977. Following intermittent negotiations, Begin and Sadat met with U.S. president Jimmy Carter at Camp David, Maryland, and signed the Camp David Accords after nearly two weeks of negotiations (September 5–17, 1978).

The accords included two framework agreements that established guidelines for both the Israel-Egypt Peace Treaty and a potentially wider Middle East peace agreement. The bilateral treaty was signed in

Washington, D.C., on March 26, 1979. Begin attended and participated in Sadat's funeral in Cairo after the Egyptian leader was assassinated by Muslim fundamentalists in October 1981.

Despite Begin's willingness to seek peace with Egypt, the other Arab states, including Syria and Jordan, remained hostile toward Israel. And Begin was uncompromising on the place of the West Bank and the Gaza Strip, seized by Israel during the Six-Day War, in the modern State of Israel. He considered them part of the historical lands given to Israel by God. Indeed, he promoted and oversaw the expansion of Jewish settlements in the West Bank and the Gaza Strip that continue to be an impediment to Palestinian-Israeli peace accords to the present day.

From May 28, 1980, to August 6, 1981, Begin served concurrently as Israel's prime minister and defense minister. When Israeli intelligence notified Begin that Iraq was close to producing weapons-grade nuclear fuel at its Osiraq/Tammuz nuclear reactor, he ordered the Israeli air force's successful destruction of the facility on June 7, 1981. Shortly thereafter he enunciated the Begin Doctrine, which held that Israel would act preemptively to counter any perceived threat from weapons of mass destruction (WMDs).

On June 30, 1981, Begin was reelected prime minister. It was soon apparent to the second Begin government that the Lebanese government was unable or unwilling to stop terrorist attacks launched from its soil. As such, in June 1982 Begin authorized Operation PEACE FOR GALILEE, the Israeli invasion of southern Lebanon. The operation was designed to drive Palestine Liberation Organization (PLO) Katyusha rockets out of the range of Israel's northern border and to destroy the terrorist infrastructure that had developed in southern Lebanon.

Although the PLO was driven from Lebanon, the Israeli presence in the country lasted three years. (A limited Israeli force remained until 2000.) The Israeli operation resulted in such a high number of Palestinian civilian deaths that worldwide public opinion turned against Israel. The failure of Operation PEACE FOR GALILEE to progress in the intended time frame and the large number of casualties on both sides weighed heavily on Begin. Tired and still mourning the recent death of his wife, he resigned as prime minister on September 15, 1983. Over the next nine years he lived quietly, if not reclusively, in Tel Aviv. Begin died of heart failure on March 9, 1992, in Tel Aviv.

Richard M. Edwards

Further Reading

Avner, Yehuda. *The Prime Ministers: An Intimate Narrative of Israeli Leadership.* New Milford, CT: Toby Press, 2010.

Begin, Menachem. *The Revolt.* Los Angeles: Nash Publishing, 1972.

Begin, Menachem. *White Nights: The Story of a Prisoner in Russia.* New York: Harper and Row, 1979.

Hurwitz, Harry, and Yisrael Medad, eds. *Peace in the Making: The Menachem Begin-Anwar Sadat Personal Correspondence.* Jerusalem: Gefen Publishing, 2011.

Hurwitz, Zvi Harry. *Begin: His Life, Words and Deeds.* Jerusalem: Gefen Publishing, 2004.

Perlmutter, Amos. *The Life and Times of Menachem Begin.* Garden City, NY: Doubleday, 1987.

Seidman, Hillel. *Menachem Begin: His Life and Legacy.* New York: Shengold, 1990.

Shilon, Avi. *Menachem Begin: A Life.* Translated by Danielle Silverberg and Yoram Sharett. New Haven, CT: Yale University Press, 2012.

Sofer, Sasson. *Begin: An Anatomy of Leadership.* New York: Blackwell, 1988.

Stein, Kenneth W. *Heroic Diplomacy: Kissinger, Sadat, Carter, Begin and the*

Quest for Arab-Israeli Peace. New York: Routledge, 1999.

Temko, Ned. *To Win or to Die: A Personal Portrait of Menachem Begin.* New York: Morrow, 1987.

Ben-Gurion, David

Born: October 16, 1886
Died: December 1, 1973

Zionist leader, defense minister (1948–1954 and 1955–1963), and prime minister of Israel (1948–1953, 1955–1963). Celebrated as Israel's "Father of the Nation," David Ben-Gurion was born David Grün in Plonsk, Poland, on October 16, 1886. Educated in

A devout Zionist while still in his teens and a guerrilla fighter in his adult years, David Ben-Gurion later delivered Israel's Declaration of Independence and has since been hailed as his nation's founding father. (USHMM)

his Zionist father's Hebrew school, as a teenager he joined the Zionist youth group Erza. He then taught at a Hebrew school in Warsaw and joined the Poalei Zion (Workers of Zion). Ben-Gurion believed that Zionism would be achieved by Jewish settlement in Palestine and by collective farming and industrialization of the land.

Putting his beliefs into action, Ben-Gurion moved to Jaffa, Palestine, in 1906 and established the first Jewish workers' commune there. He then began organizing other workers into unions. In Jerusalem, in 1910, he began writing for the newspaper *Ahdut*, publishing his first article on Zionism under the name Ben-Gurion ("son of the lion" in Hebrew).

Ben-Gurion then moved to Jerusalem and joined the editorial staff of a Hebrew-language newspaper. He left Palestine in 1912 to earn a law degree from the University of Constantinople during 1912–1914. Returning to Palestine to take up his union work, he was expelled by the Ottomans—who still controlled Palestine—in March 1915.

Settling in New York City, Ben-Gurion met Russian-born Paula Munweis, whom he married in 1917. Buoyed by the 1917 British Balfour Declaration that proposed a Jewish homeland in Palestine, Ben-Gurion joined the Jewish Legion, a volunteer British military unit formed to help defeat the Turks. In 1920, he returned to union organizing. Indeed, he helped found the Histadrut, a powerful federation of Jewish labor unions. During 1921–1935 he served as its general secretary. The Histadrut became in effect a state within British-controlled Palestine. Ben-Gurion was also a driving force behind the establishment of the Haganah, the paramilitary force of the Zionist movement that helped facilitate illegal Jewish immigration to Palestine and protect the Jewish settlements there. Within the Zionist movement in Palestine, however, he was known as a moderate who opposed the radical approach advocated by Ze'ev Jabotinsky and Menachem Begin. Briefly Ben-Gurion cooperated with Begin's Irgun Tsvai Leumi (National Military Organization) but only rarely supported violence, and then only against military targets. While Ben-Gurion agreed to Begin's plan to bomb the King David Hotel, it was only with the aim of humiliating the British. When it became apparent that the effort would result in loss of life, Ben-Gurion ordered Begin to call off the bombing, which Begin refused to do.

When it became clear after World War II that Britain was not sympathetic to the establishment of a Jewish state in Palestine, Ben-Gurion pursued other avenues to achieve Jewish statehood. He supported the United Nations' (UN) 1947 partition plan that called for separate Jewish and Arab states in Palestine. In May 1948, the UN formally partitioned Palestine, and the State of Israel was born.

Ben-Gurion was concurrently prime minister and defense minister of the new nation. Austere and ascetic, he insisted that the new state be marked by full social and political equality without regard to race, religion, or sex. As its defense minister, he immediately consolidated all the Jewish paramilitary organizations into the Israel Defense Forces (IDF), enabling them to effectively fight both the Arab Palestinians and the surrounding Arab nations.

As Israel's prime minister, Ben-Gurion promoted Jewish immigration from the Arab states (Operation MAGIC CARPET). He also oversaw establishment of the Jewish state's governmental institutions, advocated compulsory primary education, and urged the creation of new towns and cities. Deeply involved in rural development projects, he urged the establishment of new settlements, especially in the Negev. He was also one of the founders of Mapai, the political party that held power in the first three decades of the Jewish state.

Ben-Gurion retired from politics in 1953 only to return as prime minister and defense minister in 1955. His second period as prime minister coincided with the 1956 Suez Crisis in which the Israeli government worked secretly with the French and British governments to seize control of the Suez Canal and topple Egyptian president Gamal Abdel Nasser from power. Although the IDF performed admirably, heavy pressure from the U.S. government brought the withdrawal of the British, which in turn forced the French and Israelis to remove their own forces.

The last years of Ben-Gurion's premiership were marked by general Israeli prosperity and stalled secret peace talks with the Arabs. He resigned his posts in June 1963 but retained his seat in the Knesset (Israeli parliament). In 1965, he broke with the Mapai Party over Prime Minister Levi Eshkol's handling of the Lavon Affair. Ben-Gurion then formed a new party, Rafi. When it voted to merge with Mapai to form the Labor Alignment in 1968, he formed another new party, the State List. He resigned from the Knesset and left politics altogether in 1970. Among his books are *Israel: An Achieved Personal History* (1970) and *The Jews in Their Land* (1974). He spent his last years on his kibbutz. Ben-Gurion died in Tel Aviv–Jaffa on December 1, 1973.

Richard M. Edwards

Further Reading

Aronson, Schlomo. *David Ben-Gurion and the Jewish Renaissance*. Translated by Naftali Greenwood. Cambridge: Cambridge University Press, 2010.

Avner, Yehuda. *The Prime Ministers: An Intimate Narrative of Israeli Leadership*. New Milford, CT: Toby Press, 2010.

Bar-Zohar, Michel. *Ben-Gurion: The Armed Prophet*. Translated by Len Ortzen. London: Barker, 1967.

Ben-Gurion, David. *Recollections*. Edited by Thomas R. Bransten. London: Macdonald & Co., 1970.

Kurzman, Dan. *Ben-Gurion: Prophet of Fire*. New York: Simon and Schuster, 1983.

Peres, Shimon, in conversation with David Landau. *David Ben-Gurion: A Political Life*. New York: Schocken Books, 2011.

Zweig, Ronald W., ed. *David Ben-Gurion: Politics and Leadership in Israel*. Jerusalem: Y. I. Ben-Zvi, 1991.

C

Camp David Accords

A peace agreement reached between Egypt and Israel in September 1978 at Camp David, the U.S. presidential retreat in rural Maryland.

During 1977 and 1978, several remarkable events took place that set the stage for the Camp David negotiations. In autumn 1977, Egyptian president Anwar Sadat indicated his willingness to go to Israel in the cause of peace, something that no Arab leader had done since the creation of the Jewish state in 1948. On November 19, 1977, Sadat followed through on his promise, addressing the Knesset (Israeli parliament) and calling for peace between the two nations. The Israelis welcomed Sadat's bold initiative but took no immediate steps to end the state of belligerency, instead agreeing to ministerial-level meetings in preparation for final negotiations.

In February 1978, the United States entered into the equation by hosting Sadat in Washington, with both President Jimmy Carter and Congress hailing the Egyptian president as a statesman and a courageous leader. American adulation for Sadat led to greater cooperation by the Israelis, and they thus agreed to a summit meeting in September at Camp David.

During September 5–17, 1978, Carter hosted a conference that brought together Sadat and Israeli prime minister Menachem Begin and their respective staffs at Camp David. Carter participated as an active player in the resultant talks. As was expected, the discussions proved difficult. Begin insisted that Sadat separate the Palestinian issue from the peace talks, something that no Arab leader had been willing to do before. Israel also demanded that Egypt negate any former agreements with other Arab nations that called for war against Israel.

Sadat bristled at Begin's demands, which led to such acrimony between the two men that they met in person only once during the entire negotiation process. Instead, Carter shuttled between the two leaders in an effort to moderate their positions. After several days of little movement and accusations of bad faith directed mostly at Begin, however, Carter threatened to break off the talks. Faced with the possibility of being blamed for a failed peace plan, Begin finally came to the table ready to deal. He agreed to dismantle all Jewish settlements in the Sinai Peninsula and return it in its entirety to Egypt. For his part, given Begin's absolute intransigence on it, Sadat agreed to put the Palestinian issue aside and sign an agreement separate from the other Arab nations. On September 15, 1978, Carter, Sadat, and Begin announced that an agreement had been reached on two frameworks, the first for a peace treaty between Egypt and Israel and the second for a multilateral treaty dealing with the West Bank and the Gaza Strip.

The framework regarding Egypt and Israel had 11 major provisions: (1) the two nations would sign a peace treaty within three months; (2) this treaty would be implemented within two to three years after it was signed; (3) Egypt would regain full sovereignty of the Sinai to its pre–Six-Day War (1967) borders; (4) Israel would withdraw its forces from the

U.S. president Jimmy Carter signs the Camp David Peace Treaty on March 26, 1979 in Washington, D.C. (Jimmy Carter Library)

Sinai, with the first such withdrawal to occur nine months after signature of the treaty; (5) Israel was to have freedom of navigation through the Suez Canal and the Strait of Tiran; (6) a highway would be built between the Sinai and Jordan to pass near Eilat with the guarantee of free passage through Israeli territory for both nations; (7) Egyptian forces in the Sinai would be limited to one division in the area 30 miles (50 km) east of the Gulf of Suez and the Suez Canal; (8) there would be no other Egyptian forces in the Sinai; (9) Israeli forces would be restricted to four infantry battalions in the area 1.8 miles (3 km) east of the international border with Egypt; (10) United Nations (UN) forces would be positioned in certain areas; and (11) the peace between the two nations would be complete, including full diplomatic recognition and an end to any economic restrictions on the other nation's goods, with free movement of goods and people.

The second framework, officially known as the "Framework of Peace in the Middle East," was far more general and skirted major issues. It contained seven major provisions: (1) UN Security Council Resolutions 242 and 338 were recognized as holding "in all their parts" the basis for a peace settlement; (2) the peace settlement would be negotiated by Egypt, Israel, Jordan, and "the representatives of the Palestinian people"; (3) residents of the West Bank and Gaza would secure "full autonomy"; (4) Egypt, Israel, and Jordan were to agree on "modalities for establishing the elected self-governing authority" in these areas, and the Egyptian and Jordanian delegations "may include Palestinians from the West Bank and Gaza or other Palestinians as mutually agreed"; (5) a withdrawal of Israeli forces would occur, with remaining forces grouped in certain agreed-upon locations; (6) as soon as the self-governing authority ("administrative council") had been estab-lished, a five-year transitional period would begin, by the end of which the final status of the West Bank and Gaza would have been agreed to, understanding that there would be recognition of "the legitimate rights of the Palestinian people and their just require-ments"; and (7) in the transitional period, representatives of Egypt, Israel, and Jordan as well as those of the self-governing author-ity "will constitute a continuing committee" to agree on "the modalities of admission of peoples displaced from the West Bank and Gaza in 1967."

Despite a feeling of euphoria in the United States and an upward spike in Car-ter's approval ratings, the agreement in fact was a retreat from the president's own pro-gram in 1977 that called for Israeli with-drawal from the occupied lands with only minor territorial adjustments and a home-land for the Palestinian people based on self-determination rather than on autonomy under Israeli administrative control. Much was also simply left out. There was no men-tion in the framework of the future of Jeru-salem and the Golan Heights or about Israeli settlements in the West Bank and the future of the Palestine Liberation Organization (PLO), which the United States steadfastly refused to recognize.

Over the next several months, Secretary of State Cyrus Vance made numerous trips to the Middle East to finalize the agreement. The United States promised that it would help organize an international peacekeep-ing force to occupy the Sinai following the Israeli withdrawal. Washington also agreed to provide $2 billion to pay for the reloca-tion of an airfield from the Sinai to Israel and promised economic assistance to Egypt in exchange for Sadat's signature on a peace treaty.

Finally, on March 26, 1979, in a White House ceremony, Sadat and Begin shook hands again and signed a permanent peace treaty, normalizing relations between their two nations. Hopes that other Arab nations, particularly the pro-Western regimes in Jor-dan and Saudi Arabia, would soon follow Egypt's lead and sign similar agreements with Israel were quickly dashed. Indeed, the Camp David Accords produced a strong negative reaction in the Arab world, where other states and the PLO denounced the agreement and condemned Sadat for hav-ing "sold out" the Arab cause. Egypt was expelled from the Arab League, and several Middle Eastern nations broke off diplo-matic relations with Cairo. For Sadat, the consequences were literally fatal. In Octo-ber 1981 radical, Islamist Egyptian army officers who belonged to the Islamic Jihad organization, which hoped to overthrow the government and had bitterly denounced Sadat's un-Islamic rule and failure to imple-ment Islamic law, his peace overtures with Israel, and his suppression of dissidents, assassinated him as he reviewed a mili-tary parade. Not until the mid-1990s would another Arab nation, Jordan, join Egypt in normalizing relations with Israel. None-theless, the Camp David Accords were undoubtedly President Carter's greatest for-eign policy success.

Brent Geary and Spencer C. Tucker

Further Reading

Brzezinski, Zbigniew. *Power and Principle: Memoirs of the National Security Adviser, 1977–1981.* New York: Farrar, Straus and Giroux, 1985.

Carter, James E. *Keeping Faith: Memoirs of the President.* New York: Bantam, 1982.

Glad, Betty. *An Outsider in the White House: Jimmy Carter, His Advisers, and the Mak-ing of American Foreign Policy.* Ithaca, NY: Cornell University Press, 2009.

Gordis, Daniel. *Menachem Begin: The Battle for Israel's Soul*. New York: Schocken Books, 2014.

Hurwitz, Harry, and Yisrael Medad, eds. *Peace in the Making: The Menachem Begin-Anwar El-Sadat Personal Correspondence*. Jerusalem: Gefen Books, 2011.

Kamel, Mohamed Ibrahim. *The Camp David Accords*. London: KPI, 1986.

Parker, Thomas. *The Road to Camp David*. New York: Peter Lang, 1988.

Quandt, William. *Camp David: Peacemaking and Politics*. Washington, DC: Brookings Institution, 1986.

Shilon, Avi. *Menachem Begin: A Life*. New Haven, CT: Yale University Press, 2012.

Stein, Kenneth W. *Heroic Diplomacy: Kissinger, Sadat, Carter, Begin and the Quest for Arab-Israeli Peace*. New York: Routledge, 1999.

Strong, Robert A. *Working in the World: Jimmy Carter and the Making of American Foreign Policy*. Baton Rouge: Louisiana State University Press, 2000.

Telhami, Shibley. *Power and Leadership in International Bargaining: The Path to the Camp David Accords*. New York: Columbia University Press, 1990.

E

Egypt

An African and a Middle Eastern nation, Egypt encompasses 386,660 square miles and is bordered by the Mediterranean Sea to the north, Sudan to the south, Libya to the west, and the Red Sea to the east. Egypt is one of the world's oldest civilizations. Its documented history extends well back into the third millennium BC. Its strategic position and the fertility of its land have always attracted outside powers. This strategic importance only increased with the opening of the Suez Canal in 1869.

Although the canal company was predominantly French, Britain acquired the shares belonging to the Khedive of Egypt and a controlling interest in it. The British recognized the importance of the canal as its imperial lifeline to India, and a nationalist uprising in Egypt gave Britain the excuse to seize control of Egypt in 1882. Within two decades, British authority was extended to the Sudan as well.

In December 1914, following the entry of the Ottoman Empire into World War I on the side of the Central Powers, Great Britain declared Egypt a protectorate. During the war Egypt became a major British military base for operations against Turkey on the Gallipoli Peninsula and in Palestine. Cairo was also the center for British diplomacy toward the Arabs.

In 1919, anti-British riots and labor unrest erupted in Egypt. In response, in February 1922, the British ended the protectorate and declared Egypt a sovereign, independent kingdom. This was window dressing only, for Britain continued to exercise real authority through its advisers, who controlled key departments including internal security. In April 1923, King Fuad promulgated a constitution that followed Western patterns but reserved considerable rights to the Crown. Anti-British demonstrations and agitation continued. Fuad died in April 1936 and was succeeded by his 16-year-old son Farouk. Meanwhile, the threat posed to the security of the region by Italy's invasion of Ethiopia in September 1935 and long-standing Egyptian grievances regarding British policy in Egypt and the Sudan had led to negotiations between the British and Egyptian governments and a new treaty between the two nations signed on August 26, 1936.

Among the major terms of the 1936 treaty, Britain pledged to defend Egypt against outside aggression, while Egypt promised to place its facilities at Britain's disposal in case of war. Egypt agreed to a garrison of 10,000 British troops and 400 pilots in the canal zone and to provide their barracks. Britain was to evacuate all other bases except the naval base at Alexandria, which it would have for eight more years. British personnel in the Egyptian army and the police were to be withdrawn (Britain had previously controlled the armed forces and the police), but a British military mission would advise the Egyptian army to the exclusion of other foreigners. Egyptian officers were to train abroad only in Britain. Britain also promised to allow unrestricted immigration of Egyptians into the Sudan, and Egyptian troops were also allowed to return there. Britain agreed to work for the removal of the capitulations and for most-favored nation

Anchored ships are seen in Port Said harbor, Egypt, September 18, 1956, awaiting the first southbound convoy to be piloted through the Suez Canal by the Egyptians since the seizure of the canal by Egyptian president Nasser. The Greek ship *Tasmania* is in the foreground. (AP Photo)

commercial treaties, and its high commissioner was replaced by an ambassador. The treaty was to be of indefinite duration but with negotiations for any changes permitted after 20 years.

In effect, Britain retained its right to protect security through the canal and compromised on a number of other issues. Left unresolved was the question of the future of the Sudan. Egypt ratified the treaty, although there was much criticism of it. Egypt was then admitted to the League of Nations. Many of the treaty's terms, however, were set aside with the advent of World War II.

Before and during World War II, both the Egyptian Crown and Britain sought to break the power of the Wafd Party, which had been the main vehicle of Egyptian nationalism since its founding in 1919 and dominated the parliament. In February 1938, ignoring constitutional rights, the king dissolved the parliament. The Wafd remained out of power for the next four years.

During World War II there was some pro-Axis sentiment in Egypt, but the British requested and received full government cooperation against Germany. Egypt became the principal British, and later Allied, base in the Middle East with more than half a million troops stationed there, and Cairo was a center of intense diplomatic activity and the venue for a major Allied conference in the fall of 1943. During the war, the numbers of British, Australian, and New Zealand troops in the country went up dramatically, leading many Egyptians to conclude that their long struggle to escape Western dominance via negotiation was of little consequence. Wartime profiteering, increased prostitution, and alcohol and drug use accompanied the Commonwealth forces in the country.

Egyptian president Muhammad Hosni Said Mubarak arriving in the United States at Andrews Air Force Base, Maryland, on January 27, 1983. (U.S. Department of Defense)

The war set in motion profound economic changes in Egypt, and these helped prompt a dangerous increase in extremism, both leftist and rightist. On the Left the Egyptian Communist Party, although illegal, gained in influence, partly because of the heightened prestige of the Soviet Union from the war. The party sought to exploit legitimate labor grievances that had arisen from the war.

On the Right there was the powerful Muslim Brotherhood. Organized by Sheikh Hasan al-Banna in 1929, it was both staunchly pro-Islamic and anti-West and opposed the corruption of wealthy landowners in parliament. In contrast to the small Communist Party of perhaps 5,000 members, the Muslim Brotherhood had a large following ranging from 500,000 to 3 million people according to different sources. It made no secret of its distaste for the Western

use of the country to fight the Axis. In July 1946, the government moved against the Communists, arresting many of the party leaders and bringing them to trial in 1947. Most received prison terms.

The government also began a low-scale war with the Muslim Brotherhood in 1948 when it banned the organization following the assassination of a judge who had sentenced a member of the Brotherhood. The Muslim Brotherhood had developed a secret military organization since 1939 that was banned by General Guide Hasan al-Banna. After the ban, though, more violence broke out, and a member of the Brotherhood assassinated Prime Minister Mahmud al-Nuqrashi. The Egyptian secret police assassinated al-Banna in 1949 on the orders of the government, which refused to re-legalize the Brotherhood.

In the January 1950 parliamentary elections, the Wafd won 228 of 319 seats in the Chamber, and Nahas Pasha again assumed the premiership. He persuaded King Farouk to remove 17 appointed senators, replacing them with Wafd nominees and giving that party an absolute majority in both chambers.

In foreign affairs, the Egyptian government was determined to revise the 1936 treaty with Britain. The two chief points of grievance for the Egyptians were the continued presence of British troops in the country and the matter of the future of the Sudan, which Egypt sought to regain or liberate from British control. There were strong historical, cultural, ethnic (in the case of the northern Sudan), and economic ties between Egypt and the Sudan, but Egypt was most concerned about the security of its critical water supply in the Nile River, which flowed north through the Sudan into Egypt.

In October 1946, Egyptian prime minister Sidqi Pasha concluded an agreement with British foreign secretary Ernest Bevin.

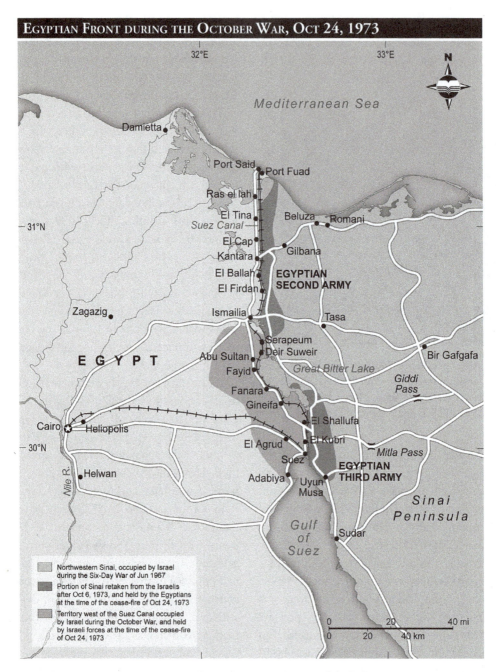

EGYPTIAN FRONT DURING THE OCTOBER WAR, OCT 24, 1973

Northwestern Sinai, occupied by Israel during the Six-Day War of Jun 1967

Portion of Sinai retaken from the Israelis after Oct 6, 1973, and held by the Egyptians at the time of the cease-fire of Oct 24, 1973

Territory west of the Suez Canal occupied by Israel during the October War, and held by Israeli forces at the time of the cease-fire of Oct 24, 1973

Map of the Egyptian Front during the October War on October 24, 1973 in the Arab-Israeli Wars.

It provided for the withdrawal of British forces from the canal zone and a formula regarding a settlement in the Sudan, by which the Sudanese themselves would determine their future government and whether the Sudan would be part of Egypt or independent.

In 1948, Egypt went to war against Israel. Egypt was able to send only a small military force to participate in the coalition of Arab states against the Jewish state, and Egyptian forces performed poorly, suffering a number of defeats. This was a source of embarrassment for Egyptians.

In the January 1950 general elections the Wafd was returned to power, resulting in talks with Britain in the winter of 1950–1951 over modification of the 1936 treaty. The Cold War produced British intransigence regarding revision, however, as Western nations regarded Egypt as their suitable base in the Middle East. As an indication of Egyptian attitudes, upon the beginning of the Korean War in June 1950, the Egyptian government announced that it would be neutral and not support the United Nations (UN) military effort there.

Discontent against the government and its policies had been steadily building. On January 19, 1952, rioting broke out at Ismailiyya, an important town and base at the north end of the Suez Canal. The British then occupied the town and evicted the local police. This led to major riots in Cairo in which hundreds of well-known establishments were put to the torch. The toll in a day of rioting on January 26 was 26 dead and 552 wounded. King Farouk, hostile to the Wafd, took advantage of this event to dismiss Nahas Pasha and his cabinet on January 27 and appoint Ali Mahir Pasha in his place.

All this created something of a political vacuum, which was filled on July 23, 1952, when a core of 13 army officers, representing a larger group that had formed in 1949, seized power in Egypt. They set up a Revolutionary Command Council (RCC) of 17 members. The chairmanship of the RCC went to Major General Mohammad Naguib, Ali Mahir headed the government, and a regency council acted for the son of King Farouk, Ahmad Fuad. The real leader of the Free Officers was Gamal Abdel Nasser, however. In 1953, when the monarchy was abolished, Nasser became deputy prime minister and minister of the interior in 1953, while Naguib became president and prime minister. The RCC made it clear that it sought to free Egypt from imperialism and feudalism and introduce a program of social justice, reform, and economic progress. On July 26, Naguib demanded that King Farouk renounce the throne and leave Egypt forthwith. Farouk departed the same day, abdicating in favor of his infant son Ahmed Fuad II. This arrangement lasted for only one year until June 1953, when the military junta terminated the monarchy and declared Egypt a republic. While Naguib was the nominal head of the revolutionary government, the real authority rested in the hands of the RCC, which was dominated by Colonel Nasser. On April 17, 1954, Nasser pushed Naguib aside and assumed full power.

During the first years after the revolution, the military leaders perceived themselves as Egyptian nationalists with the twin missions of domestic social reform and ridding the country of foreign influence. The new government also moved against the Muslim Brotherhood, which had supported their coup. In January 1954, the government ordered it dissolved and arrested 78 of its leaders. Soon the Egyptian leader announced a broader movement known as Pan-Arabism (also called Nasserism), a mix of nationalism and Pan-Arab sentiments. Nasser supported improving the lot of the common man or peasants, and after 1961 he advocated greater Arab socialism. His regime moved to carry out land reform and nationalized most banks and many commercial and industrial enterprises. The centerpiece of Nasser's economic program was to be a new high dam at Aswan in southern Egypt. This, he believed, would provide electricity sufficient for Egyptian needs, halt the often costly Nile flooding, and open new lands for crops. Despite sweeping changes or due to their incomplete realization coupled with defense spending, the Egyptian economy underperformed during most of Nasser's years in power.

While the early years after the 1952 coup saw little participation by Egypt in Arab affairs, the Aswan High Dam project and the Suez Crisis soon changed that. On October 19, 1954, shortly after coming to power, Nasser had concluded a new treaty with Britain whereby the British gave up all rights to the Suez Canal base and agreed to evacuate the canal zone entirely within 20 months. In return, Egypt promised to keep the base in combat readiness and allow the British to return in case of an attack by an outside power against Turkey or any Arab state.

Meanwhile, the United States and Britain agreed to extend financial assistance to Egypt for the Aswan High Dam project. However, when these Western powers refused to sell Nasser advanced weaponry and he concluded a massive arms deal with Czechoslovakia for Soviet-bloc weapons and then recognized the People's Republic of China (PRC), the United States cancelled its offer of aid for the dam construction. The British government followed suit. In response, on July 26, 1956, Nasser (elected president of Egypt on June 23) nationalized the Suez Canal. Nasser planned to use the revenues from the canal to pay for construction of the Aswan Dam.

In spite of the Egyptian assurances of compensation to the Suez Canal Company shareholders, Britain and France began a secret dialogue with Israel for an attack on Egypt to topple Nasser from power and reoccupy the Suez Canal Zone. The attack began on October 29, 1956, when Israeli troops invaded the Gaza Strip and the Sinai Peninsula. On October 31, 1956, British and French forces, acting to protect the canal, joined the assault. These actions enraged U.S. president Dwight D. Eisenhower, who applied significant economic pressure to secure British withdrawal, which was followed by that of France and Israel.

Meanwhile, during the fighting Nasser had ordered ships sunk in the canal to keep it from being used by the invaders. This resulted in the closure of the canal until April 1957.

There were several important ramifications of the Suez Crisis. First and foremost, it greatly bolstered Nasser's standing in the Arab world as a leader who could stand up to foreign powers, a position he would try to utilize to form Arab alliances for the remainder of his life. The conflict also resulted in the signing of a Treaty of Arab Solidarity among Egypt, Saudi Arabia, Syria, and Jordan in January 1957, as well as the Eisenhower administration's announcement of the Eisenhower Doctrine to provide both financial and military support to any nation in the Middle East in the struggle against communism.

Within a year, the solidarity movement from the Suez Crisis among the various Arab states was weakened. Some experts have called this the beginning of the Arab Cold War. However, Westerners might not appreciate Nasser's popularity throughout the region from Morocco to Iraq, not least because of his oratorical skills, which were heard over the radio. On February 1, 1958, Syria invited Nasser to join in a union known as the United Arab Republic (UAR). This created tensions in Syria, as one political faction had essentially preempted another with this invitation. Syrian opponents to the union complained of Egyptian dominance and economic changes not well suited to Syria (although the subsequent governments also embarked on land reform). Jordan also saw the UAR as a clear threat. In September 1961, the UAR dissolved after a coup swept the ruling faction in Syria out of office, and Nasser accepted the dissolution.

In the meantime, Egypt began to turn increasingly to the Soviet bloc for aid, beginning with Soviet assistance in construction of the Aswan Dam. Egypt began a war of words with Saudi Arabia that eventually emerged as a proxy struggle in Yemen. The Arab states agreed on the danger that Israel represented to them and the need to find justice for the Palestinian refugees. Egypt claimed leadership of the Pan-Arab movement in this regard and promoted cultural and intellectual expressions of Arab identity. Pan-Arabism remained very popular in the region among youths, workers, intellectuals, peasants, and professionals despite the difficulties of formally expressing it through political union. Nasser's strengthening of Egypt's political profile and regional leadership through Arabism was borne out in the country's continuing influence and mediation of crises in the region, from Jordan to Lebanon on up to the present day.

In December 1961, Nasser broke off relations with the monarchical government of Yemen and began clandestine support for a republican movement there. Saudi Arabia, meanwhile, supported the Yemeni monarchy. Finally, Egyptian armed forces intervened openly on the republican side. Egyptian troops remained in Yemen until 1967 and the Egyptian defeat in the Six-Day War. The Yemen war was both costly and deeply frustrating for Egypt. The People's Democratic Republic of Yemen was a highly progressive Marxist state that attempted modernization and reform, inspired in some ways by Nasser's Egypt. The country has since reunified.

Nasser signed a mutual defense treaty between Egypt and Syria on November 4, 1966. At the time, both Egypt and Syria were supporting guerrillas operating against Israel. Tensions in the region began to mount with this alliance, and they were exacerbated on November 13, 1966, when Israeli forces destroyed the Jordanian village of Samu, which Israel asserted had often served as

a staging area for guerrilla strikes into its territory. This action escalated already high regional tensions.

On April 7, 1967, in response to an incident on the Golan Heights, Israeli aircraft shot down seven Syria fighter jets and concluded the action by a triumphant flight over Damascus itself. On May 16, Nasser promised to come to the aid of Syria if it was attacked, and he heightened tensions by ordering several divisions closer to the Israeli border in the Sinai. On May 18, Nasser demanded the removal of the UN Emergency Force (UNEF) along the cease-fire line with Israel, and UN secretary general U Thant complied. Four days later, Nasser placed an Egyptian garrison at Sharm al-Sheikh and announced a blockade of the Straits of Tiran, effectively closing the Israeli port of Eilat. On May 30, Jordan's King Hussein signed a military alliance with Egypt.

On June 5, 1967, as tensions came to a head, Israel launched a series of well-coordinated peremptory strikes first against Egypt and then on Syria, Jordan, and Iraq. The centerpiece of this was a crippling air strike on the morning of June 5, which resulted in most of Egypt's aircraft destroyed on the ground. Soon, Israeli ground forces had driven deep into the Sinai. By June 8, after only four days of fighting, Egypt had suffered its most stunning modern military defeat. Still, the war continued for two more days. At its conclusion, the Israelis occupied the West Bank in Jordan, Syria's Golan Heights, and the entire Sinai Peninsula in Egypt. This last territorial acquisition brought Israeli troops to the Suez Canal.

In all, Egyptian losses included 10,000 enlisted men and 1,500 officers killed or wounded, with an additional 5,000 enlisted men and 500 officers taken prisoner. The Egyptians lost 600 tanks and virtually their entire air force.

The shock of the defeat lingered on for years. Nasser, stung by this sudden reversal, resigned the presidency on June 9. The Egyptian people took to the streets, however, refusing to accept his resignation and demanding that he remain in power, which he did. Indeed, Egypt's defeat in the 1967 Six-Day War led to the emergence of militant and revolutionary activity to protest the failures of the Arab states. While Egyptian political and military leaders took the first steps that might have led to the return of their lost territories, opposition groups and the Palestinians concluded that the Arab armies and governments might not be capable of victory and began planning smaller-scale military actions. Thus, the Six-Day War led directly to the War of Attrition (1968–1970).

In June 1968, Nasser's government, still smarting from the humiliation of the Six-Day War, began shelling Israeli positions on the east bank of the Suez Canal. In the meantime, the Israelis had fortified this forward position with a string of forts known as the Bar-Lev Line. The Israelis responded on October 30 with a commando raid that effectively destroyed Egypt's electrical-generating facilities. In February 1969, Egypt again initiated a series of bombardments and counterbombardments across the canal. This time, the fighting led to superpower intervention when Nasser flew to Moscow in January 1970 seeking arms and military aid. This in turn precipitated a whole new set of difficulties. The United States became involved in negotiations that finally led to a cease-fire agreement on August 7, 1970. Nasser died suddenly the next month, on September 28, 1970, after negotiating a cease-fire in the Black September violence in Jordan. He was succeeded by his vice president, Anwar Sadat.

For a brief time, Sadat continued Nasser's policies toward both the Soviet Union and Israel as he dealt with internal opposition. But before long, Sadat began to replace Nasser's supporters in the government and initiated a major turn against his predecessor's policies, both foreign and domestic. Domestically, by 1975 this included a move away from Nasser's state socialist economic policies, including changes in investment laws and import rules. These became known as the Infitah, or economic opening. Sadat sent home the Soviet and Soviet-bloc advisers in Egypt and sought increased economic aid from the West, including the United States. He also freed Islamist groups such as the Muslim Brotherhood and allowed Muslim student groups to meet in an effort to mobilize them against leftist students and elements who protested his new policies.

Sadat embarked on a concentrated program of rearmament and military reform. The new weaponry, which included large numbers of surface-to-air missiles (SAMs), was supplied mainly by the Soviet Union. After 1972, Egypt sought Western weapons and made efforts to upgrade older weapons systems. General Ismail Ali was the chief figure associated with these improvements in the Egyptian military. He undertook a series of changes in the Egyptian army designed to take advantage of its strengths while at the same time minimizing its weaknesses. These resulted in the concentration of SAMs along the Suez Canal to counter the Israeli air force. Likewise, he drastically increased the proportion of antitank weapons to deal with Israeli armor.

By 1973, Sadat had agreed to participate with Syria in a daring preemptive strike against Israel as a way to reverse the outcome of the Six-Day War. The timing of the attack, around the Jewish holiday of Yom Kippur and the Muslim observance of Ramadan, was an attempt to maximize Arab chances. The overall strategy was for Egypt and Syria to launch a concerted attack on Israel, inflict a quick but serious defeat on the Jewish state, and thus influence the negotiations for the return of the lost territories.

For their part, the Israelis were clearly overconfident in their ability to repel any Arab attack after their easy victories in the Six-Day War and their continued success in the War of Attrition. Warnings of the impending attack fell on deaf ears, and the timing of the strike caught the Israelis by surprise. They were also certain that any Arab attack could be defeated from the air. In retrospect, the Arab attack was a great humiliation for the Israeli military and intelligence communities, for the Egyptians had practiced their attack in military exercises in plain view of the Israeli army.

The actual attack began on October 13, 1973. The Egyptians were able to cross the Suez Canal and secure most of the forts of the vaunted Israeli Bar-Lev Line, while Syrian forces drove into the Golan Heights. The Egyptian plan had been to capture the Israeli defensive positions, destroy, with their missiles, the Israeli air and armor counterattacks, and wait for a negotiated settlement. But the success of the Egyptians in their crossing and their subsequent accomplishments in shooting down a number of aircraft and blunting the Israeli ground counterattack led Sadat to demand deeper offensive action. The Egyptians deviated from the original plan, and by October 15 the initiative had passed into the hands of the Israelis. The fighting raged on until October 22, when a cease-fire negotiated by the United States and the Soviet Union went into effect. From this point on, the negotiations began for a peace settlement.

Frustrated by the slow progress, Sadat decided on a radical change of course. On November 19, 1977, he flew to Israel, much to the astonishment of the world community.

His move was condemned in most Arab capitals. By going to Israel, Sadat implicitly recognized its existence. He also became the first Arab leader to do so, and it proved the turning point in the negotiations. In September 1978, Sadat and Israeli prime minister Menachem Begin signed the Camp David Peace Accords. Negotiated in part with the assistance of U.S. president Jimmy Carter, the agreements returned the Sinai Peninsula to Egypt. In return, Egypt officially recognized Israel. This historic rapprochement in effect ended Egyptian involvement in the Arab-Israeli wars. The peace accords also solidified the growing Egyptian-American alliance.

Yet the Israeli-Egyptian peace deal had negative repercussions as well. Much of the Arab world was infuriated by Sadat's seeming capitulation to the Israelis. As such, the other states cut off aid, discouraged travel to Egypt, and expelled Egypt from the Arab League. Within Egypt, the bilateral agreement with Israel had not been popular. As time went by, support for it steadily eroded, as many Egyptians blamed economic dislocations, rising factionalism, and dissatisfaction with the political scene on the Camp David settlement. Such public resentment also extended to Sadat, who had promised but not delivered political liberalization.

In 1980, a cultural agreement was signed between Egypt and Israel. Those intellectuals, journalists, physicians, athletes, and writers who braved boycotts in their professional syndicates in Egypt were disappointed to learn that even Israeli doves did not support Palestinian sovereignty. The Israeli Academic Center in Egypt brought little contact between Egyptians and Israelis. As a result, following Sadat's death the Egyptian government essentially stopped promoting cultural exchange.

As factionalism and extremism continued to rise in Egypt, Sadat's position became more difficult, and he arrested a large number of political opponents on the Left and the Right. On October 6, 1981, he was assassinated by members of the radical Islamic Jihad while in the reviewing stand during a military parade. Whereas Nasser was loudly and demonstrably mourned by the Egyptian public, Sadat was not.

Sadat was immediately succeeded by his vice president, Hosni Mubarak, who was also injured in the assassination. Mubarak, who presided over Egyptian politics from 1981 to 2011, continued Sadat's policies, although slowing economic rationalization and privatization. He also put the brakes on political liberalization that would strengthen any parts of government except for the executive or that might lead to free elections for all candidates and parties.

Under Sadat, the Arab Socialist Union, the mass political party, had begun its transformation into the National Democratic Party. Only a few small opposition parties were allowed to operate openly, including the Wafd. Mubarak continued operating through the National Democratic Party in which his son, Jamal, likewise later became a leader. Mubarak also continued Sadat's policy of cooperation with the West, and he maintained diplomatic relations with Israel except during several notable crises. Mubarak also sought to maintain a potent military establishment. He continued to modernize and upgrade it, and by 1992 the Egyptian air force was the largest in the Middle East.

During the 1991 Persian Gulf War, Mubarak joined the international coalition against the Iraqi invasion of Kuwait, and Egyptian troops were among the first to land in Kuwait at the beginning of the ground war in February 1991. As a result of its service to the coalition, Egypt received loan waivers in excess of $20 billion from the United States, Western Europe, and several Persian Gulf states.

Mubarak spoke out against the Anglo-American invasion of Iraq in 2003, believing that it would only further the growth of extremism in the region. From the late 1980s to 1999 when a truce was forged, radical and fundamentalist groups within Egypt waged low-level terrorist activities against local and national officials as well as tourists. From 2003 onward, new extremist groups not participating in the truce emerged. Many of these groups still decried the settlement with Israel. Mubarak came under pressure from Washington to denounce both Hamas and Hezbollah, although Egyptians generally supported them, and to rein in the Muslim Brotherhood, which was indeed his government's policy.

In the late 1990s, the Egyptian economy entered a period of sluggish growth and high unemployment. Tourism was adversely affected by terrorist attacks during 2004–2005. Unemployment and underemployment remained very high. Mubarak came under increasing pressure from the international community to carry out significant political reform, including an end to the emergency laws in place since Sadat's assassination that prohibited political activity or gatherings not sanctioned by the government. He also refused to permit the holding of bona fide presidential and legislative elections or provide for judicial oversight of elections. In the early 21st century, he took only halting steps to address these issues. Despite assassination attempts Mubarak refused to designate a successor, arousing fears among the opposition that he intended to pass the presidency to his son Jamal following the completion of his fifth presidential term in 2011.

In late January 2011, spontaneous street demonstrations erupted in Egypt, inspired in part by the recent success of popular protests in Tunisia in ousting that country's long-time president. Mubarak initially resorted to forcible repression, but resigned in February 2011, transferring power to the Egyptian armed forces. The military immediately dissolved parliament, suspended the constitution, and promised to lift the 30-year-old state of emergency. Protests continued throughout 2011, driven by fears that the military sought to defer implementing any reforms. In September 2011, insurgents sacked the Israeli embassy in Cairo, in retaliation for the deaths of Egyptian border guards some weeks early, in an Israeli operation in Sinai. In June 2012, Mohamed Morsi, leader of the Islamic Muslim Brotherhood, one of the most prominent opposition groups, became the first democratically elected Egyptian president, with 51.73 percent of the vote.

Morsi and his followers were far more adamantly hostile to Israel than Mubarak had been, and strongly supportive of the radical Hamas regime in Gaza. In September 2012, Egyptian militants opened fire on Israeli soldiers and civilians across the border, killing one Israeli soldier. Morsi's efforts to expand presidential powers, dismiss political rivals, and remodel Egypt on sectarian rather than secular and democratic lines soon provoked fresh protests, with millions of Egyptians participating in these in the first half of 2013. In July 2013, the Egyptian military ousted Morsi, placing Egypt under military rule once more. Adly Mansour, head of the constitutional court, was appointed interim president. Whether Egypt would again take a relatively moderate stance and encourage Palestinian-Israeli reconciliation remained unclear in early 2014. The country appeared largely preoccupied with domestic problems, bedeviled by economic difficulties, rising labor unrest, and high-profile terror attacks on security installations and personnel. In January 2014 a new constitution was approved. In late February 2014 the prime minister and cabinet resigned en masse, fuelling speculation that General Abdel-Fatah el-Sissi, the defense minister, would soon run for the presidency.

James R. Mcintyre, Paul G. Pierpaoli Jr., Spencer C. Tucker, and Sherifa Zuhur

Further Reading

Abdel-Malek, Anouar. *Egypt: Military Society, the Army Regime, the Left, and Social Change under Nasser.* New York: Random House, 1968.

Al Aswaany, Alaa. *On the State of Egypt: What Made the Revolution Inevitable.* Cairo, Egypt: American University in Cairo Press, 2011.

Al-Awadi, Hesham. *In Pursuit of Legitimacy: The Muslim Brothers and Mubarak, 1982–2000.* New York: I. B. Tauris, 2004.

Al-faqih, Abdullah. *Liberalization and Democratization in Egypt, Jordan, and Yemen: Beginnings, Development, and Decline.* Saarbrücken, Germany: VDM Verlag Dr. Müller, 2013.

Amin, Galal. *Egypt in the Era of Hosni Mubarak.* Cairo, Egypt: American University in Cairo Press, 2011.

Beattie, Kirk J. *Egypt during the Sadat Years.* New York: Palgrave Macmillan, 2000.

Bradley, John R. *After the Arab Spring: How Islamists Hijacked the Middle East Revolts.* New York: Palgrave Macmillan, 2012.

Bradley, John R. *Inside Egypt: The Land of the Pharaohs on the Brink of a Revolution.* New York: Palgrave Macmillan, 2008.

Brownlee, Jason. *Democracy Prevention: The Politics of the U.S.-Egyptian Alliance.* Cambridge: Cambridge University Press, 2012.

Burns, William J. *Economic Aid and American Policy toward Egypt, 1955–1981.* Albany: State University of New York Press, 1984.

Cook, Steven A. *The Struggle for Egypt: From Nasser to Tahrir Square.* New York: Oxford University Press, 2011.

Cooper, Chester L. *The Lion's Last Roar: Suez, 1956.* New York: Harper and Row, 1978.

Dawisha, A. I. *Egypt in the Arab World.* New York: Wiley, 1976.

Elaasar, Aladdin. *The Last Pharaoh: Mubarak and the Uncertain Future of Egypt in the Obama Age*. Boston, MA: Beacon Press, 2009.

El-Mahdi, Rabab, and Philip Marfleet, eds. *Egypt: The Moment of Change*. London: Zed Books, 2009.

Gardner, Lloyd C. *The Road to Tahrir Square: Egypt and the United States from the Rise of Nasser to the Fall of Mubarak*. New York: New Press, 2011.

Kassem, Maye. *Egyptian Politics: The Dynamics of Authoritarian Rule*. Boulder, CO: Lynne Rienner, 2004.

Khalil, Ashraf. *Liberation Square: Inside the Egyptian Revolution and the Rebirth of a Nation*. New York: St. Martin's Press, 2012.

Korn, David. A. *Stalemate: The War of Attrition and Great Power Diplomacy in the Middle East, 1967–1970*. Boulder, CO: Westview, 1992.

Lesch, Ann Mosely, and Mark Tessler. *Israel, Egypt, and the Palestinians: From Camp David to Intifada*. Bloomington: Indiana University Press, 1989.

McDermott, Anthony. *Egypt from Nasser to Mubarak: A Flawed Revolution*. London: Routledge and Kegan Paul, 1998.

Osman, Tarek. *Egypt on the Brink: From Nasser to Mubarak*. New Haven, CT: Yale University Press, 2011.

Pollack, Kenneth M. *Arabs at War: Military Effectiveness, 1948–1991*. Lincoln: University of Nebraska Press, 2002.

Stacher, Joshua. *Adaptable Autocrats: Regime Power in Egypt and Syria*. Stanford: Stanford University Press, 2012.

Stein, Ewan. *Representing Israel in Modern Egypt: Ideas, Intellectuals and Foreign Policy from Nasser to Mubarak*. New York: I. B. Tauris, 2012.

Tadros, Mariz. *The Muslim Brotherhood in Contemporary Egypt: Democracy Redefined or Confined?* New York: Routledge, 2012.

Thompson, Jason. *A History of Egypt: From Earliest Times to the Present*. Cairo, Egypt: American University in Cairo Press, 2008.

Waterbury, John. *The Egypt of Nasser and Sadat: Political Economy of Two Regimes*. Princeton, NJ: Princeton University Press, 1983.

Zahid, Mohammed. *The Muslim Brotherhood and Egypt's Succession Crisis: The Politics of Liberalisation and Reform in the Middle East*. New York: I. B. Tauris, 2010.

European Union and the Arab-Israeli Conflict

From the outset, the European Economic Community (EEC), later renamed the European Community (EC) and currently known as the European Union (EU), has had problematic relations with Israel. There are several reasons for this. First, member states of the EU have often acted unilaterally, reflecting individual rather than group priorities. Second, international developments, especially in the context of Arab-Israeli conflicts, have shifted, triggering changes in policy. Third, both Israel and its major supporter, the United States, have objected to the European body's perceived pro-Arab stance and have therefore been hesitant to allow the EU an active role in the Middle East peace process.

The EU's Israeli policies thus need to be viewed in an evolving context. By and large, however, they reflect a movement from an initially passive to a more active role in the peace process, alongside increasing efforts to consolidate economic and cultural links with both Israel and the Arab world. Central to these initiatives are the EU's Euro-Mediterranean Partnership (EMP), otherwise known as the Barcelona Process, and the European Neighborhood Policy (ENP).

The Treaty of Rome (1957), which founded the EEC, included no formal foreign policy provisions, leaving key aspects up to individual member states. Although the EEC recognized Israel as early as 1959 and by 1964 had drawn up a limited European-Israeli trade agreement, its more active role in the Middle

Palestine leader Yasser Arafat, left, with Luxembourg foreign minister and EU Council president Jacques Poos, second left, Israeli foreign minister David Levy, second right, and EU Special Envoy to the Middle East Miguel Angel Moratinos, right, at press conference following bilateral talks between Levy and Arafat on July 22, 1997. (AP Photo/Tatia Paule)

East developed slowly. During the 1967 Six-Day War, EEC policy largely reflected that of the United States, focusing on curtailing the Soviet presence and its influence on the spread of Arab nationalism. Nevertheless, the policy of individual EEC members reflected a growingly critical stance, as in 1965, when West German Chancellor Ludwig Erhard proclaimed his country's neutrality in future Arab-Israeli conflicts and in 1967 when French president Charles de Gaulle condemned Israel's decision to wage war, terminating Franco-Israeli military cooperation.

Nevertheless, it was not until the Yom Kippur War of 1973 and the subsequent Organization of Petroleum Exporting Countries (OPEC) oil embargo that the European body, now renamed the European Community, began to abandon its passive role toward Israel and the Middle East. OPEC's October 13, 1973, announcement that 11 Arab oil-producing countries would reduce oil production by 5 percent monthly, an action that would target countries viewed as supporters of Israel, created panic in Western Europe, which then depended on Arab countries for about 70–80 percent of its oil. This development led the EC to its first major collective action when on October 28, 1973, it released a communiqué calling for Israel to recognize Palestinian rights and withdraw from all territories it had occupied since the June 1967 Six-Day War.

This increasingly critical stance toward Israel continued with the EC's 1979 condemnation of Israeli settlement policy and culminated in the Venice Declaration of 1980, issued in the wake of the U.S.-sponsored Camp David Accords between Egypt and Israel. This declaration voiced EC support of United Nations (UN) Security Council Resolutions 242 and 338. While the UN resolutions, however, viewed the Palestinian problem primarily from a refugee perspective, the European declaration emphasized that the Palestinian people should be allowed to exercise their right to self-determination and that the Palestine Liberation Organization (PLO) should take part in peace negotiations. Israel strongly objected to Europe's demand that it deal with a "terrorist organization" and denounced Europe's "Munich-like capitulation to totalitarian blackmail."

The crises of 1973 further spurred the EC's foreign involvement by highlighting the importance of diplomatic exchange and trade agreements. To serve these ends, the EC expanded its political relationship with Middle Eastern countries via the Euro-Arab dialogue and set in motion its long-term goal of creating a free trade area in the Mediterranean region by implementing the Global Mediterranean Policy (GMP). The 1975 cooperation agreement with Israel aimed at mutually eliminating all customs duties on industrial goods and establishing a cooperative in the areas of finance, agriculture, and industry. By the beginning of 1977, the EC provided free access for Israeli industrial products. Correspondingly, Israel removed duties on comparable EC goods by 1989. In short, Israel had achieved a preferential status as an EC trading partner.

Nevertheless, the ongoing Arab-Israeli conflict left its mark on trade relations between Israel and Europe. In 1982, the EC condemned Israel's invasion of Lebanon as a violation of international law and placed the 1975 trade agreement on hold for a year. Similarly, the First Intifada of 1987 led the European Parliament to delay finalization of three financial and trade protocols with Israel in March 1988. These were passed only when Israel agreed to permit agricultural and manufactured goods stemming from the occupied territories to pass

unobstructed through Israeli ports en route to Europe. Before the introduction of the single market in 1992, the EC placed further pressure on Israel by delaying negotiations on a new bilateral trade agreement. Progress was made dependent upon breakthroughs in the Madrid peace process, begun in 1991. Only with the signing of the Oslo Accords in 1993 did the European body, now known as the EU, proceed with negotiations, which officially resumed in November 1995.

In spite of the EU's growing economic and political importance, however, Israel and the United States were reluctant to assign Europe a more active role in peace negotiations, as when the EU secured merely observer status in the Madrid conference of 1991, convened by the United States and Russia. The EU nevertheless began to play a leading role in multilateral working groups set up to channel financial aid to the Middle East and coordinate economic, infrastructural, social, and environmental projects. Most importantly, it headed the Regional Economic Development Working Group (REDWG) that, after the Oslo Accords and the Washington Agreements were signed in 1993, was delegated with initiatives for economic rebuilding in the occupied territories. The EU soon became the main financial supporter of the Palestinian Authority (PA), contributing more than $2 billion from 1994 to 1999.

Subsequent developments caused further deterioration in EU-Israeli relations and highlighted disunity within the EU. After the failure of the Oslo Accords, French president Jacques Chirac paid a controversial visit to East Jerusalem in 1996 and sent French delegates to negotiate a cease-fire after the Israeli shelling of southern Lebanon in April 1996. Critical of the French action, the EU reluctantly sent its own negotiating team and held talks with PLO leader

Yasser Arafat and Israeli foreign minister David Levy. Israel rebuffed the European move, while U.S. secretary of state Warren Christopher warned EU members to refrain from interfering in the peace process at such a delicate time.

The EU's next move, appointing a special envoy to the peace process, was more successful. Miguel Moratinos, the former Spanish ambassador to Israel, received a mandate to facilitate dialogue among Israelis, Palestinians, and other Arabs. Not only did he arrange a meeting between Arafat and the Israeli foreign minister in Brussels, but he was also instrumental in Israel's agreement to withdraw its troops from Hebron, where they had been stationed since the massacre of 1994. Late in 1997, Moratinos presented a code of conduct to Palestinian and Israeli representatives, calling upon the Israeli government of Benjamin Netanyahu to adhere to previous commitments and the Palestinians to combat terrorism. As another signal of increasing European involvement, in March 1998, an EU delegation headed by British foreign minister Robin Cook highlighted concerns with Israeli settlement policy and protested the Netanyahu government's refusal to open an EU-funded airport in Gaza.

Yet the EU took no part in the U.S.-led diplomacy culminating in the Wye River Memorandum of October 1998, whereby Israel agreed to withdraw from 13 percent of West Bank territory. The Washington Donors' Conference of November 30, 1998, whereby the EU and member states pledged 3.2 billion European currency units (ECUs) in support of the PA, reconfirmed Europe's role as a payer and not a major player in the Middle East peace process.

The failure of the Camp David Summit in September 2000 marked a new low in the Middle East peace process, exacerbated by the shift of focus from Palestine to Iraq in the wake of the September 11, 2001, terror attacks on the United States. Nevertheless, the Mitchell Report of April 2001, cosponsored by the United States and the EU, made recommendations for resuming negotiations, and a new diplomatic initiative resulted in the creation of the Quartet—the United States, Russia, the UN, and the EU—as a forum for advancing the peace process. By the end of 2002, the Quartet, upon European urging, had established the Road Map to Peace for a Palestinian-Israeli settlement that would lead to the establishment of two states. On April 30, 2003, the plan was presented to Israeli prime minister Ariel Sharon and Mahmoud Abbas, newly elected PA prime minister.

The first years of the 21st century, however, highlighted the EU's impotence and disunity in the ongoing conflict. Europe's credibility suffered from its failure to take a unified stand on sanctions against Israel in the wake of its renewed occupation of West Bank territory. Nevertheless, in November 2005, Israel agreed to allow the EU to maintain a Border Assistance Mission at the Rafah crossing between the Gaza Strip and Egypt. Similarly, Israel also welcomed the presence of European countries as peacekeepers after the Israeli-Hezbollah War (July–August 2006).

EU-Israeli relations underwent yet another shift with the PA's election of a Hamas government on January 25, 2006. On April 10, 2006, the EU decided to suspend direct aid to the PA, announcing that in coordination with the Middle East Quartet it would cut $600 million, which had comprised some 25 percent of the PA's total foreign aid. The United States also cut $420 million at this time, and Israel withheld about $60 million per month, also using $15 million to pay the PA's water and electricity bills, which the

PA could not pay directly. The EU instead allowed an emergency aid package of $140 million to keep the PA from collapsing, although this meant a barely functioning state.

Other indications of a possible rapprochement between the EU and Israel included the endorsement of a three-year ENP Action Plan in December 2004 and its implementation in April 2005. As part of the EMP (Barcelona Process), the agreement incorporated free trade arrangements for industrial goods, concessionary arrangements for trade in agricultural products, and the possibility for Israel to participate increasingly in key aspects of EU policies and programs. Since June 2006, the EU has provided direct assistance to the Palestinians through the temporary international mechanism (TIM). Created at the request of the Quartet and the European Council (EC), the TIM works closely with the PA Ministry of Finance to facilitate need-based assistance by international donors to the Palestinian people. Aid emphasis is in the public social services sector. In 2007, the EC committed €265 million through the TIM. Over the following six years, the EU, through the European Commission and member states, was the largest multilateral provider of financial assistance to the Palestinians, together with Norway and Switzerland.

At a March 2007 summit meeting of the Arab League, EU foreign affairs commissioner Xavier Solana endorsed the Arab Peace Initiative, a comprehensive proposal for a permanent settlement. This called for complete Israeli withdrawal from the occupied territories, the creation of an independent Palestinian state with East Jerusalem as its capital, and a "just solution" to the problem of Palestinian refugees. In return, all Arab states would sign permanent peace treaties with Israel, recognizing its existence. This proposal, first put forward by then Crown Prince Abdullah of Saudi Arabia at an Arab League meeting in 2002, had already won endorsement from all Arab League member states, plus PA president Mahmoud Abbas.

In 2008, the EU sought to enhance cooperation with the United States on the Arab-Israeli conflict, in the hope of facilitating a settlement. In 2009, the EU backed the PA plan, announced by Prime Minister Salam Fayyad, to establish a Palestinian state within two years, with its capital in Jerusalem. Eight of its 27 member states have already recognized the state of Palestine, though the organization was divided over the issue. The EU was repeatedly highly critical of Israeli military retaliation against attacks from Hamas and Hezbollah groups based in Lebanon and Gaza, characterizing these responses as "disproportionate" and "excessive" and calling for immediate cease-fires during such operations in 2008–2009 and 2012. In 2011, a classified EU working paper also recommended that the EU should address as a "core issue" the treatment of Arabs living in Israel, though EU members divided over this suggestion. In 2013, the EU adopted binding guidelines whereby, in any future agreements with the EU, the Israeli government must state that the settlements in the West Bank and East Jerusalem fall outside the state of Israel. Without such a declaration, no EU funding of any kind will be given to Israeli entities. These directives did not, however, affect funding from individual EU states to Israel. The Israeli government responded by refusing to sign any further agreements with the EU until this position had been clarified. Meanwhile, as a Quartet member, the EU continued to give strong support to continued negotiations between Israel and the PA intended to reach a final status agreement.

When U.S.-backed negotiations intended to accomplish this stalled in early 2014, across much of Europe pressure for economic sanctions and boycotts of Israel began to intensify.

Anna M. Wittmann

Further Reading

Ahlswede, Stefan. *Israel's European Policy after the Cold War*. Baden-Baden, Germany: Nomos, 2009.

Aoun, Elena. "European Foreign Policy and the Arab-Israeli Dispute: Much Ado about Nothing?" *European Foreign Affairs Review* 8 (2003): 289–312.

Cronin, David. *Europe's Alliance with Israel: Aiding the Occupation*. London: Pluto Press, 2011.

Dannreuther, Roland, ed. *European Union Foreign and Security Policy: Towards a Neighbourhood Strategy*. London: Routledge, 2004.

Gomez, Ricardo. *Negotiating the Euro-Mediterranean Partnership: Strategic Action in EU Foreign Policy?* Aldershot, UK: Ashgate, 2003.

Gorce, Paul-Marie de la. "Europe and the Arab-Israel Conflict: A Survey." *Journal of Palestine Studies* 26(3) (Spring 1997): 5–16.

Hollis, Rosemary. "Europe and the Middle East: Power by Stealth?" *International Affairs* 73(1) (January 1997): 15–29.

Miller, Rory. *Inglorious Disarray: Europe, Israel, and the Palestinians since 1967*. New York: Columbia University Press, 2011.

Musu, Constanza. *European Union Policy towards the Arab-Israeli Peace Process*. Basingstoke: Palgrave Macmillan, 2010.

Pardo, Sharon, and Joel Peters. *Israel and the European Union: A Documentary History*. Lanham, MD: Lexington Books, 2012.

Pardo, Sharon, and Joel Peters. *Uneasy Neighbors: Israel and the European Union*. Lanham, MD: Lexington Books, 2010.

Sachar, Howard Morley. *Israel and Europe: An Appraisal in History*. New York: Knopf, 1999.

Shindler, Colin. *Israel and the European Left: Between Solidarity and Delegitimization*. London: Bloomsbury, 2011.

Wistrich, Robert S. *From Ambivalence to Betrayal: The Left, the Jews, and Israel*. Lincoln: University of Nebraska Press, 2012.

F

Fayyad, Salam

Born: April 12, 1952

Palestinian politician, prime minister of the Palestinian Authority (PA) from June 2007 to December 2012 and of the State of Palestine from January to June 2013. Born in 1952 in Deir al-Ghasun, Jordan, Salam Fayyad grew up near Tulkarm in the West Bank. He graduated from Beirut University in 1975 and went on to earn a doctorate in economics from the University of Texas at Austin. He then worked for the Federal Reserve Bank of St. Louis, Missouri; taught economics at Yarmuk University in Jordan; and joined the staff of the World Bank in 1987. He lived in the United States until 1995, when he became the representative of the International Monetary Fund to the PA, a post he held until 2001. In June 2002, PA president Yasser Arafat, pressed by Western governments to clean up the vast corruption in Palestinian finances, appointed the internationally respected Fayyad to be finance minister. He held the position until December 2005, when he resigned over what he believed was an unwarranted pay increase granted to the already bloated Palestinian civil service.

Fayyad ran in the January 2006 Palestinian legislative elections as a member of a new political party, the Third Way, which won only 2.4 percent of the vote; only two of its candidates, Fayyad and Hanan Ashrawi, were elected. When Mahmoud Abbas formed a unity government with Hamas in March 2007, Fayyad agreed to become finance minister. In this post he urged Israel to release tax revenues it was withholding.

After the outbreak of fighting in the Gaza Strip and the Hamas seizure of that territory, President Abbas carried out a questionable firing of the Hamas-led ministry and on June 15, 2007, appointed the technocrat Fayyad as head of the new emergency government. A reformer who believes that ideology will not solve problems, Fayyad was in effect not only prime minister but also foreign minister and finance minister. He expressed the conviction that armed resistance was counterproductive and sought to bar anyone from carrying arms except members of the uniformed security services, a position opposed by many Palestinians. He also trimmed a number of political appointees from the bloated government payroll.

Fayyad believed that while the peace process should be ongoing, it must parallel efforts to create jobs, improve security, and loosen Israeli security restrictions that are stifling the Palestinian economy. Fayyad hoped to create in the West Bank a model of stability that would inspire Palestinians and defeat the challenge posed by Hamas. Still, he believed that the main issue remained the Palestinians gaining their freedom, something that could be resolved only by political means. On August 2009, Fayyad therefore published a detailed plan, *Palestine—Ending the Occupation, Establishing the State*, that called for the strengthening of Palestinian institutions, including establishing a stock market, building an airport, and better administrative structures, with the objective of attaining full Palestinian statehood within two years.

Palestinian prime minister Salam Fayyad smiles before a meeting of the Ad Hoc Liaison Committee for Assistance to Palestinians at United Nations headquarters on September 21, 2010. (AP Photo/Seth Wenig)

The United Nations (UN), the World Bank, and other international organizations, as well as many Palestinians, considered Fayyad responsible for major improvements in the West Bank's political infrastructure, good governance, economic performance, and security organizations. He was credited with winning the PA $200 million in aid from the U.S. Congress in 2009, and was generally considered pro-Western.

In March 2009, President Mahmoud Abbas appointed Fayyad to a second term as prime minister. Despite the refusal of Hamas in Gaza to recognize the legitimacy of his authority, Fayyad was still prime minister on January 1, 2013, when with UN backing the PA retitled itself the State of Palestine. He submitted his resignation to Abbas in March 2013. Some believed Fayyad's resignation was due to large-scale West Bank Palestinian protests in September and October 2012, sparked by economic difficulties and the rising cost of living and also inspired by the Arab Spring. At Abbas's request, Fayyad continued as interim prime minister until a new government could be formed. On June 6, 2013, the Palestinian academic and independent politician Rami Hamdallah succeeded Fayyad, but resigned two weeks later. In early 2014, the position of Palestinian prime minister was still vacant.

Spencer C. Tucker

Further Reading

Allen, Lori. *The Rise and Fall of Human Rights: Cynicism and Politics in Occupied Palestine.* Stanford: Stanford University Press, 2013.

Beschel, Robert P., Jr., Tarik Youssef, and Khalid Al-Yahya, eds. *Public Sector Reform in the Middle East and North Africa: The Lessons of Experience.* Washington, DC: World Bank Publications, 2013.

Bröning, Michael. *Political Parties in Palestine: Leadership and Thought.* New York: Palgrave Macmillan, 2013.

Bröning, Michael. *The Politics of Change in Palestine: State-Building and Non-Violent Resistance.* London: Pluto, 2011.

Davis, Rochelle, and Mimi Kirk, eds. *Palestine and the Palestinians in the 21st Century.* Bloomington: Indiana University Press, 2013.

Gelvin, James L. *The Israel-Palestine Conflict: One Hundred Years of War.* 3rd ed. Cambridge: Cambridge University Press, 2014.

Karpin, Michael. *Imperfect Compromise: A New Consensus among Israelis and Palestinians.* Washington, DC: Potomac Books, 2013.

Parsons, Nigel Craig. *The Politics of the Palestinian Authority: From Oslo to al-Aqsa.* 2nd ed. London: Routledge, 2012.

Swisher, Clayton E. *The Palestine Papers: The End of the Road?* London: Hesperus Press, 2011.

G

Gaza Strip

A 7-mile-wide, 25-mile-long, heavily populated strip of land along the Mediterranean Sea, adjacent to Egypt's Sinai Peninsula. The Gaza Strip takes its name from its principal city of Gaza. In biblical times the area that is today the Gaza Strip was the home of the Philistines, and the name Palestine is derived from Philistine.

The Gaza Strip has a border of approximately 31 miles with Israel on the northeast and east and 6.6 miles with Egypt on the southwest. It has been one of the main focal points of the Arab-Israeli conflict since 1967, when it became one of Israel's occupied territories. Although much of the strip is now under Palestinian Authority (PA) jurisdiction, borders and main roads are still controlled by Israel, and the entire area remains disputed. At the end of 2007 it had a population of some 1.5 million people.

According to a 1947 United Nations (UN) plan, which never took effect, the Gaza Strip and the West Bank were to form an independent Arab state following the dismantling of the British Mandate for Palestine. Arab leaders, however, rejected the plan and instead waged war. During the Israeli War of Independence (1948–1949), many of the Palestinian people who had lived in what had become Israel either fled or were forced into areas surrounding the new Jewish state, including Gaza. Although a Palestinian government began operating in the Gaza Strip, the 1949 armistice between Israel and Egypt that ended the war gave control of the area to Egypt, which suspended the government in 1959.

Despite the 1949 armistice, significant portions of the Israeli population believed that the Gaza Strip (along with the West Bank and parts of Lebanon and Syria) was part of biblical Eretz Israel, or Land of Israel, and therefore should be part of the modern Jewish state. After a failed attempt to gain the strip in the 1956 Sinai Campaign, Israel launched the Six-Day War in 1967. In spite of fighting a war against Egypt, Syria, and Jordan, the Jewish state was nevertheless able to take control of Gaza from Egypt. UN Security Council Resolution 242 called for Israel to withdraw from territories captured in the war, but Israel instead began constructing Jewish settlements in the Gaza Strip.

At the beginning of the 21st century, there were 25 Israeli settlements in Gaza, although in 2005 the population of about 1.4 million included a mere 8,000 Israelis. In May 1994, the historic Declaration of Principles on Interim Self-Government Arrangements (also known as the Oslo Accords) transferred some governmental services of the strip to the PA, but its status remained in dispute.

A high birthrate has contributed to the Gaza Strip's ongoing poverty, unemployment, and low standard of living. Although control of the strip's finances was also transferred to the PA in 1994, government corruption and Israeli border closures severely hindered the economy until 1998, when Israel began taking measures to ensure that border closures resulting from terrorism threats would affect cross-border trade less adversely. However, with the outbreak of the Second (al-Aqsa) Intifada in 2000, many of these measures were reversed, and the area witnessed another economic downturn.

Smoke and a ball of fire are seen after an Israeli air strike in Gaza City on November 21, 2012. Israeli aircraft pounded Gaza with at least 30 strikes overnight, hitting government ministries, smuggling tunnels, a banker's empty villa, and a Hamas-linked media office. (AP Photo/Hatem Moussa)

In 2005, Israeli prime minister Ariel Sharon's government voted to begin disengagement from the Gaza Strip, a plan that met with mixed reactions in the international community. Although the European Union (EU) and the United States supported Sharon's plan to dismantle Israeli settlements in the area and withdraw Israeli forces from many areas, the EU said that the plan did not go far enough in establishing pre-1967 borders. Many Israelis opposed the plan and supported the settlers. Palestinians, while in favor of any move that increased PA jurisdiction, complained that the plan was not comprehensive. Nonetheless, it was hoped that disengagement would mark a step in implementing the so-called Road Map to Peace in the Middle East, a peace plan brokered by the United States, the EU, Russia, and the UN.

The Israeli government began dismantling the settlements on August 15, 2005,

as planned. Although contested by the nationalist Right within Israel, by some of the Jewish community abroad, and in some confrontational events, the Israel Defense Forces (IDF) completed the process on September 12, 2005. Israel retains offshore maritime control and control of airspace over the Gaza Strip, however. At the same time, Israel withdrew from the Philadelphia Route adjacent to the strip's border with Egypt, following a pledge by Egypt that it would secure its side of the border. Palestinian militants have, however, used the Gaza Strip to fire Qassam rockets into Israeli border settlements, and Israel carried out several military campaigns in 2006 against Palestinians in Gaza both prior to the war with Hezbollah in Lebanon and that November.

An optimistic attitude prevailed in Gaza in 2005 when Israel withdrew its troops, along with 9,000 Jewish settlers. These hopes were dashed by fighting among criminal gangs and clashes between Hamas and Fatah that soon escalated and ultimately killed an estimated 160 people and wounded 800 more. On June 14, 2007, Hamas took over Gaza entirely. This brought an end to the Palestinian unity government and also brought the declaration of a state of emergency by Palestinian president Mahmoud Abbas. The resulting emergency Palestinian government excluded Hamas and was limited to the West Bank.

On June 19, 2007, Abbas cut off all ties and dialogue with Hamas, pending the return of Gaza. This left Fatah, backed by the United States, the EU, and Israel, scrambling to consolidate its control in the West Bank, while Hamas tightened its own control of Gaza and increasingly imposed its brand of religious conservatism, especially where women were concerned.

After fierce fighting between moderate Fatah and more radical Hamas Palestinian groups in Gaza, in June 2007, Hamas won complete control of Gaza, leaving President Mahmoud Abbas of the PA heading a government whose writ ran only in the West Bank. In July, Abbas announced that the PA would have no contact with Hamas and called for the stationing of international peacekeepers in and around Gaza. In September 2007, the Israeli Knesset voted unanimously to declare the Gaza Strip, where 1.4 million Palestinians lived, an "enemy entity." With aid from the West largely cut off, Hamas soon found itself under siege along with the people of Gaza. Israel and Egypt imposed an economic blockade upon Gaza, drastically restricting imports of all kinds, on the grounds that PA forces were no longer maintaining order and security there. As of the end of 2007, few of Gaza's 1.5 million people could leave Gaza for any reason. With the Egyptian border also closed, the economy was in a state of near collapse,

with Gazans unable to export products and thus incapable of paying for imports. Gaza was more isolated than ever.

Gaza became a base for rocket attacks on southern Israel, which provoked fierce Israeli retaliation. In January 2008, Israel cut down fuel supplies to Gaza and, in retaliation for the rockets, in February and early March mounted a major raid on Gaza, killing over 100 people. In response to Israel's actions, Abbas suspended peace talks with Israel. International bodies, including the UN and EU, repeatedly condemned Israel's use of force against Gaza as excessive, and opposed the blockade on humanitarian grounds, but such representations were largely ineffective. Violence diminished somewhat from June to December 2008, when a truce was in place between Hamas and Israel. Upon its expiration Hamas rocket attacks on Israel intensified. From December 27, 2008, to January 18, 2009, the IDF implemented Operation CAST LEAD AGAINST GAZA, killing over 1,300 Palestinians.

With U.S. assistance, in 2009 Egypt began construction of a barrier intended to run the entire six or seven miles of the border separating its territory from Gaza. The objective was to quarantine Egypt politically from Al Qaeda or other militants based in Gaza. In late January 2011, major popular protests began in Egypt, which soon brought the resignation of President Hosni Mubarak. Rumors were rife that Hamas operatives from Gaza tunneled past the barrier into Egypt, where they helped to destabilize the country, assisting members of Egypt's Islamist Muslim Brotherhood in that country's ongoing political struggles.

In April 2011, in Cairo, and again in February 2012 in Doha, Palestinian Fatah and Hamas representatives signed reconciliation agreements intended to resolve their disputes and lead to joint elections that would create a national unity government drawn from both Palestinian factions. Hamas leaders reportedly renounced violence against Israel and agreed to endorse Abbas's position on peace negotiations. The compromise was short-lived. By late 2013, the projected elections had still not been held. Instead, as early as July 2012 reports were circulating that, with assistance from neighboring Egypt, where President Hosni Mubarak had fallen from power and Mohamed Morsi of the Muslim Brotherhood had just become president, Hamas hoped to declare Gaza an independent state.

In March 2012, militants in Gaza launched over 300 rocket attacks on Israel, provoking major Israeli air strikes. In the November 2012 Operation PILLAR OF DEFENSE, Israel attacked over 1,500 sites in Gaza, killing 133 Palestinians, while Hamas fired almost 1,500 rockets at targets in southern Israel, including the cities of Tel Aviv and Jerusalem. Once again, PA, UN, and EU officials, together with representatives of many individual countries, unavailingly characterized Israel's actions as disproportionate. In late November 2012, President Morsi of Egypt helped to negotiate a truce between Hamas and Israel, a document that called on both sides to improve conditions for the people of Gaza, allowing jubilant Hamas representatives to claim a victory.

Such rejoicings were short-lived. In July 2013, a military coup removed President Morsi of Egypt from power, making it far less likely that Egypt would come to Gaza's assistance. Indeed, the new Egyptian government promptly imposed tight controls on its border with Gaza, shutting down the hundreds of smuggling tunnels that had allowed Gaza to survive economically. By late 2013, electricity and water supplies were disrupted and sewage pumping stations unable to function, a situation exacerbated by heavy floods

in December 2013. In early 2014, conditions continued to deteriorate, and the situation in Gaza remained unstable and unpredictable, In February 2014, a United Nations humanitarian mission visited Gaza and unavailingly urged Israel to end its rocket attacks on Gaza and drop restrictions on power and fuel supplies.

Spencer C. Tucker

Further Reading

Arrigoni, Vittorio. *Gaza: Stay Human*. Markfield, Leicestershire, UK: Kube Publishing, 2010.

Chediac, Joyce, ed. *Gaza: Symbol of Resistance*. Canton, OH: Worldview Forum, 2011.

Chomsky, Noam, and Ilan Pappé. *Gaza in Crisis: Reflections on Israel's War against the Palestinians*. 3rd ed. Chicago: Haymarket Books, 2013.

Dalsheim, Joyce. *Unsettling Gaza: Secular Liberalism, Radical Religion, and the Israeli Settlement Project*. New York: Oxford University Press, 2011.

Efrat, Elisha. *The West Bank and Gaza Strip: A Geography of Occupation and Disengagement*. New York: Routledge, 2006.

Feldman, Ilana. *Governing Gaza: Bureaucracy, Authority, and the Work of Rule, 1917–1967*. Durham, NC: Duke University Press, 2008.

Hajjar, Lisa. *Courting Conflict: The Israeli Military Court System in the West Bank and Gaza*. Berkeley: University of California Press, 2005.

Levy, Gideon. *The Punishment of Gaza*. London: Verso, 2010.

Lock, Sharyn, with Sarah Irving. *Gaza: Beneath the Bombs*. New York: Pluto, 2010.

Muhanna, Eitemad. *Agency and Gender in Gaza: Masculinity, Femininity and Family during the Second Intifada*. Farnham, Surrey: Ashgate, 2013.

Oren, Michael B. *Six Days of War: June 1967 and the Making of the Modern Middle East*. Novato, CA: Presidio, 2003.

Parsons, Nigel Craig. *The Politics of the Palestinian Authority: From Oslo to Al-Aqsa.* 2nd ed. London: Routledge, 2012.

Roy, Sara. *Hamas and Civil Society in Gaza: Engaging the Islamist Social Sector.* Princeton: Princeton University Press, 2011.

Said, Edward W. *The End of the Peace Process: Oslo and After.* New York: Vintage Books, 2001.

Schanzer, Jonathan. *Hamas vs. Fatah: The Struggle for Palestine.* New York: Palgrave Macmillan, 2008.

Shachar, Nathan. *The Gaza Strip: Its History and Politics—From the Pharaohs to the Israeli Invasion of 2009.* Eastbourne, UK: Sussex Academic Press, 2010.

Smith, Charles D. *Palestine and the Arab-Israeli Conflict: A History with Documents.* 8th ed. New York: Bedford/St. Martin's Press, 2012.

Weizman, Eyal. *The Least of All Possible Evils: Humanitarian Violence from Arendt to Gaza.* London: Verso, 2011.

H

Hamas

Islamist Palestinian organization formally founded in 1987. The stated basis for Hamas (Harakat al-Muqawama al-Islamiyya, or Movement of Islamic Resistance) is the creation of an Islamic way of life and the liberation of Palestine through Islamic resistance. Essentially, Hamas combines Islamic fundamentalism with Palestinian nationalism. Hamas gained about 30–40 percent support in the Palestinian population within five years because of its mobilization successes and the general popular desperation experienced by the Palestinian population during the First Intifada. In January 2006, Hamas won a majority in the Palestinian Authority's (PA) general legislative elections, which brought condemnation from Israel and a power struggle with PA president Mahmoud Abbas and his Fatah Party.

The word "Hamas" means courage, bravery, or zeal. But it is also an Arabic acronym for the Movement of Islamic Resistance. Hamas is an Islamist movement, as are larger and longer-established groups such as the Muslim Brotherhood and the Palestinian Islamic Jihad. The growth of Islamist movements was delayed among Palestinians because of their status as a people without a state and the tight security controls imposed by Israel, which had strengthened the more secular nationalist expression of the Palestine Liberation Organization (PLO).

The Muslim Brotherhood, established in Egypt in 1928, had set up branches in Syria; Sudan; Libya; the Gulf states; Amman in Jordan, which influenced the West Bank;

and Gaza. However, for two decades the Muslim Brotherhood focused on its religious, educational, and social missions and was quiescent politically. That changed with the First Intifada (1987). The Muslim Brotherhood advocated *dawah*, what may be called a re-Islamization of society and thought; *adala* (social justice); and an emphasis on *hakmiyya* (the sovereignty of God, as opposed to temporal rule). The Muslim Brotherhood turned to activism against Israel after Islamic Jihad had accelerated its operations during 1986 and 1987. Eventually Islamic Jihad split into three rival organizations. The new movement coming out of the Jordanian and Egyptian Muslim Brotherhood groups, unlike Islamic Jihad, retained its major programmatic emphasis on the Islamization or re-Islamization of society. As the new organization of Hamas emerged out of the Muslim Brotherhood, it was able to draw strength from the social work of Sheikh Ahmed Yassin, a physically disabled schoolteacher who had led the Islamic Assembly (al-Mujamma al-Islami), an organization influential in many mosques and at the Islamic University of Gaza.

In December 1987, Abd al-Aziz Rantisi, who was a physician at Islamic University, and former student leaders Salah Shihada and Yahya al-Sinuwwar, who had had charge of security for the Muslim Brotherhood, formed the first unit of Hamas. While Yassin gave his approval, as a cleric he was not directly connected to the new organization.

In February 1988, as a result of a key meeting in Amman involving Sheikh Abd al-Rahman al-Khalifa (the spiritual guide

Supporters of the militant Islamic group Hamas celebrate their victory in Palestinian elections on January 26, 2006, in the West Bank city of Ramallah. Hamas unseated the ruling Fatah party. (Uriel Sinai/Getty Images)

of the Jordanian Muslim Brotherhood), Ibrahiam Ghawsha (the Hamas spokesperson and Jordanian representative), Mahmud Zahar (a surgeon), Rantisi (acting as a West Bank representative), Jordanian parliament members, and the hospital director, the Brotherhood granted formal recognition to Hamas. In 1988, Hamas issued its charter. The charter condemns world Zionism and the efforts to isolate Palestine, defines the mission of the organization, and locates that mission within Palestinian, Arab, and Islamic elements. It does not condemn the West or non-Muslims but does condemn aggression against the Palestinian people, arguing for a defensive jihad. It also calls for fraternal relations with the other Palestinian nationalist groups.

Hamas is headed by a political bureau with representatives for military affairs, foreign affairs, finance, propaganda, and internal security. An advisory council, or Majlis al-Shura, is linked to the political bureau, which is also connected with all Palestinian communities; Hamas's social and charitable groups, elected members, and district committees; and the leadership in Israeli prisons.

Major attacks against Israel have been carried out by the Izz al-Din al-Qassam Brigades of Hamas. They also developed the Qassam rocket used to attack Israeli civilian settlements in the Negev Desert. However, much of Hamas's activity during the First Intifada consisted of its participation within more broadly based popular demonstrations and locally coordinated efforts at resistance, countering Israeli raids, enforcing opening of businesses, and the like.

Hamas greatly expanded by 1993 but decried the autonomy agreement between the Israelis and the PLO in Jericho and the Gaza

Strip as too limited a gain. By the time of the first elections for the PA's council in 1996, Hamas was caught in a dilemma. It had gained popularity as a resistance organization, but Oslo 1 and Oslo 2 (the Taba Accord of September 28, 1995) were meant to end the intifada. The elections would further strengthen the PLO, but if Hamas boycotted the elections and most people voted, then it would be even more isolated. Finally, Hamas's leadership rejected participation but without ruling it out in the future, and this gave the organization the ability to continue protesting Oslo.

When suicide attacks were launched to protest Israeli violence against Palestinians, Hamas was blamed for inspiring or organizing the suicide bombers, whether or not its operatives or those of the more radical Islamic Jihad were involved.

Hamas funds an extensive array of social services aimed at ameliorating the plight of the Palestinians. It provides funding for hospitals, schools, mosques, orphanages, food distribution, and aid to the families of Palestinian prisoners who, numbering more than 10,000 people, constituted an important political force. Given the PA's frequent inability to provide for such needs, Hamas stepped into the breach and in so doing endeared itself to a large number of Palestinians.

Until its electoral triumph in January 2006, Hamas received funding from a number of sources. Palestinians living abroad provided money, as did a number of private donors in the wealthy Arab oil states such as Saudi Arabia, Bahrain, and Kuwait and other states in the West. Iran has been a significant donor to Hamas. Much aid was directed to renovation of the Palestinian territories and was badly needed, and unfortunately a great deal of that rebuilding was destroyed in the Israeli campaign in the West Bank in 2002, which in turn was intended to combat the suicide bombings.

Over the years the Israel Defense Forces (IDF) has carried out targeted eliminations of a number of Hamas leaders. These include Shihada (July 23, 2002), Dr. Ibrahim Al-Makadma (August 3, 2003), Ismail Abu Shanab (August 21, 2003), Yassin (March 22, 2004), and Rantisi (April 17, 2004).

Hamas had two sets of leaders, those inside the West Bank and Gaza and those outside. The West Bank leadership is divided along the general structure into political, charitable, student, and military activities. The political leadership is usually targeted for arrests because its members can be located, unlike the secret military units. That leadership has organized very effectively before and since PLO leader Yasser Arafat's death and has become more popular than the PLO in the West Bank, an unexpected development. A current Hamas leader, Khalid Mishaal, is in Syria. Other senior Hamas leaders are there as well, and there is also some Hamas activity in refugee camps in Lebanon. Although Arafat was quickly succeeded by Abbas as the PLO leader, a sizable number of Palestinians had already begun to identify with Hamas, mainly because it was able to accomplish what the PA could not, namely, to provide for the everyday needs of the people.

Hamas won the legislative elections in January 2006. Locals had expected a victory in Gaza but not in the West Bank. Nonetheless, both Israel and the United States have steadfastly refused to recognize the Palestinian government now under the control of Hamas. The United States cut off $420 million and the European Union (EU) cut off $600 million in aid to the PA's Hamasled government, which created difficulties for ordinary Palestinians. The loss of this aid halted the delivery of supplies to hospitals and ended other services in addition to stopping the payment of salaries. To prevent total collapse, the United States and the EU promised relief funds, but these were not allowed to go through the PA. The cutoff in funds was designed to discourage Palestinian support for Hamas.

On March 17, 2007, Abbas brokered a Palestinian unity government that included members of both Hamas and Fatah in which Hamas leader Ismail Haniyeh became prime minister. Yet in May armed clashes between Hamas and Fatah escalated, and on June 14 Hamas seized control of Gaza. Abbas promptly dissolved the Hamas-led unity government and declared a state of emergency. On June 18, having been assured of EU support, he dissolved the National Security Council and swore in an emergency Palestinian government. That same day, the United States ended its 15-month embargo on the PA and resumed aid in an effort to strengthen Abbas's government, now limited to the West Bank.

On June 19, Abbas cut off all ties and dialogue with Hamas, pending the return of Gaza. By the end of 2007, Hamas had imposed a more religiously conservative regime on Gaza, which was now largely cut off economically from the rest of the world and more than ever an economic basket case. In September 2007, the Israeli Knesset voted unanimously to declare the Gaza Strip, where 1.4 million Palestinians lived, an "enemy entity." Israel and Egypt imposed an economic blockade upon Gaza, drastically restricting imports of all kinds, on the grounds that security and order were no longer being maintained there. With aid from the West largely cut off, Hamas soon found itself under siege along with the people of Gaza. Although the United Nations and European Union contended that Israeli sanctions contravened basic humanitarian standards, Israel largely ignored such caveats. Hamas leaders' own disregard for human rights within Gaza also attracted UN and EU censure.

Hamas used Gaza as a base for launching extensive rocket attacks on targets in Southern Israel, provoking harsh retaliation from Israel. In January 2008, Israel cut down fuel supplies to Gaza, and in late February and early March mounted a major raid there, killing over 100 people. Violence diminished somewhat from June to December 2008, when a truce was in place between Hamas and Israel. Upon its expiration Hamas rocket attacks on Israel intensified. From December 27, 2008, to January 18, 2009, the IDF implemented Operation CAST LEAD AGAINST GAZA, killing over 1,300 Palestinians. Further Hamas attacks in 2010 were reportedly intended to derail ongoing Israeli-Palestinian negotiations. In March 2012, militants in Gaza launched over 300 rocket attacks on Israel, provoking major Israeli air strikes. In the November 2012 Operation PILLAR OF DEFENSE, Israel attacked over 1,500 sites in Gaza, killing 133 Palestinians, while Hamas fired almost 1,500 rockets at targets in southern Israel, including the cities of Tel Aviv and Jerusalem.

In January 2009, on the expiration of his term as president, Abbas unilaterally extended his tenure, initially by a year, then indefinitely. In April 2011, in Cairo, and again in February 2012 in Doha, Fatah and Hamas representatives signed reconciliation agreements intended to bring about joint elections that would create a national unity government drawn from both Palestinian factions. Hamas leaders reportedly agreed to cease violent attacks on Israel and endorse Abbas's negotiating positions. These understandings did not last. By late 2013, the scheduled elections had still not been held. Hamas rejected Abbas's insistence that all agreements he had made as PA president must be honored. In late 2013, he remained

PA president, though Hamas refused to recognize his authority, claiming that with the expiration of Abbas's term Abdel Aziz Duwaik, speaker of the Palestine Legislative Council, should be considered now acting president.

Whatever conciliatory gestures or moves toward compromise some Hamas officials chose to make were almost invariably undercut by more extreme elements. After popular protests erupted in Egypt in January 2011, driving President Hosni Mubarak from power the following month, Hamas operatives reportedly crossed into Egypt, to assist members of the Muslim Brotherhood in the ongoing political battles in that country. Hamas personnel were also alleged to have joined the insurgents fighting against the government of President Bashar al-Assad in the civil war that began in Syria in 2011, with some reputedly killed by Syrian security forces. When U.S. president Barack Obama visited Israel and the West Bank in March 2013, he apparently hoped to broker a settlement reconciling Hamas, the PA, and Israel. Instead, Hamas directed five rockets against Israeli targets. As 2013 drew to an end, the United States and Israel both defined Hamas as a terrorist organization, subject to a wide range of sanctions. Hamas was not involved in the peace talks between the PA and Israel orchestrated by U.S. secretary of state John Kerry in the second half of 2013 and early 2014.

Harry Raymond Hueston, Paul G. Pierpaoli Jr., and Sherifa Zuhur

Further Reading

Caridi, Paola. *Hamas: From Resistance to Government.* Translated by Andrea Teti. New York: Seven Stories Press, 2012.

Chomsky, Noam and Ilan Pappé. *Gaza in Crisis: Reflections on Israel's War against the Palestinians.* London: Hamish Hamilton, 2010.

Ghanem, Assad. *Palestinian Politics after Arafat: A Failed National Movement.* Bloomington: Indiana University Press, 2010.

Gleis, Joshua L., and Benedetta Berti. *Hezbollah and Hamas: A Comparative Study.* Baltimore: Johns Hopkins University Press, 2012.

Hroub, Khaled. *Hamas: A Beginner's Guide.* Ann Arbor, MI: 2006.

Hroub, Khaled. *Hamas: Political Thought and Practice.* Washington, DC: Institute for Palestine Studies, 2000.

Legrain, Jean-François. "Hamas: Legitimate Heir of Palestinian Nationalism?" in *Political Islam: Revolution, Radicalism, or Reform,* edited by John Esposito, pp. 159–78. Boulder, CO: Lynne Rienner, 1997.

Mishal, Shaul, and Avraham Sela. *The Palestinian Hamas: Vision, Violence, and Coexistence.* New York: Columbia University Press, 2000.

Nusse, Andrea. *Muslim Palestine: The Ideology of Hamas.* London: Routledge, 1999.

Pargeter, Alison. *The Muslim Brotherhood: From Opposition to Power.* New ed. London: Saqi Books, 2013.

Parsons, Nigel Craig. *The Politics of the Palestinian Authority: From Oslo to Al-Aqsa.* 2nd ed. London: Routledge, 2012.

Pearlman, Wendy. *Violence, Nonviolence, and the Palestinian National Movement.* Cambridge: Cambridge University Press, 2011.

Roy, Sara. *Hamas and Civil Society in Gaza: Engaging the Islamist Social Sector.* Princeton: Princeton University Press, 2011.

Rubin, Barry. *The Muslim Brotherhood: The Organization and Politics of a Global Islamist Movement.* New York: Palgrave Macmillan, 2010.

Schanzer, Jonathan. *Hamas vs. Fatah: The Struggle for Palestine.* New York: Palgrave Macmillan, 2008.

Tamimi, Azzam. *Hamas: A History from Within.* 2nd ed. New York: Olive Branch Press, 2011.

Wickham, Carrie Rosefsky. *The Muslim Brotherhood: Evolution of an Islamist Movement.* Princeton, NJ: Princeton University Press, 2013.

Hezbollah

Lebanese radical Shia Islamist organization. Founded in Lebanon in 1984, Hezbollah is a major political force in Lebanon and, along with the Amal movement, a principal political party representing the Shia community in Lebanon. There have been other smaller parties by the name of Hezbollah in eastern Saudi Arabia and Iraq, and their activities have been mistakenly or deliberately associated with the Lebanese party. The Lebanese Hezbollah also operates a number of social service programs, schools, hospitals, clinics, and housing assistance programs to Lebanese Shiites. (Some Christians also attended Hezbollah's schools and ran on their electoral lists.)

A Hezbollah sentry stands under a fluttering Hezbollah flag as he scans the Israeli border at the Tziporen army post on March 2, 2003. (AFP/Getty Images)

One of the core founding groups of Hezbollah, meaning the "Party of God," actually fled from Iraq when Saddam Hussein cracked down on the Shia Islamic movement in the shrine cities. Lebanese as well as Iranians and Iraqis studied in Najaf and Karbala, and some 100 of these students returned to Beirut and became disciples of Sayyid Muhammad Husayn Fadlallah, a Lebanese cleric who was also educated in Najaf.

Meanwhile, in the midst of the ongoing civil war in Lebanon, a Shia resistance movement developed in response to Israel's invasion in 1982. Israel's first invasion of southern Lebanon had occurred in 1978, but the invasion of 1982 was more devastating to the region, with huge numbers of casualties and prisoners taken and peasants displaced.

The earliest political movement of Lebanese Shia was established under the cleric Musa al-Sadr and known as the Movement of the Dispossessed. The Shia were the largest but poorest sect in Lebanon and suffered from discrimination, underrepresentation, and a dearth of government programs or services that, despite some efforts by President Fuad Shihab, persist to this day. After al-Sadr's disappearance on a trip to Libya, his nonmilitaristic movement was subsumed by the Amal Party, which had a military wing and fought in the civil war. However, a wing of Amal, Islamic Amal led by Husayn al-Musawi, split off after it accused Amal of not resisting the Israeli invasion.

On the grounds of resistance to Israel (and its Lebanese proxies), Islamic Amal made contact with Iran's ambassador to Damascus, Akbar Muhtashimi, who had once found refuge as an Iranian dissident in the Palestinian camps in Lebanon. Iran sent between 1,000 and 1,200 Revolutionary Guards to the Bekáa Valley to aid an Islamic resistance to Israel. At a Lebanese army barracks near Baalbek, the Revolutionary

Guards began training Shia fighters identifying with the resistance, or Islamic Amal.

Fadlallah's followers now included displaced Beiruti Shia and displaced southerners, and some coordination between his group and the others began to emerge in 1984. The other strand of Hezbollah came from the Islamic Resistance in southern Lebanon led by Sheikh Raghib Harb, the imam of the village of Jibshit who was killed by the Israelis in 1984. In February 1985, Harb's supporters met and announced the formation of Hezbollah, led by Sheikh Subhi Tufayli.

Another militant Shia group was the Organization of the Islamic Jihad, led by Imad Mughniya. It was responsible for the 1983 bombings of the U.S. and French peacekeeping forces' barracks and the U.S. embassy and its annex in Beirut. This group received some support from the elements in Baalbek. Hezbollah, however, is to this day accused of bombings committed by Mughniya's group. While it had not yet officially formed, the degree of coordination or sympathy between the various militant groups operative in 1982 can only be ascertained on the level of individuals. Hezbollah stated officially that it did not commit the bombing of U.S. and French forces, but it also did not condemn those who did. Regardless, Hezbollah's continuing resistance in the south earned it great popularity with the Lebanese, whose army had split and had failed to defend the country against the Israelis.

With the Taif Agreement the Lebanese civil war should have ended, but in 1990 fighting broke out, and the next year Syria mounted a major campaign in Lebanon. The Taif Agreement did not end sectarianism or solve the problem of Muslim underrepresentation in government. Militias other than Hezbollah disbanded, but because the Lebanese government did not assent to the Israeli occupation of southern Lebanon, Hezbollah's militia remained in being.

The leadership of Hezbollah changed over time and adapted to Lebanon's realities. The multiplicity of sects in Lebanon meant that an Islamic republic there was impractical, and as a result Hezbollah ceased trying to impose the strictest Islamic rules and focused more on gaining the trust of the Lebanese community. The party's Shura Council was made up of seven clerics until 1989; from 1989 to 1991 it included three laypersons and four clerics, and since 2001 it has been entirely composed of clerics. An advisory politburo has from 11 to 14 members. Secretary General Abbas Musawi took over from Tufayli in 1991. Soon after the Israelis assassinated Musawi, Hassan Nasrallah, who had studied in Najaf and briefly in Qum, took over as secretary general.

In 1985, as a consequence of armed resistance in southern Lebanon, Israel withdrew into the so-called security zone. Just as resistance from Hezbollah provided Israel with the ready excuse to attack Lebanon, Israel's continued presence in the south funded Lebanese resentment of Israel and support for Hezbollah's armed actions. In 1996, the Israelis mounted Operation GRAPES OF WRATH against Hezbollah in south Lebanon, pounding the entire region from the air for a two-week period.

Subhi Tufayli, the former Hezbollah secretary general, opposed the party's decision to participate in the elections of 1992 and 1996. He launched the Revolt of the Hungry, demanding food and jobs for the impoverished people of the upper Bekáa, and was expelled from Hezbollah. He then began armed resistance, and the Lebanese army was called in to defeat his faction.

In May 2000, after suffering repeated attacks and numerous casualties, Israel withdrew its forces from southern Lebanon, a move that was widely interpreted as a victory for Hezbollah and boosted its popularity hugely in Lebanon and throughout the Arab world. Hezbollah disarmed in some areas of the country but refused to do so in the border area because it contests the Jewish state's control of the Shaba Farms region.

Sheikh Fadlallah survived an assassination attempt in 1985 allegedly arranged by the United States. He illustrates the Lebanonization of the Shia Islamist movement. He had moved away from Ayatollah Khomeini's doctrine of government by cleric (*wilaya al-faqih*), believing that it is not suitable in the Lebanese context, and called for dialogue with Christians. Fadlallah's stance is similar to that of Ayatollah Sistani in Iraq. He, like some of the Iraqi clerics, called for the restoration of Friday communal prayer for the Shia. He has also issued numerous reforming views, for example, decrying the abuse of women by men. Fadlallah is not, however, closely associated with Hezbollah's day-to-day policies.

Some Israeli and U.S. sources charge that Iran directly conducts the affairs of Hezbollah and provides it with essential funding. While at one time Iranian support was crucial to Hezbollah, the Revolutionary Guards were withdrawn from Lebanon for some time. The party's social and charitable services claimed independence in the late 1990s. They are supported by a volunteer service, provided by medical personnel and other professionals, and by local and external donations. Iran has certainly provided weapons to Hezbollah. Some, apparently through the Iran-Contra deal, found their way to Lebanon, and Syria has also provided freedom of movement across its common border with Lebanon as well as supply routes for weapons.

Since 2000 Hezbollah has disputed Israeli control over the Shaba Farms area, which Israel claims belongs to Syria but Syria says belongs to Lebanon. Meanwhile, pressure

began to build against Syrian influence in Lebanon with the constitutional amendment to allow Émile Lahoud (a Christian and pro-Syrian) an additional term. Assassinations of anti-Syrian, mainly Christian, figures had also periodically occurred. The turning point was the assassination of Prime Minister Rafik Hariri in February 2005. This led to significant international pressure on Syria to withdraw from Lebanon, although pro-Syrian elements remained throughout the country.

Hezbollah now found itself threatened by a new coalition of Christians and Hariri-supporting Sunnis who sought to deny its aim of greater power for the Shia in government. The two sides in this struggle were known as the March 14th Alliance, for the date of a large anti-Syrian rally, and the March 8th Alliance, for a prior and even larger rally consisting of Hezbollah and anti-Syrian Christian general Michel Aoun. These factions have been sparring since 2005 and in some ways since the civil war.

Demanding a response to the Israeli campaign against Gaza in the early summer of 2006, Hezbollah forces killed three Israeli soldiers and kidnapped two others, planning to hold them for a prisoner exchange as has occurred in the past. The Israel Defense Forces (IDF) responded with a massive campaign of air strikes throughout Lebanon, and not just on Hezbollah positions. Hezbollah responded by launching missiles into Israel, forcing much of that country's northern population into shelters. In this open warfare, the United States backed Israel. At the conflict's end, Sheikh Nasrallah's popularity surged in Lebanon and in the Arab world, and even members of the March 14th Alliance were furious over the destruction of the fragile peace in post–civil war Lebanon. Hezbollah offered cash assistance to the people of southern Lebanon displaced by the fighting and those in the southern districts of Beirut who had been struck there by the Israelis. They disbursed this aid immediately. The government offered assistance to other Lebanese, but this assistance was delayed.

In September 2006, Hezbollah and its ally Aoun began calling for a new national unity government. The existing government, dominated by the March 14th Alliance forces, refused to budge, however. Five Shia members and one Christian member of the Lebanese cabinet also resigned in response to disagreements over the proposed tribunal to investigate Syrian culpability in the Hariri assassination. At the same time, Hezbollah and Aoun argued for the right of a sizable opposition group in the cabinet to veto government decisions. Hezbollah and Aoun called for public protests, which began as gigantic sit-ins and demonstrations in the downtown district of Beirut in December 2006. There was one violent clash in December and another in January of 2007 between the supporters of the two March alliances. Meanwhile, the United Nations Interim Force in Lebanon (UNIFIL) took up position in southern Lebanon. Its mission, however, was not to disarm Hezbollah but only to prevent armed clashes between it and Israel.

Plans to establish a special international criminal tribunal for Lebanon, with headquarters in the Netherlands, progressed, albeit at glacial speed. Hezbollah had not disarmed, and sharp political divisions remained and were coupled with assassinations (alleged to be Syrian-sponsored) of leading political figures. In military clashes between the Lebanese army and Fatah al-Islam groups, centered on the Nahr al-Bared refugee camp, 169 soldiers, 289 insurgents, and 41 civilians reportedly died.

From 2006 to 2008 the largely Shia political opponents of the pro-Western prime minister, Fouad Siniora, demanded a government of national unity, over which they would enjoy a veto power. In May 2008, Hezbollah and Amal forces seized western Beirut, resulting in military clashes, ultimately resolved on May 21, 2008 by the Doha Agreement, which established a national unity government, as the opposition had demanded. In January 2011, however, this government collapsed, largely because Prime Minister Saad Hariri rejected demands from Hezbollah elements that he repudiate the international special tribunal for Lebanon, established under United Nations auspices and based in the Netherlands, which was investigating the murder of former prime minister Rafik Hariri. In 2011, the tribunal issued arrest warrants for four Hezbollah members, and top Lebanese and Syrian security officers were also implicated.

Although UN resolutions had called on Hezbollah and other militias in Lebanon to disarm as part of the settlement of the 2006 crisis, Hezbollah ignored such demands. By 2009, indeed, Hezbollah officials boasted that they possessed more and better weaponry than three years earlier. In 2010, Hezbollah claimed that the Dalit and Tamar gas fields in Israel, approximately 50 miles west of Haifa, belonged to Lebanon, and warned Israel against trying to extract gas from them. Some believed that Hezbollah took this aggressive stance in order to justify its continued failure to disarm. It was also claimed that Hezbollah was responsible for a May 2011 bombing attack in Istanbul, Turkey, aimed at the Israeli consul to Turkey.

In March 2011, a bitter sectarian civil war erupted in Syria, in which a variety of insurgents attempted to overthrow the government of President Bashar al-Assad, with whose family Hezbollah had long had close ties. Hezbollah militia units fought fiercely for al-Assad, characterizing his opponents—who included many Al Qaeda activists—as agents of a Zionist plot. Several thousand Lebanese Hezbollah militia members were believed to be fighting on al-Assad's behalf, arousing fears within Lebanon that their involvement would drag the country as a whole into the civil war in Syria. In late 2013, the war was still continuing, though the balance appeared to be tipping against al-Assad. This raised at least the possibility that the lengthy history of Syrian interference in Lebanese politics, influence generally exercised through Hezbollah, might finally be nearing an end.

Harry Raymond Hueston
and Sherifa Zuhur

Further Reading

Avon, Dominique, and Anaïs-Trissa Katchadourian. *Hezbollah: A History of the "Party of God."* Translated by Jane Marie Todd. Cambridge, MA: Harvard University Press, 2012.

Azani, Eitan. *Hezbollah: The Story of the Party of God: From Revolution to Institutionalization.* New York: Palgrave Macmillan, 2008.

Blanford, Nicholas. *Warriors of God: Inside Hezbollah's Thirty-Year Struggle against Israel.* New York: Random House, 2011.

Cambanis, Thanassis. *A Privilege to Die: Inside Hezbollah's Legions and Their Endless War against Israel.* New York: Free Press, 2010.

Gleis, Joshua L., and Benedetta Berti. *Hezbollah and Hamas: A Comparative Study.* Baltimore: Johns Hopkins University Press, 2012.

Hajjar, Sami G. *Hezbollah: Terrorism, National Liberation, or Menace?* Carlisle Barracks, PA: Strategic Studies Institute, U.S. Army War College, 2002.

Harel, Amos, and Avi Issacharoff. *34 Days: Israel, Hezbollah, and the War in Lebanon.* Translated by Ora Cummings and Moshe Tlamim. New York: Palgrave Macmillan, 2008.

Harik, Judith Palmer. *Hezbollah: The Changing Face of Terrorism.* London: Taurus, 2005.

Jaber, Hala. *Hezbollah: Born with a Vengeance.* New York: Columbia University Press, 1997.

Lebanese Political Parties: Hizbullah. Arabic documentary. Farid Assaf, Lebanese National Broadcasting Company, 2003.

Levitt, Matthew. *Hezbollah: The Global Footprint of Lebanon's Party of God.* Washington, DC: Georgetown University Press, 2013.

Newman, Barbara, and Tom Diaz. *Lightning Out of Lebanon: Hezbollah Terrorists on American Soil.* New York: Random House, 2005.

Noe, Nicholas, ed. *Voice of Hezbollah: The Statements of Sayed Hassan Nasrallah.* London: Verso Books, 2007.

Norton, Augustus R. *Hezbollah: A Short History.* Princeton: Princeton University Press, 2007.

Qassem, Naim. *Hizbullah: The Story from Within.* London: Saqi Books, 2010.

Saad-Ghorayeb, Amal. *Hizb'ullah: Politics and Religion.* London: Pluto, 2002.

Totten, Michael J. *The Road to Fatima Gate: The Beirut Spring, the Rise of Hezbollah, and the Iranian War against Israel.* New York: Encounter Books, 2011.

Zuhur, Sherifa. "Hasan Nasrallah and the Strategy of Steadfastness." *Terrorism Monitor* 4(19) (October 5, 2006).

Intifada, First

A spontaneous protest movement by Palestinians against Israeli rule and an effort to establish a Palestinian homeland through a series of demonstrations, improvised attacks, and riots. The First Intifada (literally, "shaking off") began in December 1987 and ended in 1993 with the signing of the Oslo Accords and the creation of the Palestinian Authority (PA).

The founding of Israel in 1948 created a situation in which Palestinians and citizens of the new Israeli state suddenly found themselves occupying a single body of land but under Israeli control. This basic reality would remain the most contentious issue in the region for decades to come. It also led to an emerging Palestinian national consciousness calling for Israel's destruction. Other Arab nations and the Arab world at large generally shared such anti-Israeli sentiment, and material and military support often followed suit. While the Palestinians had not resisted under the repressive measures of the 1950s and 1960s, their treatment became even worse later, especially with the ascendance of the Likud Party in Israel. Many Palestinians, and especially the young, became more convinced of the need for resistance from 1968 to the early 1970s; then just as Palestinians experienced still worse treatment, more property encroachment, and more difficulties, their leadership moved toward negotiation as a strategy. By the time of the intifada, most Palestinians had experienced or knew those who had experienced Israel's de jure or de facto draconian civil and criminal enforcement practices including torture, summary executions, mass detentions, and the destruction of property and homes.

In 1987, strained relations between Palestinians and Israelis were pushed to the limit when, on October 1, Israeli soldiers ambushed and killed seven Palestinian men from Gaza alleged to have been members of the Palestinian terrorist organization Islamic Jihad. Days later, an Israeli settler shot a Palestinian schoolgirl in the back. With violence against Israelis by Palestinians also increasing, a wider conflict may have been inevitable.

The tension only mounted as the year drew to a close. On December 4, an Israeli salesman was found murdered in Gaza. On December 6, a truck driven by the Israel Defense Forces (IDF) struck a van, killing its four Palestinian occupants. That same day, sustained and heavy violence involving several hundred Palestinians took place in the Jabalya refugee camp, where the four Palestinians who died in the traffic accident had lived. The unrest spread quickly and eventually involved other refugee camps. By the end of December, the violence had made its way to Jerusalem. The Israelis reacted with a heavy hand, which did nothing but fan the fires of Palestinian outrage. On December 22, 1987, the United Nations (UN) Security Council officially denounced the Israeli reaction to the unrest, which had taken the lives of scores of Palestinians.

The result of the escalating spiral of violence was the intifada, a series of Palestinian protests, demonstrations, and ad hoc

Ignoring pouring rain, Palestinian protesters, some with their faces covered in the traditional keffiyeh headdress, hurl rocks at Israeli Defense Forces soldiers. The confrontation
took place in Nablus in the occupied West Bank on January 12, 1988. (AP Photo)

attacks whose manifestations ranged from youths throwing rocks at Israeli troops to demonstrations by women's organizations. While quite spontaneous at first, a shadowy organization, the Unified Leadership of the Intifada, emerged, issuing directives via numbered statements. Along with a series of general strikes and boycotts, the demonstrations caused such disruption to the Israeli state that the government responded with military force. Heated tensions proved a hotbed for further violence, which led to increasingly violent reprisals on both sides. While the Palestinians had begun by relying on rocks and superior numbers under the auspices of the Unified Leadership, they were soon throwing Molotov cocktails and grenades as well as simply burning tires and using spray paint to write graffiti of the intifada. Israeli rules were such that the Palestinian flag and its colors were banned, so these were displayed by the demonstrators. In the meantime, Israeli defense minister

Yitzhak Rabin exhorted the IDF to "break the bones" of demonstrators. Rabin's tactics resulted in more international condemnation and further deterioration in an already worsening relationship with Washington. Moshe Arens, who succeeded Rabin in the Ministry of Defense in 1990, seemed better able to understand both the root of the uprising and the best ways of subduing it. Indeed, the number of Palestinians and Israelis killed declined during the period from 1990 to 1993. However, the intifada itself seemed to be running out of steam after 1990, perhaps because so many Palestinian men were in prison by then.

Despite continued violence on the part of Hamas (Islamic Resistance Movement), on September 13, 1993, Rabin, now prime minister, and Palestine Liberation Organization (PLO) chairman Yasser Arafat signed the historic Oslo Accords on the White House lawn. The accords, which brought both Rabin and Arafat the Nobel Peace

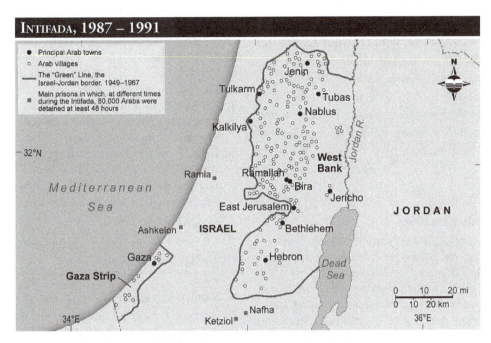

Map of the Intifada from 1987 to 1991 during the Arab-Israeli Wars.

Prize, called for a five-year transition period during which the Gaza Strip and the West Bank would be jointly controlled by Israel and the PA, with power eventually meant to be turned over to the Palestinian people.

The First Intifada caused both civil destruction and humanitarian suffering, but it also produced gains for the Palestinian people before it was brought to an end. First, it solidified and brought into focus a clear national consciousness for the Palestinian people and made statehood a clear national objective. Second, it cast Israeli policy toward Palestine in a very negative light on the world stage, especially the killing of Palestinian children. Third, to some Israelis it indicated that their primary struggle was with Palestinians and not all Arabs. Thus, it rekindled public and political dialogue on the Arab-Israeli conflict across Europe, in the United States, and in other Middle Eastern states. Fourth, the First Intifada threatened the leadership role of the PLO in Tunis, illustrating the self-mobilization of the population in

the territories, leading eventually to friction between the Tunis old guard and younger leadership. Finally, it cost Israel hundreds of millions of dollars in lost imports and tourism.

At the time the Oslo Accords were signed in September 1993, the six-year-long intifada had resulted in well over 1,000 deaths, most of them Palestinian. It is believed that approximately 1,160 Palestinians died in the uprising, of which 241 were children. On the Israeli side, 160 died, 5 of whom were children. Clearly, the IDF's inexperience in widespread riot control had contributed to the high death toll, for in the first 13 months of the intifada alone, more than 330 Palestinians were killed. Indeed, the policies and performance of the IDF split Israeli public opinion on the handling of the intifada and also invited international scrutiny.

In more recent years, continued terrorist attacks by pro-Palestinian interests and Israeli control of the Palestinian territories long beyond the time line set by the Oslo Accords and the failure of the accords to proceed have caused unrest both in the international community and in Palestinian-Israeli relations. In 2000, a new wave of violent Palestinian protest broke out and would eventually become known as the Second (al-Aqsa) Intifada.

Paul G. Pierpaoli Jr.

Further Reading

Brynen, Rex, ed. *Echoes of the Intifada: Regional Repercussions of the Palestinian-Israeli Conflict.* Boulder, CO: Westview, 1991.

Bucaille, Laetitia. *Growing Up Palestinian: Israeli Occupation and the Intifada Generation.* Princeton, NJ: Princeton University Press, 2004.

Catignani, Sergio. *Israeli Counter-Insurgency and the Intifadas: Dilemmas of a Conventional Army.* New York: Routledge, 2008.

Enderlin, Charles. *The Lost Years: Radical Islam, Intifada, and Wars in the Middle East, 2001–2006.* New York: Other Press, 2007.

Farsoum, Samih K., and Naseer H. Aruri. *Palestine and the Palestinians: A Social and Political History.* 2nd ed. Jackson, TN: Westview, 2006.

Hiltermann, Joost R. *Behind the Intifada.* Princeton, NJ: Princeton University Press, 1992.

Hudson, Michael C. *The Palestinians: New Directions.* Washington, DC: Center for Contemporary Arab Studies, Georgetown University, 1990.

Hunter, F. Robert. *The Palestinian Uprising: A War by Other Means.* Berkeley: University of California Press, 1991.

King, Mary Elizabeth. *A Quiet Revolution: The First Palestinian Intifada and Nonviolent Resistance.* New York: Nation Books, 2007.

Lockman, Zachary, and Joel Benin. *Intifada.* Boston, MA: South End Press, 1999.

Peretz, Don. *Intifada: The Palestinian Uprising.* Boulder, CO: Westview, 1990.

Pines, Ayala M. "The Palestinian Intifada and Israelis' Burnout." *Journal of Cross-Cultural Psychology* 25(4) (December 1994): 414–38.

Pratt, David. *Intifada: The Long Day of Rage.* Havertown, PA: Casemate, 2007.

Said, W. Edward. *Intifada: The Palestinian Uprising against Israeli Occupation.* Boston, MA: South End, 1989.

Schiff, Ze'ev, and Ehud Ya'ari. *Intifada: The Palestinian Uprising—Israel's Third Front.* New York: Simon and Schuster, 1990.

Schleifer, Ron. *Psychological Warfare in the Intifada: Israeli and Palestinian Media Politics and Military Strategies.* Eastbourne, UK: Sussex Academic Press, 2006.

Intifada, Second

A popular Palestinian uprising and period of enhanced Israeli-Palestinian hostilities that broke out in the year 2000 following the collapse of the Camp David peace talks that summer. The Second Intifada is also called the al-Aqsa Intifada because it began at the al-Aqsa Mosque in the Old City of Jerusalem. On September 28, 2000, Likud Party leader Ariel Sharon, accompanied by a Likud Party delegation and 1,500 police and security forces, entered and moved through the Haram al-Sharif complex, the area of Jerusalem's Old City also called the Temple Mount. The al-Aqsa Mosque and the Dome of the Rock are located there. The enclave, one of Islam's three most holy sites, is sacred to Jews as well. Many observant Jews will not walk on the Temple Mount for fear of desecrating the remnants of the Temple underneath it. Some Jewish and Christian organizations have called for the destruction of the Dome of the Rock or its transferal to an Arab country so that Jews can reclaim the site.

Sharon claimed to be investigating Israeli complaints that Muslims were damaging archeological remains below the surface of the Temple Mount. By agreement, at that time the area was then supervised by Palestinian rather than Israeli security, with Israeli tour guides handing over their charges to their Arab counterparts during the times when the area was open to non-Muslims.

Palestinians believed that Sharon's actions demonstrated Israeli contempt for limited Palestinian sovereignty and for Muslims in general. Anger began to build as a result, and soon riots and demonstrations erupted. Israeli troops launched attacks in Gaza, and on September 30, 2000, television footage showed the shooting of an unarmed 12-year-old boy, Muhammad Durrah, hiding behind his father as Israeli forces attacked. Protests then grew more violent, involving Israeli Arabs as well as Palestinians. For the first time, stores and banks were burned in Arab communities. Thousands of Israelis also attacked Arabs and destroyed Arab property in Tel Aviv and Nazareth during the Jewish holiday of Yom Kippur. On October 12, two

Israeli reservists were lynched by a mob at the Ramallah police station, further inflaming Israeli public opinion. In retaliation, Israel launched a series of air strikes against Palestinians.

On October 17, Israeli and Palestinian officials signed the Sharm al-Sheikh agreement to end the violence, but it continued nevertheless. Sharon's election as prime minister in February 2001 heightened Israel's hard-line tactics toward the Palestinians, such as the use of F-16 aircraft for the first time. Both Palestinians and Israelis admitted that the Oslo period was now over. Some Palestinians characterized their response as the warranted resistance of an embittered population that had received no positive assurances of sovereignty from years of negotiations. Others began or encouraged suicide attacks, also new to the situation; an example of this was the June

Israeli security men guard opposition leader Ariel Sharon (center) as he leaves the Temple Mount compound in east Jerusalem's Old City on September 28, 2000. (AP Photo/Eyal Warshavsky, File)

1, 2001, attack on Israelis waiting to enter a Tel Aviv discotheque and another attack on a Jerusalem restaurant on August 9, 2001. While some attacks were claimed by various Palestinian organizations, the degree of organizational control over the bombers and issues such as payments made to the so-called martyrs' families remain disputed.

These attacks in public places terrified Israelis. Those in modest economic circumstances had to use public transportation, but most malls, movie theaters, stores, and day care centers hired security guards. Israeli authorities soon began a heightened campaign of targeted killings, or assassinations, of Palestinian leaders. Some political figures began to call for complete segregation of Arabs and Israelis, even within the Green Line (the 1967 border). This would be enforced by a security wall and even population transfers, which would involve evicting Arab villagers and urban residents from Israel in some areas and forcing them to move to the West Bank.

A virulent campaign against Palestine Liberation Organization (PLO) chairman and Palestinian Authority (PA) president Yasser Arafat's leadership began in Israel with U.S. assent, complicating any negotiations between the two sides. Arafat was charged with corruption and with supporting the intifada. Israelis argued that he had actually planned it, a less than credible idea to most professional observers. However, when the Israel Defense Forces (IDF) captured the ship *Santorini* filled with weapons purchased by Ahmad Jibril, head of the Popular Front for the Liberation of Palestine (PFLP) General Command (a PLO faction that did not accept the Oslo Accords), in May 2001, and with the January 2002 capture of the *Karine-A*, a vessel carrying weapons allegedly from Iran, the anti-Arafat campaign increased.

The regional response to the al-Aqsa Intifada consisted of cautious condemnation by Egypt and Jordan, which had concluded peace agreements with Israel, and calls of outrage from other more hard-line states such as Syria. In February 2002, Saudi Arabia's crown prince Abdullah called for Arabs to fully normalize relations with Israel in return for Israeli withdrawal from the occupied territories. This plan was formally endorsed at an Arab League Summit in Beirut in March, although Israeli authorities prohibited Arafat from attending the summit. The proposal was never acknowledged by Israel.

Instead, in response to a suicide bomber's attack on the Netanya Hotel on March 28, 2002, in which 30 Israeli civilians died, the Israeli military began a major military assault on the West Bank. The PA headquarters were targeted, and international negotiations became necessary when militants took refuge in the Church of the Nativity in Bethlehem. Charges of a massacre in the IDF's onslaught on Jenin were investigated, showing a smaller death count of 55.

The Israeli military response to the intifada did not successfully convince Palestinians to relinquish their aims of sovereignty and seemed to spark more suicide attacks rather than discouraging them. In contrast, political measures and diplomacy produced some short interruptions in the violence, which gradually lengthened on the part of some Palestinian organizations and actors. In March 2003, Mahmoud Abbas, under pressure from Israel and the United States, became the first Palestinian prime minister of the PA because the United States refused to recognize or deal with Arafat. On April 30, 2003, the European Union (EU), the United States, Russia, and the United Nations (UN) announced the so-called Road Map to Peace that was to culminate in an independent Palestinian state.

The plan did not unfold as designed, however, and in response to an Israeli air strike intended to kill Abd al-Aziz Rantisi, the leader of Hamas, militants launched a bus bombing in Jerusalem. At the end of June 2003, Palestinian militants agreed to a *hudna* (truce), which lasted for seven weeks and longer on the part of certain groups. There was no formal declaration that the intifada had ceased, and additional Israeli assassinations of Palestinian leaders as well as suicide attacks continued. Nevertheless, since 2004, Hamas has respected the cease-fire, and the issues of Israeli withdrawal from Gaza, Arafat's November 2004 death, Palestinian elections, and the Israeli response to their outcome took the spotlight in late 2004 and throughout 2005.

Casualty numbers for the al-Aqsa Intifada are disputed. Approximately 1,000 Israelis had died, and 6,700 more were wounded by September 2004. By 2003, the Israelis reported that 2,124 Palestinians had been killed, but a U.S. source reported 4,099 Palestinians killed and 30,527 wounded by 2005. Israel's tourism sector suffered a considerable decline at a time in which inflation and unemployment were already problematic.

An outcome of the al-Aqsa Intifada in the global context of the September 11, 2001, terror attacks on the United States was that Israeli officials have tended to brand all Palestinian resistance, indeed all activity on behalf of Palestinians, as being terrorism. This discourse and the heightened violence have lent credence to those who call for separation rather than integration of Israelis with Arabs. Therefore, the building of the security barrier known as the Israeli Security Fence, which effectively cuts thousands of Palestinians off from their daily routes to work or school, was widely supported by Israelis. Similarly, Sharon's idea of withdrawal from Gaza was essentially funded by this idea, but his government had to confront those who were unwilling to relinquish settlements in that area.

The intifada resulted in crisis and despair among some Israeli peace activists and discouraged many independent efforts by Israelis and Palestinians to engage the other. A 2004 survey showed that the numbers of Israelis in general who believed that the 1993 Oslo Peace Accords would lead to settlements declined during the intifada, and greater numbers believed that Israel should impose a military solution on the Palestinians. Such opinions may well have shifted, however, following Israeli attacks on Lebanon in the summer of 2006, as well as the election in January 2005 of the relatively conciliatory Mahmoud Abbas as president of the PA in the West Bank.

The intifada also had deleterious effects on Palestinians who had hoped for the blossoming of normalcy in the West Bank, particularly as 85 percent of those in Gaza and 58 percent in the West Bank live in poverty. Following the outbreak of the intifada, the IDF demolished 628 housing units in which 3,983 people had lived. Less than 10 percent of these individuals were implicated in any violence or illegal activity.

Another outcome of the intifada was its highlighting of intra-Palestinian conflict. This included that between the Tunis PLO elements of the PA and the younger leaders who emerged within the occupied territories, between Fatah and Hamas, and between Fatah and the al-Aqsa Martyrs Brigades. Also evident were the difficulties of responding to Israeli demands for security when security for Palestinian citizens was not in force. Some Palestinian Israeli citizens asserted their Palestinian identity for the very first time as a result of the intifada. The conflict indubitably caused discord in the Arab world too.

Sherifa Zuhur

Further Reading

Baroud, Ramzy, et al. *The Second Palestinian Intifada: A Chronicle of a People's Struggle*. London: Pluto, 2006.

Bucaille, Laetitia. *Growing Up Palestinian: Israeli Occupation and the Intifada Generation*. Princeton, NJ: Princeton University Press, 2004.

Catignani, Sergio. *Israeli Counter-Insurgency and the Intifadas: Dilemmas of a Conventional Army*. New York: Routledge, 2008.

Dor, Danny. *Intifada Hits the Headlines: How the Israeli Press Misreported the Outbreak of the Second Palestinian Uprising*. Bloomington: Indiana University Press, 2004.

Enderlin, Charles. *The Lost Years: Radical Islam, Intifada, and Wars in the Middle East, 2001–2006*. New York: Other Press, 2007.

Hallward, Maia Carter. *Struggling for a Just Peace: Israeli and Palestinian Activism in the Second Intifada*. Gainesville: University Press of Florida, 2011.

Hallward, Maia Carter, and Julie M. Norman, eds. *Nonviolent Resistance in the Second Intifada: Activism and Advocacy*. New York: Palgrave Macmillan, 2011.

Khalidi, Walid. "The Prospects of Peace in the Middle East." *Journal of Palestine Studies* 32 (Winter 2003): 50–63.

Norman, Julie M. *The Second Palestinian Intifada: Civil Resistance*. New York: Routledge, 2010.

Pearlman, Wendy. *Occupied Voices: Stories of Everyday Life from the Second Intifada*. New York: Nation Books, 2003.

Pratt, David. *Intifada: The Long Day of Rage*. Havertown, PA: Casemate, 2007.

Reinhart, Tanya. *The Road Map to Nowhere: Israel/Palestine since 2003*. London: Verso, 2006.

Schleifer, Ron. *Psychological Warfare in the Intifada: Israeli and Palestinian Media Politics and Military Strategies*. Eastbourne, UK: Sussex Academic Press, 2006.

Shamir, Jacob, and Khalil Shikaki. *Palestinian and Israeli Public Opinion: The Public Imperative in the Second Intifada*. Bloomington: Indiana University Press, 2010.

Shulz, Helena Lindholm. "The al-Aqsa Intifada as a Result of Politics of Transition." *Arab Studies Quarterly* 24 (Fall 2002): 21–47.

Stork, Joe. "Erased in a Moment: Suicide Bombing Attacks against Israeli Civilians." *Human Rights Watch* (2002): 1–160.

Tarabay, Jamie. *A Crazy Occupation: Eyewitness to the Intifada*. Crows Nest, NSW, Australia: Allen and Unwin, 2005.

Iran

Middle Eastern nation of 636,293 square miles, slightly larger than the U.S. state of Alaska. Iran is bordered by the Persian Gulf and the Gulf of Oman to the south; Turkey, Azerbaijan, the Caspian Sea, and Armenia to the north; Afghanistan and Pakistan to the east; and Iraq to the west. Iran has long been

Followers of fundamentalist Islamic cleric Ayatollah Khomeini march in Tehran, Iran, on February 6, 1979, shortly after his return from exile. (AP Photo)

important because of its strategic location at the geographic nexus of the Middle East, Europe, and Southwest Asia. Its location captured the attention of both Britain and Russia in the 19th century, with each nation seeking to control the area. Rivalry over Iran continued in the early years of the Cold War as both the United States and the Soviet Union sought to control its oil resources.

Iran is predominantly a Shia Islam nation. However, Shiism did not become identified with the state until the Safavid Empire formed. The Shia were found in a variety of locations in the Middle East and South Asia, having originated in the Arabian Peninsula before the sect actually coalesced as such. Sunni Muslims comprise the great majority of Muslims in the Middle East and around the world, and Shia Iranians have periodically viewed the actions of Sunni-dominated governments as a direct threat to their economic, political, religious, and social well-being and independence.

In 1921, the Pahlavi dynasty was established in Iran by Shah Reza Pahlavi I, a military officer known first as Reza Khan, who led a coup against the last Qajar shah. A reformer and modernizer, Reza Shah instituted agricultural, economic, and educational reforms and began the modernization of the country's transportation system. In the end, these and other reforms threatened the status of the Shia clerics in Iran, who began to oppose the shah and his reforms. Desiring to extend the country's lengthy and imperial pre-Islamic tradition and so to include Iranians who were not from Fars (the central province), Reza Pahlavi changed the country's name from Persia to Iran in 1935.

Reza Pahlavi's lack of cooperation with the Allies during World War II led to his forced abdication in 1941 in favor of his son, Mohammad Reza Pahlavi. During the war, Iran was occupied by Soviet and British forces in the north and south of the country, respectively, and was a key conduit for lend-lease supplies. The shah's strong ties to the West over the next four decades often meant economic difficulty for Iran. For example, during World War II the British-controlled Anglo Iranian Oil Company (AIOC) artificially deflated the price of oil to reduce the cost of the war to the British economy. Certainly, the shah's popularity declined because of his ties to the West.

Mohammad Mosaddeq, a member of the National Front Party (NFP), became prime minister in 1951 and soon became the shah's most prominent critic. Mosaddeq's persistent criticism of the regime's weak position vis-à-vis Britain led him to nationalize the British-owned AIOC in 1951, which Washington chose to see as a clear example of his communist tendencies. Britain responded by imposing an embargo on Iranian oil and blocking the export of products from the formerly British properties. Because Britain was Iran's primary oil consumer, this had a considerable impact on Iran. Mosaddeq then asked the shah to grant him emergency powers that included direct control of the military. The shah refused, precipitating a domestic political crisis.

Mosaddeq understood the power of his popularity. He promptly resigned, causing widespread protests and demands that he be returned to power. Unnerved, in 1952, the shah reappointed Mosaddeq, who then took steps to consolidate his power. This included the implementation of land reforms and other measures, which to the West seemed socialist. Although Mosaddeq had not had any direct contact with the Soviets, the events in Iran were nevertheless of great concern to the United States, which feared a Soviet takeover (based on Soviet efforts to annex northern Iran at the end of World War II).

The United States refused Mosaddeq's repeated requests for financial aid because he refused to reverse the nationalization of the AIOC. By the summer of 1953, Mosaddeq's intransigence and his legalization of the leftist Tudeh Party led the United States to join Britain and the temporarily exiled shah in a covert August 1953 plot to overthrow Mosaddeq. Known as Operation AJAX, the coup against Mosaddeq was successful, and the shah was back in power by the end of August 1953. While the British were correct in viewing Mosaddeq as a threat to their position in Iran, the United States was incorrect in presuming that he was a communist. Rather, he was an Iranian nationalist who saw the income of Iranian farmers drop to $110 a year and witnessed many Iranians fall into abject poverty. He sought to ameliorate these conditions and establish a more independent foreign policy.

The decade that followed was marked by the creation in 1957 of the Sazeman-e Ettelaat va Amniyat-e Keshvar (SAVAK, National Information and Security Organization), the shah's dreaded secret police, and a number of failed economic reforms. Iranian economic policy was similar to that of many other developing nations, which showed preference to large state projects over a true free-market economy. Predictably, the largely state-run economy failed to perform as promised. This and pressure by the West finally led the shah to propose the White Revolution, which called for land reform, privatization of government-owned firms, electoral reform, women's suffrage, the nationalization of forests, rural literacy programs, and profit sharing for industrial workers. The shah hoped that such ambitious measures would spark economic growth and mitigate growing criticism of his regime. The White Revolution proved far less than revolutionary. That same year also witnessed a brutal crackdown on Iranian dissidents and fundamentalist clerics,

which did nothing to endear the shah to his own people.

Ayatollah Ruhollah Khomeini, a conservative Muslim cleric, became the shah's most prominent opponent in the early 1960s, berating the regime for its secular focus and the shah for his elaborate and regal Western lifestyle. Khomeini was especially critical of Iran's close relationship to the United States and Israel. From Khomeini's perspective, the Americans provided arms, training, and technical assistance to their key anticommunist ally in the Middle East. And Israel provided training to SAVAK, which included intelligence-gathering, interrogation, and counterterrorism techniques. Thus, when SAVAK arrested, tortured, and killed anti-regime activists, the United States and Israel were blamed along with the shah.

Khomeini's popularity prevented the shah from eliminating him but did not prevent the shah from exiling the cleric. Forced to leave Iran in 1964, Khomeini set himself apart from other Iranian clerics by refusing to compromise with the shah. While in exile Khomeini continued to denounce the shah, Zionism, and the United States in his many sermons.

As the shah's reforms failed to bring about the desired effects, leftist groups such as the Mujahideen-e Khalq and Fedayeen-e Islami Khalq joined the NFP and religious conservatives in unified opposition. The increase in oil revenue after the 1973–1974 oil crisis was insufficient to compensate for an Iranian economy teetering on insolvency and lacking clear private property rights.

During the 1970s opposition to the regime often took the form of overt acts of defiance, such as the wearing of the *hijab* by Iranian women or attending mosques whose imams openly criticized the shah. When an article critical of Khomeini ran in a Tehran newspaper in January 1978, the city's streets filled with Khomeini supporters and regime opponents. The shah's failure to quell the riots that followed only emboldened his opponents.

U.S. president Jimmy Carter's administration was repeatedly given false information by SAVAK, which misrepresented the level of civil unrest in Iran. In the end, after massive general strikes in the fall of 1978, the shah lost control of the country in January 1979 and fled. This was followed by the triumphal return of Khomeini from exile on February 1, 1979, and the establishment of a transitional government composed of the various opposition groups.

Relative moderates such as Mehdi Bazargan and Abolhasan Bani-Sadr, the first prime minister and president, respectively, after the Pahlavi collapse, were soon forced out of power by Khomeini's supporters, who firmly held the reins of power by 1980. Iran was transformed into a fundamentalist Islamic theocracy, with Khomeini as supreme faqih, the de facto national leader. It was with the support of the Revolutionary Guards—and the tacit support of Khomeini himself—that Iranian students were able to seize the U.S. embassy in Tehran on November 4, 1979, and take the Americans there hostage. The crisis endured for 444 days, paralyzing the Carter administration.

The incoming Ronald Reagan administration (1981–1989) viewed the fundamentalist regime as a threat to U.S. interests in the Middle East and to its closest ally, Israel. This led the United States to support Iraqi dictator Saddam Hussein's September 22, 1980, invasion of Iran. Initially, the Iraqi army had great success against the poorly led, disorganized, and surprised Iranians. However, Iranian zeal led to counteroffensives in 1982 that pushed the Iraqis back. The war then settled into a bloody stalemate during which the Iraqis for the most part fought from prepared defensive positions in the fashion of World War I and the Iranians

endured huge casualties while staging unsophisticated human wave attacks against prepared Iraqi positions. Khomeini viewed the war as a jihad, or holy war, and rejected any end to the fighting before the destruction of Hussein's secular government. After almost a decade of war and more than a million casualties, the Iran-Iraq War ended in 1988 with no clear victor.

Khomeini died in 1989, but a movement promoting reform did not begin until the late 1990s. Following Khomeini's death, his Islamic Religious Party continued to dominate the government bureaucracy and the policy-making apparatus. The ongoing conflict with Iraq did not limit the regime from becoming the single most important state sponsor of terrorism in the 1980s. Hezbollah traces one of its roots directly to Iran's support. Nearly two decades later, a policy of eradicating Israel and forcing the United States out of the Middle East continues to dominate Iranian foreign and military policy. This has influenced other groups, not only Hezbollah but also the secular Amal group and many other smaller militias that do not want Western intervention in the Middle East.

Israel's superior military and presumed nuclear weapons would make a direct Iranian strike against the Jewish state suicidal, but Israel has accused Iran of waging a proxy war in Gaza and Lebanon, a strategic blow to Israel well within Iran's capabilities. When Israel finally withdrew from southern Lebanon in May 2000, Iran continued, verbally at least, to support Hezbollah's struggle against Israeli encroachment of Lebanon.

The Islamic Republic of Iran has also strongly supported the Palestinian struggle against Israel and criticized the United States for its blind support of Israel. One reason for that stance is to differentiate itself from the former shah, who was an ally of Israel and an even stronger ally of the United States.

During the 1990s, U.S. president Bill Clinton attempted to pursue détente with Iran and sought to restore economic relations. Instead of accepting the U.S. offer, Saudi Shia terrorists detonated a car bomb outside the Khobar Towers housing complex at Dhahran Air Base (Saudi Arabia) in 1996. More than a dozen Americans were killed. The United States blamed Iran, but the Saudi Arabian government urged restraint and achieved a détente of sorts with Iran at that time.

Iran was accused of being a key supporter of the insurgency in Iraq following the Anglo-American invasion of that nation in 2003. Ties between Iran and insurgents are widely reported, with the regime providing weapons, training, and safe passage into Iraq. These ties go back to the Islamist opposition to Saddam Hussein, and so it is difficult to separate the Iraqi militia's self-ambitions and those of Tehran, but they are distinct. This was in addition to Iran's support for Hezbollah, which waged a bloody month-long war against Israel during July–August 2006.

In the near future, Iran is unlikely to end nearly two decades of anti-American and anti-Israeli foreign policy. The U.S. government claimed that Iran was moving toward the development of nuclear weapons and long-range missile technology needed to deliver nuclear warheads to Israel and Europe. Some Iranian clerics showed signs of increasing disapproval of the confrontational course taken by Khomeini and President Mahmoud Ahmadinejad toward the United States and Israel. A student-led reform movement that seemed to argue for the rise of moderation was not broadly supported, however.

From 2006 onward, preventing Iran from developing nuclear weapons became an increasingly salient priority of first the George W. Bush and then the Barack Obama administrations. Israel likewise regarded Iran's desire to acquire nuclear weapons—a charge denied by Iran—as a palpable threat. Iranian president Mahmoud Ahmadinejad repeatedly attacked Israel's policies, denied the Holocaust, and called for the destruction of Israel, which greatly concerned the Israelis. In an effort to halt Iran's nuclear weapons programme, from 2006, the United Nations imposed a range of economic sanctions on Iran, which were gradually tightened. The European Union acquiesced in these constraints, while the United States imposed a near total economic embargo on Iran. These measures imposed significant hardship upon Iran, leading to a major currency crisis. Netanyahu, however, considered them ineffective and repeatedly advocated air strikes on Iran's nuclear facilities, ideally in conjunction with U.S. forces but if necessary as a unilateral Israeli operation.

The election in August 2013 of the less confrontational Hassan Rouhani as president of Iran did nothing to allay Netanyahu's fears, since Ayatollah Ali Khameini, Iran's supreme leader, remained deeply hostile to Israel. Even so, in late November 2013, several major powers, including the United States, negotiated an interim six-month agreement with Iran whereby Iran froze key components of its nuclear program, in exchange for the relaxation of economic sanctions. This agreement was implemented in January 2014. In February 2014, talks opened on the framework of further negotiations intended to reach a permanent settlement, that would impose strict international controls on Iranian nuclear facilities in exchange for the unfreezing of Iranian assets held overseas.

Adam Lowther, Louis A. DiMarco,
and Paul G. Pierpaoli Jr.

Further Reading

Daniel, Elton L. *The History of Iran*. 2nd ed. Westport, CT: Greenwood, 2012.

Gheissari, Ali, and Vali Nasr. *Democracy in Iran: History and the Quest for Liberty*. New York: Oxford University Press, 2006.

Goodarzi, Jubin M. *Syria and Iran: Diplomatic Alliance and Power Politics in the Middle East*. New York: I. B. Tauris, 2008.

Katz, Yaakov, and Yoaz Hendel. *Israel vs. Iran: The Shadow War*. Washington, DC: Potomac Books, 2012.

Keddie, Nikki. *Modern Iran: Roots and Results of Revolution*. Updated ed. New Haven, CT: Yale University Press, 2006.

Kinzer, Stephen. *All the Shah's Men: An American Coup and the Roots of Middle East Terror*. Hoboken, NJ: Wiley, 2003.

Mottahedeh, Roy. *The Mantle of the Prophet: Religion and Politics in Iran*. Rev. ed. New York: Simon and Schuster, 2008.

Pappas, Theodore, ed. *Iran*. New York: Wiley, 2006.

Parsi, Trita. *Treacherous Alliance: The Secret Dealings of Israel, Iran, and the United States*. New Haven, CT: Yale University Press, 2007.

Pollack, Kenneth. *The Persian Puzzle*. New York: Random House, 2006.

Pollack, Kenneth. *Unthinkable: Iran, the Bomb, and American Strategy*. New York: Simon and Schuster, 2013.

Roshandel, Jalil, and Alethia H. Cook. *The United States and Iran*. New York: Palgrave Macmillan, 2009.

Shirazi, Saeed. *A Concise History of Iran*. Baltimore: Publish America, 2004.

St. Marie, Joseph J., and Shahdad Naghshpour. *Revolutionary Iran and the United States: Low-Intensity Conflict in the Persian Gulf*. Farnham, UK: Ashgate, 2011.

Totten, Michael J. *The Road to Fatima Gate: The Beirut Spring, the Rise of Hezbollah, and the Iranian War against Israel*. New York: Encounter Books, 2011.

Von Maltzahn, Nadia. *The Syria-Iran Axis: Cultural Diplomacy and International Relations in the Middle East*. New York: I. B. Tauris, 2013.

Iraq

Middle Eastern nation covering 168,753 square miles, slightly smaller than the U.S. state of California. Iraq borders Saudi Arabia to the west and south, Kuwait and the Persian Gulf to the south, Iran to the east, and Syria and Turkey to the north. Most important to a modern understanding of Iraq is the Arab conquest of the region (AD 633–644), which was responsible for making Iraq the culturally, ethnically, linguistically, and religiously diverse country it is today. As the capital of the Muslim Abbasid Empire shifted from Damascus to Baghdad, Iraq rose to renewed prominence with a new culture and religion. The synthesis of this empire and subsequent Muslim states with the influence of Iraq's numerous tribes remains a powerful historical aspect of life in Iraq.

The Ottoman defeat in World War I left Great Britain the new master of the former Ottoman provinces of Mosul, Baghdad, and Basra, which now form the modern state of Iraq. Independence in 1932, however, was far less than the salvation many Iraqis assumed it would be. Iraq was split between Sunni and Shia, among Arab, Kurd, and Turcoman, and between urban and rural, and deep cleavages tore at the fabric of Iraqi society.

While it lasted, the Hashemite monarchy (1921–1958) attempted to build a unified sense of identity in Iraq. Following the 1958 coup that toppled the monarchy and brought General Abdul Karim Qassem to power, Iraqi governments fell in rapid succession.

In 1940, Prime Minister Rashid Ali al-Gaylani offered to support Britain in World War II if Palestine were to be established as a state. Winston Churchill's refusal caused a split between the nationalists, who thought that Axis support would help them, and moderates such as former prime minister Nuri al-Said. The crisis led to a British and Arab Legion occupation of Baghdad and the flight of al-Gaylani and his allies from Iraq and lent support to the later Baathist anti-imperialist stance.

When Israel declared its independence on May 14, 1948, a new dimension was added to an already unstable regional situation. In the Israeli War of Independence (1948–1949), Iraq provided 3,000 troops in May 1948, adding 15,000 troops during the months that followed. Iraqi forces successfully held the Jenin-Nablus-Tulkaram triangle but singularly failed to launch an attack on Jewish forces. The failure of the allied Arab forces to succeed on the battlefield left Arab leaders with little choice but to negotiate the 1948 cease-fire.

Arab failure, as in the past, led to the persecution of Iraqi Jews, whose loyalty was suspect. The focus on internal deficiencies

of the regime was replaced by charges that the small number of Iraqi Jews had spied for Israel and were responsible for Iraq's military failure. This pattern of behavior repeated itself during the 1967 Six-Day War and the 1973 Yom Kippur War. Later, Iraqi dictator Saddam Hussein would perfect this ploy and use it on a number of occasions against other enemies to deflect attention away from his own economic, military, and political failures.

In 1955, Iraq joined the pro-Western Baghdad Pact, allying itself with Turkey, Iran, and Pakistan in a mutual defense agreement sponsored by the United States. The pact was a direct affront to the long-simmering nationalist sentiments within the Iraqi army officer corps. Indeed, the pact became the catalyst that ignited the 1958 revolution, the first in a string of coups and countercoups that would plague Iraq until the Baathists finally consolidated power in 1968. The 1958 coup was led by a secret nationalist organization known as the Free Officers Movement. On

Iraqi president Saddam Hussein (center), accompanied by aides, tours the front line in Iraqi-occupied Kuwait in January 1991. (AP Photo)

July 14, 1958, its members seized control of Baghdad and executed King Faisal II and Prime Minister al-Said. The revolutionaries then abolished the monarchy, proclaimed Iraq a republic, and sought closer ties to the Soviet Union. Colonel Qassem had led the coup, but his policies ultimately created a great many internal and external enemies.

The republican period of Iraqi history (1958–1968) was marked as one of internal conflict in which the antimonarchist factions fought among themselves. Qassem's rule of Iraq was short-lived, and he was overthrown in 1963 by a coalition of anticommunist military officers and secular Arab nationalists and Baathists who installed Colonel Abd al-Salam Arif as president and Hasan al-Bakr as prime minister. Allies in the National Council of the Revolutionary Command that took the reigns of government in February 1963 soon turned against one another, as it became clear that the military and the Baath Party fundamentally disagreed on the path that Iraq should pursue. President Arif's tenure in office ended abruptly when he was killed in a helicopter crash in 1966. His more pliable brother, Abdal-Rahman Arif, took over and served as president until 1968.

Iraq's failure to support fellow Arab states in the Six-Day War led to massive riots in Baghdad, which the regime was ineffective in suppressing. On July 17, 1968, the Baathists seized radio stations, the Ministry of Defense, and the headquarters of the Republican Guard. The Baath Party thus came to power with Hasan al-Bakr taking the posts of president, prime minister, and secretary general of the party. His cousin, Saddam Hussein, worked in the background to eliminate adversaries of the new regime. Over time, Hussein proved to be a ruthless operator whose patronage system broke down the historic bonds in Iraqi society. His network of security

organizations so thoroughly penetrated government, the military, and society that he was able to remove al-Bakr from power without a challenge. Security operatives also settled old scores with the communists and Free Officers on Hussein's behalf.

When the Yom Kippur War began in October 1973, a recently attempted coup by the brutal head of state security services, Nadhim Kzar, was still at the forefront of government efforts to purge the Baath Party. This led to Iraq playing only a minor role in the war in the form of an armored division sent to Syria. The Iraqis fought alongside the Syrians as they sought to retake the Golan Heights. The effort failed.

Defeat in the war was the third consecutive defeat for the Arabs at the hands of Israel, and it led the Iraqi regime to turn inward. This meant that the Kurds, Shiites, and communists suffered the brunt of the regime's onslaught throughout the 1970s. Survival became the focus of existence for these three groups. With the establishment of the Islamic Republic of Iran in 1979, the Iraqi regime saw a looming threat in Ayatollah Ruhollah Khomeini's Shiite-fundamentalist regime.

After Hussein assumed the presidency in 1979, his consolidation of power was complete. He launched an offensive against the southern Iranian city of Khorramshahr on September 17, 1980, sparking the Iran-Iraq War that would drag on until 1988 and would witness more than 1 million combined casualties. Neither side achieved a clear victory, and both countries saw their economies dramatically decline during the war. For Israel, however, the Iran-Iraq War was a respite that reduced foreign threats.

Exhausted, Iran and Iraq reached a ceasefire agreement in July 1988. In the aftermath of the war, Hussein turned to Saudi Arabia and Kuwait for financial assistance but was rebuffed. Under Ottoman rule, Kuwait had been part of Basra Province and only became an independent emirate during the British Mandate. This historical quirk provided Hussein with an excuse to invade Kuwait.

But Hussein had other reasons to attack Kuwait. He accused the Kuwaitis of manipulating the price of oil to the detriment of Iraq and asserted that Kuwait was illegally tapping Iraqi oil reserves by slant-drilling into Iraqi oil fields. The dictator also fumed that the Kuwaitis would not accede to debt reduction to help a struggling Iraqi economy. To Hussein's way of thinking, if the Kuwaiti emir would not provide financial relief to Iraq, then the Iraqi army would simply conquer Kuwait.

In the days leading up to the 1990 Iraqi invasion of Kuwait, the United States failed to clearly communicate its disapproval of an Iraqi invasion but instead led the Iraqis to believe that they were free to invade Kuwait. After the invasion began on August 2, 1990, the United Nations (UN) quickly condemned Iraq, and U.S. president George H.W. Bush began deploying U.S. troops to Saudi Arabia. Although the Iraqi regime was convinced that the United States would not attack, the Iraqi high command began planning for such a contingency. Part of the plan called for a massive air strike that would see Israel's major cities hit by devastating chemical weapons attacks designed to bring Israel into the war and cause other Arab nations to terminate their support of the U.S.-led coalition. The attack never materialized, but Iraq did manage to strike Israel with approximately two dozen Scud missiles in January 1991. The United States responded rapidly and deployed two Patriot missile batteries to Israel.

In the wake of a resounding coalition victory in February 1991, Iraq was reduced economically and politically by the sanctions placed on Hussein's regime and the presence of UN weapons inspectors who scoured the country for weapons of mass destruction (WMDs). Average Iraqis suffered intensely under the sanctions. The UN's Oil for Food Program was designed to bring needed medicine and food to Iraq while preventing the regime from rebuilding its WMD capabilities. Instead, Hussein built lavish palaces and exported the medical supplies and food intended for Iraqis to foreign countries. He also ruthlessly suppressed uprisings by both the Kurds and Shiites.

Iraq's link to international terrorism had begun as early as the 1980s. It was in fact the Iraqi regime that provided Abu Abbas, mastermind of the *Achille Lauro* ocean liner hijacking, safe haven in 1985. In the years that followed the Persian Gulf War, Hussein dramatically stepped up his support for terrorist organizations. Ramzi Yusef, mastermind of the 1993 World Trade Center bombing, received support from regime elements prior to traveling to the United States on a valid Iraqi passport. In addition, Abu Nidal, Abu Musab al-Zarqawi, the Popular Front for the Liberation of Palestine (PFLP), and Hamas all received financial support, training, and/or military assistance from Iraq prior to 2003. Perhaps most notoriously, Hussein allegedly sent checks for $25,000 to the families of Palestinian suicide bombers.

It was not until President George W. Bush launched Operation IRAQI FREEDOM in March 2003, with a thin multinational coalition, that direct action was taken against the Iraqi regime. Bush offered three reasons for the invasion. First, tyranny in Iraq was no longer acceptable. Second, Iraq's WMD capability was a threat to the United States and its allies. Third, Iraqi support of terrorism presented an unacceptable danger to free nations.

The vaunted Iraqi military proved to be a shell of its former self. Within three weeks, the regime collapsed. In the months that followed, however, Fedayeen Saddam as well as Iraqi Sunnis, foreign Islamists, and former members of the Baathist army began an insurgency that continues to plague Iraq and the ongoing U.S. occupation to the present.

In order to assist in the rebuilding of civil society in Iraq, the Bush administration initiated an effort to train a new Iraqi military and police force capable of taking over security operations throughout the country. This process proved far more difficult than the administration had anticipated. What became evident, however, is that some of the reasons Bush cited for going to war with Iraq were exceedingly dubious. After more than six years in Iraq, no WMDs were found. And despite Bush administration claims that Hussein had links to the terrorist organization Al Qaeda, no such relationship was established. Indeed, Hussein would have had little reason to support an Islamic extremist group, as he had ruthlessly suppressed Iraqi Islamist groups whose philosophy countered that of the Baath Party and, according to him, threatened Iraqi unity.

Iraq's relationship with Israel in the coming years is unlikely to see Iraqi state-sponsored terrorism visited upon the Jewish state, but neither is Iraq likely to become Israel's greatest ally. Among Israelis, the hope was that Iraq would focus on its domestic affairs and the rebuilding of its shattered economy, leaving Israel with one less adversary. U.S. forces left Iraq in December 2011, though the United States still has two bases and around 4,000 military personnel in the country. By early 2012, Iranian influence was alleged to be increasing in Iraq, with one Iranian military official reportedly stating that Iraq's largely Shiite government was under neighboring Iran's control. Given the deep hostility between Iran and Israel, such developments were unwelcome to Israel. Sectarian conflicts continued in Iraq, albeit at a far lower level than earlier, and in parts of the country insurgent forces were still active.

Adam Lowther, Louis A. DiMarco, and Paul G. Pierpaoli Jr.

Further Reading

Abdullah, Thabit. *A Short History of Iraq.* London: Pearson, 2003.

Cook, Jonathan. *Israel and the Clash of Civilisations: Iraq, Iran and the Plan to Remake the Middle East.* London: Pluto, 2008.

Dodge, Toby. *Inventing Iraq.* New York: Columbia University Press, 2003.

Dodge, Toby. *Iraq: From War to a New Authoritarianism.* New York: Routledge, 2013.

Ghanim, David. *Iraq's Dysfunctional Democracy.* Westport, CT: Praeger, 2011.

Karsh, Efraim. *Islamic Imperialism.* New Haven, CT: Yale University Press, 2006.

Keegan, John. *The Iraq War.* New York: Vintage Books, 2005.

Long, Jerry M. *Saddam's War of Words: Politics, Religion, and the Iraqi Invasion of Kuwait.* Austin: University of Texas Press, 2004.

Makiya, Kanan. *Republic of Fear: The Politics of Modern Iraq.* Berkeley: University of California Press, 1998.

Marr, Phoebe. *The Modern History of Iraq.* 3rd ed. Boulder, CO: Westview, 2011.

Murray, Williamson, and Robert H. Scales Jr. *The Iraq War: A Military History.* Cambridge, MA: Harvard University Press, 2003.

Nissen, Hans J., and Peter Heine. *From Mesopotamia to Iraq: A Concise History.* Chicago: Chicago University Press, 2009.

Oren, Michael B. *Six Days of War: June 1967 and the Making of the Modern Middle East.* Novato, CA: Presidio, 2003.

Pelletière, Stephen C. *Israel in the Second Iraq War: The Influence of Likud.* Santa Barbara, CA: Praeger, 2009.

Pelletiere, Stephen. *The Iran-Iraq War: Chaos in a Vacuum*. New York: Praeger, 1992.

Polk, William R. *Understanding Iraq*. New York: Harper Perennial, 2005.

Sassoon, Joseph. *Saddam Hussein's Ba'ath Party: Inside an Authoritarian Regime*. Cambridge: Cambridge University Press, 2011.

Tripp, Charles. *A History of Iraq*. 3rd ed. Cambridge: Cambridge University Press, 2007.

Woods, Kevin M. *The Mother of All Battles: Saddam Hussein's Plans for the Persian Gulf*. Annapolis, MD: Naval Institute Press, 2008.

Woods, Kevin M., David D. Palkki, and Mark E. Stout, eds. *The Saddam Tapes: The Inner Workings of a Tyrant's Regime, 1978–2001*. Cambridge: Cambridge University Press, 2011.

Israel

Israel, the only Jewish nation in the world, has an area of some 8,019 square miles (slightly larger than the U.S. state of Massachusetts) and a current population of about 7 million people. It is bordered by the eastern Mediterranean to the west, Lebanon to the north, Jordan and Syria to the east, and Egypt to the southwest. Its government is a parliamentary democracy, and the country boasts an advanced Western-style economy.

According to the Jewish Bible, the Tanakh (known as the Old Testament to Christians), Jews trace their origins to some 4,000 years ago to the prophet Abraham and his son Isaac. A series of Jewish kingdoms and states intermittently ruled Palestine or Israel for more than a millennium thereafter. Jews were the majority of the inhabitants of Palestine or, as the Jews called it, Israel (Land of God), for many centuries until the first century AD. After suppressing a series of Jewish revolts in the first century, the Romans expelled most Jews from Palestine. Over the next thousand years, Jews migrated to Western and Eastern Europe and then to the United States. Beginning at the end of the 19th century, however, a strong movement, known as Zionism, developed whereby Jews sought to return to and take up residence in Palestine.

During World War I in order to secure Jewish support for the war, the British government in 1917 issued the Balfour Declaration. Named after Foreign Secretary Arthur Balfour, it announced British support for the "establishment in Palestine of a national home for the Jewish people." At the same time, however, in order to secure Arab support against the Turks, the British government was promising support for establishment of an Arab state.

After the war, in 1920 Britain and France divided up the Middle Eastern possessions of the Ottoman Empire as League of Nations mandates. Britain secured Palestine and Iraq, while France was granted mandates in Syria and Lebanon. In 1922, Britain split Palestine into Transjordan, east of the Jordan River, and Palestine to the west.

Already a number of Jews had arrived in Palestine and settled there, purchasing Arab lands. Following World War I these numbers grew substantially, something that Palestinian Arabs viewed with alarm. The Arabs saw themselves becoming a marginalized minority in their own land. In response to continuing Jewish immigration, sporadic Arab attacks against Jews as well as British officials in Palestine occurred, escalating into the Arab Revolt of 1936–1939.

At the same time, militant Jewish groups began to agitate against what they saw as restrictive British immigration policies for Jews in Palestine. Armed militant Zionist groups such as the Lohamei Herut Israel (Stern Gang) and the Irgun Tsvai Leumi (National Military Organization) carried out

On May 14, 1948, one year after the United Nations proposed carving two separate states out of Palestine, David Ben-Gurion declares the creation of the independent state of Israel. (AFP/Getty Images)

actions against the British administration in Palestine, and in the 1930s a three-way struggle emerged that pitted the British against militant Arabs and Jews. Amid sharply increased violence, the British government attempted a delicate balancing act, made more difficult by the need to secure Arab (and also Jewish) support against Germany and Italy in World War II.

The Holocaust, the demonic Nazi scheme to exterminate the Jews during World War II, resulted in the deaths of some 6 million Jews in Europe. During the war and immediately afterward, many of the survivors sought to immigrate to Israel. For Jews, the great lesson of the war was that they could not rely on national governments or international agencies to protect them. In order to be protected, they would require their own independent state. The Holocaust also created in the West, which did little to try to save the Jews during the war, a sense of moral obligation for the

creation of a Jewish state and brought pressure on the British government to relax the prewar restrictive policies it had instituted regarding Jewish immigration into Palestine. At the same time, however, the Arabs of Palestine were adamantly opposed to any sharp increase in the number of Jews in Palestine or the creation there of a Jewish state.

Following World War II, as Jewish refugees sought to gain access to Palestine, many were forcibly turned away by British warships sent to patrol the Mediterranean coast for this very purpose. At the same time, British authorities wrestled with partitioning Palestine into Arab and Jewish states. Jews and Arabs proved intransigent, and in February 1947 after both rejected a final proposal for partition, Britain turned the problem over to the United Nations (UN).

In August 1947, the UN recommended granting Palestine its independence. The UN also developed a plan for partitioning

A section of Israel's separation barrier at the Kalandia checkpoint is seen with the West Bank town of Ramallah in the background on the outskirts of Jerusalem on April 30, 2006. (AP Photo/Kevin Frayer)

Palestine into separate Arab and Jewish states. Jerusalem was to be classified as an international area under the UN in order to preclude conflict over its status. Although the Arab population in Palestine was then 1.2 million people and the Jews numbered just 600,000, the UN plan granted the proposed Jewish state some 55 percent of the land and the Arab state only 45 percent. The Arab states rejected the partition plan, which included an economic union. The Jews generally accepted it. The UN General Assembly approved the plan in November 1947, and the British government announced that it would accept the UN recommendation and declared that the British Mandate for Palestine would end on May 15, 1948.

The Council of the Arab League announced that it was prepared to prevent the creation of a Jewish state by force if necessary, and immediately following the UN vote militant Palestinian Arabs and foreign Arab fighters began attacks against Jewish communities in Palestine, beginning the Arab-Jewish Communal War (November 30, 1947–May 14, 1948). The United States, with the world's largest Jewish population, became the chief champion and most reliable ally of a Jewish state, a position that cost it dearly in its relations with the Arab world and greatly impacted subsequent geopolitics in the Middle East and throughout the world.

The British completed their pullout on May 14, 1948, and that same day David Ben-Gurion, executive chairman and defense minister of the Jewish Agency, immediately declared the independent Jewish State of Israel. Ben-Gurion, from Mapai (Worker's Party), became the new state's first prime minister, a post he held during 1948–1953 and 1955–1963.

At first, the interests of the United States and those of the Soviet Union regarding the

Jewish state converged. U.S. recognition of Israel came only shortly before that of the Soviet Union. Moscow found common ground with the Jews in their suffering at the hands of the Nazis in World War II and also identified with the socialism espoused by the early Jewish settlers in Palestine as well as their anti-British stance. The Cold War, the reemergence of official anti-Semitism in the Soviet Union, and Moscow's desire to court the Arab states by supporting Arab nationalism against the West soon changed all that.

Immediately following Ben-Gurion's declaration of independence, the Arab armies of Egypt, Lebanon, Transjordan, Syria, and Iraq invaded Palestine, thus sparking the Israeli War of Independence (1948–1949). In the war, the Jews successfully defended their new state and defeated the Arab armies. A series of armistices in 1949 ended the war, with Israel left in control of an additional 26 percent of the land of Mandate Palestine west of the Jordan River. Transjordan, however, controlled large portions of Judea and Samaria, later known as the West Bank. The establishment of Israel and subsequent wars created some 600,000–700,000 Palestinian Arab refugees. Why these refugees fled their homes is hotly disputed. Arabs blame the Jews for expelling the Palestinian Arabs by causing mass panic and fear through warfare, terrorism, and massacres. Jews, on the other hand, insist that Arabs fled on their own or at the urging of Arab states, which incited fear and panic among Palestinian Arabs by warning darkly of imminent Jewish attacks and massacres.

Meanwhile, the Israelis set up the machinery of statehood. Mapai and its successor parties would govern Israel for the next 30 years. These were social democratic parties with strong roots in Zionism. As such, they were hawkish on defense but inclined toward moderate socialism in the socioeconomic sphere. The provisional government governed until February 14, 1949, following democratic elections on January 25, 1949, that established a unicameral parliament, later known as the Knesset, and consisted of 120 members. The executive (cabinet) was selected by the Knesset and was subject to it. Israel also adopted a system of proportional representation in which seats in the Knesset were based on the percentage of votes received. Even parties receiving relatively few votes had representatives in the Knesset. Such parties included those representing the Arab population, those espousing various degrees of Jewish orthodoxy, the communists, and Revisionist Zionist groups.

On May 11, 1949, Israel was admitted as the 59th member of the UN. Mapai remained the dominant political party after the second Knesset elections on July 30, 1951, in which a coalition government with religious parties was formed.

In 1950, Israel promulgated the so-called right of return law, which stipulated the right of any Jew to settle in Israel. In 1951 alone, 687,000 Jews arrived in Israel, some 300,000 from the Arab states. Ben-Gurion remained prime minister until 1953 and returned to that position in October 1955, remaining in office until 1963.

Israel's early years were dominated by the great challenge of absorbing and integrating into society hundreds of thousands of Jewish immigrants from different parts of the world, including Ashkenazi Jews from Eastern and Central Europe; Sephardic Jews who had fled from Spain in 1492 and settled in Muslim or Ottoman lands, including what is today Bulgaria, parts of Romania, Turkey, and the Middle East; other Middle Eastern or Oriental Jews; and those from such places as Iran, India, and Afghanistan. In addition to money raised from Jewish communities overseas, especially in the United States, and the U.S. government, financial assistance came from an unlikely source. Chancellor Konrad Adenauer of West Germany secured passage of legislation to provide billions of dollars in assistance to Israel over a 12-year period. Federal indemnification laws provided for payments to individual victims of the Holocaust.

Israel's formative years also witnessed the creation of a mixed socialist–capitalist economy. Included in the expansion and maturation of the economy were agricultural incentives and cultivating more land. The differences in terms of cultural background and socioeconomic status among these various groups of Jews initially proved a challenge for the Israeli government.

The 1949 cease-fires that ended the 1948–1949 war were not followed by peace agreements. The Arab states not only refused to recognize the existence of Israel but also refused to concede defeat in the war. By 1950, they had imposed an economic and political boycott on Israel. Throughout most of the 1950s, Israel suffered from repeated attacks and raids from neighboring Arab states as well as Palestinian Arab paramilitary and terrorist groups. Aggressive Israeli retaliation failed to stop them. The 1952 coup and revolution in Egypt led by the Free Officers further increased tension between Israel and Egypt. Indeed, Egyptian president Gamal Abdel Nasser proved to be an outspoken opponent of Israel and the West and a champion of Arab nationalism and unity. He increased the power of the Egyptian military, supported cross-border raids into Israeli territory by fedayeen (guerrilla fighters) from the Gaza Strip, and formed alliances with other Arab states. He also cultivated close ties with the Soviet Union.

In 1956, Nasser nationalized the Suez Canal, which provided the pretext for the French, British, and Israeli governments to collaborate to attack Egypt. The British sought to retake control of the canal, while the French sought to end Nasser's support of the Algerian independence movement. At the same time, Israel also saw the Suez Crisis as an opportunity to cooperate with Britain and France to check Nasser's power and influence if not overthrow him. On October 29, 1956, Israeli forces invaded the Sinai and headed for the Suez Canal. This provided the excuse for the British and the French to intervene. The U.S. government applied considerable pressure, and all three states agreed to withdraw. Israel secured the right to free navigation through the Suez Canal and on the waterways through the Straits of Tiran and the Gulf of Aqaba. The UN deployed a peacekeeping force between Egypt and Israel until 1967, when Egypt secured its departure just before the June 1967 Six-Day War.

During 1957–1967, Israel was primarily preoccupied with domestic politics, including continued agricultural and industrial development. Its border with Egypt generally remained calm, although incidents with Syria in particular increased, especially over water rights as Israel diverted water from the Jordan River to irrigate its land. This led Syria and Lebanon to divert water upstream from the Jordan River. In response to this so-called water war, Israel destroyed Lebanese and Syrian projects designed to reduce water flow downstream.

Ben-Gurion resigned as prime minister in 1963 and two years later defected from Mapai, creating a new party, the Rafi Party (Israeli Labor List). Upon Ben-Gurion's resignation, Levi Eshkol of Mapai served as prime minister until his death in 1969, when Foreign Minister Golda Meir replaced him as Israel's fourth prime minister.

On May 23, 1960, in Buenos Aires, Argentina, Israeli agents captured the fugitive Nazi official Adolf Eichmann, who had official charge of the deportation of Jews to the death camps during World War II. Spiriting Eichmann out of Argentina, Israeli agents brought him to Israel. The Israeli government then placed him on trial for crimes against humanity and the Jewish people. Convicted, he was hanged on May 31, 1962, the only time the death penalty was imposed according to Israeli law. In 1965, however, after much internal debate and controversy, Israel established formal diplomatic relations with West Germany.

On February 22, 1966, a coup brought a military government to power in Syria, committed to the Palestinian cause and the liberation of Palestine. Incidents along Israel's border with Syria increased significantly. Throughout the spring of 1967, Israel faced increasing attacks along its borders from Syria and the Palestine Liberation Organization (PLO), an organization created in 1964 to represent the Palestinian Arabs and coordinate efforts with Arab states to liberate Palestine. The PLO began mounting cross-border attacks from Jordan. By May war seemed imminent with Syria, as Egypt and Jordan announced that they had mobilized their armies. This was in reaction to what they claimed was an Israeli mobilization, and other Arab countries such as Iraq pledged to join in any war against Israel. On May 23, Egypt closed the Straits of Tiran and blockaded the Gulf of Aqaba, thereby blockading the Israeli port of Eilat.

Fearing an imminent Arab attack and invasion, Israel launched a preemptive attack on June 5, 1967, crippling the air forces of Egypt, Syria, Jordan, and Iraq. Having achieved air supremacy, Israel then easily defeated the armies of Egypt, Jordan, and Syria as well as Iraqi units. Five days later, Israel occupied the Sinai and the Gaza Strip from Egypt, the West Bank and East Jerusalem from Jordan, and the Golan Heights from Syria, doubling the amount of territory under the control of the Jewish state and providing buffer zones in the new territories. In the wake of its military victory, Israel announced that it would not withdraw from these captured territories until negotiations with the Arab states took place leading to recognition of Israel's right to exist.

Israel's military victory did not, however, lead to peace with its Arab neighbors. Humiliated by their defeat, the Arab states refused to negotiate with, recognize, or make peace with Israel, which was spelled out in the Khartoum Arab Summit Communiqué of September 1, 1967. The war united much of Israeli society and muted, if not silenced, most political disputes for several years. On January 21, 1968, the Mapai Party merged with two other socialist political parties to form the Labor Party.

In 1969, the War of Attrition began, with Egypt shelling Israeli targets in the Sinai along the Suez Canal. Israel responded by launching retaliatory raids and air strikes. Israel also constructed the Bar-Lev Line, an elaborate series of defensive fortifications to shield Israeli forces from Egyptian artillery attacks. Nasser sought Soviet military aid and support, including surface-to-air missiles (SAMs). By 1969, the euphoria from Israel's decisive 1967 victory had turned into disillusionment over rising Israeli casualties and the fact that peace still seemed elusive.

During this time, Israel also experienced increasing incidents along its border with Jordan as the PLO launched raids and attacks into Israel from Jordan, leading to retaliatory Israeli attacks. This ultimately provoked a civil war between the PLO and the Jordanian government in 1970, which culminated in the so-called Black September that brought heavy fighting involving the Jordanian army and the expulsion of the PLO from Jordan to Lebanon. During Black September, Syria sought to intervene on the side of the PLO but was deterred from doing so by Israel, which dispatched a military force to the Jordanian border as a deterrence at the request of the United States.

Beginning in 1970 with U.S. support, UN-sponsored peace talks between Egypt and Israel resulted in a cease-fire and a temporary end to the War of Attrition. But no lasting peace settlement was reached over the question of Israel's occupation of Arab territories since the 1967 war. President Nasser died in September 1970. His successor, Anwar Sadat, sought an end to the war with Israel so as to focus on Egypt's many internal problems. Frustrated at the lack of progress in the peace process, on October 6, 1973, on the Jewish high holy day of Yom Kippur, Egypt and Syria launched a surprise attack on Israel. Although both attacking powers enjoyed initial success and inflicted heavy casualties on Israeli forces, Israel, after regrouping its forces and being resupplied by the United States, repulsed the Egyptian and Syrian offensives and retained control of the Sinai and Golan Heights. Israel won the war but only after early and heavy losses. Nevertheless, the military balance between Israel and its Arab foes had shifted, and the notion of Israeli invincibility had ended.

The Yom Kippur War shook Israel's confidence and morale and proved costly in terms of lives. It also made Israel more economically dependent on the United States. In the December 1973 Knesset elections the Labor Party lost seats, and the newly formed right-wing Likud Party gained strength. Public and political fallout from the war led Prime Minister Meir to resign on April 10,

1974. She was succeeded by Yitzhak Rabin, also of the Labor Party.

A series of cease-fire talks between Israel and Egypt and between Israel and Syria now occurred, followed up by intensive shuttle diplomacy by U.S. secretary of state Henry Kissinger in 1974 to turn the cease-fire agreements into the basis for peace talks. By this time, international opinion was growing increasingly anti-Israeli as the propaganda war turned in favor of the Arabs, especially given the latter's hold over much of the world's oil supply. Israel's refusal to withdraw from occupied Arab territories seized during the Six-Day War led to the loss of much world support and sympathy especially in Africa, which viewed Israel's occupation as but another form of colonialism.

During this time, Arab states along with the PLO proved much more effective in publicizing the plight of the Palestinians. Increasing acts of terrorism by the PLO during 1970–1972 also focused world attention on the Arab-Israeli conflict and the Palestinian cause. On October 14, 1974, the UN General Assembly authorized the PLO to participate in a series of debates. Included was PLO chairman Yasser Arafat, considered a terrorist in Israel. He addressed the body, and on November 10, 1975, the General Assembly declared Zionism as racist. Rabin refused to negotiate with the PLO because it refused to recognize Israel and had proclaimed as its goal the destruction of the Jewish state.

With little loss of life, on July 4, 1976, Israeli commandos rescued Israeli airline passengers who had been kidnapped by Palestinian hijackers and taken to Entebbe, Uganda, under the protection of Ugandan dictator Idi Amin. The hijackers threatened to kill the passengers unless Palestinian terrorists in Israeli and West European prisons were released. The successful rescue of the 103 jetliner passengers proved a major morale boost for Israel and its military.

In May 1977, the Likud Party ended the Labor Party's 29-year political reign, and Menachem Begin became prime minister. Now seeking to jump-start the peace process, Sadat shocked the world by announcing on November 9, 1977, his willingness to go to Jerusalem and meet with the Israelis face-to-face to negotiate peace. Accepting an invitation by Begin to visit, Sadat arrived in Israel on November 19, the first Arab head of state to do so, effectively recognizing Israel's right to exist. During his visit, Sadat met with Begin and addressed the Knesset. Although every other Arab state refused to negotiate with Israel, after two years of negotiations mediated by U.S. president Jimmy Carter, Egypt and Israel made peace on March 26, 1979. Per the Camp David Accords, Israel withdrew from the Sinai in exchange for Egypt recognizing Israel. Discussions about the status of the Palestinians took place but the two states never achieved any common ground on this issue. Sadat's assassination on October 6, 1981, effectively ended the talks. The Arab world condemned the peace treaty with Israel, and Egypt was suspended from the Arab League.

On July 7, 1981, the Israeli Air Force bombed the Iraqi nuclear reactor at Osiraq, thwarting Iraqi efforts to acquire nuclear weapons. The next year Israel invaded Lebanon, which had been experiencing a civil war since 1975, ostensibly to defend its northern border from terrorist attacks but also to expel the PLO from Lebanon, which it did by capturing the capital of Beirut and forcing the PLO to relocate to Tunisia. This came at a terrible human cost and material destruction to Lebanese civilians, however, and Israel failed to achieve its broad policy objectives of creating a stable pro-Israeli

government in Lebanon. In 1983, Begin resigned and was replaced by fellow Likud member Yitzhak Shamir. Israel withdrew from most of Lebanon in 1986 but maintained a security zone there until May 2000, when it surrendered that territory as well.

A major Palestinian uprising—the First Intifada—erupted in 1987 in the Israeli occupied territories of the West Bank and the Gaza Strip and consumed much of Israel's military resources. The images of armed Israeli soldiers battling Palestinian children and teenagers, mostly throwing rocks, led to considerable international criticism of Israel. In 1991, following Iraq's 1990 invasion of Kuwait, Iraq targeted Israel with missiles in an ultimately unsuccessful attempt to provoke Israel to attack Iraq and cause the Arab states to withdraw from the multinational U.S.-led coalition force.

The collapse of the Soviet Union in December 1991 and the end of the Cold War brought an influx into Israel of hundreds of thousands of Jews from the Soviet Union. It also left many Arab states, previously allied with Moscow, isolated and gave the United States much more influence and leverage in the region. Accordingly, peace talks were held in 1991 and 1992 among Israel, Syria, Lebanon, Jordan, and the Palestinians. Those talks paved the way for the 1993 Oslo Accords between Israel and the PLO, stipulating the beginning of Palestinian self-rule in the West Bank and the Gaza Strip, and peace between Israel and Jordan in 1994.

Initial Israeli support for the Oslo Accords waned following a series of terrorist attacks by Hamas, a Palestinian terrorist group founded in 1987 at the beginning of the First Intifada that opposed the Oslo Accords. On November 4, 1995, a right-wing Jewish nationalist assassinated Rabin for his peace efforts with the Palestinians and willingness to cede occupied territory in the West Bank to the Palestinians. Continued Hamas terrorism led to the election as prime minister of hardliner Benjamin Netanyahu of Likud. Netanyahu refused to pursue the land-for-peace dialogue with the Palestinians. Thus, the peace process stalled. In 1999, Labor's Ehud Barak defeated Netanyahu, and in 2000 talks between Barak and Arafat, mediated by U.S. president Bill Clinton, failed to produce agreement on a Palestinian state. The collapse of these talks and the visit of Likud's Ariel Sharon to the contested religious site known to Jews as the Temple Mount and to Muslims as the Noble Sanctuary sparked the Second (al-Aqsa) Intifada. Relations between the Israelis and Palestinians tumbled downward.

Sharon was elected prime minister of Israel in March 2001 and reelected in 2003. In the face of stalled peace talks with the Palestinians, Israel had withdrawn from the Gaza Strip by September 2005, although it controlled its borders, coast, and airspace. Under Sharon, the Israeli government also began building a series of walls, or barriers, to separate Israel from most of the West Bank. These barriers are designed to defend Israel from repeated Palestinian terrorist attacks, but their construction has been criticized as a violation of international law and as an impediment to the establishment of any viable, independent Palestinian state. After Sharon suffered a massive stroke on January 4, 2006, Ehud Olmert became acting prime minister. He was formally elected to the post following the victory of his only recently formed Kadima Party in the legislative elections of April 14, 2006.

In June 2006, after a Hamas raid killed two Israeli soldiers and led to the capture of another, Israel launched a series of attacks on Hamas targets and infrastructure in the Gaza Strip. The next month, the Olmert government opted to become involved in a month-long conflict in Lebanon following an attack by Hezbollah on Israel that killed three Israeli soldiers and captured two others. Hezbollah is a large political party with a social and charitable wing but also has a militia that has received Iranian backing in the past and Syrian logistical support. This month-long conflict, which devastated southern and central Lebanon and parts of its eastern region and ruined its infrastructure, seemed to many observers a repeat of 1982, with Israel having failed to achieve its broad policy objectives and leaving Hezbollah stronger than ever.

After fierce fighting between moderate Fatah and more radical Hamas Palestinian groups in Gaza, in June 2007, Hamas won complete control of Gaza, leaving President Mahmoud Abbas of the Palestinian Authority (PA) heading a government whose writ ran only in the West Bank. In July, Abbas announced that the PA would have no contact with Hamas and called for the stationing of international peacekeepers in and around Gaza. In September 2007, the Israeli Knesset voted unanimously to declare the Gaza Strip, where 1.4 million Palestinians lived, an "enemy entity." Gaza became a base for rocket attacks on southern Israel, which provoked fierce Israeli retaliation. In January 2008, Israel cut down fuel supplies to Gaza, and in late February and early March mounted a major raid there, killing over 100 people. Violence diminished somewhat from June to December 2008, when a truce was in place between Hamas and Israel. Upon its expiration Hamas rocket attacks on Israel intensified. From December 27, 2008, to January 18, 2009, Israeli Defense Forces implemented Operation CAST LEAD AGAINST GAZA, killing over 1,300 Palestinians.

In September 2008, Olmert resigned as Israeli prime minister. Elections held in

February 2009 gave a majority to right-wing parties. Israeli voters remained keenly interested in such issues as the role of the Orthodox minority, the rights of Israeli Arabs, the fate of Israeli settlements in the West Bank, and the ups and downs of the economy. The Likud politician Benjamin Netanyahu became prime minister. Just a few weeks earlier Barack Obama had become president of the United States. In June 2009, Obama called for an Arab-Israeli rapprochement based on Arab recognition of Israel, Israel's acceptance of a Palestinian state, and a halt to any further Israeli settlements in East Jerusalem or the West Bank. Netanyahu publicly endorsed the first two demands, but his position on settlements remained ambivalent. In September 2010, direct Israeli-Palestinian talks began in Washington, with a regular timetable of fortnightly meetings.

Israel regarded Iran's desire to acquire nuclear weapons—a charge denied by Iran—as a palpable threat. Iranian president Mahmoud Ahmadinejad repeatedly attacked Israel's policies, denied the Holocaust, and called for the destruction of Israel, which greatly concerned the Israelis. In an effort to halt Iran's nuclear weapons programme, from 2006 onward the UN imposed economic sanctions on Iran, which gradually became more severe. Netanyahu, however, considered these ineffective and repeatedly advocated air strikes on Iran's nuclear facilities, ideally in conjunction with U.S. forces but if necessary as a unilateral Israeli operation. The election in August 2013 of the less controversial Hassan Rouhani as president of Iran did nothing to allay Netanyahu's fears, since Ayatollah Ali Khameini, Iran's supreme leader, remained deeply hostile to Israel.

In the second decade of the 21st century, the two nearest and direct threats to Israel remained violence from Hezbollah and other radical organizations and threats from Palestinians. The Arab Spring democracy movement did little to enhance Israel's security. The resignation of President Hosni Mubarak of Egypt in February 2011 enhanced the political position of the Muslim Brotherhood, which was predominantly hostile to Israel. In August 2011, Egyptian militants joined Palestinians in attacking southern Israel. In June 2012, Mohammed Morsi of the Muslim Brotherhood became president of Egypt, bringing further militant Egyptian assaults on Israel. Morsi's ouster by the Egyptian military in July 2013 helped to de-escalate such moves. In the Syrian civil war that began in 2011, however, Hezbollah, whose elements had for years, with backing from Syria, used Lebanon as a base to launch attacks on Israel, rallied to the support of President Bashar al-Assad of Syria, while Sunni Al Qaeda forces backed by Iran were prominent among the rebel forces. Both groups considered Israel a leading enemy.

With respect to peace with the Palestinians, the presence of several hundred thousand Israeli settlers in the West Bank, the continuance of violent attacks by Palestinians, and disputes over the precise borders of any future Palestinian state remained the principal outstanding issues of contention. In March 2012, militants in Gaza launched over 300 rocket attacks on Israel, provoking major Israeli air strikes. In the November 2012 Operation PILLAR OF DEFENSE, Israel attacked over 1,500 sites in Gaza, killing 133 Palestinians, while Hamas fired almost 1,500 rockets at targets in southern Israel, including the cities of Tel Aviv and Jerusalem. President Obama's 2012 reelection victory nonetheless brought new momentum to the peace process. In June 2013, U.S. secretary of state John Kerry encouraged the resumption of Israeli-Palestinian talks, with the objective of reaching a final status agreement on the West Bank within nine months. During that period, the Palestinians agreed not to mount appeals against Israeli policies to international agencies, in return for Israel's release of 104 Palestinian prisoners. Continuing Israeli construction of settlements nonetheless had the potential to derail these negotiations. In Gaza, by contrast, for the indefinite future no real compromise or genuine Palestinian-Israeli peace talks appeared likely even to begin.

Stefan Marc Brooks, Daniel E. Spector,
and Spencer C. Tucker

Further Reading

Aly, Abdel Monem Said, Shai Feldman, and Khalil Shikaki. *Arabs and Israelis: Conflict and Peacemaking in the Middle East*. Basingstoke: Palgrave Macmillan, 2013.

Ben-Eliezer, Uri. *Old Conflict, New War: Israel's Politics toward the Palestinians*. New York: Palgrave Macmillan, 2012.

Berry, Mike, and Greg Philo. *Israel and Palestine: Competing Histories*. London: Pluto Press, 2006.

Bregman, Ahron. *Israel's Wars: A History Since 1947*. 3rd ed. New York: Routledge, 2010.

Bunton, Martin. *The Palestinian-Israeli Conflict: A Very Short Introduction*. New York: Oxford University Press, 2013.

Byman, Daniel. *A High Price: The Triumphs and Failures of Israeli Counterterrorism*. New York: Oxford University Press, 2011.

Cohen, Avner. *The Worst-Kept Secret: Israel's Bargain with the Bomb*. New York: Columbia University Press, 2010.

Cook, Jonathan. *Disappearing Palestine: Israel's Experiments in Human Despair*. London: Zed Books, 2008.

Dershowitz, Alan M. *The Case for Israel*. New York: Wiley, 2004.

Dowty, Alan. *Israel/Palestine*. 3rd ed. Malden, MA: Polity, 2005.

Gilbert, Martin. *Israel: A History*. New York: Harper, 2008.

Hammack, Philip L. *Narrative and the Politics of Identity: The Cultural Psychology of Israeli and Palestinian Youth*. New York: Oxford University Press, 2010.

Kimmerling, Joel. *The Invention and Decline of Israeliness: State, Society, and the Military*. Berkeley: University of California Press, 2001.

Klein, Menachem. *The Shift: Israel/Palestine from Border Struggle to Ethnic Conflict*. Translated by Chaim Weitzman. New York: Columbia University Press, 2010.

Morris, Benny. *One State, Two States: Resolving the Israel/Palestine Conflict*. New Haven, CT: Yale University Press, 2009.

Pelletière, Stephen C. *Israel in the Second Iraq War: The Influence of Likud*. Santa Barbara, CA: Praeger, 2009.

Reich, Bernard. *A Brief History of Israel*. 2nd ed. New York: Checkmark Books, 2008.

Rubin, Barry M. *Israel: An Introduction*. New Haven, CT: Yale University Press, 2012.

Sachar, Howard M. *A History of Israel: From the Rise of Zionism to Our Time*. 3rd ed. New York: Knopf, 2007.

Shindler, Colin. *A History of Modern Israel*. Cambridge: Cambridge University Press, 2008.

Shlaim, Avi. *The Iron Wall: Israel and the Arab World*. New York: Norton, 2001.

Stein, Leslie. *The Making of Modern Israel: 1948–1967*. Malden, MA: Polity, 2009.

Swisher, Clayton E. *The Palestine Papers: The End of the Road?* London: Hesperus Press, 2011.

Zureik, Elia, David Lyon, and Yasmeen Abu-Laban, eds. *Surveillance and Control in Israel: Population, Territory, and Power*. New York: Routledge, 2011.

Israeli War of Independence, Overview

Conflict between the newly created State of Israel and its Arab neighbors that occurred between May 1948 and May 1949. When the Ottoman Empire was dismantled in the

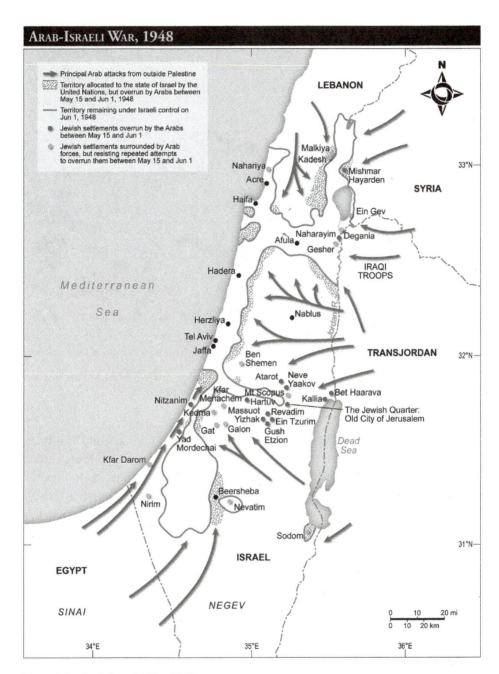

Map of the Arab-Israeli War, 1948.

wake of World War I, Great Britain received a mandate from the League of Nations over Palestine. Much of the British Mandate period (1920–1948) was spent maintaining peace among the Muslim, Jewish, and Christian populations in the region.

In the 1920s and 1930s, the region received a large influx of Jewish immigrants, many of whom were fleeing persecution in Europe. The rising number of Jewish residents spawned a violent backlash from Palestinian Arabs. This often took the form

Jewish Haganah troops are seen on patrol near the no-man's-land line in Katamon, a suburb of Jerusalem, Palestine on May 6, 1948. (AP Photo/Pringle)

of demonstrations against British policies, including a series of riots centered in Jerusalem. During the Arab Revolt of 1936–1939, Arab insurgents attacked Jewish settlements and businesses. They also boycotted British-owned businesses. Riots swept Palestine and were put down by British forces, which sometimes were augmented by Jewish auxiliary police.

Thousands of Palestinians were killed, wounded, or imprisoned during the revolt. After British forces successfully quelled the rebellion, the mandate administration adopted a decidedly pro-Jewish stance, turning a blind eye to Jewish militia forces such as Haganah, which were officially outlawed. These militia forces would prove vital when open fighting erupted between Arabs and Jews in 1948. At the same time, the British sought to enforce immigration quotas that worked against Jews finding refuge in

Palestine, even during World War II and the Holocaust. Increasingly, Jewish paramilitary forces such as the Irgun Tsvai Leumi (National Military Organization) battled the British occupiers, who arrested a number of them. The British seemed unable to please either side as the violence escalated.

World War II marked the end of colonialism in the Middle East and elsewhere. Lebanon became independent in 1943, although French troops did not leave that country until 1946, when they also departed from the French Mandate for Syria. British-controlled Transjordan and Iraq also gained independence in 1946, under King Abdullah and his half-brother King Faisal, respectively. The British remained in Palestine until November 29, 1947, when the United Nations (UN) approved a partition plan that would have created two states, one Jewish and the other Arab. Jewish and Arab leaders each criticized aspects of the partition. However, the Jewish populace of Palestine mostly supported the UN resolution as the key to an independent Jewish state. The Arabs roundly rejected the plan.

On November 30, 1947, seven Jewish inhabitants of Palestine died in three separate attacks by Arabs. Jewish militia forces retaliated, and British authorities proved unable to halt the escalating violence in the region. The British became increasingly unwilling to intervene in the growing conflict as the date of complete British withdrawal drew near. In December 1947 and January 1948, almost 1,000 Palestinian residents died in the fighting, which continued to escalate in early 1948.

Although Arabs outnumbered Jews in Palestine, Jewish forces proved better armed and organized. Arab military efforts focused on cutting communications between Jewish settlements and isolating the city of Jerusalem. Jewish counterattacks sought to control roads linking Jewish towns but could rarely open routes to Jerusalem.

With the British Mandate due to expire on May 15, 1948, and no agreement on partition, Jewish leaders declared the independence of the State of Israel on May 14, 1948. Israel promptly received diplomatic recognition from the United States and the Soviet Union but was also immediately invaded by troops from surrounding Arab nations. The Arab forces included regular units from Egypt, Iraq, Lebanon, Syria, and Transjordan, augmented by Libyan, Saudi Arabian, and Yemeni volunteers. Officially, the troops cooperated under the auspices of the Arab League, which had been formed in 1945. Nominally, King Abdullah of Transjordan was the commander in chief of the Arab armies, although cooperation among the Arab forces remained almost nonexistent throughout the war.

On May 15, 1948, the Arab League announced its intention to create the United State of Palestine, encompassing the Jewish and Arab regions created by the UN partition plan. Although the Arab invasion was denounced by the United States, the Soviet Union, and UN secretary general Trygve Lie, it found support from the Republic of China (Taiwan) and other UN member states.

On May 26, 1948, the Israeli government created the Israel Defense Forces (IDF), primarily by incorporating the irregular Jewish militias that had existed under the British Mandate, including Haganah, the Palmach, and Irgun. Although the IDF numbered fewer than 30,000 troops at its formation, by mid-July 1948 it had more than doubled in size. It continued to grow exponentially, and by the end of 1948 Israel could place more than 100,000 troops in the field. The vast majority of those troops, however, were recently arrived immigrants from the concentration camps and displaced persons camps of Europe who had little or no military training. In comparison, the combined Arab armies, which began the conflict with approximately 23,500 troops, increased to only 40,000 by July 1948 and 55,000 that October.

Despite the rapid growth in the IDF's manpower, the Arab armies had a significant superiority in heavy weapons at the beginning of the conflict. Worldwide observers opined that the Jewish state would be quickly overrun because of its almost complete lack of armored vehicles, artillery, and warplanes. The new Israeli government quickly moved to purchase weapons, however, beginning with a shipment of 25 Czechoslovakian aircraft that arrived in late May 1948. Czechoslovakia continued to provide weapons to the IDF for the remainder of the war, even during UN-mandated cease-fires that prohibited the sale of arms to any belligerent.

In the first phase of the fighting, Arab armies from Transjordan and Iraq advanced on Jerusalem with the aim of driving all Jewish inhabitants from the city. Abdullah ordered an assault on Jerusalem to begin on May 17, 1948. Two weeks of brutal house-to-house fighting followed, partially negating the Arab Legion's advantage in mobility and heavier weapons. Transjordanian troops succeeded in driving back IDF forces, but Iraqi attacks were ineffective, and soon the Iraqi force shifted to a defensive posture in the regions of Jenin and Nablus. A Syrian attack along the northern front of the war, supported by tanks and artillery, was defeated by Jewish settlers at Degania, the oldest kibbutz in Palestine. The settlers there had only light weapons, but they skillfully used terrain features and night attacks to halt the Syrian advance.

Only in the south did Arab forces make significant territorial gains. Egyptian forces captured several kibbutzim but took heavy losses in the process and bogged down near Ashdod. The first phase of the war ended when a UN-declared truce came into effect on June 11, 1948. Although the truce included an arms embargo for all belligerents, the Israelis successfully smuggled in munitions from Czechoslovakia while the four-week truce remained in effect. UN mediator Folke Bernadotte also proposed a new partition plan that was immediately rejected by both sides. When Egyptian forces resumed their attacks on July 8, the truce collapsed.

In the second phase of the war, the IDF assumed the offensive. Its primary objective was to restore Israeli command of the Tel Aviv–Jerusalem corridor. This it secured by a massive assault against Lod, which included the first Israeli use of bomber aircraft. The city, defended by Transjordanian troops augmented by Palestinian irregulars

and the Arab Liberation Army (ALA), surrendered on July 11. The next day, the IDF captured Ramla, also in the vital corridor. The IDF, however, failed to take Latrun.

With the Jerusalem sector fairly stable, the IDF launched Operation DEKEL, a major push against Syrian and Lebanese troops in lower Galilee. The IDF captured Nazareth on July 16. Only against Egyptian forces in the south did the IDF fail to make any significant progress in the July fighting.

Another UN-brokered truce went into effect on July 18. Bernadotte presented yet another partition plan, this time calling for Transjordan to annex the Arab regions, the creation of an independent Jewish state, and the establishment of Jerusalem as an international city. All belligerents again rejected the plan, and the day after Bernadotte presented his latest solution to the conflict, he was assassinated by members of the Zionist militia Lehi. The truce remained in effect, however, until October 15, when Israel ended the cease-fire with a series of offensives designed to drive out the Arab armies completely.

In the third phase of the war, the Israelis began their offensives with an assault against Egyptian forces in the Negev Desert. Operation YOAV, commanded by Yigal Allon, sought to isolate Egyptian troops along the coast from those in the Negev. It was a tremendous success, forcing the Egyptian army to abandon its forward positions and evacuate the northern Negev. On October 24, Operation HIRAM commenced in the upper Galilee region, virtually destroying the remnants of the ALA and pushing several miles into Lebanon, driving Lebanese forces completely out of Israel. A renewed assault against the Egyptians started on December 22, when IDF troops encircled Egyptian units in the Gaza Strip and attacked their positions in the Sinai

Peninsula. The Egyptians withdrew from and accepted a cease-fire effective January 7, 1949.

Once the truce went into effect, IDF troops withdrew from the Sinai and Gaza. In December 1948, the UN passed Resolution 194, which declared that refugees from the Arab-Israeli conflict should have the opportunity to return to their homes and live in peace. Those who chose not to return were to be offered compensation for their property by the government in control of that territory at the end of the conflict. The resolution never achieved its goals, and the huge population of Palestinian refugees became a lasting legal and diplomatic problem for the region.

International military observer forces occasionally were drawn into the conflict. One such clash between the British Royal Air Force and the Israeli Air Force occurred on January 7, 1949, when Royal Air Force observation aircraft overflew an Israeli convoy immediately after an attack by Egyptian aircraft. IDF troops opened fire upon the British aircraft, downing one. Three more British aircraft were shot down by Israeli interceptors. When more British planes entered the area they were attacked by Israeli warplanes, which destroyed an additional British plane and damaged another.

In 1949, Israel concluded separate armistices with each of the Arab belligerents with the exception of Iraq. On February 24, Egypt and Israel signed a cease-fire, which left Egyptian troops in occupation of the Gaza Strip. On March 23, Lebanon and Israel concluded an armistice, and the IDF withdrew from Lebanese territory. The Transjordan-Israel armistice, signed on April 3, left Transjordanian troops in control of the West Bank. On July 20, Syria agreed to a cease-fire and the creation of a demilitarized zone along the Israeli-Syrian border.

The new State of Israel now covered three-fourths of the former British Mandate for Palestine and was 50 percent larger than the land area offered in Bernadotte's original partition proposal. Israel's independence cost 6,000 Israeli lives, one-third of which were civilian casualties. Arab losses were higher. Most estimates place the number of Arabs killed at approximately 10,000. In the aftermath of the war, Jewish residents of Arab nations were expelled. Hundreds of thousands traveled to Israel or immigrated to Europe. Likewise, thousands of Palestinians left the new Israeli nation. The surprising Israeli victory humiliated the Arabs, who had expected quick and easy success. This humiliation fueled hatred for Jews in Arab nations, and this enmity, coupled with rising Arab nationalism, virtually ensured that future conflict would erupt within the region before a lasting peace could be achieved.

Paul Joseph Springer

Further Reading

Ben-Ze'ev, Efrat. *Remembering Palestine in 1948: Beyond National Narratives.* Cambridge: Cambridge University Press, 2011.

Bregman, Ahron. *Israel's Wars: A History Since 1947.* 3rd ed. New York: Routledge, 2010.

Draper, Thomas. *Israel and the Middle East.* New York: H. W. Wilson, 1983.

Gelvin, James M. *The Israel-Palestine Conflict: One Hundred Years of War.* 3rd ed. Cambridge: Cambridge University Press, 2014.

Herzog, Chaim. *The Arab-Israeli Wars: War and Peace in the Middle East from the War of Independence to Lebanon.* Westminster, MD: Random House, 1984.

La Guardia, Anton. *War without End: Israelis, Palestinians, and the Struggle for a Promised Land.* Revised and updated ed. New York: St. Martin's Press, 2003.

Lustick, Ian. *From War to War: Israel vs. the Arabs, 1948–1967.* New York: Garland, 1994.

Milstein, Uri. *History of Israel's War of Independence.* Translated by Alan Sacks. 4 vols.

Lanham, MD: University Press of America, 1996–1999.

Morris, Benny. *1948: A History of the First Arab-Israeli War*. New Haven, CT: Yale University Press, 2008.

Morris, Benny. *1948 and After: Israel and the Palestinians*. New York: Oxford University Press, 1991.

Morris, Benny. *The Birth of the Palestinian Refugee Problem Revisited*. Cambridge: Cambridge University Press, 2004.

Pappé, Ilan. *The Ethnic Cleansing of Palestine*. Oxford: Oneworld Publications, 2006.

Pollack, Kenneth M. *Arabs at War: Military Effectiveness, 1948–1991*. Lincoln: University of Nebraska Press, 2002.

Rogan, Eugene L., and Avi Shlaim, eds. *The War for Palestine: Rewriting the History of 1948*. 2nd ed. Cambridge: Cambridge University Press, 2007.

Rubin, Barry, and Thomas A. Keaney, eds. *Armed Forces in the Middle East: Politics and Strategy*. Portland, OR: Frank Cass, 2002.

Sachar, Howard Morley. *Egypt and Israel*. New York: R. Marek, 1981.

Sa'di, Ahmad H., and Lila Abu-Lughod, eds. *Nakba: Palestine, 1948, and the Claims of Memory*. New York: Columbia University Press, 2007.

Tal, David. *War in Palestine, 1948: Israeli and Arab Strategy and Diplomacy*. New York: Routledge, 2003.

J

Jordan

Middle Eastern nation covering 35,637 square miles, about the size of the U.S. state of Indiana. Jordan, officially known as the Hashemite Kingdom of Jordan, borders Israel and the West Bank to the west, Syria and the Golan Heights to the north, Iraq to the east, and Saudi Arabia to the east and south. From 1516 to 1919, Jordan was part of the Ottoman Empire. With the end of World War I and the collapse of the Ottoman Empire, Transjordan (as it was then known) became part of Britain's League of Nations mandate over Palestine in 1920. In 1921, Abdullah ibn Hussein, a member of the Hashemite dynasty, became the de facto king of Transjordan. Transjordan became a constitutional monarchy under Abdullah I, who was formally placed on the throne by the British in 1928. Nevertheless, Transjordan was still considered part of the British Mandate. That changed in May 1946 when Transjordan secured its independence.

Because Transjordan was a member of the Arab League when the State of Israel was created in May 1948, Abdullah was obliged to fight alongside his Arab neighbors against the Israelis. As with most Arabs, he flatly rejected Zionist ambitions. He gained control of the West Bank in 1949 as a result of the Israeli War of Independence (1948–1949) and officially changed his country's name to Jordan to reflect the new territories west of the Jordan River. Months later, he moved to permanently annex the West Bank, which deeply troubled Arab leaders. Many believed that the territory should have been reserved for the displaced Palestinians.

A large number of these displaced Palestinians, about 70,000 by 1949, fled to Jordan, and 280,000 Palestinians were already residing in or fled to the West Bank. The Palestinian population outnumbered the Jordanian population, and although these received citizenship, their identity and aspirations were a point of tension within Jordan. In 1951, a Palestinian assassinated Abdullah in Jerusalem, and the following year he was succeeded by his grandson, King Hussein I. Hussein ruled Jordan for the next 47 years.

A series of anti-Western uprisings in Jordan, combined with the 1956 Suez Crisis, compelled Hussein to sever military ties to Britain. The British government had taken part in the covert British–French–Israeli scheme to topple Egyptian president Gamal Abdel Nasser and wrest back control of the Suez Canal from the Egyptians.

In February 1958, Hussein formed the Arab Federation with Iraq. The king viewed this as a needed countermeasure to the newly formed United Arab Republic (UAR), formed between Egypt and Syria and dominated by Egypt's Pan-Arab nationalist President Nasser. The Arab Federation fell apart by autumn 1958, however, after the Iraqi king was overthrown in a coup. Later that same year, leaders of the UAR called for the overthrow of governments in Beirut and Amman. Hussein fought back by requesting help from the British, who dispatched troops to Jordan to quell antigovernment protests.

Hussein ibn Talal became king of Jordan as Hussein I in May 1953. (AFP/Getty Images)

The Americans had simultaneously sent troops to Lebanon to bolster its besieged Christian-led government.

Jordan's relations with the UAR remained tense. Indeed, in 1963, when a rival Jordanian government-in-exile was set up in Damascus, Syria, King Hussein declared a state of emergency. The crisis subsided when the United States and Britain publicly endorsed Hussein's rule. For good measure, the United States placed its Sixth Fleet on alert in the Mediterranean.

After the mid-1960s and more than a decade of crises and regional conflicts, Hussein turned his attention to domestic issues. He was devoted to improving the welfare of his people and launched major programs to improve literacy rates (which were very low), increase educational opportunities, bolster public health initiatives, and lower infant mortality rates. In these endeavors he was quite successful. By the late 1980s literacy rates approached 100 percent, and infant deaths were down dramatically. Jordan's economy also began to expand as the nation engaged in more trade with the outside world and as its relations with Egypt improved. Hussein also began to erect a modern and reliable transportation system and moved to modernize the country's infrastructure. Notable in all of this was that he accomplished much without resorting to overly repressive tactics. Indeed, throughout the Cold War most Jordanians enjoyed a level of freedom virtually unrivaled in the Middle East. However, the government undertook sharp responses to anti-regime elements and tensions with the Palestinian population.

By the late 1960s another Arab-Israeli conflict was in the making. After Egypt blockaded Israeli shipping in the Gulf of Aqaba in 1967, King Hussein signed a mutual defense pact with Egypt, setting aside his former differences with Nasser's government. Normally a moderating force in volatile Middle East politics, Hussein reluctantly entered the war on the side of Egypt, even as Tel Aviv was imploring him through diplomatic channels not to do so. When the June 1967 Six-Day War ended, Israel took from Jordan the entire West Bank and all of Jerusalem.

As a result of the war, thousands of Palestinians fled to Jordan from the West Bank, now controlled by Israel. Indeed, it is estimated that as many as 300,000 Palestinians poured into Jordan after June 1967, swelling the Palestinian refugee population there to almost 1 million. This massive influx severely taxed Jordanian infrastructure as well as schools, health care, and other services and engendered considerable resentment among some Jordanians. The number of Palestinians in Jordan by 1968 meant that Palestinian groups—especially resistance groups such as the fedayeen—increased their power and clout considerably within Jordan. These groups were well armed (receiving significant assistance from Syria and Egypt) and posed a serious threat to Hussein's rule. By 1970, it appeared as if the Palestinian resistance fighters were in the process of creating a Palestinian state within a state, much as they would do in Lebanon. This situation greatly alarmed King Hussein.

In early 1970, Palestinian guerrilla groups and the Palestine Liberation Organization (PLO) were already skirmishing with Jordanian troops. Open warfare erupted in June. Heretofore, the Jordanian army had been unsuccessful in its attempts to stop Palestinian attacks on Israel from taking place on Jordanian soil. Hussein also opposed the Palestinian aims of creating a Palestinian state in the West Bank, which he hoped to regain in the future.

In September 1970, after 10 days of bloody conflict, thousands of Palestinians, including the leadership of the PLO, fled Jordan for Syria and Lebanon. Hussein and his government were deeply troubled by this conflict, as were many of the Jordanians of Palestinian origin. From the Palestinian perspective the fighting and forced expulsion in September were seen as a great betrayal. Indeed, the Palestinians referred to the events of September 1970 as Black September.

The early 1970s saw continued unrest. In 1972, King Hussein tried to create a new Arab federation, which would have included the West Bank as Jordanian territory. Israel as well as most of the Arab states flatly rejected the idea. Then, in December 1972, Hussein was nearly assassinated by a Palestinian.

During the Yom Kippur War (1973) Hussein played only a minor role, ordering a limited troop deployment (one brigade) to fight in Syria. In 1974, he finally agreed to recognize the Arab League's position that the PLO was the sole representative of the Palestinian people.

Hussein strengthened relations with neighboring Syria beginning in the late 1970s, and he vigorously opposed the 1979 Israeli-Egyptian peace treaty. Jordan backed Iraq in the Iran-Iraq War (1980–1988). The 1980s was a period of economic chaos for the Jordanian people. Job creation did not keep pace with the expanding population, resulting in high unemployment. Inflation became a problem, foreign investment fell off, and exports declined. In 1989, riots occurred in southern Jordan over the lack of jobs and a government-mandated increase in basic commodities including electricity and water. These severe economic dislocations led Hussein to seek U.S. financial aid in the late 1980s. As a result, the nation's foreign debt burden grew substantially.

When King Hussein refused to condemn Iraqi dictator Saddam Hussein in the 1991 Persian Gulf War, U.S. assistance and much general Western aid was curtailed. Saudi Arabia and later Kuwait also withheld financial assistance. Jordan's economy went from bad to worse. When some 700,000 Jordanians returned to Jordan because they were now unwelcome in Kuwait and Saudi Arabia, the economic situation became truly dire. Jordan's tourism declined precipitously after 1991, oil came at a very high premium, and exports suffered enormously. By 1995, unemployment stood at 14 percent (as stated by the government), although other measures estimated that it may have been twice that. Not until 2001 did the economy begin to regain its footing. Hussein's decision to back Iraq put Jordanian-U.S. relations in a holding pattern, and his relations with other major Western powers were little better.

By 1993–1994, however, Jordanian-U.S. relations were on an upswing. The Jordanians decided to become an active partner in the Arab-Israeli peace process, and King Hussein actively supported United Nations (UN) sanctions on the Iraqi regime. On July 25, 1994, Hussein signed a historic nonbelligerent agreement with the Israelis (the Washington Declaration), which was soon followed up by the October 26, 1994, signing of the Israel-Jordan Peace Treaty. In November 1998, shortly before his death, Hussein also interceded between Israeli prime minister Benjamin Netanyahu and Palestinian leader Yasser Arafat, to persuade both to sign the Wye River Agreement on the steps toward a Palestinian-Israeli settlement.

King Hussein died in February 1999 and was succeeded by his son, King Abdullah II. Following the outbreak of the Second (al-Aqsa) Intifada in 2000, Abdullah tried to continue Jordan's role as the force of moderation in the Middle East. He attempted to keep avenues of dialogue open between the Israelis and the Palestinians and repeatedly counseled both sides that discussions and agreements were far preferable to conflict and war, advice he publicized in a 2011 book. Nevertheless, in a show of Arab solidarity, Jordan recalled its ambassador from Israel. This lasted until 2005. Although Abdullah publicly criticized the Iraq War that began in March 2003, he quietly provided assistance to the United States and Britain and partnered with the West in an attempt to bring a semblance of control to war-torn Iraq. Jordan also criticized the United States and Israel during the 2006 fighting in Lebanon. Seeking to encourage the peace process, in September 2012, Abdullah spoke out publicly at the UN, urging Israel to accept the 2002 Arab League Peace Initiative that called for total Israeli withdrawal from the West Bank and East Jerusalem and a "just settlement" for Palestinian refugees.

In the early 21st century, Jordan enjoyed a limited degree of parliamentary democracy, with most seats held by pro-government representatives. King Abdullah sought to implement economic reforms, some of them unpopular. As demonstrations spread across the Middle East during the Arab Spring, street protests began in Jordan in January 2011. The major opposition group, the Islamic Action Front, which was affiliated to the Muslim Brotherhood, demanded greater democracy and wider political representation in parliament. General elections were held in January 2013, and municipal elections in August 2013. The Islamic Action Front boycotted these, on the grounds that the electoral system favored tribal groups and reserved too few seats for political parties. Mass demonstrations in late 2012 also protested against rises in fuel prices, which were subsequently reversed. Like his father before him, both domestically and in foreign affairs Abdullah sought to maintain a balance between opposing forces.

Paul G. Pierpaoli Jr.

Further Reading

Abdullah II, King of Jordan. *Our Last Best Chance: The Pursuit of Peace in a Time of Peril*. New York: Viking, 2011.

Al-faqih, Abdullah. *Liberalization and Democratization in Egypt, Jordan, and Yemen: Beginnings, Development, and Decline*. Saarbrücken, Germany: VDM Verlag Dr. Müller, 2013.

Alon, Yoav. *The Making of Jordan: Tribes, Colonialism, and the Modern State*. New York: I. B. Tauris, 2007.

Brand, Laurie. *Jordan's Inter-Arab Relations: The Political Economy of Alliance Making*. New York: Columbia University Press, 1995.

Habib, Randa. *Hussein and Abdullah: Inside the Jordanian Royal Family*. London: Saqi Books, 2010.

Lunt, James D. *Hussein of Jordan: Searching for a Just and Lasting Peace*. New York: William Morrow, 1989.

Marshood, Nabil. *Voices from the Camps: A People's History of Palestinian Refugees in Jordan, 2006.* Lanham, MD: University Press of America, 2010.

Robins, Philip. *A History of Jordan.* Cambridge: Cambridge University Press, 2004.

Ryan, Curtis R. *Jordan in Transition: From Hussein to Abdullah.* Boulder, CO: Lynne Riener, 2002.

Salibi, Kamal S. *The Modern History of Jordan.* Rev. ed. New York: William Morrow, 1998, reprinted by I.B. Tauris, 2006.

Satloff, Robert B. *From Abdullah to Hussein: Jordan in Transition.* New York: Oxford University Press, 1993.

Shlaim, Avi. *Collusion across the Jordan: King Abdullah, the Zionist Movement, and the Partition of Palestine.* New York: Columbia University Press, 1988.

Shlaim, Avi. *Lion of Jordan: The Life of King Hussein in War and Peace.* New York: Knopf, 2008.

Wilson, Mary C. *King Abdullah, Britain and the Making of Jordan.* Cambridge: Cambridge University Press, 1988.

K

Kuwait

Monarchy in the Middle East. Kuwait, with a 1945 population of some 100,000 people, occupies 6,880 square miles, including the Kuwaiti share of the Neutral Zone defined by agreement with Saudi Arabia in 1922 and partitioned by mutual agreement in 1966. Kuwait is thus about the size of the U.S. state of Hawaii. The current population is about 2.35 million people, of whom more than half are noncitizen workers attracted by job opportunities in this oil-rich Persian Gulf nation.

Kuwait is strategically located at the northern end of the Persian Gulf. It is bordered by Saudi Arabia to the south, Iraq to the west and north, and the Persian Gulf to the east. The topography is flat, low desert, and the climate is very hot and dry. More than 95 percent of the Kuwaiti people live in urban areas, mostly along the coast. The nation's major natural resources are oil and natural gas, comprising an estimated 10 percent of the world's known reserves. There is a minor fishing industry, but oil sales make up half of Kuwait's gross domestic product (GDP) and provide 80 percent of the government's yearly revenues. The large oil reserves have sustained a relatively high per capita GDP annually and allow for extensive social services for Kuwaiti citizens.

Oil and geographic location have made Kuwait a crucial strategic state far beyond what might be expected of a country its size and population. Kuwait has been a key to British imperial interests in the Middle East, a major player in regional affairs, a staunch Cold War ally of the United States, the focus of the 1990 Persian Gulf War, and an important staging area for subsequent U.S.-led operations in Iraq.

In contrast to its current prominence, Kuwait was a remote part of the Ottoman Empire in the 18th century, largely left to manage its own affairs. This earlier insignificance is manifest in the fact that the Utub tribes that settled in the area early in the 18th century called their central town Kuwait, the Arabic diminutive for *kut*, meaning a fortress built near water. By mid-century the Utub's al-Sabah tribe, whose descendants rule Kuwait to this day, had emerged as the most prominent in the area. The al-Sabah focused on developing the local pearl beds and taking advantage of location to promote regional trade.

Recognizing the fact that any increase in the wealth of Kuwait and the al-Sabah family would attract Ottoman attention and invite closer imperial control and higher taxation, Sheikh Mubarak al-Sabah sought the protection of Britain, the major European power in the region. The result was an 1899 agreement in which Kuwait ceded control over its foreign affairs and defense to the British. In return, Kuwait agreed to eschew alliances with other powers and promised not to cede any concessions—economic or military—to any other nation. Kuwait thus became a British protectorate. This situation remained fairly stable until Britain reduced its imperial commitments after World War II. Kuwait became fully independent in June 1961.

Kuwait then aligned itself with the West—the United States in particular—in regional and international affairs. The 1979 Iranian Revolution served to further strengthen this alliance, and Kuwait became a staunch

Oil wells burning out of control darken the sky with smoke in Kuwait on March 2, 1991. The fires were set by retreating Iraqi forces during Operation Desert Storm. (U.S. Department of Defense)

supporter of Iraq during the Iran-Iraq War, which began in 1980. That support included nearly $35 billion in grants, loans, and other assistance to Iraq. After the war, which ended in 1988, Iraqi leader Saddam Hussein demanded that Kuwait forgive its loans, reasoning that Iraq had been the bulwark in the Arab world against Iran and was thus owed monetary concessions. Iraq also accused the Kuwaitis of slant-drilling for oil into Iraqi fields and then claimed that Kuwait was a lost Iraqi province, the administrative boundaries of which dated back to the defunct Ottoman Empire.

Angry with Kuwait's refusal to forgive the Iraqi debt and convinced that the kingdom was keeping oil prices artificially low by pumping too much oil, Hussein launched an invasion of Kuwait on August 2, 1990. The international response, which was divided into two stages, was strong and swift. The U.S.-led Operation DESERT SHIELD saw a large-scale military

buildup in Saudi Arabia. Then in January 1991, when Hussein steadfastly refused to withdraw from Kuwait, Operation DESERT STORM began, during which the United States led an international military coalition, including other Arab nations, to drive Iraqi forces from Kuwait. During the conflict, Hussein sought to entangle Israel in the war and unhinge the support of Arab states such as Syria and Egypt for the coalition by firing Scud surface-to-surface missiles against Israel. While this step gained him support from the Palestine Liberation Organization (PLO) as well as many Palestinians, heavy U.S. pressure on Israel prevented him from realizing his plan of drawing the Jewish state into the war. The brief war ended on February 27, 1991, with Iraq compelled to recognize Kuwaiti independence.

Thereafter, Kuwait remained a firm ally of the United States and allowed its territory to be used as a staging area for the

U.S.-led effort to oust Hussein from power in the spring of 2003. In return the United States has been restrained in any criticism of Kuwaiti internal affairs. In May 2005, however, Kuwait's parliament did grant full political rights to women. The United States maintains a significant military and naval presence in the region that protects the al-Sabah ruling family of Kuwait, which has had long experience in maintaining its position from the 19th century to the present.

Kuwait has not been a major player in the Arab-Israeli conflict. As Kuwait did not obtain independence from Britain until 1961, it did not participate in the 1948 and 1956 wars in and around Israel. After independence, Kuwait aligned itself with the Arab side in the Arab-Israeli conflict, sending small numbers of troops to fight in the 1967 and 1973 wars. These were token forces, and Kuwait focused on internal development of its oil resources. The large contingent of Palestinians in the Kuwaiti workforce were taxed by Kuwait, and these funds were then used to support Palestinian causes. Yet there was a suspicion of Palestinians as a possible source of political dissidence, as had occurred in Jordan and Lebanon in the 1970s and 1980s. PLO support for Iraq in the 1990 conflict with Iraq enraged Kuwaitis, who evicted the Palestinians after the conflict.

Kuwait has an active Islamist opposition and is wary of Shia-dominated Iran. Its relations with Yemen, which supported the 1990 invasion, also remain fragile. Kuwait's ruling house is close to that of Saudi Arabia, which offered refuge and substantial support during the 1990–1991 Gulf War. Despite its ties to the United States, Kuwait has consistently refused to recognize Israel. From 2003 to 2011, its territory served as a primary forwarding point for U.S. troops deployed to Iraq.

From June to November 2011, major political protests took place in Kuwait, with demonstrators demanding greater democracy. In late November 2011, the prime minister and the entire cabinet resigned, and in December 2011 the emir dissolved parliament and called new elections for February 2012. The elections returned the opposition to power, but in June 2012 the constitutional court declared these elections unconstitutional, since the previous parliament had not served out its term. In October 2012, the emir issued a decree dissolving the reinstated parliament, while making unspecified changes to the voting system, and calling new elections for December 2012. Politicians who opposed this were detained, but popular protests continued, despite government attempts to ban meetings of more than 20 people. After the electoral law was changed, opposition forces largely boycotted these elections.

Daniel E. Spector

Further Reading

Al-Hijji, Yacoub Yusuf. *Kuwait and the Sea: A Brief Social and Economic History*. London: Arabian Publishing, 2010.

Almdaires, Falah Abdullah. *Islamic Extremism in Kuwait: From the Muslim Brotherhood to Al-Qaeda and Other Islamic Political Groups*. New York: Routledge, 2010.

Assiri, Abdul-Reda. *Kuwait's Foreign Policy: City-State in World Politics*. Boulder, CO: Westview, 1990.

Cordesman, Anthony J. *Kuwait: Recovery and Security after the Gulf War*. Boulder, CO: Westview, 1997.

Daniels, John. *Kuwait Journey*. Luton, UK: White Crescent, 1971.

Finnie, David H. *Shifting Lines in the Sand: Kuwait's Elusive Frontier with Iraq*. Cambridge, MA: Harvard University Press, 1992.

Long, Jerry M. *Saddam's War of Words: Politics, Religion, and the Iraqi Invasion of Kuwait*. Austin: University of Texas Press, 2004.

Slot, Ben J., ed. *Kuwait: The Growth of a Historic Identity*. London: Arabian Publishing, 2003.

United States Army. *Area Handbook Series: Persian Gulf States*. Washington, DC: U.S. Government Printing Office, 1984.

L

Lebanon

Middle Eastern nation located on the eastern end of the Mediterranean Sea. Lebanon borders on Israel to the south and Syria to the east and north and covers 4,015 square miles (roughly twice the size of the U.S. state of Delaware). Lebanon's estimated 1948 population was approximately 1.5 million, but that was not based on an official government census. The only government census was conducted in 1932 when France held Lebanon as a League of Nations mandate and counted 861,399 people, which became the basis for the religious composition of the government. This gave a 6-to-5 advantage to Lebanese Christians. The unwritten *mithaq al-watani* (national pact) formalized this arrangement as well as the allocation of leadership positions to specific confessional or religious sects, with, for example, the presidency allocated to the Maronites, once considered the largest sect; the office of the prime minister allocated to the Sunni Muslims; and the speaker of parliament allocated to the Shia. This continued after independence, with subsequent population figures being estimates based on demographic trends. A U.S. Central Intelligence Agency (CIA) population estimate in 2003 put the population at 3.72 million, split 70 to 30 percent between Muslims and Christians.

The Lebanese population is further split among the Sunni, Shia, and Druze sects of Islam and the Maronite, Greek Orthodox, Greek Catholic, Armenian Orthodox, and Syriac denominations of Christianity. The Shia community contained more poor

workers and peasants, based on its concentration in the rural east and south. A belt of rural poverty also existed in the Sunni north. Certain Christian areas were also impoverished.

Lebanon's population suffered greatly during World War I, leading to high emigration in a pattern repeated during the lengthy civil war of 1975–1991. Remittances from Lebanese abroad were essential to the economy as were Beirut's services and banking. On the other hand, many areas of the country were dependent on agriculture and were farmed by peasants with small plots or who were landless and worked for large landholders. A neo-feudal system remained even after independence whereby the larger landholders, traditional chieftains, counted on the political support of their dependents. Urban counterparts operated like political bosses.

Lebanon declared its independence from France in November 1941 and became a charter member of the United Nations (UN) in 1945, the same year it joined the Arab League. Although independence and international status were welcomed by the Lebanese, sectarian tensions have continually threatened internal peace. The country essentially developed different cultures tied to some degree to educational systems: the private and greatly superior French-language system as opposed to the national system, which in later years increasingly utilized Arabic.

The 1932 census awarded the Maronite Christians a privileged place in Lebanese government. Only a Maronite may become the

Smoke rises from a Beirut television tower during the July 2006 Israel-Hezbollah conflict. (U.S. Department of Defense)

volunteers in the Arab Liberation Army fought alongside those from Syria in the north in the Israeli War of Independence (1948–1949) but were not successful. A series of battles ended with Israel in control of the Jordan River, the lakes of Galilee and Hulah, and a panhandle of territory jutting north and bordering on both Lebanon and Syria. Lebanon was not a major player in the 1956 Sinai Campaign or the 1967 Six-Day War between Israel and its Arab opponents because the Lebanese army was very small.

This did not mean that Lebanon remained at peace, however, for sectarian troubles and the evolving Cold War between the United States and the Soviet Union brought their own set of challenges. Both sides sought to support local regimes that they believed would support them in the worldwide conflict. The Suez War boosted President Gamal Abdel Nasser's popularity, and his oratory that "the Arab nation is one nation" was greeted with considerable enthusiasm by Lebanese Muslims, especially the young. In 1958, the pro-Western monarchy in Iraq fell and was replaced by a government that tilted toward the Soviet bloc. Egypt had already rejected Western support in favor of Soviet aid and was pursuing union with Syria, which still had claims to Lebanon as part of the so-called Greater Syria. Lebanon's Christian Maronite-controlled government responded to these perceived threats by requesting U.S. aid. President Dwight D. Eisenhower responded by sending U.S. marines to Beirut in the hopes of stabilizing the region. Almost simultaneously, the British sent troops to Jordan to prop up the monarchy there following an alleged coup attempt. The interventions actually heightened tensions and divisions in both nations. Lebanon is known as the Switzerland of the Middle East; however, the extreme poverty of Lebanon's countryside was a contrast to

president, only a Sunni may become the prime minister, and only a Shia may become the speaker of parliament. As demographic developments led to a Muslim majority by the 1960s, Maronite predominance came under increasing pressure from various Muslim groups. The fact that the Muslims were not a monolithic force further complicated matters. The Shia outnumbered the Sunnis, but many of the urban Sunni merchant families were far better off than the poverty-stricken Shia peasants or tobacco farmers. On top of this, the Arab cold war (or battle between conservative and military progressive states), the overall Cold War, and the ongoing Arab-Israeli conflict presented Lebanon with very serious challenges.

As a member of the Arab League, Lebanon sent troops to fight Israeli forces when the latter declared its independence in May 1948. Lebanese forces and Lebanese

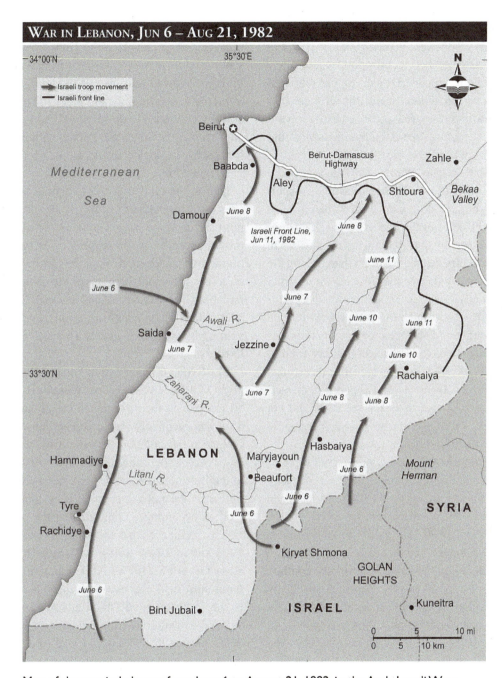

War in Lebanon, Jun 6 – Aug 21, 1982

- → Israeli troop movement
- — Israeli front line

34°00'N — 35°30'E — N

Mediterranean
Sea

Beirut
Baabda
Aley
Beirut-Damascus Highway
Zahle
Shtoura
Bekaa Valley
Damour
June 8
Israeli Front Line, Jun 11, 1982
June 8
June 11
June 6
June 7
June 10
June 11
Awali R.
Saida
June 7
Jezzine
June 10
Rachaiya
June 10
33°30'N
Zaharani R.
June 7
June 8
June 8
Hasbaiya
LEBANON
Maryjayoun
Mount Herman
Hammadiye
Litani R.
Beaufort
June 6
SYRIA
June 6
Tyre
June 6
Rachidye
June 6
Kiryat Shmona
GOLAN HEIGHTS
June 6
Bint Jubail
ISRAEL
Kuneitra

0   5   10 mi
0   5   10 km

Map of the war in Lebanon from June 6 to August 21, 1982, in the Arab-Israeli Wars.

its attraction for wealthy Arabs who came to vacation there. This mirage of Swiss neutrality belied the politics in Lebanon that simmered just under the surface. The relative degree of freedom of the press meant that political exiles of all types were present, but Lebanon was probably most important in this era as the banking and services capital of the region.

Gradually the Muslim population became the clear majority, and Lebanon could not avoid becoming involved in the Arab-Israeli conflict. After the Israeli victory in the 1948–1949 war, about 100,000 Palestinian refugees fled to Lebanon, where many Muslims supported them in carrying out hit-and-run actions against Israel. Lebanese Christians opposed these guerrilla operations, fearing that Israeli reprisals would threaten Lebanese independence.

The Six-Day War in 1967 and the Yom Kippur War in 1973 coupled with the expulsion of the Palestinians from Jordan in 1970 and 1971 (many relocating to Lebanon) increased the overall numbers of Muslims in the country. More important than tipping the sectarian balance, they fueled the conflict between Christian supporters of the political status quo and leftist and progressive and Muslim and Druze challengers to politics as usual. While the Lebanese military tried to maintain order and restrain the Palestinian guerrillas from using Lebanon as a base for attacks against Israel, the effort did not work. This led to clashes between Lebanese Christians and Muslims.

The result, ultimately, was a civil war that began in 1975, leading to the deaths of many Lebanese. In sectarian fighting between March 1975 and November 1976, 40,000 died and 100,000 more were wounded. The carnage continued. Lebanon was again brought into the larger Arab-Israeli conflict, with disastrous results. Repeated attacks by guerrillas operating in southern Lebanon brought the inevitable Israeli response. In June 1982, Israeli forces invaded Lebanon and even drove north to Beirut, which they occupied by August, leading to an agreement whereby the Palestine Liberation Organization (PLO) departed Beirut for Tunis. The conflict was temporarily ended by international agreements. But with the exodus of the Palestinian fighters and leadership, Lebanese Christian militias massacred scores of Palestinians in the Sabra and Shatila refugee camps in Beirut. Part of the truce agreement involved the United States sending U.S. marines into Beirut, and the French followed suit in 1983. Israel and Syria maintained significant forces in Lebanon and continued to do so for several years after the United States and French withdrew in response to suicide attacks on their forces in October 1983.

During the civil war, the Lebanese government was unable to carry out any of the normal functions of government, whether providing services or security, managing municipalities, or controlling the movement of goods or persons in or out of the country. Israel maintained forces and backed Lebanese allies in the south ostensibly to prevent raids and rocket attacks against Israeli territory.

The Syrian intervention in Lebanon came about in a piecemeal fashion, first with only 50 troops and then in a much larger force. This was eventually sanctioned by the Arab League as one component of the Araf Deterrent Force, supposedly under the command of the Lebanese president. Syria managed to influence the Lebanese political system as well as becoming a combatant in the civil war with alliances that shifted over time. In 1993 and in 1996, during the Israeli Operation GRAPES OF WRATH, hundreds of thousands of Lebanese fled their homes in the south to avoid Israeli attacks. Israel decided to withdraw from Lebanon in May 2000, hoping that this would lead to a stable border. Instead, the border became more dangerous for the Israelis, as Hezbollah controlled much of southern Lebanon. After 2000, Hezbollah militias were able to fortify their positions with Syrian help. Syria did withdraw its troops from Lebanon in mid-2005, and there was fleeting hope that Lebanon might enter a new era with foreign forces finally off its territory. However, those political and intelligence elements that had relied on Syria in the previous era began battling other new political forces on the scene.

Lebanon continued to be plagued by internal conflicts, including the continuing debate over the structure of its government and cabinet, which operate along outdated sectarian lines. Hezbollah had continued to arm its militia and participated in limited border hostilities with Israel during 2000–2006. In July 2006, war again erupted between Lebanon and Israel. Hezbollah by then effectively governed southern Lebanon and also had elected representatives in the national and local governments. The Lebanese refer to this 2006 conflict as the Fifth Arab-Israeli War.

On July 12, 2006, Hezbollah miscalculated the Israeli response to a raid on Israel. In addition to short-range Katyusha rocket attacks, Hezbollah raided Israeli territory and captured two Israeli soldiers. The reaction was massive and not anticipated by the Hezbollah leader, Hassan Nasrallah, who later admitted that the raid would not have been launched if he had known the likely Israeli response. The result was a month of war until a tenuous UN cease-fire was negotiated on August 14. Both sides suffered casualties and damage, although they were far more numerous on the Lebanese side. Hezbollah had about 1,000 fighters well dug into positions in southern Lebanon, backed by other militias and a civilian population that largely supported them, facing up to 30,000 Israel Defense Forces (IDF) troops.

Hezbollah fighters and militias supporting them sustained between 250 and 600 dead during the month-long war, while the Lebanese army suffered 46 dead and about 100 wounded. Israel reported 119 dead, up to 450 wounded, and 2 captured. UN observer forces in the area also suffered 7 dead and 12 wounded. The worst toll, however, was among Lebanese civilians. About 1,187 Lebanese civilians died, while 4,080 more were injured. As many as 1 million Lebanese were displaced by the fighting. Some returned to their homes after Hezbollah issued a call for them to do so, leaving some 255,986 still displaced. Israel suffered 44 civilian deaths and more than 1,300 injured as a result of cross-border attacks.

Both sides used massive amounts of ordnance in the conflict. Israel had complete control of the skies and was able to fly 12,000 sorties over Lebanese territory. In addition to Israeli artillery, the Israeli navy fired 2,500 shells against Lebanese targets. Lebanon suffered damage to its infrastructure that will require billions of dollars and many years to repair. The effective blockade imposed by Israel until September 2006 exacerbated the problems faced by Lebanon. The power of the Israeli military was not a surprise, but the robust defense put up by Hezbollah was. This militia had used its years of control over southern Lebanon to increase its stocks of weapons and prepare defensive positions. Hezbollah was able to fire 4,000 rockets into Israeli territory. These included not only the short-range Katyushas but also middle-range missiles capable of hitting Haifa and other points believed safe from the usual Hezbollah rockets. In southern Lebanon, Hezbollah was able to resist Israeli armored attacks, destroying 20 main battle tanks in two engagements. Launching what might have been a cruise missile against an Israeli warship was also a surprise.

The cease-fire called for a halt in the fighting, an end to the Israeli blockade, the deployment of UN forces to southern Lebanon to maintain peace, and the Lebanese army to aid in that effort. Whether these measures would be successful was questionable. Hezbollah soon announced that it had already restocked its missiles.

The political fallout from the summer's war manifested itself in a struggle over the Lebanese cabinet's recommendation that a tribunal be established to hear evidence on the assassination of former prime minister Rafik Hariri. Issues at stake included the future of Syria's government and future influence in Lebanon, the willingness of Lebanese leaders to compromise, the role to be played by such groups as Hezbollah, Saad Hariri's Future Party and the pro- and anti-Syrian Christian elements, and the need to diminish sectarianism as spelled out in the Taif Agreements but not achieved since the end of the Lebanese Civil War. By late 2007, the Lebanese political scene remained very much in turmoil. Plans to establish a special international criminal tribunal for Lebanon, with headquarters in the Netherlands, progressed, albeit at glacial speed. Hezbollah had not disarmed, and sharp political divisions remained and were coupled with assassinations (alleged to be Syrian-sponsored) of leading political figures. In military clashes between the Lebanese army and Fatah al-Islam groups, centered on the Nahr al-Bared refugee camp, 169 soldiers, 289 insurgents, and 41 civilians reportedly died.

From 2006 to 2008, the largely Shia political opponents of the pro-Western prime minister, Fouad Siniora, demanded a government of national unity, over which they would enjoy a veto power. In May 2008, Hezbollah and Amal forces seized western Beirut, resulting in military clashes, ultimately resolved on May 21, 2008, by the Doha Agreement, which established a national unity government, as the opposition had demanded. In January 2011, however, this government collapsed, largely because Prime Minister Saad Hariri rejected demands from Hezbollah elements that he repudiate the international special tribunal for Lebanon, established under UN auspices and based in the Netherlands, that was investigating the murder of former prime minister Rafik Hariri. In 2011, the tribunal issued arrest warrants for four Hezbollah members, and top Lebanese and Syrian security officers were also implicated.

In March 2011, civil war erupted in Syria, as insurgent elements sought to emulate the success of Arab Spring popular movements in Egypt and Tunisia in overturning authoritarian governments. Shia Hezbollah forces generally supported the government of Bashar al-Assad, which obtained arms from Iran and Russia, while Sunni Al Qaeda elements backed by Saudi Arabia and Qatar were prominent among the insurgents. Government forces wreaked brutal repression on their enemies, employing chemical weapons and devastating much of the country. Several thousand Lebanese Hezbollah militia members were believed to be fighting on al-Assad's behalf, arousing fears within Lebanon that their involvement would drag the country as a whole into the civil war in Syria.

By September 2013, over 120,000 Syrians had reportedly been killed, while 6.5 million were refugees, 2 million of whom sought safety outside Syria. By 2013, almost 700,000 of these had fled to Lebanon, straining that small country's resources, with one in six inhabitants now a refugee. Many Lebanese now resented their presence, fearing that refugees in such great numbers would inevitably disrupt the fragile sectarian balance within that country. As civil war in Syria intensified in late November 2013, Lebanon nonetheless opened its borders to many more thousands of Syrian refugees. By late 2013, the balance of war appeared to be turning against al-Assad, whose government, working through Hezbollah forces, had long treated Lebanon very much as a client state. This raised at least some possibility of opening a new and conceivably less turbulent chapter in Lebanese politics.

Daniel E. Spector and Sherifa Zuhur

Further Reading

Blanford, Nicholas. *Killing Mr. Lebanon: The Assassination of Rafik Hariri and Its Impact on the Middle East.* New York: I. B. Tauris, 2006.

Fisk, Robert. *Pity the Nation: The Abduction of Lebanon.* 4th ed. New York: Nation Books, 2002.

Gilsenan, Michael. *Lords of the Lebanese Marches: Violence and Narrative in an Arab Society.* London: I. B Tauris, 1996.

Harel, Amos, and Avi Issacharoff. *34 Days: Israel, Hezbollah, and the War in Lebanon.* Translated by Ora Cummings and Moshe Tlamim. New York: Palgrave Macmillan, 2008.

Harris, William W. *Lebanon: A History 600–2011.* New York: Oxford University Press, 2012.

Haugbolle, Sune. *War and Memory in Lebanon.* Cambridge: Cambridge University Press, 2012.

Herzog, Chaim. *The Arab-Israeli Wars: War and Peace in the Middle East from the War of Independence to Lebanon.* Westminster, MD: Random House, 1984.

Hirst, David. *Beware of Small States: Lebanon, Battleground of the Middle East.* New York: Nation Books, 2010.

Hudson, Michael. *The Precarious Republic: Political Modernization in Lebanon.* Boulder, CO: Westview, 1985.

Kerr, Michael, and Ari Knudsen, eds. *Lebanon: After the Cedar Revolution.* New York: Oxford University Press, 2013.

Mackey, Sandra. *Lebanon: A House Divided.* New York: Norton, 2006.

Mackey, Sandra. *Mirror of the Arab World: Lebanon in Conflict.* New York: Norton, 2008.

Najem, Tom. *Lebanon: The Politics of a Penetrated Society.* New York: Routledge, 2003.

Osoegawa, Taku. *Syria and Lebanon: International Relations and Diplomacy in the Middle East.* New York: I. B. Tauris, 2013.

Rabil, Robert G. *Embattled Neighbors: Syria, Israel and Lebanon.* Boulder, CO: Lynne Rienner, 2003.

Rabinovich, Itamar. *The War for Lebanon, 1970–1985.* Rev. ed. Ithaca, NY: Cornell University Press, 1985.

Salamey, Imad. *The Government and Politics of Lebanon.* New York: Routledge, 2013.

Shaery-Eisenlohr, Roschanack. *Shi'ite Lebanon: Transnational Religion and the Making of National Identities.* New York: Columbia University Press, 2011.

Totten, Michael J. *The Road to Fatima Gate: The Beirut Spring, the Rise of Hezbollah, and the Iranian War against Israel.* New York: Encounter Books, 2011.

Traboulsi, Fawwaz. *A History of Modern Lebanon.* New York: Pluto Press, 2007.

Libya

Predominantly Muslim North African nation covering 679,358 square miles. Libya borders Niger, Chad, and Sudan to the south; Tunisia and the Mediterranean Sea to the north; Algeria to the west; and Egypt to the east. The Ottoman Empire ruled Libya for much of the 19th century, but in 1907 Italy began to assert itself in the region. After a brief war with the Turks during 1911–1912, Italy gained control of Libya. A 20-year Libyan insurgency resulted, and Italy did not pacify the colony until 1931.

Libya was the site of significant fighting in the North African campaigns of World War II until it was ultimately secured by British forces in 1943. At the end of the war, Libya's status was immersed in the larger question of the fate of European colonial possessions in the Middle East and Africa.

Muammar Qaddafi was the revolutionary leader of Libya from September 1, 1969, and prime minister from January 1970, until his death at the hands of insurgents in October 2011. (Marko Kucijarov)

Ultimately, in 1949 the United Nations (UN) passed a resolution in favor of an independent Libya. Negotiations among the varied regions in Libya proved delicate. Those in and around Tripoli supported a large degree of national unity, while the more established government of Cyrenaica preferred a federal system and insisted on choosing the monarch. The process resulted in a constitutional monarchy, an elected bicameral parliament, and a federal system of government. Emir Idris of Cyrenaica was named hereditary king of Libya, and final independence was declared on December 24, 1951.

The new Kingdom of Libya had strong links to the West. Both Britain and the United States maintained military bases on its soil and helped support the state financially. Libya also had a strong Arab identity and joined the Arab League in 1953.

Arab nationalist movements grew in response to the 1948 creation of Israel, and Libya had experienced de-Arabization and a conflict of identity during the oppressive years of Italian colonization. The emergence of Gamal Abdel Nasser's Pan-Arab nationalist regime in Egypt by 1954 encouraged the growth of similar political thought in Libya, and the 1956 Suez Crisis only increased this trend. The discovery of oil in the late 1950s transformed the country, endowing it with wealth and increased geopolitical significance. Oil exports reached $1 billion by 1968.

The June 1967 Six-Day War proved a turning point for Libyan politics. On June 5, 1967, the day hostilities began, anti-Jewish and anti-Western riots broke out in Tripoli. When Nasser claimed that the Arab defeat was because of American and British assistance to Israel, Libyan oil workers refused to load Western tankers. The Libyan prime minister was forced to resign, and the king appointed a new cabinet.

In the months after the war, the government was under continued pressure from Arab nationalists. It pledged financial aid to Egypt and Jordan and demanded the closing of all foreign bases on Libyan soil (although the demand was not pressed). On July 31, 1969, a group of junior army officers seized power while the king was out of the country. The Revolution Command Council, headed by Colonel Muammar Qaddafi, took control with little opposition.

Qaddafi, an adherent of Nasser's version of Arab nationalism, stressed Arab unity, opposition to Western imperialism, and socialist economic policies. Qaddafi maintained that this agenda could be reconciled with a strong emphasis on an Islamic way of life, and an Islamic political and economic system. He rejected the Western presence in the Middle East but also communism or socialism. After Nasser's death, Qaddafi actively sought leadership in the Muslim world in the 1970s, promoting his so-called Third International Theory, a middle way between the communism of the Soviet Union and the capitalism of the West. Although he succeeded in convincing more than 30 African countries to reject relations with Israel, he never gained the confidence of certain other Muslim nations, perhaps because of his repression of the Muslim Brotherhood and other Muslim figures in Libya or more likely because of his advancement of radical causes and interference in regional politics.

Always an enemy of Zionism, Qaddafi supported Yasser Arafat's Fatah faction of the Palestine Liberation Organization (PLO) and sponsored terrorist attacks against Israel and related Western targets. As the 1970s progressed, Qaddafi voiced his support for anticolonialist movements around the world, including the Irish Republican Army (IRA); Libya also played host to a number of insurgent groups. Qaddafi also sought to build up the Libyan military and pursued significant arms purchases from France and the Soviet Union after 1970.

Internally, Qaddafi sought to remake Libyan society, insisting that a mixture of socialism and Islam would ensure social justice. He created a welfare state based on oil revenues and reformed the legal system to include elements of Koranic law (Sharia). His *Green Book* (1976) laid out his political and economic philosophy. In it he rejected representative government in favor of direct democracy. Finally, he transformed Libya's oil industry by insisting on a larger share of profits from international oil companies, setting a pattern that would be imitated by other oil-rich states.

Despite Qaddafi's radical politics, Libya and the United States avoided direct confrontation for much of the 1970s because of their economic relationship. This changed, however, when Libya vehemently opposed the 1978 Camp David Accords. Qaddafi viewed any Arab rapprochement with Israel as a betrayal. In 1977, President Jimmy Carter's administration listed Libya, Cuba, and North Korea as states that supported terrorism. U.S.-Libyan relations continued to sour. On December 2, 1979, rioters targeted the U.S. embassy in Tripoli in imitation of the attack on the U.S. embassy in Tehran earlier that year. As a result, in May 1980 the United States withdrew its diplomatic personnel from Libya.

With the election of President Ronald Reagan in 1980, relations chilled further. On May 6, 1981, the Reagan administration expelled Libyan diplomats from the United States. The administration also pursued a freedom of navigation policy and challenged Libya's 1973 claims of sovereignty over the Gulf of Sidra in the Mediterranean. On July 19, 1981, the *Nimitz* carrier battle group was patrolling near the gulf when two of the carrier's Grumman F-14 Tomcat fighters were approached and attacked by two Libyan Soviet-made Sukhoi Su-22 fighter jets. The U.S. planes evaded the attack and shot down both Libyan aircraft.

Tensions increased further, and in March 1982 the United States banned the import of Libyan oil. The sanctions had limited effect, however, as European nations did not adopt U.S. policies. Qaddafi continued to support revolutionary and terrorist activity. On April 5, 1986, an explosion in a Berlin nightclub killed 3 and injured 200, including 63 U.S. servicemen. The United States claimed Libyan involvement and retaliated with great ferocity. On April 15, 1986, U.S. Air Force and Navy planes bombed five targets in Libya. One of the targets was Qaddafi's home. He escaped injury but lost an adopted daughter in the raid.

The Reagan administration maintained that the raid resulted in significant disruptions to Libyan-supported terrorism, and such activity did decline for a number of years. However, on December 21, 1988, Pan Am Flight 103 was destroyed over Lockerbie, Scotland, by a terrorist's bomb. More than 270 died, and subsequent investigations pointed to two Libyan men as primary suspects. When the Qaddafi regime refused to extradite the men for arrest and trial, the UN imposed sanctions on Libya in 1992. U.S. confrontations with Libya continued, and a second incident over the Gulf of Sidra resulted in the destruction of two Libyan MiG-23 fighter planes in January 1989. At the end of the Cold War, the Qaddafi regime remained steadfast in its support of revolutionary movements and terrorist actions against Israel and the West.

In recent years Qaddafi had taken a more conciliatory tone with the West, including turning over the men responsible for the Pan Am bombing and paying restitution to victims' families. After the September 2001 terrorist attacks on the United States, Qaddafi issued a stinging denunciation of the acts and condemned Al Qaeda and other terrorist groups. In February 2004, Libya declared that it would renounce its weapons of mass destruction (WMD) program and comply with the Nuclear Nonproliferation Treaty. This began a thaw in relations with the United States, which resumed diplomatic relations that June and lifted all remaining economic sanctions in September 2004.

In February 2011, civil war broke out in Libya, shortly after the Arab Spring protests had overturned the governments of Egypt and Tunisia. Gaddafi's forces initially cracked down on the rebels. In March 2011, the United Nations Human Rights Council expelled Libya, while the UN Security Council established a "no-fly zone" over Libya and authorized the use of "all means necessary" to protect civilians there. NATO air strikes targeted government forces. In October 2011, the war ended in a rebel victory, with Gaddafi captured and killed in the city of Sirte. A General National Congress was elected in July 2012, with the mandate of establishing an interim government and drafting a new constitution. Factionalism and disorder nonetheless posed severe problems to the new regime's authority. In September 2012, Islamic militants attacked the U.S. consulate in Benghazi, killing the U.S. ambassador and provoking a political storm in the United States.

Robert S. Kiely

Further Reading

Burton, Fred, and Samuel M. Katz. *Under Fire: The Untold Story of the Attack in Benghazi.* New York: St. Martin's Press, 2013.

Cooley, John. *Libyan Sands: The Complete Account of Qaddafi's Revolution.* New York: Holt, Rinehart and Winston, 1982.

Hilsum, Lindsey. *Sandstorm: Libya in the Time of Revolution.* New York: Penguin, 2012.

Pargeter, Alison. *Libya: The Rise and Fall of Gaddafi.* New Haven, CT: Yale University Press, 2012.

Prashad, Vijay. *Arab Spring, Libyan Winter.* Oakland, CA: AK Press, 2012.

Simons, Geoff. *Libya and the West: From Independence to Lockerbie.* London: I. B. Tauris, 2004.

St. John, Ronald Bruce. *Libya: From Colony to Revolution.* Chino Valley, AZ: Oneworld Press, 2012.

Vandewalle, Dirk. *A History of Modern Libya.* 2nd ed. Cambridge: Cambridge University Press, 2012.

Vandewalle, Dirk. *Libya since Independence: Oil and State-Building.* Ithaca, NY: Cornell University Press, 1998.

Vandewalle, Dirk, ed. *Libya since 1969: Gaddafi's Revolution Revisited.* New York: Palgrave Macmillan, 2008.

Wright, John. *A History of Libya.* Revised and updated. New York: Columbia University Press, 2012.

M

Meir, Golda

Born: May 3, 1898
Died: December 8, 1978

Golda Meir had a varied and challenging life as an impoverished child, a pioneer in Jewish Palestine, a caring mother, and a political leader. She is remembered fondly by Jews as Israel's matriarch.

Meir was born as Goldie Mabovitz in Kiev, Ukraine, on May 3, 1898. Her parents, Moshe and Bluma (Neiditz) Mabovitz, were poor, and in 1903, her father took the family to Pinsk and decided they would immigrate to the United States. He went to the United States first and prepared for his family to follow. In the meantime, pogroms affected the Jews in Pinsk, and Meir remembered those attacks against the Jewish community—they influenced her for years to come. In 1908, Meir, along with her mother and her two sisters, arrived in the United States and joined her father in Milwaukee. She attended elementary school and high school there until she ran away from home after her mother tried to arrange a marriage for her. She lived with her sister in Denver, Colorado, where she met anarchist and Zionist intellectuals and liked the democratic socialist ideology promoted by Eugene V. Debs. In 1915, she joined Poale Zion, a Zionist group, and began making speeches to promote Jewish settlements in Palestine. She also fell in love with a Lithuanian immigrant, Morris Meyerson. Meir soon returned to Milwaukee and in 1916, completed high school.

In 1917, Meir organized demonstrations against the pogroms in Russia, and the same year, she graduated from the Teachers' Training College of Milwaukee State Normal School. Rather than teach, however, she worked full time for Poale Zion. In December, she married Meyerson yet worried he would not agree to her desire—immigrating to Palestine. At about that time, the United Kingdom, which controlled Palestine under a League of Nations mandate, issued the Balfour Declaration (1917). The Balfour Declaration, which supported a home for Jews in the Palestinian territory, and Meir's persuasiveness convinced Meyerson to leave for Palestine.

In 1921, Meir and Meyerson joined the Kibbutz Merhavia, a poor commune near Nazareth, where they raised chickens. Two years later, Meyerson decided he could not endure living on the kibbutz, and he and Meir moved to Tel Aviv. She worked in the office of the Histradut (Israel Labor Federation) and took in laundry to help make ends meet. She worked hard to raise her two children under dire economic circumstances and within a marriage that neared collapse.

In 1930, one year after Meir had been elected a delegate to the World Zionist Congress, she assumed an important role in Mapai (Labor Party). In the 1930s, she spent much time in Europe and the United States raising money for Zionism. In 1945, she separated from her husband (who died in 1951).

After World War II, the Jewish struggle for a homeland intensified, and Meir sided with David Ben-Gurion, who advocated an activist approach to circumvent British restrictions in Palestine and end British rule there. Meir,

Golda Meir was a prominent Israeli political leader and the first woman to hold the office of prime minister of Israel (1969–1974). She was forced to resign in the aftermath of the 1973 Yom Kippur (Ramadan) War, which had caught Israeli leaders by surprise. (Library of Congress)

along with Ben-Gurion and other prominent Zionists, signed the Israeli Declaration of Independence (1948) and was chosen the only female member of the provisional council of state. Under Prime Minister Ben-Gurion and President Chaim Weizmann, she served as Israel's first minister to the Soviet Union, and then in 1949, she won election to the Knesset (Parliament) under the Mapai banner. She also served as minister of labor, a position she held for seven years. In that capacity, she substantially improved housing and jobs for immigrants. It was in 1956 that she changed her last name to Meir.

Also in 1956, Meir promoted the acquisition of arms for the military as a means to offset recent weapons modernization by Egypt and Syria, a move that proved invaluable for Israel in the Suez Canal crisis later that year. Ill health forced her to resign from the cabinet in 1966, but she served as general secretary of Mapai and closely advised Prime Minister Levi Eshkol. Meir resigned as general secretary in 1968, owing to political differences with other party leaders, but not until after she had merged Mapai with several other parties to form a restructured Labor Party.

Shortly after Eshkol died in February 1969, Labor Party leaders bypassed Moshe Dayan, hero of the 1967 Six-Day War, and chose Meir as the new prime minister. She took the oath of office on March 17, 1969. Meir supported new Jewish settlements in the West Bank and peace initiatives with Egypt. At the same time, she underestimated Arab military strength, a mistake that likely contributed to Israel being poorly prepared when the Egyptians and Syrians launched a surprise attack in 1973. As Meir's popularity dropped, her Labor Party lost seats, and early in 1974, she resigned as prime minister. Meanwhile, a special committee investigating the 1973 war effort cleared her and Defense Minister Dayan of any wrongdoing. Her ardent Zionism, determination, and belief that Israel stood alone all contributed to the realization of a Jewish homeland. Suffering from leukemia, in her final weeks Meir endorsed the Camp David Accords negotiated in late 1978 by Israel's hard-line Likud prime minister Menachem Begin and Egyptian president Anwar Sadat, which marked the beginning of moves by Israel and the Arab states to negotiate a lasting peace settlement. She died on December 8, 1978.

Neil A. Hamilton

Further Reading

Avner, Yehuda. *The Prime Ministers: An Intimate Narrative of Israeli Leadership.* New Milford, CT: Toby Press, 2010.

Burkett, Elinor. *Golda.* New York: Harper, 2008.

Mann, Peggy. *Golda: The Life of Israel's Prime Minister.* New York: Coward, McCann and Geoghegan, 1971.

Martin, Ralph G. *Golda Meir: The Romantic Years.* New York: Scribner, 1988.

Meir, Golda. *My Life.* New York: Putnam, 1975.

Steinberg, Bierna S. *Women in Power: The Personalities and Leadership Styles of Indira Gandhi, Golda Meir, and Margaret Thatcher.* Montreal: McGill-Queen's University Press, 2008.

Morocco

Northwest African nation. The Kingdom of Morocco borders on the Mediterranean Sea to the north, the Atlantic Ocean to the west, Western Sahara to the south, and Algeria to the east. Morocco has an area of 172,414 square miles, slightly larger than the U.S. state of California. Morocco's 2006 population was approximately 33 million people.

Until the early 20th century, Morocco was relatively isolated from spheres of European, Middle Eastern, or sub-Sahara African influence. These circumstances resulted in a strong Berber and Arab Islamic national character. From 1912 to 1956, Morocco was both a French and Spanish protectorate. France granted independence to Morocco in 1956, although Spain continued to control the Western Sahara region until the mid-1970s and still retains the small enclaves of Cuenta and Melilla along the Mediterranean coast.

When the State of Israel was founded in May 1948, Morocco, like other countries in the Maghrib, was confronted with the considerable problem of Jewish emigration, which was to continue for the next several decades. From 1947 to 1960, approximately 50,000 Jews, or 25 percent of the Jewish population of Morocco, left the country, mostly to settle in Israel but some in Europe and the United States. Although most émigrés were poor or middle class, Jews were an important part of the country's economy. Neither the king, Mohammed V, nor the ruling Istiqlal party were anti-Jewish, and many members of the country's elite were Jewish including judges, government ministers, and university administrators. While Morocco attempted to limit emigration in opposition to the desires of the United Nations (UN) and the United States, this process nevertheless continued, frequently with the covert involvement of Israeli military forces. In 2006, the Jewish population in Morocco was estimated to be only 5,000 people.

In March 1961, Crown Prince Moulay Hassan succeeded his father, Mohammed V, as King Hassan II. He ruled for the next four decades until his death in July 1999. The king was both the nation's spiritual leader, as a direct descendent of the Prophet Muhammad, and its political head of government. Hassan, while lacking the charisma and unifying ability of his father, was nonetheless an effective leader, able to balance relations with the West, whose economic and political aid helped modernize his country, and the Middle East, whose Islamic heritage was his basis for power.

Unlike many other Arab nations, Morocco has maintained relatively amiable contacts with Israel since the early 1950s. At times these contacts have occurred directly between government representatives on matters of security and intelligence. Other times they have involved third parties such as Jewish organizations, intellectuals, journalists, and foreign diplomats seeking mutually beneficial political, economic, and cultural developments and information.

King Hassan II pursued a conciliatory foreign policy during his reign and sought to strengthen ties among Arabs and Jews,

Forging a powerful role for himself and his country through a blend of Islamic traditionalism and Western pragmatism, King Hassan II ruled Morocco for 38 years until his death in July 1999 at age 70. (Embassy of the Kingdom of Morocco)

envisioning a powerful union of states that he hoped would bring the region prosperity similar to that of Western Europe and the United States. Morocco was essentially kept isolated from the June 1967 Six-Day War, although the relationship between Israel and Morocco was tested when Morocco provided military support to Syria during the October 1973 Yom Kippur War. In October 1976, Morocco hosted a meeting with Israeli prime minister Yitzhak Rabin. The following year Morocco hosted another meeting between Israeli foreign minister Moshe Dayan and Egyptian deputy prime minister Hasan Tuhami. Both meetings served to lay the groundwork for Egyptian president Anwar Sadat's groundbreaking visit to Israel and eventually Egypt's peace agreement with Israel in 1978.

To strengthen his position in the wake of political and military opponents of his centralized authority, Hassan embarked on an effort to secure the Western Sahara, which historically had been part of Morocco, after its abandonment by Spain in 1975. To allay widespread international criticism, Moroccan officials and a delegation of Moroccan Jews visited the United States in 1978 to win support for the movement among allies of Israel in the U.S. Congress. Domestically, the social and economic disparity between urban and rural populations lessened, and education, health care, and communications all improved during Hassan's reign.

In the 1980s, Hassan worked to secure Arab recognition of Israel and an end to the Arab-Israeli conflict. In November 1981 and again in September 1982, he hosted an Arab summit to address conflicts in the region through a Saudi-sponsored peace plan. The plan called for the Israeli withdrawal from all occupied territories and the establishment of a Palestinian state. In July 1986, he held two days of talks on continued Palestinian issues with Israeli prime minister Shimon Peres. Hassan also sought to improve relationships among other Arab states. In 1984, he organized the Islamic Congress of Casablanca and created the Arabic-African Union with Libya. During the 1991 Persian Gulf War, Morocco aligned itself squarely with the United States and sent troops to defend Saudi Arabia.

Morocco expressed agreement with the principles of the 1993 Oslo Accords and received Israeli prime minister Rabin and Foreign Minister Peres in Casablanca following the signing ceremony in Washington, D.C. On September 1, 1994, Morocco and Israel established semiofficial diplomatic relations with the opening of liaison offices in Jerusalem and Rabat. These offices served to promote tourism and trade between the two countries, an issue of great economic importance to Morocco. They remained open for eight years but closed following the Palestinian uprising in 2002.

The problems of rising Islamic fundamentalism posed difficult challenges for Morocco in the late 1980s and early 1990s and continue under the leadership of Hassan's son and successor, King Mohammed VI. On May 16, 2003, 12 suicide bombers of Salafiyya Jihadiyya, an offshoot of the Moroccan Islamic Combatant Group and believed to be affiliated with Al Qaeda, killed 45 people in Casablanca in five separate bombings. Although the attack on the Jewish Sabbath ultimately killed no Jews, the targets included a Jewish social club and restaurant, a Jewish cemetery, and a Jewish-owned Italian restaurant.

In February 2011, a pro-democracy Youth Movement for Change spearheaded by young people mounted major demonstrations in Morocco, which at their peak in March mobilized 800,000 people, who demanded free elections, an end to corruption, and social justice. King Mohammed VI granted a new constitution, which gave more power to the prime minister, and parliamentary elections took place in November 2011, which returned a moderate Islamist government. Salaries of public employees were increased, but more radical activists experienced intimidation and sometimes imprisonment. As prices rose dramatically in 2012 and 2013, demonstrations continued, some

of them specifically targeting the king and his spending, and others protesting the lack of independence in the judiciary. It remained unclear just how drastic or effective these demands for change would ultimately prove.

Mark M. Sanders

Further Reading

Entelis, John P. *Culture and Counterculture in Moroccan Politics.* Boulder, CO: Westview, 1989.

Hart, David M. *Tribe and Society in Rural Morocco.* New York: Routledge, 2000.

Howe, Marvin. *Morocco: The Islamist Awakening and Other Challenges.* New York: Oxford University Press, 2005.

Laskier, Michael M. *Israel and the Maghreb: From Statehood to Oslo.* Tallahassee: Florida State University Press, 2004.

Miller, Susan Gilson. *A History of Modern Morocco.* Cambridge: Cambridge University Press, 2012.

Pennell. C. R. *Morocco: From Empire to Independence.* 2nd ed. China Valley, AZ: Oneworld Press, 2009.

Pennell, C. R. *Morocco since 1830: A History.* New York: New York University Press, 2000.

Sater, James N. *Morocco: Challenges to Tradition and Modernity.* New York: Routledge, 2010.

Willis, Michael. *Politics and Power in the Maghreb: Algeria, Tunisia and Morocco from Independence to the Arab Spring.* New York: Columbia University Press, 2012.

N

Nasser, Gamal Abdel

Born: January 16, 1918
Died: September 28, 1970

Egyptian nationalist politician, vice president (1953–1954), premier (1954–1956), and president (1956–1970). Born in Beni Mor, Egypt, on January 16, 1918, the son of a civil servant, Gamal Abdel Nasser at an early age developed great antipathy toward Britain's rule over Egypt, setting the stage for his later championing of Egyptian nationalism and Pan-Arabism. Settling on a military career, Nasser graduated from the Egyptian Royal Military Academy in 1936 and was commissioned a second lieutenant. While stationed at a post in the Sudan, he met and became friends with future Egyptian president Anwar Sadat. Based on their mutual dislike of the British, they eventually formed the foundation for a secret anti-British organization that came to be called the Free Officers.

The Free Officers recruited Egyptian military officers who wished to bring about an end to British colonial rule and to oust King Farouk II. After months of painstaking planning, the Free officers fomented a revolt against Farouk's government on July 23, 1952. Three days later, the king abdicated and fled Egypt. The British withdrew from Egypt in early 1956. Upon Farouk's abdication, a Revolutionary Command Council was established under the leadership of Major General Mohammad Naguib, with Nasser working behind the scenes. When the council declared Egypt a republic in June 1953, Naguib became its first president with Nasser as vice president. Beginning in the winter of 1954, a political power struggle ensued between Nasser and Naguib. Within months, Nasser took de facto control as president of the Revolutionary Command Council, while Naguib was allowed to continue as president of Egypt, although the latter was in reality little more than a figurehead position.

Nasser and his faction consolidated their hold on power, and after the October 1954 attempt on Nasser's life, which Nasser blamed on Naguib, Nasser ordered Naguib arrested. Using the assassination attempt to solidify his power base, Nasser became the premier of Egypt on February 25, 1955. Seven months later he also took on the title of provisional president.

Nasser quickly moved to centralize his authority, creating a tightly controlled police state in which political opponents were imprisoned, intellectuals and elites disenfranchised, and industries nationalized. In June 1956, a national election was held in which Nasser was the sole candidate for the presidency; thus, he "officially" became Egypt's second president.

In addition to seeking land reform and following quasi-socialist economic policies, Nasser sought to modernize Egyptian infrastructure. His public works projects included the building of a massive dam at Aswan, Egypt, for which he received promises of financial support from the United States as well as Great Britain. Nasser also approached the Americans about purchasing arms, ostensibly to be used against

Egyptian president Gamal Abdel Nasser acknowledges the acclaim of his supporters as he drives through Port Said, Egypt, on his way to the Navy House, where he will hoist the Egyptian flag on June 18, 1956. (AP Photo)

Israel. When the United States refused this request, Nasser turned to the Soviet Union. The Soviets saw a chance to increase their influence in the region and began negotiating an arms deal with Nasser, whereupon the United States and Britain withdrew their support for the Aswan Dam project in early July 1956. Seeing an additional opportunity to gain more influence with the Egyptians and to establish a foothold in the Middle East, the Soviet Union quickly offered to help Nasser with the Aswan Dam.

Nasser used the loss of Western financial support as a pretext to nationalize the Suez Canal on July 26, 1956. This action provoked joint French/British/Israeli military action against Egypt, beginning the Suez Crisis. Thus, on October 29, 1956, Israeli forces attacked Egypt and French and British forces attacked by air two days later.

On November 5, French and British forces landed at Port Said, further escalating the conflict. The United States, not privy to the attack, put great pressure on the Israelis as well as the French and British to withdraw, which they did on November 7.

Far from being defeated, Nasser was vindicated by the Suez Crisis, and he shrewdly used this "victory" to further consolidate his rule at home and to promote Pan-Arabism throughout the Middle East. The Suez Crisis turned Nasser into a hero of Middle East nationalism.

In pursuit of his Pan-Arab vision, Nasser established the United Arab Republic (UAR) on February 22, 1958. Consisting of only Egypt and Syria, however, the UAR fell apart when Syria withdrew on September 28, 1961. Nevertheless, Nasser continued to promote Arab nationalism and his vision of a Pan-Arab union.

Nasser's strong-arm rule began to work against him as the years progressed. Losing some of his popular appeal at home, Nasser attempted to reform the government, which was corrupt and riddled with cronyism. Instead, he was forced to crack down on his opponents who tried to aggrandize their power during the attempted reorganization. Turning his sights to foreign affairs, in an effort to play up Arab resentment toward Israel, Nasser signed a defense pact with Syria in November 1966. In early 1967, Nasser began provoking the Israelis through various different actions, including having the UN Peacekeepers removed from the border between Egypt and Israel, blockading the Gulf of Aqaba, and moving troops in to the Sinai. In retaliation, on June 5, 1967, the Israelis attacked Egypt, and Syria and Jordan. The war lasted only until June 9 and proved to be a humiliating defeat for Nasser.

Nasser's miscalculation further eroded his support in Egypt and blemished his reputation throughout the Middle East. In March 1969, he launched a War of Attrition against Israel, which resulted in many more Egyptian than Israeli casualties. In July 1970, Nasser agreed to a cease-fire arrangement put forward by U.S. secretary of state William Rogers to end the so-called War of Attrition. Now in deteriorating health, Nasser died on September 28, 1970, in Cairo.

Dallace W. Unger Jr.

Further Reading

Aburish, Saïd K. *Nasser: The Last Arab.* New York: St. Martin's Press, 2004.

Alexander, Anne. *Nasser.* London: Haus Publishing, 2004.

Cook, Steven A. *The Struggle for Egypt: From Nasser to Tahrir Square.* New York: Oxford University Press, 2011.

DuBius, Shirley Graham. *Gamal Abdel Nasser, Son of the Nile.* New York: Third Press, 1972.

Ferris, Jesse. *Nasser's Gamble: How Intervention in Yemen Caused the Six-Day War and the Decline of Egyptian Power.* Princeton, NJ: Princeton University Press, 2012.

Gardner, Lloyd C. *The Road to Tahrir Square: Egypt and the United States from the Rise of Nasser to the Fall of Mubarak.* New York: New Press, 2011.

Gordon, Joel. *Nasser's Blessed Movement: Egypt's Free Officers and the July Revolution.* New York: Oxford University Press, 1992.

Kerr, Malcolm. *The Arab Cold War: Gamal Abd al-Nasir and His Rivals.* New York: Oxford University Press, 1971.

Lacouture, Jean. *Nasser: A Biography.* New York: Knopf, 1973.

McNamara, Robert. *Britain, Nasser, and the Balance of Power in the Middle East, 1952–1967: From the Egyptian Revolution to the Six Day War.* New York: Routledge, 2003.

Nutting, Anthony. *Nasser.* London: Dutton, 1972.

Osman, Tarek. *Egypt on the Brink: From Nasser to Mubarak.* New Haven, CT: Yale University Press, 2011.

Waterbury, John. *The Egypt of Nasser and Sadat: The Political Economy of Two Regimes.* Princeton, NJ: Princeton University Press, 1983.

Oslo Accords

The agreement commonly called the Oslo Accords and formally known as the Declaration of Principles on Interim Self-Government Arrangements was signed on September 13, 1993, in Washington, D.C., by Israeli prime minister Yitzhak Rabin, Palestine Liberation Organization (PLO) chairman Yasser Arafat, and U.S. president Bill Clinton. In the Oslo Accords, the PLO, the Palestinians' major representative party and de facto government-in-exile, formally recognized Israel's right to exist and Israel's sovereignty over 78 percent of historic Palestine and pledged to end military actions against Israel. Israel, while failing to recognize Palestinian statehood, did recognize Palestinian nationhood, including the right of self-determination, and the PLO's role as the Palestinians' legitimate representative body.

The document spelled out ways in which the Palestinians could achieve a degree of autonomy in parts of the West Bank and the Gaza Strip, which had been occupied by Israeli forces since the June 1967 Six-Day War. The hope was that by the PLO's demonstration of competent self-governance and control over anti-Israel violence, the Israelis would gain the confidence needed to make a phased withdrawal from the occupied territories and grant the Palestinians an independent state alongside Israel. Similarly, it was hoped that the removal of foreign occupation forces from certain areas, increasing levels of self-government, and the prospects of a viable independent state would give the Palestinian population the incentive to end the violence against Israelis. The interim peace period was to be completed by 1998, at which time a permanent peace agreement would be signed.

Although the U.S. government became the guarantor of the Oslo Accords, Washington had little to do with the agreement itself. Soon after the election of a more moderate Israeli government in 1992, direct talks began in secret between representatives of Israel and the PLO. They were first facilitated by Norwegian nongovernmental organizations and later with the assistance of the foreign ministry. This apparently took place without the knowledge of U.S. officials, who still took the position that the PLO should not be allowed to take part in the peace process, excluding it from the stalled peace talks then going on in Washington. As the secret negotiations in Norway progressed during the summer of 1993, the Clinton administration put forward what it called a compromise proposal for Palestinian autonomy. This compromise was actually less favorable to the Palestinians than what was then being put forward by the Israelis.

The U.S. role in the Oslo process began with a historic signing ceremony on the White House lawn on September 13, 1993. The agreement had been finalized in Oslo on August 20. Given the ambiguities in the agreement, both parties agreed that the United States should be its guarantor. Indeed, the Israelis saw the U.S. government as the entity most likely to support its positions on outstanding issues, and the Palestinians saw the U.S. government as the only

President Bill Clinton (center) watches as Israeli prime minister Yitzhak Rabin (left) and Palestine Liberation Organization leader Yasser Arafat (right) shake hands at the ceremony for the signing of the historic Israeli-Palestinian Declaration of Principles (also known as the Oslo Accords) on September 13, 1993. (William J. Clinton Presidential Library)

entity capable of forcing Israel to live up to its commitments and able to move the occupying power to compromise.

Peace talks resumed in Washington in the fall of 1993 within the Oslo framework. Over the next seven years, the United States brokered a series of Israeli-Palestinian agreements that led to the withdrawal of Israeli forces from most of the Gaza Strip and parts of the West Bank. By the end of the decade, about 40 percent of the West Bank and the Gaza Strip, including most of its towns and cities, had been placed under the rule of the new Palestinian Authority (PA), headed by Arafat, and divided into dozens of noncontiguous zones wherein the Palestinians could for the first time exercise some limited autonomy within their sphere of control.

During this period, the Israeli government severely limited the mobility of Palestinians within and between the West Bank and

the Gaza Strip, dramatically expanded its expropriation of land in the occupied territories for colonization by Jewish settlers, and refused to withdraw from as much territory as promised in the U.S.-brokered disengagement agreements. In addition, the United States tended to side with the Israelis on most issues during talks regarding the disengagement process, even after a right-wing coalition that had opposed the Oslo Accords came to power in Israel in 1996. This served to alienate many Palestinians who had been initially hopeful about the peace process and hardened anti-Israeli attitudes.

Meanwhile, much of the PA proved itself to be rather inept, corrupt, and autocratic in its governance of those parts of the occupied territories under its control. The corruption alienated much of the Palestinian population, and the PA's lack of control made it difficult to suppress the growth of radical Islamic groups. On more than two dozen occasions between 1994 and 2000, Islamic extremists from the occupied Palestinian territories engaged in terrorist attacks inside Israel, killing scores of Israeli civilians and thereby hardening anti-Palestinian attitudes.

The Palestinians had hoped that the United States would broker the negotiations based on international law that forbids the expansion of any country's territory by military force and prohibits occupying powers from transferring their civilian population into occupied land. The Palestinians also hoped that U.S. officials would support a series of specific United Nations (UN) Security Council resolutions demanding that Israel honor these principles. From the Palestinians' perspective—as well as that of the UN, most U.S. allies, and most international legal experts—the onus of the burden was on Israel, as the occupying power, to make most of the compromises for peace. The Clinton administration, however, argued that the UN resolutions were no longer relevant and saw the West Bank and the Gaza Strip simply as disputed territories, thereby requiring both sides to compromise. This gave the Israelis a clear advantage in the peace process.

In signing the Oslo Accords, the Palestinians operated on the assumption that the agreement would result in concrete improvements in the lives of those in the occupied territories. They hoped that the interim period would be no more than five years and that the permanent settlement would be based on UN Security Council Resolutions 242 and 338, which called upon Israel to withdraw from the territories seized in the 1967 war. For their part, the Israelis had hoped that the Oslo Accords would lead to the emergence of a responsible Palestinian leadership and greater security. Twenty years later, these optimistic expectations had at best only been partially fulfilled. The broad overall objectives of the Oslo Accords nonetheless continued to inform still continuing negotiations intended to bring about a final Israeli-Palestinian settlement.

Stephen Zunes

Further Reading

Bauck, Petter, and Mohammed Omer, eds. *The Oslo Accords: A Critical Assessment.* Cairo: American University in Cairo Press, 2013.

Beilin, Yossi. *Touching Peace: From the Oslo Accord to a Final Agreement.* London: Weidenfeld and Nicolson, 1999.

Brown, Nathan J. *Palestinian Politics after the Oslo Accords: Resuming Arab Palestine.* Berkeley: University of California Press, 2003.

Enderlin, Charles. *Shattered Dreams: The Failure of the Peace Process in the Middle East, 1995–2002.* New York: Other Press, 2003.

Freedman, Robert Owen, ed. *The Middle East and the Peace Process: The Impact of the Oslo Accords.* Gainesville: University Press of Florida, 1998.

Gerstenfeld, Manfred. *Israel's New Future Revisited: Shattered Dreams and Harsh Realities, Twenty Years after the First Oslo Accords.* New York: RVP Press, 2013.

Golan, Galia. *Israel and Palestine: Peace Plans and Proposals from Oslo to Disengagement.* Updated ed. Princeton, NJ: Markus Wiener, 2008.

Grossman, David. *Death as a Way of Life: Israel Ten Years after Oslo.* New York: Farrar, Straus and Giroux, 2003.

Makovsky, David. *Making Peace with the PLO: The Rabin Government's Road to the Oslo Accord.* Boulder, CO: Westview, 1995.

Peres, Shimon. *The New Middle East.* New York: Henry Holt, 1993.

Said, Edward. *The End of the Peace Process: Oslo and After.* New York: Pantheon, 2000.

Watson, Geoffrey R. *The Oslo Accords: International Law and the Israeli-Palestinian Peace Agreements.* New York: Oxford University Press, 2000.

Weinberger, Peter. *Co-Opting the PLO: A Critical Reconstruction of the Oslo Accords, 1993–1995.* New York: Rowman and Littlefield, 2006.

P

Palestine Liberation Organization

A political and military organization founded in 1964 and dedicated to protecting the human and legal rights of Palestinians and creating an independent state for Palestinian Arabs in Palestine. Since the 1960s, the Munazzamat al-Tahrir Filastiniyyah (Palestine Liberation Organization, PLO) has functioned as the official mouthpiece for the Palestinian people. There are numerous factions and organizations that loosely fall under the PLO's umbrella. In addition to Fatah which is the largest of these groups, the PLO has also encompassed the Popular Front for the Liberation of Palestine (PFLP), the Democratic Front for the Liberation of Palestine (DFLP), the Palestinian People's Party, the Palestine Liberation Front (PLF), the Arab Liberation Front, al-Saiqa (Syrian Baathists), the Palestine Democratic Union, the Palestinian Popular Front Struggle, and the Palestinian Arab Front. Two groups no longer associated with the PLO include the Popular Front for the Liberation of Palestine–General Command (PFLP-GC) and the Fatah Uprising. The PLO comprises centrist-nationalist groups (such as Fatah), rightist groups, leftist groups (including communists), militant groups, and non-militant groups. It has purposely eschewed embracing any one political philosophy so as to be as inclusive as possible in its membership. The PLO has been enormously successful in attracting funding over the years. Indeed, a 1993 survey estimated the PLO's total assets at between $8 billion and $10 billion and its average yearly income at $1.5 billion to $2 billion.

The PLO was founded in 1964 by the Arab League and Egypt. Its first president was Ahmad Shukeiri. The stated purpose of the PLO was the liberation of Palestine, condemnation of Zionist imperialism, and the dissolution of Israel through the use of armed force. Throughout its existence, the PLO has often used violence to express its viewpoints and gain international attention. This has earned it the reputation of being a terrorist organization, although Palestinians and many international observers dispute that characterization. In 1988, PLO chairman Yasser Arafat—who led the organization from 1969 to 2004—renounced violence as a means to achieve Palestinian goals, but a number of PLO groups did not follow this decree and have continued to mount terrorist attacks in Israel and elsewhere.

Although the PLO has been reorganized many times since its inception, its leading governing bodies have been the Palestinian National Council (PNC), the Central Council, and the Executive Committee. The PNC has 300 members and functions as a nominal legislature. The Executive Committee has 15 members elected by the PNC and holds the PLO's real political and executive power. The Palestinian Revolutionary Forces constitute the PLO's military arm. (The Palestine Liberation Army, or PLA, a military group in Syria during the 1970s, was never part of the PLO.)

The PLO has always had a variety of viewpoints represented, some more radical and prone to violence than others, and Egyptians dominated the organization in its first years. As the 1960s wore on, fedayeen

Palestine Liberation Organization (PLO) leader Yasser Arafat talks with his supporters in Beirut, Lebanon, on July 10, 1982, following a night of fighting between the PLO and Israeli troops. (AP Photo)

organizations, groups that existed expressly to take up the armed struggle against the Israelis, became more powerful. These groups used guerrilla and paramilitary tactics to resist the encroachment of Israelis on what they considered Palestinian territory.

In 1968, Fatah took control of the PLO's activities after Arafat appeared on the cover of *Time* magazine as the chairman of the Palestinian movement. On February 3, 1969, the PNC in Cairo officially appointed Arafat chairman of the PLO. Over the next four years, Arafat had become the commander in chief of the PLO's military branch, the Palestinian Revolutionary Forces, and the political leader of the organization. He based the PLO in Jordan.

In 1968 and 1969, the PLO functioned as a well-organized unofficial state within Jordan, with its uniformed soldiers acting as a police force and collecting their own taxes. In 1968, King Hussein of Jordan and the PLO signed an agreement by which the PLO agreed that its members would stop patrolling in uniform with guns, stop searching civilian vehicles, and act as Jordanian civilian citizens. The PLO did not comply with this agreement, however, and both attacks on civilians and clashes between Palestinians and Jordanian soldiers increased. By 1970, Hussein decided that the Palestinians threatened national security and ordered his army to evict them. This led to several months of violence, during which Syria aided the Palestinians and the United States aided Jordan. The events of Black September (including an attempt on Hussein's life), several airliner hijackings by the PFLP, and a declaration of martial law in Jordan culminated with the PLO agreeing to a cease-fire on September 24 and promising to leave the country.

Arafat now relocated the PLO to Beirut, Lebanon. There Palestinians moved into existing refugee settlements. The Lebanese government tried to restrict the PLO's movements, which led to tensions, but the Palestinians used their position to launch periodic attacks across the Israeli border. Lebanese Muslims and members of Kamal Jumblatt's progressive coalition supported the Palestinian cause, seeing the Palestinians as allies in their struggle against certain Christian factions who dominated the government and the Lebanese Forces (Maronite militias). The latter disliked the PLO presence and wanted to drive the Palestinians out by force.

During the early 1970s, Arafat and the various groups that comprised the PLO often came into conflict over the proper means of achieving the organization's goals. Although Arafat agreed that a certain amount of violence against Israel was necessary to accomplish the PLO's purposes, he believed that diplomacy and compromise were also key to gaining international support. After 1968, the more politically radical groups, such as the PFLP, the DFLP, and other smaller factions, strongly disagreed because it seemed apparent that the Arab countries could not defeat Israel militarily. Such groups gained notoriety for their airplane hijackings in the late 1960s and early 1970s, carried out in Europe and the Middle East. These attacks were intended to further efforts to destroy Israel and create a socialist secular Arab society in its stead. Arafat himself condemned overseas attacks because he believed that they hurt the PLO's international image.

When the radical Black September organization killed several Israeli athletes at the Olympic Games in Munich in 1972, Arafat promptly stated that the PLO was not responsible for the attacks. Arafat closed down the Black September organization in 1973, and in 1974, he ordered the PLO to restrict its violent attacks to Israel, the Gaza Strip, and the West Bank.

In 1974, the Arab Summit recognized the PLO as the sole representative of the Palestinian people. Arafat then appeared before the United Nations (UN) that same year as the official representative of the Palestinians. Speaking before the UN General Assembly, he condemned Zionism and said that the PLO would continue to operate as freedom fighters but also said that he wanted peace. This was the first time the international community had heard directly from the PLO, and many international observers praised Arafat and came to support the Palestinian cause. The UN granted the PLO observer status on November 22, 1974.

Also in 1974, the leaders of Fatah, in the guise of the PNC, created a Ten-Point Program that set forth the PLO's goals. This program called for a secular state in Israel and Palestine that would welcome both Jews and Arabs and provide all citizens equal rights regardless of religion, race, or gender. It also called for the creation of a Palestinian Authority (PA) on free Palestinian territory. Israel rejected the Ten-Point Program. Meanwhile, the radical guerrilla groups the PFLP and the PFLP-GC, which had earlier split from the PFLP, departed from the PLO in protest of its attempt to negotiate with Israel.

In 1975, the Lebanese civil war broke out. Israel pursued a strategy of support of the Lebanese Forces, the Maronite militias who opposed the Palestinians. The PLO and Fatah joined forces with the National Front, a more left-wing coalition of Muslims, Druze, and Christians. Syria intervened at first on behalf of Muslim forces but later came to the aid of the Maronites and in the 1980s also supported the Shia militias.

On January 12, 1976, the UN Security Council voted to grant the PLO the right to participate in Security Council debates. The PLO became a full member of the Arab League that same year.

During the late 1970s, PLO members continued to enter Lebanon and maintain positions in Beirut, from which they exchanged attacks with Israel. On July 24, 1981, the PLO and Israel agreed to a cease-fire within Lebanon and on the border between Lebanon and Israel. Arafat interpreted the cease-fire agreement literally and continued to allow the PLO to attack Israel from Jordan and the West Bank. The Israelis violated the cease-fire numerous times, bombing PLO targets in Beirut. That autumn, Israeli prime minister Menachem Begin and Defense Minister Ariel Sharon planned an invasion into Lebanon to occupy southern Lebanon and territory all the way up to Beirut, where they planned to destroy the PLO. Israeli troops invaded, occupied much of southern Lebanon, and rounded up much of the male population of the area. The UN passed a resolution demanding that Israel withdraw its troops, but the United States vetoed another resolution repeating this demand. The United States demanded that the PLO withdraw from Lebanon. Sharon ordered the bombing of West Beirut beginning on June 15. The UN once again demanded that Israel withdraw, but the United States again vetoed the resolution.

On August 12, 1982, the two sides agreed to another cease-fire in which both the PLO and Israel would leave Lebanon. As a result, about 15,000 Palestinian militants left Lebanon by September 1. The Israelis, however, claimed that PLO members were still hiding in Beirut and returned to the city on September 16, killing several hundred Palestinians, none of whom were known to be PLO members. Sharon resigned as defense minister after the Sabra and Shatila massacres, which were carried out by Lebanese Christian militias with Israeli foreknowledge and approval.

Arafat and many surviving PLO members spent most of the 1980s in Tunisia rebuilding the organization, which had been severely damaged by the fighting in Beirut. During this time, Iraq and Saudi Arabia donated substantial sums of money to the organization. But relations between the PLO and Israel remained intractably bad. The Israel Defense Forces (IDF) bombed the PLO headquarters in Tunis in 1985, an attack that killed 73 people.

In December 1987, the First Intifada broke out spontaneously in the West Bank and Gaza, surprising Israelis with its intensity. On November 15, 1988, the PLO officially declared the formation of the State of Palestine. The PLO claimed all of Palestine as defined by the former British Mandate. However, the PLO had decided to seek a two-state solution. That December Arafat spoke before the UN, promising to end terrorism and to recognize Israel in exchange for the Israeli withdrawal from the occupied territories, according to UN Security Council Resolution 242. This was a distinct change from the PLO's previous position of insisting on the destruction of Israel. The PNC symbolically elected Arafat president of the new Palestinian state on April 2, 1989.

Arafat and the Israelis began conducting peace negotiations at the Madrid Conference in 1991. Although the talks were temporarily set back when Arafat and the PLO supported Iraq in the 1991 Persian Gulf War, over the next two years the two parties held a number of secret discussions. These negotiations led to the 1993 Oslo Accords in which Israel agreed to Palestinian self-rule in the Gaza Strip and the West Bank and Arafat officially recognized the existence of the State of Israel. Despite the condemnation of many Palestinian nationalists, the peace process appeared to be progressing apace. Israeli troops withdrew from the Gaza Strip and Jericho in May 1994.

In 1994, the PLO established a Negotiations Affairs Department (NAD) in Gaza to implement the Interim Agreement. Mahmoud Abbas, then secretary general of the PLO Executive Committee, headed the NAD until April 2003, when the Palestinian Legislative Council chose him as the first prime minister of the PA. He was replaced by Saeb Erakat. The Gaza office of NAD handled Israeli affairs, agreements between Israel and Palestine, colonization, and refugees. It also kept careful track of Israeli expansion into Palestinian territory. The NAD also opened an office in Ramallah to handle the implementation of the Interim Agreement and prepare the Palestinian position for negotiations toward permanent status. The government of the United Kingdom began assisting the NAD with its preparation for permanent status talks in 1998.

In 1996, the PNC agreed to remove from the PLO charter all language calling for armed violence aimed at destroying Israel, and Arafat sent U.S. president Bill Clinton a letter listing language to be removed, although the PLO has dragged its feet on this. The organization claimed that it was waiting for the establishment of the Palestinian state, when it would replace the charter with a constitution.

Arafat was elected leader of the new PA in January 1996. The peace process began unraveling later that year, however, after rightist hard-liner Benjamin Netanyahu was elected prime minister of Israel. Netanyahu distrusted Arafat and condemned the PLO as a terrorist organization responsible for numerous suicide bombings on Israeli citizens. The accord collapsed completely in 2000 after Arafat and Israeli prime minister Ehud Barak failed to come to an agreement at a Camp David meeting facilitated by Clinton. After that, the Second (al-Aqsa) Intifada began when Palestinians, already experiencing the intractability of the Israeli government, saw Ariel Sharon lead security

forces onto the Haram al-Sharif. During that period, suicide bombings increased. These attacks were in some instances claimed by Islamic Jihad of Palestine (PIJ), Hamas sympathizers, and other groups. Arafat and the PLO disavowed any support for such attacks. But whether right or wrong, the Israeli media continued to state or suggest that Arafat clandestinely supported the work of the terrorists.

Arafat died on November 11, 2004. There was much dissension over the succession, but Abbas eventually came to represent the PLO's largest faction, Fatah. In December 2004, he called for an end to the violence associated with the Second Intifada that began in September 2000. In January 2005, he was elected president of the PA but has struggled to keep the PLO together and Fatah from losing its political and financial clout. In the January 2006 PA parliamentary elections, Abbas and Fatah were dealt a serious blow when Hamas captured a significant majority of seats. An even greater blow apparently came in June 2007 when Hamas seized control of Gaza.

Following the Hamas takeover of Gaza on June 14, Abbas dissolved the Hamas-led unity government and declared a state of emergency. On June 18, having been assured of European Union support, he dissolved the National Security Council and swore in an emergency Palestinian government. That same day, the United States ended its 15-month embargo on the PA and resumed aid in an effort to strengthen Abbas's government, which was now limited to the West Bank. On June 19, Abbas cut off all ties and dialogue with Hamas, pending the return of Gaza. In a further move to strengthen the perceived moderate Abbas, on July 1, Israel restored financial ties to the PA. Hamas, by contrast, remained largely isolated, although repeated Israeli military retribution against

Gaza for rocket attacks on Israeli territory, together with an Israeli economic blockade of Gaza, were the subject of international protests. In April 2011 in Cairo, and again in February 2012 in Doha, Fatah and Hamas representatives signed reconciliation agreements intended to restore Hamas membership in the PLO. They called for joint elections that would create a national unity government drawn from both Palestinian factions. By late 2013, such elections had still not taken place.

Abbas, effectively the acceptable face of the Palestinian cause, continued negotiations with Israel and the international community, invariably seeking to expand the scope of the PA's authority and operational independence. In January 2009, on the expiration of his term as president, Abbas unilaterally extended his tenure, initially by a year, then indefinitely. In late 2013, he remained president, though Hamas-controlled Gaza considered that his term had expired and refused to recognize his authority. Abbas had, however, succeeded in inching closer to winning international recognition for a Palestinian state. In November 2012, the UN General Assembly granted the PA nonobserver state status, meaning that Palestine could join treaties and specialized UN agencies, exercise jurisdiction over airspace and territorial waters, and pursue cases in the international criminal court. The UN also permitted the PA to use the designation "State of Palestine" in official communications.

Amy Hackney Blackwell

Further Reading

Abbas, Mahmoud. *Through Secret Channels: The Road to Oslo; Senior PLO Leader Abu Mazen's Revealing Story of the Negotiations with Israel*. Reading, UK: Garnet, 1997.

Aburish, Said K. *Arafat: From Defender to Dictator*. New York: Bloomsbury, 1998.

Baracskay, Daniel. *The Palestine Liberation Organization: Terrorism and Prospects for Peace in the Holy Land*. Santa Barbara, CA: Praeger, 2011.

Bunton, Martin. *The Palestinian-Israeli Conflict: A Very Short Introduction*. New York: Oxford University Press, 2013.

Chamberlin, Paul Thomas. *The Global Offensive: The United States, the Palestine Liberation Organization, and the Making of the Post-Cold War Order*. New York: Oxford University Press, 2012.

Cobban, Helena. *The Palestinian Liberation Organisation: People, Power, and Politics*. Cambridge: Cambridge University Press, 1984.

Gabriel, Richard. *Operation Peace for Galilee: The Israeli-PLO War in Lebanon*. New York: Farrar, Straus and Giroux, 1985.

Harms, Gregory, and Todd Ferry. *The Palestine-Israel Conflict: A Basic Introduction*. 3rd ed. London: Pluto, 2012.

Hart, Alan. *Arafat: A Political Biography*. Rev. ed. London: Sidgwick and Jackson, 1994.

Jamal, Amal. *The Palestinian National Movement: Politics of Contention, 1967–2005*. Bloomington: Indiana University Press, 2005.

Kimmerling, Baruch, and Josel S. Migdal. *The Palestinian People: A History*. Cambridge, MA: Harvard University Press, 2003.

Kushner, Arlene. *Disclosed: Inside the Palestinian Authority and the PLO*. Philadelphia: Pavilion, 2004.

Livingstone, Neil C., and David Haley. *Inside the PLO*. New York: William Morrow, 1990.

Norton, Augustus R. *The International Relations of the Palestine Liberation Organization*. Carbondale, IL: Southern Illinois University Press, 1989.

Pearlman, Wendy. *Violence, Nonviolence, and the Palestinian National Movement*. Cambridge: Cambridge University Press, 2011.

Rubin, Barry M. *Revolution until Victory? The Politics and History of the PLO*. Cambridge, MA: Harvard University Press, 1994.

Rubin, Barry M. *The Transformation of Palestinian Politics: From Revolution to State-Building*. Cambridge, MA: Harvard University Press, 1999.

Rubin, Barry, and Judith Colp Rubin. *Yasir Arafat: A Political Biography.* New York: Oxford University Press, 2003.

Schanzer, Jonathan. *State of Failure: Yasser Arafat, Mahmoud Abbas, and the Unmaking of the Palestinian State.* Basingstoke: Palgrave Macmillan, 2013.

Walker, Tony, and Andrew Gowers. *Arafat: The Biography.* London: Virgin Books, 2005.

Palestinian Authority

The Palestinian Authority (PA) is an interim self-governing entity authorized by the 1993 Oslo Accords and established in 1994 to govern what would be the Palestinian autonomous regions of the West Bank and the Gaza Strip and what Palestinians specified as a future autonomous state. The Oslo Accords were finalized after a series of secret meetings between Israel and the Palestine Liberation Organization (PLO). The accords scheduled incremental Israeli withdrawals from the designated territories as refined in ensuing agreements. Israel, as scheduled, withdrew from Jericho on May 13, 1994; the Gaza Strip on May 18, 1994; Janin on November 13, 1995; Tulkarem and Nablus on December 11, 1995; Qalqiliyya on December 16, 1995; Bethlehem on December 21, 1995; Ramallah on December 27, 1995; and 80 percent of Hebron on January 17, 1997.

The autonomous areas were chosen so that the PA would govern 91 percent of the Palestinian populace. The PA was given control over 85 percent of the Gaza Strip. (The Jewish settlements comprised the other 15 percent.) Prime Minister Ariel Sharon

Palestinian security forces loyal to Palestinian Authority President Mahmoud Abbas, left, stand guard in front of Hamas supporters during a demonstration at the entrance to the Palestinian Legislative Council in the West Bank in the West Bank town of Ramallah on June 14, 2006. (AP Photo/Kevin Frayer)

imposed an Israeli withdrawal from these settlements in August 2005 despite some governmental and popular opposition and in the absence of any agreement with the Palestinians. The PA was initially given control over 39.7 percent of the West Bank.

The Oslo Accords specified that the PA would have control over all civilian- and security-related issues in most of the urban areas of the autonomous regions, termed "Area A," but would have control over only civilian affairs in certain rural areas, termed "Area B." By 1997, the urban areas under the control of the PA included most of the major Arab population centers in the West Bank, excepting East Jerusalem. Israel retained control over all travel, civilian affairs, and security in "Area C"; all of the remaining disputed territories; all Israeli settlements and military installations and access to them in all of the autonomous regions; the Jordan Valley; connecting roads between Palestinian communities; and any common borders.

The PA's elected presidency is its highest-ranking political office. The Palestinian Legislative Council (PLC), representing the Gaza Strip and the West Bank, was originally composed of 88 elected members but now has 132. It elects a member from its ranks for the president to declare as prime minister, an office first created by the PLC in March 2003. The prime minister ostensibly reports to the president. Even though the president and prime minister share power, in theory at least the preponderance of power rests with the prime minister. The prime minister, with the approval of the PLC, chooses a cabinet that runs the PA's government agencies. As chief of the national security services, the prime minister also directs the PA's security forces. The president, as the head of state, represents the PA in negotiations with governmental entities apart from the PA.

The PA is headquartered in Ramallah and seats the PLC in Gaza City. Since the death of President Yasser Arafat in November 2004, the ability of the PA to govern has been challenged by various Palestinian subgroups, and the PA is also constrained by the Israeli government and military. This conflict was made clear following the January 2006 PLC elections, when Hamas won a majority of seats. A Hamas prime minister, Ismail Haniyeh, was then chosen to govern with the previously elected Fatah PA president, Mahmoud Abbas.

The PA regulates businesses within its borders and levies taxes and duties that are collected for it by Israel and then are distributed back to it by Israel. It is responsible for social services, education, and health care within the regions it governs and represents the Palestinians in all negotiations with Israel. The PA is also responsible for publicly denouncing, discouraging, and stopping any Palestinian terrorism against Israel. Attempts to carry out this mandate, however, have placed the PA at odds with groups within its own ranks.

Funding for the PA comes from the duties and taxes levied and distributed as well as in the form of aid from Western nations, Russia, and some Arab states. Most Western aid was cut off, however, after the 2006 election of a Hamas-oriented PLC. This meant that the PA could not in fact provide many of the educational, health care, and other social services under its mandate. Most of the PA budget is dedicated to paying its employees, who also went unpaid for months, especially its police and security agencies. The lack of sufficient indigenous sources of income and resources coupled with a history of corruption and patronage together with the freezing of donor funds left the PA with insufficient funds to meet its basic responsibilities. These gaps have been filled in part by groups such as Hamas, which although cut off from most sources of external funding and prevented by the Israelis from operating their normal charitable associations, still obtain in-country contributions and provide volunteer services, as from physicians or instructors who donate their time.

The Oslo Accords limit the PA to an official uniformed security force (police force) totaling 30,000 personnel. Although the PA officially claims a force under that number, external sources estimate the true size at 40,000–80,000 men. The force is also restricted to armored cars and a limited number of automatic weapons, but external estimates judge its capabilities to be much more powerful.

The unemployment rate and number of people living below the regional poverty level was substantial in the Palestinian autonomous regions before the creation of the PA. However, continued violence and curfews, the Israeli security fence, and strict Israeli border control have cost jobs within the region and prevented others from the region from entering Israel where they were historically employed as guest workers. In the mid-2000s the Israeli government cut back severely on the number of work permits issued to workers from the PA areas. In 2012, around 20,000 Palestinians were thought to be legally employed and a further 10,000 working illegally in the West Bank Israeli settlements; in Israel proper, around 60,000 had work permits and perhaps 20,000 more were there illegally as 'ghost workers.' These figures represented a substantial decline from earlier levels.

The Oslo Accords envisioned the withdrawal of Israel from the proposed autonomous regions and the transfer of administrative responsibilities to the PA during a five-year interim to be followed by a second phase that would have begun in 1999 and would develop a permanent solution to the problem. However, despite repeated final status agreements signed at the 2000 Camp David Summit and the 2001 Taba Summit and the 2003 Geneva Draft Permanent Status Agreement, an official peace agreement between Israel and the PA remains elusive.

The issues that remain are the same issues that existed before the PA, including the status of Jerusalem, the Palestinian right of return, recognition of the right of Israel to exist, security issues, economic issues, and borders. Actual negotiations over the status of Jerusalem were postponed, and in fact this issue has not yet been settled. The PA also remains committed to the creation of a Palestinian state with its capital in Jerusalem. The Oslo period was at first accompanied by more Israeli travel to Arab countries and the grassroots formations of cousins' clubs, or discussion groups for Palestinians and Israelis, and generally advanced the pro-peace faction within Israel and among the Palestinians. The sporadic violence and then suicide bombings from 1996 troubled many, but the spirit of Oslo did not truly break down until the Second (al-Aqsa) Intifada.

Following the signing of the Oslo Accords, Arafat immediately returned to the region from his exile in Tunisia and in 1994 appointed a 19-member interim PA until elections could be held. The elections were delayed for 18 months beyond the intended date. As with most events in the Middle East, the reasons for the delay depend upon one's perspective. The Israelis asserted that Arafat caused the delay so that he had time to regain control over the area, allowing him to control the election and select those who might run in it. The interim PA asserted that the delay was prompted by the need to develop an administrative system from scratch, the logistics of setting up an election, and Israeli intransigence in dealing with Arafat.

The elections for the presidency and the 88-member PLC occurred on January 20, 1996. Arafat was elected president of the PA, and his Fatah party was represented by 55 of the 88 PLC members in March 1996.

Additional areas of the West Bank were placed under PA control in 1997 as Israel continued its phased withdrawals. Israel agreed to additional withdrawals as part of the October 23, 1998, Wye River Agreement, but the continued failure of the PA to enforce the agreed-upon security provisions of the agreement caused the Israelis to halt their withdrawals. The agreement allowed the PA to open the Gaza International Airport in Rafah, although Israel maintained control over its security so that the facility could not be used to launch terrorist attacks or import weapons. The airport opened in November 1998 but was closed and then completely razed by Israel in December 2001 following the outbreak of the Second Intifada.

The signing of the Oslo Accords and the creation of the PA effectively ended the violence of the First Intifada (1987–1993). The Second Intifada began in September of 2000 after Israeli politician Sharon brought troops onto the Haram al-Sharif (Temple Mount). The intifada ended most of the discussions concerning the implementation of the Oslo Accords, for as the violence increased and suicide bombings became more prevalent, Israel responded by attacking PA infrastructure and facilities and reoccupying territory previously ceded to the PA. Israel also added to the tension by doubling the number of Jewish settlements in the West Bank between 1991 and 2001. Whether it was a valid reason or not, the violence of the intifada was used as the reason for the PA's delay of its scheduled 2001 PA presidential and legislative elections.

The PLC created the position of prime minister in March 2003 and named Abbas to the position, which he held from March to October 2003. Although considered a moderate, he was a longtime PLO associate of Arafat. Arafat saw the addition of a PA prime minister as weakening his position as PA president, and tension between the two seemed to escalate. By this point, both Israel and the United States had cut off all contact with Arafat and dealt only with Abbas, further isolating the PA president. A short lull in the cycle of Palestinian violence and Israeli reprisals soon ended, and Abbas resigned. Abbas's appointed successor, Ahmad Quray (Qurei), also battled with Arafat over the administration of the PA and the control of the PA security forces, but Arafat remained firmly in control of both the PLO and the PA.

Although he never formally assumed the title, Rawhi Fattuh, then PLC speaker of the House, became the interim PA president following Arafat's death on November 11, 2004. Fattuh assumed the duties of the office until Abbas, who had been elected PLO chairman after Arafat's death, was elected president of the PA on January 9, 2005, with 62.3 percent of the vote.

Although Abbas's attempts to reengage the U.S. Road Map to Peace proposal were challenged by most of the militant Palestinian groups, he and Israeli prime minister Sharon agreed in an early 2005 summit to suspend hostilities. This agreement effectively ended the Second Intifada and led to the March 2005 reestablishment of PA control of Jericho and a few northern West Bank towns over which Israel had reassumed control during the conflict.

While continuing to encourage new settlements in the West Bank and against the extremely vocal opposition of the Israeli settlers, Sharon began a unilateral withdrawal of all Israeli military and civilians from the Gaza Strip in August 2005. The withdrawal and razing of the settlements, completed on September 12, 2005, ceded control of all of Gaza to the PA. While the PA gained control of the territory and benefited from the appearance of having successfully negotiated a withdrawal on quite favorable terms to the PA, the jobs lost when Israeli farms and industries no longer provided employment drove more than 75 percent of the population of the Gaza Strip below the poverty line.

A pledge of $50 million and continued support of a free Palestinian state from the United States in May 2005 coupled with the Israeli withdrawal from Gaza led Abbas to set PLC elections for January 25, 2006. However, when Hamas did well in local elections (December 15, 2005), Abbas sought to no avail to postpone the PLC election.

Violence continued within Gaza and against Israel after the withdrawal. Abbas's power as PA president dissipated rapidly when Sharon experienced a debilitating stroke on January 4, 2006, that ended his premiership. The elections that Abbas had called but could not cancel led to a Hamas majority in the expanded 132-seat PLC. Although Abbas remained as PA president, his party's hold on the PA was weakened. Hamas selected Ismail Haniyeh as the new PA prime minister, and he formed a new PA government while Abbas remained as PA president. Israel's opposition to Hamas due to its previously stated refusal to recognize the right of Israel to exist caused the European Union (EU) and the United States to withhold their financial support that together totaled approximately $1 billion in 2005 alone. Some nations, including Canada, also terminated aid. Other nations did not terminate aid, but it remained frozen.

This aid withdrawal and the worsening unemployment situation exacerbated the PA's economic crisis and stoked tensions between Fatah and Hamas. The security and military situation drastically worsened after funds and political encouragement were received by some elements in Fatah who aimed to displace Hamas. Hamas operatives dug a tunnel from inside Gaza to an IDF border outpost inside Israeli territory and captured an Israeli soldier in June 2006, taking him back into Gaza. Israel responded by invading Gaza and arresting PA leaders, primarily members of Hamas.

The already-weak PA economic and security conditions worsened as the political friction between Fatah and Hamas grew and the potential for civil war seemed palpable. Abbas called for early parliamentary elections, which many Palestinians rejected as a gambit to undo the previous Hamas electoral victory. Instead, a truce was negotiated in Mecca between Fatah and Hamas representatives in February 2007.

On March 17, 2007, Abbas managed to put together a Palestinian unity government that included both Hamas and Fatah. In it, Hamas leader Ismail Haniyeh became prime minister. Despite the agreement, in May violence between Hamas and Fatah escalated. Then on June 14 in an unexpected move, Hamas fighters seized control of Gaza. In retaliation, Abbas dissolved the Hamas-led unity government and declared a state of emergency. On June 18, having been assured of EU support, Abbas dissolved the National Security Council and swore in an emergency Palestinian government. Concurrently, the United States ended its 15-month embargo on the PA and resumed aid to it in an effort to strengthen Abbas's government, which was now limited only to the West Bank. On June 19, Abbas cut off all ties and dialogue with Hamas, pending the return of Gaza. In a further move to strengthen the perceived moderate Abbas, Israel restored financial ties to the PA on July 1. The situation in

Gaza remained stalemated, with the Hamas authorities increasingly isolated economically and diplomatically. In April 2011 in Cairo, and again in February 2012 in Doha, Fatah and Hamas representatives signed reconciliation agreements intended to bring about joint elections that would create a national unity government drawn from both Palestinian factions. By late 2013, such elections had still not been held. Hamas rejected Abbas's insistence that all agreements he had made as PA president must be honored.

Abbas, as the acceptable face of the Palestinian cause, continued negotiations with Israel and the international community, invariably seeking to expand the scope of the PA's authority and operational independence. In March 2008, after Israel threatened retaliation against rocket attacks from Gaza, Abbas suspended peace talks with Israel. In January 2009, on the expiration of his term as president, Abbas unilaterally extended his tenure, initially by a year, then indefinitely. He continued high-profile diplomatic activities intended to bolster his quest for an independent Palestinian state, hosting a visit in May 2009 by Pope Benedict XVI, who endorsed this objective, and visiting sympathetic nations, including Canada, Bolivia, and Japan.

In late 2013, Abbas remained PA president, though Hamas-controlled Gaza steadfastly refused to recognize his authority. Even so, in his persona as the Palestinian people's representative, Abbas consistently protested against repeated and heavy-handed Israeli measures, including military incursions in February and March 2008, and again in the December 2008–January 2009 Operation CAST LEAD, massive airstrikes in March 2012 and in the November 2012 Operation PILLAR OF FIRE, and economic blockades, intended to retaliate against Hamas rocket and other attacks on Israel and prevent further such assaults.

Abbas, meanwhile, succeeded in inching closer to winning international recognition for a Palestinian state, on terms acceptable to the PA. The UN, the EU, and many nations sympathetic to the Palestinian cause—though not the United States—frequently spoke out publicly against Israel's continued construction of settlements in the West Bank and the continued Israeli repression of Palestinians, especially in Gaza and also in the West Bank. Increasing numbers of states accorded international recognition to the PA on a bilateral basis. In November 2012, the United Nations General Assembly granted the PA nonobserver state status, meaning that Palestine could join treaties and specialized UN agencies, exercise jurisdiction over airspace and territorial waters, and pursue cases in the international criminal court. The UN also permitted the PA to use the designation "State of Palestine" in official communications.

A few months after U.S. president Barack Obama began his second term of office, in July 2013, U.S. secretary of state John Kerry prevailed upon Abbas and Israel's prime minister Benyamin Netanyahu to resume direct talks, with the objective of reaching a complete settlement of all matters dividing the West Bank Palestinian Authority and Israel within nine months. Despite difficulties over new Israeli settlements, in November 2013, Abbas expressed faith that this timetable was attainable, anticipating that, at least for the West Bank based PA, full Palestinian statehood was a goal that could be realized in the foreseeable future. In early 2014, it remained uncertain whether such optimistic expectations would finally bear fruit or whether, like so many previous hopes for a permanent settlement, they would once again merely prove exercises in futility.

Richard M. Edwards

Further Reading

Abbas, Mahmoud. *Through Secret Channels: The Road to Oslo; Senior PLO Leader Abu Mazen's Revealing Story of the Negotiations with Israel*. Reading, UK: Garnet, 1997.

Ben-Eliezer, Uri. *Old Conflict, New War: Israel's Politics toward the Palestinians*. New York: Palgrave Macmillan, 2012.

Bröning, Michael. *The Politics of Change in Palestine: State-Building and Non-Violent Resistance*. London: Pluto, 2011.

Chamberlin, Paul Thomas. *The Global Offensive: The United States, the Palestine Liberation Organization, and the Making of the Post-Cold War Order*. New York: Oxford University Press, 2012.

Chomsky, Noam and Ilan Pappé. *Gaza in Crisis: Reflections on Israel's War against the Palestinians*. London: Hamish Hamilton, 2010.

Gelvin, James M. *The Israel-Palestine Conflict: One Hundred Years of War*. 3rd ed. Cambridge: Cambridge University Press, 2014.

Ghanem, Assad. *Palestinian Politics after Arafat: A Failed National Movement*. Bloomington: Indiana University Press, 2010.

Hall, John G. *Palestinian Authority: Creation of the Modern Middle East*. Langhorne, PA: Chelsea House, 2002.

Hammack, Philip L. *Narrative and the Politics of Identity: The Cultural Psychology of Israeli and Palestinian Youth*. New York: Oxford University Press, 2010.

Khalidi, Rashid. *Palestinian Identity: The Construction of Modern National Consciousness*. Rev. ed. New York: Columbia University Press, 2009.

Khalidi, Rashid. *The Iron Cage: The Story of the Palestinian Struggle for Statehood*. Boston, MA: Beacon Press, 2006.

Klein, Menachem. *The Shift: Israel/Palestine from Border Struggle to Ethnic Conflict*. Translated by Chaim Weitzman. New York: Columbia University Press, 2010.

Makdisi, Sari. *Palestine Inside Out: An Everyday Occupation*. New York: Norton, 2008.

Makovsky, David. *Making Peace with the PLO: The Rabin Government's Road to the Oslo Accord*. Boulder, CO: Westview, 1996.

Massad, Joseph. *The Persistence of the Palestinian Question: Essays on Zionism and the Palestinians*. New York: Routledge, 2006.

Meir, Litvak, ed. *Palestinian Collective Memory and National Identity*. New York: Palgrave Macmillan, 2009.

Pappé, Ilan. *A History of Modern Palestine: One Land, Two Peoples*. Cambridge: Cambridge University Press, 2003.

Parsons, Nigel Craig. *The Politics of the Palestinian Authority: From Oslo to Al-Aqsa*. 2nd ed. London: Routledge, 2012.

Schanzer, Jonathan. *Hamas vs. Fatah: The Struggle for Palestine*. New York: Palgrave Macmillan, 2008.

Swisher, Clayton E. *The Palestine Papers: The End of the Road?* London: Hesperus Press, 2011.

Zureik, Elia, David Lyon, and Yasmeen Abu-Laban, eds. *Surveillance and Control in Israel: Population, Territory, and Power*. New York: Routledge, 2011.

Persian Gulf War

A conflict between Iraq and an international coalition of 34 nations mandated by the United Nations (UN) and led by the United States. The Persian Gulf War was sparked by Iraq's August 2, 1990, invasion and subsequent occupation of Kuwait, which was met with immediate economic sanctions by the UN against Iraq. The war commenced on January 17, 1991, with a heavy aerial attack against key Iraqi assets, including its air force, antiaircraft facilities, and command, control, and communications centers. The ground war began on February 24. Declaring a cease-fire on February 27, President George H. W. Bush announced the liberation of Kuwait, and the war thus ended.

Relations between Iraq and Kuwait had been strained for some time. Despite improvement during the Iran-Iraq War (1980–1988), when Kuwait assisted Iraq

U.S. Army UH-60A Blackhawk helicopters and one AH-64A Apache helicopter, second from right, taking off during Operation DESERT SHIELD in August, 1990. (U.S. Department of Defense)

with loans and diplomatic support, relations worsened when Iraqi president Saddam Hussein, who had launched a costly reconstruction program, demanded that Kuwait forgive its share of Iraq's war debt and help with other payments. Also at issue was oil. As Hussein tried to increase the price of the commodity by slackening production within the Organization of Petroleum Exporting Countries (OPEC), Kuwait undercut his plans by increasing its own production. Kuwait's alleged slant-drilling into Iraqi oil fields also rankled Hussein. Meanwhile, Washington miscalculated Hussein's intentions and sent mixed signals as to its possible action.

Iraqi forces invaded Kuwait shortly after midnight on August 2, 1990. About 150,000 Iraqi soldiers with almost 2,000 tanks easily overwhelmed the unprepared and inexperienced Kuwaiti forces, which numbered only about 20,000 men. By dawn, Iraq had assumed control of Kuwait City, the capital,

and was soon in complete control of the small country.

The Iraqis initially posed as liberators, hoping to appeal to Kuwaiti democrats who opposed the ruling Sabah monarchy. When this claim attracted neither Kuwaiti nor international support, it was dropped. In place of the Sabahs, most of whom fled during the invasion, Iraq installed a puppet government.

The UN Security Council and the Arab League immediately condemned the Iraqi invasion and imposed an economic embargo that prohibited nearly all trade with Iraq. Iraq responded to the sanctions by formally annexing Kuwait on August 8, prompting the exiled Sabah family to call for a stronger international response to evict Iraqi forces from their homeland. In response, the UN passed a total of 12 resolutions condemning the invasion.

After consulting with U.S. secretary of defense Dick Cheney, King Fahd of Saudi

Arabia invited U.S. troops onto Saudi soil. The Americans and their West European allies were now concerned about the Iraqi threat to the Saudi oil fields. Other Arab countries, including Egypt, Syria, and the smaller states along the Persian Gulf, also joined the growing coalition, fearing that even if Iraq's conquests stopped at Kuwait, Iraq could still intimidate the rest of the region.

Beginning a week after the Iraqi takeover of Kuwait and continuing for several months, a large international force gathered in Saudi Arabia. The United States sent more than 500,000 troops, and more than 200,000 additional troops came from Saudi Arabia, the United Kingdom, France, Kuwait, Egypt, Syria, Senegal, Niger, Morocco, Bangladesh, Pakistan, the United Arab Emirates, Qatar, Oman, and Bahrain. Other countries, including Canada, Italy, Australia, Belgium, Denmark, Greece, Norway, Portugal, Spain, Czechoslovakia, New Zealand, the Netherlands, Poland, and South Korea, contributed ships, air forces, and medical units. Still other countries made other contributions. Turkey allowed air bases on its territory to be used by coalition planes, and Japan and Germany lent financial support.

On November 29, with coalition forces massing in Saudi Arabia and Iraq making no signs of retreat, the UN Security Council passed a resolution authorizing the use of "all necessary means" to force Iraq from Kuwait if Iraq remained in the country after January 15, 1991. The Iraqis flatly rejected the ultimatum. Soon after the vote, the United States agreed to a direct meeting between Secretary of State James Baker and Iraq's foreign minister, Tariq Aziz. The two sides met on January 9, 1991. Neither side offered to compromise. The United States underscored the ultimatum, and the Iraqis refused to comply with it, even threatening to attack Israel.

When the UN deadline of January 15 passed without an Iraqi withdrawal, the coalition forces had reached a strength of 700,000 troops. President Bush, in consultation with the other key leaders of the coalition, waited two days after the UN deadline before ordering the coalition to commence operations against Iraq. In the early morning hours of January 17, 1991, coalition forces began a massive U.S.-led air attack on Iraqi targets.

The air assault, which had been named Operation DESERT STORM, had three goals: to neutralize Iraqi air assets, to disrupt command and control, and to weaken ground forces in and around Kuwait. After five and a half weeks of intense bombing and more than 10,000 sorties by coalition planes, Iraq's forces were severely damaged.

In an attempt to pry the coalition apart, Iraq fired Scud missiles at both Saudi Arabia and Israel, which especially disrupted Israeli civilian life. Iraq could thus portray its Arab adversaries as fighting on the side of Israel. The strategy failed to split the coalition, in part because the Israeli government did not retaliate.

The ground war, code-named Operation DESERT SABRE, began at 8:00 p.m. on February 24 with a massive ground offensive. This was launched northward from northeastern Saudi Arabia into Kuwait and southern Iraq. The main U.S. armored thrust drove deep, some 120 miles into Iraq, and struck the Iraqi armored reserves from the rear. This maneuver surrounded Kuwait, encircling the Iraqi forces there and allowing coalition forces (mainly Arab) to move up the coast and take Kuwait City. Some Iraqi units resisted, but the coalition offensive advanced more quickly than anticipated. Thousands of Iraqi troops surrendered. Others deserted. Iraq then focused its efforts on withdrawing its elite units and sabotaging

Kuwaiti infrastructure and industry. Many oil wells were set on fire, creating huge oil lakes, thick black smoke, and other environmental damage. The coalition forces destroyed most of Iraq's elite Republican Guard units when they tried to make a stand south of Basra in southeastern Iraq.

On February 27, with the collapse of Iraqi resistance and the recapture of Kuwait, the coalition's stated goals had been achieved. President Bush declared a cease-fire, to go into effect on February 28. The land war had lasted precisely 100 hours. The cease-fire came shortly before coalition forces would have surrounded Iraqi forces. On March 2, the UN Security Council issued a resolution laying down the conditions for the cease-fire, which were accepted by Iraq in a meeting of military commanders on March 3. They agreed to pay reparations to Kuwait, reveal the location and extent of Iraqi stockpiles of chemical and biological weapons, and eliminate weapons of mass destruction (WMDs).

President Bush's decision to terminate the ground war so soon was criticized because it allowed the escape of a large amount of military equipment and personnel, which were later used to suppress the postwar rebellion of Shiite and Kurdish citizens. Bush asserted that the war had accomplished its mandate. More extensive aims, such as overthrowing the Iraqi government or destroying Iraqi forces, did not have the support of all coalition members. Most Arab members, for example, believed that the war was fought to restore one Arab country, not to destroy another.

In terms of casualty counts, the outcome of the Persian Gulf War was very one-sided. The number of Iraqi combat casualties is very much in dispute, and estimates range from 10,000 to 100,000 Iraqis killed. Western military experts now seem to agree that Iraq sustained between 20,000 and 35,000 casualties. Coalition losses were extremely light by comparison: 240 killed in action, 148 of whom were Americans. The number of coalition wounded totaled around 900, of whom 467 were Americans. In military terms, the campaign was clearly successful. Politically, however, the outcome of the war was more clouded. The end of the fighting left Hussein still in power with a large part of his combat capability intact.

James H. Willbanks

Further Reading

Allison, William Thomas. *The Gulf War, 1990–91*. New York: Palgrave Macmillan, 2012.

Atkinson, Rick. *Crusade: The Untold Story of the Persian Gulf War*. New York: Mariner Books, 1994.

De la Billière, Sir Peter. *Storm Command: A Personal Account of the Gulf War*. New York: HarperCollins, 1992.

Finlan, Alastair. *The Gulf War, 1991*. Oxford, UK: Osprey, 2004.

Gause, F. Gregory, III. *The International Relations of the Persian Gulf*. Cambridge: Cambridge University Press, 2009.

Gordon, Michael R., and Bernard E. Trainor. *The Generals' War*. Boston, MA: Little, Brown, 1995.

Khaled bin Sultan. *Desert Warrior: A Personal View of the Gulf War by the Joint Forces Commander*. New York: Perennial, 1996.

Long, Jerry M. *Saddam's War of Words: Politics, Religion, and the Iraqi Invasion of Kuwait*. Austin: University of Texas Press, 2004.

Marolda, Edward J., and Robert J. Schneller, Jr. *Shield and Sword: The United States Navy and the Persian Gulf War*. Annapolis, MD: Naval Institute Press, 2001.

Pollack, Kenneth M. *Arabs at War: Military Effectiveness, 1948–1991*. Lincoln: University of Nebraska Press, 2002.

Schwarzkopf, Norman H. *It Doesn't Take a Hero*. New York: Bantam, 1992.

Woods, Kevin M. *The Mother of All Battles: Saddam Hussein's Plans for the Persian Gulf*. Annapolis, MD: Naval Institute Press, 2008.

R

Rabin, Yitzhak

Born: March 1, 1922
Died: November 4, 1995

Israeli army general, diplomat, leader of the Labor Party, and prime minister of Israel (1974–1977 and 1992–1995). Born in Jerusalem on March 1, 1922, Yitzhak Rabin moved with his family to Tel Aviv the following year. He attended the Kadoori Agricultural High School, graduating in 1940. He then went to work at the Kibbutz Ramat Yochanan, where he joined the Palmach, an elite fighting unit of Haganah, the Jewish self-defense organization that ultimately became the Israel Defense Forces (IDF).

In 1944, Rabin was second-in-command of a Palmach battalion and fought against the British Mandate authorities. He was arrested by the British in June 1946 and spent six months in prison. He became chief operations officer of the Palmach in 1947.

Rabin spent the next 20 years fighting for Israel as a member of the IDF. During the 1948–1949 Israeli War of Independence he commanded the Harel Brigade and fought for Jerusalem. He participated in the armistice talks and served as a deputy to Yigal Allon.

During 1956–1959, Rabin headed the Northern Command. During 1959–1961, he was chief of operations, and during 1961–1964, he was deputy chief of staff of the IDF. On January 1, 1964, he became IDF chief of staff and held this position during the Six-Day War in 1967. Following the Israeli capture of the Old City of Jerusalem in the war, he was one of the first to visit the city, delivering what became a famous speech on the top of Mount Scopus at the Hebrew University.

On January 1, 1968, Rabin retired from the army and shortly thereafter was named Israeli ambassador to the United States. He held this position until the spring of 1973, when he returned to Israel and joined the Labor Party. He was elected to the Knesset (Israeli parliament) in December 1973. Prime Minister Golda Meir appointed Rabin to her cabinet as minister of labor in April 1974. Meir retired as prime minister in May 1974, and Rabin took her place on June 2.

As prime minister, Rabin concentrated on improving the economy, solving social problems, and strengthening the IDF. He also sought to improve relations with the United States, which played a key role in mediating disengagement agreements with Israel, Egypt, and Syria in 1974. Egypt and Israel signed an interim agreement in 1975. That same year Israel and the United States signed their first memorandum of understanding. The best-known event of Rabin's first term as prime minister was the July 3–4, 1976, rescue of hostages of Air France Flight 139 held at Entebbe, Uganda.

In March 1977, Rabin was forced to resign as prime minister following the revelation that his wife Leah held bank accounts in the United States, which was at that time against Israeli law. Menachem Begin replaced him, and Rabin was praised for his integrity and honesty in resigning.

Between 1977 and 1984, Rabin served in the Knesset as a member of the Labor

Yitzhak Rabin, Israeli army general, diplomat, leader of the Labor Party, and prime minister of Israel (1974–1977 and 1992–1995). (Israel Government Press Office)

Party and sat on the Foreign Affairs and Defense Committee. He published his memoirs, *Service Notebook*, in 1979. He served as minister of defense in the national unity governments between 1984 and 1990. In 1985, he proposed that IDF forces withdraw from Lebanon and establish a security zone to protect the settlements along the northern border of Israel.

In February 1992, Rabin was elected chairman of the Labor Party in its first nationwide primary. He led the party to victory in the June elections. He became prime minister for the second time that July. In an effort to achieve peace in the Middle East, he signed a joint Declaration of Principles with Palestine Liberation Organization (PLO) chairman Yasser Arafat, shaking hands with him on September

13, 1993, during the Oslo Peace Accords. This agreement created the Palestinian Authority (PA) and gave it some control over the West Bank and the Gaza Strip. Rabin, Arafat, and Shimon Peres shared the 1994 Nobel Peace Prize for their efforts to achieve peace. In 1995, Rabin continued his negotiations, signing an agreement with Arafat expanding Palestinian autonomy in the West Bank.

A number of ultraconservative Israelis believed that Rabin had betrayed the nation by negotiating with the Palestinians and giving away land they considered rightfully theirs. On November 4, 1995, right-wing extremist Yigal Amir shot Rabin after a peace rally in Kings of Israel Square, afterward renamed Yitzhak Rabin Square. Rabin died of his wounds soon afterward in Ichilov Hospital in Tel Aviv. November 4 has since become a national memorial day for Israelis. Numerous squares, streets, and public foundations have been named for Rabin, who is revered by many for his efforts on behalf of peace.

Amy Hackney Blackwell

Further Reading

Avner, Yehuda. *The Prime Ministers: An Intimate Narrative of Israeli Leadership*. New Milford, CT: Toby Press, 2010.

Freedman, Robert Owen, ed. *Israel under Rabin*. Boulder, CO: Westview, 1995.

Horovitz, David, ed. *Shalom, Friend: The Life and Legacy of Yitzhak Rabin*. New York: Newmarket Press, 1996.

Inbar, Efraim. *Rabin and Israel's National Security*. Baltimore, MD: Johns Hopkins University Press, 1999.

Kurzman, Dan. *Soldier of Peace: The Life of Yitzhak Rabin, 1922–1995*. New York: HarperCollins, 1998.

Makovsky, David. *Making Peace with the PLO: The Rabin Government's Road to the Oslo Accord*. Boulder, CO: Westview, 1996.

Rabin, Leah. *Rabin: Our Life, His Legacy.* New York: G. P. Putnam's Sons, 1997.

Rabin, Yitzhak. *The Rabin Memoirs.* Expanded ed. Berkeley: University of California Press, 1996.

Slater, Robert. *Rabin of Israel.* Rev. ed. New York: St. Martin's Press, 1993.

Tessler, Mark. *A History of the Israeli-Palestinian Conflict.* 2nd ed. Bloomington: Indiana University Press, 2009.

Vinitzky-Seroussi, Vered. *Yitzhak Rabin's Assassination and the Dilemmas of Commemoration.* Albany: State University of New York Press, 2009.

S

Sadat, Anwar

Egyptian nationalist leader, vice president (1966–1970), and president of Egypt (1970–1981). Born on December 25, 1918, in Mit Abu al-Kum, near Tala in the Minufiyya province of Egypt, Muhammad Anwar Sadat attended the Royal Egyptian Military Academy, from which he graduated in 1938 as a second lieutenant. Early on he supported the Misr al-Fatat (an Islamist youth party) and the Muslim Brotherhood. His first posting was in the Sudan, where he met fellow nationalist and future Egyptian president Gamal Abdel Nasser. Stemming from their mutual disdain of the continuing British influence over the Egyptian government, Sadat joined with Nasser in forming the secret organization that would eventually be called the Free Officers Movement, comprising young Egyptian military officers dedicated to ousting the British and replacing the government of King Farouk.

Sadat joined the organization in 1950 and helped Nasser plan the July 23, 1952, Free Officers' bloodless revolution against King Farouk. Farouk was forced to abdicate and departed Egypt on July 26. In February 1955 Nasser became prime minister, and seven months later he became president. Sadat, meanwhile, served loyally under Nasser, a trusted member of his government. In 1969, Colonel Sadat became vice president of Egypt. After Nasser's death in September 1970, Sadat became temporary president, and then was elected president by the National Assembly on October 7. This decision was later confirmed in a popular vote.

In domestic affairs, despite professing his adherence to Nasser's policies, Sadat soon began to move away from Nasser's Leftist positions. The new regime was not much more politically liberal than its predecessor, however, so dissenters had virtually no avenue to dispute the changes in direction. In 1976, Sadat ran unopposed for a second six-year term as president and was confirmed. The Egyptian economy had been adversely affected by Nasser's government takeover of large industries and corporations. Sadat now began a new economic policy intended to encourage joint investments by foreigners and Egyptians and attempted to privatize some industries, to encourage expansion of the private sector, and to win foreign investment from oil-rich Arab states, the United States, and other Western nations.

In foreign affairs, Sadat improved ties with the Arab Gulf states. This relationship had several intended and unintended effects, including growing legitimacy for and support given to Islamist groups in Egypt and aid granted to the Egyptian government. Many wealthy Gulf Arabs preferred to vacation in Egypt, where socially conservative mores were corruptible by riches. This trend came under criticism from the Islamist groups, however. The Camp David Accords largely ended this relationship when Egypt was ousted from the Arab League.

In his early years in power, Sadat sought to develop a common policy toward Israel. Libyan strongman Muammar Qaddafi earnestly sought an Egyptian–Syrian–Libyan federation, an agreement for which was signed in Damascus in August 1971. Warm

Anwar Sadat, president of Egypt from 1970 until his assassination in 1981. (U.S. Department of Defense)

relations with Libya were short-lived, however, and in April 1974, Cairo announced that it had discovered a plot to overthrow the Egyptian government and pointed to Qaddafi as the mastermind behind it.

When Sadat became president, Egypt's once robust relationship with the Soviet Union was already showing signs of serious strain. In fact, Nasser had been moving away from the Soviet Union at the time of his death. Part of the reason for this had been the failure of the Soviet Union, then preoccupied by supporting India during the latter's war with Pakistan, to sell advanced weapons systems to Egypt. On July 18, 1972, a frustrated Sadat ordered the expulsion of all Soviet military advisers and experts from Egypt, placing all their bases in the country under Egyptian control.

Meanwhile, Sadat did all he could to prepare Egypt for war, especially by increasing military training. He privately expressed the view to United Nations (UN) envoy Gunnar

Jarring that he was willing to recognize the State of Israel and even to sign a peace treaty with the Jewish state but that the precondition for this was the return of all territory conquered by Israel to Egypt and the Palestinians. Sadat feared that the recent situation of no war and no peace might endure indefinitely and that the world would ultimately come to accept this as a permanent situation, giving Israel de facto control over the annexed territories. Sadat believed that the only way to change this was for him to initiate a new war, which in turn would produce an international crisis that would force the world to deal with the situation once and for all.

Over a protracted period, Egyptian forces engaged the Israelis in low-level skirmishing across the Suez Canal. Then, on October 6, 1973 (Yom Kippur, the Jewish Day of Atonement), Sadat launched a massive cross-canal attack that caught the Israeli government and military completely by surprise, partly because of its timing. He had carefully coordinated his plans with Syria in order to oblige the Israelis to fight a two-front war. In the Yom Kippur War, Syrian forces simultaneously struck Israel in the north along the Golan Heights. The war ended with Israeli forces poised to achieve total victory. On the Golan Heights front, Israeli forces held fort during desperate fighting and then counterattacked deep into Syria. Against Egypt, they had rallied from early setbacks, crossed the canal, and were in position to drive on Cairo. However, the Egyptians had achieved a psychological victory with the initial Egyptian crossing of the canal. This and the relatively satisfactory cease-fire brokered by the United States and the Soviet Union earned Sadat great respect among his people and in the Arab world.

Painfully aware that only the United States could elicit any substantive concessions from Israel, Sadat completely severed relations with the Soviet Union in March 1976 and began working with the Americans toward a peace settlement with the Israelis. In a courageous move, on November 19, 1977, Sadat traveled to Jerusalem on a two-day visit, the first Arab leader to make an official trip to the Jewish state. He met with Prime Minister Menachem Begin and even addressed the Israeli Knesset. In September 1978, Sadat signed the Camp David Accords. This agreement and the peace treaty of March 1979 produced a comprehensive peace agreement with Israel. The accords were highly unpopular in the Arab world and rapidly became less popular in Egypt.

Although the Camp David Accords and the peace treaty of March 1979 were, in the long run, beneficial for Egypt, which with its larger army had borne the brunt of much of the previous three wars, many in the Arab world considered them a great betrayal and Sadat a traitor. In September 1981, his government cracked down on extremist Muslim organizations and also on many other non-Islamist and liberal opponents of the president, in the process arresting more than 1,600 people. Sadat's strong-arm tactics angered many in the Arab community and only exacerbated his problems, which included economic stagnation and charges that he had quashed dissident voices through force.

On October 6, 1981, Sadat was assassinated in Cairo while reviewing a military parade commemorating the Yom Kippur War. His assassins were radical Islamist army officers who belonged to the Islamic Jihad organization, which hoped to overthrow the government and had bitterly denounced Sadat's un-Islamic rule and failure to implement Islamic law, his peace overtures with Israel, and his suppression of dissidents. Hosni Mubarak succeeded Sadat in office.

Dallace W. Unger Jr., Spencer C. Tucker, and Sherifa Zuhur

Further Reading

Beattie, Kirk J. *Egypt during the Sadat Years*. New York: Palgrave Macmillan, 2000.

Cook, Steven A. *The Struggle for Egypt: From Nasser to Tahrir Square*. New York: Oxford University Press, 2011.

Finklestone, Joseph. *Anwar Sadat: Visionary Who Dared*. Portland, OR: Frank Cass, 1996.

Gardner, Lloyd C. *The Road to Tahrir Square: Egypt and the United States from the Rise of Nasser to the Fall of Mubarak*. New York: New Press, 2011.

Haykal, Muhammad Hasanayn. *Autumn of Fury: The Assassination of Sadat*. New York: Random House, 1983.

Hirst, David, and Irene Beeson. *Sadat*. London: Faber and Faber, 1981.

Hurwitz, Harry, and Yisrael Medad, eds. *Peace in the Making: The Menachem Begin-Anwar Sadat Personal Correspondence*. Jerusalem: Gefen Publishing, 2011.

Lippman, Thomas W. *Egypt after Nasser: Sadat, Peace, and the Mirage of Prosperity*. New York: Paragon House, 1989.

Osman, Tarek. *Egypt on the Brink: From Nasser to Mubarak*. New Haven, CT: Yale University Press, 2011.

Sadat, Anwar. *In Search of Identity: An Autobiography*. New York: Harper and Row, 1978.

Stein, Kenneth W. *Heroic Diplomacy: Kissinger, Sadat, Carter, Begin and the Quest for Arab-Israeli Peace*. New York: Routledge, 1999.

Waterbury, John. *The Egypt of Nasser and Sadat: The Political Economy of Two Regimes*. Princeton, NJ: Princeton University Press, 1983.

Saudi Arabia

Middle Eastern nation located on the Arabian Peninsula. The Kingdom of Saudi Arabia, founded in 1932, covers 756,981 square miles, nearly three times the area of the U.S. state of Texas. Saudi Arabia borders

King Abd al-Aziz al-Saud (Ibn Saud) of Saudi Arabia seated with others at a banquet. (Library of Congress)

on Jordan, Iraq, and Kuwait to the north; the Persian Gulf, Qatar, and United Arab Emirates to the east; Oman and Yemen to the south; and the Red Sea to the west.

Saudi Arabia has been dominated by its ruling family, the House of Saud, for all of its modern history. King Abd al-Aziz al-Saud, known as Ibn Saud, the founding monarch, ruled until his death in 1953. All succeeding kings have been his sons, of which he had 48. The House of Saud has historical ties to the descendants of Muhammad abd al-Wahhab, the founder of Wahhabism (a sect of Islam), and as a result Saudi Arabian law and society are based on the Hanbali school of Islamic law and Wahhabi interpretations. Indeed, the Koran serves as the basic constitution for Saudi Arabia.

The role of Ibn Saud in Saudi Arabia cannot be overstated. The state grew inexorably as a result of his domination of the Arabian

Peninsula in the early 20th century as the Ottoman Empire declined. After the end of World War I, he consolidated his position and became king in 1925. The realm was renamed the Kingdom of Saudi Arabia seven years later. The fortunes of the kingdom were transformed with the discovery of petroleum in the 1930s. The nation's vast oil reserves would bring with them trillions of dollars of revenue and turn the kingdom into one of the world's wealthiest nations. After the 1960s, at which point the influence of foreign oil companies was on the wane, Saudi Arabia's oil assets gave the kingdom a great deal of geopolitical clout as well.

Initially, U.S. oil companies (Chevron in particular) played the leading role in oil exploration and formed a partnership with the Saudi monarchy, paying royalties for the right to extract and ship Saudi oil. The importance of oil during World War II enhanced the Saudi-U.S. relationship, and in 1944 the Arab-American Oil Corporation (ARAMCO) was formed. President Franklin Roosevelt helped to cement the growing relationship when he met with Ibn Saud on February 14, 1945, aboard the heavy cruiser USS *Quincy*. The Saudi monarchy maintained close economic and strategic ties to the United States throughout the remainder of the century.

Nevertheless, the Israeli issue greatly complicated U.S.-Saudi relations. The Saudis firmly objected to the 1948 formation of Israel, opposed the displacement of Palestinian Arabs, and played a minor military role in the Israeli War of Independence (1948–1949). Opposition to Israel became a central theme of Saudi foreign policy, and as with other Arab nations, the Saudis refused to recognize Israel for the remainder of the 20th century. However, strong U.S. ties led Saudi diplomacy to depart significantly from that of the other leading Arab states. Because of the growing strategic importance of the Middle East and its oil reserves to Cold War geopolitics, both the United States and the Soviet Union sought increased influence in the region. The Soviets endorsed the rise of secular, socialist, Arab nationalist regimes in Egypt, Iraq, and Syria, and Soviet military assistance was crucial to these nations in their ongoing struggle with Israel. The United States countered these Soviet moves by tightening its links to the royal regimes in Iran and Saudi Arabia, which included vast arms sales.

In 1962, civil war broke out in Yemen when a nationalist faction supported by Egyptian president Gamal Abdel Nasser sought to overthrow the royal government there. Despite previous rivalries with the ruling house of Yemen, the Saudis gave financial support and military assistance to the Yemeni monarchy. Egypt and Saudi Arabia thus confronted each other directly in the conflict. The devoutly Muslim House of Saud opposed the rise of secular, socialist Arab nationalism and refused to tolerate the spread of Nasser's Pan-Arabism in the region. In addition, the respective affiliations of Egypt and Saudi Arabia with the Soviet Union and the United States turned the Yemeni civil war into a regional theater of Cold War confrontation.

The resounding victory of Israel in the June 1967 Six-Day War brought warmer relations between Saudi Arabia and the various Arab nationalist states, especially Egypt. As U.S. support for Israel increased, the Saudis sought to influence U.S. policy in favor of the Arabs. This conflict ultimately laid the foundation for the 1973 oil embargo. Saudi oil was largely controlled by U.S.-owned oil companies until the early 1970s. At that point, the House of Saud negotiated the gradual takeover of ARAMCO by Saudi interests. By 1973, the transfer of control

had begun. When Egypt and Syria attacked Israel in October 1973 prompting the Yom Kippur War, Saudi Arabia's King Faisal obtained U.S. president Richard M. Nixon's assurances of U.S. nonintervention.

The Israelis suffered severe reversals in the opening stages of the conflict, however, prompting Nixon to send U.S. military aid to Israel on October 19. The next day, working through the Organization of Petroleum Exporting Countries (OPEC), the Saudi government implemented an oil embargo directed mainly at the United States. The embargo hobbled the already weak U.S. economy, created inflationary pressures, and decimated the U.S. automobile and steel industries. U.S. fuel prices rose 40 percent during the five months of the crisis. The net result was a major economic recession coupled with high inflation (sometimes referred to as stagflation). Even after the embargo ended, oil prices remained high for the remainder of the decade.

Saudi Arabia emerged from the crisis as the clear leader of OPEC and with renewed respect in the Arab world. Massive increases in oil revenues (from $5 billion per year in 1972 to $119 billion per year in 1981) transformed Saudi Arabia into an affluent, cosmopolitan, urbanized society with generous government subsidies and programs for its citizens and no taxation. However, the House of Saud maintained strict control over Saudi society, culture, and law. Saudi Arabia remained an absolute monarchy until 1992, when the royal family promulgated the nation's basic law following the 1991 Persian Gulf War.

The U.S.-Saudi relationship eventually recovered and remained close. Indeed, Saudi Arabia often used its influence in OPEC to keep oil prices artificially low from the mid-1980s to the late 1990s. However, the Saudis continued to oppose the State of Israel.

Saudi relations with Egypt declined precipitously after the signing of the Camp David Accords between Israel and Egypt in 1978. The Saudis objected to any individual peace deals with Israel that did not settle the entire Arab-Israeli conflict and address the plight of the Palestinian Arabs and the refugees of the 1948–1949 war. In 1981, King Fahd proposed a peace plan based on a Palestinian state in the West Bank and the Gaza Strip, removal of Israeli settlements in those areas, and a plan to address the needs of Palestinian refugees. Indeed, Saudi Arabia became a primary source of economic aid for the Palestine Liberation Organization (PLO) after the Camp David Accords. While the PLO's support for Saddam Hussein during the Persian Gulf War of 1991 effectively curtailed Saudi financial support for Fatah, the regime in Riyadh did not change its position on a comprehensive peace and in 2002 proposed another comprehensive plan to which the Israeli government did not respond.

During the Persian Gulf War the Saudis took the unusual step of allowing some 500,000 troops to use its territory as the main staging area for a strike against Iraq, which had invaded and annexed Kuwait in August 1990. The decision caused a negative reaction among the ultraconservatives and morals police in Saudi Arabia, and consequently the king had to rein them in. The conservatives argued that the foreigners were defiling Islamic traditions and law. But the troop deployment was seen in Riyadh as a necessary evil of sorts, as Iraqi dictator Hussein could not be trusted to end his land grab in Kuwait.

After the September 11, 2001, terrorist attacks on the United States, which involved 15 Saudi Arabian nationals or citizens, U.S.-Saudi relations took a nosedive. The Saudis disapproved of the 2003 Iraq War and refused to allow their territory as a base of operations for the invasion. In August 2003, just five months after the war began, all remaining U.S. troops were withdrawn from the kingdom. During 2003–2005, a series of attacks by Al Qaeda on the Arabian Peninsula killed Saudis and Westerners. These included the bombing in May and November 2003 of two housing compounds for foreign workers in Saudi Arabia that resulted in many deaths (including Americans) and an attack on the U.S. consulate in Jeddah. Despite these developments, the Saudis repeatedly dedicated themselves to fighting the so-called war on terror, and the Saudi government continued to work with the Americans in the areas of counterterrorism and counterintelligence. Saudi efforts to suppress Al Qaeda were largely successful, but political instability in neighboring Yemen facilitated the ability of Al Qaeda elements opposed to the Saudi monarchy to find sanctuary there. In 2009, Saudi and Yemeni Al Qaeda forces merged to form Al Qaeda in the Arabian Peninsula (AQAP), launching numerous attacks on targets within Yemen, Saudi Arabia, and beyond, and demanding holy war against Israel. Paradoxically, however, from 2011 onward, the Saudis backed Al Qaeda insurgents fighting a civil war against Syrian president Bashar al-Assad's government, considering these less objectionable than the Shiite Hezbollah forces supporting him.

The Saudis also sought to resolve the Israeli-Palestinian conflict. At an Arab League meeting in Beirut in March 2002, Crown Prince Abdullah of Saudi Arabia put forward the Arab Peace Initiative, a comprehensive proposal for a permanent settlement. This called for complete Israeli withdrawal from the occupied territories, the creation of an independent Palestinian state with East Jerusalem as its capital, and a "just solution" to the problem of Palestinian refugees. In return, all Arab states would sign permanent peace treaties with Israel, recognizing its existence. The Arab League unanimously accepted this proposal, albeit with reservations on the part of some states, including Syria, on the right of the Palestinians to continue armed resistance. The Hamas-orchestrated Passover Massacre in Netanya, Israel, a suicide bombing in which 30 people died and 170 were injured, took place on March 27, the same day this initiative was announced. Abdullah and the Palestinian Authority (PA), which endorsed this plan, condemned the attack. Saudi Arabia provided massive economic assistance to the PA.

Meeting in March 2007 in Riyadh, hosted by Abdullah, now king of Saudi Arabia, the Arab League reaffirmed its commitment to this initiative. UN secretary general Ban Ki-moon and European Union foreign policy commissioner Xavier Solana, both of whom attended this meeting, also endorsed it, as did PA president Mahmoud Abbas, though the Hamas representative abstained. At the same gathering, Abdullah condemned the continuing U.S. and British occupation of Iraq and called for an end to the Israeli blockade of Hamas-controlled Gaza.

Little progress on the Arab Peace Initiative occurred during the first administration of U.S. president Barack Obama, but in July 2013, U.S. secretary of state John Kerry sought to revive it, persuading Israel and Palestine to reopen negotiations aimed at reaching a final settlement within nine months. The Arab League supported this initiative. By October 2013, however, Abdullah was expressing great frustration over the U.S. failure to move decisively to overturn President Bashar al-Assad's government in Syria, or to prevent Shiite Iran acquiring nuclear weapons that might threaten Sunni Saudi Arabia's internal stability and regional position. Given these preoccupations, facilitating an Israeli-Palestinian settlement slipped down to become only a second-rank priority for Saudi leaders. Shared concerns that the interim agreement on nuclear weapons that several other powers, including the United States, negotiated with Iran in late 2013 was inadequate and ineffective led Saudi Arabia and Israel to draw closer to each other in early 2014.

Robert S. Kiely

Further Reading

Al-Rasheed, Madawi. *A History of Saudi Arabia*. 2nd ed. Cambridge: Cambridge University Press, 2010.

Bronson, Rachel. *Thicker than Oil: America's Uneasy Partnership with Saudi Arabia*. New York: Oxford University Press, 2006.

Gardner, Lloyd C. *Three Kings: The Rise of an American Empire in the Middle East after World War II*. New York: New Press, 2009.

Hegghammer, Thomas. *Jihad in Saudi Arabia: Violence and Pan-Islamism since 1979*. Cambridge: Cambridge University Press, 2010.

Hertog, Steffen. *Princes, Brokers, and Bureaucrats: Oil and the State in Saudi Arabia*. Ithaca, NY: Cornell University Press, 2010.

Hourani, Albert, and Malise Ruthven. *A History of the Arab Peoples*. 2nd ed. Cambridge, MA: Harvard University Press, 2010.

House, Karen Elliott. *On Saudi Arabia: Its People, Past, Religion, Fault Lines—And Future*. New York: Knopf, 2012.

Lacey, Robert. *Inside the Kingdom: Kings, Clerics, Modernists, Terrorists, and the Struggle for Saudi Arabia*. New York: Viking, 2009.

Lippman, Thomas W. *Saudi Arabia on the Edge: The Uncertain Future of an American Ally*. Washington, DC: Potomac Books, 2012.

Schwartz, Stephen. *The Two Faces of Islam: The House of Sa'ud from Tradition to Terror*. New York: Doubleday, 2002.

Weston, Mark. *Prophets and Princes: Saudi Arabia from Muhammad to the Present*. New York: Wiley, 2008.

Wynbrandt, James. *A Brief History of Saudi Arabia*. 2nd ed. New York: Checkmark Books, 2010.

Zuhur, Sherifa. *Saudi Arabia: Islamic Threat, Political Reform and the Global War on Terror*. Carlisle Barracks, PA: Strategic Studies Institute, 2005.

Sharon, Ariel

Born: February 27, 1928
Died: January 11, 2014

Israeli army general, politician, and prime minister (2001–2006). Ariel Sharon was born as Ariel Scheinermann (also known by the diminutive Arik) on February 27, 1928, in Kfar Malal, Palestine, to Russian immigrants. In 1942, at age 14, he joined the Gadna, the paramilitary youth organization of the Haganah, the Jewish defense force that protected kibbutzim (collective-farming settlements) from Arab attacks.

Sharon commanded an infantry company in the Alexandroni Brigade during the Israeli War of Independence (1948–1949); while engaged in an effort to relieve the besieged Jewish population of Jerusalem during the Second Battle of Latrun, he was severely wounded by Jordanian forces. Following the war he founded and commanded a special commando unit (Unit 101) that specialized in reconnaissance, intelligence gathering, and retaliatory raids designed to punish and deter Palestinian and Arab protagonists while enhancing Israeli morale.

Sharon was criticized for targeting both Arab soldiers and noncombatants and condemned for the killing of 69 civilians, half of whom were women and children, during a raid on the West Bank village of Qibya in

Israeli prime minister Ariel Sharon pauses during a news conference in his Jerusalem office on May 16, 2004. (AP Photo/Oded Balilty, File)

the fall of 1953. In an effort to end the criticism, in 1954, Unit 101 was merged into the 202nd Paratrooper Brigade. However, it continued to attack military and civilian targets, including the Kalkiliya police station raid in October 1956.

During the 1956 Suez Crisis, Sharon commanded the 202nd Brigade in the Israeli invasion of the Sinai Peninsula, capturing the strategically important Mitla Pass at the onset. Later he received heavy criticism for capturing the pass rather than merely holding the ground east of it—taking over the pass had claimed 38 Israeli lives. This incident hindered Sharon's military advancement during the next several years.

After studying at the British Staff College in Camberley, England, in 1957, Sharon commanded an infantry brigade and then the Israeli Army Infantry School. In 1962, he earned his bachelor of law degree from the Hebrew University of Jerusalem. He was appointed chief of staff of the Northern Command in 1964 and then in 1966 headed the Israel Defense Forces (IDF) Training Department.

Sharon was promoted to major general just before the 1967 Six-Day War, when forces under his command again took the Mitla Pass. He assumed leadership of the Southern Command in 1969. He retired from the IDF in June 1972 only to be recalled to command the armored division that crossed the Suez Canal into Egypt at the end of the 1973 Yom Kippur War. His direction of that crossing, and the subsequent encirclement of Egyptian forces, is widely considered one of the masterpieces of tactical command in modern mobile warfare.

Sharon helped found the Likud Party in September 1973 and was elected to the Knesset in December 1973. He resigned in 1975 to serve as security adviser to Prime Minister Yitzhak Rabin until 1977 and then

became minister of agriculture in Likud prime minster Menachem Begin's first government (1977–1981). In this position Sharon actively promoted the construction of Jewish settlements in the occupied Arab territories. In June 1981, he became Begin's minister of defense, and in this position he designed and carried out Israel's 1982 invasion of Lebanon, known as Operation PEACE FOR GALILEE because the ostensible intent was to force the Palestine Liberation Organization's (PLO) Katyusha rockets out of the range of Israel's northern border and to destroy the terrorist infrastructure there. Sharon and Begin deliberately expanded the invasion to include a drive against Beirut. Although the PLO was driven from Lebanon, the invasion intensified the Lebanese civil war, allowing Syria to become entrenched in the politics of that country. The Israeli presence in force lasted three years (a limited Israeli force remained until 2000) and resulted in such a high number of Palestinian civilian deaths that worldwide public opinion turned against Israel. Following the September 1982 massacre of Palestinians at the Sabra and Shatila refugee camps by Israel's Lebanese Christian Phalangist allies, Sharon was found to be indirectly responsible for failing to provide adequate protection for the refugees and thus resigned as Begin's minister of defense. This event overshadowed Sharon's diplomatic rapprochement with a number of African nations and his role in developing the first strategic cooperation agreement with the United States (1981), Operation MOSES (1984), and a free trade agreement with the United States (1985).

Sharon served in various Israeli governments as a minister without portfolio (1983–1984), minister of industry and trade (1984–1990), and minister of construction and housing and chairman of the ministerial committee on immigration and absorption (1990–1992). The latter post allowed him to double the number of Jewish settlements throughout the West Bank and the Gaza Strip during his tenure in office. He hoped that these settlements would not only provide a strategic buffer for Israel proper but would also reduce the possibility of the return of these territories (Judea and Samaria) to Palestinian Arabs.

Sharon then served on the Knesset's Foreign Affairs and Defense Committee (1992–1996) and as minister of national infrastructure (1996–1998) under Likud prime minister Benjamin Netanyahu. As foreign minister (1998–1999), Sharon led Israel's permanent status negotiations with the Palestinian Authority (PA) and sought to promote long-term solutions to the region's water disputes and inadequacies.

Sharon assumed the leadership of the Likud Party after Ehud Barak's victory in the general elections of May 1999 led to the resignation of Prime Minister Netanyahu. The failure of Barak's land-for-peace initiative at the Camp David Summit in 2000 coupled with the collapse of his governing coalition and the eruption of Palestinian violence led to Barak's defeat by Sharon in the general election of February 2001, even though much of the civil violence was precipitated by Sharon's visit to the Temple Mount on September 28, 2000. The ensuing violence was known as the Second (al-Aqsa) Intifada (2000–2004).

Palestinians charged that as prime minister, Sharon pursued a policy of confrontation and nonnegotiation. On July 2004, he also angered the French government when he called for French Jews to emigrate for Israel following an upswing in anti-Semitic incidents in France. With 600,000 Jews, France had the largest Jewish population after the United States and Israel.

In 2004, Sharon began a bold policy of disengagement, or unilateral withdrawal, from the Gaza Strip, a policy opposed by his own Likud Party but supported by the Labor Party, the U.S. government, and many European nations. In January 2005, Labor Party leader Shimon Peres accepted the position of vice premier in Sharon's unity government that included members of Likud, Labor, Meimad, and United Torah Judaism. Sharon completed the withdrawal from Gaza of all Israeli settlers on August 30, 2005, and the destruction of all Israeli settlements and the complete withdrawal of the Israeli military on September 11, 2005.

Sharon narrowly defeated a challenge to his leadership of Likud by Netanyahu on September 27, 2005, and then on November 21, 2005, resigned his Likud position, dissolved parliament, formed a new center-right party known as Kadima (Forward), and set new elections for March 2006. On December 18, 2005, Sharon was hospitalized for what was thought to be a minor ischemic stroke and shortly thereafter was released anticipating surgery to repair a newly discovered hole in the atrial septum of his heart. He suffered a massive cerebral hemorrhage at his Negev ranch (Havat Hashikmim) on January 4, 2006, before the surgery could be accomplished. He underwent several brain surgeries at Jerusalem's Hadassah Hospital, but for eight years remained in a persistent vegetative state with little potential for the recovery of cognitive function, finally dying of heart failure on January 11, 2014. On April 11, 2006, the Israeli cabinet declared Sharon incapacitated and ended his prime ministership three days later, naming Ehud Olmert as interim prime minister, a position made official after Kadima won the most Knesset seats in the national election. Perhaps the most controversial of Sharon's projects as prime minister was a security wall designed to separate and secure Israel proper from territory to be ceded to the Palestinians.

Richard M. Edwards

Further Reading

Avner, Yehuda. *The Prime Ministers: An Intimate Narrative of Israeli Leadership*. New Milford, CT: Toby Press, 2010.

Bloom, Gadi, and Nir Hefez. *Ariel Sharon: A Life*. Translated by Mitch Ginsbury. New York: Random House, 2006.

Finkelstein, Norman H. *Ariel Sharon*. Minneapolis, MN: First Avenue Editions, 2005.

Gelvin, James L. *The Israel-Palestine Conflict: One Hundred Years of War*. 3rd ed. New York: Cambridge University Press, 2014.

Kimmerling, Baruch. *Politicide: Ariel Sharon's War against the Palestinians*. London: Verso, 2003.

Matthews, Mark. *The Lost Years: Sharon, Bush, and Failure in the Middle East*. New York: Nation Books, 2007.

Miller, Anita, Jordan Miller, and Sigalit Zetouni. *Sharon: Israel's Warrior-Politician*. Chicago: Academy Chicago Publishers, 2002.

Sharon, Ariel, and David Chanoff. *Warrior: An Autobiography*. 2nd ed. New York: Simon and Schuster, 2001.

Sharon, Gilad. *Sharon: The Life of a Leader*. New York: Harper, 2011.

Six-Day War

By May 1967, long-simmering tensions between Israel and its Arab neighbors brought the Middle East to the brink of yet another war, known as the Six-Day War. While Israel's Arab neighbors still clamored for its destruction and refused to recognize it as a sovereign state because of the occupation of the West Bank and the Gaza Strip and the dispossession of the Palestinians, military setbacks in 1948 and 1956 had left even the most belligerent Arab leaders reluctant to directly engage Israel in a contest of force. Instead, they allowed the conflict to proceed via low-intensity state-sponsored terrorist attacks against Israel. Yasser Arafat's Palestinian Fatah movement led the way. Operating from Syria's Golan Heights, Fatah and other insurgents staged daily attacks against Israeli farmers living in the north.

For years Israel managed the undeclared war on a retaliatory basis, staging its own overt and covert counterstrikes on guerrilla camps and villages in the Golan Heights and in Jordan. An Arab attempt to divert the flow of the Jordan River and seriously reduce Israel's water supply resulted in a series of Israel Defense Forces (IDF) attacks against the diversion sites in Syria in 1965.

On November 13, 1966, the IDF launched a large-scale attack against Es Samu in Jordan, a Palestinian refugee village that the Israelis believed was a base for Syrian terrorists. On April 7, 1967, a major aerial battle over the Golan Heights resulted in the downing of six Syrian MiG-21s. The ongoing cycle of strikes back and forth across the border seemingly had become institutionalized by the late spring of 1967.

With the United States heavily engaged in Vietnam, the leaders of the Soviet Union saw an opportunity to alter the balance of power in the Middle East to favor their own client states, including Egypt and Syria. On May 13, 1967, the Soviets provided the Egyptians an intelligence report falsely indicating that Israeli forces were building up along the Syrian border. The motivation behind the Soviet disinformation campaign also may have been an attempt to create problems for West Germany, then a strong supporter of Israel.

Egyptian president Gamal Abdel Nasser, mindful of the Israeli attack 11 years earlier and fearful of a future attack but also unrealistically hoping to get the best of Israel,

Israeli Commander Motta Gur and his troops survey Jerusalem's Old City before launching their attack during the Six Day War in June, 1967. (AP Photo/Government Press Office)

announced that Egypt would stand alongside Syria in the present crisis. Israel's protestations that the Soviet report was untrue fell on deaf ears, as there was little reason for the Egyptians to believe the Israelis. Politically, Nasser sought to exploit the situation as much as his Soviet sponsors, and he would not allow the opportunity to pass. Scholars disagree over whether Nasser actually intended to go to war. Most believe that he thought he could bluff his way through the crisis without actual recourse to arms, extricating himself diplomatically.

Nasser met with members of the Arab press and proposed closing the Strait of Tiran to Israeli shipping, a step that would severely disrupt the Israeli economy. Nasser certainly should have known that Israel, which used the straits as its primary access to the Arabian Sea and the Far East, could not allow it to be closed and would be forced to react militarily. Nasser probably assumed that the United States would refuse

to support Israel and that the Soviet Union in turn would support Egypt and its allies.

Initially, Nasser's gambit appears to have been as much bluff as substance. If his threat to close the straits forced Israel to withdraw its allegedly mounting forces along the Syrian border, he could emerge as a regional hero without even risking a military confrontation. If the Israelis did not react, he could close the straits and force Israel to take the next step, in which case he still could play the part of hero and protector of the Arab world. Nasser's options, however, disappeared on May 22 when Egyptian minister of defense Field Marshal Abdel Hakim Amer, acting under the president's orders, directed Egyptian forces to close the Strait of Tiran the next day. Knowing full well that Israel would have to go to war to reopen the straits, Nasser issued orders for the Egyptian military to prepare for war. Any negotiation or compromise over the situation alleged to be developing along the Syrian border was now moot.

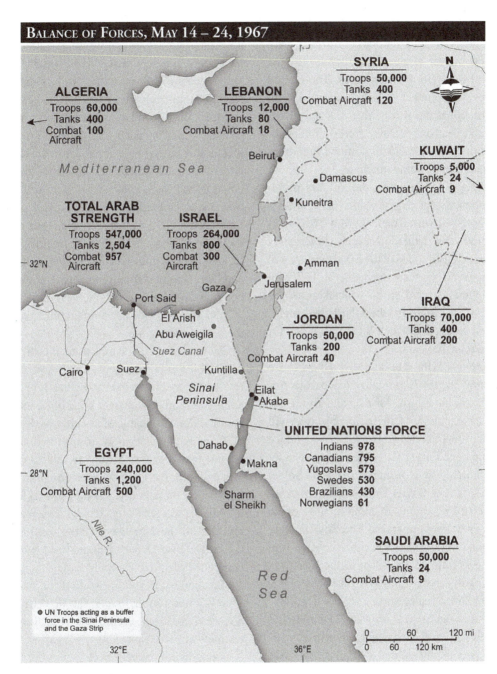

BALANCE OF FORCES, MAY 14 – 24, 1967

ALGERIA
Troops 60,000
Tanks 400
Combat 100
Aircraft

LEBANON
Troops 12,000
Tanks 80
Combat Aircraft 18

SYRIA
Troops 50,000
Tanks 400
Combat Aircraft 120

N

Mediterranean Sea

Beirut

Damascus

Kuneitra

KUWAIT
Troops 5,000
Tanks 24
Combat Aircraft 9

TOTAL ARAB STRENGTH
Troops 547,000
Tanks 2,504
Combat 957
Aircraft

ISRAEL
Troops 264,000
Tanks 800
Combat 300
Aircraft

Amman

32°N

Gaza

Jerusalem

Port Said

El Arish

Abu Aweigila

Suez Canal

Cairo   Suez

Kuntilla

Sinai Peninsula

Eilat
Akaba

JORDAN
Troops 50,000
Tanks 200
Combat Aircraft 40

IRAQ
Troops 70,000
Tanks 400
Combat Aircraft 200

EGYPT
Troops 240,000
Tanks 1,200
Combat Aircraft 500

28°N

Dahab

Makna

Sharm
el Sheikh

UNITED NATIONS FORCE
Indians 978
Canadians 795
Yugoslavs 579
Swedes 530
Brazilians 430
Norwegians 61

Nile R.

Red Sea

SAUDI ARABIA
Troops 50,000
Tanks 24
Combat Aircraft 9

● UN Troops acting as a buffer
force in the Sinai Peninsula
and the Gaza Strip

0   60   120 mi
0   60   120 km

32°E   36°E

Map of the balance of forces from May 14 to May 24, 1967, in the Arab-Israeli Wars.

Israel, meanwhile, continued to maintain its innocence regarding affairs with Syria but simultaneously signaled its determination to keep open the Strait of Tiran. Hoping to find an international solution to the crisis, Israel sent Foreign Minister Abba Eban to Washington on May 26. President Lyndon B. Johnson, however, had little to offer. On the one hand, Johnson steadfastly refused to assist Israel if it initiated hostilities. On the other hand, the U.S. promise to look for a coalition of international partners to help in keeping the straits open offered only the remotest possibility of success. The United States supported a British proposal for an international maritime force, but only Britain and the Netherlands offered to contribute ships to it. Israel's diplomatic initiatives appeared to be going nowhere.

In Egypt, meanwhile, the military mobilizations swept Nasser and his generals closer to war with Israel. On May 16, Nasser ordered the United Nations Emergency Force (UNEF) to leave the Sinai, and United Nations (UN) secretary general U Thant complied. Formed at the conclusion of the Suez Crisis in 1956, the UNEF had maintained a relatively demilitarized Sinai for more than 10 years.

Jordan's King Hussein arrived in Cairo on May 30, 1967, to finalize a tripartite alliance among Egypt, Jordan, and Syria. As Nasser declared, "Our basic objective will be the destruction of Israel." The alliance strengthened Egypt's position, but Nasser encountered new obstacles from his Soviet sponsors. The Soviet Union, having first set the chain of events in motion, now urged Nasser to show restraint. The Soviets were responding to a direct hotline message sent to the Kremlin by President Johnson on May 26. In a discussion similar to that between the Israeli ambassador and the Johnson administration, the Soviets on May 27 insisted to the Egyptians that they not strike first.

Nasser countered that a surprise first strike by Israel could neutralize Egypt's numerical superiority. The Soviets remained firm. Despite having Israel surrounded—Syria to the north, Jordan to the east, and Egypt to the south—and outnumbered, Egypt and its allies would have to wait for Israel to initiate hostilities. Meanwhile, other Arab states, including Iraq, Algeria, and Sudan, began mobilizing.

Egypt and Israel both subsequently played a waiting game in which Egypt appeared to have the advantage. Each day brought the Israeli economy closer to the brink of disaster. The mobilization for war alone had a catastrophic impact on Israel's economy, which ground to a near halt as all males between the ages of 16 and 55 entered active service. Israel recognized that the waiting game could defeat the country even more readily than a war. Unlike Israel's economy, that of Egypt remained unaffected by the closing of the Strait of Tiran. Nonetheless, the prospect of war was destabilizing to Egypt, whose economy was in difficult times with peasant complaints, riots, and inconclusive reforms. A war, if it proved disastrous, could mean the end of the regime.

On June 2, 1967, Israel tried the diplomatic route one final time, sending a special envoy to meet again with the Johnson administration. The distant hope of an international flotilla capable of keeping the Strait of Tiran open had by now disappeared altogether, with Japan and Canada reluctant to join and with the United States unwilling to take action unilaterally. Perhaps to reassure its Middle Eastern ally, the United States revealed to the Israeli envoy the results of a U.S. Defense Department analysis, which concluded that Israel could defeat Egypt, Jordan, and Syria within two to three weeks even if it allowed them to strike first. Israel, however, could not continue to wait for its enemies to strike first.

Following a heated exchange with his advisers on June 4, Israeli prime minister Levi Eshkol finally authorized a preemptive strike against Egypt despite the absence of U.S. support for such an action. For weeks Egypt had moved large numbers of armored units into the Sinai Peninsula in preparation for a clash with Israel. Israeli defense minister Moshe Dayan and IDF chief of staff

Yitzhak Rabin, however, planned to bypass Egypt's armor and strike instead at its air force. If Israel could neutralize or even seriously degrade Egyptian airpower, Dayan and Rabin were confident that Israel would prevail in the Sinai.

The Egyptian army had a nominal strength of 150,000 men, but more than 50,000 of its best troops were tied down in the civil war in Yemen. Nasser must have realized the impact of this and, for that reason, probably did not plan to enter into a war. The IDF had a core force of 50,000 highly trained troops plus more than 200,000 mobilized reservists. The Israeli air force (IAF) had only about 200 combat aircraft against 420 Egyptian planes, mostly relatively modern Soviet models. The IAF's chief advantage lay in its highly trained and efficient ground crews' ability to turn their aircraft around very quickly after each sortie, allowing each IAF aircraft to launch up to four times per day as opposed to the one or two sorties per day on average for aircraft in the Arab air forces.

At dawn on the morning of June 5, 180 Israeli aircraft launched against targets in Egypt and the Sinai. Coming in low and out of the sun to avoid Egyptian radar and visual detection, the Israeli strike force caught the Egyptians by surprise. Trapped on the ground when the IAF began to bomb and strafe the airfields, Egyptian aircraft were sitting ducks. Within minutes, all of Egypt's airfields were under attack. By noon, Egypt had lost more than 300 aircraft and 100 pilots. The Israelis lost only 19 aircraft.

The loss of Egypt's air force had an immediate and dramatic impact on the balance of power. The Egyptian forces in the Sinai consisted of some 100,000 troops, more than 900 tanks, 1,100 armored personnel carriers, and 1,000 artillery pieces, all organized into seven divisions. The IDF fielded some

70,000 troops and 700 tanks organized into three armored divisions under the IDF's Southern Command. Although Egypt outnumbered the Israelis on the ground, the absence of air support left Egyptian armor extremely vulnerable to Israeli attacks from above. Egypt suffered tremendous losses. When the IDF armored division under Major General Ariel Sharon broke through at Abu Ageila, Egypt's Marshal Amer ordered a general withdrawal, but the damage was already done. Israel thoroughly routed the Egyptians. By the end of the fighting in the Sinai, Egypt had lost 80 percent of its military equipment and 11,500 troops killed, 20,000 wounded, and 5,500 captured. The IDF had, by contrast, lost only 338 troops.

The war might have ended with Egypt losing the Sinai Peninsula and the Gaza Strip were it not for the critical lack of communications between Egypt and Jordan. Shortly after the surprise attack on the Egyptian airfields, Israel notified Jordan's King Hussein that its conflict lay with Egypt and that it had no interest in Jordan so long as Hussein kept his forces out of the fray. Simultaneously, however, Hussein received Egyptian state-run radio broadcasts claiming staggering victories and predicting the end of the Israeli nation. Hussein decided that the Israeli communiqué was a desperate ploy and ordered his forces to attack the Israeli-held West Jerusalem. Only then did Nasser admit to his ally what actually was occurring in the Sinai. By then it was too late for Hussein to withdraw from the conflict.

Israeli prime minister Eshkol ordered the IDF to attack on June 6 to seize all of Jerusalem, including the Old City, and force the Jordanian military completely out of the West Bank. The Jordanian army had 55,000 troops and 300 Western-built tanks, organized into 11 brigades. The Jordanian air force, however, had only 20 relatively obsolescent British aircraft. IDF's Central Command had only five brigades.

Israeli air superiority was decisive once more. Within days Israel successfully pushed the Jordanian forces back across the Jordan River. Israeli paratroopers entered the Old City of Jerusalem on June 7. The defeat was a staggering blow to Jordan, with almost 7,000 dead and more than 12,000 wounded; the Israeli deaths were only about 300. King Hussein called upon Nasser for help, but the Egyptian president, his military machine little more than broken and twisted wreckage, could offer little assistance. Nasser did, however, offer a ruse that if successful might have brought the Soviet Union to the rescue.

Since Israel had struck first, Egypt could claim to have honored its earlier agreement with the Soviets. The agreement, however, failed to specify what support, if any, the Soviets would provide. Nasser assured Hussein that the Soviet Union would waste no time becoming involved if it believed that the United States already had done so. Thus emerged what some later dubbed the "Great Lie." In calling upon the Soviets for support, Nasser alleged that the United States had led the initial air strikes against Egypt. King Hussein supported Nasser's claim, and the war appeared on the verge of becoming a major Cold War superpower confrontation.

The Soviets were disappointed that their plans to change the Middle East balance of power had failed. Israel now controlled the Sinai Peninsula, the Gaza Strip, and the West Bank and had sent its forces north to the Golan Heights. Initially giving credence to the Egyptian claim that the Americans had been involved, the Soviet Union planned to defend Syria. Soviet help in retaking the West Bank and Sinai would follow.

When the Johnson administration learned that the Soviets were mobilizing air units for possible commitment to the region, President Johnson ordered the *Independence* carrier group in the Mediterranean to alter course and head for Israel. Then, in one of the most controversial incidents of the war, on June 8, IAF aircraft attacked and nearly sunk USS *Liberty*, a U.S. electronic intelligence ship operating just outside of Egypt's territorial waters, 13 nautical miles off El Arish. The Israelis later claimed that they had committed a tragic error amid the fog of war, but much about the incident still remains unclear.

The U.S. message to the Soviet Union was unequivocal. If the Soviets sought to raise the stakes, the United States would match them. Neither superpower relished the prospect of direct confrontation—the Cuban Missile Crisis had taken place a scant five years earlier—but neither wanted to be perceived as weak. For the United States, that meant standing firm against the Soviets publicly while pursuing diplomatic alternatives through the UN. In resorting to the UN, the Johnson administration sought to end the conflict multilaterally before it could escalate.

While the Israeli ambassador to the UN had little trouble justifying Israel's actions against Egypt, the UN demanded an immediate withdrawal from the West Bank and an end to hostilities with Syria in the Golan Heights. Arab delegates demanded an Israeli withdrawal on all fronts of the war.

For Israel, however, the opportunity to seize control of the strategic Golan Heights and thereby deny its use as a terrorist staging area was too important to pass up. Consequently, Eshkol ordered his country's UN ambassador to stall for time and to claim that Israel had no further designs on Arab territory. When President Johnson demanded that the Israeli ambassador convey the U.S. insistence to withdraw from the Golan Heights, Eshkol shrewdly claimed to be unable to understand the message because of problems with the phone lines.

As the situation stabilized on the IDF's southern and central fronts, Dayan was able to turn his attention to the Golan Heights and Syria. The IAF had already destroyed some two-thirds of the Syrian air force in a series of air strikes executed on the evening of June 5. The Syrians had 75,000 troops organized into nine brigades. The IDF's Northern Command attacked with four brigades, and by June 9, they had broken through to the Golan Heights' high ground. By the morning of June 10, Israel controlled the Golan Heights, having lost only 141 soldiers. The Syrians suffered loses with 2,500 dead, 5,000 wounded, and almost all of their tanks and artillery that had been on the Golan Heights.

Having occupied the Sinai, the Gaza Strip, the West Bank, and the Golan Heights, Israel prepared to face the UN. With the fighting over, the United States and the Soviet Union pulled back from the brink. By this point, Soviet intelligence had concluded that the U.S. carrier group in the Mediterranean had been too far removed to have participated in the early morning attacks of June 5, 1967, as Nasser had claimed. It had been the IAF's impressive sortie turnaround rate that had contributed significantly to the initial belief that more than just the 200 Israeli aircraft had been involved in the first day's strikes.

The Soviets' ensuing coolness toward their Middle Eastern allies for having maneuvered them into a direct confrontation with the United States ensured that Soviet support for recovering the lost territories would be a very long time in coming. The Soviet Union did, however, sever diplomatic relations with Israel, and Soviet-sponsored regimes in Eastern Europe quickly followed suit. Although yet another cease-fire officially ended the 1967 conflict, the first

formal peace treaty between Israel and an Arab nation remained 12 years in the future.

The defeat was regarded as an utter disaster both in Egypt and the Arab world. In Egypt, Nasser resigned but then was returned to power by popular intervention. He then blamed his military advisers for the debacle. In the Arab world, people were so angry that they entered into a new stage of resistance against their own governments and elites. The defeat also led to a militant period of irregular armed struggle against Israel.

The war between the Arabs and the Israelis meanwhile simply entered another stage, later called the War of Attrition. As the protracted fighting dragged on, the diplomats continued to wrangle. Arab and Soviet demands that Israel return the captured territories did not subside with the signing of the cease-fire. By the end of the year the UN passed Resolution 242, which called upon the Israelis to return the captured territories. The resolution also stipulated that the Arab nations should negotiate and sign peace treaties with Israel. Neither the Israelis nor the Arab states, however, were in much of a mood for compromise.

Israel argued that because of its national security requirements it should not be required to return the territories. By more than doubling the territory under its control, Israel for the first time now had viable geographic buffer zones between it and most of its Arab enemies. Meaningful peace treaties would have to precede any discussion of territorial returns. The Arab states predictably countered that they would not consider peace treaties until after Israel returned the territories. Israel retorted that no nation had ever willingly returned territory that it had captured in a war, and Israel ignored Resolution 242 until the 1993 Oslo Agreements.

The Six-Day War had four long-term effects. First, Egypt and Syria quickly resumed the low-intensity conflict that had preceded the war, often using state-sponsored terrorism to execute attacks too risky for their own militaries. Israel's relations with its immediate neighbors had come full circle.

Second, outraged by UN impotence and Arab reluctance to confront Israel's superior military, armed groups such as Arafat's Fatah along with disorganized refugees called for a revolution. The armed groups and their political counterparts argued about tactics and methodology, with the most radical, violent, and antielitist elements holding sway for approximately the next six years. This was the origin of the high-profile media-focused attacks mounted by various Palestinian groups.

Third, Israel's control of the contested territories greatly complicated the long-term prospects for peace. Right-wing Israelis and ultraorthodox Jews considered a surrender of land that had belonged to biblical Israel (i.e., the West Bank and the Gaza Strip) to be completely out of the question. This, in turn, created a huge problem for Israel in retaining its essential identity as both a Jewish state and a democracy. With some 600,000 more Arabs now under Israeli control and with long-term demographic trends in the region favoring the Arabs, their inclusion in the nation's political process would eventually undercut the state's Jewish character. However, denying the Arabs full political rights would also erode Israel's democratic foundations.

Fourth, Israeli settlements subsequently established in the occupied territories have since become a force of their own and a major fault line in Israeli domestic politics. To this day the settlements cast a long shadow over any prospects of trading land for peace with the Arabs.

During the 40 years following the Six-Day War, the Gaza Strip, the West Bank, and the Golan Heights remained under Israeli control. Israel formally annexed East Jerusalem and the Golan Heights, although no other nations have given formal recognition to these actions. Under the Camp David Accords, Israel returned the Sinai Peninsula to Egypt in 1978. The Israelis finally withdrew from Gaza in 2005 but continued to launch military incursions against terrorist groups as they thought necessary.

While Israel, Egypt, and Jordan are finally officially at peace, Syria's relations with Israel remain strained at best, given Syria's support for radical Islamic Hezbollah activists in Lebanon, who since 2011 have become influential backers of President Bashar al-Assad in Syria's civil war. The West Bank and the Gaza Strip became breeding grounds for anti-Israeli sentiment and direct action, most notably the First Intifada (1987–1993) and the Second (al-Aqsa) Intifada (2000–2004). The West Bank is now under Palestinian Authority administration, with prospects that it may develop into a Palestinian state. Even so, the construction of new Israeli settlements in Palestinian territory has continued, and their existence constitutes an obstacle to reaching a final status agreement.

All Israeli forces and settlers withdrew from Gaza in September 2005, handing over official control to Palestinians. After fierce fighting, in June 2007 radical Hamas forces wrested control of Gaza from the more moderate Fatah, whereupon the Palestinian Authority broke all ties with Gaza. Gaza quickly became a launching pad for Hamas rocket attacks on southern Israel, as well as attempts to tunnel into Israeli territory, provoking Israeli military incursions in 2008 and 2009, and major Israeli airstrikes in 2009 and 2012. By early 2014, antagonism and hostilities between Gaza and Israel seemed liable to continue indefinitely.

Bryan E. Vizzini and David T. Zabecki

Further Reading

Bowen, Jeremy. *Six Days: How the 1967 War Shaped the Middle East*. New York: Thomas Dunne, 2005.

Bregman, Ahron. *Israel's Wars: A History Since 1947*. 3rd ed. New York: Routledge, 2010.

Dunstan, Simon. *The Six Day War 1967: Jordan and Syria*. Oxford: Osprey, 2009.

Dunstan, Simon. *The Six Day War 1967: Sinai*. Oxford: Osprey, 2009.

Ferris, Jesse. *Nasser's Gamble: How Intervention in Yemen Caused the Six-Day War and the Decline of Egyptian Power*. Princeton, NJ: Princeton University Press, 2012.

Finkelstein, Norman G. *The Rise and Fall of Palestine: A Personal Account of the Intifada Years*. Minneapolis: University of Minnesota Press, 1996.

Friedman, Thomas. *From Beirut to Jerusalem*. New York: Anchor Books, 1995.

Ginor, Isabelle, and Gideon Remez. *Foxbats Over Dimona: The Soviets' Nuclear Gamble in the Six Day War*. New Haven, CT: Yale University Press, 2007.

Goldschmidt, Arthur. *Modern Egypt: The Formation of a Nation State*. Boulder, CO: Westview, 2004.

Hammel, Eric. *Six Days in June: How Israel Won the 1967 Arab-Israeli War*. New York: Scribner's, 1992.

Herzog, Chaim. *The Arab-Israeli Wars: War and Peace in the Middle East from the War of Independence to Lebanon*. Westminster, MD: Random House, 1984.

Morris, Benny. *Righteous Victims: A History of the Zionist-Arab Conflict, 1881–2001*. New York: Vintage Books, 2001.

Netanyahu, Benjamin. *A Durable Peace: Israel and Its Place among the Nations*. New York: Warner, 2000.

Ochsenwald, William, and Sydney Nettleson Fisher. *The Middle East: A History*. 7th ed. Boston, MA: McGraw Hill, 2010.

Oren, Michael B. *Six Days of War: June 1967 and the Making of the Modern Middle East*. Novato, CA: Presidio, 2003.

Ro'i, Yacov. *The Soviet Union and the June 1967 Six Day War*. Stanford: Stanford University Press, 2008.

Soviet Union and Russia, Middle East Policy

Geography and oil made the Middle East a crucial arena of Cold War competition. The foreign policy of the Soviet Union in the region sought to reduce British, French, and American influence and gain dominance for itself. The Soviets supported Arab states for geopolitical reasons, such as access to the Mediterranean Sea, the Suez Canal, and the Indian Ocean, and for ideological reasons because the Arabs shared Soviet opposition to Western imperialism and colonialism. The Soviets backed the Arab side during the various Arab-Israeli wars for political as well as ideological reasons and sought to keep the region polarized to preserve Egyptian and Syrian dependence on the Soviet Union. Soviet efforts to dominate the Middle East failed due to vigorous U.S. counteraction and ended when the Soviet Union collapsed in 1991.

Soviet-Egyptian ceremonies at the Aswan High Dam project, in the late 1950s. (Bettmann/Corbis)

With the monument to Egypt's unknown soldier in the background, Soviet-built Sam-6 anti-aircraft missiles are on display during a military parade in Cairo, on October 7, 1976, the third anniversary of the start of the 1973 war with Israel. (AP Photo)

Since 1991 Russia, a nation hobbled by financial crises and political turmoil, has taken a far more pragmatic and reactive stand in the Middle East. This does not mean, however, that the Soviet successor state had abdicated its strategic or economic interests and commitments in the region. Since the late 1990s, in fact, the Kremlin had shown a renewed interest in the region. But this has not been driven by the old Soviet ideologies. Rather, it is based upon economic imperatives as well as traditional Russian conceptions of security and international power.

The primary vehicle of Soviet influence was military aid, sometimes transferred using East Europeans as deniable proxies. Soviet arms were available in large quantities, at low prices, and on favorable credit terms. The Soviet Union was the chief military patron of Egypt (1955–1973), Syria (after 1958), Iraq (after 1958), Libya (after 1974), Algeria (after 1962), Somalia (1962–1977), Ethiopia (after 1977), North and South Yemen (after 1967), and Afghanistan (after 1973). During the Iran-Iraq War (1980–1988), the Soviets supplied both Iraq and Iran via intermediaries. The Soviets provided advisers to their clients, obtained air and naval basing rights in the region, and deployed combat forces in Egypt (1970–1972) and Afghanistan (1979–1989).

The Soviets had negligible influence in the Middle East before World War II. After that war decisively weakened Britain and France, the Soviets hoped to gain influence in the region but had limited means at their disposal. They decided to support the Zionist movement in order to weaken British power and create tensions between the United States and Britain but also in part because of the common suffering of the war that had claimed up to 27 million

Soviet citizens and 6 million Jews. In 1947, Soviet diplomats supported the partition of Palestine, which led to the creation of Israel in 1948. To strengthen Israel, the Soviets transferred Jews from Soviet-occupied territories to Poland, fully expecting them to emigrate. The Soviets instructed Poland, Czechoslovakia, Romania, and Hungary to permit Jewish emigration. From 1948 to 1951, more than 302,000 Jews emigrated from Eastern Europe to Israel. Israel's Jewish population was only 806,000 in 1948, so this was a vital demographic boost.

At Soviet direction, Czechoslovakia provided $22 million in arms to Israel in 1948, including 50,000 rifles, 6,000 machine guns, 90 million rounds of ammunition, and Supermarine Spitfire and Avia S-199 fighter aircraft. Czech arms played a crucial role in securing air superiority over Israel and halting Arab ground advances in the Israeli War of Independence (1948–1949).

The Soviets may have initially contemplated a strategic alliance with Israel. However, relations deteriorated with the onset of the Cold War when Soviet dictator Joseph Stalin launched an anti-Semitic, anti-Western propaganda campaign. In late 1952, Soviet security services manufactured an alleged conspiracy of Jewish doctors to poison Soviet leaders, and in this atmosphere the Soviet Union broke relations with Israel. Official anti-Semitism eased with the death of Stalin in March 1953. Diplomatic relations with Israel were restored, but Israel had shifted permanently into the Western camp.

In 1955, the United Kingdom signed the Baghdad Pact, a defense alliance with Iraq, Turkey, Pakistan, and Iran. The alliance's ostensible purpose was to contain Soviet advances to the south, yet ironically the Baghdad Pact prompted Egypt, Syria, and Yemen to seek closer relations with the Soviet Union.

In the 1950s the United States, Britain, and France sought to maintain an Arab-Israeli arms balance and would not sell advanced weapons to Egypt. Egyptian president Gamal Abdel Nasser approached the Soviets, who agreed in September 1955 to supply arms via Czechoslovakia. The Egyptian-Soviet arms deal included 230 tanks, 200 armored personnel carriers, 100 self-propelled guns, 500 artillery pieces, several hundred MiG-15 jet fighters, 50 Il-28 jet bombers, transport aircraft, and assorted naval vessels. This development greatly alarmed Israel as well as Britain and France, which had their own difficulties with Nasser.

Anglo-French tensions with Egypt came to a head in 1956. The United States withdrew funding from the proposed Aswan High Dam project, forcing Egypt to nationalize the Suez Canal. The British, French, and Israelis invaded Egypt in October in order to regain control of the canal and overthrow Nasser. At that time the Soviets were busy crushing the Hungarian Uprising and in any case had little military capability to intervene on Egypt's behalf. However, the Soviets sent diplomatic notes with veiled threats of force against Britain and France unless they withdrew from Egypt and proposed a joint U.S.-Soviet military intervention to halt the fighting. Washington rebuffed Soviet threats, rejected the proposal for joint action, and employed political and economic pressure to force Britain and France to abandon their occupation. After the Suez Crisis, the Soviets portrayed themselves as Egypt's friend and protector even though their bluster had risked nothing and achieved little. During the brief war, British, French, and Israeli forces destroyed large quantities of Soviet-supplied equipment at little cost to themselves. The Soviets attributed this discreditable performance to poorly trained Egyptian operators.

The British and French defeat at Suez facilitated increased Soviet influence in the Middle East. The Soviets agreed to replenish Egypt's lost equipment and supplied more modern MiG-17 and MiG-19 fighters. In 1963, Egypt received first-line T-54/55 tanks, MiG-21 supersonic fighters, Tu-16 bombers, and SA-2 surface-to-air missiles (SAMs). The Soviets provided similar modern equipment to the progressive regimes in Syria and Iraq, the latter of whose pro-British government was overthrown in 1958. Some 1,300 Soviet and East European advisers trained Egyptian forces to use the new equipment. The number of Soviet tanks and combat aircraft given to the Arabs vastly exceeded Western supplies to Israel, not least because the United States refused to supply significant quantities of modern equipment to Israel before 1967.

Soviet strategy in the Middle East from 1965 to 1973 was subordinate to Soviet strategy toward Indochina. In response to the escalating war in Vietnam after 1965, the Soviets supplied many tens of thousands of tons of weapons and equipment to Hanoi. The overland supply route from the Soviet Union across China to North Vietnam was not secure due to Sino-Soviet antagonism and the turmoil created by China's Great Proletarian Cultural Revolution. Nor could supplies travel via Vladivostok given the limited capacity of the Trans-Siberian Railroad and the need to increase Soviet forces in the Far East to confront China. Thus, the Soviets shipped supplies to North Vietnam primarily via the Black Sea port of Odessa. The sea route from Odessa to Haiphong via the Cape of Good Hope was more than twice as long as the route via the Suez Canal. Closing the Suez Canal would thus more than halve the quantity of supplies the Soviets could deliver. From 1965 to 1967, the Soviets sought to prevent Egyptian-Israeli conflict, which would likely close the Suez Canal. After the 1967 Six-Day War closed the canal, the Soviets urgently sought to reopen it both by demanding Israeli withdrawal from the canal zone and by arming Egypt in order to open the canal by force.

The argument that the Soviets instigated the Six-Day War or encouraged Arab aggression in 1967 defies logic. The Soviets needed to keep the Suez Canal open. Furthermore, Egyptian and Syrian forces had not yet received all the weapons or training that the Soviets intended to provide. About a third of Egypt's army (55,000 troops, including the best units) was deployed in Yemen and was unavailable to fight Israel. When tensions rose in May 1967, the Soviets warned Egypt that Israel planned to attack Syria. Possibly, the Soviets hoped that a display of Egyptian resolve would deter Israel from striking Syria, but if so this backfired. Nasser's decision to close the Strait of Tiran, to order United Nations (UN) peacekeepers to leave the Sinai, and to mobilize Egyptian forces simply induced Israel to crush Egypt. On May 26, 1967, the Soviets pressured Egypt and Syria to moderate their rhetoric and prevent armed conflict with Israel by whatever means necessary, but this came too late to prevent Israeli action.

Soviet behavior during the Six-Day War was restrained. The Soviets expressed resolute support for the Arabs but did not resupply them or risk confrontation with the United States. The Soviets only threatened overt involvement on June 10 when they feared that Israel would take Damascus and overthrow the Syrian government. They broke relations with Israel and alerted their airborne divisions for deployment, but intervention proved unnecessary when Israel accepted a cease-fire.

After the Six-Day War, the Soviets replaced Egypt's and Syria's lost equipment and dispatched huge quantities of arms to Sudan, Iraq, and Yemen. The Soviets sent 13,000 military advisers to Egypt in late 1967—rising to 20,000 in 1970—with advisers attached to every Egyptian unit down to battalion level. The Soviets demanded an overhaul of the Egyptian high command, and thousands of Egyptian officers visited the Soviet Union for training. Diplomatically, the Soviets continued to insist that Israel withdraw from the canal zone without preconditions. Washington responded that a comprehensive solution to the Arab-Israeli conflict must precede Israeli withdrawal from occupied territories. The Soviets and the East Europeans began to train, fund, and equip terrorist organizations such as the Palestine Liberation Organization (PLO) and the Popular Front for the Liberation of Palestine (PFLP) in order to harass Israel, Western Europe, and the United States.

In April 1969, Egypt launched the War of Attrition, which sought to avoid major ground combat while causing continual Israeli casualties. Israel countered with air strikes that destroyed Egypt's air defenses in the canal zone. When this did not force Egypt to desist, Israel began deep-penetration raids throughout Egypt. Egypt then convinced the Soviets to take control of Egypt's air defenses. More than 12,000 Soviet operators manned air defenses that included 85 SA-2 and SA-3 missile sites, radar-guided artillery pieces, and more than 100 MiG-21 fighters with Soviet pilots. Although initially restricted to defense of the Nile River Valley, in July 1970, the Soviets began moving SAM batteries closer to the Suez Canal, creating the prospect that Egyptian forces could cross the canal under this umbrella. The United States equipped Israeli aircraft with advanced electronic countermeasures and air-to-surface missiles to defeat the SAM threat.

The effort to put a SAM umbrella over the Suez Canal coincided with a crisis in Jordan. In September 1970, King Hussein violently suppressed increasingly uncontrollable Palestinian guerrilla groups. In response, the Soviets sponsored a Syrian invasion of Jordan. Soviet advisers planned the operation and accompanied Syrian tanks until they crossed the border. The Soviets hoped that either Israel would intervene, which would discredit Hussein, or that the Americans would intervene, which would discredit the United States in the Arab world. However, the Jordanian air force smashed Syria's tank columns, making outside intervention unnecessary.

After Nasser's death in September 1970, Egypt's new president, Anwar Sadat, sought to improve relations with Israel and the United States. When the Soviets tried to influence the Egyptian succession struggle in favor of pro-Soviet vice president Ali Sabri, Sadat dismissed and arrested Sabri. More than 100 pro-Soviet officials were purged from the Egyptian government in the Corrective Revolution of May 1971. To prevent a complete break in relations, the Soviets demanded—and obtained—a Soviet-Egyptian Treaty of Friendship. The treaty restricted the Soviet role in Egypt to providing military aid and training, and Egypt agreed not to join any anti-Soviet alliance.

Having lost influence in Egypt, the Soviets tried to strengthen their relations with other Arab states through arms deliveries to Syria, Iraq, Somalia, North and South Yemen, and Sudan. This effort succeeded except in Sudan, where the government followed Sadat's lead in purging local communists. Desperate Sudanese communists launched a coup attempt but were crushed. Soviet military advisers were then expelled.

Sadat understood that the Soviets preferred to perpetuate Arab-Israeli antagonism in order to keep Egypt isolated and dependent on the Soviet Union. He also knew that only the Americans could deliver a political settlement with Israel and the return of the Sinai to Egyptian control. Sadat hoped that Washington could broker a political solution, but U.S. efforts to do so in 1971 and 1972 foundered on Israeli intransigence. Sadat signaled his independence and desire for improved relations with the United States—for example, he expelled Soviet military advisers in July 1972—but could not completely burn his bridges with the Soviets because he needed Soviet arms. Sadat's strategy was to prepare for a limited war in the expectation that victory would enable Washington to force Israel to accept a peace agreement and withdraw from the Sinai. Sadat informed the Soviets in February 1973 that he intended to attack Israel, and he demanded their support. The Soviets had little choice but to agree since failure to support Egypt would destroy Soviet influence in the Middle East. Furthermore, reopening the Suez Canal would facilitate arming Hanoi for a future attack on South Vietnam.

From late June 1967 until early 1973, the Soviets gave Egypt sufficient weaponry to defend itself but not advanced offensive weapons. The Egyptians were especially displeased that the Soviets did not provide their latest MiG-23 and MiG-25 fighters to counter Israeli F-4 Phantoms. Before the October 1973 Yom Kippur War, the Soviets provided first-line T-62 tanks and large numbers of antiaircraft and antitank missiles, which would enable Egypt to take and hold a bridgehead on the east bank of the Suez against Israeli air and armored counterattacks. Syria and Iraq also received significant quantities of Soviet weapons before the war.

The main Soviet objective before and during the Yom Kippur War was to ensure that the region remained polarized. This required either stampeding Israel into a preemptive attack on Egypt that would make Sadat's goal of a limited victory over Israel impossible or prodding Washington into a premature display of full support for Israel that would ruin Washington's credibility as an honest broker. Moscow tried to provoke Israeli preemption by circulating warnings in the communist press that an attack was imminent and by evacuating Soviet civilians from Egypt and Syria. These gambits failed, not least because the United States sternly warned Israel not to preempt.

Once the war began, the Soviets sought a cease-fire at the point of maximum Arab gain—when Egypt had taken the east bank of the canal and Syria had taken the Golan Heights—but this effort failed. Israel quickly counterattacked the Syrians, and Moscow asked Egypt to advance in order to divert Israeli attention. The Soviets also began resupplying Syria and Egypt by air and sea and alerted their airborne divisions for deployment to Damascus. Israel, however, stopped short of Damascus and shifted its forces south to inflict a catastrophic defeat on the Egyptians, who had advanced into the Sinai beyond their air-defense umbrella. Israeli forces then crossed the Suez Canal and threatened to destroy Egyptian forces trapped on the east bank. The UN Security Council called for a cease-fire on October 22, 1973, but Israel disregarded this and continued encircling the Egyptians. The Soviets proposed sending joint U.S.-Soviet military contingents to enforce the cease-fire and threatened to act unilaterally if the United States refused. To emphasize their determination, the Soviets made further preparations to deploy airborne forces, and Soviet troops in Egypt fired two Scud ballistic missiles into Israel. At this point there was a real prospect of renewed fighting and the commitment to nuclear weapons. Washington raised its military alert level, informed Moscow of its willingness to cooperate in maintaining a cease-fire (although not with U.S. troops), asked Sadat to withdraw his request for superpower military intervention (which he did), and demanded that Israel cease operations (which, under extreme duress, it eventually did).

The Yom Kippur War yielded only one positive result for Moscow: the opening of the Suez Canal. Otherwise, the outcome was profoundly negative. Washington reestablished ties with Egypt and excluded Moscow from any substantive role in the Egyptian-Israeli peace process. Moscow's only recourse was to strengthen ties with Syria and to forge a relationship with Libya, which bought $20 billion in Soviet arms from 1974 to 1985.

In 1974, Iran began a determined effort to shift Afghanistan into its orbit. With Iranian assistance, Afghan president Mohammed Daoud lessened his dependence on Moscow and attempted to suppress Afghan communists. To arrest this trend, in April 1978, Moscow approved a coup that killed Daoud and installed Noor Mohammed Taraki. Afterward, the Soviet political and military presence in Afghanistan rapidly escalated.

U.S. efforts to guide Iran from autocracy to constitutional monarchy in the late 1970s completely failed, and Mohammad Reza Shah Pahlavi abdicated in early 1979. Major U.S. forces began gathering in the region, and the Soviets, perceiving a geopolitical opportunity, warned the Americans not to intervene militarily in Iran. The crisis in Iran coincided with an anticommunist revolt in Afghanistan that the Afghan government was unable to quell. After Hafizullah Amin assassinated Taraki and became president of Afghanistan in September 1979, the Soviets decided on military action there. In December 1979, 80,000 Soviet troops invaded Afghanistan—and Amin was executed—in order to suppress the revolt and deter a U.S. invasion of Iran, which the Soviets mistakenly believed was imminent.

The Soviet army originally intended to garrison key points and allow the Afghan army to fight the resistance but was soon drawn into combat itself. Soviet equipment and tactics designed for conventional opponents proved poorly suited to fighting guerrillas in rugged Afghan terrain. The Soviet-Afghan War resulted in 15,000 Soviet deaths, with 470,000 sick and wounded over a 10-year period. Afterward, Afghanistan sank into civil war. From a larger perspective, the Soviet war in Afghanistan galvanized U.S. leadership toward a global anti-Soviet crusade. The Afghan debacle was in fact a major factor in the collapse of the Soviet Union.

Before 1979 Iraq was a long-standing Soviet client, receiving 90 percent of its arms from Soviet sources, while Iran was a U.S.-armed client. The fall of the shah of Iran caused Iraq to improve relations with Saudi Arabia, Jordan, and the United States, while Iran strengthened its relations with Syria, Libya, and the Soviets. After Iraq invaded Iran in September 1980, the Soviets tried to manipulate the conflict to bring a pro-Soviet regime to power in Iran. The Soviets believed that Iran's war with Iraq, Iran's need for Soviet arms to fight that war, the presence of Soviet troops in Afghanistan, and U.S. forces in the Persian Gulf would create irresistible pressure on Tehran to turn to Moscow to solve its problems and escape hostile encirclement.

Soviet strategy required time to come to fruition. Moreover, prolonged conflict would weaken Iran and, because Iran could not obtain Western arms, increase its dependence on the Soviet Union. Thus, the Soviets armed both sides to protract the fighting. Some regard Iraq as an U.S. puppet during the Iran-Iraq War. In fact, the Soviet bloc and its clients provided the vast majority of Iraq's tanks, armored personnel carriers, artillery, small arms, and combat aircraft. At the same time, Soviet clients—Syria, Libya, North Korea, Cuba, and Vietnam—supplied Iran with arms that played a critical role in blunting the initial Iraqi offensive and allowing Iran to counterattack. The Soviets backed Iranian communist resistance groups that three times attempted to overthrow the Khomeini regime, but each time the coups were brutally suppressed. Ultimately, Soviet strategy did not succeed. Only after the end of the Iran-Iraq War, the death of Khomeini, and the Soviet withdrawal from Afghanistan were the Iranians willing to accept a close relationship with Moscow (which persists to this day).

Syrian alignment with Iran in the 1980s created fear of a Syrian attack that Iraq, fully engaged against Iran, could not withstand. The Soviets did not intend to authorize such Syrian action, but Israel, with U.S. backing, moved to pin down the Syrians in any case. After Iran expelled the Iraqis from Iranian soil in May 1982 and began driving into Iraq, Israel launched a powerful incursion into Lebanon, mauling Syrian forces there. The deployment of the multinational force in Lebanon further fixed Syrian attention in the West and eased pressure on the Iraqi rear. The minimum Soviet goal during the Syrian-Israeli confrontation was to ensure that Israel did not destroy Syria, although the Soviets took no direct steps to support Syria or counter Israel in Lebanon itself. After the destruction of Syrian air defenses in 1982, the Soviets rebuilt it with the more modern SA-5 SAMs and provided additional modern weapons such as Su-24 and MiG-29 aircraft and T-72 tanks. Soviet military presence in Syria peaked with 13,000 Soviet and East European advisers in 1984 and declined after 1985.

The Soviets were on the defensive worldwide from 1985 to 1991. This was driven by serious internal economic dislocations, the disastrous Soviet intervention and occupation of Afghanistan, and Soviet leader Mikhail Gorbachev's efforts to reform Soviet society and government (glasnost and perestroika). In the Middle East, the Soviets' willingness to provide unstinting military largesse to their clients declined, and the Soviets sought to extract themselves from the Afghan quagmire. Diplomatically, the Soviets improved relations with Egypt, Israel, Saudi Arabia, and the Gulf states in the late 1980s and joined the UN consensus in condemning Iraq's invasion of Kuwait in August 1990.

Indeed, Soviet cooperation completely changed the character of the U.S. confrontation with Iraq during 1990–1991 that culminated in the 1991 Persian Gulf War. The Kremlin declined to aid—or even shield—its regional client as it had done during the Cold War. The Persian Gulf War would have in fact been unimaginable at the height of the U.S.-Soviet Cold War rivalry. The movement of major U.S. forces from Germany to Saudi Arabia most certainly would not have been possible during the Cold War. The Soviets attempted to persuade Iraqi strongman Saddam Hussein to withdraw unscathed from Kuwait, but he obstinately refused a diplomatic solution. Thus, the Soviets did not block the use of force in January and February 1991. The Soviet collapse in December 1991 ended four decades of bipolar superpower competition in the Middle East and ushered in a less peaceful and unpredictable era in the region.

With the familiar bipolarity of the Cold War now gone, nations in the Middle East are far less likely to heed Great Power admonitions to exercise restraint. The lack of restraining forces on Middle Eastern states has literally sent some of them into centrifugal chaos. Both religious and political radicalism have been on the rise, and few regional governments have been able to contain them entirely. This turn of events has been key to the rise of terrorism—both regionally and worldwide—and sectarian violence. Nowhere is this more apparent than in war-torn Iraq, where Shiites, Sunnis, and Kurds battle it out to win supremacy in a nation that Anglo-American forces have been unable to pacify or control. In addition, perceived U.S. hegemony in the Middle East since the fall of the Soviet Union has begun to look far more menacing without the countervailing power of the Soviet Union.

Under Russian presidents Boris Yeltsin and Vladimir Putin, Russian policy in the Middle East largely eschewed the ideologically oriented prescriptions of the communist era. Russian policies now tend to be grounded in pragmatism. Much to the annoyance and occasional chagrin of the West, the Russians have cultivated relations with Middle East nations that are both friendly to and antipathetic to the West. Indeed, Russian diplomats have played a masterful juggling act by maintaining relations with Syria and Iran while at the same time keeping relations with Washington and London on a relatively even keel. To showcase this ecumenical approach, in 2005, Putin visited Israel, Egypt, and the Palestinian Authority (PA) territories. In January 2005, Syrian president Bashar al-Assad traveled to Moscow on an official state visit. Clearly, the Kremlin was hedging its bets by attempting to stay on firm footing with a number of diverse regimes in the Middle East.

Russia has been supportive of the Israeli-Palestinian peace process since 1993 and has courted positive relations with Tel Aviv. Because of the large number of Israeli Jews from Russia (some 30 percent of Israel's population is now of Russian origin), there has been a natural affinity between the two nations. Russian businesses have also benefited from economic ties with Israel. With the United Nations, the European Union, and the United States, Russia was the fourth of the Middle East quartet of powers established in 2002 with the objective of facilitating an Israeli-Palestinian settlement.

Relations between Moscow and Tel Aviv have not been without tension, however, as the Kremlin's support of Iran and Syria has at times caused much dismay among Israeli policymakers.

Since the 1990s, the Kremlin has engaged in major economic and technology deals with Iran, as Russian-Iranian ties owe much to the two nations' proximity and shared geopolitical interests. Indeed, Iran concluded a major arms agreement and became Russia's third-largest arms client (after China and India) in the 1990s. Iran purchased advanced weapons, including Kilo-class submarines, T-72 tanks, S-300 SAMs, and Su-24 and MiG-29 aircraft. Iran also acquired the rights to produce Russian weapons. Iranian officers attended Russian military schools, and Russian advisers trained Iranian forces in the use of Russian weapons. In 1995, under U.S. pressure, Russia agreed not to conclude any new arms deals with Iran, but Putin abrogated this agreement in 2000. A particular U.S. concern has been the transfer of nuclear and missile technology. Russia sold Iran important missile components and manufacturing technologies in the 1990s and trained Iranian scientists in ballistics, aeronautic design, booster design, and missile guidance. Iranian Shahab ballistic missiles were derived from Soviet SS-4 and SS-5 designs. In 1995, Russia obtained a contract to build a nuclear power plant at Bushehr and despite U.S. protests remained determined to finish the project. Russia subsequently agreed to provide fuel for Bushehr and to build additional reactors in Iran.

The Russians notably abstained from voting when the International Atomic Energy Agency (IAEA) found Iran in noncompliance with Nuclear Non-Proliferation Treaty safeguards on uranium enrichment and reprocessing in September 2005 and opposed referring the issue to the UN Security Council. Russia consistently opposed the imposition of sanctions on Iran and sought to protract negotiations for as long as possible. Moreover, in late 2006, Russia began delivering advanced Tor-M1 air defense missiles to Iran that would seriously complicate any military action to destroy Iran's nuclear facilities. Moscow's repeated dilution of U.S. efforts to enact UN sanctions against Iran for its nuclear program only added to the tension. Russia supplied Iran with the material needed to build its first nuclear power plant. By November 2013, however, Russia had acquiesced in a range of international economic sanctions against Iran, and seemed ready to join with other major powers in reaching a settlement with Iran that would impose strict international controls on Iranian nuclear facilities in exchange for the unfreezing of Iranian assets held overseas.

In recent years Russian ties to Syria were strengthened. In 2005, President Putin seemed to support the position of Hezbollah in Lebanon, which is heavily funded by the Syrians and Iranians (who in turn have received weapons systems and armaments from Russia). Moscow's links with Iran, Syria, and Hezbollah strained relations with Washington during the George W. Bush and Barack Obama administrations. During the Israeli-Hezbollah Lebanon War in the summer of 2006, the Putin government did not openly oppose the Israeli incursion into southern Lebanon. Nevertheless, Hezbollah obtained Russian-made Spandrel, Kornet, and Vampir antitank missiles from Syria

and Iran. These missiles played a major role in blunting Israel's armored offensive. Once more, the Kremlin was attempting to hedge its bets by staying out of any direct conflict in the region. But behind the scenes, it played an important role while attempting to appear neutral. There can be little doubt that Moscow had known from the very beginning that the armaments it sold to the Syrians and Iranians were going to end up in the hands of groups such as Hezbollah.

When civil war broke out in Syria in 2011, initially Russia firmly backed President Bashar al-Assad's regime, supplying weapons to the Syrian government and vetoing UN efforts to impose sanctions on Syria should the government continue its violent repression of insurgents. By mid-2013, however, Putin and other Russian leaders had withdrawn all Russian military personnel from Syria. Acknowledging that the authoritarian policies of Assad's regime were largely responsible for the civil war, Russian officials suggested that Syria's chemical weapons be placed under international control and destroyed, and advocated the opening of negotiations among the parties concerned.

In the early 21st century, some right-wingers in the United States began to assert that Russia was seeking to revive the Soviet Union's hegemonic policies in the Middle East. This seemed unlikely. Moscow's ever-decreasing military power and its shaky economic underpinnings will more than likely guarantee the continuation of the cautious, pragmatic approach in the region for some time to come.

James D. Perry and Paul G. Pierpaoli Jr.

Further Reading

Bar-Siman-Tov, Yaacov. *Israel, the Superpowers, and the War in the Middle East.* New York: Praeger, 1987.

Belopolsky, Helen. *Russia and the Challengers: Russian Alignment with China, Iran and Iraq in the Unipolar Era*. Basingstoke: Palgrave Macmillan, 2009.

Cobban, Helena. *The Superpowers and the Syrian-Israeli Conflict*. Westport, CT: Praeger, 1991.

Cronin, Stephanie, ed. *Iranian-Russian Encounters: Empires and Revolutions since 1800*. New York: Routledge, 2012.

Daigle, Craig. *The Limits of Détente: The United States, the Soviet Union, and the Arab-Israeli Conflict, 1969–1973*. New Haven, CT: Yale University Press, 2012.

Freedman, Robert O. *Soviet Policy toward Israel under Gorbachev*. New York: Praeger, 1991.

Ginor, Isabelle, and Gideon Remez. *Foxbats Over Dimona: The Soviets' Nuclear Gamble in the Six Day War*. New Haven, CT: Yale University Press, 2007.

Golan, Galia. *Soviet Policies in the Middle East: From World War II to Gorbachev*. Cambridge: Cambridge University Press, 1990.

Hiro, Dilip. *The Longest War: The Iran-Iraq Military Conflict*. London: Routledge, 1991.

Horowitz, Brian, and Shai Ginsburg, eds. *Bounded Mind and Soul: Russia and Israel, 1880–2010*. Bloomington, IN: Slavica, 2013.

Israelyan, Victor. *Inside the Kremlin during the Yom Kippur War*. University Park: Pennsylvania State University Press, 1995.

Korn, David A. *Stalemate: The War of Attrition and Great Power Diplomacy in the Middle East, 1967–1970*. Boulder, CO: Westview, 1992.

Lazin, Frederick A. *The Struggle for Soviet Jewry in American Politics: Israel versus the American Jewish Establishment*. Lanham, MD: Lexington Books, 2005.

Lynch, Allen C. *Vladimir Putin and Russian Statecraft*. Washington, DC: Potomac Books, 2011.

Oren, Michael B. *Six Days of War: June 1967 and the Making of the Modern Middle East*. Novato, CA: Presidio, 2003.

Pollack, Kenneth M. *Arabs at War: Military Effectiveness, 1948–1991*. Lincoln: University of Nebraska Press, 2002.

Primakov, E. M. *Russia and the Arabs: Behind the Scenes in the Middle East from the Cold War to the Present*. New York: Basic Books, 2009.

Ro'i, Yaacov. *The Soviet Union and the June 1967 Six Day War*. Stanford: Stanford University Press, 2008.

Ro'i, Yaacov, ed. *The Jewish Movement in the Soviet Union*. Washington, DC, and Stanford: Wilson Center Press and Stanford University Press, 2012.

Rumer, Eugene. *Dangerous Drift: Russia's Middle East Policy*. Washington, DC: Washington Institute for Near East Policy, 2000.

Smolansky, Oles M., and Bettie M. Smolansky. *The USSR and Iraq: The Soviet Quest for Influence*. Durham, NC: Duke University Press, 1991.

Thornton, Richard. *The Carter Years*. New York: Paragon House, 1991.

Thornton, Richard. *The Nixon-Kissinger Years*. New York: Paragon House, 1989.

Suez Crisis

The Suez Crisis was one of the major events of both the Cold War and the Arab-Israeli wars. It ended Britain's pretensions to be a world superpower and fatally weakened Britain's hold on what remained of its empire. It also placed a dangerous strain on U.S.-Soviet relations, strengthened the position of Egyptian leader Gamal Abdel Nasser throughout the Middle East, and distracted world attention from the concurrent Soviet military intervention in the Hungarian Revolution.

The Suez Crisis had its origins in the development plans of Gamal Abdel Nasser. In 1952, a reformist and anti-British coup d'état in Egypt, led by young army officers, toppled the government of King Farouk I. During the months that followed, Nasser emerged as the strongman and ultimately became president of Egypt. Nasser hoped to

Tanks on the beach, after being landed off the coast of Port Said during the Suez Crisis, 1956. (Popperfoto/Getty Images)

enhance his prestige and improve the quality of life for his nation's burgeoning population by carrying out long-discussed plans to construct a high dam on the upper Nile River south of Aswan to provide electric power. To finance the project, Nasser sought assistance from the Western powers. But Nasser had also been endeavoring to build up and modernize the Egyptian military. Toward that end he had sought to acquire modern weapons from the United States and other Western nations. When the U.S. government refused to supply the advanced arms, which it believed might be used against the State of Israel, in 1955, Nasser turned to the communist bloc. In September 1955, with Soviet encouragement, he reached a barter arrangement with Czechoslovakia for substantial quantities of weapons, including jet aircraft and tanks, in return for Egyptian cotton.

This arms deal impacted on the Aswan High Dam construction project for which Nasser had sought Western financing. In December 1955, Washington declared its willingness to lend $56 million for financing the dam, while Britain pledged $14 million and the World Bank $200 million. The condition to the aid was that Egypt provide matching funds and that it not accept Soviet assistance.

Nasser was unhappy with the attached strings. With Nasser expecting a Soviet offer of assistance, the controlled Egyptian press launched an all-out propaganda offensive against the West, especially the United States. But when no Soviet offer was forthcoming, Nasser finally accepted the Western aid package on July 17, 1956. Much to his chagrin, two days later U.S. secretary of state John Foster Dulles announced that it had been withdrawn. Britain immediately followed suit. The official U.S. reasons were that Egypt had failed to reach agreement with the Sudan over the dam (most of the vast lake created by the dam would be in Sudanese territory), and the Egyptian part

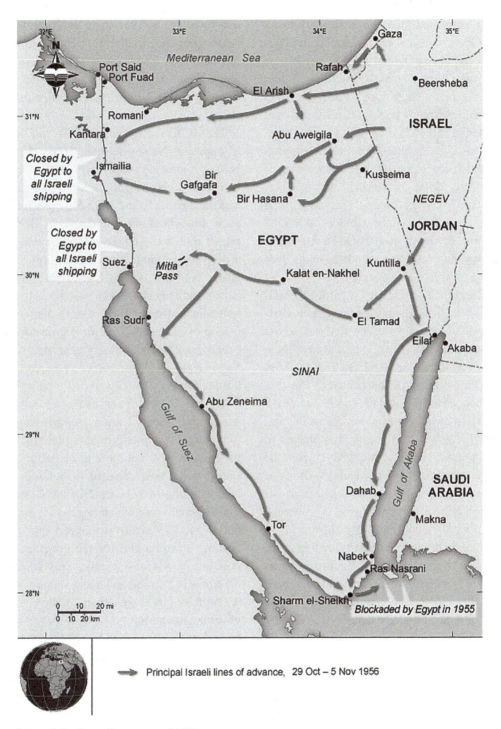

Map of the Sinai Campaign of 1956.

of the financing for the project had become uncertain. The real reasons were objections from some U.S. congressmen, especially Southerners fearful of competition from Egyptian cotton, and Dulles's determination to teach Nasser and other neutralists a lesson. Dulles was angry over Nasser's flirtation with the communist bloc, including the arms purchases, and was especially upset over Egypt's recent recognition of the People's Republic of China (PRC).

Nasser's response to this humiliating rebuff came a week later on July 26 when he nationalized the Suez Canal. He had contemplated such a move for some time, but the U.S. decision prompted its timing. In 1955, the canal produced net revenues of nearly $100 million, of which Egypt received only $2 million. Seizure of the canal would not only provide additional funding for the Aswan High Dam project, but it would make Nasser a hero in the eyes of many Arab nationalists.

The British government regarded the sea-level Suez Canal, which connected the eastern Mediterranean with the Red Sea across Egyptian territory, as its lifeline to Middle Eastern oil and the Far East. Indeed, fully 60 percent of all oil consumed in Western Europe passed through the canal. The canal, built by a private company headed by Frenchman Ferdinand de Lesseps, had opened to much fanfare in 1869. It quickly altered the trade routes of the world, and two-thirds of the tonnage passing through the canal was British. Khedive Ismail Pasha, who owned 44 percent of the company shares, found himself in dire financial straits, and, in 1875, the British government stepped in and purchased his shares. In 1878, Britain acquired the island of Cyprus north of Egypt from the Ottoman Empire, further strengthening its position in the eastern Mediterranean north of Egypt. The British also increased their role in Egyptian financial affairs, and, in 1882, they intervened militarily in Egypt, promising to depart once order had been restored. Britain remained in Egypt and in effect controlled its affairs through World War II.

In 1954, Nasser, determined to end British influence in Egypt, succeeded in renegotiating the 1936 treaty with the British to force the withdrawal of British troops from the Suez Canal Zone. The last British forces departed the canal zone on June 13, only six weeks before Nasser nationalized the canal.

The British government took the lead in opposing Nasser. London believed that Nasser's growing popularity in the Arab world was encouraging Arab nationalism and threatening to undermine British influence throughout the Middle East. British prime minister Anthony Eden developed a deep and abiding hatred of the Egyptian leader. For Eden, ousting Nasser from power became nothing short of an obsession. In the immediate aftermath of Nasser's nationalization of the canal, the British government called up 200,000 military reservists and dispatched military resources to the eastern Mediterranean.

The French government also had good reason to seek Nasser's removal. Paris sought to protect its own long-standing interests in the Middle East, but more to the point, the French were now engaged in fighting the National Liberation Front (NLF) in Algeria. The Algerian War, which began in November 1954, had greatly expanded and had become an imbroglio for the government, now led by Socialist premier Guy Mollet. Nasser was a strong and vocal supporter of the NLF, and there were many in the French government and military who believed that overthrowing him would greatly enhance French chances of winning the Algerian War. This position found considerable support when on October 18, 1956, the French intercepted the Egyptian ship *Athos* and found it loaded with arms and documents proving Egyptian support for the NLF.

Israel formed the third leg in the triad of powers arrayed against Nasser. Egypt had instituted a blockade of Israeli ships at the

Gulf of Aqaba, Israel's outlet to the Indian Ocean. Also, Egypt had never recognized the Jewish state and indeed remained at war with it following the Israeli War of Independence (1948–1949). In 1955, Israel mounted half a dozen cross-border raids, while Egypt carried out its own raids into Israeli territory by fedayeen (guerrilla fighters).

Over the months that followed Egyptian nationalization of the Suez Canal, the community of interest among British, French, and Israeli leaders developed into secret planning for a joint military operation to topple Nasser. The U.S. government was not consulted and indeed opposed the use of force. The British and French governments either did not understand the U.S. attitude or, if they did, believed that Washington would give approval after the fact to policies undertaken by its major allies, which the latter believed to be absolutely necessary.

The British government first tried diplomacy. Two conferences in London attended by the representatives of 24 nations using the canal failed to produce agreement on a course of action, and Egypt refused to participate. A proposal by Secretary of State Dulles for a canal users' club of nations failed, as did an appeal to the United Nations (UN) Security Council. On October 1, Dulles announced that the United States was disassociating itself from British and French actions in the Middle East and asserted that the United States intended to play a more independent role.

Meanwhile, secret talks were going forward, first between the British and French for joint military action against Egypt. Military representatives of the two governments met in London on August 10 and hammered out the details of a joint military plan known as "Musketeer" that would involve occupation of both Alexandria and Port Said. The French then brought the Israeli government

in on the plan, and General Maurice Challe, deputy chief of staff of the French air force, undertook a secret trip to the Middle East to meet with Israeli government and military leaders. The Israelis were at first skeptical about British and French support. They also had no intention of moving as far as the canal itself. The Israelis stated that their plan was merely to send light detachments to link up with British and French forces. They also insisted that British and French military intervention occur simultaneously with their own attack.

General André Beaufre, the designated French military commander for the operation, then came up with a new plan. Under it, the Israelis would initiate hostilities against Egypt in order to provide the pretext for military intervention by French and British forces to protect the canal. This action would technically be in accord with the terms of the 1954 treaty between Egypt and Britain that had given Britain the right to send forces to occupy the Suez Canal Zone in the event of an attack against Egypt by a third power.

On October 23, Mollet and French foreign minister Christian Pineau met in the Paris suburbs at Sèvres with Israeli prime minister David Ben-Gurion, Defense Minister Shimon Peres, and chief of the Israeli General Staff Lieutenant General Moshe Dayan. The French agreed to provide additional air cover for Israel. French ships supposedly searching for Egyptian arms shipments to the Algerian rebels would move to the Israeli coast immediately, and French Mystère aircraft flown by French pilots would be repositioned in Israel. That afternoon British foreign secretary Selwyn Lloyd and Foreign Office undersecretary of state Patrick Dean joined the discussions. The British, while staunchly pro-intervention, were deeply concerned about their position in the Arab world and were not anxious to be seen in collusion with the Israelis. Thus, an Israeli strike toward the canal through the Sinai would enable the British to have it both ways: they could join the French in demanding of Nasser the right to protect the canal. When he refused, as he certainly would, they could join the French in destroying the Egyptian air force, eliminating the one possible threat to Israeli success on the ground. All parties agreed to this new plan, dubbed the "Treaty of Sèvres" and signed by Dean, Pineau, and Ben-Gurion.

On October 23, meanwhile, unrest began in Hungary. The next day Soviet tanks entered Budapest to put down what had become the Hungarian Revolution. French and British planners were delighted at this international distraction that seemed to provide them a degree of freedom of action.

On the afternoon of October 29 Israeli forces began Operation KADESH, the invasion of the Sinai Peninsula. Sixteen C-47 transports took off from Israeli fields, each with a paratroop platoon. The objective of the 395-man paratroop battalion was the key Mitla Pass, 156 miles from the Israeli border and only 45 miles from the canal. Meanwhile the remainder of Colonel Ariel Sharon's 202nd Parachute Brigade would race for the pass in French-provided trucks, linking up with the paratroopers within 36 hours. This operation was designed to trigger a major Egyptian response and threaten the canal in order to trigger the planned British-French response.

The announced objective of Operation KADESH was the eradication of the fedayeen bases, but it was begun so as to appear to the Egyptians as if it was the beginning of an all-out war. Dayan's detailed plan called for nothing less than a week-long lightning advance that would end with Israeli forces securing the entire Sinai and a total victory over Egypt. The destruction of Nasser's prestige in the Arab world and final Egyptian recognition of the impossibility of an Arab military victory over Israel were the goals rather than destruction of the Egyptian army or acquisition of its new Soviet equipment.

A day later, October 30, the British and French governments issued an ultimatum, nominally to both the Egyptian and Israeli governments but in reality only to Egypt, expressing the need to separate the combatants and demanding the right to provide for the security of the Suez Canal. The ultimatum called on both sides to withdraw their forces 10 miles from the canal and gave them 12 hours to reply. The Israelis, of course, immediately accepted the ultimatum, while the Egyptians just as promptly rejected it.

At dusk on October 31, British and French aircraft struck Egyptian airfields and military installations from bases on Cyprus and Malta and from aircraft carriers. The aircraft attacked four Egyptian bases that day and nine the next. On November 1, meanwhile, a British and French naval task force sailed from Malta to join with other ships at Cyprus. In all, the allied landing force numbered some 80,000 men: 50,000 British and 30,000 French. There were 100 British and 30 French warships, including 7 aircraft carriers (5 British) and the French battleship *Jean Bart*, hundreds of landing craft, and some 80 merchant ships carrying 20,000 vehicles and stores. Yet when Eden reported to the House of Commons on events, he encountered a surprisingly strong negative reaction from the opposition Labour Party.

Also, following the initial British and French military action, the Egyptians immediately sank a number of ships in the canal to make it unusable. The Israelis, meanwhile, swept across the Sinai in only four days against ineffective Egyptian forces. Finally, on November 5, British and French paratroopers carried out a vertical envelopment of Port Said, Egypt, at the Mediterranean terminus of the canal, while at the same time French and British destroyers carried out a shore bombardment against those targets likely to impede a landing. Early on November 6, British troops began coming ashore at Port Said and the French at Port Fuad. A single day of fighting saw the ports in allied hands. French and British forces then began a virtually unopposed advance southward along the canal.

President Dwight D. Eisenhower had already entered the picture. On October 31, he described the British attack as "taken in error." He was personally furious at Eden over events and is supposed to have asked when he first telephoned the British leader, "Anthony, have you gone out of your mind?" The United States applied immediate and heavy financial threats, both on a bilateral basis and through the International Monetary Fund, to bring the British government to heel. Eisenhower also refused any further dealings with Eden personally.

The Soviets, preoccupied by Hungary, took some five days to come to the conclusion that the United States was actually opposing the British and French action. On November 5, Moscow threatened to send "volunteers" to Egypt. This proved a further embarrassment for the British government, but it was U.S. pressure that was decisive. Nonetheless, the world beheld the strange spectacle of the United States cooperating with the Soviet Union to condemn Britain and France in the UN Security Council and call for an end to the use of force. Although Britain and France vetoed the Security Council resolution, the matter was referred to the General Assembly, which demanded a cease-fire and withdrawal.

Israel and Egypt agreed to a cease-fire on November 4. At midnight on November 6, the day of the U.S. presidential election, the British and French governments also accepted a cease-fire, the French only with the greatest reluctance. By the time the cease-fire went into effect, the French and British controlled about half of the canal's length. French and British losses in the operation were 33 dead and 129 wounded. Egyptian losses are unknown.

A 4,000-man UN Emergency Force (UNEF) authorized on November 4 and made up of contingents from the Scandinavian countries, Brazil, Colombia, India, and Indonesia then arrived in Egypt to take up positions to keep Israeli and Egyptian forces separated. At the end of November the British and French governments both agreed to withdraw their forces from Egypt by December 22 and, on December 1, Eisenhower announced that he had instructed U.S. oil companies to resume shipping supplies to both Britain and France. Under pressure from both the United States and the UN, Israel withdrew its forces from the Sinai, to include the Gaza Strip, during February 5–March 6, 1957. A UN observer force of 3,500 men then took up station in Gaza, at Sharm al-Sheikh, and along the Sinai border. Although Israel had been assured that Egyptian forces would not return to Gaza, they were there within 48 hours of the Israeli withdrawal.

Nasser and Arab self-confidence were the chief beneficiaries of the crisis. The abysmal performance of Egyptian military forces in the crisis was forgotten in Nasser's ultimate triumph. Nasser found his prestige dramatically increased throughout the Arab world. Israel also benefited. The presence of the UN force guaranteed an end to the fedayeen raids, and Israel had also broken the Egyptian blockade of the Gulf of Aqaba, although its ships could still not transit the

Suez Canal. The crisis also enhanced Soviet prestige in the Middle East, and the UN emerged with enhanced prestige, helping to boost world confidence in that organization.

The Suez Crisis ended Eden's political career. Ill and under tremendous criticism in parliament from the Labour Party, he resigned from office in January 1957. Events also placed a serious, albeit temporary, strain on U.S.-British relations. More importantly, they revealed the serious limitations in British military strength. Indeed, observers are unanimous in declaring 1956 a seminal date in British imperial history that marked the effective end of Britain's tenure as a great power. The events had less impact in France. Mollet left office in May 1957 but not as a result of the Suez intervention. The crisis was costly to both Britain and France in economic terms, for Saudi Arabia had halted oil shipments to both countries.

Finally, the Suez Crisis could not have come at a worse time for the West because the event diverted world attention from the concurrent brutal Soviet military intervention in Hungary. Eisenhower believed, rightly or wrongly, that without the Suez diversion there would have been far stronger Western reaction to the Soviet invasion of its satellite.

Spencer C. Tucker

Further Reading

Aridan, Natan. *Britain, Israel and Anglo-Jewry 1949–57*. New York: Routledge, 2004.

Beaufre, André. *The Suez Expedition, 1956*. Translated by Richard Barry. New York: Praeger, 1969.

Bregman, Ahron. *Israel's Wars: A History Since 1947*. 3rd ed. New York: Routledge, 2010.

Cooper, Chester L. *The Lion's Last Roar: Suez, 1956*. New York: Harper and Row, 1978.

Eden, Anthony. *The Suez Crisis of 1956*. Boston, MA: Beacon Press, 1968.

Freiberger, Steven Z. *Dawn over Suez: The Rise of American Power in the Middle East, 1953–1957*. Chicago: Ivan R. Dee, 1992.

Gorst, Anthony, and Lewis Johnman. *The Suez Crisis*. London: Routledge, 1997.

Hahn, Peter. *The United States, Great Britain, and Egypt, 1945–1956: Strategy and Diplomacy in the Early Cold War*. Chapel Hill: University of North Carolina Press, 1991.

Kelly, Saul, and Anthony Gorst, eds. *Whitehall and the Suez Crisis*. London: Routledge, 2000.

Kingseed, Cole C. *Eisenhower and the Suez Crisis of 1956*. Baton Rouge: Louisiana State University Press, 1995.

Kunz, Diane B. *The Economic Diplomacy of the Suez Crisis*. Chapel Hill: University of North Carolina Press, 1991.

Kyle, Keith. *Suez: Britain's End of Empire in the Middle East*. New ed. London: I.B. Tauris, 2011.

Levey, Zach. *Israel and the Western Powers, 1952–1960*. Chapel Hill: University of North Carolina Press, 2011.

Louis, William R., and Roger Owen, eds. *Suez, 1956: The Crisis and Its Consequences*. New York: Oxford University Press, 1989.

Lucas, W. Scott. *Divided We Stand: Britain, the United States and the Suez Crisis*. Rev. ed. London: Spectre, 1996.

Morris, Benny. *Israel's Border Wars, 1949–1956: Arab Infiltration, Israeli Retaliation, and the Countdown to the Suez War*. Oxford, UK: Clarendon, 1993.

Nichols, David A. *Eisenhower, 1956: The President's Year of Crisis—Suez and the Brink of War*. New York: Simon and Schuster, 2011.

Turner, Barry. *Suez 1956: The Inside Story of the First Oil War*. New York: Hodder and Stoughton, 2006.

Varble, Derek. *The Suez Crisis, 1956*. London: Osprey, 2003.

Syria

Arab nation in the Middle East covering 71,498 square miles, just slightly larger than the U.S. state of North Dakota. The Syrian Arab Republic borders on Jordan and Israel to the south, Lebanon and the Mediterranean Sea to the west, Turkey to the north, and

Syrians gather at Ein al-Teineh, southern Damascus, Syria, on February 14, 2009. They came together opposite to the occupied village of Majdal Shams, in the background, in the Golan Heights, to protest the 27th anniversary of the Israeli annexation of the Heights. (AP Photo/Bassem Tellawi)

Iraq to the east. For much of its history Syria was dominated by larger powers. Syria was part of the Ottoman Empire until the end of World War I, and the country's economy and educational system had left its populace in relative destitution. In 1920, France received a League of Nations mandate over both Syria and neighboring Lebanon.

French rule resulted in repeated uprisings, particularly among the Druze. After a tortuous series of negotiations and anti-French violence in the late 1920s, Syria was granted considerable autonomy in 1936. Following the defeat of France by Germany in June 1940, Syria was controlled by the Vichy French government headed by Marshal Henri Philippe Pétain. It appointed General Henri Dentz as high commissioner to Syria with a cabinet headed by Khalid al-Azm. Pétain ordered Dentz to allow German and Italian aircraft landing rights in Syria on

their way to support Radhid Ali's regime in Iraq.

This situation was intolerable to the Allies. British, Australian, and Free French forces as well as the Transjordan Arab Legion crossed from Palestine into Lebanon and Syria in June 1941. By mid-July they were fully in control of both Syria and Lebanon. Syria was then turned over to the Free French authorities. Although the French recognized Syrian independence, they continued to occupy the country, declared martial law, imposed strict press censorship, and arrested political subversives.

In July 1943, under pressure from its allies, the Free French government-in-exile announced new elections. A nationalist government came to power that August, electing as president Syrian nationalist Shukri al-Quwatli. France granted Syria independence on January 1, 1944, but the country

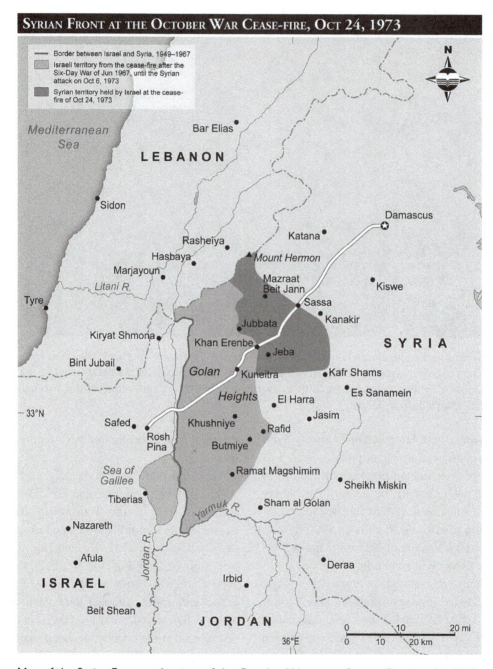

SYRIAN FRONT AT THE OCTOBER WAR CEASE-FIRE, OCT 24, 1973

— Border between Israel and Syria, 1949–1967

Israeli territory from the cease-fire after the
Six-Day War of Jun 1967, until the Syrian
attack on Oct 6, 1973

Syrian territory held by Israel at the cease-
fire of Oct 24, 1973

N

Mediterranean
Sea

Bar Elias

LEBANON

Damascus

Sidon

Katana

Rasheiya

Mount Hermon

Hasbaya

Mazraat
Beit Jann

Marjayoun

Kiswe

Litani R.

Sassa

Tyre

Kanakir

Jubbata

Kiryat Shmona

Khan Erenbe

SYRIA

Jeba

Bint Jubail

Golan

Kuneitra

Kafr Shams

Heights

Es Sanamein

El Harra

33°N

Jasim

Safed

Khushniye

Rafid

Rosh
Pina

Butmiye

Sea of
Galilee

Ramat Magshimim

Tiberias

Sheikh Miskin

Sham al Golan

Nazareth

Yarmuk R.

Jordan R.

Afula

Deraa

ISRAEL

Irbid

Beit Shean

JORDAN

0   10   20 mi

0   10   20 km

36°E

Map of the Syrian Front at the time of the October War cease-fire on October 24, 1973.

remained under Allied occupation for the remainder of the war. In February 1945, Syria declared war on the Axis powers and then the next month became a member of the United Nations (UN).

In early May 1945, anti-French demonstrations erupted throughout Syria, whereupon French forces bombarded Damascus, killing 400 people before the British intervened. A UN resolution in February 1946 called on France to evacuate the country, and by mid-April all French and British forces were off Syrian soil. Evacuation Day, April 17, is still celebrated as a Syrian national holiday.

On March 22, 1945, Syria cofounded the Arab League, which advocated Pan-Arab nationalism but without the consolidation of states and the resultant problems that such a movement would have witnessed. The Arab League was also aimed at blocking the creation of a Jewish state in Palestine, which the Syrians strongly opposed.

Syria played a relatively small role in the failed Israeli War of Independence (1948–1949) that arose from the creation of the Jewish state in May 1948. At the beginning of the fighting, Syria had only some 4,500 troops to commit, almost all of whom were dispatched to the Syrian-Palestinian border. Just six days into the fighting, Syrian troops had been repelled, with heavy casualties. News of the Syrian defeat spread rapidly and many Syrians blamed al-Quwatli for the setback. Al-Quwatli reacted by firing his defense minister and chief of staff. As time progressed, however, Syrian troops enjoyed some success and managed to occupy a small strip of Palestinian territory along the border. They also occupied a small piece of land in northeastern Palestine. After these initial successes, the small Syrian military contingent remained rather inactive for the rest of 1948. For al-Quwatli, whose popularity was quickly eroding, the chief issue of the 1948–1949 war was whether Syria would fight alongside other Arab nations in a show of Pan-Arabism or whether it would fight to retain its Syrian identity. In so doing, he diluted the Syrian effort against the Israelis and engendered opponents in other Arab states.

The Israeli victory in the war and disagreements over Syria's potential union with Iraq torpedoed al-Quwatli's government.

There were three separate coups in 1949, the last one headed by Lieutenant Colonel Adib al-Shishakli, who governed with a heavy hand until 1954. In 1952, after a series of lengthy talks, al-Shishakli agreed in principle with a U.S. offer that would have brought $400 million of aid to Syria in exchange for Syria's settling of as many as 500,000 displaced Palestinians. The plan was doomed from the start, however, as many Syrians—especially those on the political Left—decried the plan as an attempt to deny Palestinians their right of return to Palestine, which by now had UN backing.

Al-Shishakli was ousted in 1954, and late that year elections were held to determine the makeup of the new government, which would now be civilian. In the end, a three-party coalition (People's Party, National Party, and Baath Party) emerged with National Party chief Sabri al-Asali as its head. The coalition was a shaky one, and political instability plagued the new government. In the succeeding years the Baathists, who combined Arab nationalism with socialist economic policies, became the most powerful political force in Syria, and Syria gradually entered into economic and military agreements with the Soviet Union.

In February 1958, Syria and Egypt joined to form the United Arab Republic (UAR), with Syrian political parties supposed to refrain from all political activity. Complete Egyptian domination of the UAR forced yet another coup against the Syrian government in September 1961. Carried out by military officers, the coup promptly pulled Syria out of the UAR and established the Syrian Arab Republic. In December 1961, elections for a national assembly were held, and the body chose two conservative People's Party members to lead the new regime. However, another coup in late 1962 again toppled the government.

In 1963, a joint Baath-military government came to power. The new government nationalized most industrial and large commercial concerns and engaged in land reforms that redistributed land to the peasants. Meanwhile, Syria continued to cultivate relations with the Soviet bloc. A schism in the Baath Party resulted in more instability and, in 1966, the radical wing of the party staged a coup and installed Yussuf Zayan as prime minister. Nur al-Din al-Atasi became president. This new regime tightened Syria's ties with both the Soviets and Egyptians.

Syria fought Israel yet again in the June 1967 Six-Day War, with disastrous consequences. This time, its defeat included the loss of the Golan Heights to the Israelis. The outcome of the war eviscerated the ruling government, and when Syrian forces had to pull back after attempting to aid the Palestinians in Jordan during Black September (1970), the scene had been set for yet another change of government. On November 13, 1970, General Hafez al-Assad, the minister of defense, seized power in a bloodless coup. Al-Assad referred to it as the corrective resolution, which essentially ousted from power civilian Baathists in favor of the military Baathists. An ardent Baathi nationalist, al-Assad sought to strengthen ties to other Arab states, deemphasize Syrian reliance on the Soviet Union, and defeat Israel.

In early 1971, al-Assad was elected president and immediately began to consolidate his power. He would rule the country until his death in 2000. During the early years of his presidency, he modernized the Syrian army and engaged in modest economic reforms, while the Baath Party gained even more strength. Befitting his Baathist philosophy, the state played a central role in economic planning and implementation. Al-Assad's tactics could be brutal, and there was little room for dissent or democracy in Syria.

Syria joined with Egypt against Israel in the October 1973 Yom Kippur War. At the beginning of the fighting, Syria launched a massive ground attack that included 1,500 tanks (900 in the initial attack and 600 in reserve) and 144 batteries of artillery in an attempt to retake the Golan Heights. After some initial success and although their forces this time fought quite well, the Syrian attackers were finally driven back beyond their original positions. Syria did not take the Golan Heights, although it did regain control over a small portion of it as a result of U.S.-led negotiations after the war.

In the late 1970s and 1980s, Sunni Muslim fundamentalists began challenging the government's authoritarian rule, as the Sunni majority greatly resented the way they were treated by Alawites who had settled in the larger cities. The Islamic parties opposed the Baath Party's secular outlook. From 1976 to 1982, urban areas all across Syria became hotbeds of political unrest. Al-Assad's brother brutally crushed a February 1982 uprising by the Muslim Brotherhood in Hama, and troops killed as many as 30,000 people.

Al-Assad also sent his army into Lebanon in 1976, ostensibly as a peacekeeping force during the civil war there. The troops stayed on, however, with al-Assad siding at certain times with the progressive Christian, Druze, and Muslim forces and then later with certain Christian militias. By the mid-1980s Syrian forces in Lebanon played a dominating military and political role there. In 1990, the conflict was declared to have ended, although Syrian troops were not withdrawn from Lebanon until 2005. As a result of the long Syrian presence in Lebanon, many thousands of Syrians moved into Lebanon after the civil war to seek work. Syrian produce was cheaper than that grown in Lebanon, and smuggling continued from

Lebanon into Syria. In 1994, the Lebanese government granted citizenship to 250,000 Syrians, a move that was, for obvious reasons, controversial among the Lebanese people.

At the same time, the 1980s saw the al-Assad regime taking harder-line Arab positions and moving closer to the Soviets. Al-Assad's get-tough approach in regional politics included funding and encouragement of terrorism both in the Middle East and internationally. Al-Assad, who was always in the end a pragmatist, sought to ameliorate relations with the West as the Soviet Union began to implode in 1990. When Iraq invaded Kuwait in August 1990, al-Assad was the first Arab leader to denounce the attack. His government also provided 20,000 troops to the international coalition that defeated Iraqi forces in the 1991 Persian Gulf War. Al-Assad's frontline position in the war reflected both his desire to strengthen relations with the West and his strong dislike of Iraqi dictator Saddam Hussein. For although Hussein was a Baathist—at least in name—he was also a direct threat to al-Assad, who saw himself as the pivotal leader in the region.

In 1991, al-Assad's government entered into peace negotiations with Israel, although the process broke down with no firm agreement in January 2000. Al-Assad died unexpectedly in June 2000 after 30 years in power. He was succeeded by his son, Bashar al-Assad, who had been carefully groomed as the heir apparent after the death of his brother Basil in 1993. Allegedly a free market proponent, the younger al-Assad attempted some economic reforms, but the process has been fraught with setbacks and obstacles. In 1998, 65 percent of all Syrian revenues came from petroleum products. The younger al-Assad also promised both political and democratic reform, but neither has come to fruition.

After the September 11, 2001, terror attacks against the United States, Syria pledged its cooperation in the so-called war on terror. But with the beginning of the 2003 Iraq War, which al-Assad refused to support, U.S.-Syrian relations sharply deteriorated. Syria's continued support, or at least hosting of militant Palestinian groups and terrorist organizations such as Hezbollah, let alone the insurgents fighting U.S. and coalition troops in Iraq, all further strained relations with the United States. And although Syrian troops were out of Lebanon by 2005, considerable evidence suggested that the Syrians continued to involve themselves in the internal politics of that nation. Indeed, most observers agree that Syrian operatives were responsible for the assassination of former Lebanese prime minister Rafik Hariri in February 2005 as well as other assassinations of leading Lebanese figures into late 2007. For several years, the Syrian government continued to back Hezbollah elements demanding a national unity government in Lebanon, over which they would possess a veto power.

In March 2011, sectarian civil war began in Syria, as insurgent elements sought to emulate the success of Arab Spring popular movements in Egypt and Tunisia in overturning authoritarian governments. Shia Hezbollah forces generally supported the government of Bashar al-Assad, which obtained arms from Iran and Russia, while Sunni Al Qaeda elements backed by Saudi Arabia and Qatar were prominent among the insurgents. Government forces wreaked brutal repression on their enemies, employing chemical weapons and devastating much of the country. By September 2013, over 120,000 Syrians had reportedly been killed, while 6.5 million were refugees, 2 million of whom sought safety outside Syria. As fighting continued with no real conclusion in sight, by the final months of 2013, even the Russian government was modifying its early support for Bashar al-Assad. Acknowledging that the authoritarian policies of Assad's regime were largely responsible for the civil war, Russian officials suggested that Syria's chemical weapons be placed under international control and destroyed, and advocated the opening of negotiations among the various parties concerned and their international sponsors. With international encouragements, peace talks among the various factions began in January 2014, but by late February 2014, little progress had been made in these negotiations. Given the prominence of radical Islamic forces on both sides of the civil war, it seemed quite probable, however, that whatever regime eventually emerged in Syria would be no more sympathetic toward Israel than the al-Assad family and their Hezbollah allies in Lebanon had for many years shown themselves. Whether any new Syrian government would emulate its predecessor in seeking to dominate Lebanon remained impossible to predict.

Paul G. Pierpaoli Jr.

Further Reading

Ajami, Fouad. *The Syrian Rebellion*. Stanford, CA: Hoover Institution Press, 2012.

Deeb, Marius. *Syria's Terrorist War on Lebanon and the Peace Process*. New York: Palgrave Macmillan, 2003.

Goodarzi Jubin M. *Syria and Iran: Diplomatic Alliance and Power Politics in the Middle East*. New York: I. B. Tauris, 2008.

Hokayem, Emile. *Syria's Uprising and the Fracturing of the Levant*. New York: Routledge, 2013.

Lawson, Fred. H., ed. *Demystifying Syria*. London: Saqi Books, 2010.

Lefevre, Raphael. *Ashes of Hama: The Muslim Brotherhood in Syria*. New York: Oxford University Press, 2013.

Lesch, David W. *Syria: The Fall of the House of Assad*. New updated ed. New Haven, CT: Yale University Press, 2013.

Lesch, David W. *The New Lion of Damascus: Bashar Al-Assad and Modern Syria*. New Haven, CT: Yale University Press, 2005.

Maoz, Moshe, and Avner Yaniv, eds. *Syria under Assad: Domestic Constraints and Regional Risks*. London: Croom Helm, 1987.

Osoegawa, Taku. *Syria and Lebanon: International Relations and Diplomacy in the Middle East*. New York: I. B. Tauris, 2013.

Owen, Roger. *The Rise and Fall of Arab Presidents for Life*. Cambridge, MA: Harvard University Press, 2012.

Pipes, Daniel. *Greater Syria: The History of an Ambition*. New York: Oxford University Press, 1990.

Rabil, Robert J. *Embattled Neighbors: Syria, Israel, and Lebanon*. Boulder, CO: Lynne Rienner, 2003.

Roberts, David. *The Ba'ath and the Creation of Modern Syria*. New York: St. Martin's Press, 1987.

Seale, Patrick. *Assad of Syria: The Struggle for the Middle East*. Berkeley: University of California Press, 1988.

Shaaban, Bouthaina. *Damascus Diary: An Inside Account of Hafez al-Assad's Peace Diplomacy, 1990–2000*. Boulder, CO: Lynne Rienner, 2012.

Stacher, Joshua. *Adaptable Autocrats: Regime Power in Egypt and Syria*. Stanford: Stanford University Press, 2012.

Starr, Steven. *Revolt in Syria: Eye-Witness to the Uprising*. New York: Columbia University Press, 2012.

Van Dam, Nikolaos. *The Struggle for Power in Syria: Politics and Society under Assad and the Ba'th Party*. Rev. and updated ed. London: I. B. Tauris, 2011.

Von Maltzahn, Nadia. *The Syria-Iran Axis: Cultural Diplomacy and International Relations in the Middle East*. New York: I. B. Tauris, 2013.

T

Tunisia

North African nation. The Republic of Tunisia, an overwhelmingly Sunni Muslim nation, covers 63,170 square miles, about twice the size of the U.S. state of South Carolina. Tunisia borders Algeria to the west, Libya to the south, and the Mediterranean Sea to the east and north. Tunisia had a 2006 population of approximately 10 million people.

Until the late 19th century, Tunisia was dominated by various larger powers as well as Arab and Berber dynasties. In 1881, the French signed an agreement with the bey, the local Tunisian ruler, establishing a French protectorate there. Prior to that, Tunisia had been part of the Ottoman Empire. Tunisian society and culture were greatly affected by the long period of French colonial rule, which did not officially end until 1956.

Following World War II, a strong nationalist movement in Tunisia engaged in a protracted struggle against French colonial rule. When the State of Israel was founded in May 1948, the Jewish population of Tunisia numbered approximately 85,000 persons. Of these, nearly 15 percent emigrated during the following four years. On March 20, 1956, following arduous, delicate, and behind-the-scenes negotiations, an independence protocol was signed by French foreign minister Christian Paul Francis Pineau and Tunisian prime minister Tahar ben Amara. Some 6,500 Jews left Tunisia during the year following its independence from France, leaving the country with a population of 58,000 Jewish citizens.

On July 25, 1957, the Tunisian Constituent Assembly ousted the bey, Muhammad VIII al-Amin, who was sympathetic to France and had long been unpopular. It also declared the formation of the Tunisian republic and elected Habib Bourguiba as president. Bourguiba, who would rule until 1987, was decidedly pro-Western in his outlook and foreign policy. He maintained cordial communications with Israeli officials, although this was not made public until years later. In discussions of common interests and subsequent public statements, he made known his opinion that Arab states should accept the existence of Israel and pertinent United Nations (UN) resolutions as a condition for solving the Palestinian problem.

Bourguiba's efforts to transform Tunisia into a modern democratic state had the backing of the majority of young Westernized Tunisian intellectuals. His main political support came from the well-organized Neo-Destour Party, which he had founded in 1934 and which constituted the country's chief political force. The Bourguiba administration was very tolerant of its Jewish citizens, always distinguishing between the unpopular policies of the State of Israel and the Jewish population living in the country. Bourguiba was not without political rivals, however. Early in his presidency he was strongly challenged by Salah ben Youssef, who leaned toward Egypt and Pan-Arabism and championed the continuation of Tunisia's ancient Islamic traditions.

But Tunisia has always aligned itself squarely with the West and has been

Protesters chant slogans against President Zine al-Abidine Ben Ali in Tunis on January 14, 2011. (AP Photo/Christophe Ena, File)

considered a strong American ally. During the June 1967 Six-Day War, for example, Bourguiba refused to sever relations with the United States over its support of Israel, despite considerable pressure to do so from other Arab states. Tunisia also faced hostility from Egyptian leader Gamal Abdel Nasser with whom Bourguiba often found himself at odds, even going so far as to briefly sever diplomatic relations in October 1966. During the Six-Day War, there were many anti-Jewish demonstrations and attacks on Jewish citizens, property, and synagogues throughout Tunisia. Bourguiba severely rebuked such events.

In spite of Bourguiba's support of Western-style democracy, his regime exerted strong centralized authority. The economy was closely controlled by Tunis, and as fears of Islamic fundamentalism increased, especially after the late 1970s, the government increasingly relied on censorship, illegal detentions, and other decidedly undemocratic schemes to smother radical movements.

As the country increasingly lost influence among its Arab neighbors, Tunisia's stance on Israel hardened and was often marked by contradictory and paradoxical policies. For instance, Tunisia supported the October 1973 Egyptian-Syrian attack on Israel that sparked the Yom Kippur War and sent close to 1,000 combatants to fight, despite historically urging a diplomatic solution to Arab-Israeli conflicts. Although Tunisia distanced itself from the Middle East's continued problems throughout the rest of the decade, from 1979 to 1989, Tunis served as the headquarters of the Arab League when the organization suspended Egypt's membership and abandoned Cairo following President Anwar Sadat's peace agreement with Israel.

In 1982, Tunisia reluctantly allowed the Palestine Liberation Organization (PLO) to move the majority of its operations from Beirut to Tunis after Israel's invasion of Lebanon. On October 1, 1985, Israel killed 68 Palestinians and injured many more in the bombing of a Palestinian compound in a Tunis suburb. The bombing was Israel's response to the murder of three of its citizens in Cyprus for which the PLO claimed responsibility. On April 16, 1988, Israeli commandos killed the PLO's second-in-command, Khalil al-Wazir (Abu Jihad), at his home in Tunis.

Bourguiba's heavy-handed rule and frail health combined to bring about his ouster on November 7, 1987. General Zine al-Abidine Ben Ali carried out a bloodless coup and succeeded him as president. Under Ben Ali's tenure, Tunisia had taken a moderate, nonaligned stance in its foreign relations.

Following the PLO's acceptance of Israel's right to exist in December 1988, the organization left Tunis and returned to the Middle East, much to the relief of Tunisia. Domestically, it has sought to defuse rising pressures for a more open political system while at the same time dealing with increased Islamic fundamentalist activities and growing anti-Western sentiments.

In April 1996, Tunisia followed the lead of Morocco and opened a liaison office in Tel Aviv to strengthen cultural ties to Israel, especially with respect to Jewish tourism. While the rise of Israel's conservative Likud Party strained emerging Tunisian-Israeli relations over the next several years, on February 6, 2000, Tunisia's secretary of state met with the Israeli foreign minister in Tel Aviv, marking the first ever visit of such high-ranking officials.

The 21st century witnessed another cooling of relations between Israel and Tunisia. At the 2002 Arab Summit in Beirut, President Ben Ali supported the peace plan that called for an independent Palestinian state with Jerusalem as its capital and the return of all occupied territories. In 2004, he won a fourth five-year term.

In December 2010, the authoritarian nature of President Ben Ali's rule, lack of human and political rights, widespread corruption, high unemployment, and inflation sparked massive popular protests, the beginning of the Arab Spring, in which demonstrations rapidly spread across the Arab world. One month later, in January 2011, Ben Ali resigned, and other members of the ruling party were eventually banned from holding further office. Special police who had specialized in repressing dissent also disbanded. A transitional government was established.

In October 2011, the Ennahda or Renaissance Party, a moderate Islamist political grouping, won 90 out of 217 seats in the new Constituent Assembly, which elected Moncef Marzouki, a longtime human rights activist and dissident, as president in December 2011. In March 2012, the Ennahda Party committed itself to maintaining Tunisia as a secular state rather than implementing Muslim Sharia law, a stance welcomed by secular parties and criticized by hard-line Islamist groups.

Mark M. Sanders

Further Reading

Abadi, Jacob. *Tunisia since the Arab Conquest: The Saga of a Westernized Muslim State*. London: Ithaca Press, 2013.

Alexander, Christopher. *Tunisia: Stability and Reform in the Modern Maghreb*. New York: Routledge, 2010.

Geyer, Georgie Anne. *Tunisia: The Story of a Country that Works*. London: Stacey International, 2002.

Hibou, Beatrice. *The Force of Obedience: The Political Economy of Repression in Tunisia*. Translated by Andrew Brown. London: Polity, 2011.

King, Stephen J. *Liberalization against Democracy: The Local Politics of Economic Reform in Tunisia*. Bloomington: Indiana University Press, 2003.

Laskier, Michael M. *Israel and the Maghreb: From Statehood to Oslo*. Tallahassee: Florida State University Press, 2004.

Perkins, Kenneth. *A History of Modern Tunisia*. 2nd ed. New York: Cambridge University Press, 2014.

Willis, Michael. *Politics and Power in the Maghreb: Algeria, Tunisia and Morocco from Independence to the Arab Spring*. New York: Columbia University Press, 2012.

U

United Kingdom, Middle East Policy

Until 1914, the United Kingdom was, on the whole, content to exercise only informal influence in the Middle East. Only the small Crown Colonies of Aden and Cyprus (acquired in 1839 and 1878, respectively) were British in a strictly legal sense. The emirates along the southeastern coast of the Arabian Peninsula, from Qatar in the Persian Gulf to Muscat and Oman, were bound to Britain by defensive treaties. Aden, important to Britain with its port and fueling capacity, was actually under the rule of the British government of India, and Britain held protectorates over West Aden and East Aden. British leaders perceived the strongest area power, the moribund regime of the Ottomans, more as a dependent satellite than as an adversary and it therefore enjoyed British protection from predatory neighbors such as czarist Russia.

The major exception to this hands-off approach was Egypt, occupied in 1882 in response to a nationalist coup and thereafter incorporated into the British imperial sphere under the veil of a puppet monarchy. With the opening of the Suez Canal in 1869, the old route from Europe to the Indies via the Cape of Good Hope had become obsolete, and with the majority of traffic passing through the canal of British registry, London deemed it a vital British interest to defend the maritime artery running through the Straits of Gibraltar to Port Alexandria and from there along the Red Sea corridor to Aden and the long transoceanic voyage to India.

The security of this line of communication and transportation remained one of the core components of Britain's foreign policy, and control of Egypt's canal zone, which was eventually to become the world's largest military base, was thought crucial to imperial defense. The British, who had originally promised only a short-term intervention to stabilize Egypt's faltering government and secure the extensive financial assets owned by European investors throughout the country, made periodic noises about leaving when conditions allowed. But with each passing year, the occupation grew more permanent.

An accident of geography made Egypt crucial to British interests, and an accident of geology would make the Middle East as a whole the geopolitical key to the 20th century. The otherwise economically worthless deserts of Arabia sat atop the world's largest reservoirs of crude petroleum, the energy resource that would eventually replace coal as the most critical strategic resource on the planet. The long-term significance of this was already becoming clear before the outbreak of World War I. In 1911, Winston Churchill, at the time first lord of the Admiralty, took the critical step of beginning the changeover of the Royal Navy from coal to more efficient oil-burning engines. Three years later, he seized the prescient opportunity of buying a government majority shareholding in the Anglo-Persian Oil Company, which was busy exploiting its newly drilled fields in what is today southwestern Iran. The economic and military implications of the Middle East's oil reserves would, by 1945, come to dominate the region's political fortunes.

British troops patrol Port Said, Egypt, during the Anglo-French invasion of the Suez Canal area on November 8, 1956. (AP Photo)

Britain's traditional approach to Middle Eastern affairs ended in October 1914 when the Ottoman Empire's leaders took that country into World War I on the side of the Central Powers. Britain declared Egypt a formal protectorate and launched an extensive military effort across the eastern Mediterranean and the Fertile Crescent. The war there began badly for the British. An ambitious but poorly executed naval effort to force the Dardanelles, followed by the landing of an expeditionary force on the Gallipoli Peninsula, both in 1915, ended in ignominious evacuation, and there was another humiliating failure in Mesopotamia the following year when an Anglo-Indian expeditionary force moving up the Tigris and Euphrates was besieged and forced to surrender at Kut. But in early 1917, following reinforcement and a change of command, the Mesopotamian advance recovered its momentum, reaching and capturing Baghdad. British troops under Lieutenant General Sir

Edmund Allenby launched a successful offensive from Egypt into Palestine, breaking the stubborn Ottoman line of resistance at the Third Battle of Gaza. Allenby entered Jerusalem on December 11, 1917, the first Christian general to seize the city since the Crusades. The following year, the Ottoman Empire imploded.

Britain's victory in World War I created new regional opportunities but also problems in the Middle East. In May 1916, Foreign Office envoy Mark Sykes had drawn up with his French counterpart François Georges Picot a plan to divide the former Ottoman territories in the Middle East. Britain would directly control Mesopotamia, France would control Lebanon and much of southern Anatolia, and the rest of the region would be carved up into informal spheres of European control. This, however, contradicted a promise already made by the high commissioner in Egypt to the sharif of Mecca, Hussein ibn Ali, that if the Arab

British troops and units from other coalition countries gather for review by King Fahd of Saudi Arabia. (U.S. Department of Defense)

chieftains revolted against Ottoman rule, the British would sponsor an independent Arab state in the Middle East at the end of the war. To complicate things further, in 1917, Foreign Secretary Arthur Balfour had announced in his famous declaration that a postwar homeland would be established for the Jewish people in Palestine.

The final result was an untidy compromise. As a consequence of the Paris Peace Conference at the end of the war, Britain and France were awarded a number of mandate colonies under the auspices of the League of Nations. France received control over Syria and Lebanon. Britain received three mandate territories. Two of these, Iraq and Transjordan, were parceled out to the Hashemite princes Faisal and Abdullah, respectively, as consolation for the failure to create a Pan-Arab state. Palestine, the third, became the responsibility of the Colonial Office in London. Kuwait, at the mouth of the Mesopotamian delta, was detached from Iraq and declared a direct British protectorate.

The propping up of this shaky inheritance proved to be one of the British Empire's most intractable security problems of the 1920s onward. Nationalist feelings, both Arab and Zionist, had been permanently stirred up across the region by the rhetoric of Wilsonianism at the Paris peace talks, and tempers flared given the widespread belief that the colonial powers had betrayed legitimate national aspirations for their own selfish benefit. A popular revolt in Iraq during 1920–1922 was suppressed by the innovative (although later controversial) employment of military aircraft in so-called aerial policing by the Royal Air Force (RAF). In the spring of 1919, urban riots against British rule in Egypt led to a general uprising in which British troops killed hundreds of protestors. Although the protectorate was formally abandoned and a state of Egyptian independence declared in 1922—later modified by the Anglo-Egyptian Treaty of 1936—Britain retained control of key political and economic aspects of the country's life, and this transparently quasi-colonial situation continued to offend Egyptian national pride.

The situation in Palestine was if anything even worse. Britain was committed to the stewardship of a Jewish national homeland in the mandate, although the level of political autonomy that it would enjoy was not defined, and Britain insisted that "the civil and religious rights of existing non-Jewish communities" had to be left undisturbed, a demand that was easier to make than enforce. Jewish immigration quickly became the dominant issue. More than 100,000 Jews arrived in Palestine from Europe during the 1920s, and there were large transfers of land ownership as these migrants bought property from absentee landlords, displacing the Arab tenants who had traditionally worked the fields and orchards. As the resentment of the Arab fellahin (peasants and agricultural laborers) grew, the British authorities attempted to alleviate the tension by introducing immigration quotas. This angered Jewish residents and did little to heal the growing sectarian divide across the mandate.

Sporadic armed conflict between the two communities simmered until, in August 1929, 67 Jews were murdered by rioters in Hebron. This shocking event eroded what little confidence Jewish leaders had in a binational compromise future for the region and led to the rapid expansion of the paramilitary Jewish self-defense force known as the Haganah. For their part the British continued their increasingly unsuccessful policy of keeping the peace, trying to favor neither side and thereby alienating both. A British inquiry into the Arab riots, the Shaw Commission, acknowledged that previous government statements about the future of the mandate had been unhelpfully vague and contradictory, with politicians too eager to tell each community what it wanted to hear. But the subsequent 1930 Passfield white paper could only suggest new and ultimately ineffectual restrictions on future Jewish land purchases.

The failure of Britain's efforts at de-escalation became clear in the spring of 1936 when a full-scale Arab revolt broke out across Palestine in protest against continuing Jewish immigration and land purchase. More than 20,000 British security troops spent three years suppressing the rebellion (often in unofficial cooperation with the Haganah) in a counterinsurgency that was marked by often brutal policing tactics and the suspension of civil liberties. During the revolt the remaining economic ties between the Arab and Jewish communities were mostly severed, hampering the chance of any reconciliation between the two factions. Although in 1939 the revolt petered out, its containment did nothing to resolve the fundamental tensions that still plagued the mandate's political life.

Prime Minister Neville Chamberlain's government sought an opportunity to bring a final negotiated end to the conflict. Its first proposal was an Arab-Jewish summit, the 1939 St. James Conference, but this proved a failure because Arab representatives refused to even recognize the negotiating legitimacy of their Jewish counterparts. Forced to come up with a settlement of its own, Chamberlain's administration drafted a new white paper later that year. It promised the creation within 10 years of an independent Palestinian state to be jointly governed by Arabs and Jews. More significant for the short term, however, it limited future Jewish immigration into the mandate to 75,000 people for the next five years.

The white paper infuriated Jewish settlers while failing to satisfy Arabs, and it was only the outbreak of World War II that forestalled a more vigorous reaction to its proposals. Given the virulent anti-Semitism of Nazi Germany, mainstream Jewish organizations in Palestine were understandably willing to freeze the dispute for the duration of the war, although more extreme terrorist cells such as the Lohamei Herut Israel (also known as Lehi or the Stern Gang) refused to abandon their struggle. In 1944, Lehi would assassinate Lord Moyne, the resident minister in Cairo and one of the most senior British officials in the region.

Britain faced multiple challenges to its military power in the Middle East during the war. An Italian army invaded Egypt in the fall of 1940 and, although this assault was expelled in a spectacular counteroffensive into Libya the following year, the fortunes of the desert war would soon be dramatically reversed in favor of the Axis by the arrival of the German Afrika Korps. Behind the front line, sedition openly flourished. In May 1941, British troops returned to Iraq (which had received independence nine years earlier) when a pro-German cabinet overthrew King Faisal II's government, headed by the regent Abd al-Ilah, and this performance repeated itself in Vichy-held French Syria a few weeks later and, in cooperation with the Soviet Union, in Iran in August. In July 1942, at a particularly desperate moment in the battle against German general Erwin Rommel, Egypt's king Farouk was ordered at gunpoint to dissolve his government and appoint a premier more accommodating toward British interests. Not until 1943 were North Africa and the Middle East secured by the Allies.

In 1945, the incoming Labour Party prime minister Clement Attlee and his foreign secretary, Ernest Bevin, faced the paradox that while the diplomatic importance of the Middle East had never been greater and Britain's nominal control over the region never stronger, the country was far less capable of exerting imperial authority than it had been before the war. According to the map, Britain's assets were impressive. Not only did it control a swath of occupied territory from Egypt to Iran, but the clearing out of Italian dictator Benito Mussolini's African colonies had left Britain in control of former Italian Somaliland, Eritrea, Tripolitania, and Cyrenaica. Only the vast and empty Arabian desert, ruled since 1927 by the Wahhabist House of Saud, remained—at least to some extent—outside the British orbit.

Britain's finances and manpower had, however, been exhausted by six years of war. The United States was now quite clearly the much stronger of the two powers, and it was evident to everyone—including Arab nationalists restless for greater autonomy and a fairer share of oil revenues—that the British Empire was on the decline. But Bevin refused to submit to despondency. In a September 1945 memorandum, he laid out his plan for a revitalized imperial role in the Middle East. While recognizing that gunboat diplomacy and informal rule through pliable puppet monarchs was no longer a feasible strategy, he proposed a new and more equitable set of partnerships that were to be based on British-funded economic development and Cold War defense cooperation. Bevin saw the Middle East as the keystone of his anti-Soviet strategy, with the Suez Canal base securing oil shipments to the West and long-range bomber airfields in Palestine threatening the Soviet Union's southern flank in the event of war.

Bevin's plans were bold but ultimately unrealistic. Insofar as Palestine in particular was concerned, they ignored the fact that the war had completely changed the character of Jewish politics in Europe. The Nazi so-called Final Solution had killed an estimated 6 million Jews and left at least 250,000 survivors of Hitler's death camps stranded in refugee facilities across the continent. Many of these displaced persons (DPs) sought to immigrate to Palestine in defiance of the white paper quotas, and although British troops succeeded in intercepting and detaining many of them, the war-weary public back in the United Kingdom had little stomach for the distasteful spectacle of its soldiers imprisoning recent survivors of the Holocaust in new prisons. World sympathy for the DPs was strong particularly in the United States, where the new president, Harry Truman, was under pressure to use enhanced U.S. diplomatic leverage to change British policy in Palestine.

Britain's ability to maintain control of the region was also under pressure. Toward the end of the war Jewish militant groups such as the Irgun Tsvai Leumi (National Military Organization) had restarted their paramilitary campaigns against mandate rule, and a vicious insurgency campaign broke out that culminated in the July 1946 bombing of the King David Hotel, the British military headquarters in Jerusalem, in which 91 people died. In a period of rapid postwar demobilization and a dire manpower shortage at home, it was difficult to justify the presence of large numbers of British personnel in a province that looked increasingly headed toward civil war.

The Labour government's main political initiative was the 1946 Anglo-American Committee of Inquiry, which proposed the creation of a single binational state and the immediate entry of 100,000 Jewish DPs into Palestine. Although Attlee's administration was much more enthusiastic about the former recommendation than the latter, it cautiously welcomed the committee's findings, but President Truman torpedoed the delicate negotiation process when he made a blunt statement implying that the larger immigration quota was the only significant element to the report. Britain's determination to find a binational solution to Palestine came to an end the following February when, beleaguered by the mounting violence in the mandate, Attlee's government announced that it was referring the problem back to the United Nations (UN). In November 1947, the UN voted for partition, a vote on which the United Kingdom abstained. The following May, Britain abruptly withdrew its last remaining personnel from the mandate, precipitating the outbreak of the first Arab-Israeli war, the Israeli War of Independence (1948–1949). Britain expected the Arab League to win this conflict and would no doubt have welcomed the emergence of an independent Palestinian entity from the post-mandate wreckage, but any chance of such a scenario was ruined by the poor military showing of the Arabs in the war.

The creation of the State of Israel in May 1948 greatly complicated Britain's subsequent Middle East policy. Recognition that the Jewish state was—however imperfectly—the region's only practicing democracy, a powerful anti-Soviet bastion, and a valued client of the United States had to be balanced against the British desire not to inflame Arab sensibilities elsewhere. Cold War Anglo-Israeli relations were characterized by periods of cooperation interspersed with diplomatic prickliness, with Tel Aviv critical of what it saw as Britain's too-cozy attitude toward the Arabs and with London frustrated by the Israeli failure to settle the Palestinian question once and for all.

The 10 years that followed the end of World War II saw Britain's gradual withdrawal from many of its formal Middle East suzerainties. Nevertheless, it sought to retain key advisory links with the successor states, particularly with regard to oil exploration and defense issues. The success of this policy was mixed. In March 1946, the Transjordanian mandate was peacefully abolished, and two years later Emir Abdullah declared himself monarch of the new Anglophile Kingdom of Jordan. That same year, Britain negotiated the Treaty of Portsmouth, an attempt to define its ongoing security relationship with Iraq, particularly with regard to the retention of RAF bases there. The treaty failed, however, to appease Iraqi nationalists and was never ratified by Baghdad. Worse than this disappointment was the 1951 crisis in Iran, when populist prime minister Mohammad Mosaddeq nationalized the assets of the Anglo-Iranian Oil Company (AIOC), which forced a tense standoff with the British government. The crisis was relieved only when Mosaddeq was toppled from office through the covert actions of the U.S. Central Intelligence Agency (CIA) and Britain's Secret Intelligence Service (MI6).

British Petroleum (BP), a reconstruction of the AIOC, retained a 40 percent share in Iranian oil production in the postcrisis settlement, but the net result was Iran's shift into an American rather than exclusively British sphere of influence, a pervasive theme of the postwar period.

That increasing U.S. involvement in Middle Eastern affairs might not always be in Britain's best interests was illustrated by the rise to power of Gamal Abdel Nasser in Egypt following the 1952 officers' coup that dethroned King Farouk. Violent protests had been brewing in Egypt even during the last days of the Hashemite monarchy because of Britain's procrastination over its withdrawal from the canal zone, originally scheduled to take place in 1949 but persistently delayed. London initially hoped to find in Nasser a more willing partner than Farouk, conceding an October 1954 treaty with Nasser that finalized the cession of the Suez base and offering to help fund the Aswan High Dam project.

However, in 1955 when Britain organized the anti-Soviet Baghdad Pact—also known as the Central Treaty Organization (CENTO)—with Turkey, Iran, Iraq, and Pakistan, an outraged Nasser denounced the agreement as neoimperialist and sought a rearmament deal with the Soviet Union. British prime minister Anthony Eden then followed the U.S. lead in withdrawing British assistance for the Aswan High Dam project. Egypt promptly nationalized the Anglo-French Suez Canal Company as compensation. Secret negotiations followed among Israel (already involved in an undeclared sniping war with Egypt) and the aggrieved British and French, and a plan was concocted to invade Egypt and unseat Nasser. Israel would invade the Sinai Peninsula, giving the European powers the excuse to intervene and seize the canal zone

as neutral peacemakers. Because Nasser's refusal to accept this intervention was more or less guaranteed, the expeditionary force would then have a legal pretext to crush the Egyptian regime.

Israel duly attacked on October 29, 1956, and a few days later a mainly British amphibious force supported by strong airpower assaulted Port Said. Although militarily successful, the invasion was a diplomatic disaster for Britain, and when the Soviet Union threatened to intervene on Nasser's side, President Dwight D. Eisenhower's administration used its financial muscle to force the British into a cease-fire and a humiliating evacuation. The Suez Crisis was the last occasion in which Britain attempted a unilateral military solution to a Middle Eastern crisis and marked the collapse of Britain's already-tottering prestige in the region. During the crisis, CENTO proved ineffective in advancing British interests. As early as 1959, Iraq had dropped out of the organization following its republican revolution, and the pact was unable to influence the course of the Arab-Israeli conflict.

With the winding down of Britain's military presence in Jordan and the granting of independence to Kuwait in 1961, the only remaining remnants of empire were now along the Arabian shoreline. The old garrison town of Aden had, with the loss of Suez, become Britain's primary defense base in the Middle East, and although London recognized that its days as a Crown Colony were numbered, it was determined that any successor state should be friendly toward British interests. In January 1963, Prime Minister Harold Macmillan's government united Aden and the old Yemeni protectorate into the Federation of South Arabia (FOSA), which was promised independence within five years. However, terrorist resistance by the Egyptian-backed National Liberation

Front prevented a peaceful transition of power, and after a fruitless campaign to pacify civil unrest, British troops abandoned the territory in November 1967. The failure to retain the Aden bridgehead coupled with parlous financial problems at home (set off in part by the rise in international oil prices after the 1967 Six-Day War) necessitated a comprehensive British defense review. This resulted in the decision to withdraw all remaining British forces east of Suez by the end of 1971. The political consequence of this decision for the Middle East was the reorganization of Britain's old Persian Gulf protectorates. Thus, they transformed themselves into the United Arab Emirates (UAE), and Qatar and Bahrain (which could not agree on a unified constitution with their UAE neighbors) became independent polities.

The end of empire did not of course end Britain's relationship with the Middle East. As one of the West's principal oil importers and a major supplier of advanced technology, Great Britain inevitably continued to display a strong interest in regional affairs. Although after the Suez debacle Britain no longer sought a leading role in the Arab-Israeli conflict, its position as a permanent member of the UN Security Council gave its opinions inherent significance. In general, Britain followed the lead of the United States throughout the remainder of the Cold War. But, bearing in mind its historical ties with the Arabian Peninsula, it was less publicly emphatic in its support of Israel.

Until 1990 the story of Britain's military disengagement from the region followed a clear and consistent narrative. This was rudely reversed, however, with the Iraqi invasion of Kuwait in August 1990. Great Britain actively contributed to all of the U.S.-led multinational operations that followed it, including DESERT SHIELD and DESERT STORM. It also took part in the various airborne policing campaigns of Iraq in the 1990s, including Operation DESERT FOX, an air campaign launched in December 1998 designed to destroy suspected sites where weapons of mass destruction (WMDs) were allegedly being developed. After the September 11, 2001, terrorist attacks on the United States, Britain stood closely with its ally across the Atlantic and fully supported the operations to rid Afghanistan of the Taliban regime, contributing substantially to NATO operations in that country. The unseating of Iraqi dictator Saddam Hussein's regime in Operation IRAQI FREEDOM (2003)—given the more prosaic title TELIC by British forces—likewise involved direct involvement of British troops. British intervention in Iraq was politically unpopular, with major public demonstrations against it in London and other British cities. It also brought major Islamic terrorist attacks by suicide bombers on the London underground and buses in July 2003, while car bombs targeted several airports in 2007.

British forces nonetheless continued operations in both Iraq and Afghanistan, incurring a total of 179 military fatalities in Iraq and, by April 2014, 448 in Afghanistan. In September 2007, British troops withdrew from their last base in Basra to an airport garrison on the outskirts of the city, and half of the 5,000 British troops remaining in Iraq were scheduled to return home by spring 2008. After eight years, in 2011, the last British troops left Iraq. By the end of 2013, some 5,000 British military personnel were still left in Afghanistan, scheduled to depart in 2014. Britain also maintained a substantial air and naval presence throughout the Persian Gulf area, an epilogue that would have seemed bizarre to those witnessing the lowering of the last Union Jacks in the region 35 years earlier.

As a member of the UN and European Union (EU), Britain supported the Israeli-Palestinian peace negotiations. In June 2007, former Labour prime minister Tony Blair, who had been the driving force behind British intervention in Iraq, became the Middle East Quartet representative, heading up the office established in 2002 by the EU, UN, Russia, and the United States to facilitate the implementation of the Israeli-Palestinian peace process and promote economic and political development in the West Bank and Gaza. Several Quartet advisers were also seconded from the British government. From 2006 onward, Britain also joined the United States in supporting the imposition of extensive UN and EU sanctions on Iran, should that country continue its efforts to develop nuclear weapons that might be used against Israel.

Alan Allport

Further Reading

Abadi, Jacob. *Britain's Withdrawal from the Middle East, 1947–1971*. Middlesex, UK: Kingston, 1983.

Almog, Orna. *Britain, Israel, and the United States, 1955–1958: Beyond Suez*. New York: Routledge, 2002.

Anderson, Scott. *Lawrence in Arabia: War, Deceit, Imperial Folly and the Making of the Modern Middle East*. New York: Doubleday, 2013.

Aridan, Natan. *Britain, Israel and Anglo-Jewry 1949–57*. New York: Routledge, 2004.

Balfour-Paul, Glen. *The End of Empire in the Middle East*. New York: Cambridge University Press, 1991.

Barr, James. *A Line in the Sand: The Anglo-French Struggle for the Middle East, 1914–1948*. New York: Norton, 2012.

Brenchley, Frank. *Britain, the Six-Day War and Its Aftermath*. London: I. B. Tauris, 2005.

Butler, Daniel Allen. *Shadow of the Sultan's Realm: The Destruction of the Ottoman Empire and the Creation of the Modern Middle East*. Washington, DC: Potomac Books, 2011.

Cohen, Michael J. *Britain's Moment in Palestine: Retrospect and Perspectives, 1917–1948*. New York: Routledge, 2014.

Cohen, Michael J., and Martin Kolinsky, eds. *The Demise of the British Empire in the Middle East*. London: Frank Cass, 1998.

Ford, Roger. *Eden to Armageddon: World War I in the Middle East*. Glendale Heights, IL: Pegasus, 2010.

Fromkin, David. *A Peace to End All Peace: The Fall of the Ottoman Empire and the Creation of the Modern Middle East*. New York: Avon, 1989.

Golani, Motti. *Palestine between Politics and Terror, 1945–1947*. Waltham, MA: Brandeis University Press, 2013.

Greenwood, Sean. *Britain and the Cold War, 1945–91*. New York: Macmillan, 2000.

Hamilton, Jill. *God, Guns and Israel: Britain, the First World War and the Jews in the Holy City*. Stroud: Sutton, 2005.

Levey, Zach. *Israel and the Western Powers, 1952–1960*. Chapel Hill: University of North Carolina Press, 2011.

Lewis, Geoffrey. *Balfour and Weizmann: The Zionist, the Zealot, and the Emergence of Israel*. London: Bloomsbury, 2009.

Louis, William Roger. *The British Empire in the Middle East, 1945–1951: Arab Nationalism, the United States, and Postwar Imperialism*. New York: Oxford University Press, 1984.

Miller, Rory. *Britain, Palestine, and Empire: The Mandate Years*. Farnham, UK: Ashgate, 2010.

Ovendale, Ritchie. *Britain, the United States, and the Transfer of Power in the Middle East, 1945–1962*. Leicester, UK: Leicester University Press, 1996.

Peterson, Tore. *The Middle East between the Great Powers: Anglo-American Conflict and Cooperation, 1952–57*. New York: Macmillan, 2000.

Podeh, Elie, and Zach Levey, eds. *Britain and the Middle East: From Imperial Power to Junior Partner*. Brighton: Sussex Academic Press, 2008.

Reid, Walter. *Empire of Sand: How Britain Shaped the Middle East*. Edinburgh, Scotland: Birlinn, 2011.

Schneer, Jonathan. *The Balfour Declaration: The Origins of the Arab-Israeli Conflict*. New York: Random House, 2010.

Segev, Tom. *One Palestine, Complete: Jews and Arabs under the British Mandate*. New York: Henry Holt, 2000.

Shepherd, Naomi. *Ploughing Sand: British Rule in Palestine, 1917–1948*. New Brunswick, NJ: Rutgers University Press, 1999.

Smith, Simon C. *Ending Empire in the Middle East: Britain, the United States, and Post-war Decolonization, 1945–1973*. New York: Routledge, 2013.

United Nations, Role of

The United Nations (UN) was created by 50 founding countries on October 24, 1945, as the successor to the post–World War I League of Nations (formed in 1919). The UN inherited the so-called Palestine question when London informed the UN on February 14, 1947, that Great Britain would no longer administer the British Mandate for Palestine that had been formally granted by the League of Nations on September 29, 1923.

The UN Special Commission on Palestine (UNSCOP) was formed on May 13, 1947, and its 11 member states voted unanimously to terminate British administration of mandatory Palestine. On August 31, 1947, a majority of UNSCOP, 7 of 11 members, recommended that Palestine be partitioned into a Jewish state and an Arab state, with Jerusalem and Bethlehem remaining neutral. This recommendation was accepted by the UN General Assembly on November 29, 1947. Jews in Palestine agreed to the partition plan, but the Arab spokesmen rebuffed it.

On March 12, 1948, UNSCOP informed the UN that it believed that dissolution would bring chaos and war to the region

Yugoslav troops of the United Nations Emergency Forces (UNEF) on patrol at El Arish, Egypt, in 1957. (Corel)

UN secretary general Ban Ki-moon, left, stands with Palestinian Prime Minister Salam Fayyad, during a tour of the West Bank city of Ramallah on March 20, 2010. (AP Photo/Mohamad Torokman, Pool)

and, on March 18, recommended that the UN attempt to maintain order and peace by assuming temporary trusteeship over Palestine from the British. The UN responded by creating the Truce Commission for Palestine (April 23, 1948) to assist the UN Security Council in bringing peace and order to Palestine as per UN Resolution 46 (April 17, 1948).

The mandate was dissolved, partition was enacted, and the independent Jewish State of Israel was created at midnight Palestine time on May 14, 1948. Egypt, Syria, Jordan, Lebanon, and Iraq attacked Israel on May 15, and the UN dissolved UNSCOP on May 20 in the belief that an appointed mediator, Count Folke Bernadotte, UN mediator on Palestine (UNMP) and president of the Swedish Red Cross working with the Truce Commission, had a better chance at bringing peace to the region.

On May 29, 1948, the UN Security Council called a four-week truce under the supervision of a UNMP and an international military observer team eventually known as United Nations Truce Supervision Organization (UNTSO). The truce lasted from June 11 until July 8. The Security Council initiated a second truce on July 15. The territories assigned to Palestine captured by the Israelis and the territory of the newly created Israel from 1948 to 1950 are well documented, but the number of Palestinian refugees who fled or were expelled from Jerusalem and other areas is disputed. The estimates range from the Israeli total of 400,000 to the Arab estimate of 950,000 to 1 million. The official UN estimate is 711,000.

Count Bernadotte was assassinated on September 17, 1948. The UNMP was then replaced by the UN Conciliation Commission for Palestine (UNCCP) headquartered in Jerusalem (January 1949), created by General Assembly Resolution 194 (III) on December 11, 1948. The UNCCP attempted to reach a settlement between the Arab states (Egypt, Saudi Arabia, the Hashemite Kingdom of Jordan, Iraq, Syria, and Lebanon), Israel, and

UN PARTITION PLAN, 1947

LEBANON

SYRIA

Hanita

Matzuva

Eilon

Nahariya

Gaaton

Acre

Yehiam

Safed

Haifa

Sea of
Galilee

Kfar
Hahoresh

Mediterranean

Sea

Jenin

Hadera

Nablus

Jordan R.

Tel Aviv

Ben
Shemen

Java

Atarot

Kfar
Menachem

Hartuv

Neve Yaakov

Bet Haatava

Nitzanim

Kallia

Kedma

Galon

Gat

Ein Tzurim

Yad Mordechai

Gush Etzion

Revadim

Hebron

Kfar Darom

Massout
Yitzhak

*Dead
Sea*

Nirim

Beersheba

Negev

El Arish

E G Y P T

Sinai

Peninsula

TRANSJORDAN

- - - Boundary of the British
Palestine Mandate, 1922–1947

Proposed Jewish State

Proposed Arab State

⊙ Jewish Settlements to be
included in the Arab State

Jerusalem and its Suberbs
(to be an International Zone)

0   10   20 mi

0 10 20 km

Eilat

Akaba

34°E

36°E

33°N

32°N

31°N

30°N

N

Map of the 1947 UN partition plan of Palestine.

the displaced Palestinians. Although armistice agreements were signed from February to July 1949 between Israel and Egypt, Jordan, Lebanon, and Syria, the UNCCP concluded after meeting with the concerned parties from March 21 through November 1951 that the entities involved were unwilling to comply with paragraph 11 of Resolution 194 (III) concerning Palestinian refugees and that reconciliation would be difficult to effectuate.

During 1952–1966, the UNCCP also determined the final valuations for approximately

453,000 abandoned or seized Arab-owned land parcels as well as Arab disposable property lost. The UNCCP completed its work in 1966 except for brief annual reports that it submits to the General Assembly and the maintenance of the property valuations and records on which the valuations were based. The General Assembly's 1996 Resolution 51/129 authorized that all necessary means should be taken to "preserve and modernize the existing records" of the UNCCP. The UNCCP annual report to the General Assembly generates an annual resolution regretting that Resolution 194 (III), paragraph 11, concerning the repatriation or compensation of the refugees has not been accomplished and requesting that the UNCCP continue its efforts and annual reporting until such time that its original mandate is completely fulfilled.

Israel became a full member of the UN on May 11, 1949. The UN Relief and Works Agency for Palestine Refugees (UNRWA) began operation on May 1, 1951, after it was created on December 8, 1948, by UN General Assembly Resolution 302 (IV) to replace the UN Relief for Palestine Refugees (UNRPR) created on November 19, 1948, by Resolution 212 (III). The UNRWA was and still is the main provider of education, health, relief, social services, and other basic services to more than 4.3 million Palestinian refugees and their descendants who were displaced by Arab-Israeli wars during 1948–1949, 1956, 1967, 1973, 1982, and 2006 and Palestinian-Israeli conflicts such as the First Intifada (1987–1993) and the Second (al-Aqsa) Intifada (2000–2005). Although most refugees fall under the purview of the Office of the UN High Commissioner for Refugees (UNHCR) headquartered in Geneva, Switzerland, most Palestinian refugees are the responsibility of the UNRWA. The responsibility for all Palestinian refugees within Israel was the

UNRWA's from 1948 until it was appropriated by Israel in 1952.

The UNRWA had an initial budget of $50 million but is the largest UN operation in the Middle East in the 21st century, employing 22,000 people in 900 facilities including the 59 camps with 1.3 million residents in the Gaza Strip, the West Bank, Jordan, Lebanon, and Syria. The UNRWA's mandate must be periodically renewed by the General Assembly.

The UNRPR was envisioned as a short-term agency coordinating the activities of international relief nongovernmental organizations (NGOs) that, along with other UN agencies such as the UN International Children's Emergency Fund (UNICEF), World Health Organization (WHO), Food and Agriculture Organization (FAO), and the International Refugee Organization were providing the direct relief services to the displaced Palestinians until what the UN anticipated would be a quick resolution of the Israeli-Palestinian crisis. The UN created the UNRWA when it became clear that there was to be no quick resolution of the displaced Palestinians. The UNRWA was headquartered in Beirut from 1950 to 1978 and in Vienna from 1978 to 1996 before it moved to Gaza in the Palestinian territories in 1996.

The UNRWA provides relief services to the Palestinian refugee camps in the Gaza Strip, the West Bank, Jordan, Lebanon, and Syria but does not participate in the administration of the camps. Half of the UNRWA's budget and two-thirds of its staff are committed to operating 647 elementary and secondary schools and 8 vocational training centers. The UNRWA also operates 122 health centers and provides environmental health services for the refugee camps. The agency develops infrastructure for the camps and provides loan assistance for enterprise development for all Palestinian refugees.

The UN helped end the 1956 Suez Crisis involving Egypt, Israel, France, and the United Kingdom by calling a cease-fire and deploying in November 1956 the UN's first peacekeeping force, the United Nations Emergency Force (UNEF). Egypt expelled UNEF from the buffer zone in the Sinai Peninsula in July 1967, however, and Israel responded to this and other provocations by launching the 1967 Six-Day War (June 5–10). Israel gained control of East Jerusalem, the West Bank, the Gaza Strip, the Sinai Peninsula, and the Golan Heights, and an additional 500,000 Palestinian refugees fled from these areas. On November 22, 1967, Security Council Resolution 242 urged both Israeli withdrawal from these territories and the correlative recognition of Israel as a state having the right to exist. Egypt and Jordan accepted the resolution contingent on the Israeli withdrawal, Syria and the Palestine Liberation Organization (PLO) rejected the resolution, and Israel accepted the resolution with the caveat that withdrawal was contingent on direct negotiations with the involved Arab states and the finalization of a comprehensive peace treaty.

Security Council Resolution 252 (1968) called on Israel to rescind its absorption and administration of East Jerusalem and return it to international administration. General Assembly Resolution 2443 (XXIII) of December 1968 created the three-member (Sri Lanka, Senegal, and Malaysia) Special Committee to Investigate Israeli Practices Affecting the Human Rights of the Palestinian People and Other Arabs of the Occupied Territories, also known as the Special Committee. The Special Committee was tasked with reporting on Israel's regard of the essential and inalienable human rights of the Palestinians and other Arabs under Israeli control, any Israeli looting of Palestinian and Arab real or disposable property,

and any pillaging of Palestinian and Arab cultural and holy places. The Special Committee began submitting annual reports to the General Assembly in 1970 and then in 1989 began submitting two additional reports each year.

In 1972, UNTSO initiated a cease-fire and observation operation in southern Lebanon after Israel responded to PLO cross-border incursions by attacking PLO refugee camps in Lebanon.

The Security Council addressed the October 1973 Yom Kippur War by adopting Resolution 338 reaffirming Resolution 242 and the need for negotiations leading to "a just and durable peace in the Middle East." The Security Council cease-fire went into effect on October 23 and was followed on October 24 with the establishment of the second UN Emergency Force (UNEF II), which supervised the disengagement of Israeli and Egyptian forces. The mission of the UNEF ended with the 1979 Israel-Egypt Peace Treaty based on the 1978 Camp David Accords. In December 1973, the UN convened an International Peace Conference in Geneva that led in part to the disengagement agreements between Egypt and Israel (January 1974 and October 1975) and between Syria and Israel (May 1974). The UN created the UN Disengagement Force (UNDOF) to monitor the disengagement agreement between Israel and Syria.

In 1974, the UN granted the PLO observer status as the representative of the Palestinian people and on November 22 reaffirmed the inalienable rights of the Palestinian people to self-determination, national independence and sovereignty, and the right to return to their homes and property, a reaffirmation that continues to be made annually. In 1975, the General Assembly created the Committee on the Exercise of the Inalienable Rights of the Palestinian People (CEIRPP), also known as the Palestinian Rights Committee, and tasked it with developing a program that would enable the Palestinians to exercise these rights.

The PLO increased its incursions into northern Israel from the end of 1976 to early 1978. Israel responded by invading southern Lebanon in March 1978. The Lebanese government requested that the Security Council create the UN Interim Force in Lebanon (UNIFIL) to monitor the withdrawal of the Israel Defense Forces (IDF) from Lebanon and then to help restore peace, security, and Lebanese authority over southern Lebanon. The IDF withdrew in June 1978 and bypassed UNIFIL by creating a security zone roughly 62 miles long and 6–12 miles wide in southern Lebanon defended by the 2,000 member South Lebanon Army (SLA) backed by Israel.

On March 22, 1979, the Security Council and General Assembly determined in Resolution 446 that Israeli settlements in Palestinian areas captured since 1967 were against the 1949 Fourth Geneva Convention, had no legal basis, and created a great obstacle to a comprehensive peace in the area. The resolution also created a commission composed of Bolivia, Portugal, and Zambia tasked with investigating these settlements. The commission submitted reports in July 1979, December 1979, and November 1980 affirming that the settlement policy constituted a serious impediment to the establishment of a comprehensive peace agreement. It was after the first two reports that Israel began the process of making Jerusalem its capital. Security Council Resolution 476 (June 1980) called on Israel to follow all previous UN resolutions on the status of Jerusalem and was followed by Resolution 478 (August 1980) urging all UN member states not to establish diplomatic missions in Jerusalem. The assertion of Resolution 446

that Israeli settlements in these areas contravened the Geneva Convention was reaffirmed in December 1980 and in subsequent years.

During 1980–1982 the Lebanese Civil War intensified, and fighting increased throughout the country. Fearing the growing influence and power of the Syrians and the PLO in Lebanon and following the PLO attacks on Israeli diplomats in London and Paris, Israel invaded Lebanon on June 6, 1982. The Israeli invasion, known as Operation PEACE FOR GALILEE, was planned to move the PLO's Katyusha rockets out of the range of Israel's northern border and to destroy the terrorist infrastructure that had developed in Lebanon. The IDF bypassed or overran the UNIFIL positions, and the Security Council called for a cease-fire and the withdrawal of the IDF (Resolution 509). Israel continued its operation and eventually surrounded and blockaded Beirut. From June through August 1982, the Security Council demanded that Israel lift the blockade and withdraw. The Security Council also deployed UN military observers known as Observer Group Beirut to monitor the conflict.

At the request of the Lebanese government, a multinational force evacuated PLO forces from Beirut. This evacuation was achieved on September 1, 1982, and the multinational force withdrew over the next two weeks. Israel moved into West Beirut following the assassination of Lebanon's president-elect Bashir Gemayal on September 14, 1982. On September 17, 700–3,500 Palestinian civilians, including women and children, were massacred in the refugee camps of Sabra and Shatila by Lebanese Christian Phalangist forces along with some members of the SLA. A new multinational force reentered the area but failed to resolve the conflict, and all elements of this force withdrew by early 1984. In December 1983, PLO forces and PLO chairman Yasser Arafat were evacuated from Tripoli in northern Lebanon on ships flying the UN flag.

The General Assembly convened the International Conference on the Question of Palestine, which met in Geneva from August 29 to September 7, 1983, despite opposition from Israel, the United States, and other countries. The conference, attended by 137 UN states and the PLO, adopted a Declaration on Palestine and approved a Program of Action for the Achievement of Palestinian Rights that included opposition to future Israeli settlements in the occupied territories, opposition to any change in status of Jerusalem, the right of all states to have internationally recognized secure borders, and respect for the inalienable rights of the Palestinian people.

Even though the PLO had been driven from Lebanon, the Israeli presence in force lasted until 2000 and resulted in such a high number of Palestinian civilian deaths that worldwide public opinion turned against Israel. A treaty ending the engagement was signed on May 17, 1983, only to be revoked by the Lebanese under Syrian pressure soon after Israeli prime minister Menachem Begin resigned. Israel continued to garrison soldiers and to operate in consort with the SLA in the southern security zone.

The First Intifada (1987–1993) erupted in December 1987. The Palestinian violence and the response of the Israelis were monitored by CEIRPP, the Special Committee, and the UNRWA. The UN was particularly disturbed by Palestinian deportations from the occupied territories and responded with Resolutions 607 and 608 in January 1988, Resolution 636 in July 1989, and Resolution 641 in August 1989 demanding that Israel cease and desist from deportations and allow the deportees to return.

The PLO's Palestinian National Council (PNC) meeting in Algiers formally created the State of Palestine in November 1988 in accordance with UN Resolution 181 (II). The General Assembly acknowledged the proclamation in December 1988 when the General Assembly changed the name of the UN delegation representing the Palestinian people from the "PLO" to "Palestine" and reaffirmed the borders of Palestine to be those preceding the 1967 war. From 1988 through 1990, the Security Council repeatedly condemned Israel for its disregard of the UN directions concerning Israel's handling of the First Intifada. In February 1993, the UN Commission on Human Rights appointed a Special Rapporteur on human rights violations in the occupied Palestinian and Arab territories.

The General Assembly supported the 1993 Oslo Accords, officially called the Declaration of Principles on Interim Self-Government Arrangements or simply the Declaration of Principles (DOP), and sought to actively participate in the ensuing peace process. The Oslo Accords and the creation of the Palestinian Authority (PA) effectively ended the violence of the First Intifada. The UN increased economic support to the Palestinians, established the High-Level Task Force on the Socioeconomic Development of the Gaza Strip and Jericho; hosted a donor conference on October 1, 1993, in Washington, D.C., known as the Conference to Support Middle East Peace; and in June 1994 created the UN Special Coordinator (UNSCO) to enhance interagency cooperation. UNSCO was tasked with coordinating all UN and NGO operations in the West Bank and Gaza, representing the UN at donor coordination meetings and meetings concerning the Palestinian-Israeli Peace Accords, assisting the PA in its administration of international donations, and implementing the DOP as requested by the involved parties.

Three important events occurred in 1995 and 1996. First, the Israeli-Palestinian (PLO) Interim Agreement on the West Bank and the Gaza Strip (September 28, 1995), also known as Oslo II or Taba, directed the continuing redeployment of the IDF. Second, Israeli prime minister Yitzhak Rabin was assassinated on November 4, 1995. And third, Yasser Arafat was elected as the first president of the PA.

The UN secretary general participated in the Summit of Peacemakers in Sharm al-Sheikh, Egypt, in March 1996 that condemned violence in the Middle East. The UN along with Norway also facilitated talks between Arafat and Israeli prime minister Benjamin Netanyahu on September 4, 1996. The secretary general monitored the construction of new Israeli settlements in the occupied territories during this time and reported in June 1997 that the construction continued in spite of UN protestations. The General Assembly increased its scrutiny of Israeli actions in East Jerusalem and the Palestinian territories during 1997–1998 as Israel continued its redeployment per the 1997 Hebron Protocol. The General Assembly continued to express concern over what it determined to be persistent Israeli violations of the Geneva Convention.

The General Assembly enhanced Palestine's observer status on July 7, 1998, in Resolution 52/250 by expanding Palestine's rights and privileges of participation in the General Assembly. The UN played no role in the 1998 Wye River Memorandum signed by Netanyahu and Arafat.

On February 9, 1999, the General Assembly again declared that all legislative and administrative actions taken by Israel, called the "occupying power," in the areas it seized in 1967 were illegal, invalid, null,

and void. The General Assembly convened a conference on July 15, 1999, concerning alleged continuing Israeli violations of the Geneva Convention. UNSCO was reconfigured in September 1999 into the Office of the Special Coordinator for the Middle East Peace Process and Personal Representative of the Secretary-General to the Palestine Liberation Organization and the Palestinian Authority. The Special Coordinator's Office was tasked with representing the UN secretary general in all matters relating to the Middle East peace process.

The Special Rapporteur issued a report on the status of human rights in the Palestinian territories on March 15, 2000, asserting that Israeli settlement activity continued unabated through 1999 and that Israeli occupation forces conducted numerous punitive and violent demolitions of Palestinian homes and forcible evictions of entire Palestinian villages. The CEIRPP concurred and asserted (as it has annually) that Israel's settlement policy is a serious impediment to the establishment of a final comprehensive peace accord.

The July 2000 Camp David talks between Israel and the PA ended with no progress despite Israel's withdrawal of its forces from Lebanon on April 17, 2000, in full accord with Security Council Resolutions 425 (1978) and 426 (1978). The General Assembly asserted again on October 20, 2000, that all Israeli settlements in areas occupied since 1967 were illegal and an impediment to peace. On December 1, 2000, the General Assembly reaffirmed that all actions taken by Israel relative to what the UN deemed "occupied" East Jerusalem were illegal, invalid, null, and void.

The Second (al-Aqsa) Intifada began in September 2000 in Jerusalem after Israel's Likud Party opposition politician Ariel Sharon in the company of security forces visited the al-Aqsa Mosque. After demonstrations broke out, larger ones were met with violence by Israeli forces in the West Bank and Gaza. Security Council Resolution 1322 (2000) condemned all acts of violence and specifically condemned excessive force by Israel in dealing with the Palestinian uprising. The CEIRPP met in October 2000 and urged the UN to remain engaged in the peace process and to continue monitoring the conflict and safeguarding the inalienable rights of the Palestinian people. The intifada ended most discussions concerning the implementation of the DOP framework. As the violence increased and as suicide bombings became more prevalent, Israel responded by attacking PA infrastructure and facilities and reoccupied territory ceded to the PA. Israel also added to the tension by allowing the number of Jewish settlements in the West Bank to more than double the Israeli population within the autonomous region.

Although the Security Council considered deploying a UN observer group in the Palestinian territories in March 2001, the UN made no progress in resolving the conflict or the tangential issues. Mahmoud Abbas was elected president of the PA on January 9, 2005, after Arafat's death on November 11, 2004. The intifada essentially ended following a summit between Abbas and Israeli prime minister Ariel Sharon in early 2005. Despite Israeli withdrawals from Gaza and the Jericho area, Abbas's position was severely weakened when his Fatah party lost control of the Palestinian Legislative Council (PLC) to Hamas in the January 2006 elections. The United States, Canada, and the European Union (EU) withdrew financial support for the PA due to Hamas's unwillingness to recognize Israel's right to exist, and the UN was unable to make up the financial shortfall.

War raged again in Lebanon from July 12 to August 14, 2006, when Israel and Hezbollah fought in what is known in Lebanon as the July War and in Israel as the Second Lebanon War. Security Council Resolution 1701, passed on August 11, 2006, called for an end to militias in Lebanon, the withdrawal of Israeli forces from Lebanon, and the deployment of Lebanese soldiers and an enhanced UNIFIL in southern Lebanon. Unfortunately, the largest segment of the Lebanese population saw Resolution 1701 as a U.S.- and Israeli-supported mandate against Hezbollah that aimed to support only one side of the Lebanese government. In 2006, UN Security Council Resolution 1664, authorized the establishment of a Special Tribunal for Lebanon, an international criminal court based in the Netherlands, to investigate the assassination of former Lebanese prime minister Rafik Hariri. This tribunal came into existence in March 2009.

As one of the international Quartet group, also including the EU, the United States, and Russia, that came together in 2002 to encourage continuing negotiations between Israel and Palestinians, the UN remained permanently involved in the peace process. At a March 2007 summit meeting of the Arab League, UN secretary general Ban Ki-moon endorsed the Arab Peace Initiative, a comprehensive proposal for a permanent settlement. This called for complete Israeli withdrawal from the occupied territories, the creation of an independent Palestinian state with East Jerusalem as its capital, and a "just solution" to the problem of Palestinian refugees. In return, all Arab states would sign permanent peace treaties with Israel, recognizing its existence. This proposal, first put forward by then Crown Prince Abdullah of Saudi Arabia at an Arab League meeting in 2002, had already won endorsement from all Arab League member states, plus PA president Mahmoud Abbas.

After fierce fighting between moderate Fatah and more radical Hamas Palestinian groups in Gaza, in June 2007, Hamas won complete control of Gaza, leaving Abbas heading a PA government whose writ ran only in the West Bank. In July, Abbas announced that the PA would have no contact with Hamas, a split that allowed the revival of negotiations between the PA and Israel. Meanwhile, UN relief and economic agencies sought to provide welfare and development assistance to Palestinians in both the West Bank and Gaza Strip.

In 2009, the UN Human Rights Commission established a fact-finding mission, headed by the South African jurist Richard Goldstone, to investigate human rights abuses and breaches of international humanitarian law in the Palestinian territories, especially the Gaza Strip. The report, released in September 2009, held both the IDF and Palestinian militants responsible war crimes and possibly crimes against humanity. It urged both sides to investigate their own conduct, or else face proceedings from an international criminal court. Hamas initially rejected the report, but afterward switched its position, urging other powers to embrace it, while Israel, which had already refused to cooperate with the mission, rejected its findings. By substantial majorities, the UN Human Rights Commission and UN General Assembly endorsed the report, demanding further investigations, but neither Israel nor Hamas implemented these recommendations.

The UN continued to criticize the continued existence and extension of Israeli settlements. In February 2011, the United States vetoed a Security Council Resolution condemning as illegal all Israeli settlements in the occupied territories since 1967. In January 2012 a UN fact-finding mission published a report stating that Israeli settlements in the West Bank had not only resulted in numerous infractions of Palestinian human rights, but violated international law, warning that unless Israel withdrew from these settlements it might face international criminal proceedings.

UN measures to check Iranian efforts to develop nuclear weapons were rather more in accord with Israeli and U.S. priorities. In an effort to halt Iran's nuclear weapons programme, from 2006 the UN imposed a range of economic sanctions on Iran, which were gradually tightened. The EU acquiesced in these constraints, while the United States imposed a near total economic embargo on Iran. These measures imposed significant hardship upon Iran, leading to a major currency crisis. In late 2013, Iran and six other powers, including the United States, reached an interim agreement, whereby Iran froze several aspects of its nuclear program for six months, in exchange for the relaxation of economic sanctions. In early 2014, talks on negotiations intended to leader to a long-term agreement on nuclear weapons were opened.

The UN was broadly sympathetic to Palestinian efforts to attain full statehood. In April 2011, the UN's coordinator for the Middle East process issued a report praising aspects of the PA's administration as entirely adequate for an "independent state." In September 2011, the PA applied for UN membership, as a step toward winning recognition as an independent state. In November 2011, the PA won membership of the cultural agency UNESCO, prompting the United States and Israel to withdraw their funding for that body, which in turn meant that in November 2013 each lost its own UNESCO membership. Over United States and Israeli protests, in November 2012, UN General Assembly 67/19 resolution granted the PA nonmember observer state status, with restricted voting rights in specific areas. Palestine could join treaties and specialized UN agencies, exercise jurisdiction over airspace and territorial waters, and pursue cases in the international criminal court. The UN also permitted the PA to use the designation "State of Palestine" in official communications.

To general applause, in November 2013, the Palestinian ambassador cast his first General Assembly vote, for an international criminal court justice. Urged by U.S. secretary of state John Kerry, in July 2013, Israel and the PA resumed negotiations intended to reach a full status agreement within nine months. During that period, the PA agreed to defer efforts to seek full UN membership or to submit appeals against Israeli policies to international agencies. The Palestinians of the West Bank were nonetheless moving ever closer to winning much coveted formal recognition as an independent state.

Richard M. Edwards

Further Reading

Beker, Avi. *The United Nations and Israel: From Recognition to Reprehension*. Lanham, MD: Lexington Books, 1988.

Berry, Mike, and Greg Philo. *Israel and Palestine: Competing Histories*. London: Pluto, 2006.

Caplan, Neil. *Futile Diplomacy: The United Nations, the Great Powers and Middle East Peacemaking, 1948–1954*. New York: Routledge, 1997.

Caplan, Neil. *The Israel-Palestine Conflict: Contested Histories*. New York: Wiley-Blackwell, 2009.

Di Mauro, Danilo. *The UN and the Arab-Israeli Conflict: American Hegemony and UN Intervention since 1947*. New York: Routledge, 2012.

Gelvin, James L. *The Israel-Palestine Conflict: One Hundred Years of War*. 3rd ed. New York: Cambridge University Press, 2014.

Grobman, Alex. *Nations United: How the United Nations Undermines Israel and the West*. Green Forest, AR: Balfour, 2006.

Hanafi, Sari, Leila Hilal, and Lex Takkenberg. *UNRWA and Palestinian Refugees: From Relief and Works to Human Development*. New York: Routledge, 2014.

Harms, Gregory, and Todd Ferry. *The Palestine-Israel Conflict: A Basic Introduction*. London: Pluto, 2005.

Horowitz, Adam, Lizzy Ratner, and Philip Weiss, eds. *The Goldstone Report: The Legacy of the Landmark Investigation of the Gaza Conflict*. New York: Nation Books, 2011.

Meisler, Stanley. *The United Nations: A History*. 2nd ed. New York: Grove Press, 2011.

Mingst, Karen A., and Margaret P. Karns. *United Nations in the Twenty-First Century*. 4th ed. Boulder, CO: Westview, 2011.

Pappé, Ilan. *A History of Modern Palestine: One Land, Two Peoples*. Cambridge: Cambridge University Press, 2003.

Pelcovits, Nathan A. *The Long Armistice: UN Peacekeeping and the Arab-Israeli Conflict, 1948–1960*. Boulder, CO: Westview, 1993.

Pogany, Istvan. *The Security Council and the Arab-Israeli Conflict*. London: Palgrave Macmillan, 1984.

Ross-Nazzal, James. *The U.S. Veto and the Polemics of the Question of Palestine in the United Nations Security Council, 1947–2007*. Lewistown, PA: Edwin Mellen, 2008.

United Nations, ed. *Basic Facts about the United Nations*. New York: United Nations, 2004.

United Nations, ed. *Palestinians (the Work of the Committee on the Exercise of the Inalienable Rights of the Palestinian People)*. New York: United Nations, 1997.

United Nations, ed. *The Origins and Evolution of the Palestine Problem, 1917–1988*. New York: United Nations, 1990.

United Nations, ed. *The Question of Palestine and the United Nations*. Rev. ed. New York: United Nations, 2008.

United States, Middle East Policy

U.S. interest in the Middle East from a strategic perspective did not begin until the early 1940s, when the exigencies of World War II dictated that it pay increased

Members of the U.S. Navy assigned to a mobile construction battalion patrol a Fallujah street one day before the January 30, 2005, national elections in Iraq. (U.S. Navy)

attention to that region. Before that time, the U.S. government expressed little interest in the Middle East. It maintained only loose diplomatic and political relations with the region, deferring to the British and the French, who controlled the area after World War I. In the early 20th century, U.S. petroleum companies had secured oil concessions in Iraq, Kuwait, Bahrain, and Saudi Arabia, but that was the extent of U.S. involvement until World War II. Worried about German and Italian efforts to seize oil fields and the strategic Suez Canal, the Americans assisted and fought with the British in defeating German and Italian forces in North Africa during 1941–1942. From this point on, securing the Middle Eastern oil fields became a major foreign policy objective of the United States.

In early 1943, as the tide of the war began to turn in favor of the Allies and the Axis threat to the Middle East receded, the United States began to challenge European colonialism in the region. President Franklin D. Roosevelt and his successor, Harry S. Truman, supported in principle the independence of Arab states in the Middle East. The government of Prime Minister Winston Churchill objected to the U.S. position, but by the end of war, bankrupt and war weary, the new Labour government of Clement Attlee was willing to release its hold on much of the region, although it retained a considerable interest in Egypt and the Suez Canal. With the onset of the Cold War, the British government increasingly deferred to the United States. For their part, the Americans sought to fill the power vacuum in the Middle East following the end of British and French rule and to challenge efforts by the Soviet Union to project its power and influence in the region.

The U.S. government sought to deny Soviet efforts to gain control of the Persian Gulf's oil fields, to acquire military bases and especially a port in the region, and to sponsor or promote procommunist or Soviet-inclined regimes. The creation of the Jewish State of Israel in May 1948 greatly complicated the politics of the Middle East and U.S. foreign policy, as it sparked the enduring Arab-Israeli conflict. It also put the United States in a delicate and arguably untenable position. Washington supported Israel but at the same time sought to maintain friendly relations with Arab states, whose support for the Palestinians conflicted with close U.S. ties with Israel.

Owing to the strategic location of Greece and Turkey to the Middle East and the Mediterranean Sea, both countries became a part of U.S. Middle East policy in 1947. Bankrupt and facing severe domestic troubles from the war, Britain announced that it was abandoning its military and financial support for Greece against communist insurgents and its efforts to protect Turkey against Soviet encroachments. This prompted the United States in March 1947 to assume Britain's responsibilities in these nations. As such, the U.S. Congress appropriated $400 million in aid and secured the pro-Western governments of both countries. Thus, the Truman Doctrine, which pledged U.S. assistance to any nation fighting communism, began in the Middle East.

After including Greece and Turkey in the North Atlantic Treaty Organization (NATO), the United States sought to create a similar collective security arrangement for the Middle East proper. Initially known as the Baghdad Pact and signed in 1955, after an Iraqi nationalist government seized power in July 1958, it was renamed the Central Treaty Organization (CENTO) and then included Iran, Turkey, and Pakistan. Because of the weak military positions of its members, however, both the Baghdad Pact and CENTO had serious limitations as deterrents: to Soviet aggression. In addition, once Iraq withdrew from the Baghdad Pact in 1958, none of the remaining members were Arab states. Even Arab countries friendly to the United States, such as Saudi Arabia, refused to align with

either organization, preferring to maintain their independence and avoid being seen as U.S. puppets and accused of serving American and, in the view of many Arabs, neocolonial and imperial interests.

Iran also figured prominently as an U.S. ally until the 1979 revolution there. In August 1953, U.S. and British intelligence agencies engineered a coup that deposed the nationalist prime minister of Iran, Mohammad Mosaddeq, after he nationalized the Anglo-American Oil Company. The bloodless coup restored to full power the pro-Western shah Mohammad Reza Pahlavi II. In the ensuing decades, the United States equipped the shah's military with advanced weapons and trained his secret police, the Sazeman-e Ettelaat va Amniyat-e Keshvar (SAVAK, National Information and Security Organization), to consolidate and secure the shah's power and crush all political dissent. Indeed, by the early to mid-1970s, Iran was the bulwark of U.S. foreign policy in the Middle East. In 1979, an Islamic fundamentalist revolution deposed the shah and installed a theocratic government, which because of staunch U.S. support for the shah was rabidly anti-American. The United States and Iran remain bitter rivals to this day, and as recently as 2003 President George W. Bush labeled Iran a member of the so-called axis of evil along with North Korea and Saddam Hussein's Iraq. Preventing Iran from acquiring nuclear weapons became a high priority for both Bush and his Democratic successor, President Barack Obama, in part because these weapons might be used against Israel.

Successive U.S. administrations regarded Israel as an important ally against Soviet efforts to influence the region. This was particularly the case after 1953, when the Soviet Union under Nikita Khrushchev actively sought to challenge and undermine U.S.

influence in the region by fostering closer ties and providing economic and military aid to Arab states such as Egypt, Syria, and Iraq.

The United States has enjoyed a close and strong relationship with Israel since 1948. Various reasons explain this special relationship, as it is sometimes called. Humanitarian factors—guilt over the Holocaust and the sympathy it created for both its victims and survivors—was a major reason behind U.S. support for the establishment of Israel. In addition, the fact that Americans regarded Jews arriving in Palestine as settlers or pioneers, much like the early English colonists to North America, almost certainly elicited a sense of communion. Culturally, despite obvious differences in faith, because many Jews were Westernized and thus viewed as less foreign or alien than Arabs, this fostered a sense of cultural affinity among many Americans. Also, the establishment of a democratic government in Israel created an instant political bond between both nations. Many Evangelical Christians supported the establishment of Israel and remain among its staunchest defenders. Finally, along with his Christian faith, electoral considerations certainly played a role in President Truman's decision to recognize Israel in 1948. Indeed, the powerful Jewish bloc of voters clearly contributed to his reelection that November. Since then, the political and financial success of Jewish interest groups—such as the American Israeli Public Affairs Committee (AIPAC)—continues to exert major influence on both Congress and the White House, far surpassing the influence of the Arab states. Given Israel's strategic location and growing military might, Washington believed that the Jewish state would become the regional power and offer an effective way to check Soviet ambitions. Not surprisingly, over time many Arab states either allied themselves or at least fostered closer ties with the Soviet Union because of the strong U.S. support for Israel.

Although the United States has provided economic assistance to Israel since its inception, until the late 1960s France was Israel's main patron and supplier of military aid. The United States remained decidedly neutral or aloof from the Arab-Israeli conflict until the late 1960s. After the June 1967 Six-Day War, however, U.S. president Lyndon B. Johnson fostered much closer ties with Israel, and the United States became its main supplier of military weapons, thereby establishing the precedent for subsequent U.S. military sales to the Jewish state, a policy that has continued to this day. Acting on the belief that by the late 1960s many Arab states, particularly Egypt and Syria, had decisively drifted into the Soviet orbit, Washington established much closer ties with Tel Aviv. The Soviets, meanwhile, severed diplomatic relations with Israel in 1967. In this context, Israel became a far more important ally to the Americans and was a key player in its foreign policy. During the October 1973 Yom Kippur War, the United States mounted a major airlift to resupply Israel's besieged military after it suffered heavy casualties in the opening days of the war following the surprise Egyptian-Syrian attack.

With respect to the Arab-Israeli conflict, the United States has generally been very supportive of Israel despite sometimes pressuring Israel to negotiate with its Arab neighbors or relinquish its control of occupied Arab lands. Such was the case during the 1956 Suez Crisis, when President Dwight D. Eisenhower ordered the Israelis to pull back from the Suez Canal. It was also evident in the late 1970s, when President Jimmy Carter sought to secure a peace treaty—the 1978 Camp David Accords—between Israel and Egypt that brought Israel's withdrawal from the Sinai, which it had captured in 1967. By the 1980s, U.S. aid to Israel was approximately $3 billion annually, and Washington continued its policy of equipping Israel with some of the most advanced weapons to assure its military superiority. It also implemented a free trade agreement in 1985 eliminating all tariffs between both countries.

At the same time, however, over Israeli objections, the United States has repeatedly sold military weapons to friendly Arab states, particularly Egypt and Saudi Arabia. Saudi Arabia figured prominently in U.S. foreign policy owing to its large oil reserves and generally pro-American leaders. As early as 1943, in fact, the United States provided military aid to the kingdom and constructed an air base at Dhahran. U.S. policymakers especially relished King Ibn Saud's anticommunism.

One area of noticeable friction between the United States and Israel, particularly during the late 1980s and 1990s, was the Israeli policy of constructing settlements in the occupied Arab territories of the Gaza Strip and the West Bank. In 1989, U.S. secretary of state James Baker went so far as to denounce Israel's expansionist policies, and President George H. W. Bush refused to grant loans to Israel if such funds were to be used to construct Israeli settlements in the occupied territories. This caused significant friction with Israeli prime minister Yitzhak Shamir.

Iraq's invasion of Kuwait on August 2, 1990, led the United States to organize a multinational coalition to compel Iraq's withdrawal and, following the failure of diplomacy, launch Operation DESERT STORM, a sustained air and then ground offensive that routed and expelled the Iraqi military from Kuwait in late February 1991. The decision of the United States to repel Iraq's invasion of Kuwait was prompted by the fear that Iraq might invade Saudi Arabia and seize its northern oil fields located near the border with Kuwait. If Iraq were allowed to retain control of Kuwait's

vast oil reserves, much less seize those of Saudi Arabia, Iraq would control a large share of the world's oil supply and thus potentially might engage in oil blackmail. Highly dependent upon Middle Eastern oil for its economy, the United States was unwilling to allow the free flow of oil to be threatened. Arab states were members of the coalition against Iraq, and for that reason the United States put heavy pressure on Israel not to attack Iraq in response to Iraqi Scud surface-to-surface missiles launched against Israel. Washington feared that if Israel entered the war, the Arab states would leave the coalition. The United States supplied Patriot missiles to Israel and was able, despite the missile attacks, to keep the Jewish state from intervening.

The September 11, 2001, terrorist attacks on the United States committed President Bush to waging the so-called war on terror against the terrorist organization Al Qaeda and other terrorist groups and any country that harbors or supports them. The Americans launched an attack and invasion of Afghanistan in early October 2001 (Operation ENDURING FREE-DOM) to overthrow the Taliban government that had offered sanctuary to the Al Qaeda terrorist network. By December, the Taliban had been routed, but the extent of Al Qaeda's losses remains unknown. A provisional government for Afghanistan was established that same month followed by democratic elections for president in 2004 and for the legislature in 2005. A recent escalation in Taliban attacks in Afghanistan has raised fears of a resurgent threat posed by the Taliban. In April 2014 there were over 30,000 U.S. troops in Afghanistan, U.S. troops in Afghanistan along with 40,000 troops from NATO member countries. These troops remained active in defending the country and government against Taliban and Al Qaeda forces.

In March 2003, the United States and Great Britain invaded Iraq—with a weak coalition of several other nations—and overthrew Hussein's government. President Bush justified the invasion by alleging Hussein's pursuit of weapons of mass destruction (WMDs) and ties to terrorism, including Al Qaeda. Following the end of the Persian Gulf War in 1991, per United Nations (UN) Resolution 687 (April 3, 1991) Hussein agreed to disable all of his WMDs. After 12 years of defiance and violating 10 subsequent UN resolutions demanding Iraqi disarmament, Bush justified the invasion as the only way to enforce the will of the UN and assure that Iraq would never pose a threat to the region.

The U.S. government claimed that Iraq had failed to disarm and remained in possession of stockpiles of WMDs, including biological, chemical, and nuclear materials. In the aftermath of the war, however, no major stockpiles of WMDs were located. Nor have any direct links between Hussein and Al Qaeda ever been determined. This subsequently led critics of the Bush administration to suggest that the president at the very least deliberately exaggerated the threat posed by Iraq to convince Congress and the U.S. public to support the war. Defenders of the administration pointed out that before the war many of these same critics believed that Hussein had not disarmed and remained a threat. The Bush administration failed, however, to persuade the UN to authorize military action against Iraq and invaded Iraq on March 20, 2003. While most of the world denounced the invasion as illegal, the Bush administration defended its actions, claiming that UN Resolution 687 authorized any state "to use all necessary means … to restore international peace and security in the area." What has become abundantly clear, however, is that U.S. intelligence gathering and the interpretation of that intelligence leading up to the war were deeply flawed.

As to the claim that Iraq had ties with Al Qaeda, in his 2003 State of the Union address Bush declared that "Saddam Hussein aids and protects terrorists, including members of Al Qaeda," and warned that he might even supply WMDs to Al Qaeda. Bush therefore sought to link the overthrow of Hussein with the war on terror. No links between Al Qaeda and Hussein have yet been uncovered. In the absence of finding stockpiles of WMDs, Bush recast the reason for going to war from one of disarming Hussein to promoting democracy in Iraq. In a speech on September 11, 2006, he equated the war on terror with the U.S. struggle against fascism during World War II.

Less than one month after the invasion of Iraq, Hussein's government fell. Although the war resulted in a seemingly quick and decisive victory with limited resistance from Iraq's military, the aftermath of the invasion proved far more problematic and bloody. U.S. forces faced much difficulty and were criticized for not aggressively restoring order in the wake of the collapse of Hussein's government. They were also blamed for allowing mass looting, including that of military depots, providing a significant source of ammunition and weapons for the subsequent insurgency. The disbanding of the Iraqi army immediately after the war was regarded as another critical mistake contributing to the disorder, if not anarchy, in the country.

By the summer of 2003 remnants of Hussein's military forces began attacking U.S. forces, leading to an insurgency characterized by guerrilla warfare and acts of terrorism including hundreds of car bombings. In response, a series of U.S. military operations was launched to suppress the insurgency, which also included radical Islamist militias in Iraq. Elections were held in January 2005 to select an assembly to draft a new constitution followed by elections in December of that year to seat a new parliament. Despite the establishment of a democratically elected government, and the withdrawal of the last U.S. forces in 2011—though 4,000 U.S. troops remained on two bases in Iraq—violence continued, often escalating into inter-sectarian conflict, mainly between Sunnis and Shias. From 2005 onward, relations between Iraq and Iran greatly improved; ironically, the U.S. military intervention ultimately dramatically enhanced Iranian influence over Iraq. Critics of the war in Iraq contended that it not only distracted the nation from the war on terror but actually made the United States less safe because the war served as a rallying call for Islamic terrorism. Meanwhile, the United States also faced a challenge from Iran in a generally held belief that Iran is seeking to acquire nuclear weapons. Resolution to that crisis remains elusive.

The United States has consistently favored the land-for-peace option to resolving the Arab-Israeli conflict and regards states that sponsor or support terrorism against Israel (such as Syria and Iran) as enemies of peace. Following the Persian Gulf War of 1991, the Middle East peace process accelerated with the hosting of the Madrid Peace Conference followed by the signing of the Oslo Peace Accords on September 13, 1993, between Israel and the Palestine Liberation Organization (PLO) and a peace treaty between Israel and Jordan in 1994. Subsequent negotiations between Israel and the Palestinians sought but largely failed to build on the Oslo Accords, despite active U.S. sponsorship and participation in such talks by U.S. presidents Bill Clinton and George W. Bush. Under President George W. Bush, the United States supported an independent Palestinian state but insisted that parties such as Hamas must formally recognize Israel and cease all talk of resistance and that all acts of terrorism against Israel must end.

The 2007 split between Hamas-controlled Gaza and the more conciliatory Fatah-run Palestinian Authority in the West Bank at first seemed to block further progress, but in practice made it simpler for U.S. officials to encourage the peace process further. Speaking at Cairo University, in June 2009, President Barack Obama called for renewed negotiations between the Palestinian Authority and Israel. During his first term these lost momentum, undermined by new Israeli settlements in the West Bank and military hostilities between Gaza and Israel. In June 2013, however, U.S. secretary of state John Kerry encouraged the resumption of talks, with the objective of reaching a final status agreement on the West Bank within nine months. By February 2014, although talks were still continuing, it seemed increasingly unlikely that this deadline would be met. Kerry publicly warned that, if agreement on a two-state settlement was not reached, the possibility was growing that private American businesses and individuals would sanction Israel by boycotting Israeli goods and services and divesting themselves of investments in Israel.

Stefan Marc Brooks

Further Reading

Abrams, Elliott. *Tested by Zion: The Bush Administration and the Israeli-Palestinian Conflict.* New York: Cambridge University Press, 2013.

Bass, Warren. *Support Any Friend: Kennedy's Middle East and the Making of the U.S.-Israel Alliance.* New York: Oxford University Press, 2003.

Buckley, Mary, et al. *The Bush Doctrine and the War on Terrorism: Global Reactions, Global Consequences.* New York: Routledge, 2006.

Chamberlin, Paul Thomas. *The Global Offensive: The United States, the Palestine*

Liberation Organization, and the Making of the Post-Cold War Order. New York: Oxford University Press, 2012.

Citino, Matthew J. From Arab Nationalism to OPEC: Eisenhower, King Saud, and the Making of U.S.-Saudi Relations. 2nd ed. Bloomington: Indiana University Press, 2002.

Clark, Victoria. Allies for Armageddon: The Rise of Christian Zionism. New Haven, CT: Yale University Press, 2007.

Fisk, Robert. The Great War for Civilization: The Conquest of the Middle East. New York: Knopf, 2005.

Freedman, Lawrence. A Choice of Enemies: America Confronts the Middle East. New York: PublicAffairs, 2008.

Gaddis, John Lewis. Surprise, Security and the American Experience. Cambridge: Harvard University Press, 2005.

Gardner, Lloyd C. Three Kings: The Rise of an American Empire in the Middle East after World War II. New York: New Press, 2009.

Gerges, Fawaz A. Obama and the Middle East: The End of America's Moment. Basingstoke: Palgrave Macmillan, 2012.

Hahn, Peter L. Crisis and Crossfire: The United States and the Middle East since 1945. Dulles, VA: Potomac Books, 2005.

Hurst, Steven. The United States and Iraq since 1979: Hegemony, Oil, and War. Edinburgh, Scotland: Edinburgh University Press, 2010.

Jacobs, Matthew F. Imagining the Middle East: The Building of an American Foreign Policy, 1918–1967. Chapel Hill: University of North Carolina Press, 2011.

Khalidi, Rashid. Resurrecting Empire: Western Footprints and America's Perilous Path in the Middle East. Boston, MA: Beacon Press, 2004.

Khalidi, Rashid. Sowing Crisis: The Cold War and American Dominance in the Middle East. Boston, MA: Beacon Press, 2009.

Kurtzer, Daniel C., Scott B. Lasensky, William B. Quandt, Steven L. Spiegel, and Shibley Z. Telhami. The Peace Puzzle: America's Quest for Arab-Israeli Peace, 1989–2011. Ithaca, NY: Cornell University Press, 2013.

Lesch, David W., and Mark L. Haas, eds. The Middle East and the United States: History, Politics, and Ideologies. 5th ed. Boulder, CO: Westview, 2013.

Levey, Zach. Israel and the Western Powers, 1952–1960. Chapel Hill: University of North Carolina Press, 2011.

Little, Douglas. American Orientalism: The United States and the Middle East. 3rd ed. Chapel Hill: University of North Carolina Press, 2008.

Makdisi, Ussama. Faith Misplaced: The Broken Promise of U.S.-Arab Relations: 1800–2001. New York: Public Affairs, 2010.

McAlister, Melani. Epic Encounters: Culture, Media, and U.S. Interests in the Middle East since 1945. Berkeley: University of California Press, 2001.

Palmer, Michael A. Guardians of the Gulf: A History of America's Expanding Role in the Persian Gulf, 1883–1992. New York: Free Press, 1992.

Parsi, Trita. Treacherous Alliance: The Secret Dealings of Israel, Iran, and the United States. New Haven, CT: Yale University Press, 2007.

Quandt, William B. Peace Process: American Diplomacy and the Arab-Israeli Peace Process since 1967. 3rd ed. Washington, DC: Brookings Institution Press, and Berkeley: University of California Press, 2005.

Spector, Stephen. Evangelicals and Israel: The Rise of American Christian Zionism. New York: Oxford University Press, 2008.

Spiegel, Stephen. The Other Arab-Israeli Conflict: Making America's Middle East Policy, from Truman to Reagan. Chicago: University of Chicago Press, 1986.

Stein, Kenneth W. Heroic Diplomacy: Kissinger, Sadat, Carter, Begin and the Quest for Arab-Israeli Peace. New York: Routledge, 1999.

Terry, Janice. U.S. Foreign Policy in the Middle East: The Role of Lobbies and Special Interest Groups. London: Pluto, 2005.

Tyler, Patrick. A World of Trouble: The White House and the Middle East—From the Cold War to the War on Terror. New York: Farrar, Straus and Giroux, 2008.

Yaqub, Salim. Containing Arab Nationalism: The Eisenhower Doctrine and the Middle East. Chapel Hill: University of North Carolina Press, 2006.

Yemen

Middle Eastern nation located in the southern part of the Arabian Peninsula with an estimated 2006 population of 21.45 million people. Yemen borders Saudi Arabia to the north, Oman to the east, the Arabian Sea and the Gulf of Aden to the south, and the Red Sea to the west. Not far off the western and southern coasts of the country are the East African nations of Eritrea, Djibouti, and Somalia. Yemen's total area encompasses 203,846 square miles. Much of the country can be characterized as a desert. Topographically, Yemen features a narrow strip of coastal plains and low hills immediately behind them that give way to high mountains. High desert plains farther east descend to hot desert in the interior. The nation's chief resources include oil, marble, fish, minor coal deposits, gold, lead, nickel, and copper. The bulk of Yemen's arable land is located in the west and comprises less than 3 percent of the entire land mass.

Yemen's population is overwhelmingly Muslim and of Arabic descent, and Arabic is the official language. Of the nation's Muslims, about 52 percent are Sunni Muslims and 48 percent are Shia Muslims. The Sunnis live principally in the south and southeastern part of the country. Yemen has one of the world's highest birthrates, and as a result its population as a whole is quite young. Indeed, some 46 percent of the population is 14 years old and under, while less than 3 percent is older than 65. The median age is 16.

The Ottoman Empire controlled some or most of Yemen sporadically between the 1500s and 1918, when the empire crumbled as a result of World War I. Ottoman influence was most keen in northern Yemen. In the south, imams tended to control the local scene but were usually overseen to some extent by the central authorities in Constantinople (Istanbul).

Yemen had been divided into North Yemen and South Yemen since 1918. In 1918, North Yemen won its independence from the Ottoman Empire and finally became a republic in 1962, which precipitated an eight-year-long civil war. The conflict pitted royalists of the Mutawakkilite Kingdom of Yemen against republicans. Before 1962, the ruling imams in North Yemen pursued an isolationist foreign policy. North Yemen did have commercial and cultural ties with Saudi Arabia, however. In the late 1950s, the Chinese and Soviets attempted to lure North Yemen into their orbit with technological missions. By the early 1960s, North Yemen had become dependent upon Egypt for financial and technical support. Later still, the Saudis supplanted the Egyptians as the main conduit of support. During the civil war the Saudis backed the royalists, while Egypt and the Soviet Union aided the republicans. In the 1970s and 1980s, many Yemenis from the north found jobs in neighboring Saudi Arabia, boosting North Yemen's flagging economy.

Until 1967, the British dominated the south, having established a protectorate in Aden in 1839. Soon the British created a formal colony that incorporated Aden and southern Yemen, giving the British great command of the region's strategic waterways. After World

Yemeni Royalist forces man a recoilless rifle on the crest of Algenat Alout in 1964 during the civil war. (Hulton Archive/Getty Images)

War II, however, Yemenis in the south came to greatly resent the British presence, and with Egyptian assistance they soon organized an anti-British insurgency. Several attacks against British interests sponsored by Egypt's government under Gamal Abdel Nasser in addition to insurgents from the north essentially forced the British out in 1967. The former British colony of Aden then became South Yemen. After 1967, when South Yemen declared itself a Marxist state (with ties to the Soviet Union), it maintained tense—and sometimes hostile— relations with its conservative Arab neighbors. In addition to the ongoing conflict with the north, southern Yemeni insurgents engaged the Saudis in military actions first in 1969 and again in 1973. They also openly aided the Dhofar rebellion in Oman.

In 1970, the South Yemen government declared a Marxist state and aligned itself squarely with the Soviet Union. As a result, several hundred thousand Yemenis from the south fled to North Yemen, overwhelming

that nation's resources. The south did nothing to stop the mass exodus. This precipitated a virtual civil war between north and south that endured for 20 years. Not until 1990 did the two states reconcile, forming a single state known as the Republic of Yemen. Subsequently, groups in the south mounted several unsuccessful attempts to secede from the republic. The most serious secessionist move came in 1994.

After the 1990 unification, the Republic of Yemen generally pursued a pragmatic foreign policy. It is a member of the Non-Aligned Movement, a signatory to the Nuclear Non-Proliferation Treaty, and attempted to stay impartial during the 1991 Persian Gulf War and subsequent wars in the Middle East. Its noncommittal stance in these areas, however, has not endeared it to the Gulf states or Western nations.

Yemen is a representative republic with a popularly elected president and a prime minister appointed by the president. The executive branch shares power with the bicameral legislature. The legal system in Yemen is a mix of Islamic law, Turkish law (a vestige of the Ottoman Empire), English common law, and local tribal dictates. Nevertheless, Islamic laws almost always take precedence in accordance with the Koran. With the 1990 unification Ali Abdullah Saleh, who had been president of North Yemen since 1978, became president of the Republic of Yemen.

Yemen is among the poorest nations in the Arab world. The long civil war of 1962 to 1970 wrought great havoc on an already struggling economy, and the agricultural sector was badly hit by periodic droughts. Coffee production, once a mainstay among northern Yemeni crops, declined dramatically. The Port of Aden in the south suffered dramatic curtailments in its cargo handling after the 1967 Six-Day War and the British exit that same year. After 1990, the return of hundreds of thousands of Yemenis from other Gulf states due to Yemen's nonalignment in the Persian Gulf War generated staggering unemployment. Reduced aid from other nations at this time and a brief secessionist movement in 1994 conspired to keep Yemen's economy depressed. Yemen possesses significant oil deposits, but they are not of the same quality as Persian Gulf oil and so have not brought in a windfall profit. Yemen does have major natural gas reserves, but that industry remains underdeveloped. The Yemeni government waged constant battle against high inflation, excessive spending, widespread corruption, and Islamist militants.

By the late 1990s, the Al Qaeda radical Islamic terrorist group was active in Yemen. In October 2000, suicide bombers mounted an attack in Aden harbor on the U.S. naval vessel *USS Cole*, killing 17 U.S. military personnel. Saleh assured U.S. president George W. Bush of Yemen's support in the War on Terror. In June 2004, a Shia insurgency against the government began. When fuel prices soared in 2005, violent protests ensued. In 2007 and 2008, suicide bombers attacked foreign tourists and businesses, diplomats, and Yemeni government officials and police. In 2009, Al Qaeda personnel in Yemen and Saudi Arabia merged, to form Al Qaeda in the Arabian Peninsula (AQAP), many of whose members had previously been imprisoned at the U.S. Guantánamo Bay facility. Besides launching attacks on Saudi and Yemeni targets, AQAP called for renewed holy war against Israel and the imposition of a blockade on all sea traffic with Israel. In 2009 and 2010, Yemen's government launched a new offensive against the Shiite insurgents, a campaign in which AQAP groups assisted Yemeni military forces. From 2009 onward, the United States launched air strikes and drone attacks against suspected AQAP targets in Yemen.

Inspired by successful protests in Tunisia, from late January 2011, demonstrators took to Yemen's streets, orchestrating "days of rage" or "days of anger" against corruption, economic difficulties, and human rights abuses, and demanding the resignation of President Saleh. Ultimately, in November 2011, after mediation by Saudi Arabia and the Gulf Cooperation Council, Saleh agreed to do so. His vice president, Abd al-Rab Mansur al-Hadi, replaced him, running unopposed in presidential elections held in February 2012, and winning a two-year term. Hadi formed a government of national unity, entrusted with drawing up a new constitution. On the day Hadi was sworn in AQAP mounted a suicide attack on the presidential palace, killing 26. President Barack Obama deployed U.S. military, intelligence, and Special Forces personnel to Yemen and stepped up economic assistance. By late 2012, the government had succeeded in driving back AQAP forces and regained control of the Shabwah governorate. The situation in Yemen nonetheless remained fragile, offering potential for Islamic militants to mount operations whose violence would spill over beyond Yemen's borders, destabilizing other parts of the inflammable region.

Paul G. Pierpaoli Jr.

Further Reading

Al-faqih, Abdullah. *Liberalization and Democratization in Egypt, Jordan, and Yemen: Beginnings, Development, and Decline.* Saarbrücken, Germany: VDM Verlag Dr. Müller, 2013.

Boucek, Christopher, and Marina Ottaway, eds. *Yemen on the Brink.* Washington, DC: Carnegie Endowment for International Peace, 2010.

Clark, Victoria. *Yemen: Dancing on the Heads of Snakes.* New Haven, CT: Yale University Press, 2010.

Day, Stephen W. *Regionalism and Rebellion in Yemen: A Troubled National Union.* Cambridge: Cambridge University Press, 2012.

Dresch, Paul. *A History of Modern Yemen.* New York: Cambridge University Press, 2001.

Hull, Edmund J. *High-Value Target: Countering Al Qaeda in Yemen.* Washington, DC: Potomac Books, 2011.

Johnsen, Gregory D. *The Last Refuge: Yemen, Al-Qaeda, and America's War in Arabia.* New York: Norton, 2012.

Jones, Clive. *Britain and the Yemen Civil War.* London: Sussex Academic, 2004.

Mackintosh-Smith, Martin. *Yemen: The Unknown Arabia.* Woodstock, NY: Overlook, 2001.

Phillips, Sarah. *Yemen and the Politics of Permanent Crisis.* New York: Routledge, 2011.

Yom Kippur War

Arab-Israeli conflict that occurred from October 6 to October 26, 1973, so-named because it began with a coordinated Egyptian-Syrian surprise attack against Israel on the Jewish holy day of Yom Kippur (Day of Atonement.) The war is therefore also known as the War of Atonement or, for Muslims, the Ramadan War because it began during the holy month of Ramadan.

An Israeli convoy advances into Syria under a barrage of shellfire during the Yom Kippur War, 1973. (Popperfoto/Getty Images)

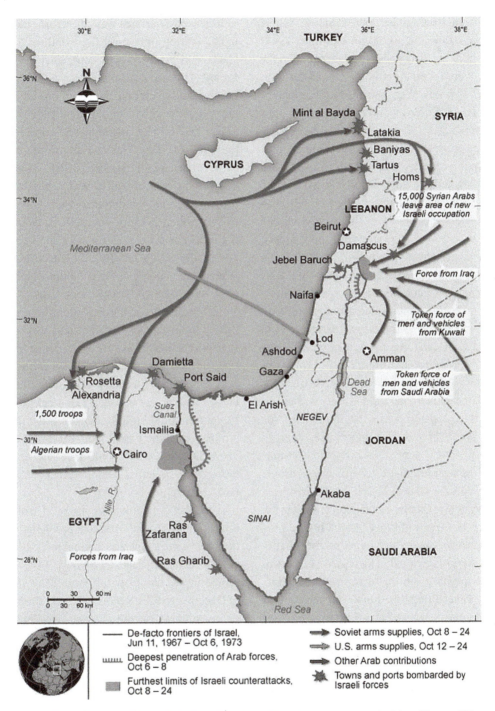

Map of the October War, 1973. The October War, also known as the Yom Kippur War, forced the United States to put Arab-Israeli relations at the forefront of its foreign relations policy.

In addition to the long-standing issues of the Arab-Israeli conflict dating to 1948, the more pressing causes of the Yom Kippur War were inherent in the results of the June 1967 Six-Day War. During that campaign, the Israel Defense Forces (IDF) not only humiliated the Arab armies but also seized large portions of Syrian, Jordanian, and Egyptian territory. Possession of the Golan Heights and the Sinai Peninsula gave Israel much-needed strategic depth, but this was absolutely intolerable to the highly nationalistic regimes in Damascus and Cairo. Israel's continued occupation of these lands transformed the abstract grievances of Palestinian rights into a deeply resented insult to the Arab governments and armies involved.

Paradoxically, therefore, Israel's very success in 1967 had made it more difficult, both politically and emotionally, for Arab leaders to reach a negotiated settlement with the Israelis. Israel naturally wished to use these territories as a bargaining chip for a possible diplomatic compromise, whereas its opponents demanded complete evacuation as a prerequisite to any negotiations. In addition, these Israeli-held territories brought with them a constant drain on the reservist Israeli military, which had to provide forces to defend large sectors that it had never previously possessed. In particular, the 35 positions of the so-called Bar-Lev Line along the Suez Canal required garrisons to provide early warning and deter Egyptian infiltrations. Moreover, the distance between Israel proper and the canal meant that in the event of war Israeli reserve units would take several days to mobilize and reach the southern front. For Egypt, a constant state of semimobilization in combination with the loss of revenues from the Suez Canal placed enormous strains on the economy, increasing pressure to resolve the situation at all costs.

Renewed warfare was therefore inevitable, waiting only until the frontline Arab states had rearmed and reorganized their forces. The question in 1973 was how the Arabs could overcome the enormous advantages possessed by the IDF. The 1956 Suez Crisis and Sinai Campaign and especially the 1967 Six-Day War had shown the IDF to be a master of flexible, offensive warfare reminiscent of World War II blitzkrieg tactics. Although individual Arab soldiers had exhibited bravery and skill in defending fixed positions in those wars, they could not easily match the Israelis' mechanized maneuvers, and few Arab pilots had the experience of their Israeli counterparts.

The problem for the Egyptians was further complicated by the fact that they had to begin their offensive by crossing the Suez Canal, whose concrete-lined banks and adjacent sand walls made the canal difficult to breach with heavy vehicles. Long before the Egyptians could build bridges to bring their armor across the canal, their first waves of dismounted infantry would face counterattacks from the lethal combination of Israeli tanks and fighter-bombers.

A number of people were involved in planning solutions to these tactical problems, but the most significant was undoubtedly Lieutenant General Saad el-Shazly, Egyptian armed forces chief of staff from May 1971 to December 1973. Recognizing the strength of his soldiers on the defensive, el-Shazly developed a bold program to provide his assault infantry with as many man-portable antitank and antiaircraft missiles as possible. Particularly important in this regard was the AT-3 Sagger antitank guided missile (ATGM), Soviet designation 9M14, a wire-guided weapon that could be "flown" by the operator to kill tanks at a range of up to two miles. El-Shazly stripped the rest of the Egyptian army of such weapons in order to give his attacking brigades all the missiles they could carry forward. He also planned five different crossings on a wide front, with the troops rushing forward to assume shallow but coherent bridgeheads that could defeat the first Israeli armored counterattacks, giving Egyptian forces time to bring their armored vehicles across the canal. Thus, while conducting an offensive at the operational level, at the tactical level the Egyptians planned to stand on the defensive, forcing the IDF to attack them with little opportunity for outflanking maneuvers.

To span the Suez Canal, the Egyptians formed 40 battalions of assault and bridging engineers. A junior engineer officer suggested that to achieve an immediate breach of the huge sand walls that Israel had built on the eastern side of the canal, the attackers should use high-pressure water cannon rather than explosives or earthmoving equipment. During the event, 450 British- and German-made pumps enabled the attackers to create 60 gaps in the sand wall during the first six hours of the campaign.

At a time when most of his contemporaries still sought a single war of annihilation against Israel, el-Shazly decided to conduct a limited offensive, one that would capitalize on the abilities of his troops and shake the IDF's confidence in its own invincibility. Thus, Operation THE HIGH MINARETS intended to penetrate no more than six miles east of the Suez Canal. This meant that in order to attack the Egyptians, the Israeli air force would have to fly inside the overlapping range fans of the SA-2 and SA-3 air defense missiles located on the western bank of the canal. As they crossed the canal, Egyptian units took with them not only ATGMs but also a variety of more mobile air defense weapons, including the man-portable SA-7 missile and the vehicle-mounted ZSU-23–4 guns and SAM-6 missiles.

Working together, these Soviet-supplied weapons posed an integrated air defense capability that would degrade or neutralize the Israeli advantage in fighter-bombers.

Although there was general agreement on this first phase of the operation, most Egyptian officials expected far more from the war. In particular, the Egyptians had promised their Syrian allies that they would quickly move forward to the Sinai passes, denying Israel any defensible terrain in the desert. El-Shazly consistently opposed such plans because a deep advance would leave behind the air defense umbrella and tightly coordinated defensive positions that gave the Egyptians their initial advantages. Instead, el-Shazly envisaged forcing Israel to choose between a long stalemated war that it could not afford, unacceptably high casualties to retake the canal, or peace negotiations.

For its part, the Syrian plan was more conventional, relying on multiple attack echelons, each consisting of two to three mechanized or armored divisions, to overwhelm the IDF in the occupied Golan Heights before Israeli reserves could arrive. The leading brigades of infantry would cross the Israeli antitank ditch on foot, to be followed by vehicle-launched bridges to permit the tanks to cross. This concept was a highly stylized and overly centralized version of the offensive tactics that the Soviet army had taught to its Arab allies. From the beginning, therefore, Damascus was pushing for a total victory, a serious divergence from the Egyptian plans. Again, an integrated Soviet-manufactured air defense system, including 15 batteries of the mobile SA-6, would shelter the Syrian ground advance. Given the shallow (approximately 12.5 miles) depth of the IDF enclave on the Golan Heights, this plan appeared more feasible than an equivalent Egyptian effort to retake the entire Sinai.

Yet these plans would have been pointless had Israeli intelligence agencies detected Arab preparations in time to mobilize and counterattack. Indeed, the Egyptian intelligence services predicted that Israel would have unambiguous warning of the attack 15 days before it began. Therefore, planning and preparations for the attack included unprecedented secrecy and deception efforts. In this regard, it is worth noting that the 1973 attack was the first major conflict in which the Arab armed forces had actually planned their attacks and conducted those attacks at a time and place of their own choosing. It was also the first war in which the different Arab states coordinated their operations. This coordination was responsible for the unusual H-hour of 2:00 p.m., which was a compromise between the Syrian desire to attack at dawn and the Egyptian desire to conduct most of the canal crossing in darkness.

From August 21 to 24, 1973, the Syrian and Egyptian military planners met in civilian clothes for final staff talks regarding the approaching offensive, code-named Operation BADR after the AD 624 victory of the Prophet Muhammad. As a result of this meeting, the military commanders proposed a series of appropriate dates for the attack from which Presidents Anwar Sadat of Egypt and Hafez al-Assad of Syria chose October 6 as the starting date.

During the remaining weeks of intensive preparations, all concerned continued routine activities in public. Egypt in particular desensitized the Israelis by a series of field exercises and no fewer than 22 practice mobilizations and demobilizations of reservists during 1973. A major Egyptian troop concentration had passed without incident in the spring of 1973, further desensitizing observers. Meanwhile, the Egyptian General Staff maintained secrecy to the point that it did not inform its division commanders until three days before the attack.

Despite such tight security by the Egyptians, Israel's lack of strategic warning has been the subject of much debate. As early as January 1971, IDF chief of staff General David Elazar had recognized that the diplomatic stalemate virtually impelled the Arabs to attack. The only error was in estimating when that attack would occur. Fundamentally, the problem was a classic example of the intelligence conundrum of enemy capabilities versus intentions. In late September and early October 1973, Israeli and U.S. intelligence reports clearly identified the fact that the Arab armies were fully mobilized and concentrated in attack positions. Indeed, the head of the IDF's Northern Command, Major General Yitzhak Hofi, reportedly concluded by mid-September that Syria was capable of attacking at any time without additional warning indications.

However, with certain exceptions, the Israeli intelligence and leadership structure was convinced that the Arab states did not intend to launch a war, because in Israeli eyes Syria knew that it could not win alone and Egypt supposedly felt too vulnerable to Israeli air attacks on its economy and population. Israeli leaders assumed that their opponents shared IDF views about the likely outcome of an immediate war. Indeed, the Israeli director of military intelligence, Major General Eliezer Zeira, was so convinced of this interpretation that he repeatedly delayed reporting key information to his superiors and downplayed the significance of the reports he did present. Thus, as recently as the day before the attack, Zeira estimated that a general attack was still improbable, although as a precaution the regular Israeli army moved to its highest state of alert on October 5.

During those final 24 hours before the war began, sufficient intelligence indications appeared to make the threat of attack seem real. In particular, after Sadat and al-Assad informed their Soviet military advisers that an attack was imminent, during October 4–6, Soviet aircraft urgently evacuated the families of their personnel from both countries. King Hussein of Jordan provided several specific warnings, as did one of Israel's highest human intelligence sources in Egypt. By the morning of October 6, therefore, the IDF belatedly began mobilization. The Israeli air force also prepared a preemptive strike against Arab targets, but low clouds made it impossible to strike the Golan Heights, and eventually Prime Minister Golda Meir cancelled the attack. She reportedly told U.S. ambassador to Israel Kenneth Keating that Israel wanted to avoid any accusation that it was responsible for the war.

As a result, the IDF began the conflict with only its active duty forces on the frontiers. Although IDF security makes exact order of battle analysis difficult, the overall weakness of these forces was obvious. The normal garrison on the Golan Heights was built around the 188th Brigade, which was deployed by platoons of three tanks each to support the infantry strong points, occupied in many cases by paratroopers, along the cease-fire line. As the threat of war loomed on October 5, this force received reinforcements including the famous 7th Armored Brigade and at least portions of the 1st (Golani) Infantry Brigade. These units were at full strength, but in the crisis the troops, airlifted from other parts of Israel, had to draw new vehicles while their commanders studied the unfamiliar terrain. Moreover, at least two companies of the 7th Brigade were composed of conscripts still undergoing initial training as tank crewmen. Overall, there were 177 IDF Centurion tanks and 44 artillery pieces on the Golan Heights, as compared to 700 T-55s and extensive artillery found in just the first echelon of Syrian attackers.

The Sinai was almost equally weak. The positions of the Bar-Lev Line required 800–3,000 infantrymen to occupy effectively, but at the time of the attack the positions contained only about 460 reservists, many of them middle-aged. These positions were poorly maintained, with wire obstacles buried by drifting sand and with shortages of ammunition. Behind them stood Major General Avraham Mandler's 252nd Armored Division. Major General Shmuel Gonen was the overall southern commander. Gonen had assumed command recently and was unaware of accurate intelligence concerning the wide frontage of the Egyptian attack plan. Although Mandler had 291 tanks and 48 artillery pieces, these troops expected the Egyptians to attack at dusk and were thus far from the canal when the attack began in midafternoon. In addition, the IDF had placed a low priority on mechanized infantry after the success of the tank–fighter-bomber team in 1967.

Consequently, many infantry troops were still in the mobilizing reserves, while tank units were in the habit of maneuvering without infantry support. Most mechanized infantry still rode in World War II era M3 half-tracks, and the field artillery branch was almost equally neglected. The IDF plan for emergency defense in the south, Operation DOVECOTE, called for one battalion (36–40 tanks) from each of the three armored brigades to immediately advance to firing positions near the canal in order to break up any attack and support the Bar-Lev Line.

The initial attack began on both fronts with air strikes at 2:00 p.m. on October 6 followed immediately by brief artillery barrages to suppress the defenders in fortified positions. Preceded by reconnaissance engineers and commandos, the first wave of infantry crossed the canal in assault boats at 2:15 p.m. Subsequent waves followed every 15 minutes, so that 23,500 men—the assault elements of five infantry divisions—had crossed the canal by 4:15 p.m. The commandos and initial infantry troops shattered the quick-reaction IDF tank units, which had not trained to deal with ATGMs. Additional losses followed as the Israelis repeatedly attempted to relieve and evacuate the Bar-Lev positions. The first floating bridge was completed by 8:30 that night, beginning the flow of tanks and heavy weapons. Only in the south did the Egyptians have difficulties. There, the different soil opposite the 19th Infantry Division meant that the water cannon turned the protective walls into impenetrable mud, restricting the number of crossing points. Meanwhile, an amphibious brigade successfully crossed the Great Bitter Lake, but its lightly armored vehicles suffered heavily when they tried to reach the Gidi Pass in mid-Sinai.

IDF tank crews quickly learned to disturb ATGM gunners' aim by weaving rapidly while firing at the gunners' positions. Still, in the first day the Egyptian army achieved its objectives at a cost of only 280 killed. That evening, more commandos were airlifted forward to ambush arriving IDF reserve and supply columns. Although the Israelis shot down 20 of the 48 helicopters involved, these commandos seriously disrupted Israeli movements. On the coastal road alone, at least 21 Israelis died before they neutralized the tenacious commandos.

Matters for Israel were even worse on the Golan Heights. General Hofi and his chief of staff were both absent for meetings when the attack began, so the two tank brigades operated almost independently. Moreover, only two battalions defended the flatter, open southern portion of the Golan Heights, and in most instances these battalions were dispersed in small groups, trying to defend every inch of the Golan Heights territory rather than blocking major penetrations. While IDF commanders reported stopping the attackers in their sectors, they were unaware of large forces infiltrating between those sectors and advancing to the rear. Indeed, by the early evening of the first day, the 5th Syrian Infantry Division had in effect broken through in the south but turned its forces northward toward Nafakh, seeking to outflank the defenders rather than pushing forward into Israel. During this period both sides created epics of individual gallantry, such as that of Lieutenant Zvika Greengold whose single tank delayed the Syrian flanking movement for hours along the Tapline Road. Although equipped with infrared vision devices, many of the Syrian units were untrained for night fighting, causing them to pause in the darkness. Moreover, despite the bravery of individual Syrian soldiers, many of their commanders were slow to respond to changing situations.

At the start of the war, Syrian commandos had captured the key IDF observation point on Mount Hermon but failed to execute their plan to interdict the flow of reserves across the Jordan River bridges. That night, Israeli brigadier general Rafael Eitan's 36th Armored Division headquarters assumed tactical responsibility for the Golan Heights. During the next two days, the 7th Armored Brigade and reinforcements fought the attackers to a standstill on the northern Golan Heights, destroying more than 260 tanks of the 7th Syrian Infantry Division and following echelons. On October 9, the remnants of the 7th Brigade performed another miracle, halting two Syrian tank brigades including the T-62s of the Presidential Guard Brigade, which outnumbered the Israelis four to one.

Only seven original tanks of the 7th Brigade remained after that battle.

The Israeli air force suffered heavily, losing 49 aircraft in the first four days in large measure because it was unable to eliminate enemy air defense batteries. Instead, Defense Minister Moshe Dayan repeatedly changed priorities, insisting that the air force attack Syrian spearheads and Egyptian bridges to gain time until the reserves were mobilized. Although the latter attacks were effective, the Egyptians rapidly replaced damaged sections of their floating bridges. Only at sea did Israel enjoy its usual dominance, using electronic countermeasures to negate Arab Styx missiles.

On October 8, a poorly coordinated IDF counterattack by two armored divisions failed painfully in the Sinai, due as much to excessive optimism by General Gonen as to Egyptian defensive capabilities. Yet on that and the following day two reserve armored divisions, Major General Dan Laner's 240th Division and Major General Moshe Peled's 146th Division, successfully retook the southern and central Golan Heights despite the dogged defense of Colonel Tawfiq Juhni's 1st Syrian Armored Division around Hushniyah. By darkness on October 10, Israel had destroyed some 870 Syrian tanks and retaken its prewar positions except for Mount Hermon. Still, the Syrian army had withdrawn in good order. Fearing that an early cease-fire would leave Israel with a net loss in territory, Prime Minister Meir ordered an offensive into Syria to begin on October 11.

This offensive, in combination with Israeli air attacks against Syrian command and infrastructure targets, changed the course of the war. Damascus appealed to Cairo to divert Israeli attention by a renewed attack, and President Sadat overruled his field commanders, ordering the Egyptian army to leave its air defense umbrella and advance to the Sinai passes on the morning of October 14. This attack by three understrength divisions, the 4th Armored and 6th Mechanized in the south and the 21st Armored in the north, was a predictable disaster, costing Egypt 250 tanks in a few hours. More significantly, it disrupted the integrity of Egypt's bridgehead defenses while committing most of the operational reserve.

Once these armored units (less one brigade of the 4th Division) crossed the Suez Canal going eastward, it was politically impossible for them to reverse course and defend the western bank. As a result, beginning on the evening of October 15, the IDF, led by Major General Ariel Sharon's 143rd Armored Division, was able to launch Operation GAZELLE, breaking through to the canal and pushing Colonel Danny Matt's 247th Paratroop Brigade across just north of Great Bitter Lake. Although the Egyptians attempted to pinch off this penetration by attacks on the eastern side of the canal, those attacks failed. Instead, over the next several days, elements of the 143rd and 146th Armored Divisions crossed the canal and fanned out, disrupting the Egyptian air defense network by attacking individual batteries on the ground. Egyptian artillery took a considerable toll on Israeli engineers, who nonetheless maintained bridges across the canal. For days, Sadat refused to recall units from the east, and in fact senior Egyptian commanders were not informed of the threat until several days after the initial crossing.

The Egyptian failure was compounded by continued defeats in Syria, where the IDF continued to push toward Damascus while engaging other Arab forces as they arrived to fight. In the early morning of October 13, Laner's 240th Armored Division decimated the Iraqi 3rd Armored Division and repulsed the Jordanian 40th Armored Brigade. The Arab armies continued to fight bravely, but coordination among those armies was not always effective.

From the beginning of the conflict, the Soviet Union had attempted to impose a cease-fire, at first because it expected the Arabs to be defeated and later to preserve their gains. Sadat had refused such initiatives until the Israeli crossing endangered his forces. Meanwhile, U.S. secretary of state Henry Kissinger tried to delay cease-fire negotiations in order to afford Israel time to regain its initial positions. By mid-October such a cease-fire appeared imminent, accelerating the two IDF offensives.

At the same time, Kissinger had to persuade his own government and especially Secretary of Defense James R. Schlesinger that Israel urgently needed replacement tanks, aircraft, and ammunition. Many officials suspected a trick, but Kissinger argued that an IDF defeat would appear to be an U.S. defeat as well. President Richard Nixon decisively supported Kissinger. Beginning on October 13, the United States defied Arab reactions, sending a total of 567 transport aircraft sorties moving 22,000 tons of supplies. Seventy-two fighter aircraft were also flown to Israel, while two Israeli ships moved 65 M-60 tanks, 23 M-109 howitzers, and 400 M-54 trucks from West Germany. Many of these vehicles arrived too late for immediate use, but the knowledge that they were on the way permitted the IDF to use all its available stocks in battle. The Soviet Union responded with 15,000 tons airlifted to replace the losses of its client states.

On October 22, the United Nations (UN) Security Council approved a cease-fire, but the agreement failed as each side blamed the other for violations. Regardless of who was at fault, the IDF used this excuse to push southward on the western bank of the canal, cutting off the Third Egyptian army from its supplies. With the air defense umbrella ruptured, the Israeli air force could again excel in both air-to-surface and air-to-air operations, downing almost 100 Egyptian aircraft at a loss of only 3 Israeli planes. In defeat, the Egyptians continued to fight in a disciplined manner, and a combination of soldiers and local militia thwarted Israeli efforts to seize Suez City, at the southern end of the canal, on October 23 and 25.

The continued fighting, with the Third Army stranded and the IDF approaching Damascus, provoked a superpower confrontation at the end of the war. The Soviet Union had alerted some of its forces at the start of hostilities and reportedly increased the readiness of certain airborne units after an Israeli victory became apparent. On October 24, Soviet leader Leonid Brezhnev sent President Nixon a note threatening unilateral action if the United States did not join with him in curbing the Israelis. Kissinger had already told the Israelis that their further incursions violated the spirit of his agreements with Moscow, but this new message prompted the United States to alert its nuclear forces to Defense Condition (DefCon) 3 at 11:41 p.m. on October 24. Although Brezhnev's true intentions have never been established, the situation was defused peacefully when, after repeated UN Security Council resolutions, the fighting finally halted on October 26. Even then, Israel refused to permit resupply of the stricken Third Army until Egypt returned all prisoners.

Overall, Israel suffered at least 2,687 killed and 7,251 wounded. Some 314 more were taken prisoner. This compares to combined Arab losses that exceeded 15,400 dead, 42,000 wounded, and 8,400 prisoners.

Although like the previous conflicts the Yom Kippur War ended with Israeli victories, General el-Shazly's larger objectives were clearly accomplished. Because the Arabs rather than the Israelis had the advantages of preparation and surprise, the fighting value of the opposing sides was much closer than in previous conflicts. Egypt in particular had demonstrated that Israel could not occupy the Sinai indefinitely, thereby establishing the psychological preconditions for successful peace negotiations in 1978.

The conflict also contributed to Middle Eastern disenchantment with the superpowers. The Soviet Union had shown itself unwilling or unable to give the Arabs weapons equal in quality to those that the United States had provided to Israel. However, the open U.S. support for Israel offended many Arab governments and led directly to the crippling oil embargo by Arab nations during late 1973 and early 1974. That imbroglio wrought havoc on already-weak U.S. and West European economies and saw the near quadrupling of petroleum prices in the span of only a few months.

Jonathan M. House

Further Reading

Adan, Avraham. *On the Banks of the Suez: An Israeli General's Personal Account of the Yom Kippur War*. Novato, CA: Presidio, 1980.

Asher, Dani, and Moshe Tlamim. *The Egyptian Strategy for the Yom Kippur War: An Analysis*. Jefferson, NC: McFarland, 2009.

Asher, Jerry, with Eric Hammel. *Duel for the Golan: The 100-Hour Battle that Saved Israel*. New York: William Morrow, 1987.

Bar-Joseph, Uri. *The Watchman Fell Asleep: The Surprise of Yom Kippur and Its Sources*. Albany: State University of New York Press, 2005.

Boyne, Walter. *The Two O'Clock War: The 1973 Yom Kippur Conflict and the Airlift that Saved Israel*. New York: St. Martin's Press, 2002.

Bregman, Ahron. *Israel's Wars: A History since 1947*. 3rd ed. New York: Routledge, 2010.

Dunstan, Simon. *The Yom Kippur War, 1973*. 2 vols. Westport, CT: Praeger, 2005.

El Shazly, Saad. *The Crossing of the Suez*. San Francisco: American Mideast Research, 1980.

Gamasy, Mohamed Abdul Ghani el-. *The October War: Memoirs of Field Marshal El-Gamasy of Egypt*. Translated by Gillian Potter, Nadra Morcos, and Rosette Frances. Cairo, Egypt: American University in Cairo Press, 1993.

Gawrych, George W. *The 1973 Arab-Israeli War: The Albatross of Decisive Victory*. Leavenworth Papers No. 21. Fort Leavenworth, KS: Combat Studies Institute, 1996.

Heikal, Mohammed Hasanyn. *The Road to Ramadan*. New York: Quadrangle/New York Times Book, 1975.

Herzog, Chaim. *War of Atonement: The Inside Story of the Yom Kippur War*. Haverford, PA: Casemate, 2010.

House, Jonathan M. *Toward Combined Arms Warfare: A Survey of 20th Century Tactics, Doctrine, and Organization*. Fort Leavenworth, KS: U.S. Army Command and General Staff College, 1984.

Kahalani, Avigdor. "Israeli Defense of the Golan." *Military Review* 59(10) (October 1979): 2–13.

Kahalani, Avigdor. *The Heights of Courage: A Tank Leader's War on the Golan*. Westport, CT: Praeger, 1992.

Kahana, Ephraim. "Early Warning versus Concept: The Case of the Yom Kippur War, 1973." *Intelligence and National Security* 17 (Summer 2002): 81–104.

Pollack, Kenneth M. *Arabs at War: Military Effectiveness, 1948–1991*. Lincoln: University of Nebraska Press, 2002.

Rabinovich, Abraham. *The Yom Kippur War: The Epic Encounter that Transformed the Middle East*. New York: Schocken, 2005.

Z

Zionism

Zionism holds that Jews constitute a people and a nation. As a political movement, it supports the creation of a homeland for the Jewish people. Zionism began in the late 19th century, arising out of the general movement of nationalism and increased anti-Semitism. It soon became a well-organized and well-funded settlement movement focused on Palestine, which many Jews believe was the ancient homeland granted them by God. Zionism eventually contributed directly to the formation of the State of Israel and continued to influence the politics of Israeli Jews for the rest of the 20th century and beyond.

The word "Zionism" derives from Mount Zion, the high ground in Jerusalem just south of the Temple Mount and the traditional burial place of King David. The term was first used in 1890 by Austrian Jew Nathan Birmbaum. Zionists found justification for their movement in the Hebrew Bible (and Christian Old Testament) account of God giving the Land of Israel to the Israelites in perpetuity and from the long-standing belief of Diaspora Jews that they would one day return to the Holy Land. Zionism also grew out of the rise of nationalism in the 19th century, as various European nations developed national identities and political systems. Many Jews at that time had a secular view of their Judaism. They abandoned their religious practices but embraced the concept of Jews as a people and a nation that deserved a national homeland. Other ideas, such as socialism and rationalism, also influenced early Zionists. Zionism was

fueled by the persecution of Jews in many places in Europe, most notably the Russian Empire. Jews came to believe, with some justification, that only a Jewish state could protect them.

Although other locations were suggested, Palestine seemed to be the obvious choice for the establishment of a Jewish nation. It had biblical connotations, and many Jews believed that it was their historical homeland. In 1862, Moses Hess wrote *Rome and Jerusalem*, which urged Jews to settle in Palestine in an agrarian socialist state. Hess and other writers, such as Ber Borochov and Nahum Syrkin, believed that Jews had become weak and downtrodden as a result of their centuries of working as merchants and pawnbrokers and that they needed to redeem themselves with healthful outdoor labor and socialism. Zionism and socialism often went hand in hand in the late 1800s and early 1900s. Many Jews looked on the creation of a Jewish state as an opportunity for them to build an ideal society, a religious community founded on the principles of socialism. This belief coalesced in a movement known as Labor Zionism, which held that the creation of a Jewish state must necessarily be part of a class struggle in which Jews would become agriculturists, living on collective socialist farms known as kibbutzim.

From the late 1870s through 1882, some Russian Jews went to Palestine, then a part of the Ottoman Empire, there to establish small farms in a movement that became known as the First Aliya. Beginning in 1882, thousands of Russian Jews immigrated to Palestine, fleeing from pogroms and Czar Alexander

Theodor Herzl at the Second Zionist Congress in Basel, 1897–1898. (Singer, Isadore, ed. *The Jewish Encyclopedia*, 1901)

III's 1882 anti-Semitic May Laws. These settlers called themselves Biluim, after a verse from the book of Isaiah. Their goal was to establish a Jewish national homeland in the land they called Israel. These first settlers nearly starved during their attempt to support themselves on land without adequate freshwater, and many of them left. Baron Edmond de Rothschild provided the remaining settlers with money to establish a winery, which soon became successful. The settlers also used his money to found the town of Zichron Yaakov.

In 1894, the Dreyfus Affair in France, which triggered an explosion of anti-Semitism in that country, persuaded many European Jews that anti-Semitism was a growing problem, even in the supposedly enlightened Western Europe. Theodor Herzl, a Jewish-Austrian journalist who covered the trial, became a staunch supporter of Zionism in the course of the Dreyfus Affair. In 1896, Herzl wrote *Der Judenstaat* (*The Jewish State*), in which he called for the Jews to create their own homeland either in Palestine or in Argentina.

In 1897, Herzl organized the First Zionist Congress in Switzerland. It created the Zionist Organization (ZO), the goal of which was to raise money and buy land in Palestine so that Jews could settle there. Herzl was the group's first president. The group spent the next 52 years purchasing land and creating governmental procedures for the new Israeli state. It was later renamed the World Zionist Organization (WZO).

All Jews were allowed to join the ZO. People from countries all over the world came to the group's congresses, which were held every two years between 1897 and 1946. Members assembled in delegations according to ideology instead of geographic origin. Some Zionists were ardent socialists or communists. Many were vehemently secular or even atheists. Others had more religious leanings.

The ZO organized the Jewish Colonial Trust to handle financial matters. The Jewish

National Fund, created in 1901, took responsibility for purchasing land. The Anglo-Palestine Bank, established in 1903, provided financial services for settlers. Gradually the group created an infrastructure for the Jewish homeland that made the process of settling in Palestine easier than it had been in the 1800s.

In the early years of the 20th century, Zionists debated whether Palestine was the ideal location for the Jewish homeland. In 1903, the British government proposed a Jewish homeland in modern Kenya. This plan was known as the British Uganda Program. Herzl suggested this to the Sixth Zionist Congress as a temporary safe haven for Russian Jews, but the Russian Jews themselves disliked the idea, and the Seventh Zionist Congress abandoned the idea in 1905. The Jewish Territorialist Organization wanted to create a Jewish homeland wherever it could, but it disbanded in 1917. In the 1930s, the Soviet Union created a Jewish Autonomous Republic in the Far Eastern Federal District, but few Jews wanted to move there. For the most part, Palestine remained the sole focus of the Zionist movement.

During the early 1900s, many small groups of settlers went to Palestine. A number arrived there following the 1905 Revolution in Russia. Leaders such as Joseph Baratz and other settlers pooled their money, added to it contributions from Jews all over the world, and founded kibbutzim on plots of land that they lived on and farmed collectively. By 1914, there were kibbutzim throughout Palestine. Residents shared all work and all profits and governed themselves democratically.

Cultural Zionists looked on the settlement movement as an opportunity to create a unique Jewish culture. Many Jews were quite critical of Jewish culture in the late 19th century, which they saw as downtrodden and weak after centuries of diaspora. Some Zionist thinkers such as Asher Ginsberg and Eliezer Ben Yehudah thought that Palestine would be the ideal place to revive Hebrew language and culture, allowing Jews to replace their Germanic Yiddish language and speak to one another in a uniquely Jewish language that would unite diverse groups of Jews. Herzl wanted German to be the official language of Palestine, but most settlers and Zionists supported the use of Hebrew. Tel Aviv, founded in 1909, was the first city to make Hebrew its official language.

The United Kingdom was an important ally in the creation of the Jewish state. Jews were generally made welcome in Britain in the early 20th century, and many British people appreciated Jewish culture. During World War I, the British government sought to mobilize the support of Jews for the war effort and, in 1917, British foreign secretary Arthur Balfour issued a statement (known as the Balfour Declaration) in which the British government expressed its support for the establishment of a Jewish homeland (not a state) in Palestine.

In Balfour's declaration, he said that a Jewish homeland should not harm the civil rights of non-Jewish people already living in Palestine. Zionists realized that the Muslim Arabs already living in Palestine would become a source of conflict, but many of them chose to ignore the issue or to suggest that Jewish immigration could only benefit the current residents. Zionist leaders such as Israel Zangwill concocted slogans such as "A land without a people, for a people without a land," which deliberately glossed over the presence of people in the land in question.

In the early days of settlement (the 1880s and earlier) Arabs did not object to the incursion of Jews. The first Jewish settlers had been unable to farm successfully, so they ended up hiring Arab laborers to work their farms. In the 1890s, however, as Arabs began to realize what the Zionists intended, they grew concerned about losing their farmland and water. The socialist agrarian settlers of the early 1900s did not employ Arabs because their whole raison d'être was to encourage Jews to work the land themselves. This, the Balfour Declaration, the partitioning of Palestine in 1918, and their increasing landless status and poverty all prompted Palestinian Arabs to agitate for a state of their own. Also around this time, some Zionists suggested that Palestinian Arabs should be expelled from the country or should be made to accept the Jewish presence through armed force.

In the early 1920s, the ZO, having reached the conclusion that socialism was the only way to distribute available economic resources among a rapidly growing group of Jewish immigrants, decided that Jewish settlement in Palestine should be socialist. During the 1920s, David Ben-Gurion, a leader of Histadrut, the Jewish Labor Zionist trade union that dominated Jewish Palestine, officially opposed the use of force against Arabs, claiming that it would be unnecessary because Arabs would soon decide that Zionism was good for them. In private, however, he said that conflict was inevitable because Arabs would never accept Zionist settlement. In the late 1930s, Ben-Gurion and the Labor Zionists supported the idea of a Jewish state with no Arabs in it, the existing Arabs having been removed forcibly.

Zionism became somewhat more popular after the creation of the British Mandate for Palestine in 1922. Increasing numbers of Jews moved to Palestine, as the ZO and other Zionist organizations raised money and lobbied the British government not to allow the Palestinian Arabs to create their own state. Palestinian nationalism also increased during this time, as the Muslims saw their land and livelihood increasingly threatened by Jewish newcomers.

Zionism was made up of many different streams. "General Zionism" is the term used to describe the general or transcending beliefs held in common by all Zionists exemplified by the goals of the ZO. General Zionism sought unity by placing the importance of the Jewish homeland above class, party, political, social, religious, or personal interests. Political Zionism centered on the creation of a legal and political entity in Palestine, the existence and sovereignty of which would be sanctioned by the great world powers.

Socialist Zionism asserted that the fusion of Zionist and socialist ideals in Palestine would create a labor-based communal society (socialism) that would transform Palestine and become an attractive haven for the downtrodden of world Jewry. Socialist Zionism eventually evolved into the Labor Zionism of Ben-Gurion. Although the Socialist Zionists and the Labor Zionists were more ethnic Jews than religious Jews, both respected Jewish religious traditions as part of their national heritage.

Labor Zionism believed that the best foundation for a Jewish state was a strong economy and shared economic opportunity that benefited all of the society's members, such as collective settlements (kibbutzim). Labor Zionism generally believed that Arabs in Palestine should and could be encouraged to transfer out of Palestine.

Practical Zionism asserted that the best way to achieve the Zionist goal was through a massive immigration movement (aliya). The aliya would be oriented toward settling both rural and urban areas and the creation of industries, educational institutions, and social services.

Messianic Zionism effectively ignored the practical and simply asserted that the Jewish state would come to be and would last because it was part of the original divine decree given to Abraham, a promise on which those settling in Palestine could depend. Religious Zionism asserted that the formation of an ethnic Jewish state with no religious heart would be temporary. Religious Zionism argued that the only Jewish state that would survive and attract other Jews would be one that wove a conservative Torah-based Jewish religion into its political and social fabric. In other words, the state should be based on the commandments and laws of the Torah. Spiritual Zionism agreed with Religious Zionism but asserted further that the then-prevalent form of Judaism in the Zionist movement, the more liberal and intellectual Ashkenazic Judaism, had lost its guiding spirit. Spiritual Zionism believed that Palestine could not practically hold all of world Jewry, and even if it could, a Jewish state would not elevate the social and economic status of Jews, nor would it end persecution. Spiritual Zionism advocated a modest settlement plan and the formation of a national spiritual center in Palestine instead of a Jewish political state. Chaim Weizmann's Synthetic Zionism combined political, social, practical, and ethno-religious Judaism into a single entity that tried to incorporate all of the different ideals into a Jewish state reflecting all of the concerns of the Zionist spectrum.

Revisionist Zionism argued that the British Mandate for Palestine should be revised to create a sovereign Jewish state encompassing both sides of the Jordan River. Revisionist Zionists also held that Zionism should shift its emphasis from social and economic development in Palestine to the immediate creation of a Jewish state aligned with Great Britain.

Not all Jews supported the Zionist movement, of course. Some socialist Jews disliked the idea of a state because it smacked of un-socialistic nationalism. Communist Jews in Russia also rejected the idea of a Jewish state in Palestine. Many Jews believed that there was no need for a Jewish homeland because Jews could live perfectly well in other nations, such as the United States. American Jews argued that the United States was the Jewish homeland.

All these arguments changed after Adolf Hitler came to power in Germany in 1933. The United States, formerly so welcoming to Jews, closed its doors to Jewish immigration. Jews became refugees in the Europe that they had formerly considered a perfectly adequate home. Increasing numbers of Jews moved to Palestine in the 1930s, but this angered Palestinian Arabs. After riots broke out, in 1939, the British government restricted Jewish immigration to Palestine. Jews living in Palestine armed themselves and began fighting the Arabs and launching attacks on British targets.

After World War II, Zionism experienced a huge upsurge of popularity and support thanks to the horrific events of the Holocaust, Hitler's attempt to exterminate the Jews in Europe. The United States was one of the strongest backers of the formation of a Jewish state in Palestine. Jews themselves were almost unanimous in their support for the creation of Israel. Following the failure of British partition efforts, in 1947, the United Nations (UN) voted to create two states within Palestine, one Arab and one Jewish, with Jerusalem as a shared possession. The Jews accepted the plan, but the Palestinian Arabs rejected it. With the British withdrawal, Jewish leaders in Palestine declared the independent State of Israel on May 14, 1948.

Once the Jewish homeland was established, Israeli leaders turned their attention to expelling Arab agitators, welcoming a new influx of Jewish settlers, and organizing the Israel Defense Forces (IDF). International Zionist organizations continued their support for Israel, raising money and sponsoring immigration and development. In 1960, the ZO became the WZO, dedicated to making Israel the center of Jewish life, preserving Jewish identity, and protecting the rights of Jews around the world.

Amy Hackney Blackwell

Further Reading

Beinart, Peter. *The Crisis of Zionism*. New York: Times Books, 2012.

Brenner, Michael. *Zionism: A Brief History*. Translated by Shelley L. Frisch. Princeton, NJ: Marcus Wiener, 2003.

Butler, Judith. *Parting Ways: Jewishness and the Critique of Zionism*. New York: Columbia University Press, 2012.

Engel, David. *Zionism*. New York: Longman, 2009.

Hart, Alan. *Zionism: The Real Enemy of the Jews*. 3 vols. Atlanta, GA: Clarity Press, 2005.

Hertzberg, Arthur, ed. *The Zionist Idea: A Historical Analysis and Reader*. Philadelphia: Jewish Publication Society, 1997.

Herzl, Theodor. *The Jewish State*. Mineola, NY: Dover, 1989.

Laqueur, Walter. *A History of Zionism: From the French Revolution to the Establishment of the State of Israel*. Reprint ed. New York: Schocken, 2003.

Massad, Joseph. *The Persistence of the Palestinian Question: Essays on Zionism and the Palestinians*. New York: Routledge, 2006.

Netanyahu, Benzion. *The Founding Fathers of Zionism*. Toronto: Balfour Books, 2012.

Pappé, Ilan. *A History of Modern Palestine: One Land, Two Peoples*. Cambridge: Cambridge University Press, 2003.

Petras, James F. *Zionism, Militarism, and the Decline of US Power*. Atlanta, GA: Clarity Press, 2008.

Pianko, Noam. *Zionism and the Roads Not Taken: Rawidowicz, Kaplan, Kohn*. Bloomington: Indiana University Press, 2010.

Rose, John. *The Myths of Zionism*. London: Pluto, 2004.

Primary Source Documents

Balfour Declaration, 1917

World War I gave considerable impetus to Zionist demands for the establishment of a Jewish state or homeland in Palestine, then part of the Ottoman Empire. At least some British statesmen were sympathetic, in part because of the romantic fascination that the Zionist idea exercised upon some individuals, notably British foreign secretary Arthur James Balfour. More practical considerations also impelled them. British leaders were anxious to win support from Jewish elements in countries with which they were at war. They also sought to win over the politically influential Jewish lobby in the United States, initially a key neutral state and eventually a vital ally whose economic and manpower resources proved crucial in bringing about an Allied victory. Lobbying efforts by Chaim Weizmann, a leading Zionist and biochemist whose scientific research was of great value to the Allied efforts, also proved persuasive to British leaders. On November 2, 1917, Balfour wrote an official letter to Lord Rothschild, a prominent British Zionist figure. Although its terms were somewhat ambivalent, this brief communication offered Jews a homeland in Palestine, a development that eventually led to the creation of the State of Israel in 1948. Correctly or not, Sharif Hussein of Mecca, a key Arab leader and British ally in the revolt against Turkey, believed that he too had been promised this territory, a source of lasting bitterness among Arab leaders and peoples. After World War I, Palestine would become a British mandate under the League of Nations, and Arab and Jewish settlers would begin a lengthy struggle over which element should predominate in this territory.

November 2, 1917
Dear Lord Rothschild,

I have much pleasure in conveying to you, on behalf of His Majesty's Government, the following declaration of sympathy with Jewish Zionist aspirations which has been submitted to, and approved by, the Cabinet.

His Majesty's Government view with favour the establishment in Palestine of a national home for the Jewish people, and will use their best endeavours to facilitate the achievement of this object, it being clearly understood that nothing shall be done which may prejudice the civil and religious rights of existing non-Jewish communities in Palestine, or the rights and political status enjoyed by Jews in any other country.

I should be grateful if you would bring this declaration to the knowledge of the Zionist Federation.

Signed: Arthur James Balfour

Source: "Letter of Foreign Minister Balfour to Lord Rothschild," *The Times* (London), November 2, 1917.

United Nations General Assembly Resolution 181, Future Government of Palestine [Excerpt], November 29, 1947

After lengthy debate, on November 29, 1947, the United Nations (UN) General Assembly voted on the plan to partition Palestine into independent Arab and Jewish states put forward in the report of the United Nations Special Committee on Palestine (UNSCOP). Both the Soviet Union and the United States voted in favor of UN General Assembly Resolution 181, which described this plan, as did 31 other UN member states. Thirteen member states, including all the Arab states, voted in opposition: Afghanistan, Cuba, Egypt, Greece, India, Iran, Iraq, Lebanon,

Pakistan, Saudi Arabia, Syria, Turkey, and Yemen. Ten member states, including the United Kingdom and several Latin American states as well as Yugoslavia and China, abstained. Besides advocating the partition of Palestine into Arab and Jewish states and ending the British mandate no later than August 1948 (sooner if possible), Resolution 181 also supported the creation of a zone under international administration that would include the highly religiously significant towns of Jerusalem and Bethlehem. The Jewish state included a substantial Arab minority, 45 percent of the total population, whereas only 1 percent of the inhabitants of the proposed Arab state would be Jewish. The bulk of Jews and Jewish groups in Palestine supported the partition, whereas it was highly unpopular with the Arabs within Palestine, most of whom refused to accept it. Arab attacks on Jewish individuals and businesses began almost immediately. Other Arab nations also declined to endorse the plan, sought to challenge it in the International Court of Justice, and passed resolutions at the November and December 1947 meetings of the Arab League that envisaged taking military action to prevent fulfillment of the resolution. The British government, still the mandatory power, declined to try to implement partition on the grounds that it did not have the support of both parties involved and also refused to share the administration of Palestine with the UN Palestine Commission in the transitional period up to May 15, 1948. Jewish residents of areas in Palestine designated as part of the Arab state, together with inhabitants of Arab states elsewhere in the region, mostly fled to those regions earmarked to form the Jewish state, while Arab refugees likewise left what they feared would soon be hostile Jewish territories. All anticipated that as soon as the mandate ended, the bitter internecine Arab-Jewish fighting that began virtually as soon as Resolution 181 was passed would intensify, and that Arab nations would attack the new State of Israel.

The General Assembly,

[...]

Recommends to the United Kingdom, as the mandatory Power for Palestine, and to all other Members of the United Nations the adoption and implementation, with regard to the future Government of Palestine, of the Plan of Partition with Economic Union set out below;

Requests that

(a) The Security Council take the necessary measures as provided for in the plan for its implementation;

(b) The Security Council consider, if circumstances during the transitional period require such consideration, whether the situation in Palestine constitutes a threat to the peace. If it decides that such a threat exists, and in order to maintain international peace and security, the Security Council should supplement the authorization of the General Assembly by taking measures, under Articles 39 and 41 of the Charter, to empower the United Nations Commission, as provided in this resolution, to exercise in Palestine the functions which are assigned to it by this resolution; . . .

Calls upon the inhabitants of Palestine to take such steps as may be necessary on their part to put this plan into effect;

Appeals to all Governments and all peoples to refrain from taking any action which might hamper or delay the carrying out of these recommendations;

[. . .]

Plan of Partition with Economic Union

Part I.—Future Constitution and Government of Palestine

A. Termination of Mandate, Partition and Independence

1. The Mandate for Palestine shall terminate as soon as possible but in any case not later than 1 August 1948. . . .

2. Independent Arab and Jewish States and the Special International Regime for the

City of Jerusalem, set forth in part III of this Plan, shall come into existence in Palestine two months after the evacuation of the armed forces of the mandatory Power has been completed but in any case not later than 1 October 1948. The boundaries of the Arab State, the Jewish State, and the City of Jerusalem shall be as described in Parts II and III below. . . .

B. Steps Preparatory to Independence

1. A Commission shall be set up consisting of one representative of each of five Member States. The Members represented on the Commission shall be elected by the General Assembly on as broad a basis, geographically and otherwise, as possible.

2. The administration of Palestine shall, as the mandatory Power withdraws its armed forces, be progressively turned over to the Commission, which shall act in conformity with the recommendations of the General Assembly, under the guidance of the Security Council. The mandatory Power shall to the fullest possible extent coordinate its plans for withdrawal with the plans of the Commission to take over and administer areas which have been evacuated. . . .

3. On its arrival in Palestine the Commission shall proceed to carry out measures for the establishment of the frontiers of the Arab and Jewish States and the City of Jerusalem in accordance with the general lines of the recommendations of the General Assembly on the partition of Palestine. Nevertheless, the boundaries as described in part II of this Plan are to be modified in such a way that village areas as a rule will not be divided by state boundaries unless pressing reasons make that necessary.

[. . .]

7. The Commission shall instruct the Provisional Councils of Government of both the Arab and Jewish States, after their formation, to proceed to the establishment of administrative organs of government, central and local.

[. . .]

9. The Provisional Council of Government of each State shall, not later than two months after the withdrawal of the armed forces of the mandatory Power, hold elections to the Constituent Assembly which shall be conducted on democratic lines.

[. . .]

10. The Constituent Assembly of each State shall draft a democratic constitution for its State and choose a provisional government to succeed the Provisional Council of Government appointed by the Commission. The Constitutions of the States shall embody Chapters 1 and 2 of the Declaration provided for in section C below and include, *inter alia*, provisions for:

a. Establishing in each State a legislative body elected by universal suffrage and by secret ballot on the basis of proportional representation, and an executive body responsible to the legislature;

b. Settling all international disputes in which the State may be involved by peaceful means in such a manner that international peace and security, and justice, are not endangered;

c. Accepting the obligation of the State to refrain in its international relations from the threat or use of force against the territorial integrity or political independence of any State, or in any other manner inconsistent with the purposes of the United Nations;

d. Guaranteeing to all persons equal and non-discriminatory rights in civil, political, economic and religious matters and the enjoyment of human rights and fundamental freedoms, including freedom of religion, language, speech and publication, education, assembly and association;

e. Preserving freedom of transit and visit for all residents and citizens of the other State in Palestine and the City of Jerusalem, subject to considerations of national security, provided that each State shall control residence within its borders.

[. . .]

D. Economic Union and Transit

1. The Provisional Council of Government of each State shall enter into an undertaking with respect to Economic Union and Transit. This undertaking shall be drafted by the Commission provided for in section B, paragraph 1, utilizing to the greatest possible extent the advice and cooperation of representative organizations and bodies from each of the proposed States. It shall contain provisions to establish the Economic Union of Palestine and provide for other matters of common interest. If by 1 April 1948 the Provisional Councils of Government have not entered into the undertaking, the undertaking shall be put into force by the Commission.

The Economic Union of Palestine

2. The objectives of the Economic Union of Palestine shall be:

(a) A customs union;

(b) A joint currency system providing for a single foreign exchange rate;

(c) Operation in the common interest on a non-discriminatory basis of railways; inter-State highways; postal, telephone and telegraphic services, and ports and airports involved in international trade and commerce;

(d) Joint economic development, especially in respect of irrigation, land reclamation and soil conservation;

(e) Access for both States and for the City of Jerusalem on a non-discriminatory basis to water and power facilities.

[. . .]

11. There shall be a common customs tariff with complete freedom of trade between the States, and between the States and the City of Jerusalem.

[. . .]

Freedom of Transit and Visit

18. The undertaking shall contain provisions preserving freedom of transit and visit for all residents or citizens of both States and of the City of Jerusalem, subject to security considerations; provided that each State and the City shall control residence within its borders.

[. . .]

F. Admission to Membership in the United Nations

When the independence of either the Arab or the Jewish State as envisaged in this plan has become effective and the declaration and undertaking, as envisaged in this plan, have been signed by either of them, sympathetic consideration should be given to its application for admission to membership in the United Nations in accordance with article 4 of the Charter of the United Nations.

[. . .]

Part III.—City of Jerusalem

A. Special Regime

The City of Jerusalem shall be established as a *corpus separatum* under a special international regime and shall be administered by the United Nations. The Trusteeship Council shall be designated to discharge the responsibilities of the Administering Authority on behalf of the United Nations. . . .

C. Statute of the City

The Trusteeship Council shall, within five months of the approval of the present plan, elaborate and approve a detailed statute of the City which shall contain, *inter alia*, the substance of the following provisions:

1. Government machinery; special objectives.

The Administering Authority in discharging its administrative obligations shall pursue the following special objectives:

(a) To protect and to preserve the unique spiritual and religious interests located in the city of the three great monotheistic faiths throughout the world, Christian, Jewish and Moslem; to this end to ensure that order and peace, and especially religious peace, reign in Jerusalem;

(b) To foster cooperation among all the inhabitants of the city in their own interests as well as in order to encourage and support the peaceful development of the mutual relations between the two Palestinian peoples throughout the Holy Land; to promote the security, well-being and any constructive measures of development of the residents having regard to the special circumstances and customs of the various peoples and communities.

[. . .]

4. Security measures.

(a) The City of Jerusalem shall be demilitarized; its neutrality shall be declared and preserved, and no para-military formations, exercises or activities shall be permitted within its borders. . . .

[. . .]

8. Freedom of transit and visit; control of residents.

Subject to considerations of security, and of economic welfare as determined by the Governor under the directions of the Trusteeship Council, freedom of entry into, and residence within, the borders of the City shall be guaranteed for the residents or citizens of the Arab and Jewish States. Immigration into, and residence within, the borders of the city for nationals of other States shall be controlled by the Governor under the directions of the Trusteeship Council. . . .

13. Holy Places.

(a) Existing rights in respect of Holy Places and religious buildings or sites shall not be denied or impaired.

(b) Free access to the Holy Places and religious buildings or sites and the free exercise of worship shall be secured in conformity with existing rights and subject to the requirements of public order and decorum.

(c) Holy Places and religious buildings or sites shall be preserved. No act shall be permitted which may in any way impair their sacred character. . . .

[. . .]

Source: United Nations General Assembly Official Records, 2nd Sess., *Future Government of Palestine*, G.A. Res. 181 (II), November 29, 1947.

The Declaration of the Establishment of the State of Israel, May 14, 1948

On May 14, 1948, a few hours before the withdrawal of British troops from the Palestine Mandate, the National Council, consisting of representatives of Palestine's Jewish inhabitants and of the Zionists, met in Tel Aviv and approved the declaration of independence of the new state of Israel, or Eretz Israel. The declaration invoked the sufferings of Jews in Europe during the Nazi Holocaust and the efforts of Jewish fighters during World War II. After recalling the endorsement that the United Nations (UN) had given to the creation of a Jewish state, the authors proclaimed the existence of the new State of Israel. From midnight that evening, the declaration established a Provisional State Council, based on the existing National Council, to hold authority until elections could be held under a constitution still to be drawn up. The declaration proclaimed Israel's intention of living in peace with all. The authors of this declaration nonetheless undoubtedly knew that the withdrawal of British troops would prove the signal for immediate attack by the armed forces of Transjordan, Egypt, Syria, and other neighboring Arab countries and that the attainment of peace would depend on their ability to wield the sword.

ERETZ-ISRAEL [(Hebrew)—the Land of Israel, Palestine] was the birthplace of the Jewish people. Here their spiritual, religious and political identity was shaped. Here they first attained to statehood, created cultural values of national and universal significance and gave to the world the eternal Book of Books.

After being forcibly exiled from their land, the people kept faith with it throughout their Dispersion and never ceased to pray and hope for their return to it and for the restoration in it of their political freedom.

Impelled by this historic and traditional attachment, Jews strove in every successive generation to re-establish themselves in their ancient homeland. In recent decades they returned in their masses. Pioneers, ma'pilim [(Hebrew)—immigrants coming to Eretz-Israel in defiance of restrictive legislation] and defenders, they made deserts bloom, revived the Hebrew language, built villages and towns, and created a thriving community controlling its own economy and culture, loving peace but knowing how to defend itself, bringing the blessings of progress to all the country's inhabitants, and aspiring towards independent nationhood.

In the year 5657 (1897), at the summons of the spiritual father of the Jewish State, Theodor Herzl, the First Zionist Congress convened and proclaimed the right of the Jewish people to national rebirth in its own country.

This right was recognized in the Balfour Declaration of the 2nd November, 1917, and reaffirmed in the Mandate of the League of Nations which, in particular, gave international sanction to the historic connection between the Jewish people and Eretz-Israel and to the right of the Jewish people to rebuild its National Home.

The catastrophe which recently befell the Jewish people—the massacre of millions of Jews in Europe—was another clear demonstration of the urgency of solving the problem of its homelessness by re-establishing in Eretz-Israel the Jewish State, which would open the gates of the homeland wide to every Jew and confer upon the Jewish people the status of a fully privileged member of the comity of nations.

Survivors of the Nazi holocaust in Europe, as well as Jews from other parts of the world, continued to migrate to Eretz-Israel, undaunted by difficulties, restrictions and dangers, and never ceased to assert their right to a life of dignity, freedom and honest toil in their national homeland.

In the Second World War, the Jewish community of this country contributed its full share to the struggle of the freedom- and peace-loving nations against the forces of Nazi wickedness and, by the blood of its soldiers and its war effort, gained the right to be reckoned among the peoples who founded the United Nations.

On the 29th November, 1947, the United Nations General Assembly passed a resolution calling for the establishment of a Jewish State in Eretz-Israel; the General Assembly required the inhabitants of Eretz-Israel to take such steps as were necessary on their part for the implementation of that resolution. This recognition by the United Nations of the right of the Jewish people to establish their State is irrevocable.

This right is the natural right of the Jewish people to be masters of their own fate, like all other nations, in their own sovereign State.

ACCORDINGLY WE, MEMBERS OF THE PEOPLE'S COUNCIL, REPRE-SENTATIVES OF THE JEWISH COM-MUNITY OF ERETZ-ISRAEL AND OF THE ZIONIST MOVEMENT, ARE HERE ASSEMBLED ON THE DAY OF THE TERMINATION OF THE BRIT-ISH MANDATE OVER ERETZ-ISRAEL AND, BY VIRTUE OF OUR NATURAL AND HISTORIC RIGHT AND ON THE STRENGTH OF THE RESOLUTION OF THE UNITED NATIONS GENERAL ASSEMBLY, HEREBY DECLARE THE ESTABLISHMENT OF A JEWISH STATE IN ERETZ-ISRAEL, TO BE KNOWN AS THE STATE OF ISRAEL.

WE DECLARE that, with effect from the moment of the termination of the Mandate being tonight, the eve of Sabbath, the 6th Iyar, 5708 (15th May, 1948), until the establishment of the elected, regular author-ities of the State in accordance with the Constitution which shall be adopted by the Elected Constituent Assembly not later than the 1st October 1948, the People's Council shall act as a Provisional Council of State, and its executive organ, the People's Admin-istration, shall be the Provisional Govern-ment of the Jewish State, to be called "Israel."

THE STATE OF ISRAEL will be open for Jewish immigration and for the Ingath-ering of the Exiles; it will foster the devel-opment of the country for the benefit of all its inhabitants; it will be based on freedom, justice and peace as envisaged by the proph-ets of Israel; it will ensure complete equality of social and political rights to all its inhab-itants irrespective of religion, race or sex; it will guarantee freedom of religion, con-science, language, education and culture; it will safeguard the Holy Places of all reli-gions; and it will be faithful to the principles of the Charter of the United Nations.

THE STATE OF ISRAEL is prepared to cooperate with the agencies and represen-tatives of the United Nations in implement-ing the resolution of the General Assembly of the 29th November, 1947, and will take steps to bring about the economic union of the whole of Eretz-Israel.

WE APPEAL to the United Nations to assist the Jewish people in the building-up of its State and to receive the State of Israel into the comity of nations.

WE APPEAL—in the very midst of the onslaught launched against us now for months—to the Arab inhabitants of the State of Israel to preserve peace and participate in the upbuilding of the State on the basis of full and equal citizenship and due representation in all its provisional and permanent institutions.

WE EXTEND our hand to all neighbour-ing states and their peoples in an offer of peace and good neighbourliness, and appeal to them to establish bonds of cooperation and mutual help with the sovereign Jewish people settled in its own land. The State of Israel is prepared to do its share in a common effort for the advancement of the entire Middle East.

WE APPEAL to the Jewish people throughout the Diaspora to rally round the Jews of Eretz-Israel in the tasks of immigration and upbuilding and to stand by them in the great struggle for the realization of the age-old dream—the redemption of Israel.

PLACING OUR TRUST IN THE "ROCK OF ISRAEL," WE AFFIX OUR SIGNATURES TO THIS PROCLAMATION AT THIS SESSION OF THE PROVISIONAL COUNCIL OF STATE, ON THE SOIL OF THE HOMELAND, IN THE CITY OF TEL-AVIV, ON THIS SABBATH EVE, THE 5TH DAY OF IYAR, 5708 (14TH MAY, 1948).

David Ben-Gurion
Daniel Auster
Mordekhai Bentov
Yitzchak Ben Zvi
Eliyahu Berligne
Fritz Bernstein
Rabbi Wolf Gold
Meir Grabovsky
Yitzchak Gruenbaum
Dr. Abraham Granovsky
Eliyahu Dobkin
Meir Wilner-Kovner
Zerach Wahrhaftig
Herzl Vardi
Rachel Cohen
Rabbi Kalman Kahana
Saadia Kobashi
Rabbi Yitzchak Meir Levin
Meir David Loewenstein
Zvi Luria
Golda Myerson
Nachum Nir

Zvi Segal
Rabbi Yehuda Leib Hacohen Fishman
David Zvi Pinkas
Aharon Zisling
Moshe Kolodny
Eliezer Kaplan
Abraham Katznelson
Felix Rosenblueth
David Remez
Berl Repetur
Mordekhai Shattner
Ben Zion Sternberg
Bekhor Shitreet
Moshe Shapira
Moshe Shertok

Source: The Declaration of the Establishment of the State of Israel, May 14, 1948, Israel Ministry of Foreign Affairs. Published in the *Official Gazette*, No. 1 of the 5th, Iyar, 5708 (14th May, 1948).

U.S. Recognition of Israel, May 14, 1948

After World War II, Zionists, often citing the deaths of 6 million European Jews at the hands of Hitler's Germany, pushed for an independent Jewish state. Against the advice of Secretary of State George Marshall, who feared that creating such an entity would permanently alienate Arab countries throughout the oil-rich Middle East, President Harry S. Truman supported its creation. Truman, an avid reader of history, had a romantic respect for the Jewish people's dedication to the restoration of the ancient state of Israel and also felt that they deserved compensation for their wartime sufferings. As soon as the State of Israel came into existence, Truman recognized it.

Text of Letter from the Agent of the Provisional Government of Israel to the President of the U.S.

[Released to the Press by the White House on May 15]

My Dear Mr. President:

I have the honor to notify you that the state of Israel has been proclaimed as an independent republic within frontiers approved by the General Assembly of the United Nations in its Resolution of November 29, 1947, and that a provisional government has been charged to assume the rights and duties of government for preserving law and order within the boundaries of Israel, for defending the state against external aggression, and for discharging the obligations of Israel to the other nations of the world in accordance with international law. The Act of Independence will become effective at one minute after six o'clock on the evening of 14 May 1948, Washington time.

With full knowledge of the deep bond of sympathy which has existed and has been strengthened over the past thirty years between the Government of the United States and the Jewish people of Palestine, I have been authorized by the provisional government of the new state to tender this message and to express the hope that your government will recognize and will welcome Israel into the community of nations.

Very respectfully yours,

Eliahu Epstein

Agent, Provisional Government of Israel

Statement by President Truman [Released to the press by the White House on May 14]

This Government has been informed that a Jewish state has been proclaimed in Palestine, and recognition has been requested by the provisional government thereof.

The United States recognizes the provisional government as the *de facto* authority of the new State of Israel.

Source: "Israel Proclaimed as an Independent Republic," *Department of State Bulletin* 18(464) (1948): 673.

Arab League Statement, May 15, 1948

The same night that British forces withdrew from the Palestine mandate and the State of Israel was proclaimed, Arab League forces from Egypt, Syria, Lebanon, Iraq, and Transjordan invaded the new state. The Egyptian foreign minister informed the United Nations (UN) Security Council that their purpose in doing so was to restore law and order. On May 15, 1948, the Arab League issued a statement proclaiming that its forces were entering Palestine to protect the rights of its Arab inhabitants.

1. Palestine was part of the former Ottoman Empire, subject to its law and represented in its parliament. The overwhelming majority of the population of Palestine were Arabs. There was in it a small minority of Jews that enjoyed the same rights and bore the same responsibilities as the [other] inhabitants, and did not suffer any ill-treatment on account of its religious beliefs. The holy places were inviolable and the freedom of access to them was guaranteed.

2. The Arabs have always asked for their freedom and independence. On the outbreak of the First World War, and when the Allies declared that they were fighting for the liberation of peoples, the Arabs joined them and fought on their side with a view to realizing their national aspirations and obtaining their independence. England pledged herself to recognize the independence of the Arab countries in Asia, including Palestine. The Arabs played a remarkable part in the achievement of final victory and the Allies have admitted this.

3. In 1917 England issued a declaration in which she expressed her sympathy with the establishment of a national home for the Jews in Palestine. When

the Arabs knew of this they protested against it, but England reassured them by affirming to them that this would not prejudice the right of their countries to freedom and independence or affect the political status of the Arabs in Palestine. Notwithstanding the legally void character of this declaration, it was interpreted by England to aim at no more than the establishment of a spiritual centre for the Jews in Palestine, and to conceal no ulterior political aims, such as the establishment of a Jewish State. The same thing was declared by the Jewish leaders.

4. When the war came to an end England did not keep her promise. Indeed, the Allies placed Palestine under the Mandate system and entrusted England with [the task of carrying it out], in accordance with a document providing for the administration of the country, in the interests of its inhabitants and its preparation for the independence which the Covenant of the League of Nations recognized that Palestine was qualified to have.

5. England administered Palestine in a manner which enabled the Jews to flood it with immigrants and helped them to settle in the country. [This was so] notwithstanding the fact that it was proved that the density of the population in Palestine had exceeded the economic capacity of the country to absorb additional immigrants. England did not pay regard to the interests or rights of the Arab inhabitants, the lawful owners of the country. Although they used to express, by various means, their concern and indignation on account of this state of affairs which was harmful to their being and their future, they [invariably] were met by indifference, imprisonment and oppression.

6. As Palestine is an Arab country, situated in the heart of the Arab countries and attached to the Arab world by various ties—spiritual, historical, and strategic— the Arab countries, and even the Eastern ones, governments as well as peoples, have concerned themselves with the problem of Palestine and have raised it to the international level. When the General Assembly of the United Nations issued, on November 29, 1947, its recommendation concerning the solution of the Palestine problem, on the basis of the establishment of an Arab State and of another Jewish [state] in [Palestine] together with placing the City of Jerusalem under the trusteeship of the United Nations, the Arab States drew attention to the injustice implied in this solution [affecting] the right of the people of Palestine to immediate independence, as well as democratic principles and the provisions of the Covenant of the League of Nations and [the Charter] of the United Nations. [These States also] declared the Arabs' rejection of [that solution] and that it would not be possible to carry it out by peaceful means, and that its forcible imposition would constitute a threat to peace and security in this area.

The warnings and expectations of the Arab States have, indeed, proved to be true, as disturbances were soon widespread throughout Palestine. The Arabs clashed with the Jews, and the two [parties] proceeded to fight each other and shed each other's blood. Whereupon the United Nations began to realize the danger of recommending the partition [of Palestine] and is still looking for a way out of this state of affairs.

10. Now that the British mandate over Palestine has come to an end, without there being a legitimate constitutional

authority in the country, which would safeguard the maintenance of security and respect for law and which would protect the lives and properties of the inhabitants, the Governments of the Arab States declare the following:

First: That the rule of Palestine should revert to its inhabitants, in accordance with the provisions of the Covenant of the League of Nations and [the Charter] of the United Nations and that [the Palestinians] should alone have the right to determine their future.

Second: Security and order in Palestine have become disrupted. The Zionist aggression resulted in the exodus of more than a quarter of a million of its Arab inhabitants from their homes and in taking refuge in the neighbouring Arab countries. . . .

After the termination of the British mandate over Palestine the British authorities are no longer responsible for security in the country, except to the degree affecting their withdrawing forces, and [only] in the areas in which these forces happen to be at the time of withdrawal as announced by [these authorities]. This state of affairs would render Palestine without any governmental machinery capable of restoring order and the rule of law to the country, and of protecting the lives and properties of the inhabitants.

Third: This state of affairs is threatening to spread to the neighbouring Arab countries, where feeling is running high because of the events in Palestine. The Governments of the Member States of the Arab League and the United Nations are exceedingly worried and deeply concerned about this state of affairs. . . .

Fifth: The Governments of the Arab States, as members of the Arab League, a regional organization within the meaning of the provisions of Chapter VIII of the Charter of the United Nations, are responsible for maintaining peace and security in their area. These Governments view the events taking place in Palestine as a threat to peace and security in the area as a whole and [also] in each of them taken separately.

Sixth: Therefore, as security in Palestine is a sacred trust in the hands of the Arab States, and in order to put an end to this state of affairs and to prevent it from becoming aggravated or from turning into [a state of] chaos, the extent of which no one can foretell; in order to stop the spreading of disturbances and disorder in Palestine to the neighbouring Arab countries; in order to fill the gap brought about in the governmental machinery in Palestine as a result of the termination of the mandate and the non-establishment of a lawful successor authority, the Governments of the Arab States have found themselves compelled to intervene in Palestine solely in order to help its inhabitants restore peace and security and the rule of justice and law to their country, and in order to prevent bloodshed.

Seventh: The Governments of the Arab States recognize that the independence of Palestine, which has so far been suppressed by the British Mandate, has become an accomplished fact for the lawful inhabitants of Palestine. They alone, by virtue of their absolute sovereignty, have the right to provide their country with laws and governmental institutions. They alone should exercise the attributes of their independence, through their own means and without any kind of foreign interference, immediately after peace, security, and the rule of law have been restored to the country.

At that time the intervention of the Arab states will cease, and the independent State of Palestine will cooperate with the [other member] States of the Arab League in order to bring peace, security and prosperity to this part of the world.

The Governments of the Arab States emphasize, on this occasion, what they have already declared before the London Conference and the United Nations, that the only solution of the Palestine problem is the establishment of a unitary Palestinian State, in accordance with democratic principles, whereby its inhabitants will enjoy complete equality before the law, [and whereby] minorities will be assured of all the guarantees recognized in democratic constitutional countries and [whereby] the holy places will be preserved and the rights of access thereto guaranteed. . . .

Source: United Nations Security Council Official Records, S/745, May 15, 1948.

Palestine Liberation Organization, Draft Constitution [Excerpt], 1963

Well before World War II, other Arab states had shown deep interest in the situation in Palestine. The Israeli War of Independence (1948–1949), however, destroyed the independent Palestinian state that the United Nations (UN) partition plan had envisaged, as Palestinian Arabs were driven out of their homes and often confined to refugee camps. While the assorted Arab states

still professed deep concern over the fate of the Palestinians and unrelenting hostility to Israel, Palestinians felt a need to establish their own organization. During the 1950s, various clandestine and unofficial guerrilla groups of young Palestinian refugees who pledged to attack Israel by all means possible emerged in Syria, Egypt, and Kuwait, the most prominent among them probably being Fatah (the Palestinian National Liberation Organization), a student organization founded in 1958 in Kuwait. At an Arab Summit Conference held in 1963, Egypt encouraged the formation of an official body to represent the interests of Palestinians, a decision that led to the creation of the Palestine Liberation Organization (PLO) in May 1964. The PLO's charter was drafted by Ahmed Shukairy, a lawyer whose original home was Palestine and who later served as a UN representative for both Saudi Arabia and Syria. The PLO was to represent Palestine officially in the Arab League and was to work for the liberation of Palestine. The PLO's charter left it vague precisely what kind of ultimate territorial outcome it sought and whether the total destruction of Israel was its objective, although the latter was implied in Article 4. Article 19, which authorized the establishment of "[p]rivate Palestinian [military] contingents," effectively authorized armed struggle against Israel and its supporters, using terrorist tactics if necessary.

1. In accordance with this constitution, an organisation known as "The Palestine Liberation Organization" shall be formed, and shall launch its responsibilities in accordance with the principles of the National Charter and clauses of this constitution.

2. All the Palestinians are natural members in the Liberation Organization exercising their duty in the liberation of their homeland in accordance with their abilities and efficiency.

3. The Palestinian people shall form the larger base for this Organization; and

the Organization, after its creation, shall work closely and constantly with the Palestine people for the sake of their organization and mobilization so they may be able to assume their responsibility in the liberation of their country.

4. Until suitable conditions are available for holding free general elections among all the Palestinians and in all the countries in which they reside, the Liberation Organization shall be set up in accordance with the rules set in this constitution.

5. Measures listed in this constitution shall be taken for the convocation of a Palestinian General Assembly in which shall be represented all Palestinian factions, emigrants and residents, including organisations, societies, unions, trade unions and representatives of [Palestinian] public opinions of various ideological trends; this assembly shall be called The National Assembly of the Palestine Liberation Organization.

6. In preparation and facilitation of work of the assembly, the Palestinian representative at the Arab League [i.e., Ahmed Shukairy] shall, after holding consultations with various Palestinian factions, form:

a)—A Preparatory Committee in every Arab country hosting a minimum of 10,000 Palestinians; the mission of each one of these committees is to prepare lists according to which Palestinian candidates in the respective Arab country will be chosen as members of the assembly; these committees shall also prepare studies and proposals which may help the assembly carry out its work; these studies and proposals shall be presented to the Coordination Committee listed below.

b)—A Coordination Committee, with headquarters in Jerusalem; the mission of this committee shall be to issue invitations to the assembly, adopt all necessary measures for the holding of the assembly, and coordinate all proposals and studies as well as lists of candidates to the assembly, as specified in the clause above; also the committee shall prepare a provisional agenda—or as a whole, undertake all that is required for the holding and success of the assembly in the execution of its mission.

7. The National Assembly shall be held once every two years; its venue rotates between Jerusalem and Gaza; the National Assembly shall meet for the first time on May 14, 1964, in the city of Jerusalem.

[. . .]

18. The Arab states shall avail the sons of Palestine the opportunity of enlisting in their regular armies on the widest scale possible.

19. Private Palestinian contingents shall be formed in accordance with the military needs and plans decided by the Unified Arab Military Command in agreement and cooperation with the concerned Arab states.

20. A Fund, to be known as "The National Palestinian Fund," shall be established to finance operations of the Executive Committee: the Fund shall have a Board of Directors whose members shall be elected by the National Assembly.

Source: Walter Laqueur and Barry Rubin, eds., *The Israel-Arab Reader: A Documentary History of the Middle East Conflict* (New York: Penguin, 2001), 93–96.

United Nations Security Council Resolution 242, November 22, 1967

Five months after the Six-Day War ended, after lengthy discussions in the United Nations (UN) General Assembly and the Security Council, the latter body passed Resolution 242, which would form the basis of all subsequent peace plans. Effectively, the resolution called upon Israel to withdraw from most of the territory it had occupied during the war in return for a comprehensive peace settlement in which all states in the Middle East recognized each other's right to exist and agreed to respect each other's borders. It also called for "a just settlement of the refugee problem" without stating what this might imply. The resolution was largely drafted by the U.S. and British UN representatives, Arthur Goldberg and Lord Caradon, respectively, and all five Security Council permanent members voted for it. Both Israel and the Arab states as well as the Palestine Liberation Organization (PLO) claimed that the other was in breach of this resolution, justifying their own failure to observe its provisions: Israel because most Arab states were still nominally in a state of war and refused to recognize its own existence, and the Arab states and PLO because Israel had not withdrawn from the occupied territories. The PLO rejected Resolution 242 outright. Between 1967 and 1973, UN special envoy Gunnar Jarring held protracted but ultimately fruitless talks with Israel, Egypt, Jordan, and Lebanon (Syria refused even to participate) on the potential implementation of Resolution 242, negotiations dramatically concluded by the 1973 Yom Kippur War.

The Security Council,

Expressing its continuing concern with the grave situation in the Middle East,

Emphasizing the inadmissibility of the acquisition of territory by war and the need to work for a just and lasting peace in which every State in the area can live in security,

Emphasizing further that all Member States in their acceptance of the Charter of the United Nations have undertaken a commitment to act in accordance with Article 2 of the Charter,

1. *Affirms* that the fulfillment of Charter principles requires the establishment of a just and lasting peace in the Middle East which should include the application of both the following principles:
   (i) Withdrawal of Israeli armed forces from territories occupied in the recent conflict;
   (ii) Termination of all claims or states of belligerency and respect for and acknowledgement of the sovereignty, territorial integrity and political independence of every State in the area and their right to live in peace within secure and recognized boundaries free from threats or acts of force;

2. *Affirms further* the necessity
   (a) For guaranteeing freedom of navigation through international waterways in the area;
   (b) For achieving a just settlement of the refugee problem;
   (c) For guaranteeing the territorial inviolability and political independence of every State in the area, through measures including the establishment of demilitarized zones;

3. *Requests* the Secretary-General to designate a Special Representative to proceed to the Middle East to establish and maintain contacts with the States concerned in order to promote agreement and assist efforts to achieve a peaceful and accepted settlement in accordance with the provisions and principles in this resolution;

4. *Requests* the Secretary-General to report to the Security Council on the progress of the efforts of the Special Representative as soon as possible.

Source: United Nations Security Council Official Records, S.C. Res. 242, November 22, 1967.

United Nations Security Council Resolution 338, October 22, 1973

As both sides in the Yom Kippur War decided to agree to a cease-fire, the United Nations (UN) Security Council passed a resolution ordering the cessation of hostilities within 12 hours. In addition, the UN called upon all parties to begin peace negotiations using as a basis the earlier UN Security Council Resolution 242, which called upon the Arab states to recognize Israel's existence and make lasting peace with that country in exchange for the return of most of the territories Israel had taken in both wars. The resolution also urged solving the Palestinian refugee issue and the internationalization of the city of Jerusalem. In July 1974, the Palestine Liberation Organization (PLO) once again rejected Resolution 242. The resolution would nonetheless form the basis of protracted subsequent efforts to negotiate an Arab-Israeli peace settlement. Meanwhile, all states involved would in future be decidedly more cautious in launching full-scale war. Over the next three decades the focus of the Arab-Israeli question increasingly switched to securing the Palestinian refugees a state of their own.

The Security Council,

1. *Calls upon* all parties to the present fighting to cease all firing and terminate all military activity immediately, no later than 12 hours after the moment of the adoption of this decision, in the positions they now occupy;
2. *Calls upon* all parties concerned to start immediately after the cease-fire the implementation of Security Council Resolution 242 (1967) in all of its parts;
3. *Decides* that, immediately and concurrently with the cease-fire, negotiations start between the parties concerned under appropriate auspices aimed at establishing a just and durable peace in the Middle East.

Source: United Nations Security Council Official Records, S.C. Res. 337, August 15, 1973.

Framework for Peace in the Middle East, September 17, 1978

U.S. president Jimmy Carter came to office in 1977 determined to seek a lasting Middle East peace settlement, one that would reconcile the warring parties. In November 1977, Egyptian president Anwar Sadat visited Israel, meeting with Israeli prime minister Menachem Begin and making a much publicized address to the Israeli Knesset calling for peace. Even so, negotiations between Israel and Egypt for a peace treaty that would end the formal state of war between the two countries, the legacy of four Arab-Israeli conflicts, soon broke down. After a hiatus of some months, Carter, who had made peace in the Middle East a high priority of his administration's foreign policy objectives, stepped in and invited both Sadat and Begin to attend a summit meeting with Carter in the United States. The Camp David Accords established an agreement under whose terms the two countries could work to secure peace in the Middle East. The Camp David Accords explicitly stated that the framework it laid out was intended as a model not just for the Israeli-Egyptian peace agreement but also for similar treaties with Israel's other Arab neighbors. It reaffirmed the principles of United Nations (UN) Security Council Resolutions 242 and 334 and the need to establish secure and recognized borders for all states involved, including Israel. The Camp David Accords envisaged that Israel would grant Palestinian Arabs in the occupied West Bank and Gaza substantial autonomy, arrangements that conceivably might ultimately lead to the establishment of a Palestinian state, and that Israel would withdraw from the Sinai Peninsula, but Egypt would largely demilitarize the area, with a border zone to be controlled by UN forces. Both Egypt and Israel gained substantially, enhancing their military security and receiving lavish economic assistance from the United States. As before, however, other Arab leaders and nations publicly repudiated and condemned these accords and denounced Sadat as a traitor to the broader Arab cause.

Muhammad Anwar al-Sadat, President of the Arab Republic of Egypt, and Menachem Begin, Prime Minister of Israel, met with Jimmy Carter, President of the United States of America, at Camp David from September 5 to September 17, 1978, and have agreed on the following framework for peace in the Middle East. They invite other parties to the Arab-Israel conflict to adhere to it.

Preamble

The search for peace in the Middle East must be guided by the following:

The agreed basis for a peaceful settlement of the conflict between Israel and its neighbors is United Nations Security Council Resolution 242, in all its parts.

After four wars during 30 years, despite intensive human efforts, the Middle East, which is the cradle of civilization and the birthplace of three great religions, does not enjoy the blessings of peace. The people of the Middle East yearn for peace so that the vast human and natural resources of the region can be turned to the pursuits of peace and so that this area can become a model for coexistence and cooperation among nations.

The historic initiative of President Sadat in visiting Jerusalem and the reception accorded to him by the parliament, government and people of Israel, and the reciprocal visit of Prime Minister Begin to Ismailia,

the peace proposals made by both leaders, as well as the warm reception of these missions by the peoples of both countries, have created an unprecedented opportunity for peace which must not be lost if this generation and future generations are to be spared the tragedies of war.

The provisions of the Charter of the United Nations and the other accepted norms of international law and legitimacy now provide accepted standards for the conduct of relations among all states.

To achieve a relationship of peace, in the spirit of Article 2 of the United Nations Charter, future negotiations between Israel and any neighbor prepared to negotiate peace and security with it are necessary for the purpose of carrying out all the provisions and principles of Resolutions 242 and 338.

Peace requires respect for the sovereignty, territorial integrity and political independence of every state in the area and their right to live in peace within secure and recognized boundaries free from threats or acts of force. Progress toward that goal can accelerate movement toward a new era of reconciliation in the Middle East marked by cooperation in promoting economic development, in maintaining stability and in assuring security.

Security is enhanced by a relationship of peace and by cooperation between nations which enjoy normal relations. . . .

Framework

Taking these factors into account, the parties are determined to reach a just, comprehensive, and durable settlement of the Middle East conflict through the conclusion of peace treaties based on Security Council resolutions 242 and 338 in all their parts. Their purpose is to achieve peace and good neighborly relations. They recognize that for peace to endure, it must involve all those

who have been most deeply affected by
the conflict. They therefore agree that this
framework, as appropriate, is intended by
them to constitute a basis for peace not only
between Egypt and Israel, but also between
Israel and each of its other neighbors which
is prepared to negotiate peace with Israel on
this basis. With that objective in mind, they
have agreed to proceed as follows:

A. West Bank and Gaza

1. Egypt, Israel, Jordan and the representatives of the Palestinian people should
   participate in negotiations on the resolution of the Palestinian problem in all its
   aspects. To achieve that objective, negotiations relating to the West Bank and
   Gaza should proceed in three stages:
   a. Egypt and Israel agree that, in order
      to ensure a peaceful and orderly
      transfer of authority, and taking
      into account the security concerns
      of all the parties, there should be
      transitional arrangements for the
      West Bank and Gaza for a period
      not exceeding five years. In order to
      provide full autonomy to the inhab-
      itants, under these arrangements the
      Israeli military government and its
      civilian administration will be with-
      drawn as soon as a self-governing
      authority has been freely elected
      by the inhabitants of these areas to
      replace the existing military gov-
      ernment. To negotiate the details of
      a transitional arrangement, Jordan
      will be invited to join the negotia-
      tions on the basis of this framework.
      These new arrangements should
      give due consideration both to the
      principle of self-government by the
      inhabitants of these territories and
      to the legitimate security concerns
      of the parties involved.

b. Egypt, Israel, and Jordan will agree
   on the modalities for establishing
   elected self-governing authority in
   the West Bank and Gaza. The delegations of Egypt and Jordan may
   include Palestinians from the West
   Bank and Gaza or other Palestinians as mutually agreed. The parties
   will negotiate an agreement which
   will define the powers and responsibilities of the self-governing
   authority to be exercised in the
   West Bank and Gaza. A withdrawal
   of Israeli armed forces will take
   place and there will be a redeployment of the remaining Israeli forces
   into specified security locations.
   The agreement will also include
   arrangements for assuring internal
   and external security and public
   order. A strong local police force
   will be established, which may
   include Jordanian citizens. In addition, Israeli and Jordanian forces
   will participate in joint patrols and
   in the manning of control posts to
   assure the security of the borders.
c. When the self-governing authority (administrative council) in the
   West Bank and Gaza is established
   and inaugurated, the transitional
   period of five years will begin. As
   soon as possible, but not later than
   the third year after the beginning of
   the transitional period, negotiations
   will take place to determine the
   final status of the West Bank and
   Gaza and its relationship with its
   neighbors and to conclude a peace
   treaty between Israel and Jordan by
   the end of the transitional period.
   These negotiations will be conducted among Egypt, Israel, Jordan
   and the elected representatives of

the inhabitants of the West Bank and Gaza. Two separate but related committees will be convened, one committee, consisting of representatives of the four parties which will negotiate and agree on the final status of the West Bank and Gaza, and its relationship with its neighbors, and the second committee, consisting of representatives of Israel and representatives of Jordan to be joined by the elected representatives of the inhabitants of the West Bank and Gaza, to negotiate the peace treaty between Israel and Jordan, taking into account the agreement reached on the final status of the West Bank and Gaza. The negotiations shall be based on all the provisions and principles of UN Security Council Resolution 242. The negotiations will resolve, among other matters, the location of the boundaries and the nature of the security arrangements. The solution from the negotiations must also recognize the legitimate right of the Palestinian peoples and their just requirements. In this way, the Palestinians will participate in the determination of their own future through:

i.   The negotiations among Egypt, Israel, Jordan and the representatives of the inhabitants of the West Bank and Gaza to agree on the final status of the West Bank and Gaza and other outstanding issues by the end of the transitional period.

ii. Submitting their agreements to a vote by the elected representatives of the inhabitants of the West Bank and Gaza.

iii. Providing for the elected representatives of the inhabitants of the West Bank and Gaza to decide how they shall govern themselves consistent with the provisions of their agreement.

iv. Participating as stated above in the work of the committee negotiating the peace treaty between Israel and Jordan.

d.   All necessary measures will be taken and provisions made to assure the security of Israel and its neighbors during the transitional period and beyond. . . .

f.   Egypt and Israel will work with each other and with other interested parties to establish agreed procedures for a prompt, just and permanent implementation of the resolution of the refugee problem.

B. Egypt-Israel

1. Egypt-Israel undertake not to resort to the threat or the use of force to settle disputes. Any disputes shall be settled by peaceful means in accordance with the provisions of Article 33 of the U.N. Charter.

2. In order to achieve peace between them, the parties agree to negotiate in good faith with a goal of concluding within three months from the signing of the Framework a peace treaty between them while inviting the other parties to the conflict to proceed simultaneously to negotiate and conclude similar peace treaties with a view to achieving a comprehensive peace in the area. The Framework for the Conclusion of a Peace Treaty between Egypt and Israel will govern the peace negotiations between them. The parties will agree on the modalities and the timetable for the implementation of their obligations under the treaty.

C. Associated Principles

1. Egypt and Israel state that the principles and provisions described below should apply to peace treaties between Israel and each of its neighbors—Egypt, Jordan, Syria and Lebanon.

2. Signatories shall establish among themselves relationships normal to states at peace with one another. To this end, they should undertake to abide by all the provisions of the U.N. Charter. Steps to be taken in this respect include:

   a. full recognition;

   b. abolishing economic boycotts;

   c. guaranteeing that under their jurisdiction the citizens of the other parties shall enjoy the protection of the due process of law.

3. Signatories should explore possibilities for economic development in the context of final peace treaties, with the objective of contributing to the atmosphere of peace, cooperation and friendship which is their common goal.

4. Claims commissions may be established for the mutual settlement of all financial claims.

5. The United States shall be invited to participate in the talks on matters related to the modalities of the implementation of the agreements and working out the timetable for the carrying out of the obligations of the parties.

6. The United Nations Security Council shall be requested to endorse the peace treaties and ensure that their provisions shall not be violated. The permanent members of the Security Council shall be requested to underwrite the peace treaties and ensure respect for their provisions. They shall be requested to conform their policies and actions with the undertakings contained in this Framework.

For the Government of Israel: Menachem Begin

For the Government of the Arab Republic of Egypt: Muhammed Anwar al-Sadat

Witnessed by Jimmy Carter, President of the United States of America

Source: "A Framework for Peace in the Middle East Agreed at Camp David," *Department of State Bulletin* 78(2019) (1978): 7–10.

Israel-Egypt Peace Treaty, March 26, 1979

In the face of fierce Arab League and Palestine Liberation Organization (PLO) opposition, the Camp David Peace Treaty, also known as the Egyptian-Israeli Peace Treaty, was signed in 1979 as an outcome of the 1978 Camp David Summit Conference, which negotiated a framework for peace between Israel and Egypt. The treaty ended the state of war between Egypt and Israel and established a fixed boundary between the two, setting aside the status of the Gaza Strip—home to numerous Palestine refugees—for future resolution. The two states also opened full diplomatic relations, exchanging ambassadors. In accordance with the treaty, the following year Israel returned most of the Sinai Peninsula to Egypt, a process completed in 1982. Western leaders and commentators greeted the treaty enthusiastically. Even relatively hard-line Israeli leaders, such as former prime minister Golda Meir, welcomed it, stating that it would ensure that their grandchildren could live in peace. Carter and others hoped that the peace treaty would encourage the subsequent negotiation of similar agreements between Israel and other Arab states, breaking the logjam blocking the conclusion of lasting Middle East peace settlements. In practice, fellow Arab states boycotted Egypt for making peace with Israel. In October 1981, moreover, Muslim extremist gunmen who resented the peace treaty assassinated Sadat, chief Egyptian architect of the Camp David Accords, while he was watching a military parade in Cairo, an ominous warning to any Arab leader who might be tempted to emulate Sadat's efforts for peace.

Preamble

The Government of the Arab Republic of Egypt and the Government of the State of Israel; Convinced of the urgent necessity of the establishment of a just, comprehensive and lasting peace in the Middle East in accordance with Security Council Resolution 242 and Resolution 338; Reaffirming their adherence to the 'Framework for Peace in the Middle East Agreed at Camp David,' dated September 17, 1978. . . . Agree to the following provisions:

Article I

1. The state of war between the Parties will be terminated and peace will be established between them upon the exchange of instruments of ratification of this Treaty.
2. Israel will withdraw all its armed forces and civilians from the Sinai behind the international boundary between Egypt and mandated Palestine . . . and Egypt will resume the exercise of its full sovereignty over the Sinai.
3. Upon completion of the interim withdrawal . . . the Parties will establish normal and friendly relations. . . .

Article II

The permanent boundary between Egypt and Israel is the recognized international boundary between Egypt and the former mandated territory of Palestine . . . without prejudice to the issue of the Gaza Strip. . . .

Article IV

1. In order to provide maximum security for both Parties on the basis of reciprocity, agreed security arrangements will be established including limited force zones in Egyptian and Israeli territory, and United Nations forces and observers . . . and other security arrangements the Parties may agree upon. . . .

Article V

1. Ships of Israel, and cargoes destined for or coming from Israel, shall enjoy the right of free passage through the Suez Canal and its approaches through the Gulf of Suez and the Mediterranean Sea. . . . Israeli nationals, vessels and cargoes, as well as persons, vessels and cargoes destined for or coming from Israel, shall be accorded non-discriminatory treatment in all matters connected with usage of the canal.
2. The Parties consider the Strait of Tiran and the Gulf of Aqaba to be international waterways open to all nations for unimpeded and nonsuspendable freedom of navigation and overflight. The Parties will respect each other's right to navigation and overflight for access to either country through the Strait of Tiran and the Gulf of Aqaba.

[Annex I describes the details of Israeli withdrawal from the Sinai Peninsula over a three-year period. It also establishes several zones in the Sinai and surrounding territory in Egypt and Israel and the restricted distribution of military forces in these areas, including the distribution of United Nations forces.]

[Annex II is a map of the Sinai Peninsula and the agreed upon boundary between Egypt and Israel.]

[Annex III sets the terms for the normalization of relations between Egypt and Israel in regard to diplomacy, economics and trade, culture, the freedom of movement of the citizens of each nation, transportation and communication, human rights, and territorial waters.]

Source: "Treaty of Peace between the Arab Republic of Egypt and the State of Israel," *Department of State Bulletin* 79(2026) (1979): 3–14.

Yasser Arafat, Declaration on Terrorism [Excerpt], November 7, 1985

In 1985, in the wake of a terrorist attack on the cruise ship *Achille Lauro*, in which a U.S. citizen died, an episode with the potential to derail ongoing Jordanian–Palestine Liberation Army (PLO) efforts to open a dialogue on permanent peace with Israel, PLO chairman Yasser Arafat stated publicly the PLO's opposition to the use "of all forms of terrorism" and to operations outside the territory of "Palestine." His declaration did not mean that Israel would be immune to attack, since Arafat carefully reserved the Palestinians' right "to resist the Israeli occupation of its land by all available means." He warned, however, that "terrorist operations" elsewhere were counterproductive, since these would merely "hurt the cause of the Palestinian people." Arafat's stance marked another milestone in his gradual embrace of more moderate and accommodating positions, the product, perhaps, of his desire, after decades of struggle, to win back a genuine territorial base for the Palestinians.

The Palestinian people has and continues to struggle to liberate its occupied land, to exercise its right to self-determination, and to establish a state as a necessary condition for achieving a just and lasting peace in the region in which all peoples would coexist, free from acts of terrorism or subjugation. . . .

[. . .]

As an impetus to the efforts which have been exerted to convene an international peace conference, the PLO announces its criticism and condemnation of all acts of terrorism, whether they be those in which states become involved or those committed by individuals or groups against the innocent and defenseless, wherever they may be.

The PLO reaffirms its declaration issued in 1974 which condemned all operations outside [Palestine] and all forms of terrorism. And it restates the adherence of all its groups and institutions to that declaration. Beginning today, the PLO will take all measures to deter violators.

In view of the fact that this adherence cannot be achieved unilaterally, it is up to the international community to force Israel to stop all of its acts of terrorism both inside and outside [Palestine].

In this context, the PLO stresses its insistence upon the right of the Palestinian people to resist the Israeli occupation of its land by all available means, with the goal of achieving withdrawal from its land. For the right to resist foreign occupation is a legitimate right, not abrogated by the UN Charter, which calls for disavowing the use of force or threatening to use it to settle conflicts, and which considers the resort to force a violation of its principles and goals. The right of the Palestinian people to resist the occupation in the occupied territories has been stressed in numerous UN resolutions and in the rules of the Geneva Convention.

Events underline the certainty that terrorist operations committed outside [Palestine] hurt the cause of the Palestinian people and distort its legitimate struggle for freedom. From another perspective, these events deepen our conviction that terminating the occupation and putting limits on its policies is the one way to achieve peace and security in the region. For in the end, our goal is achieving a just, comprehensive, and lasting peace which will safeguard the affirmation of the enduring national rights of the Palestinian people in order to establish a safe society everywhere.

Source: "Cairo Declaration on the PLO and Terrorism as Read by PLO Chairman Yasir Arafat, Cairo, 7 November 1985," *Journal of Palestine Studies* 15(58) (1986): 214–16.

Program of Hezbollah [Excerpt], February 16, 1986

As the Palestine Liberation Organization (PLO) moved, however tentatively, toward accommodation with Israel, more radical anti-Israeli groups emerged within the Arab world, their fervor fueled by the growing strength of Islamic fundamentalism. In 1979, a theocratic government headed by the Shia Muslim cleric Ayatollah Ruhollah Khomeini seized power in Iran. Deeply resentful of 25 years of past U.S. support for the deposed Mohammad Reza Shah Pahlavi of Iran, the new Iranian government assailed the United States as the "great Satan." Among the groups competing for power within Lebanon were at least two Shiite factions that received support from Iran and also from Syria, Lebanon's dominant neighbor. Hezbollah was the more extreme of the two. Unlike the largely secular PLO, Hezbollah members prided themselves on their strict adherence to Islamic principles, which, they claimed, demanded that they wage jihad, or holy war, against Israel and also against Phalangist forces in Lebanon. The Hezbollah platform, inspired by the group's mentor, Sheikh Muhammad Hussein Fadlallah, was first published in February 1985 in Beirut. Hezbollah sought to expel all U.S., Western, and Israeli forces from Lebanon and also rejected the United Nations (UN) peacekeeping force. In addition, Hezbollah sought the complete destruction of Israel. The organization's emergence meant that Arab and Islamic opposition to Israel was becoming increasingly multipolar and that the PLO now had more radical rivals.

Our Identity

We are often asked: Who are we, the Hizballah, and what is our identity? We are the sons of the *umma* (Muslim community)—the party of God (Hizb Allah) the vanguard of which was made victorious by God in Iran. There the vanguard succeeded to lay down the bases of a Muslim state which plays a central role in the world. We obey the orders of one leader, wise and just, that of our tutor and *faqih* (jurist) who fulfills all the necessary conditions: Ruhollah Musawi Khomeini. God save him!

By virtue of the above, we do not constitute an organized and closed party in Lebanon, nor are we a tight political cadre. We are an *umma* linked to the Muslims of the whole world by the solid doctrinal and religious connection of Islam, whose message God wanted to be fulfilled by the Seal of the Prophets, i.e., Muhammad. This is why whatever touches or strikes the Muslims in Afghanistan, Iraq, the Philippines and elsewhere reverberates throughout the whole Muslim *umma* of which we are an integral part. Our behavior is dictated to us by legal principles laid down by the light of an overall political conception defined by the leading jurist (*wilayat al-faqih*).

As for our culture, it is based on the Holy Koran, the Sunna and the legal rulings of the *faqih* who is our source of imitation (*marja' al-taqlid*). Our culture is crystal clear. It is not complicated and is accessible to all.

No one can imagine the importance of our military potential as our military apparatus is not separate from our overall social fabric. Each of us is a fighting soldier. And when it becomes necessary to carry out the Holy War, each of us takes up his assignment in the fight in accordance with the injunctions of the Law, and that in the framework of the mission carried out under the tutelage of the Commanding Jurist.

Our Fight

The US has tried, through its local agents, to persuade the people that those who crushed their arrogance in Lebanon and frustrated their conspiracy against the oppressed (*mustad'afin*) were nothing but a bunch of fanatic terrorists whose sole aim is to dynamite bars and destroy slot machines. Such suggestions cannot and will not mislead our *umma*, for the whole world knows that whoever wishes to oppose the US, that arrogant superpower, cannot indulge in marginal acts which may make it deviate from its major objective. We combat abomination and we shall tear out its very roots, its primary roots, which are the US. All attempts made to drive us into marginal actions will fail, especially as our determination to fight the US is solid.

We declare openly and loudly that we are an *umma* which fears God only and is by no means ready to tolerate injustice, aggression and humiliation. America, its Atlantic Pact allies, and the Zionist entity in the holy land of Palestine, attacked us and continue to do so without respite. Their aim is to make us eat dust continually. This is why we are, more and more, in a state of permanent alert in order to repel aggression and defend our religion, our existence, our dignity. They invaded our country, destroyed our villages, slit the throats of our children, violated our sanctuaries and appointed masters over our people who committed the worst massacres against our *umma*. They do not cease to give support to these allies of Israel, and do not enable us to decide our future according to our own wishes.

[. . .]

Our people could not bear any more treachery. It decided to oppose infidelity—be it French, American or Israeli—by striking at their headquarters and launching a veritable war of resistance against the Occupation forces. Finally, the enemy had to decide to retreat by stages.

Our Objectives

Let us put it truthfully: the sons of Hizballah know who are their major enemies in the Middle East—the Phalanges, Israel, France and the US. The sons of our *umma* are now in a state of growing confrontation with them, and will remain so until the realization of the following three objectives:

(a) to expel the Americans, the French and their allies definitely from Lebanon, putting an end to any colonialist entity on our land;

(b) to submit the Phalanges to a just power and bring them all to justice for the crimes they have perpetrated against Muslims and Christians;

(c) to permit all the sons of our people to determine their future and to choose in all the liberty the form of government they desire. We call upon all of them to pick the option of Islamic government which, alone, is capable of guaranteeing justice and liberty for all. Only an Islamic regime can stop any further tentative attempts of imperialistic infiltration into our country.

These are Lebanon's objectives; those are its enemies. As for our friends, they are all the world's oppressed peoples. Our friends are also those who combat our enemies and who defend us from their evil. Towards these friends, individuals as well as organizations, we turn and say:

Friends, wherever you are in Lebanon . . . we are in agreement with you on the great and necessary objectives: destroying American hegemony in our land; putting an end to the burdensome Israeli Occupation; beating back all the Phalangists' attempts to monopolize power and administration. . . .

This is the minimum that we can accept in order to be able to accede by legal means to realize our ambitions, to save Lebanon from its dependence upon East and West, to put an end to foreign occupation and to adopt a regime freely wanted by the people of Lebanon.

[. . .]

World Scene

We reject both the USSR and the US, both Capitalism and Communism, for both are incapable of laying the foundations for a just society.

With special vehemence we reject UNIFIL as they were sent by world arrogance to occupy areas evacuated by Israel and serve for the latter as a buffer zone. They should be treated much like the Zionists. . . .

[. . .]

The Necessity for the Destruction of Israel

We see in Israel the vanguard of the United States in our Islamic world. It is the hated enemy that must be fought until the hated ones get what they deserve. This enemy is the greatest danger to our future generations and to the destiny of our lands, particularly as it glorifies the ideas of settlement and expansion, initiated in Palestine, and yearning outward to the extension of the Great Israel, from the Euphrates to the Nile.

Our primary assumption in our fight against Israel states that the Zionist entity is aggressive from its inception, and built on lands wrested from their owners, at the expense of the rights of the Muslim people. Therefore our struggle will end only when this entity is obliterated. We recognize no treaty with it, no cease fire, and no peace agreements, whether separate or consolidated.

We vigorously condemn all plans for negotiation with Israel, and regard all negotiators as enemies, for the reason that such negotiation is nothing but the recognition of the legitimacy of the Zionist occupation of Palestine. Therefore we oppose and reject the Camp David Agreements, the proposals of King Fahd, the Fez and Reagan plan, Brezhnev's and the French-Egyptian proposals, and all other programs that include the recognition (even the implied recognition) of the Zionist entity.

Source: "The Hizballah Program," *Jerusalem Quarterly* 48 (Fall 1988): 111–16.

Communiqué of the Intifada, January 8, 1988

By the mid-1980s, the frustration of Palestinians in the occupied territories was growing as faith in the perennially stalemated peace process declined, Israeli settlements expanded, and the prospect of any kind of Palestinian state was perpetually receding. Palestinians in the occupied territories had high birthrates and only limited access to land for either housing or agriculture, and unemployment was rising. Many still lived in camps. Without elections, they lacked any political voice. Although the Palestine Liberation Organization (PLO) quickly claimed credit for the First Intifada, its origins were apparently spontaneous. It was sparked by rioting that broke out near the Jabalya camp in Gaza, home to 60,000 refugees, when four Palestinians were killed in a traffic accident in early December 1987. Israeli troops shot dead an 18-year-old Palestinian man who was throwing stones, and the situation snowballed. Riots broke out in camps across the occupied territories, particularly among teenage youths who threw stones and sometimes grenades or Molotov cocktails, to which Israeli forces often responded with bullets. The intifada continued until the Oslo Accords were signed in 1993, by which time 1,162 Palestinians, including 241 children, and 160 Israelis had died. The intifada, especially the large number of fatalities among young people under age 16, refocused foreign attention on the Palestinians and put the issue of their future firmly back on the international agenda, making the plight of the Palestinians an increasing embarrassment to Israel. European countries began to give extensive financial support to the Palestinians and their institutions. Communiqués clandestinely distributed among the Palestinians conveyed the sense of excitement, purpose, and solidarity that emerged among the Palestinian community in the intifada's early days, reenergizing people who had almost lost faith in themselves and, eventually, revitalizing long-stalled peace negotiations.

In the name of God, the merciful, the compassionate.

Our people's glorious uprising continues. We affirm the need to express solidarity with our people wherever they are. We continue to be loyal to the pure blood of our martyrs and to our detained brothers. We also reiterate our rejection of the occupation and its policy of repression, represented in the policy of deportation, mass arrests, curfews, and the demolition of houses.

We reaffirm the need to achieve further cohesion with our revolution and our heroic masses. We also stress our abidance by the call of the PLO, the Palestinian people's legitimate and sole representative, and the need to pursue the bountiful offerings and the heroic uprising. For all these reasons, we address the following call:

All sectors of our heroic people in every location should abide by the call for a general and comprehensive strike until Wednesday evening, 13 January 1988. The strike covers all public and private trade utilities, the Palestinian workers and public transportation. Abidance by the comprehensive strike must be complete. The slogan of the strike will be: Down with occupation; long live Palestine as a free and Arab country.

Brother workers, your abidance by the strike by not going to work and to plants is real support for the glorious uprising, a sanctioning of the pure blood of our martyrs, a support for the call to liberate our prisoners, and an act that will help keep our brother deportees in their homeland.

Brother businessmen and grocers, you must fully abide by the call for a comprehensive

strike during the period of the strike. Your abidance by previous strikes is one of the most splendid images of solidarity and sacrifice for the sake of rendering our heroic people's stand a success.

We will do our best to protect the interests of our honest businessmen against measures the Zionist occupation force may resort to against you. We warn against the consequences of becoming involved with some of the occupation authorities' henchmen who will seek to make you open your businesses. We promise you that we will punish such traitor businessmen in the not too distant future. Let us proceed united to forge victory.

Brother owners of taxi companies, we will not forget your honorable and splendid stand of supporting and implementing the comprehensive strike on the day of Palestinian steadfastness. We pin our hopes on you to support and make the comprehensive strike a success. We warn some bus companies against the consequences of not abiding by the call for the strike, as this will make them liable to revolutionary punishment.

Brother doctors and pharmacists, you must be on emergency status to offer assistance to those of our kinfolk who are ill. The brother pharmacists must carry out their duties normally. The brother doctors must place the doctor badge in a way that can be clearly identified.

General warning: We would like to warn people that walking in the streets will not be safe in view of the measures that will be taken to make the comprehensive strike a success. We warn that viscous material will be poured on main and secondary streets and everywhere, in addition to the roadblocks and the strike groups that will be deployed throughout the occupied homeland.

Circular: The struggler and brother members of the popular committees and the men of the uprising who are deployed in all the working locations should work to support and assist our people within the available means, particularly the needy families of our people. The strike groups and the popular uprising groups must completely abide by the working program, which is in their possession. Let us proceed united and loudly chant: Down with occupation; long live Palestine as a free and Arab country.

Source: Zachary Lockman and Joel Beinin, eds., *Intifada: The Palestinian Uprising against Israeli Occupation* (Boston, MA: South End Press, 1989), 328–29. Used by permission of South End Press.

Hamas Charter, Defining the Hamas Movement [Excerpt], August 18, 1988

As the Palestine Liberation Organization (PLO) moved closer to opening genuine negotiations with Israel and accepting, however grudgingly, the right to existence of its longtime enemy, more militant Islamic-influenced elements among the Palestinians and other Arabs dissented, establishing the Islamic Resistance Movement, usually known as Hamas. The organization evolved from the Islamic Mujama group, established in 1973 in Gaza with Israeli encouragement as a Muslim welfare group that was itself an offshoot of the Muslim Brotherhood, a Palestinian organization established in 1946 to encourage the development of a religious outlook within Palestinian society. The fundamentalist Muslim resurgence of the 1980s, fueled by the establishment of an Islamic government in Iran in 1979, encouraged the Mujama to take a harder line in asserting strict Islamic principles and tenets among the Gazan population. In February 1988, soon after the First Intifada began, the Mujama established Hamas so that its members could join in the uprising. The lengthy Hamas charter, promulgated in August 1988, took a far more uncompromising line than Arafat was now embracing. Hamas claimed that all Palestine, including Israeli territory, was a sacred Islamic trust, none of which could or should be abandoned. Islamic Sharia, or religious law, ought to prevail throughout Palestine. The struggle against Israel could not end until Israel had been totally destroyed. Hamas embraced violence and terror as the only methods that could accomplish its objectives.

The ideological tenets
Article 1

The path of the Islamic Resistance Movement is the path of Islam, from which it draws its principles, concepts, terms and worldview with regard to life and man. It turns to [Islam] when religious rulings are required and asks [Islam] for inspiration to guide its steps.

The relationship between the Islamic Resistance Movement and the Muslim Brotherhood
Article 2

The Islamic Resistance Movement is the branch of the Muslim Brotherhood in Palestine. The Muslim Brotherhood is a global organization and the largest Islamic movement in modem times. It excels in profound understanding and has an exact, fully comprehensive perception of all Islamic concepts in all areas of life: understanding and thought, politics and economics, education and social affairs, law and government, spreading Islam and teaching, art and the media, by that which is hidden and by martyrdom and in the other areas of life . . .

Strategy and means The strategy of the Islamic Resistance Movement Palestine is Islamic Waqf [Religious Endowment] land
Article 11

The Islamic Resistance Movement believes that the land of Palestine is a religious Islamic endowment for all Muslims until Resurrection Day. It is forbidden to relinquish it or any part of it or give it up or any part of it. It does not belong to any Arab country, or to all the Arab countries, or to any king or president, or kings or presidents, or to any organization or organizations, whether they are Palestinian or Arab, because Palestine is sacred Islamic endowment land and belongs to Muslims until Resurrection Day. Its legal status is in accordance with Islamic law. . . .

Peaceful solutions, diplomatic initiatives and international conferences
Article 13

Initiatives, the so-called peaceful solutions and international conferences to find a solution to the Palestinian problem, contradict the Islamic Resistance Movement's ideological position. Giving up any part whatsoever of [the land of] Palestine is like ignoring a part of [the Muslim] faith.

[. . .]

There is no solution to the Palestinian problem except jihad. As for international initiatives, suggestions and conferences, they are an empty waste of time and complete nonsense. . . .

The jihad for the sake of liberating Palestine is a personal duty
Article 15

The day enemies steal part of Muslim land, jihad [becomes] the personal duty of every Muslim. With regard to the usurpation of Palestine by the Jews, it is a must to fly the banner of jihad. That means the propagation of Islamic awareness among the masses—locally [in Palestine], the Arab world and the Muslim world. The spirit of jihad must be disseminated within the [Islamic] nation, the enemies must be engaged in battle and [every Muslim must] join the ranks of the jihad warriors [mujahideen]. . . .

The forces that support the enemy
Article 22

[Our] enemies planned their deeds well for a long time [and managed] to achieve whatever they have, employing the factors influencing the course of events. Therefore, they acted to pile up huge amounts of influential material resources, which they utilized to fulfill their dream. Thus [the Jews], by means of their money, have taken over the international communications media: the news agencies, newspapers, publishing houses, broadcasting stations, etc. . . . In fact, they were behind the First World War, through which they achieved the abolishment of the Islamic Caliphate, made a profit and took over many of the sources of wealth. They [also] got the Balfour Declaration and established the League of the United [*sic*] Nations to enable them to rule the world. They were also behind the Second World War, in which they made immense profits by buying and selling military equipment, and also prepared the ground for the founding of their [own] state. They ordered the establishment of the United Nations and the Security Council [*sic*] which replaced the League of the United [*sic*] Nations, to be able to use it to rule the world. No war takes place anywhere in the world without [the Jews] behind the scenes having a hand in it. . . .

In fact, the forces of imperialism in the capitalist west and Communist east support the [Zionist] enemy as stoutly as possible with both material and manpower. They alternate with one another [in giving support]. . . .

Arab and Islamic states and governments
Article 28

[. . .]

[T]he Arab states bordering Israel are required to open their borders to the jihad warriors belonging to the Arab/Muslim nations, so that they may fulfill their role and join their efforts to those of the Muslim brethren in Palestine.

With regard to the other Arab/Muslim nations, they are required to facilitate the passage of the jihad warriors through their territory, which is the very least they can do.

Source: "The Hamas Charter (1988)," Intelligence Terrorism Information Center, http://www.terror ism-info.org.il.

James A. Baker, Five-Point Peace Plan, October 10, 1989

During 1989, U.S. government officials became increasingly irritated by the stubborn Israeli refusal to include Palestinians in any peace negotiations. With President Hosni Mubarak's energetic support and involvement, Egypt was at this time playing a key role in talks with Israel on the peace process. Eventually, in October 1989, U.S. secretary of state James A. Baker III publicly endorsed a proposal that Israeli and Palestinian delegations should meet in Cairo, Egypt's capital, to begin direct talks on the Israeli proposal to hold Palestinian elections in the occupied territories. The U.S. government offered to serve as a facilitator for this encounter and proposed that the Egyptian and Israeli foreign ministers meet with Baker within two weeks to iron out any remaining details. In ongoing talks with U.S. officials, PLO leader Yasser Arafat, seeking enhanced Palestinian input in the peace talks, had endorsed this proposal, which marked a departure from his earlier insistence that the PLO be recognized as the only legitimate representative of Palestinians in the occupied territories. Baker's proposal intentionally left room for the Palestinian delegation to include not just Palestinians from the occupied territories but also from elsewhere, including disputed East Jerusalem and other countries. With its most important sponsor clearly determined on this, pressure was steadily growing for Israel to deal directly with the Palestinians, a move that Israeli leaders feared might ultimately force them to recognize and work with the PLO.

Five Point Peace Plan
James A. Baker
October 10, 1989

1. The United States understands that because Egypt and Israel have been working hard on the peace process; there is agreement that an Israel delegation should conduct a dialogue with a Palestinian delegation in Cairo.
2. The United States understands that Egypt cannot substitute itself for the Palestinians and Egypt will consult with Palestinians on all aspects of that dialogue. Egypt will also consult with Israel and the United States.
3. The United States understands that Israel will attend the dialogue only after a satisfactory list of Palestinians has been worked out.
4. The United States understands that the Government of Israel will come to the dialogue on the basis of the Israeli Government's May 14 initiative. The United States further understands that Palestinians will come to the dialogue prepared to discuss elections and the negotiating process in accordance with Israel's initiative. The United States understands, therefore, that Palestinians would be free to raise issues that relate to their opinions on how to make elections and the negotiating process succeed.
5. In order to facilitate this process, the United States proposes that the Foreign Ministers of Israel, Egypt, and the United States meet in Washington within two weeks.

Source: U.S. Department of State. Secretary of State James A. Baker's Five Point Peace Plan. Issued December 6, 1989.

Oslo Declaration of Principles [Excerpt], September 13, 1993

Four days after Palestine Liberation Organization (PLO) chairman Yasser Arafat and Israeli prime minister Yitzhak Rabin exchanged letters formally recognizing the status of both Israel and the PLO, they signed the Oslo Declaration on the future of the occupied territories of Gaza and the West Bank. The new accords called for the establishment of a "Palestinian Interim Self-Government Authority" in these areas for a transitional period not to exceed five years, after which their status would be determined by a permanent settlement based on the principles of United Nations (UN) Security Council Resolutions 242 and 338. U.S. president Bill Clinton, who flew to Oslo to attend the signing of these accords and was photographed with one arm around Arafat and the other around Rabin, hailed the accords as "the dawn of a new era" and a "new beginning." The Oslo Accords nonetheless left many salient issues open or ambivalent. It was never clear whether the ultimate objective of the "final status" agreement to be negotiated in the future would be an independent Palestinian state. The fate of the Israeli settlements in these areas was yet to be determined, and Israel still reserved to itself jurisdiction over and protection of Israeli settlers in the occupied territories, a provision that could easily justify the continuing presence of Israeli troops there. All these questions left ample room for bitter disagreement.

The Government of the State of Israel and the P.L.O. team (in the Jordanian-Palestinian delegation to the Middle East Peace Conference) (the "Palestinian Delegation"), representing the Palestinian people, agree that it is time to put an end to decades of confrontation and conflict, recognize their mutual legitimate and political rights, and strive to live in peaceful coexistence and mutual dignity and security and achieve a just, lasting and comprehensive peace settlement and historic reconciliation through the agreed political process. Accordingly, the two sides agree to the following principles:

Article I

Aim of the Negotiations

The aim of the Israeli-Palestinian negotiations within the current Middle East peace process is, among other things, to establish a Palestinian Interim Self-Government Authority, the elected Council (the "Council"), for the Palestinian people in the West Bank and the Gaza Strip, for a transitional period not exceeding five years, leading to a permanent settlement based on Security Council Resolutions 242 and 338.

It is understood that the interim arrangements are an integral part of the whole peace process and that the negotiations on the permanent status will lead to the implementation of Security Council Resolutions 242 and 338.

Article II

Framework for the Interim Period

The agreed framework for the interim period is set forth in this Declaration of Principles.

Article III

Elections

In order that the Palestinian people in the West Bank and Gaza Strip may govern themselves according to democratic principles, direct, free and general political elections will be held for the Council under agreed supervision and international observation, while the Palestinian police will ensure public order.

An agreement will be concluded on the exact mode and conditions of the elections in accordance with the protocol attached as Annex I, with the goal of holding the elections not later than nine months after the entry into force of this Declaration of Principles.

These elections will constitute a significant interim preparatory step toward the realization of the legitimate rights of the Palestinian people and their just requirements.

Article IV

Jurisdiction

Jurisdiction of the Council will cover West Bank and Gaza Strip territory, except for issues that will be negotiated in the permanent status negotiations. The two sides view the West Bank and the Gaza Strip as a single territorial unit, whose integrity will be preserved during the interim period.

Article V

Transitional Period and Permanent Status Negotiations

The five-year transitional period will begin upon the withdrawal from the Gaza Strip and Jericho area.

Permanent status negotiations will commence as soon as possible, but not later than the beginning of the third year of the interim period, between the Government of Israel and the Palestinian people representatives.

It is understood that these negotiations shall cover remaining issues, including: Jerusalem, refugees, settlements, security arrangements, borders, relations and cooperation with other neighbors, and other issues of common interest.

The two parties agree that the outcome of the permanent status negotiations should not be prejudiced or preempted by agreements reached for the interim period.

Article VI

Preparatory Transfer of Powers and Responsibilities

Upon the entry into force of this Declaration of Principles and the withdrawal from the Gaza Strip and the Jericho area, a transfer of authority from the Israeli military government and its Civil Administration to the authorised Palestinians for this task, as detailed herein, will commence. This transfer of authority will be of a preparatory nature until the inauguration of the Council.

Immediately after the entry into force of this Declaration of Principles and the withdrawal from the Gaza Strip and Jericho area, with the view to promoting economic development in the West Bank and Gaza Strip, authority will be transferred to the Palestinians on the following spheres: education and culture, health, social welfare, direct taxation, and tourism. The Palestinian side will commence in building the Palestinian police force, as agreed upon. Pending the inauguration of the Council, the two parties may negotiate the transfer of additional powers and responsibilities, as agreed upon.

Article VII

Interim Agreement

The Israeli and Palestinian delegations will negotiate an agreement on the interim period (the "Interim Agreement").

The Interim Agreement shall specify, among other things, the structure of the Council, the number of its members, and the transfer of powers and responsibilities from the Israeli military government and its Civil Administration to the Council. The Interim Agreement shall also specify the Council's executive authority, legislative authority in accordance with Article IX below, and the independent Palestinian judicial organs.

The Interim Agreement shall include arrangements, to be implemented upon the inauguration of the Council, for the assumption by the Council of all of the powers and responsibilities transferred previously in accordance with Article VI above.

In order to enable the Council to promote economic growth, upon its inauguration, the Council will establish, among other things, a Palestinian Electricity Authority, a Gaza Sea Port Authority, a Palestinian Development

Bank, a Palestinian Export Promotion Board, a Palestinian Environmental Authority, a Palestinian Land Authority and a Palestinian Water Administration Authority, and any other Authorities agreed upon, in accordance with the Interim Agreement that will specify their powers and responsibilities.

After the inauguration of the Council, the Civil Administration will be dissolved, and the Israeli military government will be withdrawn.

Article VIII

Public Order and Security

In order to guarantee public order and internal security for the Palestinians of the West Bank and the Gaza Strip, the Council will establish a strong police force, while Israel will continue to carry the responsibility for defending against external threats, as well as the responsibility for overall security of Israelis for the purpose of safeguarding their internal security and public order.

Article IX

Laws and Military Orders

The Council will be empowered to legislate, in accordance with the Interim Agreement, within all authorities transferred to it.

Both parties will review jointly laws and military orders presently in force in remaining spheres.

[. . .]

Article XIII

Redeployment of Israeli Forces

After the entry into force of this Declaration of Principles, and not later than the eve of elections for the Council, a redeployment of Israeli military forces in the West Bank and the Gaza Strip will take place, in addition to withdrawal of Israeli forces carried out in accordance with Article XIV.

In redeploying its military forces, Israel will be guided by the principle that its military forces should be redeployed outside populated areas.

Further redeployments to specified locations will be gradually implemented commensurate with the assumption of responsibility for public order and internal security by the Palestinian police force pursuant to Article VIII above.

Article XIV

Israeli withdrawal from the Gaza Strip and Jericho Area

Israel will withdraw from the Gaza Strip and Jericho area, as detailed in the protocol attached as Annex II.

Source: "Declaration of Principles on Interim Self-Government Arrangements, September 13, 1993," Israel Ministry of Foreign Affairs, http://www.mfa.gov.il/MFA/ForeignPolicy/Peace/Guide/Pages/Declaration%20of%20Principles.aspx.

Yitzhak Rabin's Last Speech, Peace Rally, Kings of Israel Square, Tel Aviv, November 4, 1995

Even though the 1995 Oslo Interim Agreements permitted Israeli forces to maintain effective control of much of the West Bank and the Gaza Strip and the Israeli government continued to expand new settlements in the West Bank and East Jerusalem, they were anathema to many conservative Israeli politicians, extremist settlers, and ultraorthodox Jews. The issue polarized the Israeli population. In the fall of 1995, right-wing Israelis held massive demonstrations against the interim agreements and any Israeli withdrawals from West Bank territories. Moderate Israelis likewise organized huge rallies in favor of peace, and Prime Minister Yitzhak Rabin agreed to appear at a peace demonstration in Tel Aviv, scheduled for November 4, 1995. Rabin, who one year earlier had shared the Nobel Peace Prize with Israel's foreign minister, Shimon Peres, and Palestine Liberation Organization (PLO) chairman Yasser Arafat, again spoke eloquently in favor of the peace process as the only way of ensuring Israel's long-term survival. He also assailed those ultraorthodox and right-wing Israeli critics of the interim agreements who advocated the use of violence against their architects, himself included, warning that such behavior was "undermining the very foundations of Israeli democracy." Ironically, during the rally he was assassinated by Yigal Amir, an orthodox and deeply anti-Arab Jewish student of theology and a former Israeli soldier who believed that Rabin's policies were endangering Israel and therefore justified his death as a threat to state security. The assassination, revealing as it did the depths of political divisions, extremism, and hatred within the country, shocked Israel and the international community. For supporters of the peace process, Rabin became a posthumous icon and martyr, the earlier ambiguities and reservations of his policies forgotten.

I want to thank each and every one of you who stood up here against violence and for peace. This government, which I have the privilege to lead, together with my friend Shimon Peres, decided to give peace a chance. A peace that will solve most of the problems of the State of Israel. I was a military man for twenty-seven years. I fought as long as there were no prospects for peace. Today I believe that there are prospects for peace, great prospects. We must take advantage of it for the sake of those standing here, and for the sake of those who do not stand here. And they are many among our people.

I have always believed that the majority of the people want peace, are prepared to take risks for peace. And you here, by showing up at this rally, prove it, along with the many who did not make it here, that the people truly want peace and oppose violence.

Violence is undermining the very foundations of Israeli democracy. It must be condemned, denounced, and isolated. This is not the way of the State of Israel. Controversies may arise in a democracy, but the decision must be reached through democratic elections, just as it happened in 1992, when we were given the mandate to do what we are doing, and to continue to do it.

. . . . [P]eace is attainable, a peace that will provide an opportunity for a progressive society and economy. Peace exists first and foremost in our prayers, but not only in prayers. Peace is what the Jewish People aspire to, a true aspiration.

Peace entails difficulties, even pain. Israel knows no path devoid of pain. But the path of peace is preferable to the path of war. I say this to you as one who was a military man and minister of defense, and who saw the pain of the families of IDF soldiers. It is for their sake, and for the sake of our children and grandchildren, that I want this government to exert every effort, exhaust every opportunity, to promote and to reach a comprehensive peace.

This rally must send a message to the Israeli public, to the Jewish community throughout the world, to many, many in the Arab world and in the entire world, that the people of Israel want peace, support peace, and for that, I thank you very much.

Source: U.S. Congress, "Anniversary of the Death of Israeli Prime Minister Yitzak Rabin," *Congressional Record*, November 19, 2003, H11628, http://www.congress.gov/cgi-bin/query/z?r108 :H19NO3–0068.

Wye River Memorandum [Excerpt], October 23, 1998

Determined to reinvigorate the Israeli-Palestinian peace process, in the fall of 1998 U.S. president Bill Clinton's administration pressured the reluctant but beleaguered Israeli prime minister Benjamin Netanyahu to follow up on the statements in the appendices to the Hebron Accords with a definite timetable for the three promised Israeli troop redeployments. Israeli and Palestinian representatives met at Wye Plantation, Maryland, and spent nine days in fraught and tense negotiations. Clinton attended portions of the meeting and the final ceremony. King Hussein of Jordan, undergoing treatment for the cancer of which he died early in 1999, also made a poignant appearance at the signing ceremony in which he begged those present to think of their children's future, saying: "There has been enough destruction. Enough death. Enough waste." The Palestinian Authority (PA) and Israel eventually concluded an agreement setting a timetable for further troop redeployments, most of which were never implemented. The Palestinians promised to take active measures to prevent and punish terrorism and violence directed at Israel and its forces and to cooperate closely with Israeli military and security forces. They also promised to amend the Palestinian National Charter by removing those clauses that sought Israel's destruction and endorsed the use of terrorism and violence. Israel also permitted the Palestinians to open an airport in Gaza and to open talks on establishing a corridor to allow safe passage from Gaza to the West Bank, ending the separation of the constituent occupied areas under the PA. The agreement promised to begin negotiations over the permanent status of the occupied territories almost immediately and complete them as originally scheduled by the following May, a timetable that all present knew was unlikely to be feasible. In addition, both sides stated that they would not "initiate or take any step that will change the status of the West Bank and the Gaza Strip," a provision the continuing Israeli commitment to new settlements constantly breached. Although it represented a paper triumph for U.S. optimism over Israeli intransigence, the prospects for the agreement's genuine implementation were poor.

I. Further Redeployments

A. *Phase One and Two Further Redeployments*

1. Pursuant to the Interim Agreement and subsequent agreements, the Israeli side's implementation of the first and second F.R.D. will consist of the transfer to the Palestinian side of 13% from Area C as follows:

   1% to Area (A) 12% to Area (B)

   The Palestinian side has informed that it will allocate an area/areas amounting to 3% from the above Area (B) to be designated as Green Areas and/or Nature Reserves. The Palestinian side has further informed that they will act according to the established scientific standards, and that therefore there will be no changes in the status of these areas, without prejudice to the rights of the existing inhabitants in these areas including Bedouins; while these standards do not allow new construction in these areas, existing roads and buildings may be maintained.

   The Israeli side will retain in these Green Areas/Nature Reserves the overriding security responsibility for the purpose of protecting Israelis and confronting the threat of terrorism. Activities and movements of the Palestinian Police forces may be carried out after coordination and confirmation; the Israeli side will respond to such requests expeditiously.

2. As part of the foregoing implementation of the first and second F.R.D., 14.2% from Area (B) will become Area (A).

B. *Third Phase of Further Redeployments*

With regard to the terms of the Interim Agreement and of Secretary Christopher's letters to the two sides of January 17, 1997 relating to the further redeployment process, there will be a committee to address this question. The United States will be briefed regularly.

II. Security

In the provisions on security arrangements of the Interim Agreement, the Palestinian side agreed to take all measures necessary in order to prevent acts of terrorism, crime and hostilities directed against the Israeli side, against individuals falling under the Israeli side's authority and against their property, just as the Israeli side agreed to take all measures necessary in order to prevent acts of terrorism, crime and hostilities directed against the Palestinian side, against individuals falling under the Palestinian side's authority and against their property. The two sides also agreed to take legal measures against offenders within their jurisdiction and to prevent incitement against each other by any organizations, groups or individuals within their jurisdiction. . . .

B. Security Cooperation

The two sides agree that their security cooperation will be based on a spirit of partnership and will include, among other things, the following steps:

1. Bilateral Cooperation
   There will be full bilateral security cooperation between the two sides which will be continuous, intensive and comprehensive. . . .
2. *PLO Charter*

The Executive Committee of the Palestine Liberation Organization and the Palestinian Central Council will reaffirm the letter of 22 January 1998 from PLO Chairman Yasir Arafat to President Clinton concerning the nullification of the Palestinian National Charter provisions that are inconsistent with the letters exchanged between the PLO and the Government of Israel on 9–10 September 1993. PLO Chairman Arafat, the Speaker of the Palestine National Council, and the Speaker of the Palestinian Council will invite the members of the PNC, as well as the members of the Central Council, the Council, and the Palestinian Heads of Ministries to a meeting to be addressed by President Clinton to reaffirm their support for the peace process and the aforementioned decisions of the Executive Committee and the Central Council.

[. . .]

IV. Permanent Status Negotiations

The two sides will immediately resume permanent status negotiations on an accelerated basis and will make a determined effort to achieve the mutual goal of reaching an agreement by May 4, 1999. The negotiations will be continuous and without interruption. The United States has expressed its willingness to facilitate these negotiations.

V. Unilateral Actions

Recognizing the necessity to create a positive environment for the negotiations, neither side shall initiate or take any step that will change the status of the West Bank and the Gaza Strip in accordance with the Interim Agreement.

Source: "Wye River Memorandum," U.S. Department of State, http://www.state.gov/www/regions/nea/981023_interim_agmt.html.

Quartet Joint Statement, July 16, 2002

One result of U.S. secretary of state Colin Powell's Middle East peace mission of April 2002 was the foundation of the international coalition that would orchestrate the new process. After visiting the Middle East, he proceeded to Madrid and met representatives from the

European Union (EU), the United Nations (UN), and Russia. Initially the group, christened the Quartet, planned to organize a Middle East peace conference, to begin in summer 2002. That gathering was not held, but representatives of the four sponsors met in New York in July 2002. They endorsed the prescriptions laid out in President George W. Bush's speech the previous month, including a commitment to the existence of two neighboring states, one Israeli and one Palestinian, and his demand for major Palestinian economic and political reforms, notably the creation of new democratic institutions and the holding of free elections in the near future. The International Task Force on Reform, comprising representatives from the Quartet group plus Japan, Norway, the World Bank, and the International Monetary Fund (IMF), had already been established to develop and implement a comprehensive reform program. The Quartet also endorsed a major overhaul of the Palestinian security apparatus. The Israelis were asked to relax the restrictions on the free movement of Palestinians, release frozen tax revenues, and "stop all new settlement activity." The Quartet called on both sides to renew dialogue with each other. Facilitating a Palestinian-Israeli settlement had clearly once again moved close to the top of the international agenda.

United Nations Secretary-General Kofi Annan, Russian Foreign Minister Igor Ivanov, U.S. Secretary of State Colin L. Powell, Danish Foreign Minister Per Stig Moeller, High Representative for European Common Foreign and Security Policy Javier Solana and European Commissioner for External Affairs Chris Patten met in New York today. The Quartet members reviewed the situation in the Middle East and agreed to continue close consultations, as expressed in the Madrid Declaration, to which the Quartet remains fully committed, to promote a just, comprehensive, and lasting settlement of the Middle East conflict. The Quartet expresses its support for the convening of a

further international Ministerial meeting at an appropriate time. . . .

Consistent with President Bush's June 24 statement, the UN, EU and Russia express their strong support for the goal of achieving a final Israeli-Palestinian settlement which, with intensive effort on security and reform by all, could be reached within three years from now. The UN, EU and Russia welcome President Bush's commitment to active U.S. leadership toward that goal. The Quartet remains committed to implementing the vision of two states, Israel and an independent, viable and democratic Palestine, living side by side in peace and security, as affirmed by UN Security Council Resolution 1397. . . . To assist progress toward these shared goals, the Quartet agreed on the importance of a coordinated international campaign to support Palestinian efforts at political and economic reform. The Quartet welcomes and encourages the strong Palestinian interest in fundamental reform, including the Palestinian 100-Day Reform Program. It also welcomes the willingness of regional states and the international community to assist the Palestinians to build institutions of good government, and to create a new governing framework of working democracy, in preparation for statehood. For these objectives to be realized, it is essential that well-prepared, free, open and democratic elections take place. The new international Task Force on Reform, which is comprised of representatives of the U.S., EU, UN Secretary General, Russia, Japan, Norway, the World Bank and the International Monetary Fund, and which works under the auspices of the Quartet, will strive to develop and implement a comprehensive action plan for reform. . . . Implementation of an action plan, with appropriate benchmarks for progress on reform measures, should lead to the establishment of a democratic Palestinian state characterized by the rule of law, separation of powers, and a vibrant free market economy that can best serve the interests of its people. The Quartet also commits itself to continuing to assist the parties in efforts to renew dialogue, and welcomes in this regard the recent high-level ministerial meetings between Israelis and Palestinians on the issues of security, economics and reform.

The Quartet agreed on the critical need to build new and efficient Palestinian security capabilities on sound bases of unified command, and transparency and accountability with regard to resources and conduct. Restructuring security institutions to serve these goals should lead to improvement in Palestinian security performance, which is essential to progress on other aspects of institutional transformation and realization of a Palestinian state committed to combating terror.

In this context, the Quartet notes Israel's vital stake in the success of Palestinian reform. The Quartet calls upon Israel to take concrete steps to support the emergence of a viable Palestinian state. Recognizing Israel's legitimate security concerns, these steps include immediate measures to ease the internal closures in certain areas and, as security improves through reciprocal steps, withdrawal of Israeli forces to their pre-September 28, 2000 positions. Moreover, frozen tax revenues should be released. In this connection, a more transparent and accountable mechanism is being put into place. In addition, consistent with the Mitchell Committee's recommendations, Israel should stop all new settlement activity. Israel must also ensure full, safe and unfettered access for international and humanitarian personnel.

The Quartet reaffirms that there must be a negotiated permanent settlement based on UN Security Council resolutions 242 and 338. There can be no military solution to the conflict; Israelis and Palestinians must address the core issues that divide them, through sustained negotiations, if there is to be real and lasting peace and security. The Israeli occupation that began in 1967 must end, and Israel must have secure and recognized borders. The Quartet further reaffirms its commitment to the goal of a comprehensive regional peace between Israel and Lebanon, and Israel and Syria, based upon Resolutions 242 and 338, the Madrid terms of reference, and the principle of land for peace.

Source: "Middle East Quartet Statement, July 16, 2002," U.S. Department of State, http://2001–2009 .state.gov/p/nea/rt/15205.htm.

Road Map to Peace, April 30, 2003

In May 2003, immediately after the inauguration of new Palestinian Authority (PA) prime minister Mahmoud Abbas, the U.S. government released the latest and fullest version of the Road Map to Peace drawn up by the Quartet grouping of the United States, Russia, the European Union (EU), and the United Nations (UN). The United States insisted that both Israel and the Palestinians accept the entire plan. Despite this stipulation, Israel accepted the plan but only with 14 reservations of its own. The PA accepted the plan without reservations. The Road Map to Peace was supposed to offer a fairly precise schedule to end violence and terror; withdraw Israeli troops from Palestinian territory; establish a more democratic, open, and efficient government in Palestinian territory on principles to be enshrined in a new constitution; hold Palestinian elections; freeze new Israeli settlement activity in the occupied territories and remove illegal settlements; establish provisional borders for a Palestinian state; and hold an international peace conference to reach a final Palestinian-Israeli settlement establishing two states, Israel and a Palestinian state, that would accept each other's existence within mutually agreed boundaries. By 2013, progress had been made in terms of Palestinian free elections and reforms, and a new constitution had been drafted. Israeli forces had withdrawn from Gaza, and some illegal settlements had been destroyed. Even so, Palestinians were deeply split, with Mahmoud Abbas and Fatah of the Palestinian National Authority governing the West Bank and more radical Hamas militants controlling Gaza. The peace process had yet to progress beyond the first stage of the Road Map to Peace.

A Performance-Based Roadmap to a Permanent Two-State Solution to the Israeli-Palestinian Conflict

The following is a performance-based and goal-driven roadmap, with clear phases, timelines, target dates, and benchmarks aiming at progress through reciprocal steps by the two parties in the political, security, economic, humanitarian, and institution-building fields, under the auspices of the Quartet [the United States, European Union, United Nations, and Russia]. The destination is a final and comprehensive settlement of the Israel-Palestinian conflict by 2005, as presented in President Bush's speech of 24 June, and welcomed by the EU, Russia and the UN in the 16 July and 17 September Quartet Ministerial statements.

A two state solution to the Israeli-Palestinian conflict will only be achieved through an end to violence and terrorism, when the Palestinian people have a leadership acting decisively against terror and willing and able to build a practicing democracy based on tolerance and liberty, and through Israel's readiness to do what is necessary for a democratic Palestinian state to be established, and a clear, unambiguous acceptance by both parties of the goal of a negotiated settlement as described below. The Quartet will assist and facilitate implementation of the plan, starting in Phase I, including direct discussions between the parties as required. The

plan establishes a realistic timeline for implementation. However, as a performance-based plan, progress will require and depend upon the good faith efforts of the parties, and their compliance with each of the obligations outlined below. Should the parties perform their obligations rapidly, progress within and through the phases may come sooner than indicated in the plan. Non-compliance with obligations will impede progress.

A settlement, negotiated between the parties, will result in the emergence of an independent, democratic, and viable Palestinian state living side by side in peace and security with Israel and its other neighbors. The settlement will resolve the Israel-Palestinian conflict, and end the occupation that began in 1967, based on the foundations of the Madrid Conference, the principle of land for peace, UNSCRs 242, 338 and 1397, agreements previously reached by the parties, and the initiative of Saudi Crown Prince Abdullah—endorsed by the Beirut Arab League Summit—calling for acceptance of Israel as a neighbor living in peace and security, in the context of a comprehensive settlement. This initiative is a vital element of international efforts to promote a comprehensive peace on all tracks, including the Syrian-Israeli and Lebanese-Israeli tracks.

The Quartet will meet regularly at senior levels to evaluate the parties' performance on implementation of the plan. In each phase, the parties are expected to perform their obligations in parallel, unless otherwise indicated.

Phase I: Ending Terror and Violence, Normalizing Palestinian Life, and Building Palestinian Institutions— Present to May 2003

In Phase I, the Palestinians immediately undertake an unconditional cessation of violence according to the steps outlined below;

such action should be accompanied by supportive measures undertaken by Israel. Palestinians and Israelis resume security cooperation based on the Tenet work plan to end violence, terrorism, and incitement through restructured and effective Palestinian security services. Palestinians undertake comprehensive political reform in preparation for statehood, including drafting a Palestinian constitution, and free, fair and open elections upon the basis of those measures. Israel takes all necessary steps to help normalize Palestinian life. Israel withdraws from Palestinian areas occupied from September 28, 2000 and the two sides restore the status quo that existed at that time, as security performance and cooperation progress. Israel also freezes all settlement activity, consistent with the Mitchell report.

At the outset of Phase I:

— Palestinian leadership issues unequivocal statement reiterating Israel's right to exist in peace and security and calling for an immediate and unconditional cease-fire to end armed activity and all acts of violence against Israelis anywhere. All official Palestinian institutions end incitement against Israel.

— Israeli leadership issues unequivocal statement affirming its commitment to the two-state vision of an independent, viable, sovereign Palestinian state living in peace and security alongside Israel, as expressed by President Bush, and calling for an immediate end to violence against Palestinians everywhere. All official Israeli institutions end incitement against Palestinians.

Security

— Palestinians declare an unequivocal end to violence and terrorism and undertake visible efforts on the ground to arrest, disrupt, and restrain individuals and groups conducting and planning violent attacks on Israelis anywhere.

— Rebuilt and refocused Palestinian Authority security apparatus begins sustained, targeted, and effective operations aimed at confronting all those engaged in terror and dismantlement of terrorist capabilities and infrastructure. This includes commencing confiscation of illegal weapons and consolidation of security authority, free of association with terror and corruption.

— GOI takes no actions undermining trust, including deportations, attacks on civilians; confiscation and/or demolition of Palestinian homes and property, as a punitive measure or to facilitate Israeli construction; destruction of Palestinian institutions and infrastructure; and other measures specified in the Tenet work plan.

— Relying on existing mechanisms and on-the-ground resources, Quartet representatives begin informal monitoring and consult with the parties on establishment of a formal monitoring mechanism and its implementation.

— Implementation, as previously agreed, of U.S. rebuilding, training and resumed security cooperation plan in collaboration with outside oversight board (U.S.-Egypt-Jordan). Quartet support for efforts to achieve a lasting, comprehensive cease-fire.

• All Palestinian security organizations are consolidated into three services reporting to an empowered Interior Minister.

• Restructured/retrained Palestinian security forces and IDF counterparts progressively resume security cooperation and other undertakings in implementation of the Tenet work plan, including regular senior-level meetings, with the participation of U.S. security officials.

— Arab states cut off public and private funding and all other forms of support for groups supporting and engaging in violence and terror.

— All donors providing budgetary support for the Palestinians channel these funds through the Palestinian Ministry of Finance's Single Treasury Account.

— As comprehensive security performance moves forward, IDF withdraws progressively from areas occupied since September 28, 2000 and the two sides restore the status quo that existed prior to September 28, 2000. Palestinian security forces redeploy to areas vacated by IDF.

Palestinian Institution-Building

— Immediate action on credible process to produce draft constitution for Palestinian statehood. As rapidly as possible, constitutional committee circulates draft Palestinian constitution, based on strong parliamentary democracy and cabinet with empowered prime minister, for public comment/debate. Constitutional committee proposes draft document for submission after elections for approval by appropriate Palestinian institutions.

— Appointment of interim prime minister or cabinet with empowered executive authority/decision-making body.

— GOI fully facilitates travel of Palestinian officials for PLC and Cabinet sessions, internationally supervised security retraining, electoral and other reform activity, and other supportive measures related to the reform efforts.

— Continued appointment of Palestinian ministers empowered to undertake fundamental reform. Completion of further

steps to achieve genuine separation of powers, including any necessary Palestinian legal reforms for this purpose.

— Establishment of independent Palestinian election commission. PLC reviews and revises election law.

— Palestinian performance on judicial, administrative, and economic benchmarks, as established by the International Task Force on Palestinian Reform.

— As early as possible, and based upon the above measures and in the context of open debate and transparent candidate selection/electoral campaign based on a free, multi-party process, Palestinians hold free, open, and fair elections.

— GOI facilitates Task Force election assistance, registration of voters, movement of candidates and voting officials. Support for NGOs involved in the election process.

— GOI reopens Palestinian Chamber of Commerce and other closed Palestinian institutions in East Jerusalem based on a commitment that these institutions operate strictly in accordance with prior agreements between the parties.

Humanitarian Response

— Israel takes measures to improve the humanitarian situation. Israel and Palestinians implement in full all recommendations of the Bertini report to improve humanitarian conditions, lifting curfews and easing restrictions on movement of persons and goods, and allowing full, safe, and unfettered access of international and humanitarian personnel.

— AHLC reviews the humanitarian situation and prospects for economic development in the West Bank and Gaza and launches a major donor assistance effort, including to the reform effort.

— GOI and PA continue revenue clearance process and transfer of funds, including arrears, in accordance with agreed, transparent monitoring mechanism.

Civil Society

— Continued donor support, including increased funding through PVOs/NGOs, for people to people programs, private sector development and civil society initiatives.

Settlements

— GOI immediately dismantles settlement outposts erected since March 2001.

— Consistent with the Mitchell Report, GOI freezes all settlement activity (including natural growth of settlements).

Phase II: Transition—June 2003–December 2003

In the second phase, efforts are focused on the option of creating an independent Palestinian state with provisional borders and attributes of sovereignty, based on the new constitution, as a way station to a permanent status settlement. As has been noted, this goal can be achieved when the Palestinian people have a leadership acting decisively against terror, willing and able to build a practicing democracy based on tolerance and liberty. With such a leadership, reformed civil institutions and security structures, the Palestinians will have the active support of the Quartet and the broader international community in establishing an independent, viable, state.

Progress into Phase II will be based upon the consensus judgment of the Quartet of whether conditions are appropriate to proceed, taking into account performance of both parties. Furthering and sustaining efforts to normalize Palestinian lives and build Palestinian institutions, Phase II starts after Palestinian elections and ends with possible creation of an independent Palestinian state with provisional borders in 2003. Its primary goals are continued comprehensive security performance and effective security cooperation, continued normalization of Palestinian life and institution-building, further building on and sustaining of the goals outlined in Phase I, ratification of a democratic Palestinian constitution, formal establishment of office of prime minister, consolidation of political reform, and the creation of a Palestinian state with provisional borders.

— INTERNATIONAL CONFERENCE: Convened by the Quartet, in consultation with the parties, immediately after the successful conclusion of Palestinian elections, to support Palestinian economic recovery and launch a process, leading to establishment of an independent Palestinian state with provisional borders.

- Such a meeting would be inclusive, based on the goal of a comprehensive Middle East peace (including between Israel and Syria, and Israel and Lebanon), and based on the principles described in the preamble to this document.
- Arab states restore pre-intifada links to Israel (trade offices, etc.).
- Revival of multilateral engagement on issues including regional water resources, environment, economic development, refugees, and arms control issues.

— New constitution for democratic, independent Palestinian state is finalized and approved by appropriate Palestinian institutions. Further elections, if required, should follow approval of the new constitution.

— Empowered reform cabinet with office of prime minister formally established, consistent with draft constitution.

— Continued comprehensive security performance, including effective security cooperation on the bases laid out in Phase I.

— Creation of an independent Palestinian state with provisional borders through a process of Israeli-Palestinian engagement, launched by the international conference. As part of this process, implementation of prior agreements, to enhance maximum territorial contiguity, including further action on settlements in conjunction with establishment of a Palestinian state with provisional borders.

— Enhanced international role in monitoring transition, with the active, sustained, and operational support of the Quartet.

— Quartet members promote international recognition of Palestinian state, including possible UN membership.

Phase III: Permanent Status Agreement and End of the Israeli-Palestinian Conflict—2004–2005

Progress into Phase III, based on consensus judgment of Quartet, and taking into account actions of both parties and Quartet monitoring. Phase III objectives are consolidation of reform and stabilization of Palestinian institutions, sustained, effective Palestinian security performance, and Israeli-Palestinian negotiations aimed at a permanent status agreement in 2005.

— SECOND INTERNATIONAL CONFERENCE: Convened by Quartet, in consultation with the parties, at beginning of 2004 to endorse agreement reached on an independent Palestinian state with provisional borders and formally to launch a process with the active,

sustained, and operational support of the Quartet, leading to a final, permanent status resolution in 2005, including on borders, Jerusalem, refugees, settlements; and, to support progress toward a comprehensive Middle East settlement between Israel and Lebanon and Israel and Syria, to be achieved as soon as possible.

— Continued comprehensive, effective progress on the reform agenda laid out by the Task Force in preparation for final status agreement.

— Continued sustained and effective security performance, and sustained, effective security cooperation on the bases laid out in Phase I.

— International efforts to facilitate reform and stabilize Palestinian institutions and the Palestinian economy, in preparation for final status agreement.

— Parties reach final and comprehensive permanent status agreement that ends the Israel-Palestinian conflict in 2005, through a settlement negotiated between the parties based on UNSCR 242, 338, and 1397, that ends the occupation that began in 1967, and includes an agreed, just, fair, and realistic solution to the refugee issue, and a negotiated resolution on the status of Jerusalem that takes into account the political and religious concerns of both sides, and protects the religious interests of Jews, Christians, and Muslims worldwide, and fulfills the vision of two states, Israel and sovereign, independent, democratic and viable Palestine, living side-by-side in peace and security.

— Arab state acceptance of full normal relations with Israel and security for all the states of the region in the context of a comprehensive Arab-Israeli peace.

Source: Distributed by the Office of International Information Programs, U.S. Department of State, http://avalon.law.yale.edu/21st_century/roadmap.asp.

Mahmoud Abbas, Inaugural Speech as President of the Palestinian Authority [Excerpt], January 15, 2005

Longtime Palestine Liberation Organization (PLO) and Palestinian Authority (PA) president Yasser Arafat died in the fall of 2004, opening the way for new movement in the peace process. Mahmoud Abbas, leader of the Fatah group within the PLO who had served six rather ineffective months as PA prime minister in 2003, was the front-runner to succeed Arafat. Abbas, chairman of the PLO Executive Committee, was a moderate who favored an end to violence and resumption of the stalled Quartet Road Map to Peace. He was also a strong supporter of greater democracy and constitutional reform within the PA. In January 2005, in elections largely boycotted by Hamas, the Palestinian group that staunchly opposed any recognition of or compromise with Israel and was pledged to the destruction of the Israeli state, Abbas was elected PA president, winning 62 percent of the vote. Israeli forces had, however, detained or restricted the movements of some of his rivals, and the Abbas campaign had virtually monopolized Palestinian television coverage of the election. In his inaugural speech, Abbas nonetheless celebrated the fact that democratic elections had been held and the rule of law upheld within the Palestinian territories. He urged the resumption of negotiations under the Quartet's peace plan to bring about the final creation of a Palestinian state, one committed to coexistence with Israel, and called for an end to the Second (al-Aqsa) Intifada and the renunciation by Palestinians of the use of violence and terror against Israeli targets. He also demanded that Israel show its good faith by ending "assassinations, the siege on our towns, arrests, land confiscations, settlement activity and the separation wall."

[. . .]

As I address you today, I am full of pride over the Palestinian people's exceptional democratic achievement. Our people have stood in the face of the occupation to say— first and foremost to ourselves but also to the whole world—that no matter how great the challenges may be, we will not give up on our national project. . . . That no matter how many obstacles may stand in our way, we will not be deterred from advancing our democratic process. The winner in these elections is the great Palestinian people who have created this democratic epic and who will safeguard it.

[. . .]

Today, the results of the elections are final, and our great people have passed this important test. [. . .]

— The people have spoken for the end of occupation and the democratic choice
— for the continuation and consolidation of development and reform in all its forms,
— The people have voted for the rule of law, order, pluralism, the peaceful transfer of authority, and equality for all,
— The people have chosen just peace, ending the occupation, and coexistence based on equality and international legitimacy.

The greatest challenge before us, and the fundamental task facing us is national liberation. The task of ending the occupation, establishing the Palestinian state on the 1967 borders, with Jerusalem as its capital, and reaching a just and agreed solution to the refugee problem on the basis of international legitimacy [resolutions], first and foremost [the UN General Assembly] resolution 194 (of 1949) and the Beirut Arab Summit Resolution [in 2002].

To achieve these national goals, we will remain committed to the PLO's strategic choice: the choice of achieving just peace and our national goals through negotiations. The path to these goals is what we and the world have agreed upon in the Road Map. We have repeatedly stated that we are committed to our responsibilities in the Road Map. We will implement our obligations as a matter of Palestinian national interest. In return, Israel has to implement its obligations.

Our hand is extended towards an Israeli partner for making peace. But partnership is not through words but rather deeds. It is through ending assassinations, the siege on our towns, arrests, land confiscations, settlement activity and the separation wall. Partnership cannot be achieved by dictation, and peace cannot be reached by partial or interim solutions. Peace can only be achieved by working together to reach a permanent status solution that deals with all of the outstanding issues, and which turns a new page on the basis of two neighboring states.

I would like to stress here that we are fully prepared to resume permanent status negotiations, and that we are politically ready to reach a comprehensive agreement over all of the issues.

From this forum, and on this day, I say to the Israeli leadership and to the Israeli people: we are two peoples destined to live side by side, and to share this land between us. The only alternative to peace is the continuation of the occupation and the conflict. Let us start implementing the Road Map, and—in parallel—let us start discussing the permanent status issues so that we can end, once and for all, the conflict between us.

[...]

As we at the Palestinian Authority express our readiness to implement all of our Road Map obligations, we expect all other parties to implement theirs. It is not reasonable that only we are required to take action while settlements continue, or while the Wall expands within Palestinian land to separate Palestinian from Palestinian, and to destroy the livelihoods of hundreds of thousands of our people, or while closures, the siege, arrests, and other violations continue against our people, spreading despair, frustration, and loss of hope.

Today, it is up to the world to give our people hope, and it is up to the world not to repeat the same mistakes that sabotaged many initiatives and positive efforts in the past. In particular, I direct this call to all of the leaders of the Quartet members, and to all those committed to re-launching the peace process, and particularly to the US as the main player in this context.

[...]

Source: Mahmoud Abbas, "Inauguration of Palestinian President Mahmoud Abbas, 15 January, 2005," Electronic Intifada, http://electronicintifada.net/content/abbas-sworn-pa-president/1993.

Ariel Sharon, Speech at the United Nations Assembly [Excerpt], September 15, 2005

A few days after the completion of Israel's disengagement from Gaza, Prime Minister Ariel Sharon addressed the United Nations (UN). His speech was brief and somewhat unspecific but, particularly given his past record as a hardliner, was also relatively moderate and tactful. Recalling his lengthy career in the military, Sharon urged the Palestinians to seek "reconciliation and compromise" and "embark on the path which leads to peace and understanding between our people." Describing eloquently and emotionally just how much the territory of Israel meant to him personally and how difficult he would find it to relinquish any of its soil to others, he nonetheless declared that the Palestinians were "also entitled to freedom and to a national, sovereign existence in a state of their own." He called upon the Palestinians to end policies tolerating the use of terrorist tactics and the incitement of hatred against Israel. Sharon emphasized that Israel would defend itself in whatever ways were necessary and praised the security fence for its role in protecting Israelis and saving lives. He also stressed that he would not compromise on "the right of the State of Israel to exist as a Jewish state, with defensible borders, in full security and without threats and terror." Having established his hard-line credentials, however, he urged Palestinian leaders to seize the "window of opportunity" that implementation of the Disengagement Plan in Gaza now offered for resuming progress under the Road Map to Peace and working toward peace that would benefit both Palestinians and Israelis. Sharon's speech was tough but not bombastic in tone and, by making few specific demands or pledges, left room for maneuver on peace terms. Tactfully, he omitted any mention of the anarchy that broke out in Gaza immediately after the Israeli disengagement, even though this might have been used to cast doubt on Palestinian fitness for self-rule. He also forbore to complain that Hamas candidates were running for office in Palestinian elections even though, under the Oslo Accords, the party's opposition to making peace with Israel or accepting Israel's existence should have excluded it from the polls. Given his past record as a military hawk, Sharon might have had the credentials to move for a compromise peace settlement with the Palestinians and simply ride out conservative Israeli opposition to this. Already in his late seventies, he could act decisively and take risks for peace with few worries about the impact on his political future. In early January 2006, however, Sharon suffered a massive stroke that left him incapacitated, and after three months the Israeli cabinet declared him incompetent to continue in office. If a window of opportunity for Palestinian-Israeli peace genuinely existed, Sharon would not be the one to open it.

I, as someone whose path of life led him to be a fighter and commander in all Israel's wars, reach out today to our Palestinian neighbors in a call for reconciliation and compromise to end the bloody conflict, and embark on the path which leads to peace and understanding between our peoples. I view this as my calling and my primary mission for the coming years.

The land of Israel is precious to me, precious to us, the Jewish people, more than anything. Relinquishing any part of our forefathers' legacy is heartbreaking, as difficult as the parting of the Red Sea. Every inch of land, every hill and valley, every stream and rock, is saturated with Jewish history, replete with memories.

[. . .]

I say these things to you because they are the essence of my Jewish consciousness, and of my belief in the eternal and unimpeachable right of the people of Israel to the Land of Israel. However, I say this here also to emphasize the immensity of the pain I feel deep in my heart at the recognition that we have to make concessions for the sake of peace between us and our Palestinian neighbors.

The right of the Jewish people to the Land of Israel does not mean disregarding the rights of others in the land. The Palestinians will always be our neighbors. We respect them, and have no aspirations to rule over them. They are also entitled to freedom and to a national, sovereign existence in a state of their own.

This week, the last Israeli soldier left the Gaza Strip, and military law there was ended. The State of Israel proved that it is ready to make painful concessions in order to resolve the conflict with the Palestinians. The decision to disengage was very difficult for me, and involves a heavy personal price. However, it is the absolute recognition that it is the right path for the future of Israel that guided me. Israeli society is undergoing a difficult crisis as a result of the Disengagement, and now needs to heal the rifts.

Now it is the Palestinians' turn to prove their desire for peace. The end of Israeli control over and responsibility for the Gaza Strip allows the Palestinians, if they so wish, to develop their economy and build a peace-seeking society, which is developed, free, law-abiding, transparent, and which adheres to democratic principles. The most important test the Palestinian leadership will face is in fulfilling their commitment to put an end to terror and its infrastructures, eliminate the anarchic regime of armed gangs, and cease the incitement and indoctrination of hatred towards Israel and the Jews.

Until they do so—Israel will know how to defend itself from the horrors of terrorism. This is why we built the Security Fence, and we will continue to build it until it is completed, as would any other country defending its citizens. The Security Fence prevents terrorists and murderers from arriving in city centers on a daily basis and targeting citizens on their way to work, children on their way to school and families sitting together in restaurants. This Fence is vitally indispensable. This Fence saves lives!

The successful implementation of the Disengagement Plan opens up a window of opportunity for advancing towards peace, in accordance with the sequence of the Roadmap. The State of Israel is committed to the Roadmap and to the implementation of the Sharm El-Sheikh understandings. And I hope that it will be possible, through them, to renew the political process.

I am among those who believe that it is possible to reach a fair compromise and coexistence in good neighborly relations between Jews and Arabs. However, I must emphasize one fact: there will be *no* compromise on the right of the State of Israel to exist as a Jewish state, with defensible borders, in full security and without threats and terror.

I call on the Palestinian leadership to show determination and leadership, and to eliminate terror, violence and the culture of hatred from our relations. I am certain that it is in our power to present our peoples with a new and promising horizon, a horizon of hope.

[. . .]

Source: Ariel Sharon, "Statement of Israel, 2005 UN World Summit," United Nations, http://www.un.org/webcast/summit2005/statements15.html.

President Barack Obama, Address at Cairo University, June 4, 2009

During his presidential campaign, Barack Obama stated his intention, if he was elected, of reaching out to the Muslim world in a spirit of conciliation and partnership. In his early months in office the new president was preoccupied with immediate problems. In early June 2009, at Cairo University in Egypt, Obama finally delivered a major and much-anticipated comprehensive address on relations between the United States and the Muslim world. It included proposals for settling the Arab-Israeli conflict that followed the now traditional U.S. proposals of mutual acceptance and concessions on the part of both Israel and the Palestinians. Obama's address helped to win him the Nobel Peace Prize, but did little to defuse tensions between Israel and the Palestinians.

Remarks by the President on a New Beginning
Cairo University
Cairo, Egypt
PRESIDENT OBAMA:
The second major source of tension that we need to discuss is the situation between Israelis, Palestinians and the Arab world.

America's strong bonds with Israel are well known. This bond is unbreakable. It is based upon cultural and historical ties, and the recognition that the aspiration for a Jewish homeland is rooted in a tragic history that cannot be denied.

Around the world, the Jewish people were persecuted for centuries, and anti-Semitism in Europe culminated in an unprecedented Holocaust. Tomorrow, I will visit Buchenwald, which was part of a network of camps where Jews were enslaved, tortured, shot and gassed to death by the Third Reich. Six million Jews were killed—more than the entire Jewish population of Israel today. Denying that fact is baseless, it is ignorant, and it is hateful. Threatening Israel with destruction—or repeating vile stereotypes about Jews—is deeply wrong, and only serves to evoke in the minds of Israelis this most painful of memories while preventing the peace that the people of this region deserve.

On the other hand, it is also undeniable that the Palestinian people—Muslims and Christians—have suffered in pursuit of a homeland. For more than 60 years they've endured the pain of dislocation. Many wait in refugee camps in the West Bank, Gaza, and neighboring lands for a life of peace and security that they have never been able to lead. They endure the daily humiliations—large and small—that come with occupation. So let there be no doubt: The situation for the Palestinian people is intolerable. And America will not turn our backs on the legitimate Palestinian aspiration for dignity, opportunity, and a state of their own. [Applause.]

For decades then, there has been a stalemate: two peoples with legitimate aspirations, each with a painful history that makes compromise elusive. It's easy to point fingers—for Palestinians to point to the displacement brought about by Israel's founding, and for Israelis to point to the constant hostility and attacks throughout its history from within its borders as well as

beyond. But if we see this conflict only from one side or the other, then we will be blind to the truth: The only resolution is for the aspirations of both sides to be met through two states, where Israelis and Palestinians each live in peace and security. [Applause.]

That is in Israel's interest, Palestine's interest, America's interest, and the world's interest. And that is why I intend to personally pursue this outcome with all the patience and dedication that the task requires. [Applause.] The obligations—the obligations that the parties have agreed to under the road map are clear. For peace to come, it is time for them—and all of us— to live up to our responsibilities.

Palestinians must abandon violence. Resistance through violence and killing is wrong and it does not succeed. . . .

Now is the time for Palestinians to focus on what they can build. The Palestinian Authority must develop its capacity to govern, with institutions that serve the needs of its people. Hamas does have support among some Palestinians, but they also have to recognize they have responsibilities. To play a role in fulfilling Palestinian aspirations, to unify the Palestinian people, Hamas must put an end to violence, recognize past agreements, recognize Israel's right to exist.

At the same time, Israelis must acknowledge that just as Israel's right to exist cannot be denied, neither can Palestine's. The United States does not accept the legitimacy of continued Israeli settlements. [Applause.] This construction violates previous agreements and undermines efforts to achieve peace. It is time for these settlements to stop. [Applause.]

And Israel must also live up to its obligation to ensure that Palestinians can live and work and develop their society. Just as it devastates Palestinian families, the continuing humanitarian crisis in Gaza does not serve Israel's security; neither does the continuing lack of opportunity in the West Bank. Progress in the daily lives of the Palestinian people must be a critical part of a road to peace, and Israel must take concrete steps to enable such progress.

And finally, the Arab states must recognize that the Arab Peace Initiative was an important beginning, but not the end of their responsibilities. The Arab-Israeli conflict should no longer be used to distract the people of Arab nations from other problems. Instead, it must be a cause for action to help the Palestinian people develop the institutions that will sustain their state, to recognize Israel's legitimacy, and to choose progress over a self-defeating focus on the past.

America will align our policies with those who pursue peace, and we will say in public what we say in private to Israelis and Palestinians and Arabs. [Applause.] We cannot impose peace. But privately, many Muslims recognize that Israel will not go away. Likewise, many Israelis recognize the need for a Palestinian state. It is time for us to act on what everyone knows to be true.

Too many tears have been shed. Too much blood has been shed. All of us have a responsibility to work for the day when the mothers of Israelis and Palestinians can see their children grow up without fear; when the Holy Land of the three great faiths is the place of peace that God intended it to be; when Jerusalem is a secure and lasting home for Jews and Christians and Muslims, and a place for all of the children of Abraham to mingle peacefully together as in the story of Isra—[applause]—as in the story of Isra, when Moses, Jesus, and Mohammed, peace be upon them, joined in prayer.

Source: Barack Obama, "Remarks by the President on a New Beginning," The White House, http://www.whitehouse.gov/the_press_office/Remarks-by-the-President-at-Cairo-University-6–04–09/.

Palestinian National Authority, "Palestine: Ending the Occupation, Establishing the State," Program of the Thirteenth Government, August 23, 2009

In August 2009, Salem Fayyad, prime minister of the Palestinian National Authority, submitted a plan that envisaged the creation within two years of a fully independent Palestinian state, comprising both Gaza—then under Hamas rule—and the West Bank. The Fayyad plan envisaged a viable, "independent, progressive, democratic and modern Arab state" that would be characterized by liberal values and internal good governance, one that would have East Jerusalem as its capital. More than four years later, Fayyad's hopes had not yet been fulfilled. Hamas still controlled the Gaza Strip, which was increasingly run as a one-party, Islamic state, while the Palestinian National Authority held power in the West Bank. Given the effective partitioning of Palestinian territories, the United Nations had still to recognize an independent Palestinian state.

Foreword

This document presents the program of the 13th government of the Palestinian National Authority. The program, which sets out our national goals and government policies, centers around the objective of building strong state institutions capable of providing, equitably and effectively, for the needs of our citizens, despite the occupation. We believe that full commitment to this state-building endeavor will advance our highest national priority of ending the occupation, thereby enabling us to live in freedom and dignity in a country of our own.
[. . .]

Introduction

The supreme goal of the national liberation cause, led by the Palestine Liberation

Organization (PLO), the sole legitimate representative of the Palestinian people, is to end the occupation, establish a sovereign and independent state on the 1967 borders with Jerusalem as its capital, and reach a just and agreed solution for Palestinian refugees in accordance with relevant international resolutions, and UN General Assembly Resolution 194 in particular. The Palestinian Declaration of Independence of 1988, and the Oslo Declaration of Principles of 1993, affirmed the willingness of the Palestinian people to reach an historic compromise to end the occupation of the Palestinian territory since 1967, and secure Palestinian self-determination in an independent, sovereign state with Jerusalem as its capital. As the natural extension of the PLO, the Palestinian National Authority (PNA) is devoting all of its energy and capacity to realizing this national goal. Since 1993, we have made significant progress in building institutions to protect and serve our citizens. We have continued on this upward path in spite of the ongoing occupation, siege and military action against our people, including land confiscation, house demolitions, and military incursions. The path has been long and hard and the patience of our people has been sorely tested. Out of respect for our citizens, and in recognition of their desire to live free and peaceful lives under national independence, we must answer their demand to see the fruits of the state-building project. Against this background, the Palestinian government is struggling determinedly against a hostile occupation regime, employing all of its energies and available resources, most especially the capacities of our people, to complete the process of building institutions of the independent State of Palestine in order to establish a *de facto* state apparatus within the next two years. It is time now for the illegal occupation to end and for the Palestinian people to enjoy security, safety, freedom and independence.

The Government calls upon our people, including all political parties and civil society, to realize this fundamental objective and unite behind the state-building agenda over the next two years. We want to work in partnership with all our citizens to build the institutions of a free, democratic and stable State of Palestine that adheres to the principles of human rights and equality under the law, without discrimination on any grounds whatsoever. Together we must confront the whole world with the reality that Palestinians are united and steadfast in their determination to remain on their homeland, end the occupation, and achieve their freedom and independence. The world should hear loudly and clearly, from all corners of our society, that the occupation is the true impediment which has frustrated our efforts to realize the stability, prosperity and progress of our people and our right to freedom, independence and decent life. The world should also know that we are not prepared to continue living under a brutal occupation and siege that flouts not only the law, but also the principles of natural justice and human decency.

The window of opportunity to secure a viable two-state solution is now mortally threatened by Israel's settlement policy, the continuation of which will undermine the remaining opportunity of building an independent Palestinian State on the Palestinian territory occupied in 1967. The PNA therefore calls upon the people of Israel and their leaders, as well as leaders and citizens across the world, to ensure that a just peace prevails in the Middle East. This peace cannot be attained unless our people gain their national rights as defined by international resolutions including their right to live freely and decently in an independent state.

We are a partner for peace. Like all other peoples of the world, we aspire to live in peace, secure prosperity for our people, and bring stability to our region. But, like all peoples, we also seek justice. This cannot be achieved unless our people attain their legitimate, national rights as prescribed by international resolutions and implicit in the two-state solution. The PNA has made remarkable progress in establishing the rule of law and delivering public services under the occupation regime and in spite of the obstacles it has constructed. For its part Israel must immediately begin dismantling these obstacles, which undermine PNA's efforts. Israel must dismantle the infrastructure of the occupation and create the space for international efforts to reach a just and lasting peace.

Notwithstanding our people's suffering from Israel's policies and actions, the 13th Government is determined to dedicate efforts to building the Palestinian state. Based upon a Palestinian vision of the tasks that must be completed to build the State of Palestine, the Government hereby sets forth and communicates to our people, and all nations and friends in the international community, the basic principles of its program to translate this vision into a solid reality.

The establishment of a Palestinian state within two years is not only possible, it is essential. The establishment of this state is fundamental to security, stability and peace in the region. It will be a state that builds bridges with all the people of the world, not walls to deny them the joy of visiting this sacred land. It will be an emblem and protector of peace, tolerance and prosperity in this troubled region. Our Declaration of Independence, issued forth by the Palestinian National Council in 1988, called upon all peace-and-freedom-loving peoples and states to assist us in achieving our goal of an independent and sovereign Palestinian state. Twenty years on, we reiterate that call in anticipation of the good will and support of our Arab brethren and the international community of nations. We hope that they will continue to assist and support us to achieve this supreme goal.

Our Vision of the State of Palestine

Palestine is an independent Arab state with full sovereignty over the West Bank and the Gaza Strip on the 1967 borders, with Jerusalem as its capital. Palestine, the cradle of civilization and of the three monotheistic religions, will shine as a beacon of humanitarian values and religious tolerance across the world.

Palestine is a state which values highly its social capital, social cohesion and solidarity, and its Arab culture. The state will forever be a peace loving state that rejects violence; it is committed to peaceful co-existence with the world community of nations.

Palestine will be a stable democratic state with a multi-party political system. Transfer of governing authority is smooth, peaceful and regular in accordance with the will of the people, expressed through free and fair elections conducted in accordance with the law.

The state of Palestine respects human rights and guarantees equal rights and duties for all citizens. Its people live in safety and security under the rule of law, safeguarded by an independent judiciary and professional security services.

Source: United Nations Information System on the Question of Palestine, http://unispal.un.org /UNISPAL.NSF/0/A013B65A5984E6718525 76B800581931.

APPENDIX: HISTORICAL DILEMMAS IN THE ARAB-ISRAELI CONFLICT

A Right to Palestine

How Has the Debate over the "Right" to Palestine Shaped the Arab-Israeli Conflict?

Since the beginning of the 20th century, tensions have existed between the Arab and Jewish populations living in the area once known as Palestine. This turmoil grew into full-scale warfare with Israel's declaration of independence on May 14, 1948. But rather than conclusively ending the conflict, the Israeli War of Independence only deepened both sides' determination and added a new dimension to hostilities—hundreds of thousands of Palestinian Arabs were now refugees. Since that time, mutual distrust and incendiary rhetoric and actions on both sides have created an Arab-Israeli conflict that is both complex and deeply emotional for all involved. With the establishment of a cooperative peace proving extremely difficult, the debate on Palestine has frequently turned to the question of which side—Arab or Jewish—has the greater claim to the area.

The perspectives that follow explore this issue from two very different perspectives. In the first essay, Dr. Sherifa Zuhur posits that Palestinians—a group that includes Muslims, Christians, and some Jews—have a claim to land in Palestine based on historical precedent and continuous ownership. She argues that the Israelis, by contrast, gained territory through conquest and the illegal seizure of land and property legitimately owned by Palestinians. The territorial ambitions of Israel during subsequent wars and the nation's continued unwillingness to recognize the legitimacy of Palestinian claims and even a Palestinian identity have fueled the ongoing Arab-Israeli conflict. In the second perspective, Dr. David Tal asserts that, as the birthplace of the Jewish identity and the site of its first religious and political institutions, Eretz Israel (the Land of Israel) continued to serve as a spiritual anchor for the world's Jewish population even after the Diaspora. Tal points out that with the birth of the modern nation-state and anti-Semitism, it was only logical that Zionists would turn to Palestine to fulfill their desire for self-determination and safety within the modern world.

Perspective 1: Palestinian Rights to Their Land, Property, and National Sovereignty

The Palestinians can trace their ancestry back to the ancient Canaanites referred to in the Old Testament, who predated the Hebrew tribes in the land of Canaan. They are also descended from other groups that invaded or settled Palestine and intermarried with the inhabitants. The Palestinian common identity was based on continuous tenure and residence in the territory of Palestine. Palestinians, who were not allowed to identify themselves by this name and were simply dubbed "Arabs" by the Israeli government, may be Muslims, Christian, or Druze (who consider themselves Muslim). Under the Palestinian definition of national identity, the members of the small Jewish community that was able to return to Jerusalem in ancient times and resided there prior to World War I are also considered Palestinian, like their Muslim and Christian counterparts. However, the many Jews who traveled to and settled in Palestine as part of the work of Zionist organizations were not natives of this land.

Palestinians' claim to their land and property is religious as well as historic. Palestine contains many places holy to Muslims and Druze, including the tombs of various holy and historic Muslim figures. Palestinians, who cannot move freely around historic Palestine, are denied access to many sites, including the tomb of Abu Huraira, while others are closed. Some, such as the tomb of the prophet Abraham (from whom Muslims, like Jews, claim descent), are shared and uneasily used by the two religious groups. No place is more sacred in Palestine to Muslims than Jerusalem. From there, the Prophet Muhammad ascended to visit Heaven, and subsequent Muslim Umayyad rulers who conquered the city in the seventh century established the Dome of the Rock and al-Aqsa Mosques on that site. Palestinians were denied control of this area, known as the Haram al-Sharif, until the signing of the 1993 Oslo Accords, and their legal control over the walkway leading to the Wailing Wall, which was a religious endowment, was wrested from them. To Palestinian Christians, the Via Dolorosa, down which Jesus walked to his crucifixion at Golgotha; his birthplace in Bethlehem; the site of Mary's annunciation in Nazareth; and

various locations near the Sea of Galilee are all sacred. In addition to homes, farms, and land, many other public areas of Palestine were legally owned by Palestinians (and, in some cases, other Arab Muslims) as *waqf*, or endowed properties created for religious purposes. These endowments were never supposed to be claimed or appropriated by governments, yet were seized and administered by Israeli officials and councils.

Israel, which accords full citizenship rights only to Jews, claimed rights to Palestine through conquest: first in 1948, and then through occupation of the West Bank and Gaza after 1967. A constant, multidimensional policy of illegal land appropriations has negatively impacted Palestinians. The Palestinians who fled their properties in terror after the massacre at Deir Yassin in April 1948 or who were physically forced out of their neighborhoods and villages retained keys and deeds to their properties and lands, yet they were never allowed to return, despite legal judgments in their favor. Additional lands were systematically taken from the Palestinians by military force, military law, and other forms of appropriation. These actions followed decades of Zionist efforts during the British Mandate period to acquire lands possessed by absentee landlords. Other methods included Israeli seizure of peasants' land held in a legal form of collective tenure and of lands irregularly registered or not occupied, continuously tilled, or belonging to the many large Bedouin tribes. While Palestinians were forced into a diaspora by the state of Israel and never permitted to return, under the 1951 Law of Return any Jew in the world—even some of dubious religious background—could claim Israeli citizenship and rights superior to those of Palestinians. Meanwhile, Palestinian refugees remained in a nebulous legal status, unable to return to their lands and prevented from becoming citizens of

Arab states (a policy intended to bolster their legal rights to their own land). This situation persisted even after Israel signed the Oslo Accords. Thus far, Israelis have not acknowledged the right of any Palestinian, even UN-registered refugees, to return to their lands, even in symbolic or token numbers. Nor have they considered providing reparations. In sum, the Palestinians' claim to their own land and to national sovereignty is based on history, religious claims, international law, and, notably, continuous tenure.

The disposition of the so-called Jewish Question—the plight of Jews in Europe who were discriminated against and subjected to pogroms and genocide under Adolf Hitler—was "solved" by creating an enormous humanitarian problem. A Jewish diaspora should not have been replaced with a Palestinian one. The British recognized this dilemma, as did the United Nations (UN). The British supported the Zionists' quest for a homeland, but stipulated that this should not be at the expense of the native inhabitants of Palestine. They noted the unequal resources of the Zionists as compared to the increasingly poorly developed Palestinian areas and tried to limit Jewish immigration. The UN proposed a partition that neither side would agree to. Then, during the 1948 war (known as "the Catastrophe" among Palestinians), Jewish military forces depopulated many areas of historic Palestine and subsequently focused on obtaining territories and property in other key areas. A series of UN resolutions declared the illegality of Israeli actions, particularly during the 1967 Six-Day War, when Israel seized control of the West Bank from Jordan, Gaza from Egypt, and the Golan Heights from Syria. Palestinian despair over the situation, coupled with the treatment they received from Israel, was the cause of terrorist activities in the late 1960s and 1970s, political organizing toward diplomatic efforts

after 1974, popular uprisings in the First and Second (al-Aqsa) Intifadas, and suicide attacks and factional violence between Palestinian factions. Palestinians have been imprisoned in huge numbers for political activities, which has only embittered them or hardened their resolve to seek justice.

The crystallizing of modern Palestinian identity—recognizable in dialect, music, and historic and contemporary cultural output, owes much to the national crisis. Certain Israelis have refused to recognize any separate Palestinian identity because this would support the latter's national claim. Yet Palestinian identity has become ever more distinct as refugees struggle to survive and as Palestinians in Israel and the Occupied Territories are increasingly cut off from contact with the Arab world.

Sherifa Zuhur

Perspective 2: The Jewish People's Historical Right to Palestine

The Jewish people became a nation about 3,000 years ago in the area on the eastern shores of the Mediterranean they called Eretz Israel, the Land of Israel, also known as Palestine. It was in the Land of Israel that the Jews created and developed their unique identity. That identity was based on their adherence to monotheism and Judaism, which led spiritually to the composition of the Bible and politically to the creation of their own national institutions. These materialized around the two temples built in Jerusalem, the first by King Solomon and the second by those who returned from Babylon.

Jerusalem and the temples were the spiritual center of the ancient Kingdoms of Judah and the modern Israel. The first temple was destroyed by Nebuchadnezzar in 586 BC, and many Jews were exiled to Babylon. Seventy years later, the Persian king Cyrus the Great permitted exiled Jews to restore the temple, and later a Jewish independent entity was recreated. Between the years 66 BCE and 130 CE, generals of the Roman Empire were engaged in fighting against the Jews. In the year 70 BC, the Romans destroyed the Jewish temple and forced tens of thousands of Jews to leave the country. The Bar Kokhba Revolt (132–135 CE) led to the final Roman offensive against the Jews. With the defeat of the rebels, the Romans reduced Jerusalem to shambles. Wishing to completely obliterate the Jewish entity, an atypical act on their part, the Romans renamed Jerusalem Aelia Capitolina and called the rest of the country Syria-Palestine after the Philistines, a tribe that lived to the south along the coast.

The attempts to erase the Jewish identity, however, failed. Judaism had had a strong territorial dimension, but with the loss of their homeland the Jews transformed, now basing their identity on spirituality. They made religion alone the center of their lives, while Eretz Israel became a source of spiritual longing. For centuries, Jewish communities maintained their identity through adherence to their ancient texts and traditions, praying the same prayers in the same language and thereby preserving the memory of their homeland.

Resorting to spiritualism allowed the Jews to preserve their identity even without having their own homeland. For centuries, a certain political reality made such an existence in foreign territories possible. Even when they were subjected to persecution as the result of varying degrees of anti-Jewish sentiment (particularly prevalent in the Christian world), the nature of medieval and early-modern political institutions enabled Jews to live among non-Jews. Two major developments, however, forced the Jews to reevaluate their position. The first was the

emergence of the modern nation-state and the second was the emergence of modern anti-Semitism.

In a process that had begun in the 16th century in Western Europe and had reached its peak in the 19th century, a new sociopolitical structure and ideology had emerged, the modern nation and nationalism. The emerging centralized and bureaucratic nation-state became a source of identity for the people living within its boundaries, giving rise to the concept of nationalism. Concurrently, a new form of hatred toward Jews emerged, one that was based on pseudo-science. Modern anti-Semitism presupposed that people could be divided along racial lines and that Jews were a distinct race, rather than the bearers of a common religion.

These two developments had a major effect on Jewish history in several ways. It was no longer possible to keep the rigid and exclusive social structure that had characterized Jewish communities since the departure into exile. The modern bureaucratic nation-state undermined the authority of Jewish leaders (rabbis), as did the growing urbanization of the modern industrialized nation. It became harder and harder to maintain the tight structure of the Jewish community, but the alternative proved to be just as difficult. While some Jews resisted the trends of change and tried to adhere to their traditional ways of life, others tried to assimilate through the abandonment of the unique characteristics of Jewish communal life. This latter course of action gave rise to the expression "be a Jew in your home and a man in the street." Both choices proved problematic. Attempts to maintain the Jewish social structure in Central and Eastern Europe were stymied by the growing power of bureaucratic states. Anti-Semitism proved to be a major obstacle preventing assimilation, as evidenced by events such as the pogroms in czarist Russia during the second half of the

19th century and the Dreyfus Affair in France during the 1890s.

One reaction to this state of affairs was the emergence of Zionism. Because nationalism and the nation-state had become the proper, and only, way for people with a common history and heritage to live their lives in the 19th- and early 20th-century world, it was only natural for the Zionists to endorse this same path as a means to solve "the Jewish Problem." Through the League of Nations, the international community endorsed the Zionist solution and acknowledged the Jewish right to self-determination.

The natural place for the Zionists to actualize their dream of self-determination was the Land of Israel, the place where Jews had first lived as an independent people. Following the dismemberment of the multinational Ottoman Empire after World War I and the British occupation of the region in 1917, the Zionist movement sought to materialize Jewish spiritualism. Palestine was defined as being res nullius, without a ruler, and the League of Nations provided the British Empire with a mandate over the area, commissioning it with the task of helping the Jews build their national home in Palestine.

The Jewish right to Palestine is thus based on Jewish history. The Jews became a nation in the Land of Israel, long before the modern term was known. Although forced into exile, the Jews had never spiritually abandoned their homeland. The history of the Jews and of the Land of Israel converged again with the rise of nationalism and the concept of self-determination. With the approval and support of the international community, Jews could once again live as an independent and free people in the place where they first formed their unique identity and established their political and religious institutions.

David Tal

Print Resources

Aruri, Naseer Hasan, ed. *Palestinian Refugees: The Right of Return*. London: Pluto, 2001.

Ateek, Naim, Hilary Rantisi, and Kent Wilkens. *Our Story: The Palestinians*. Jerusalem: Sabeel Ecumenical Liberation Theology Center, 2000.

Ayaad, Abdelaziz A. *Arab Nationalism and the Palestinians, 1850–1939*. Jerusalem: PASSIA, 1999.

Cohen, Aharon. *Israel and the Arab World*. New York: Funk and Wagnalls, 1970.

Dowty, Alan. *Israel/Palestine*. Malden, MA: Polity, 2005.

Ginat, Joseph, Edward J. Perkins, and Hassan bin Talal, eds. *Palestinian Refugees: Traditional Positions and New Solutions*. Norman: University of Oklahoma Press, 2002.

Harris, Ron. *The History of Law in a Multi-Cultural Society: Israel 1917–1967*. Aldershot, UK: Ashgate, 2002.

Hertzberg, Arthur, ed. *The Zionist Idea: A Historical Analysis and Reader*. Philadelphia, PA: Jewish Publication Society, 1997.

Pappé, Ilan. *A History of Modern Palestine: One Land, Two Peoples*. Cambridge: Cambridge University Press, 2003.

Smith, Charles D. *Palestine and the Arab-Israeli Conflict: A History with Documents*. 8th ed. New York: Bedford/St. Martin's Press, 2012.

United Nations. *The Right of Return of the Palestinian People*. New York: United Nations, 1979.

U.S. Support of Israel

How Has U.S. Support of Israel Played a Key Role in Ensuring the Existence of the Jewish State?

The United States' commitment to Israel is a long and often complex one. From its support of early Zionists to the sale of weapons to the brokering of peace agreements, the United States has helped to influence the course of events in the Middle East for more than half a century. It has acted both through its own foreign policies and by influencing other nations and organizations. As Israel's closest ally, it has helped the small nation prosper. Critics have argued, however, that this support has only helped to exacerbate the Arab-Israeli conflict. Others have suggested that the United States' reasons for supporting Israel have not always been as straightforward as they might appear.

In the two defining moments that follow, Dr. Larry Simpson examines two critical moments during the Arab-Israeli conflict in which the United States has played a major role. The first, President Harry S. Truman's support for the formation of the State of Israel, helped ensure the creation of a homeland in Palestine for the Jewish people. Israel's declaration of statehood, however, immediately triggered the first of a number of conflicts between that nation and its Arab neighbors. In the second defining moment, Dr. Simpson explores the nature of U.S.

involvement in the 1973 Yom Kippur War. This involvement included both the sale of weapons to the embattled Israelis and, later, efforts by President Richard Nixon and Henry Kissinger to negotiate peace. These essays shed light on both how and why the United States has aided Israel over the years.

Defining Moment 1: Harry Truman's Recognition of Israel

On May 14, 1948, Israel came into being. Eleven minutes after the Zionist leader, David Ben-Gurion, proclaimed its creation, the United States became the first country in the world to extend de facto recognition to the new Jewish state. The catalyst behind these events was U.S. president Harry Truman, without whom these dramatic events likely would never have occurred.

Before 1948, the lands that would become Israel were part of British-ruled Palestine. The United Kingdom had conquered the area during World War I and had encouraged Jews to establish a homeland in Palestine as part of the 1917 Balfour Declaration. Conflict soon arose, however, between the indigenous Arab population and the Jewish community. There were sporadic and escalating incidents of violence between the two subject groups that eventually culminated in a civil war that lasted from 1936 to 1939. On the eve of World

War II, British authorities yielded to Arab demands to restrict Jewish immigration and land acquisitions, and Palestine remained relatively quiet during the ensuing global conflict. Yet as World War II neared its end, Zionist underground troops waged a campaign of assassinations and bombings directed mainly at British officials, and the conflict again spun out of control. Zionists demanded that survivors of Adolf Hitler's Final Solution be permitted to go to Israel while London sought to uphold immigration restrictions in the face of strong Arab opposition to the influx of Jews.

With this background, Truman intervened on the side of the Zionists. Truman, who was sympathetic to the plight of European Jewry and Zionist determination but also concerned to maintain the political support of U.S. Jews, called for the immediate entry of 100,000 displaced Jews into Palestine. While there was bipartisan support for the Zionists in the U.S. Congress, the U.S. foreign policy establishment proved more reluctant to back Zionist aspirations, especially for the establishment of a Jewish state. Officials at the State Department and War Department in particular were concerned about alienating the Arabs of the Middle East and thus destabilizing the region. As the Cold War developed and the United States moved into confrontation with the Soviet Union, there was fear that the Soviets would exploit an important geopolitical area that held huge petroleum reserves that were important to Europe's and Washington's strategic interests. Support for the Zionists also undermined Anglo-American relations as the British had to deal with the difficult problem of Palestine. Indeed, Truman's support of Jewish immigration into Palestine led a frustrated Ernest Bevin, Great Britain's foreign secretary, to wonder aloud whether the U.S. president favored this policy in order to keep too many Jews from entering New York.

Ultimately, policy makers in London and Washington tried to put their differences aside and come up with a solution to the issue of Palestine's future. They organized a Joint Anglo-American Commission of Inquiry that unanimously recommended the admission of the displaced persons at once as well as the creation of a binational state under international supervision. When that plan foundered, the two Western powers created the Morrison–Grady Commission to address the intractable problem. This second group proposed the establishment of a single, federated Arab-Jewish state. Truman at first seemed inclined to go along with this recommendation, but then changed his mind when faced with intense lobbying by pro-Zionist groups. Just before midterm Congressional elections in October 1946 and on the eve of the Yom Kippur holiday, the president expressed support for a Jewish state, and thus torpedoed the compromise. Following a failed London Conference in January 1947, the British government, which had held Palestine under a League of Nations mandate, decided to turn the problem over to the United Nations (UN).

While it was the international body that gave legal sanction for the creation of Israel, it was Truman who made it happen. Following a fact-finding investigation into the Palestine issue by the UN Special Commission on Palestine, a majority plan recommended the partition of Palestine into an Arab state, a Jewish one, and an area to be administered by the UN. As the General Assembly considered Resolution 181, which would create the Jewish state, U.S. officials pressured several small countries into supporting the measure and helped it garner the necessary two-thirds vote required for its adoption in November 1947. Then, as Palestine lurched into civil war between Arabs and Jews, it was Truman who stayed the course against State Department recommendations to support a temporary UN trusteeship over the disputed land. While Washington would honor a UN arms embargo and leave it to the fledgling Jewish state to overcome the internal resistance and invasion by neighboring states, Truman would extend de jure recognition to Israel at the cessation of the first Arab-Israeli war in 1949.

Larry Simpson

Defining Moment 2: Watergate and the Yom Kippur War

In October 1973, U.S. president Richard Nixon faced two crises. In the Middle East, Egyptian and Syrian forces had on October 6 surprised the Israelis as well as U.S. intelligence services and launched a major war. Meanwhile, back in the United States, a beleaguered Nixon administration was embroiled in the Watergate scandal that would eventually bring about the president's fall.

The first days of fighting in the Yom Kippur War, as the conflict was known since the Arabs attacked on the Jewish Day of Atonement, went very badly for the Israelis. The Egyptians successfully crossed the Suez Canal, overwhelmed Israeli defensive positions along the Bar-Lev line, and repelled Israeli counterattacks while Syrian armor penetrated the Golan Heights and appeared poised to strike into the heart of Israel. The Israelis suffered staggering losses in men and equipment. While Moscow began to resupply its Arab surrogates on the 10th, the Nixon administration faced a crisis at home as Vice President Spiro Agnew was forced to resign from office after pleading nolo contendere on charges of tax evasion from the time he was governor of Maryland. The United States ultimately did rearm the

Israelis in an operation larger than the entire Berlin Airlift. Although the weapons arrived too late to be employed in the actual fighting, their imminent arrival allowed the Israelis to free up their last reserves and so turn the tide in the war.

Yet, one week into the war, the outcome was definitely uncertain. While the Israelis managed to overcome the Syrians by the 12th, Egypt still had the initiative in the Sinai. That changed when the Israelis repulsed a major Egyptian offensive two days later. On the 16th, the tables were turned on the Egyptians when Ariel Sharon led an armor column across the Suez Canal and threatened to envelop the Third Egyptian Army. In the next few days, oil-rich Arab countries came to the aid of the Syrians and Egyptians by curtailing petroleum production and imposing an embargo on Israel's supporters. With that as background, Nixon's secretary of state, Henry Kissinger, flew to Moscow on the 20th to arrange a cease-fire.

Complicating matters, however, were events associated with Watergate. While Kissinger was beginning delicate negotiations with the Soviet leaders, Attorney General Elliot Richardson resigned from office after refusing to dismiss Archibald Cox, the Watergate special prosecutor, on Nixon's orders. Nixon managed to remove Cox in what became known as the "Saturday Night Massacre," but at the cost of appearing to be trying to obstruct justice. Perhaps seeing a chance for immediate redemption, Nixon sent a note to Kissinger telling him to seek a comprehensive Middle East settlement with Moscow. A distraught Kissinger felt that the president's orders were overly restricting and that they ran counter to the U.S. objective of denying Soviet influence in the Middle East.

Soviet leader Leonid Brezhnev might have exploited the opening that Nixon gave him had it not been for the fact that while negotiations continued, the Israelis were completing the encirclement of the Third Army. Thus, Washington and Moscow agreed to a cease-fire in place and the Soviets accepted the U.S. terms for what would eventually become United Nations Resolution 338 on the 22nd. While fighting continued and the situation almost got out of control when the Soviets considered intervening in the conflict, the war finally came to an end on October 28, 1973. In the meantime, domestic U.S. political considerations had nearly brought about a much different conclusion to the Arab-Israeli war.

Larry Simpson

Print Resources

Christison, Kathleen. *Perceptions of Palestine: Their Influence on U.S. Middle East Policy.* Berkeley: University of California Press, 1999.

Davidson, Lawrence. *America's Palestine: Patterns of Popular and Official Perceptions, 1917–1948.* Gainesville: University Press of Florida, 2001.

Dowty, Alan. *Middle East Crisis: U.S. Decision-Making in 1958, 1970, and 1973.* Berkeley, University of California Press, 1984.

Neff, Donald. *Fallen Pillars: U.S. Policy towards Palestine and Israel since 1945.* Washington, DC: The Institute for Palestine Studies, 1995.

Shadid, Mohammed Khalil. *The United States and the Palestinians.* New York: St. Martin's Press, 1981.

Slonim, Shlomo. *Jerusalem in America's Foreign Policy, 1947–1997.* The Hague: Kluwer Law International, 1998.

Suleiman, Michael W., ed. *U.S. Policy on Palestine from Wilson to Clinton.* Normal, IL: AAUG Press, 1994.

United States. Congress House Committee on Appropriations. Department of Defense Appropriations for 1975: Part 1, Hearing. 93rd Congress, 2nd session. Washington, DC: Government Printing Office, 1974.

United States. Public Papers of President Richard Nixon. Special Message to the Congress Requesting Emergency Security Assistance Funding for Israel and Cambodia. Washington, DC: Government Printing Office, 1973.

Wilson, Evan M. *Decision on Palestine: How the U.S. Came to Recognize Israel.* Stanford, CA: Hoover Institution, 1979.

Military Maneuvers

How Did the Israeli and Egyptian Militaries Try to Get the Upper Hand in the Ongoing Arab-Israeli Conflict?

Since the Arab-Israeli conflict began with Israel's declaration of independence in 1948, both the Jewish state and its Arab neighbors have both been both the perpetrators and the victims of military attacks. Although each side has in certain cases sought to end periods of fighting through diplomatic means, each has also used deception and extensive military planning to lull the other side into a false sense of security. And, during times of relative peace, all the major players in this conflict have worked to maneuver themselves for maximum advantage in preparation for a resumption of hostilities, which many see as inevitable.

In the two defining moments that follow, Dr. Larry Simpson analyzes two key events in the ongoing conflict between the Arab nations and Israel, seeking to explain how each side has sought to militarily gain the upper hand in this long series of wars. In the first essay, he highlights Israel's stunning success in the early hours of the June 1967 Six-Day War. Through careful planning, the Israeli air force (IAF) was able to essentially destroy the Egyptian air force in a surprise attack. In the second essay, Dr. Simpson discusses Operation BADR, the Egyptian crossing of the Suez Canal, at the beginning

of the 1973 Yom Kippur War. Like Operation FOCUS, the Egyptian attack was the result of extensive planning and coordination. Although eventually defeated, the Egyptians and their Syrian allies achieved stunning victories at the beginning of the war. These successes helped dispel the myth of Israeli military invulnerability.

Defining Moment 1: Operation FOCUS and the Six-Day War

On the morning of June 5, 1967, the Israeli air force (IAF) achieved one of the most stunning successes in modern warfare. In a mere three hours, the Israelis achieved air superiority by destroying the Egyptian air force on the ground in what was truly an unparalleled victory. The first two waves against Egypt were followed by sorties against targets in Syria, Jordan, and western Iraq. All told, the IAF plan, designated Operation FOCUS ("Moked" in Hebrew), resulted in the loss of 450 Arab aircraft. Its brilliant execution ensured that there would be no challenge to Israel's ground forces from the air during the six days of fighting that followed.

Operation FOCUS was the result of years of preparation. It relied on up-to-date and precise intelligence. The plan envisioned carrying out a first-strike maneuver against Egypt, the most formidable of Israel's foes, in which IAF fighters would take off from airfields all over

Israel and fly at very low altitude while under radio silence to targets in the Sinai and east of the Suez Canal. The goal was to remain undetected until the last moment, at which time the Israeli aircraft would suddenly gain altitude and execute their missions. Rather than attacking at dawn, the IAF waited until the Egyptian pilots had returned to base from their morning patrols and were having breakfast. The Israelis chose to attack the Egyptians from the north and west, rather than flying directly to their targets from the east as their enemies expected. IAF planes would first bomb runways, leaving them cratered and thus unusable. The pilots would then turn to bombing and strafing the Egyptian aircraft to destroy as many as possible on the ground.

The IAF pilots, who were among the best in the world, were very well trained for this mission, and each squadron knew its particular objectives by heart. The operation was complex and required intricate coordination based on an excellent system of command and control. Moreover, IAF ground crews also practiced their jobs repeatedly so that they were able to reduce turnaround time between each wave and get fighters aloft as quickly as possible. Finally, Operation FOCUS was bold. The IAF would send 170 high-performance aircraft against Egypt in the first wave, leaving only a dozen fighters behind to fly combat air patrols in defense of the homeland.

The IAF achieved complete tactical surprise even in the midst of a protracted prewar crisis. The Arab militaries were mobilized and in a state of high readiness, yet they were caught unprepared when the Israelis struck. The first wave of IAF planes struck 11 Egyptian airfields and rendered most of them unserviceable. It destroyed 189 aircraft, or nearly half of the Egyptian inventory, while losing only 10 of its own. With the destruction of other Egyptian airfields and more than 100 additional aircraft

(with the loss of only a single Israeli fighter) in the second wave, the IAF removed any aerial threat from Egypt. Two additional waves targeted airfields in Jordan, Syria, and western Iraq and also had great success in crippling the Arab air forces while losing just six more IAF planes. After the first day of battle and the brilliant success of Operation FOCUS, the IAF could concentrate on close air support and other missions in support of Israel's ground forces.

Larry Simpson

Defining Moment 2: Operation BADR and the Yom Kippur War

When Egypt attacked Israel just after noon on October 6, 1973, it caught the Israelis almost completely by surprise. While Egyptian president Anwar Sadat had declared 1973 "the year of decision" and had threatened to invade Israel if it did not return the lands it had taken during the Six-Day War, he had done so before in 1971 and 1972 as well. Thus, the overly self-confident Israelis were lulled into a false sense of security. The Israel Defense Forces (IDF) had weathered Egyptian artillery barrages during the War of Attrition and felt safe behind the Bar-Lev Line, which consisted of a series of 17 maozim, or strong points, manned by 500 troops along the eastern side of the Suez Canal. That illusion would vanish on Yom Kippur, the holiest day of the year for Jews, with the Egyptian attack, coordinated with the Syrians far to the northeast in the Golan Heights.

Egyptian military objectives fit well with Sadat's desire to gain a limited victory and negotiate with the Israelis from a position of strength. The Egyptian plan, codenamed Operation BADR, was the work of Egyptian minister of war General Ahmed Ismail and his chief of staff, General Saad El Shazly. Rather than seeking the destruction of Israel, they well understood the limitations of the Egyptian military and therefore opted for a radical change in objectives by seeking only what was deemed obtainable. The idea was to cross the Suez Canal, overwhelm IDF positions on the east bank with a force of 80,000 soldiers, advance 10 to 15 kilometers to a low ridgeline, and then stop and prepare a line of defenses to withstand Israeli counterattacks. As the Egyptians and their allies had the advantage of numbers, they hoped to draw the Israelis into a war of attrition that would wear down their enemy and force a peace dictated by Cairo.

The Egyptian generals planned Operation BADR down to the minutest detail. They chose to attack when they would have long hours of moonlight and when the waters in the canal would be at their calmest. The offensive would begin not only when the Israelis were celebrating a holiday, but during the propitious Muslim month of Ramadan. The Egyptians employed deception as well. Egyptian "sources" spread disinformation about Arab disunity and about problems with the surface-to-air missiles (SAMs) purchased from the Soviet Union. These missiles were critical, as a mass of SAM batteries would provide a missile umbrella that would counter the threat posed to Egypt's exposed ground forces by the Israeli air force (IAF). The Egyptians managed to hide their mass mobilization for the invasion behind seemingly routine military exercises. They borrowed Soviet techniques to allow their engineers to rapidly construct a series of bridges across the canal. Then, the Egyptians used fire hoses attached to powerful water pumps to punch large holes through the sand dunes on the Israeli side so as to allow armor thrusts into Israeli territory. Finally, they purchased Sagger antitank missiles and trained their soldiers well using these to repel IDF armor attacks.

The result of this intense preparation was a brilliant opening to the Yom Kippur War. During the first two days of the conflict, the Egyptians scored stunning successes while the Israelis suffered serious losses. The Egyptian Army overwhelmed the Bar-Lev Line, inflicted heavy casualties on Israeli ground forces, destroyed many tanks, and shot down many of the Israeli aircraft that came to support the beleaguered IDF troops on the east bank of the Suez Canal. Only when the Egyptians tried to advance beyond their SAM umbrella and when sufficient numbers of Israeli reserves arrived in the Sinai did the tide of battle change in Israel's favor.

Larry Simpson

Print Resources

Adan, Avraham. *On the Banks of the Suez: An Israeli General's Personal Account of the Yom Kippur War*. San Rafael, CA: Presidio Press, 1980.

Bickerton, Ian J., and Carla L. Klausner. *A Concise History of the Arab-Israeli Conflict*. 6th ed. Upper Saddle River, NJ: Prentice Hall, 2009.

Bregman, Ahron. *Israel's Wars: A History since 1947*. 3rd ed. London: Routledge, 2010.

Friedman, Thomas L. *From Beirut to Jerusalem*. New York: Anchor, 1990.

Herzog, Chaim. *The Arab-Israeli Wars: War and Peace in the Middle East*. New York: Random House, 1982.

Morris, Benny. *Righteous Victims: A History of the Zionist-Arab Conflict, 1881–2001*. New York: Vintage Books, 2002.

Oren, Michael B. *Six Days of War: June 1967 and the Making of the Modern Middle East*. New York: Oxford University Press, 2002.

Pollack, Kenneth M. *Arabs at War: Military Effectiveness, 1948–1991*. Lincoln: University of Nebraska Press, 2002.

Schiff, Zeev. *A History of the Israeli Army: 1874 to the Present*. New York: Macmillan, 1985.

Smith, Charles D. *Palestine and the Arab-Israeli Conflict: A History with Documents*. 8th ed. New York: Bedford/St. Martin's Press, 2012.

Chronology

3300–1550 BC Early and Middle Canaanite Periods. Semitic-speaking Canaanites come from the area of present-day Lebanon, although other groups also settle in the area of Palestine, including those possibly from the Arabian Peninsula.

1240–1200 BC The Twelve Tribes of Israel under the leadership of Joshua conquer Canaan after wandering for 40 years following their escape from Egyptian bondage, as described in the Book of Exodus.

1180–1150 BC About the time of the Twelve Tribes' conquest of Canaan, the ancient Philistines also conquer the southern coast and adopt Canaanite culture. One theory is that the Philistines were one of the groups known as the Sea People.

539 BC King Cyrus the Great of Persia conquers the Babylonians and allows a small group of Jews to return to Judah and rebuild Jerusalem.

521 BC King Darius I of Persia allows the construction of the Second Temple under the prophets Haggai and Zechariah. Ezra restores the temple rituals, while Nehemiah, the cup-bearer to Artaxerxes I, returns to Jerusalem and rebuilds the walls of Jerusalem.

333 BC Alexander the Great of Macedonia conquers Persia, bringing Palestine under Greek rule.

142–63 BC A Jewish state is established under the Hasmonean dynasty and expands into Samaria, Galilee, Idumea, and the lands beyond the Jordan River.

63 BC The Romans under Pompey the Great conquer Judah, overthrow the Hasmonean dynasty, and rename the area Judea.

AD 26–36   The Romans consolidate their rule over the eastern Mediterranean. Caesarea is made the capital of Syria under the control of the governor Quirinius. Pontius Pilate serves as procurator of Judea and presides over the crucifixion of Jesus Christ.

41–44   The Roman emperor Claudius appoints Herod Agrippa I as king of the Jews. On his death in 44, Herod Agrippa II becomes king of the Jews.

66–73   The First Jewish Revolt takes place. The Romans under Vespasian destroy Jerusalem and the Second Temple in AD 70 after a 134-day siege. The last pocket of Jewish resistance ends in the stronghold of Masada in AD 73. The crushing of the revolt results in the Second Diaspora of the Jews. There would not be another Jewish state until the mid-20th century.

132–135   The Romans crush the Simon Bar Kokhba Revolt. The Jewish population is evicted from Jerusalem, which is reconstructed as a pagan city and renamed Aelia Capitolina. Judea is renamed Palaestina. More of the Jewish population is dispersed throughout the Roman Empire.

312   Emperor Constantine converts to Christianity. He allows the Jews to visit Jerusalem and mark the anniversary of the destruction of the Temple.

361–363   Emperor Flavius Claudius Julianus, known as Julian the Apostate, allows the Jews to resettle in Jerusalem.

622   The Prophet Muhammad flees from Mecca to Medina in the Hegira, or emigration, that marks the official beginning of Islam.

637   Khalid ibn Walid, Muslim general of the Umayyad caliph Umar ibn Khattab, conquers Jerusalem.

640–647   Palestine, a district of Syria, is controlled by the Umayyad caliphate until the Abbasid Revolution (747–750).

750–878   Palestine is under the Abbasid caliphate.

878–969   The Tulunid and Ilkhshid dynasties rule Palestine.

970–972   Until 1073, the Fatimid dynasty, whose rulers were Shia Muslims, rule Palestine from Egypt.

1071   The Seljuk Turks conquer Jerusalem.

1098   Fatimid rulers reconquer Jerusalem.

1099   Christian Crusaders from Europe invade Palestine and conquer Jaffa and Jerusalem. The Latin

Kingdom of Jerusalem is established.

1291–1517 The Mamluks conquer Acre, ending the Crusader states, and govern Syria and Egypt.

1516 Forces of the Ottoman Empire overthrow the Mamluk Sultanate and capture Syria, including Jerusalem, and Gaza. Egypt formally becomes a part of the Ottoman Empire in 1517, although the Mamluks remain powerful in Egypt, Baghdad, and other locations.

1535–1538 Sultan Suleiman the Magnificent orders the reconstruction of Jerusalem. In doing so, he seals the Golden Gate, where the Jewish Messiah was to enter.

1705 The Ottoman Empire restricts Jewish immigration after Judah the Pious and 1,000 immigrants settle in Jerusalem. By 1844, there are 7,120 Jews in Jerusalem along with 5,760 Muslims and 3,390 Christians.

1882–1904 First wave of Jewish immigration to Palestine. The Jewish population of Palestine reaches 24,000 out of a total 400,000 as a result of immigration by East European Jews. By 1895, the population almost doubles to 47,000 out of 500,000.

1891 Palestinian notables protest Jewish immigration.

1897 The First Zionist Congress, organized by Theodor Herzl, convenes in Basel (Basle), Switzerland. The World Zionist Organization (WZO) emerges from the First Zionist Congress with the stated intention of establishing a Jewish homeland in Palestine.

June 28, 1914 Archduke Franz Ferdinand and his wife are assassinated in Sarajevo, Bosnia-Herzegovina. In less than two months Austria-Hungary, Britain, France, Germany, and Russia rush into war, which would become the most devastating in history to date.

November 4, 1914 The Ottoman Empire formally enters World War I on the side of the Central Powers.

1915–1916 Correspondence between Sharif Hussein of Mecca and Sir Henry McMahon, British high commissioner of Egypt, promises Arabs an independent kingdom in certain areas in return for their support against the Ottoman armies in World War I.

1916 Sharif Hussein leads an Arab revolt against the Ottoman Empire and declares himself the king of the Arabs.

May 16, 1916 Britain and France agree to the secret Sykes–Picot Agreement, which divides the Near East and areas of the Middle East between them.

November 2, 1917 The Balfour Declaration is issued by the British government and supports the establishment of a Jewish homeland in Palestine.

December 1917 The British army under General Sir Edmund Allenby enters Jerusalem. All of Palestine falls under Allied control by September 1918.

January 18–21, 1919–January 1920 A peace conference is held in Paris and prepares treaties including the Treaty of Sèvres that deals with the former Ottoman Empire.

August 10, 1920 The Treaty of Sèvres is signed and formally dissolves the Ottoman Empire. The treaty is revised in the Treaty of Lausanne on July 24, 1923. The former Ottoman territories in the Middle East are partitioned into League of Nations mandates under Britain and France. Britain occupies Palestine, Transjordan, and Iraq, while France gains control of Lebanon and Syria.

1920 The British begin to implement the Balfour Declaration. Herbert Samuel is appointed the high commissioner over Palestine and seeks to elicit Jewish, Muslim, and Christian participation. Arab riots break out against the British Mandate for Palestine, and the Histadrut, or Jewish labor federation, is founded.

1921 The British appoint Faisal, son of Sharif Hussein, as king of Iraq and his other son, Abdullah, as the ruler of Transjordan.

March 1921 The Haganah is founded. At first, it is an untrained militia that guards Jewish lands and repels attacks by Palestinian Arabs, but after 1929 it becomes a trained underground militia.

1922 The first census conducted by the British in Palestine counts the population as 757,182, of which 78 percent are Muslim Arabs, 9.6 percent are Christian Arabs, and 11 percent are Jewish, primarily new immigrants.

August 1923 The British Mandate for Palestine formally begins.

1924–1928 A wave of Jewish immigrants arrives in Palestine.

1933 Adolf Hitler gains power in Germany. The rise of the Nazis prompts a mass emigration of Jews from Europe and into Palestine.

1936   The Arab Revolt of 1936–1939 breaks out against the British and Zionists. About 20,000 troops are sent to Palestine. Some 5,000 Arabs are killed, and thousands more are injured and arrested. The revolt is crushed only with assistance from Jewish groups.

1937   The Peel Royal Commission concludes that there is no hope for Jewish and Arab coexistence and recommends the partition of Palestine.

1939   The White Paper of 1939, also known as the MacDonald White Paper, calls for the establishment of an independent Palestinian state jointly governed by Jews and Arabs within 10 years. It limits Jewish immigration to 75,000 persons over five years. For the first time land transfers from Arabs to Jews are to be limited due to the growing number of landless and impoverished Arabs. The paper contrasts a Jewish "state," which the British feel should not be imposed against the will of the Arab population, with the Jewish "national home" as promised in the Balfour Declaration. The Zionists and Arab leadership reject the white paper. World War II (1939–1945) erupts. The Nazis carry out the Holocaust in their attempt to systematically obliterate European Jews.

1942   The Biltmore eight-point program is issued at the Extraordinary Zionist Conference. The program rejects the 1939 White Paper and calls for an independent Jewish state in all of Palestine and also stipulates that the Jewish Agency control immigration into the country.

1945   The Arab League is formed amid Jewish illegal immigration in Palestine. Jewish groups pressure the British government to allow Holocaust victims to settle in Palestine by sending refugee ships, forcing a confrontation with the Royal Navy.

1947   The majority of the United Nations Special Commission on Palestine (UNSCOP) recommends the partition of Palestine into Jewish and Arab states with Jerusalem as a neutral site, while a minority recommends a nonpartitioned nation.

Thirteen member states including six Arab nations vote against United Nations (UN) Resolution 181 (a slightly different partition plan), arguing that 36 percent of the Arab population would be under Jewish control. The Arab states try to seek remedy at the International Court of Justice and are outvoted. Fighting then begins between Jewish and Palestinian groups.

April 25, 1948 Lebanon, Syria, Iraq, Transjordan, and Egypt agree to invade Palestine. These countries mobilize for an attack on the Jewish regions in Palestine. King Abdullah of Transjordan becomes the nominal leader of the Arab forces, which fight only in a limited area.

April 30, 1948 Haganah captures western Jerusalem and expels all Palestinians.

May 14, 1948 The independence of Israel is proclaimed. David Ben-Gurion becomes the first prime minister of the State of Israel.

May 14, 1948– January 7, 1949 *Israeli War of Independence*

May 20, 1948 Count Folke Bernadotte of Sweden is appointed by the UN Security Council as a mediator between the Jews and Arabs.

June 11–July 9, 1948 After three weeks, Bernadotte negotiates a truce between both sides that is welcomed by the Israelis and opposed by the Arabs. The truce allows the Israelis to regroup their forces, which grow to 49,000 troops. On June 20, a UN police force of 49 guards arrives from New York.

July 9–18, 1948 The Second Battle for Jerusalem ends in failure, as the Israelis are rebuffed by the Arab Legion.

July 18–October 15, 1948 A second truce is declared between Israel and the Arabs. During the truce, the Israeli army grows to 90,000 troops, giving Israel a numerical advantage over the Arabs.

September 17, 1948 Israel's success in the war causes many Israelis to oppose Bernadotte's efforts at a negotiated peace with the Arabs, which would have meant returning territories conquered during the conflict. Bernadotte is assassinated by three men from the Stern Gang. Dr. Ralph Bunche succeeds him as UN negotiator.

September 29– October 15, 1948 On the southern border with Egypt, neither side adheres closely to the cease-fire. The Israelis launch an offensive to cut Egyptian communications and to open a line of communications into the Negev region.

October 19–21, 1948 Israel launches its Beersheba offensive. The Israelis are successful in opening lines of communication with the Negev. On October 19, the Israelis seize Huleiqat, which disrupts Egyptian communications, and capture Beersheba on October 21. Israeli success in these areas leaves the Egyptians at Hebron and Faluja isolated.

November 30, 1948 Israel and Transjordan declare a cease-fire.

December 1, 1948 King Abdullah declares himself king of Arab Palestine and the Union of Transjordan and Arab Palestine at Amman.

November 30, 1948 The Israelis, Syrians, and Lebanese declare a cease-fire.

December 20, 1948– January 7, 1949 Israel launches its Sinai Offensive (Operation HOREF) with the goal of knocking Egypt out of the war. Israel surrounds Rafah on December 22, Asluj on December 25, and Auja on December 27. The Israelis have a column going toward Rafah, and another column takes Abu Ageila

on December 28. The Israelis head toward El Arish and seize an airfield and surrounding villages. The Egyptians, however, halt their advance on December 29.

January 7, 1949 The Egyptians ask for an armistice, which is granted by the Israelis.

February–June 1949 Israel signs separate armistice agreements with Egypt, Lebanon, Jordan, and Syria. Israel acquires 50 percent more territory than originally provided in the UN partition plan. According to UN figures, an estimated 710,000 Palestinians flee or are evicted from Jewish-held areas. Egypt gains control of Gaza, and Jordan holds the West Bank. As part of a secret agreement with Israel, Jordan later annexes the West Bank.

March 7–10, 1949 The Israel Defense Forces (IDF) capture the southern Negev, including Eilat, without difficulty in Operation UVDA.

April 27– September 1949 Representatives from Israel and Arab states meet at the Lausanne Conference. Although the conference is largely a failure, Israel gains a working recognition by Arab states. Both sides accept UN resolutions.

1950	The Israeli Knesset passes the Law of Return, specifying that any Jew who wishes to settle in the State of Israel will be granted immediate citizenship.
July 23, 1952	Free Officers seize control of Egypt, and the July Revolution ends the monarchy.
October 19, 1954	Britain and Egypt sign an agreement whereby British troops withdraw from the Suez Canal.
February 1955	Israel launches Operation HETZ SHAHOR (black arrow) against Egypt for incursions into Israel. The operation kills 38 Egyptians and causes Nasser to reconsider his plans toward Israel.
September 27, 1955	Egypt signs an arms deal with Czechoslovakia. The Israeli government is alarmed, and discussion of preemptive military action begins.

1956 Suez Crisis (Suez or Sinai War), October 29–November 6, 1956

Background

June 13, 1956	British troops leave the Suez Canal Zone.
July 4–26, 1956	Tensions flare along Israel's borders with Jordan and along the Gaza Strip. UN secretary general Dag Hammarskjöld visits the Middle East to restore the cease-fire between Egypt and Israel, first brokered at the end of the Israeli War for Independence (1948–1949).
July 18, 1956	Secretary of State John Foster Dulles announces that the United States will withdraw its financial support to Egypt for the construction of the Aswan High Dam.
July 26, 1956	President Nasser nationalizes the Suez Canal Company.
August 16–30, 1956	Violence erupts along Israel's borders with Egypt and Jordan. This raises fears that another Middle Eastern war will erupt.
October 5, 1956	Britain and France propose to the UN Security Council that the Suez Canal be placed under international control. The Soviet Union vetoes the proposal.
October 24, 1956	Israel, Britain, and France agree to take military action against Egypt at a secret meeting in Sevrès and coordinate their strategies. Britain and France will demand that Israel withdraw from the Suez Canal. Israeli forces will then move on the canal, and upon Nasser's sure refusal to withdraw, Britain and France will

intervene militarily to save the canal from Israeli occupation.

Operations

October 29, 1956 Israel invades the Sinai.

October 30, 1956 The governments of Britain and France send an ultimatum that calls for Israel and Egypt to cease hostilities and withdraw from the Suez Canal and propose an Anglo-French occupation of Port Said, Ismailiyya, and Suez to ensure international access. As expected, Egypt rejects the ultimatum, and an Anglo-French force leaves Malta for Egypt.

October 31, 1956 Britain and France bomb airfields on the Suez Canal.

October 31, 1956 The British bombard Egyptian air bases. Nasser orders Egyptian forces to withdraw from the Sinai.

November 2, 1956 The 11th Infantry Brigade under Colonel Aharon Doron captures the northern Gaza Strip, including the city of Gaza. The Egyptian forces not surrounded by the Israelis complete their withdrawal from Sinai.

November 2, 1956 The UN calls for a cease-fire between Egypt and Israel. Egypt accepts the UN call for a cease-fire, but Britain and France continue to bomb Egyptian airfields and military installations.

November 3–4, 1956 Israel initially accepts the UN's call for a cease-fire. The British and French, however, pressure Ben-Gurion to continue hostilities since a cease-fire would negate intervention at the Suez Canal.

November 5, 1956 The Israelis mount their first assault on Sharm al-Sheikh after midnight but are stopped by a minefield and Egyptian resistance. At 5:30 a.m. the Israelis resume their attack with air and mortar support, leading to the capture of Sharm al-Sheikh.

March 23, 1957 The Suez Canal reopens to traffic.

July 15, 1958 The United States sends 14,000 troops to Lebanon in Operation BLUE BAT to shore up the government of President Camille Chamoun against his internal opposition.

October 23, 1958 The Soviet Union approves a loan to Egypt to finance the Aswan High Dam.

November 18, 1958 Israel begins the National Water Carrier Project to divert water from the Sea of Galilee, which will deplete the Jordan River.

1959	Yasser Arafat and other Palestinian leaders found Fatah, the reverse acronym of Harakat al-Tahrir al-Watani according to Salah Khalaf. However, another source dates the origins of the movement to late 1957.
January 13–17, 1964	The First Arab Summit convenes at Cairo. The Arab states condemn Israel's diversion of the Jordan River and try to formulate a response to it, hinting at diversion of its headwaters. The summit also welcomes the African Unity Charter and supports the Arab struggle and the struggle against imperialism.
May 1964	The Palestine Liberation Organization (PLO) is officially founded, as announced by the new Palestinian National Council. The PLO is headed by Ahmad Shukeiri.
September 13, 1964	The Second Arab Summit is held at Alexandria and focuses on the strengthening of Arab military forces with the goal of liberating Palestine from Israel. Israel submits its concerns to the UN Security Council.

Six-Day War, June 5–10, 1967

Preliminary Moves

May 16, 1967	Egypt declares a state of emergency.
May 17, 1967	Egypt and Syria declare their readiness for combat, and Jordan begins mobilization.
May 18, 1967	Troops in Syria and Egypt are placed on maximum alert, and Kuwait announces its mobilization.
May 19, 1967	The UN Emergency Force (UNEF) troops withdraw from Sinai.
May 20, 1967	Israel completes a partial mobilization of forces.
May 23, 1967	Saudi Arabia begins mobilization of its troops.
May 24, 1967	Jordan completes its mobilization.
May 28, 1967	Sudan mobilizes its troops.
May 29, 1967	Egypt receives units from Algeria.
May 30, 1967	Egypt and Jordan sign the Mutual Security Treaty.
May 31, 1967	Iraqi troops move into Jordan.

The Sinai Front

June 5, 1967	Israel launches a preemptive air strike against Egypt's air bases, destroying its air force. Later in the day, the

Israelis destroy the Jordanian and Syrian air forces while destroying Iraqi air units in Mosul.

June 6, 1967 Egyptian troops in Gaza surrender. The Egyptian field marshal Abdel Hakim Amer orders all units in the Sinai to withdraw.

June 8, 1967 Egyptian armored units attempt to provide cover for ground forces withdrawing from the Sinai. The Sinai is firmly under the control of the Israeli army.

The Jordanian Front

The Battle for Jerusalem

June 5, 1967 The Jordanians begin firing on Israel from Jerusalem. Israeli general Uzi Narkiss begins the offensive against Jerusalem with three brigades under Colonel Mordechai Gur. The Israelis surround the Old City, which is defended by Jordanian brigadier Ata Ali.

June 7, 1967 Gur's forces storm the Old City, while the Jordanians withdraw. The Israelis subsequently capture Bethlehem, Hebron, and Etzion.

The Battle of Jenin-Nablus

June 5, 1967 Major General David Elazar sends one division

and an armored brigade toward Jenin, capturing it after fierce combat the next day.

June 7, 1967 The Israelis advance toward Nablus despite Jordanian counterattacks and seize it. The Jordanians withdraw across the Jordan River, and both Israel and Jordan call for a cease-fire by the UN.

The Syrian Front

June 5–8, 1967 The Syrians control the Golan Heights with six brigades and six more in reserve. Elazar engages in artillery duels against the Syrians for four days.

June 8, 1967 The UN calls for a cease-fire.

June 10, 1967 Israeli forces capture the Golan Heights from Syria. Israel and Syria soon enter into a cease-fire.

The Naval War

June 7, 1967 An Israeli task force captures Egyptian fortifications at Sharm al-Sheikh. This allows naval vessels to travel unobstructed through the Strait of Tiran to the Red Sea.

August–September 1967 The Arab Summit convenes in Khartoum and votes against peace or negotiations with Israel.

November 22, 1967	Security Council Resolution 242 calls for Israeli withdrawal and for peace.
1967	Seizure of Palestinian land in the West Bank and Gaza by Israel for military and security requirements.
1968	The Popular Front for the Liberation of Palestine (PFLP) is formed.
June 1968	The War of Attrition between Egypt and Israel begins. Egypt launches attacks because of Israel's failure to withdraw from the Sinai Peninsula in accordance with UN Resolution 242. Egypt first violates the 1967 cease-fire along the Suez Canal.
1968–1970	Israel begins to build settlements in the West Bank, East Jerusalem, the Gaza Strip, and the Golan Heights.
February 1–4, 1969	The Fifth Palestinian National Council (PNC) convenes in Cairo. Arafat becomes the chair of the Executive Committee. The PNC calls for a "secular democratic state" for Muslims, Christians, and Jews in Palestine.
February 18, 1969	The PFLP attacks an El Al airplane in Zurich.
February 20, 1969	The PFLP launches a bomb attack on a supermarket in Jerusalem.
February 24, 1969	Israel launches an air strike against two Fatah camps near Damascus, inflicting heavy casualties. The PFLP declares its intention to overthrow King Hussein of Jordan, whom it sees as a Western puppet.
December 9, 1969	U.S. secretary of state William Rogers proposes an Israeli-Egyptian settlement, which is rejected by both countries.
August 7, 1970	The War of Attrition between Israel and Egypt ends with a cease-fire after pressure from the superpowers.
September 1970	Fighting between King Hussein of Jordan's forces and Palestinian guerrillas begins. The period is known as Black September for its violence and the expulsion of Palestinian fighters from Jordan. President Nasser of Egypt helps to negotiate the end of this conflict. A terrorist organization subsequently adopts the name Black September.
May 30, 1972 1972	The PFLP and the Japanese Red Army launch an attack at Lod Airport, killing 27.
September 5,	Black September massacres the Israeli Olympic team in Munich. Israel launches a

major manhunt for the assassins.

Yom Kippur War, October 6–24, 1973

Preliminary Moves

September 26, 1973

Egypt and Syria conduct military maneuvers. Israel is placed on alert, and an armored brigade is dispatched to the Golan Heights.

October 4–5, 1973

Sadat expels 15,000 Soviet advisers and all dependants. This is part of his reshaping of Egyptian foreign and domestic policies and is also aimed at Nasserists.

October 6, 1973

General Eliezer Zeira, Israeli director of intelligence, warns Lieutenant General David Elazar of an imminent attack, but Prime Minister Meir decides not to launch a preemptive strike.

Sinai Front

October 6, 1973

Egypt sends a massive air strike against Israeli artillery and command positions. At the same time, the Egyptians bombard the Bar-Lev Line along the Suez Canal, and the Syrians attack from the Golan Heights. Israel gives priority to fighting the Syrians in the Golan Heights.

October 6–7, 1973

Egyptian forces move 8,500 tanks across the Suez Canal. Two Israeli armored divisions under General Ariel Sharon and Avraham Adan are mobilized.

October 9, 1973

The Soviet Union begins to send supplies to Syria and Egypt through Hungary and Yugoslavia.

October 13, 1973

Operation NICKEL GLASS, a U.S. effort to airlift supplies to Israel, begins.

October 13, 1973

The United States augments the Israeli airlifts by sending U.S. C5A transport planes to Israel through the Azores. Between October 14 and 21, the United States airlifts 20,000 tons of supplies against 15,000 tons from the Soviet Union.

October 15–16, 1973

The Israelis mount an offensive across the Suez Canal. General Ariel Sharon strikes between the Second Army and the Third Army and establishes a bridgehead with a brigade of paratroopers.

October 17, 1973

Arab members of the Organization of Petroleum Exporting Countries (OPEC) embargo oil shipments to any nation supporting Israel. The embargo results in a full-blown energy crisis in much of the West and wreaks havoc on Western economies.

October 22, 1973
Egypt and Israel agree to a cease-fire, which is soon broken. Israel deploys reinforcements to the Suez Canal.

October 23–24, 1973
The Israelis make an attempt to take Suez but are unsuccessful.

October 24, 1973
Egypt and Israel agree to a second cease-fire.

Golan Heights Front

October 6, 1973
Syria conducts a massive air strike against Israeli positions on the Golan Heights.

October 6–7, 1973
The Syrian 5th Mechanized Division breaks through the Israeli 188th Armored Brigade. In two days, the 188th Armored Brigade is practically destroyed. The Syrians surround the Israeli Golan Heights command post. The 5th Mechanized Division halts its progress to resupply.

October 8–9, 1973
The Israeli 7th Armored Division conducts a counterattack and drives back the Syrian 1st and 5th Divisions toward the original line. The Syrians suffer heavy tank losses. The 7th Brigade repulses another Syrian attack north of Quneitra.

October 10–12, 1973
The Israelis conduct a counteroffensive north of the Quneitra–Damascus Road. Three Israeli divisions break through the first and second Syrian lines of defense near Sasa, close to Damascus. The Israelis halt their advance and redeploy their forces to the Sinai front.

October 22, 1973
Fighting ceases between the Israelis and the Syrians.

October 24, 1973
The Soviet Union places seven airborne divisions on alert to be ready to be sent to Egypt.

October 25, 1973
U.S. secretary of state Henry Kissinger announces that the United States has placed its forces—including its nuclear assets—on precautionary alert based on the possibility that the Soviet Union might intervene in the Middle East, implying that the United States will respond in such an eventuality.

October 27, 1973
The UN Security Council votes to establish a peacekeeping force to enforce the cease-fire in the Sinai Peninsula and the Golan Heights. The decision by the Security Council to establish the UNEF defuses superpower tensions in the Middle East.

November 11, 1973 Egypt and Israel agree to exchange prisoners of war on the cease-fire line. In all, 241 Israelis and 8,031 Egyptians are returned to their respective countries. However, talks between both countries break down because neither will agree on disengagement.

January 18, 1974 Israel and Egypt agree on a disengagement plan after a week of shuttle diplomacy by Kissinger. Israeli troops agree to withdraw within 40 days from their position to a line 15–20 kilometers from the Suez Canal, while the Egyptians will remain on the east bank of the canal. A buffer zone is to be established and will be patrolled by the UNEF. The Israeli withdrawal begins on January 24 and is completed by March 4.

February 28, 1974 The United States and Egypt resume diplomatic relations.

March 18, 1974 The OPEC oil embargo against the United States comes to an end. April–May 1974 Palestinian guerrillas engage in attacks from Lebanon into Israel.

May 31, 1974 Israel and Syria agree to disengage their forces after 32 days of shuttle diplomacy by Kissinger between Jerusalem and Damascus. Israel relinquishes all territory taken from Syria in the Yom Kippur War, two small strips taken in 1967, and the town of Quneitra but retains all of the Golan Heights. A cease-fire line, to be patrolled by the UNEF, is established between both countries.

July 1974 The Twelfth Palestinian National Council votes to establish sovereignty "on every part of Palestinian land to be liberated."

September 1974 The UN General Assembly debates the question of Palestine, voting 82 in favor, 4 against, and 20 abstentions for inviting PLO chairman Arafat to New York to address the body.

October 28, 1974 The Arab Summit at Rabat, Morocco, recognizes the PLO as the legitimate representative of the Palestinian people.

November 10, 1975 The UN General Assembly adopts Resolution 3379, which determines that Zionism is a "form of racism and racial discrimination" that countermands the UN's Declaration on the Elimination of All Forms of Racial Discrimination. Resolution 3379 is revoked by Resolution 46/86 on December 16, 1991.

1975   The Lebanese Civil War begins.

1976   The PLO makes gains in municipal elections in the West Bank.

July 4, 1976   Hijacking of an Air France flight from Israel by Palestinian and German terrorists to Entebbe Airport in Uganda. Israel carries out a rescue mission and frees 100 hostage passengers, but 1 Israeli soldier, 45 Ugandans, 3 hostages, and the hijackers are killed.

May 1977   The Likud Party under Menachem Begin wins the Knesset election. Begin promotes and expands the building of Jewish settlements in the West Bank, which he considers to be the liberated territories of Judea and Samaria.

November 19, 1977   Sadat shocks the Arab world and pleases the West when he travels to Jerusalem and addresses the Israeli Knesset. There he emphasizes that true peace in the Middle East will not be possible without a solution for the Palestinians.

September 5–17, 1978   The Camp David Accords, mediated by President Jimmy Carter, take place between Begin and Sadat. Sadat and Begin draft the Framework for the Conclusion of a Peace between Egypt and Israel, which establishes normal relations between both countries. Sadat and Begin are awarded the Nobel Peace Prize in December. The Camp David Accords are condemned throughout the Arab world as a betrayal of the Palestinian people.

March 26, 1979   Sadat and Begin sign the Treaty of Peace between the Arab Republic of Egypt and the State of Israel.

March 31, 1979   Egypt is expelled from the Arab League, and its headquarters move from Cairo to Tunis.

May 25, 1979   Israel begins its withdrawal from Sinai.

1980   Israel and Egypt normalize relations by exchanging ambassadors. Israel officially annexes all of Jerusalem.

July 17, 1981   Israel bombs Beirut, killing more than 450 Lebanese and Palestinians after a week of fighting that includes a naval attack as well. The PLO headquarters in West Beirut is targeted, although not exclusively.

September 1981 Egyptian authorities arrest more than 1,600 activists, intellectuals, and political figures.

October 6, 1981 Sadat is assassinated by army officers who are members of the Jihad organization while he views the October 6 victory celebration that commemorates the Ramadan War. Hosni Mubarak succeeds him as president of Egypt.

December 14, 1981 Israel announces the annexation of the Golan Heights in defiance of the U.S. position that returning the Golan Heights is a prerequisite for peace with Syria.

April 1982 Israel withdraws the last of its troops from the Sinai.

Israeli Invasion of Lebanon, 1982

June 4–5, 1982 Israel bombs Palestinian refugee camps and other targets in Beirut and southern Lebanon, killing 45 people. The Palestinians launch mortar and artillery attacks on northern Israel.

June 6, 1982 Israel launches an invasion of Lebanon called Operation PEACE FOR GALILEE. The goal is to create a 40-kilometer security zone in southern Lebanon. However, since the Israelis push far beyond that limit, it appears that the goal is to evict all Palestinians and bolster a Lebanese government more favorable to Israeli interests. Some 17,825 Lebanese, Palestinians, and Syrians are killed.

August 12, 1982 Israel announces a cease-fire.

August 13, 1982 The PLO announces its evacuation from Beirut, transporting its guerrilla fighters by land and sea to other sympathetic Arab states.

September 1, 1982 President Ronald Reagan proposes a peace plan calling for self-government in the West Bank and Gaza. The Israelis reject the plan.

September 14, 1982 Lebanese president Bashir Jumayyil is assassinated. Israel halts its withdrawal from Lebanon and reoccupies West Beirut.

September 16–18, 1982 The refugee camps of Sabra and Shatila are attacked by the Phalangists, a right-wing Lebanese militia group in association with the Israelis. The Phalangists massacre between 800 and 2,000 civilians with assistance from the Israeli army. News of the massacre sparks protests and a demonstration by 400,000 people in Tel Aviv, and international outcries prompt an inquiry by Begin. The occupation of southern Lebanon sparks a resistance movement and results in the formation of Islamic Amal and eventually Hezbollah.

September 28–29, 1982

Israel withdraws from West Beirut. A multinational force of American, French, Italian, and British troops arrives.

February 1983

The inquiry on Sabra and Shatila results in the dismissal of Sharon as defense minister and the resignation of Begin as prime minister. Yitzhak Shamir succeeds Begin as prime minister.

October 23, 1983

French and U.S. bases are attacked by Shiite suicide car bombers, causing the deaths of 78 French and 241 U.S. marines.

February 8, 1984

Reagan announces the redeployment of U.S. marines to ships offshore followed by British, French, and Italians troops. This ends the multinational force in Lebanon.

First Intifada, 1987–1993

December 8, 1987

An Israeli civilian truck crashes into a car at the Jabalya refugee camp in the Gaza Strip. Four

Palestinian passengers in the car are killed instantly, and the others are injured. Palestinians accuse the Israelis of deliberately attacking them in retaliation for the stabbing of an Israeli in Gaza two days earlier. As the victims are buried, thousands of protesters storm an Israeli military outpost in Jabalya.

December 9, 1987

Palestinian civilians stay home from work, and demonstrations take place throughout Gaza and the West Bank. This is the beginning of a period of protracted all-out confrontation between the IDF and Palestinians.

January–March 1988

The Unified National Leadership of the intifada issues communiqués and establishes popular and neighborhood committees. This formalizes the uprising.

February–June 1988

Palestinians boycott Israeli products. Israelis jail Palestinians in response, imposing heavy fines while seizing and disposing of equipment, furnishings, and goods from local stores, factories, and even homes.

July 1988

King Hussein renounces all claims to the West Bank and acknowledges the PLO's authority over Palestine.

December 13, 1988   Arafat addresses the UN General Assembly in Geneva, Switzerland. He announces his acceptance of Security Council Resolution 242, which affirms the right of every nation in the Middle East to peace and security and thus recognizes Israel's right to exist.

1990   A large influx of Jews to Israel from the former Soviet Union begins.

February 16, 1990   Members of Hamas mount a campaign of murder against Israeli soldiers by abducting them and killing them.

The Persian Gulf War, August 2, 1990–March 6, 1991

August 2, 1990   Iraq invades and occupies Kuwait with 100,000 troops, arousing fears that Hussein will then invade Saudi Arabia.

August 8, 1990   Hussein announces the annexation of Kuwait by Iraq. Because of Arafat's support of Hussein, the Gulf states interrupt funds to the PLO.

January 9, 1991   U.S. secretary of state James Baker meets with Iraqi deputy prime minister and foreign minister Tariq Aziz in Geneva and gives him President George H. W. Bush's message ordering Hussein to withdraw immediately and unconditionally from Kuwait. A similar plea by UN secretary general Javier Perez de Cuellar goes unheeded.

January 16, 1991   The United States, leader of an international coalition that includes most Western and Arab states, begins its air campaign against Iraq. Between January 18 and February 25, Iraq launches missile attacks over Israeli targets such as Tel Aviv. In all, 39 Scud missiles are launched. The United States assures its Arab allies that Israel would have no role in the Persian Gulf War and impresses upon the Israelis the importance of restraint.

February 24, 1991   The ground campaign begins.

February 27, 1991   The ground campaign ends after Hussein agrees to a cease-fire on U.S. terms.

March 3, 1991   The Persian Gulf War closes after Iraqi acceptance of a UN-brokered cease-fire agreement. Kuwait severs ties with the PLO and expels or pressures most of the 450,000 Palestinians there to leave.

1993   Israel drastically restricts
Palestinian travel from
the West Bank and
Gaza (except for East
Jerusalem) to Israel,
constituting the start of
constant closures and
restrictions on Palestinian
movements.

**Oslo Accords, September 13, 1993–
July 25, 2000**

January 1993   Secret talks in Oslo begin
between Israel and the
PLO.

**September 13,
1993**   Rabin, Peres, and Arafat
sign the Oslo Declaration
of Principles at a White
House ceremony over
which President Clinton
presides.

July 1, 1994   Arafat returns to Gaza
for the first time in 25
years. He then establishes
the Palestinian Interim
Self-Governing Authority
in Gaza and Jericho as
part of the Oslo Declara-
tion of Principles.

May 1995   The Palestinian Authority (PA) gains control of
banking, energy, industry,
labor, and securities in
the West Bank.

**September 28,
1995**   President Clinton, Hosni
Mubarak, and King Hus-
sein meet in Washington,
D.C., to encourage fur-
ther negotiations between
Israel and the Palestinians
regarding the West Bank.

This results in the signing
of the Palestinian-Israeli
Interim Agreement on
the West Bank and the
Gaza Strip, also known as
Oslo II. According to the
terms, Israel will with-
draw troops from much of
the West Bank by March
30, 1996, and hand them
over to Palestinian political institutions. The area
is divided into Areas A,
B, and C. In turn, the Palestinians will eliminate
all language pertaining to
Israel's destruction from
their National Charter.
This is accomplished on
May 4, 1996.

**January 20,
1996**   The West Bank and
Gaza hold elections for
the Palestinian Council.
Arafat's leadership in the
PLO is confirmed by the
elections. Fatah emerges
as the victorious party,
having won the most seats.

April 11, 1996   Israel launches Operation
GRAPES OF WRATH,
bombing Hezbollah bases
in southern Lebanon as
well as southern neigh-
borhoods of Beirut and
locations in the Bekáa
Valley.

April 26, 1996   The United States negotiates a truce and promotes
an agreement in which
Hezbollah will not attack
civilians in northern
Israel but has a right to

resist the Israeli occupation of southern Lebanon. Lebanon and Syria do not sign the agreement.

September 23–24, 1996 Palestinian riots over Israeli archaeological excavations on the Temple Mount break out in East Jerusalem, Ramallah, and Bethlehem. Israelis and Palestinian police exchange fire.

September 25, 1996 The PA calls for a general strike in the West Bank. Clashes and riots break out in Gaza.

September 27, 1996 Rioting subsides throughout the West Bank and Gaza. In all, 84 Palestinians and 15 Israeli soldiers are killed.

October 1998 Netanyahu and Arafat draft the Wye River Agreement. Israel will make further pullouts from the West Bank, giving Palestinians control over 40 percent of the territory. The agreement makes Arafat responsible for security in the region with assistance from the CIA. The Wye River Agreement comes under heavy criticism by both Palestinians and Israelis.

December 13, 1998 President Clinton makes a three-day visit to the Middle East to endorse his support of the Wye River Agreement.

During a visit to Gaza, he addresses the Palestinian National Council and watches it confirm the official removal of clauses for Israel's destruction from its National Charter.

May 22–24, 2000 Israel withdraws troops from southern Lebanon after 18 years. The withdrawal takes place not as planned but due to the collapse of the South Lebanon Army and Israelis under Hezbollah's fire. Lebanon declares May 25 an annual national holiday, Resistance and Liberation Day.

Second (al-Aqsa) Intifada, 2000–2004

September 28, 2000 Sharon visits the Haram al-Sharif (Temple Mount), inciting violence by Palestinians from rock throwing to demonstrations in the Second (al-Aqsa) Intifada, which lasts until 2004. Israeli settlers retaliate against Palestinians. In the violence that ensues through October, 15 Israeli Arabs, 3,000 Palestinians, and 1,000 Israelis are killed.

February 6, 2001 Sharon is elected prime minister and promises peace and security.

April 17, 2001 The Israeli army reoccupies territory ceded to the PA in Gaza under the Oslo Accords.

September 11, 2001

The Islamic terrorist group Al Qaeda, headed by Osama bin Laden, hijacks four U.S. airliners. Two of the hijacked planes strike the World Trade Center in New York City. A third hits the Pentagon in Washington, D.C. A fourth, allegedly bound for the White House, crashes in Somerset, Pennsylvania. Nearly 3,000 people die in the attacks. President George W. Bush begins the so-called war on terror soon afterward.

December 13,

The Israeli Army attacks Arafat's compound.

March–April 2002

Israel initiates Operation DEFENSIVE WALL in retaliation for the suicide bombings of the previous year. Palestinian leaders, including Marwan Barghuti, are arrested, and Arafat is surrounded in his compound in Ramallah by Israeli troops while they attack it and the city. Israeli forces surround the Church of the Nativity in Bethlehem where militants are hiding. Suspicions of atrocities arise from the Israeli assault on the refugee camp in Jenin where 50 people, including civilians, are killed. Israel refuses to cooperate with a UN investigation.

May 2002

Israel lifts its sieges of Arafat's compound in Ramallah and the Church of the Nativity. The head of the PFLP orchestrates a suicide attack from his cell in Jericho.

May 30, 2002

Arafat signs the Basic Law, which implements reforms in the government of the PA.

June 24, 2002

Bush gives a speech calling for Israeli withdrawal from the occupied territories, the establishment of a Palestinian state, and reforms within the PA as well as for Palestinians to replace Arafat with another leader. Israel sends troops to the West Bank with the exception of Jericho.

January 28, 2003

Israeli elections result in a victory for Likud and continue the premiership of Sharon.

February 2003

Israel mounts offensives in the Gaza Strip and Nablus.

March 10, 2003

The Central Council of the PLO in Ramallah approves Arafat's proposal to choose a prime minister, Abu Mazen (Mahmoud Abbas), as part of Israeli and U.S. pressure to reform the PA.

March 19, 2003 The United States launches its invasion

of Iraq after Saddam Hussein's repeated lack of cooperation with UN nuclear weapons inspectors.

April 9, 2003 Baghdad falls to the United States, and Hussein's regime falls after a quarter of a century in power.

April 24, 2003 Abbas becomes prime minister of the PA. The Quartet, consisting of the United States, Britain, Russia, and Spain, encourages further PA reforms and the Road Map to Peace. Israel also backs Abbas.

September 10, 2003 Suicide bombers kill 15 in Israel. Israeli forces surround Arafat's compound the next day.

November 24, 2003 Sharon announces the Disengagement Plan calling for a unilateral withdrawal of Israeli forces if the Road Map to Peace fails to end terrorism.

April 17, 2004 Hamas leader Abd al-Aziz Rantisi is assassinated by the IDF.

November 11, 2004 Arafat dies. Prime Minister Qurei assumes control of the PA, former prime minister Abbas heads the PLO, and Foreign Minister Farouk Qaddumi takes over the leadership of Fatah.

January 9, 2005 Abbas is elected president of the PA.

February 8, 2005 Sharon, Abbas, Mubarak, and King Abdullah II of Jordan meet at the Sharm al-Sheikh Conference to call for an end to violence. Israel agrees to release 900 Palestinian prisoners, and Egypt and Jordan agree to return ambassadors to Israel. The Second (al-Aqsa) Intifada, which has killed more than 4,000 Palestinians and more than 1,000 Israelis, is declared over.

February 20, 2005 The Israeli cabinet approves a plan for disengagement.

March 16, 2005 Palestinian militant groups agree to a cease-fire in order to participate in May elections for the Palestinian Legislative Council. Israel pulls out of Jericho.

August 15, 2005 Israel begins its evacuation of settlements in Gaza and the West Bank.

September 1, 2005 The last Israeli soldiers leave Gaza, handing over control of the settlements to Palestinians by September 12.

September 15, 2005 Sharon addresses the UN and calls for peace and recognition of Palestinian rights while reaffirming Israel's claim on a united Jerusalem and its determination to fight terror.

October 2005	Palestinian elections are held. Fatah wins 55 seats, and Hamas wins 24 seats.
November 2005	Sharon leaves the Likud Party and forms the Kadima.

The Second Lebanon War, Summer 2006

June 25, 2006	An Israeli soldier is captured in Gaza. The Israeli government demands his release and begins a military campaign against Lebanon as well as Gaza, which they had evacuated only the previous summer. Palestinian militants begin launching rockets into Israel.
August 2006	Olmert's cabinet authorizes a ground campaign 30 kilometers into Lebanon after a bombing campaign that consisted of 8,700 sorties and destroyed 74 roads, 146 bridges, and 100,000 homes in Lebanon. At the same time, Hezbollah launches rockets into Israel. About 1 million Lebanese take flight. The UN Security Council issues Resolutions 1559 and 1680 to call for an end to the hostilities and the disarming of Hezbollah.
August 14, 2006	A UN-brokered cease-fire takes effect.
December 2006–February 2007	Fighting between Hamas and Fatah results in more than 80 Palestinian deaths.
February 2007	The Mecca summit meeting produces an agreement between Fatah and Hamas, which form a Palestinian unity government.
June 14, 2007	After several days of struggle with Fatah, Hamas gains complete control of the Gaza Strip.
June 17, 2007	Abbas swears in a new emergency cabinet as a result of the Hamas takeover. All 11 members are independents. Salam Fayyad is named as the new interim prime minister.
July 9, 2007	Abbas announces that the PA will not have contact with Hamas and calls for international peacekeepers to be stationed in and around Gaza.
September 19, 2007	The Knesset votes unanimously to declare the Gaza Strip, home to some 1.4 million Palestinians, an "enemy entity."
November 26–28, 2007	United States convenes Middle East Summit at Annapolis, Maryland. Israelis and Palestinians agree to implement Roadmap, with U.S. monitoring, and to negotiate continuously with the objective of reaching a

final status agreement by December 2008.

January 2008 George W. Bush tours the Middle East. The Israeli government issues contradictory declarations on West Bank settlements and East Jerusalem.

January 20, 2008 Israel cuts fuel supplies to Gaza in retaliation for rocket attacks. Hamas shuts down Gaza power plant supplying about 20 percent of Gaza's electricity, provoking international outcry against Israel.

February 27– March 3, 2008 Major Israeli raid on Gaza kills over 100.

June 19, 2008 Israel-Hamas truce in Gaza.

July 28, 2008 Fatah arrests around 50 Hamas activists in West Bank.

September 27, 2008 Ehud Olmert resigns as Israeli prime minister, due to financial improprieties.

November 4, 2008 Barack Obama elected president of United States, raising Arab hopes for radical changes in U.S. Middle East policy.

November 4–9, 2008 IDF discover tunnel under construction from Gaza into Israel and launch raid to destroy it, killing 6 Hamas gunmen. Hamas retaliates with several days of rocket attacks on Israel.

December 19, 2008 Israel-Hamas truce expires. Hamas steps up rocket attacks on Israel.

December 27, 2008– January 18, 2009 Israel launches Operation CAST LEAD against Gaza, killing over 1300 Palestinians, for 13 Israeli dead. Hamas increases rocket attacks on Israel, broadening targets.

January 14, 2009 Abass's term of office as PA president expires and is extended. The West Bank government and Israel continue to recognize him as president, whereas the Hamas-controlled Gaza government does not.

January 18, 2009 Cease-fire in Operation CAST LEAD, though sporadic rocket attacks and IDF retaliation continue.

February 10, 2009 Israeli elections give majority to right-wing parties. Benjamin Netanyahu becomes prime minister, heading a coalition government.

June 4, 2009 President Barack Obama speaks at Cairo University, calling for Arab-Israeli rapprochement, an end to new Israeli settlement construction in the West Bank, Arab recognition of Israel, and Israeli acceptance of a Palestinian state.

June 14, 2009 Netanyahu endorses Obama's demand that Israel support creation of a Palestinian state, but refuses to end construction of settlements. Palestinians refuse to begin peace talks with Israel until all new Israeli construction in West Bank and Jerusalem ceases.

August 26, 2009 With European Union backing, PA issues plan to declare a state unilaterally within two years: *Palestine: Ending the Occupation, Establishing the State.*

November 2009 Netanyahu announces settlement freeze will end on September 26, 2010.

June 9, 2010 UN Security Council imposes sanctions on Iran, due to Iranian refusal to curtail its nuclear program.

June–July 2010 Israel eases blockade of Gaza.

September 2, 2010 Direct Israeli-Palestinian talks open in Washington, D.C., with regular meetings scheduled at fortnightly intervals.

December 18, 2010 Arab Spring begins with protests in Tunisia, which spread to Egypt, Algeria, Bahrain, Jordan, Libya, Morocco, Oman, Syria, and Yemen.

February 11, 2011 President Hosni Mubarak of Egypt resigns.

March 2011 Civil war begins in Syria.

May 2, 2011 On the instructions of President Barack Obama, US Naval Special Warfare and Development Group and CIA personnel mount a covert operation to track down and kill Osama bin Laden in Abbottabad, Pakistan.

August 18, 2011 Egyptian and Palestinian militants attack southern Israel, killing eight Israelis and five Egyptian soldiers.

September 2011 PA seeks UN recognition of Palestine statehood.

November 2011 Palestine wins membership of UNESCO, but UN vote on statehood is deferred.

March 9–15, 2012 Major clashes between Gaza and Israel, with over 300 rocket attacks on Israel from Gaza. Israel retaliates with air strikes on weapons' facilities in Gaza.

June 17, 2012 Mohammed Morsi of the Muslim Brotherhood becomes president of Egypt.

September 21, 2012 Egyptian militants open cross-border fire on Israeli soldiers and civilians, killing one soldier.

November 14–21, 2012 Israel strikes over 1,500 sites in Gaza, in Operation PILLAR OF DEFENSE, killing 133 Palestinians. Hamas fires almost 1,500 rockets at targets in southern Israel, including Tel Aviv and Jerusalem.

November 29, 2012   UN General Assembly Resolution 67/19 grants Palestine nonmember observer state status.

November 2012–July 2013   Massive and growing protests by Egyptians against Morsi's authoritarian and Islamist rule and new constitution.

July 3, 2013   Egyptian military ousts President Mohammed Morsi of Egypt.

July 22, 2013   In response to Hezbollah support for President Bashar al-Assad in Syria's ongoing civil war, the European Union adds Hezbollah's military wing to its terrorism blacklist, allowing the freezing of Hezbollah financial assets.

July 29, 2013   With encouragement from U.S. secretary of state John Kerry, Israel and Palestine reopen direct talks, intended to reach a final status agreement within nine months.

October 30–31, 2013   Israeli aircraft attack Syrian military targets, seeking to deny weapons to Hezbollah forces supporting the Syrian government.

Dino E. Buenviaje, David T. Zabecki,
Sherifa Zuhur, and Priscilla Roberts

Selected Bibliography

Abbas, Mahmoud. *Through Secret Channels: The Road to Oslo; Senior PLO Leader Abu Mazen's Revealing Story of the Negotiations with Israel*. Reading, UK: Garnet, 1997.

Abu Amr, Ziad. *Islamic Fundamentalisms in the West Bank and Gaza: Muslim Brotherhood and Islamic Jihad*. Bloomington: Indiana University Press, 1994.

Abu Amr, Ziad. *The Intifada: Causes and Factors of Continuity*. 2nd ed. Jerusalem: PASSIA, 1994.

Abu Nowar, Maan. *The Jordanian-Israeli War, 1948–1951: A History of the Hashemite Kingdom of Jordan*. Reading, UK: Ithaca Press, 2002.

Aburish, Said K. *Arafat: From Defender to Dictator*. New York: Bloomsbury, 1998.

Aburish, Said K. *Cry Palestine: Inside the West Bank*. Boulder, CO: Westview, 1993.

Aburish, Said K. *Nasser: The Last Arab*. New York: St. Martin's Press, 2004.

Achcar, Gilbert. *The Arabs and the Holocaust: The Arab-Israeli War of Narratives*. New York: Metropolitan Books, 2010.

Ali, Jaffer. *Palestine and the Middle East: A Chronicle of Passion and Politics*. Tempe, AZ: Dandelion Books, 2003.

Alimi, Eitan. *The First Palestinian Intifada and Israeli Society: Political Opportunities, Framing Processes, and Contentious Politics*. London: Routledge, 2006.

Allen, Peter. *The Yom Kippur War*. New York: Scribner, 1982.

Aly, Abdel Monem Said, Shai Feldman, and Khalil Shikaki. *Arabs and Israelis: Conflict and Peacemaking in the Middle East*. Basingstoke: Palgrave Macmillan, 2013.

Asmar, Marwan. *Intifada II: Media & Politics*. Amman: Ad Dustour Commercial Presses, 2001.

Avner, Yehuda. *The Prime Ministers: An Intimate Narrative of Israeli Leadership*. Jerusalem: Toby Press, 2010.

Bailey, Sydney D. *Four Arab-Israeli Wars and the Peace Process*. New York: St. Martin's Press, 1982.

Bar-On, Mordechai, ed. *A Never-Ending Conflict: A Guide to Israeli Military History*. Westport, CT: Praeger, 2004.

Baroud, Ramzy, et al. *The Second Palestinian Intifada: A Chronicle of a People's Struggle*. London: Pluto, 2006.

Bar-Siman-Tov, Yaacov. *The Israel-Egyptian War of Attrition, 1969–1970: A Case-Study of Limited Local War*. New York: Columbia University Press, 1980.

Bar-Zohar, Michael, and Nissim Mishal. *Mossad: The Greatest Missions of the Israeli Secret Service*. New York: Ecco, 2012.

Bawley, Dan, and Eliahu Salpeter. *Fire in Beirut: Israel's War in Lebanon with the PLO*. Briarcliff Manor, NY: Stein and Day, 1984.

Beaufre, André. *The Suez Expedition, 1956*. Translated by Richard Barry. New York: Praeger, 1969.

Begin, Menachem. *The Revolt*. Los Angeles: Nash Publishing, 1972.

Beilin, Yossi. *Israel: A Concise Political History*. New York: St. Martin's Press, 1992.

Beilin, Yossi. *The Path to Geneva: The Quest for a Permanent Agreement, 1996–2004.* New York: RDV Books, 2004.

Beinin, Joel. *Was the Red Flag Flying There? Marxist Politics and the Arab-Israeli Conflict in Egypt and Israel, 1948–1965.* Berkeley: University of California Press, 1990.

Beinin, Joel, and Rebecca L. Stein. *The Struggle for Sovereignty: Palestine and Israel, 1993–2005.* Stanford, CA: Stanford University Press, 2006.

Beitler, Ruth Margolies. *The Path to Mass Rebellion: An Analysis of Two Intifadas.* New York: Lexington Books, 2004.

Ben-Gurion, David. *Israel: Years of Challenge.* New York: Holt, 1963.

Bennis, Phyllis. *Understanding the Palestinian-Israeli Conflict: A Primer.* 2nd ed. Lowell, MA: TARI, 2003.

Bennis, Phyllis, and Neal Cassidy. *From Stones to Statehood: The Palestinian Uprising.* Brooklyn, NY: Olive Branch, 1990.

Benvenisti, Meron. *Intimate Enemies: Jews and Arabs in a Shared Land.* Berkeley: University of California Press, 1995.

Berberoglu, Berch. *Power and Stability in the Middle East.* London: Zed, 1989.

Berberoglu, Berch. *Turmoil in the Middle East.* Albany, NY: SUNY Press, 1999.

Bergen, Kathy, David Neuhaus, and Ghassan Rubeiz. *Justice and the Intifada: Palestinians and Israelis Speak Out.* New York: Friendship Press, 1991.

Bernadotte, Folke. *To Jerusalem.* London: Hodder, 1951.

Berry, Mike, and Greg Philo. *Israel and Palestine: Competing Histories.* London: Pluto, 2006.

Biale, David, ed. *Cultures of the Jews: A New History.* New York: Schocken, 2002.

Bishara, Marwan. *Palestine/Israel: Peace or Apartheid: Occupation, Terrorism and the Future.* New York: Zed, 2002.

Bix, Herbert P. *The Occupied Territories under Israeli Rule: On the Origins of the Intifada.* Sheffield, UK: University of Sheffield, 1991.

Black, Ian, and Benny Morris. *Israel's Secret Wars: A History of Israel's Intelligence Services.* New York: Grove, 1991.

Blincoe, Nicholas. *Peace under Fire: Israel/ Palestine and the International Solidarity Movement.* London: Verso, 2004.

Blum, Howard. *The Eve of Destruction: The Untold Story of the Yom Kippur War.* New York: Perennial Books, 2004.

Bowen, Jeremy. *Six Days: How the 1967 War Shaped the Middle East.* New York: Thomas Dunne, 2005.

Boyle, Francis. *Palestine, Palestinians and International Law.* Atlanta: Clarity, 2003.

Boyne, Walter J. *The Yom Kippur War and the Airlift Strike That Saved Israel.* New York: St. Martin's Griffin, 2003.

Brand, Laurie A. *Palestinians in the Arab World: Institution Building and the Search for State.* New York: Columbia University Press, 1988.

Bregman, Ahron. *A History of Israel.* New York: Palgrave Macmillan, 2003.

Bregman, Ahron. *Israel's Wars: A History since 1947.* 3rd ed. New York: Routledge, 2010.

Brenchley, Frank. *Britain, the Six-Day War and Its Aftermath.* London: I. B. Tauris, 2005.

Bröning, Michael. *The Politics of Change in Palestine: State-Building and Non-Violent Resistance.* London: Pluto, 2011.

Brown, Nathan J. *Palestinian Politics after the Oslo Accords: Resuming Arab Palestine.* Berkeley: University of California Press, 2003.

Brynen, Rex. *Echoes of the Intifada: Regional Repercussions of the Palestinian-Israeli Conflict.* Boulder, CO: Westview, 1991.

Bucaille, Laetitia. *Growing Up Palestinian: Israeli Occupation and the Intifada Generation.* Princeton, NJ: Princeton University Press, 2004.

Bunton, Martin. *The Palestinian-Israeli Conflict: A Very Short Introduction.* New York: Oxford University Press, 2013.

Carey, Roane. *The New Intifada: Resisting Israel's Apartheid.* London: Verso, 2001.

Carlton, David. *Britain and the Suez Crisis.* Oxford, UK: Blackwell, 1989.

Chaitani, Youssef. *Dissension among Allies: Ernest Bevin and Palestine Policy between Whitehall and the White House, 1945–47.* London: Saqi, 2002.

Chamberlin, Paul Thomas. *The Global Offensive: The United States, the Palestine Liberation Organization, and the Making of the Post-Cold War Order*. New York: Oxford University Press, 2012.

Chomsky, Noam. *Middle East Illusions*. Lanham, MD: Rowman and Littlefield, 2003.

Claire, Rodger W. *Raid on the Sun: Inside Israel's Secret Campaign that Denied Saddam the Bomb*. New York: Broadway, 2004.

Clark, Victoria. *Allies for Armageddon: The Rise of Christian Zionism*. New Haven, CT: Yale University Press, 2007.

Cobban, Helena. *The Palestinian Liberation Organisation: People, Power and Politics*. New York: Cambridge University Press, 1984.

Cohen, Michael J. *Palestine and the Great Powers, 1945–1948*. Princeton, NJ: Princeton University Press, 1982.

Cohen, Michael J. *Truman and Israel*. Berkeley: University of California Press, 1990.

Cohen, Mitchell. *Zion and State: Nation, Class, and the Shaping of Modern Israel*. New York: Columbia University Press, 1992.

Collins, John. *Occupied by Memory: The Intifada Generation and the Palestinian State of Emergency*. New York: New York University Press, 2004.

Collins, Larry, and Dominique Lapierre. *O Jerusalem!* New York: Simon and Schuster, 1972.

Crosbie, Sylvia K. *A Tacit Alliance: France and Israel from Suez to the Six-Day War*. Princeton, NJ: Princeton University Press, 1974.

Darraj, Susan Muaddi. *Bashar Al-Assad*. New York: Chelsea House, 2005.

Darraj, Susan Muaddi. *Hosni Mubarak*. New York: Chelsea House, 2007.

Davis, M. Thomas. *40 km into Lebanon: Israel's 1982 Invasion*. Washington, DC: National Defense University Press, 1987.

Dayan, Moshe. *Breakthrough*. New York: Knopf, 1981.

Dayan, Moshe. *Diary of the Sinai Campaign*. Cambridge, MA: Da Capo, 1991.

Dershowitz, Alan M. *The Case for Israel*. New York: Wiley, 2004.

Drury, Richard Toshiyuki, Robert C. Winn, and Michael O'Connor. *Plowshares and Swords: The Economics of Occupation in the West Bank*. Boston, MA: Beacon, 1992.

Dumper, Michael. *The Politics of Sacred Space: The Old City of Jerusalem in the Middle East Conflict*. Boulder, CO: Lynne Rienner, 2002.

Dunstan, Simon. *The Yom Kippur War, 1973*. 2 vols. Westport, CT: Praeger, 2005.

Eban, Abba. *Abba Eban: An Autobiography*. New York: Random House, 1977.

Eden, Anthony. *The Suez Crisis of 1956*. Boston, MA: Beacon, 1968.

El-Awaisi, Abd al-Fattah. *The Muslim Brothers and the Palestine Question, 1928–1947*. New York: I. B. Tauris, 1998.

Emerson, Gloria. *Gaza: A Year in the Intifada; a Personal Account from an Occupied Land*. New York: Atlantic Monthly Press, 1991.

Espy, Richard. *The Politics of the Olympic Games*. Berkeley: University of California Press, 1979.

Evron, Yair. *War and Intervention in Lebanon: The Israeli-Syrian Deterrence Dialogue*. Baltimore: Johns Hopkins University Press, 1987.

Farsoum, Samih K., and Naseer H. Aruri. *Palestine and the Palestinians: A Social and Political History*. 2nd ed. Jackson, TN: Westview, 2006.

Fawcett, Louise. *International Relations of the Middle East*. 3rd ed. Oxford: Oxford University Press, 2013.

Finkelstein, Norman G. *Image and Reality of the Israel-Palestine Conflict*. 3rd ed. London: Verso, 2008.

Finkelstein, Norman G. *The Rise and Fall of Palestine: A Personal Account of the Intifada Years*. Minneapolis: University of Minnesota Press, 1996.

Fischbach, Michael R. *Records of Dispossession: Palestinian Refugee Property and the Arab-Israeli Conflict*. New York: Columbia University Press, 2003.

Fisk, Robert. *Pity the Nation: Lebanon at War*. Oxford: Oxford University Press, 2001.

Freedman, Lawrence. *A Choice of Enemies: America Confronts the Middle East*. New York: PublicAffairs, 2008.

Freedman, Robert Owen. *The Intifada: Its Impact on Israel, the Arab World, and the Superpowers*. Miami: FL: International University Press, 1991.

Freedman, Robert Owen, ed. *The Middle East and the Peace Process: The Impact of the Oslo Accords*. Gainesville: University Press of Florida, 1998.

Friedman, Thomas. *From Beirut to Jerusalem*. New York: Anchor Books, 1995.

Gabriel, Richard. *Operation Peace for Galilee: The Israeli-PLO War in Lebanon*. New York: Farrar, Straus and Giroux, 1985.

Gardner, Lloyd C. *Three Kings: The Rise of an American Empire in the Middle East after World War II*. New York: New Press, 2009.

Gat, Moshe. *Britain and the Conflict in the Middle East, 1964–1967: The Coming of the Six-Day War*. Westport, CT: Praeger, 2003.

Gelber, Yoav. *Israeli-Jordanian Dialogue, 1948–1953: Cooperation, Conspiracy, or Collusion?* Brighton, UK: Sussex Academic, 2004.

Gelvin, James L. *The Israel-Palestine Conflict: One Hundred Years of War*. 3rd ed. Cambridge: Cambridge University Press, 2014.

Gelvin, James L. *The Modern Middle East: A History*. 3rd ed. New York: Oxford University Press, 2011.

Gerges, Fawaz A. *Obama and the Middle East: The End of America's Moment*. Basingstoke: Palgrave Macmillan, 2012.

Ghabra, Shafiq. *Palestinians in Kuwait: The Family and Politics of Survival*. Boulder, CO: Westview, 1987.

Ghanem, Assad. *Palestinian Politics after Arafat: A Failed National Movement*. Bloomington: Indiana University Press, 2010.

Giacaman, George, and Dag Jorund Lonning, eds. *After Oslo: New Realities, Old Problems*. Chicago: Pluto, 1998.

Glubb, John Bagot. *A Soldier with the Arabs*. New York: Harper and Brothers, 1959.

Golan, Galia. *Israel and Palestine: Peace Plans and Proposals from Oslo to Disengagement*. Updated ed. Princeton, NJ: Markus Wiener, 2008.

Golan, Matti. *The Road to Peace: A Biography of Shimon Peres*. New York: Warner Books, 1989.

Gold, Steven J. *The Israeli Diaspora*. Seattle: University of Washington Press, 2002.

Gordon, Hayim, Rivca Gordon, and Taher Shriteh. *Beyond Intifada: Narratives of Freedom Fighters in the Gaza Strip*. New York: Praeger, 2003.

Goremberg, Gershom. *The Accidental Empire: Israel and the Birth of Settlements, 1967–1977*. New York: Times Books, 2006.

Gorst, Anthony, and Lewis Johnman. *The Suez Crisis*. London: Routledge, 1997.

Gowers, Andrew, and Tony Walker. *Behind the Myth: Yasser Arafat and the Palestinian Revolution*. New York: Olive Branch, 1992.

Greffenius, Steven. *The Logic of Conflict: Making War and Peace in the Middle East*. Armonk, NY: M. E. Sharpe, 1993.

Hahn, Peter. *Caught in the Middle East: U.S. Policy toward the Arab-Israeli Conflict, 1945–1961*. Chapel Hill: University of North Carolina, 2004.

Hahn, Peter. *The United States, Great Britain, and Egypt, 1945–1956: Strategy and Diplomacy in the Early Cold War*. Chapel Hill: University of North Carolina Press, 1991.

Hall, John G. *Palestinian Authority: Creation of the Modern Middle East*. Langhorne, PA: Chelsea House, 2002.

Hammel, Eric. *Six Days in June: How Israel Won the 1967 Arab-Israeli War*. New York: Scribner, 1992.

Hammer, Joshua. *A Season in Bethlehem: Unholy War in a Sacred Place*. New York: Free Press, 2004.

Hammer, Julianne. *Palestinians Born in Exile: Diaspora and the Search for a Homeland*. Cairo, Egypt: American University in Cairo Press, 2005.

Harik, Judith Palmer. *Hezbollah: The Changing Face of Terrorism*. London: I. B. Tauris, 2005.

Harms, Gregory, and Todd Ferry. *The Palestine-Israel Conflict: A Basic Introduction*. 3rd ed. London: Pluto, 2012.

Hart, Alan. *Arafat: A Political Biography*. Rev. ed. London: Sidgwick and Jackson, 1994.

Hatina, Meir. *Islam and Salvation in Palestine: The Islamic Jihad Movement*. Syracuse, NY: Syracuse University Press, 2001.

Herzog, Chaim. *The Arab-Israeli Wars: War and Peace in the Middle East from the War of Independence to Lebanon*. Rev. and updated ed. Westminster, MD: Random House, 1984.

Herzog, Chaim. *The War of Atonement: The Inside Story of the Yom Kippur War*. London: Greenhill, 2003.

Heydemann, Steven, ed. *War, Institutions and Social Change in the Middle East*. Berkeley: University of California Press, 2000.

Hill, Christopher. *Olympic Politics*. 2nd ed. Manchester, UK: Manchester University Press, 1996.

Hiltermann, Joost R. *Behind the Intifada: Labor and Women's Movements in the Occupied Territories*. Princeton, NJ: Princeton University Press, 1991.

Hirst, David, and Irene Beeson. *Sadat*. London: Faber and Faber, 1981.

Holt, Maria. *Half the People: Women, History and the Palestinian Intifada*. East Jerusalem: PASSIA, 1992.

Horovitz, David Phillip. *Shalom, Friend: The Life and Legacy of Yitzhak Rabin*. New York: Newmarket Press, 1996.

Horovitz, David Phillip. *Still Life with Bombers: Israel in the Age of Terrorism*. New York: Knopf, 2004.

Hroub, Khaled. *Hamas: A Beginner's Guide*. 2nd ed. London: Pluto, 2010.

Hroub, Khaled. *Hamas: Political Thought and Practice*. Washington, DC: Institute for Palestine Studies, 2000.

Hunter, F. Robert. *The Palestinian Uprising: A War by Other Means*. Berkeley: University of California Press, 1991.

Hunter, Robert E., and Seth G. Jones. *Building a Successful Palestinian State: Security*. Santa Monica, CA: RAND, 2006.

Ichilov, Orit. *Political Learning and Citizenship Education under Conflict: The Political Socialization of Israeli and Palestinian Youngsters*. London: Routledge, 2004.

Israelyan, Victor. *Inside the Kremlin during the Yom Kippur War*. University Park: Pennsylvania State University Press, 1995.

Jaber, Hala. *Hezbollah: Born with a Vengeance*. New York: Columbia University Press, 1997.

Jansen, Michael E. *The Battle of Beirut: Why Israel Invaded Lebanon*. Boston, MA: South End Press, 1983.

Jones, Clive. *Between Terrorism and Civil War: The Al-Aqsa Intifada*. London: Routledge, 2005.

Kaspit, Ben Kafir Ilan. *Netanyahu: The Road to Power*. London: Vision, 1999.

Kassem, Maye. *Egyptian Politics: The Dynamics of Authoritarian Rule*. Boulder, CO: Lynne Rienner, 2004.

Katz, Yaakov. *Israel vs. Iran: The Shadow War*. Washington, DC: Potomac Books, 2012.

Kedourie, Elie, and Sylvia Kedourie. *Zionism and Arabism in Palestine and Israel*. London: Frank J. Cass, 1982.

Kelly, Saul, and Anthony Gorst, eds. *Whitehall and the Suez Crisis*. London: Routledge, 2000.

Khalidi, Rashid. *Palestinian Identity: The Construction of Modern National Consciousness*. New York: Columbia University Press, 1997.

Khalidi, Rashid. *Under Siege: P.L.O. Decisionmaking during the 1982 War*. New York: Columbia University Press, 1986.

Khomeini, Imam. *Islam and Revolution*. Translated by Hamid Algar. Berkeley: Mizan, 1981.

Khouri, Fred J. *The Arab-Israeli Dilemma*. 3rd ed. Syracuse, NY: Syracuse University Press, 1985.

Kidron, Peretz. *Refusenik! Israel's Soldiers of Conscience*. London: Zed, 2004.

Kimmerling, Baruch. *Politicide: Ariel Sharon's Wars against the Palestinians*. London: Verso, 2003.

Kimmerling, Baruch, and Josel S. Migdal. *The Palestinian People: A History*. Cambridge, MA: Harvard University Press, 2003.

Klein, Menachem. *Jerusalem: The Contested City*. Translated by Haim Watzman. New York: New York University Press, 2001.

Klein, Menachem. *The Shift: Israel/Palestine from Border Struggle to Ethnic Conflict.* Translated by Chaim Weitzman. New York: Columbia University Press, 2010.

Koch, Howard Everard. *Permanent War: A Reappraisal of the Arab Israeli War.* Stanford, CA: Koch, 1973.

Korn, David A. *Stalemate: The War of Attrition and Great Power Diplomacy in the Middle East, 1967–1970.* Boulder, CO: Westview, 1992.

Kurtzer, Daniel C., Scott B. Lasensky, William B. Quandt, Steven L. Spiegel, and Shibley Z. Telhami. *The Peace Puzzle: America's Quest for Arab-Israeli Peace, 1989–2011.* Ithaca, NY: Cornell University Press, 2013.

Kurzman, Dan. *Ben-Gurion, Prophet of Fire.* New York: Simon and Schuster, 1983.

Lacouture, Jean. *Nasser, a Biography.* New York: Knopf, 1973.

Lamb, Franklin P., and John E. Dockham. *Israel's War in Lebanon: Eyewitness Chronicles of the Invasion and Occupation.* 2nd ed. Boston, MA: South End Press, 1984.

Lawrence, T. E. *Seven Pillars of Wisdom.* 1936. Reprint, New York: Anchor, 1991.

Lenczowski, George. *American Presidents and the Middle East.* Durham, NC: Duke University Press, 1990.

Lesch, David W. *The Middle East and the United States: A Historical and Political Reassessment.* New York: Perseus, 2006.

Levey, Zach. *Israel and the Western Powers, 1952–1960.* Chapel Hill: University of North Carolina Press, 2011.

Lewis, Bernard. *The Crisis of Islam: Holy War and Unholy Terror.* London: Orion, 2004.

Lewis, Bernard. *The End of Modern History in the Middle East.* Stanford, CA: Hoover Institution Press, 2011.

Lewis, Bernard. *What Went Wrong? The Clash between Islam and Modernity in the Middle East.* New York: Oxford University Press, 2002.

Livingstone, Neil C., and David Haley. *Inside the PLO.* New York: William Morrow, 1990.

Lockman, Zachary. *Comrades and Enemies: Arab and Jewish Workers in Palestine, 1906–1948.* Berkeley: University of California Press, 1996.

Louis, William Roger. *The British Empire in the Middle East, 1945–1951: Arab Nationalism, the United States, and Postwar Imperialism.* New York: Oxford University Press, 1984.

Louis, William R., and Roger Owen, eds. *Suez, 1956: The Crisis and Its Consequences.* New York: Oxford University Press, 1989.

Lukacs, Yehuda Battah Abdalla M. *The Arab-Israeli Conflict: Two Decades of Change.* Boulder, CO: Westview, 1988.

Lustick, Ian. *Arabs in the Jewish State: Israel's Control of a National Minority.* Austin: University of Texas Press, 1980.

Lustick, Ian. *From War to War: Israel vs. the Arabs, 1948–1967.* New York: Garland, 1994.

Maddy-Weitzman, Bruce, and Shimon Shamir. *The Camp David Summit: What Went Wrong? Americans, Israelis, and Palestinians Analyze the Failure of the Boldest Attempt Ever to Resolve the Palestinian-Israeli Conflict.* Sussex, UK: Sussex Academic, 2005.

Makovsky, David. *A Defensible Fence: Fighting Terror and Enabling a Two-State Solution.* Washington, DC: Washington Institute for Near East Policy, 2004.

Makovsky, David. *Making Peace with the PLO: The Rabin Government's Road to the Oslo Accord.* Boulder, CO: Westview, 1996.

Mandelbaum, Michael. *Israel and the Occupied Territories: A Personal Report on the Uprising.* New York: Council on Foreign Relations, 1988.

Mann, Peggy. *Golda: The Life of Israel's Prime Minister.* New York: Coward, McCann and Geoghegan, 1971.

Martin, Ralph G. *Golda: Golda Meir, the Romantic Years.* New York: Scribner, 1988.

Masters, Bruce. *The Arabs of the Ottoman Empire, 1516–1918: A Social and Cultural History.* Cambridge: Cambridge University Press, 2013.

Mattar, Philip. *The Mufti of Jerusalem*. New York: Columbia University Press, 1988.

Matthews, Elizabeth, ed. *The Israel-Palestine Conflict: Parallel Discourses*. New York: Routledge, 2011.

McCormack, Timothy L. H. *Self-Defense in International Law: The Israeli Raid on the Iraqi Nuclear Reactor*. New York: St. Martin's Press, 1996.

McDowall, David. *Palestine and Israel: The Uprising and Beyond*. London: I. B. Tauris, 1989.

McHugo, John. *A Concise History of the Arabs*. London: Saqi, 2013.

McNamara, Robert. *Britain, Nasser and the Balance of Power in the Middle East, 1952–1967: From the Egyptian Revolution to the Six-Day War*. New York: Frank Cass, 2003.

Mearsheimer, John J., and Stephen M. Walt. *The Israel Lobby and U.S. Foreign Policy*. New York: Farrar, Straus and Giroux, 2008.

Meir, Golda. *My Life*. New York: Putnam, 1975.

Meisler, Stanley. *The United Nations: A History*. 2nd ed. New York: Grove Press, 2011.

Meital, Yoram. *Peace in Tatters: Israel, Palestine, and the Middle East*. Boulder, CO: Lynne Rienner, 2006.

Miller, Aaron David. *The Much Too Promised Land: America's Elusive Search for Arab-Israeli Peace*. New York: Bantam, 2008.

Miller, Anita, Jordan Miller, and Sigalit Zetouni. *Sharon: Israel's Warrior-Politician*. Chicago: Academy Chicago Publishers, 2002.

Milton-Edwards, Beverly. *Islamic Politics in Palestine*. London: I. B. Tauris, 1996.

Mingst, Karen A., and Margaret P. Karns. *The United Nations in the Twenty-First Century*. 4th ed. Boulder, CO: Westview, 2011.

Mishal, Shaul, and Avraham Sela. *The Palestinian Hamas: Vision, Violence, and Coexistence*. New York: Columbia University Press, 2000.

Morris, Benny. *1948: A History of the First Arab-Israeli War*. New Haven, CT: Yale University Press, 2008.

Morris, Benny. *1948 and After: Israel and the Palestinians*. New York: Oxford University Press, 1991.

Morris, Benny. *Israel's Border Wars, 1949–1956: Arab Infiltration, Israeli Retaliation, and the Countdown to the Suez War*. Oxford, UK: Clarendon, 1993.

Morris, Benny. *One State, Two States: Resolving the Israel/Palestine Conflict*. New Haven, CT: Yale University Press, 2009.

Morris, Benny. *Righteous Victims: A History of the Zionist-Arab Conflict, 1881–2001*. New York: Vintage Books, 2001.

Morris, Benny. *The Birth of the Palestinian Refugee Problem Revisited*. Cambridge: Cambridge University Press, 2004.

Morris, Benny. *The Road to Jerusalem: Glubb Pasha, Palestine and the Jews*. New York: Tauris, 2002.

Nakdimon, Shelomoh. *First Strike: The Exclusive Story of How Israel Foiled Iraq's Attempt to Get the Bomb*. New York: Summit Books, 1987.

Nusse, Andrea. *Muslim Palestine: The Ideology of Hamas*. London: Routledge, 1999.

O'Ballance, Edgar. *The Arab-Israeli War, 1948*. London: Faber, 1956.

O'Ballance, Edgar. *The Palestinian Intifada*. New York: St. Martin's Press, 1998.

Oren, Michael B. *Power, Faith, and Fantasy: America in the Middle East, 1776 to the Present*. New York: Norton, 2007.

Oren, Michael B. *Six Days of War: June 1967 and the Making of the Modern Middle East*. Novato, CA: Presidio, 2003.

Pappé, Ilan. *A History of Modern Palestine: One Land, Two Peoples*. Cambridge: Cambridge University Press, 2003.

Pappé, Ilan. *Britain and the Arab-Israeli Conflict, 1948–51*. Basingstoke, UK: Palgrave, 1988.

Pappé, Ilan. *The Ethnic Cleansing of Palestine*. Oxford: Oneworld Publications, 2006.

Pappé, Ilan. *The Forgotten Palestinians: A History of the Palestinians in Israel*. New Haven, CT: Yale University Press, 2011.

Pappé, Ilan. *The Israel/Palestine Question: Rewriting Histories*. Minneapolis: Augsburg, 1999.

Parker, Richard Bordeaux. *The Politics of Miscalculation in the Middle East.* Bloomington: Indiana University Press, 1993.

Parker, Richard Bordeaux, ed. *The Six-Day War: A Retrospective.* Gainesville: University Press of Florida, 1996.

Parsi, Trita. *Treacherous Alliance: The Secret Dealings of Israel, Iran, and the United States.* New Haven, CT: Yale University Press, 2007.

Parsons, Nigel Craig. *The Politics of the Palestinian Authority: From Oslo to Al-Aqsa.* 2nd ed. London: Routledge, 2012.

Pearlman, Wendy. *Occupied Voices: Stories of Everyday Life from the Second Intifada.* New York: Thunder's Mouth Press/ Nation Books, 2003.

Pearlman, Wendy. *Violence, Nonviolence, and the Palestinian National Movement.* Cambridge: Cambridge University Press, 2011.

Pelletiere, Stephen C. *Israel in the Second Iraq War: The Influence of Likud.* Santa Barbara, CA: Praeger, 2009.

Peres, Shimon. *Battling for Peace: A Memoir.* Edited by David Landau. New York: Random House, 1995.

Perlmutter, Amos. *The Life and Times of Menachem Begin.* Garden City, NY: Doubleday, 1987.

Petran, Tabitha. *The Struggle over Lebanon.* New York: Monthly Review Press, 1987.

Pollock, David. *The Politics of Pressure: American Arms and Israeli Policy since the Six Day War.* Westport, CT: Greenwood, 1982.

Pollack, Kenneth M. *Arabs at War: Military Effectiveness, 1948–1991.* Lincoln: University of Nebraska Press, 2002.

Quandt, William B. *Peace Process: American Diplomacy and the Arab-Israeli Peace Process since 1967.* 3rd ed. Washington, DC: Brookings Institution Press, and Berkeley: University of California Press, 2005.

Rabil, Robert G. *Embattled Neighbors: Syria, Israel and Lebanon.* Boulder, CO: Lynne Rienner, 2003.

Rabin, Lea. *Rabin: Our Life, His Legacy.* New York: Putnam, 1997.

Rabin, Yitzhak. *The Rabin Memoirs.* 1st English-language ed. Boston, MA: Little, Brown, 1979.

Rabinovich, Abraham. *The Yom Kippur War: The Epic Encounter that Transformed the Middle East.* New York: Schocken, 2005.

Rabinovich, Itamar. *The War for Lebanon, 1970–1985.* Rev. ed. Ithaca, NY: Cornell University Press, 1986.

Raviv, Dan, and Yossi Melman. *Spies against Armageddon: Inside Israel's Secret Wars.* Seacliff, NY: Levant Books, 2012.

Reinhart, Tanya. *The Road Map to Nowhere: Israel/Palestine since 2003.* London: Verso, 2006.

Robinson, Glenn E. *Building a Palestinian State: The Incomplete Revolution.* Bloomington: Indiana University Press, 1997.

Roosevelt, Kermit. *Arabs, Oil, and History.* New York: Harper and Brothers, 1949.

Roth, Stephen J. *The Impact of the Six-Day War: A Twenty-Year Assessment.* London: Palgrave Macmillan, 1988.

Roy, Sara. *Failing Peace: Gaza and the Palestinian-Israeli Conflict.* Ann Arbor, MI: Pluto, 2006.

Rubenberg, Cheryl. *The Palestinians: In Search of a Just Peace.* Boulder, CO: Lynne Rienner, 2003.

Rubin, Barry. *The Muslim Brotherhood: The Organization and Politics of a Global Islamist Movement.* New York: Palgrave Macmillan, 2010.

Rubin, Barry, and Thomas A. Keaney, eds. *Armed Forces in the Middle East: Politics and Strategy.* Portland, OR: Frank Cass, 2002.

Rubin, Barry M. *Israel: An Introduction.* New Haven, CT: Yale University Press, 2012.

Rubin, Barry M. *Revolution until Victory? The Politics and History of the PLO.* Cambridge, MA: Harvard University Press, 1994.

Rubin, Barry M. *The Transformation of Palestinian Politics: From Revolution to State-Building.* Cambridge, MA: Harvard University Press, 1999.

Saad-Ghorayeb. *Hizbu'llah: Politics & Religion.* London: Pluto, 2002.

Sachar, Howard Morley. *A History of Israel: From the Rise of Zionism to Our Time.* 3rd ed. New York: Knopf, 2007.

Sachar, Howard Morley. *Egypt and Israel.* New York: R. Marek, 1981.

Sadat, Anwar. *In Search of Identity: An Autobiography.* New York: Harper and Row, 1978.

Sadat, Anwar. *Revolt on the Nile.* London: Wingate, 1957.

Said, Edward W. *Intifada: The Palestinian Uprising against Israeli Occupation.* Boston, MA: South End Press, 1989.

Said, Edward W. *Out of Place: A Memoir.* New York: Knopf, 1999.

Said, Edward W. *Peace and Its Discontents: Essays on Palestine in the Middle East Process.* New York: Vintage Books, 1995.

Said, Edward W. *The Question of Palestine.* New York: Vintage Books, 1992.

Said, Edward W., and Christopher Hitchens, eds. *Blaming the Victims: Spurious Scholarship and the Palestinian Question.* London: Verso, 2001.

Sayigh, Rosemary. *Palestinians from Peasants to Revolutionaries.* London: Zed, 1979.

Sayigh, Yezid. *Armed Struggle and the Search for State: The Palestine National Movement, 1949–1993.* New York: Oxford University Press, 2000.

Schneer, Jonathan. *The Balfour Declaration: The Origins of the Arab-Israeli Conflict.* New York: Random House, 2010.

Schulze, Kirsten E. *Israel's Covert Diplomacy in Lebanon.* New York: St. Martin's Press, 1998.

Sela, Avraham, and Moshe Ma'oz. *The PLO and Israel: From Armed Conflict to Political Solution, 1964–1994.* Basingstoke: Macmillan, 1997.

Segev, Tom. *One Palestine, Complete: Jews and Arabs under the British Mandate.* New York: Owl Books, 2001.

Shamir, Yitzhak. *Summing Up: An Autobiography.* London: Orion, 1994.

Sharon, Ariel, and David Chanoff. *Warrior: An Autobiography.* 2nd ed. New York: Simon and Schuster, 2001.

Sheffer, Gabriel. *Moshe Sharett: Biography of a Political Moderate.* New York: Oxford University Press, 1996.

Shepherd, Naomi. *Ploughing Sand: British Rule in Palestine, 1917–1948.* New Brunswick, NJ: Rutgers University Press, 1999.

Shindler, Colin. *A History of Modern Israel.* 2nd ed. Cambridge: Cambridge University Press, 2013.

Shindler, Colin. *Israel and the European Left: Between Solidarity and Delegitimization.* London: Bloomsbury, 2011.

Shindler, Colin. *Ploughshares into Swords? Israelis and Jews in the Shadow of the Intifada.* New York: St. Martin's Press, 1991.

Shlaim, Avi. *The Iron Wall: Israel and the Arab World.* New York: Norton, 2001.

Smith, Charles D. *Palestine and the Arab-Israeli Conflict: A History with Documents.* 8th ed. New York: Bedford/St. Martin's Press, 2012.

Smith, Simon C. *Ending Empire in the Middle East: Britain, the United States, and Post-war Decolonization, 1945–1973.* New York: Routledge, 2013.

Sofer, Amon. *Rivers of Fire: The Conflict over Water in the Middle East.* Lanham, MD: Rowman and Littlefield, 1999.

Sorkin, Michael. *Against the Wall: Israel's Barrier to Peace.* New York: New Press: 2005.

Spector, Stephen. *Evangelicals and Israel: The Rise of American Christian Zionism.* New York: Oxford University Press, 2008.

Stein, Kenneth W. *Heroic Diplomacy: Kissinger, Sadat, Carter, Begin and the Quest for Arab-Israeli Peace.* New York: Routledge, 1999.

Stein, Leslie. *The Making of Modern Israel: 1948–1967.* Cambridge: Polity Press, 2009.

Stephens, Robert Henry. *Nasser: A Political Biography.* New York: Simon and Schuster, 1972.

Sullivan, George. *Sadat: The Man Who Changed Mid-East History.* New York: Walker, 1981.

Swisher, Clayton E. *The Palestine Papers: The End of the Road?* London: Hesperus Press, 2011.

Swisher, Clayton E. *The Truth about Camp David: The Untold Story about the Collapse of the Middle East Peace Process.* New York: Thunder's Mouth/Nation Books, 2004.

Telhami, Shibley. *Power and Leadership in International Bargaining: The Path to the Camp David Accords.* New York: Columbia University, 1990.

Teveth, Shabtai. *Ben-Gurion: The Burning Ground, 1886–1948.* Boston, MA: Houghton Mifflin, 1987.

Thomas, Gordon. *Gideon's Spies: The Secret History of the Mossad.* 6th ed. New York: St. Martin's Press, 2012.

Thompson, Elizabeth F. *Justice Interrupted: The Struggle for Constitutional Government in the Middle East.* Cambridge, MA: Harvard University Press, 2013.

Tyler, Patrick. *Fortress Israel: The Inside Story of the Military Elite Who Run the Country—and Why They Can't Make Peace.* New York: Farrar, Straus and Giroux, 2012.

Usher, Graham. *Palestine in Crisis: The Struggle for Peace and Political Independence after Oslo.* London: Pluto, 1995.

Van Creveld, Martin. *Military Lessons of the Yom Kippur War.* London: Sage, 1976.

Van Creveld, Martin. *The Sword and the Olive: A Critical History of the Israeli Defense Force.* New York: PublicAffairs, 2002.

Vidino, Lorenzo. *The New Muslim Brotherhood in the West.* New York: Columbia University Press, 2010.

Wagner, Heather Lehr. *King Abdullah II.* New York: Chelsea House, 2005.

Wallach, Janet, and John Wallach. *Arafat: In the Eyes of the Beholder.* Rocklin, CA: Prima, 1991.

Warschawski, Michel. *On the Border.* Boston, MA: South End Press, 2005.

Weinberger, Peter. *Co-opting the PLO: A Critical Reconstruction of the Oslo Accords, 1993–1995.* New York: Rowman and Littlefield, 2006.

Weizmann, Chaim. *Trial and Error: The Autobiography of Chaim Weizmann.* New York: Harper, 1949.

Wistrich, Robert S. *From Ambivalence to Betrayal: The Left, the Jews, and Israel.* Lincoln University of Nebraska Press, 2012.

Yamani, Mai. *Cradle of Islam: The Hijaz and the Quest for Arabian Identity.* London: I. B. Tauris, 2004.

Web Sites

Middle East Research and Information Project. http://www.merip.org.

MidEastWeb. http://www.mideastweb.org.

Palestine History.com. http://www.palestine-history.com.

The National Security Archive. http://www2.gwu.edu/~nsarchiv/index.html.

U.S. Department of State Office of the Historian Web Site. http://history.state.gov.

Wilson Center Cold War International History Project. http://www.wilsoncenter.org/program/cold-war-international-history-project.

Television and Film

Death in Gaza (2006). HBO Studios.

Encounter Point (2007). Typecast Pictures.

Gaza Strip (2002). Typecast Pictures.

Journey to the Occupied Lands: A West Bank Retrospective (2005). PBS.

Occupation 101: Voices of the Silenced Majority (2006). Trip'ol'ii Productions.

Six Days in June: The War that Redefined the Middle East (2007). PBS.

The 50 Years War: Israel and the Arabs (2000). PBS.

List of Contributors

Editor

Priscilla Roberts

Associate Professor of History, School of Humanities

Honorary Director, Centre of American Studies

University of Hong Kong

Contributors

Alan Allport

Assistant Professor of Modern British History

Syracuse University

Amy Hackney Blackwell

Independent Scholar

Stefan Marc Brooks

Associate Professor of Political Science

Lindsey Wilson College

Dino E. Buenviaje

PhD Student, History

University of California, Riverside

Louis A. DiMarco

Associate Professor of Military History

U.S. Army Command and General Staff College, Fort Leavenworth

Richard M. Edwards

Senior Lecturer of Philosophy

University of Wisconsin Colleges, Sheboygan

Elun Gabriel

Associate Professor of European History

St. Lawrence University

Neil A. Hamilton

Professor of History

Spring Hill College

Jonathan M. House

William A. Stofft Professor of Military History

U.S. Army Command & General Staff College, Fort Leavenworth

Harry Raymond Hueston

Associate Professor of Criminal Justice

West Texas A&M University

Robert S. Kiely

Illinois Mathematics and Science Academy

Adam Lowther

Research Professor

Air Force Research Institute

James R. McIntyre
Assistant Professor of History
Moraine Valley Community College

James D. Perry
Senior Analyst, Northrop Grumman

Paul G. Pierpaoli Jr.
Fellow, Military History
Military History, ABC-CLIO

Priscilla Roberts
Associate Professor of History, School of Humanities
Honorary Director, Centre of American Studies
University of Hong Kong

Mark M. Sanders
Associate Professor-Librarian
East Carolina University

Larry Simpson
Professor of History
High Point University

Daniel E. Spector
Historian
U.S. Army Chemical Corps, Retired

Paul Joseph Springer
Professor of Comparative Military Studies
Air Command and Staff College, Maxwell Air Force Base

Nancy L. Stockdale
Associate Professor of Middle Eastern History
University of North Texas

David Tal
Kahanoff Chair Professor of Israeli Studies
University of Calgary

Spencer C. Tucker
Senior Fellow
Military History, ABC-CLIO

Dallace W. Unger Jr.
Writer and Historian

Bryan E. Vizzini
Associate Professor of History
West Texas A&M University

James H. Willbanks
Director
Department of Military History
U.S. Army Command and General Staff College, Fort Leavenworth

Anna M. Wittmann
Professor of English and Film Studies
University of Alberta

David T. Zabecki
Major General
Army of the United States, Retired

Sherifa Zuhur
Independent Scholar

Stephen Zunes
Professor of Politics and International Studies
University of San Francisco

About the Editor

Priscilla Roberts read history as an undergraduate at King's College, Cambridge, where she also earned her PhD. She then spent four years in the United States on a variety of fellowships, including one year at Princeton University on a Rotary graduate studentship and a year as a visiting research fellow at the Smithsonian Institution, Washington, D.C. She then moved to the University of Hong Kong, where she is now an associate professor of history. She is also honorary director of the University of Hong Kong's Centre of American Studies. Dr. Roberts spent the year 2003 at George Washington University as a Fulbright Scholar and has received numerous other academic awards for research in the United States, Great Britain, and Australia. She specializes in 20th-century diplomatic and international history.

Index

Note: Page numbers in **bold** indicate main entries; those in *italics* indicate photos.